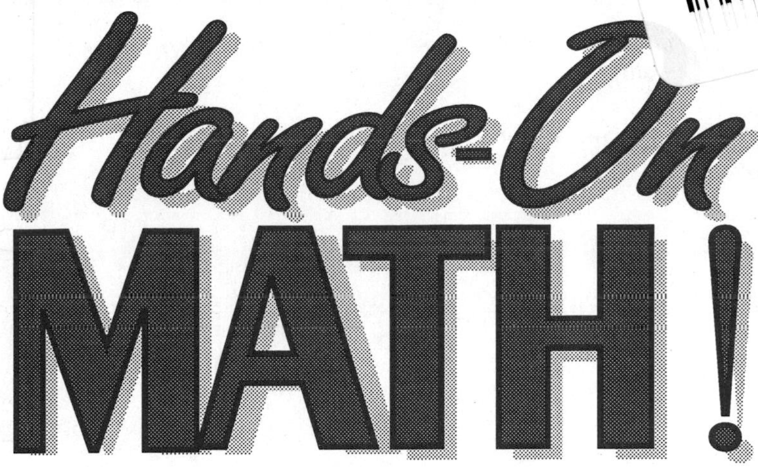

Ready-to-Use Games & Activities for Grades 4-8

FRANCES M. THOMPSON

THE CENTER FOR APPLIED RESEARCH
IN EDUCATION
West Nyack, NY 10994

On the World Wide Web at http://www.phdirect.com

Library of Congress Cataloging-in-Publication Data

Thompson, Frances McBroom.
Hands-on math! : ready-to-use games & activities for grades 4-8 / Frances McBroom Thompson.
p. cm.
ISBN 0-87628-383-0 : Spiral—ISBN 0-87628-388-1 : Paper
1. Mathematics—Study and teaching (Elementary). I. Title.
QA135.5.T498 1994 94-6162
372.7'044—dc20 CIP

Printed in the United States of America

10 9 8 7 6 (S) 10 9 8 7 6 5 4 3 2 1 (P)

ISBN 0-87628-383-0 (S) ISBN 0-87628-388-1 (P)

THE CENTER FOR APPLIED RESEARCH IN EDUCATION
West Nyack, NY 10994

On the World Wide Web at http://www.phdirect.com

This special collection of *Hands-On Math* activities is dedicated to:

. . . the young mathematics students and their teachers who so graciously opened their classrooms and candidly responded to me so that new ideas and techniques might be explored;

. . . my undergraduate and graduate students desirous of teaching, whose insatiable curiosity and trust motivated me to seek more effective methods of instruction that would increase their success in mathematics;

. . . my family—husband Claude and teenaged sons, Landon and Brooks—who cheered me through the long hours of preparing the final manuscript and who never seemed to tire of eating out!

ABOUT THE AUTHOR

Frances McBroom Thompson has been exploring the many varieties of manipulative materials available for mathematics instruction since 1973. Her investigations have often taken her into the classroom at all grade levels in an effort to provide successful learning experiences for students of all ability levels.

Frances regularly contributes articles on mathematics teaching to professional education journals and conducts workshops for inservice teachers at the elementary and secondary levels. She has published *Five-Minute Challenges* and *More Five-Minute Challenges,* two activity books in secondary problem solving, and has co-authored *Holt Math 1000* and *Holt Essential Math,* two general mathematics textbooks for high school students. She has also developed training materials for K–6 mathematics teachers with the Texas Education Agency.

She has taught mathematics full-time at the junior and senior high school levels in Texas and California and has served as a K–12 mathematics specialist in both Georgia and Texas. Frances holds a bachelor's degree in mathematics education from Abilene Christian University (Texas) and a master's degree in mathematics from the University of Texas at Austin. Her doctoral degree is in mathematics education from the University of Georgia at Athens. She presently serves on the mathematics faculty of Texas Woman's University in Denton, Texas, where she offers undergraduate and graduate courses in mathematics and mathematics teaching.

ABOUT THIS BOOK

Hands-On Math! has been written to provide specific, "hands-on" games and activities for classroom teachers to use with their students in *grades 4 through 8*. It contains instructional sequences that have been developed for a large variety of teaching objectives. Patterns, relations, and functions, along with geometry, probability, standard written algorithms, and other mathematical strands have been included. Within each individual strand, teaching objectives are ordered according to increasing difficulty. The arrangement indirectly reflects grade level in that earlier objectives will be more commonly taught in grades 4 and 5, whereas later objectives will be found more often in curriculums for grades 7 and 8. No effort has been made to assign objectives to specific grade levels, however, since this varies from state to state, as well as from district to district.

INSTRUCTIONAL SEQUENCING

Learning is a growth process that proceeds from the concrete to the abstract. It cannot be rushed. Learning also requires active participation of the learner and involvement of multiple senses. To reflect this natural growth process, each individual sequence included in this book has been designed to contain a *manipulatives* lesson, a lesson that uses *diagrams or pictorial models,* and finally a *cooperative activity* that allows students to explore a new concept further in a supportive environment before working independently and abstractly with the concept. The three-part format of each sequence supports the recent recommendations of the National Council of Teachers of Mathematics regarding mathematics instruction. Research findings of the author and many others have greatly influenced the use of manipulatives and pictorial diagrams in all the sequences. The positive effects of cooperative learning combined with problem-solving situations have also been incorporated within each cooperative activity.

LANGUAGE DEVELOPMENT THROUGH COMMUNICATION AND MODELING

The instructional sequences are appropriate for students of all abilities, including the mathematically gifted and learning disabled. All children need experiences with physical and pictorial models by which they can reflect on and clarify their thinking about new ideas and situations. Working with models encourages students to explore relationships and assists them in expressing their newly found ideas first through informal language, then through mathematical language and written symbols. From their experiences with various models, students develop mental images, which are vital if students are to effectively understand symbolic notation that they will use later on. In the instructional sequences students are often asked to look for patterns, both geometric and numeric, and to formulate generalizations when possible. They are encouraged to describe their findings in their own words on paper and to share these observations with others. Estimations and mental computations are also applied when appropriate.

STRUCTURE OF LESSONS

The three components or lessons of each instructional sequence must be presented in the order given. Manipulative explorations must come first, followed by work with diagrams. The pictorial lesson, along with the cooperative activity, provides the time needed by some students to fully assimilate the new concept. For others, these last two components provide freedom to explore the concept more deeply.

An effort has been made to keep the implementation of the lessons manageable and feasible for most classroom situations. An approximate time length will be suggested for each lesson; this will vary from class to class, however, and will ultimately depend on the teacher's overall goals for the lesson and observed student need. All materials needed for each activity or lesson will be listed or described at the beginning of the activity. Most suggested manipulatives are inexpensive and accessible to most teachers. In many cases, alternatives to commercial materials are suggested. Ideas for packaging the manipulatives are also given.

LEARNER EXPECTATIONS

In past decades in the United States, mathematics instruction has focused on rote memorization of concepts, skills, and formulas. As a result, far too many students are unable to apply their mathematical knowledge in the real world. Such rote learning is not easily retained and teachers often find themselves reteaching ideas covered in the previous year's curriculum. The use of manipulatives and diagrams to develop new concepts has proved to be more effective for increasing retention in students than *rule-giving,* rote memory techniques. Physical and pictorial models are also quite useful for remediation. Older students previously exposed to a mathematical concept will sometimes object to remediation with manipulatives, but they quickly change their attitudes when they begin to experience success in learning. When instruction is correlated with the natural growth process of learning, most students will progress necessarily and will attain the power to think and reason mathematically, a quality needed by all citizens in this world of constantly changing technology.

Frances McBroom Thompson

CONTENTS

CHAPTER 1

NUMBER AND NUMBER RELATIONSHIPS

CHAPTER 3
DEVELOPMENT OF WRITTEN ALGORITHMS

CHAPTER 5
MEASUREMENT

CHAPTER 7
NUMBER THEORY

CHAPTER 8
ALGEBRAIC THINKING

CHAPTER 1

NUMBER AND NUMBER RELATIONSHIPS

INTRODUCTION

This chapter introduces students to many number concepts and relationships. Students are shown how to determine whether one number is larger than another, how to compare fractions, and how to round off whole numbers, mixed numbers, and fractions to whole numbers. Through hands-on activities and games, students learn decimal concepts, such as tenths and hundredths. They also are introduced to the concept of percent, learn how to find equivalent fractions, and discover the relationships among fractions, decimals, and percents. In addition, students acquire the necessary tools to understand the ratio concept as well as equivalent ratios and proportions.

OBJECTIVE 1: Order four-digit and five-digit whole numbers.

Activity 1: WHICH IS MORE?

(Concrete Action)

Materials: Small counters (5 colors)
Base 10 frames (ones to ten thousands)
Pencils

Management: Partners (30 minutes)

Directions:

1. Give each pair of students a base 10 frame and 10 counters in each of 5 colors. The frames can be drawn on 8.5" × 14" paper. Each frame should consist of five columns with headings. Assign a different color to each place value column on the frame by placing a counter having a column's color on the heading of that column.

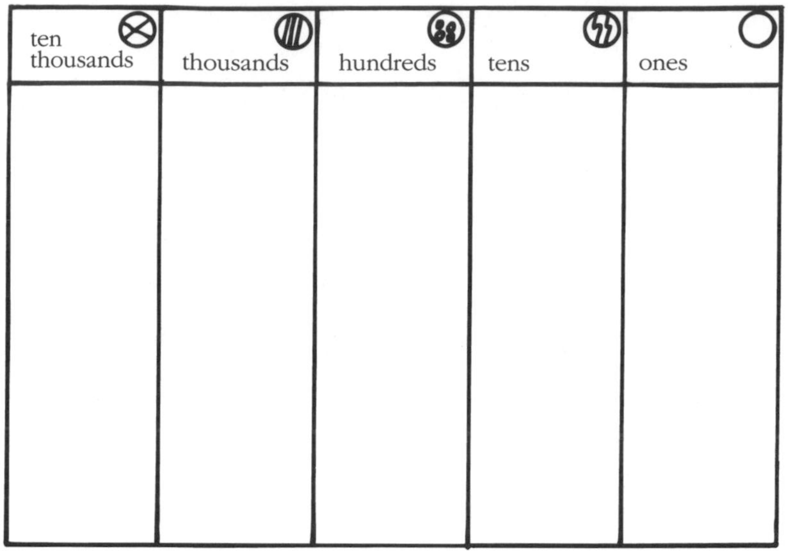

ten thousands	thousands	hundreds	tens	ones

NOTE: Circles with different designs indicate counters of different colors.

2. Have partners show 2,583 on their base 10 frame by placing the appropriate counters in the upper half of each column of the frame.

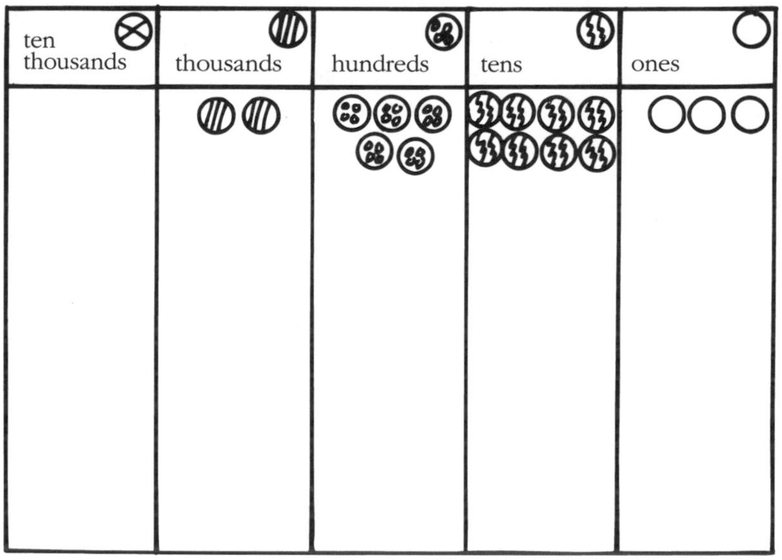

ten thousands	thousands	hundreds	tens	ones

3. Have them also show 2,740 on their frame by placing counters in the lower half of each column.

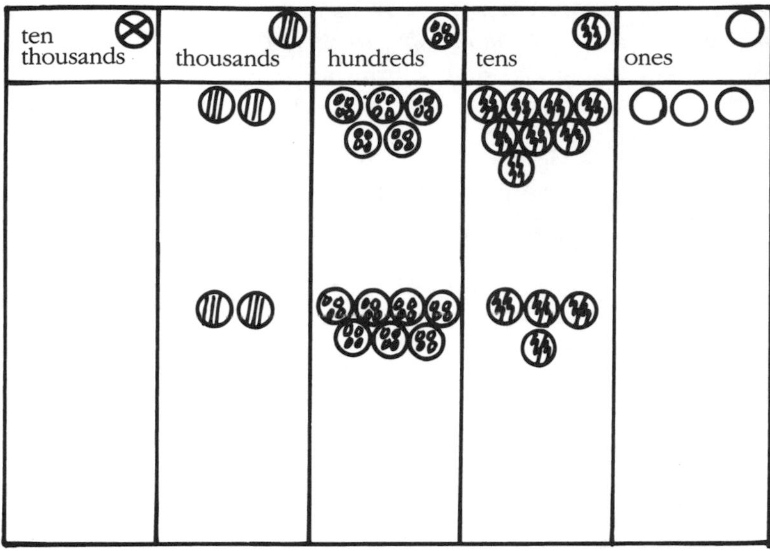

4. Ask students to locate the column of highest place value that contains counters for at least one of the two numbers displayed. They should then compare the amount of counters for each number found in that column. In this example, each number has 2 counters in the thousands column.

5. Since the thousands amounts are the same, have students compare the amounts in the next column to the right—the hundreds column. The top number has 5 counters or 5 hundreds and the bottom number has 7 counters or 7 hundreds.

6. So the number with 7 hundreds, i.e., 2,740, is greater than 2,583. Write on the chalkboard the two symbolic notations that represent the numerical order of the two numbers: *2,583 < 2,740* and *2,740 > 2,583*. Have different students read the two number sentences, starting at the left each time: *Two thousand, five hundred eighty-three is less than two thousand, seven hundred forty* and *two thousand, seven hundred forty is greater than two thousand, five hundred eighty-three.*

7. If a student suggests that 2,583 should be greater because it has 8 tens (the next place value after the thousands and hundreds) and 2,740 only has 4 tens, tell the student to match one number's thousands and hundreds counters to the corresponding counters of the second number.

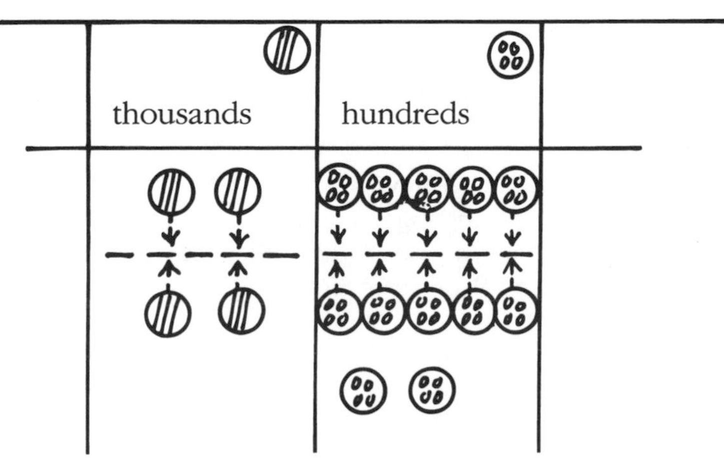

8. The larger number has 2 counters in the hundreds column still unmatched. Ask: *Which is more: 2 hundreds 4 tens (from the larger number) or 8 tens (from the smaller number)?* Hopefully, students will recognize that 2 hundreds and 4 tens equal 24 tens, which is greater than 8 tens. If necessary, trade the 2 hundreds counters for 20 tens counters so that students can actually see the 24 tens.

9. Now write several pairs of numbers on the chalkboard for the students to compare. Here are some possible pairs to use:

2,781—2,745	4,508—4,356	25,162—23,807
30,512—28,075	5,623—5,631	47,260—47,515

10. Have students build each given pair of numbers on their base 10 frames. They should compare the counters in each column, starting at the left, in order to find the *largest* place value where one number has more counters than the other number does. The number with more counters at that point is then the larger number. Students should write a number sentence that states the order they have found for the two numbers. Allow them to choose which symbol they wish to use: < or >.

11. If any students have reasoning difficulties like that discussed in steps 7 and 8, have them follow a similar matching process to find the error in their thinking.

12. If time permits, have partners create pairs of numbers for each other to compare on their base 10 frames.

13. When all are finished, have different students read the number sentences they have written, correctly reading the sentences from left to right.

Activity 2: DRAW TO ORDER

(Pictorial Action)

Materials: Comparison Worksheet NNR-1.2
Pencils
Counters
Base 10 frames from Activity 1 (optional)

Management: Partners (20–30 minutes)

Directions:

1. Give each pair of students a Comparison Worksheet. Some students may find it helpful to continue using the counters and base 10 frames from Activity 1; this is acceptable. Have them first build each pair of numbers with the counters, then draw pictures of the counters on their worksheet frames.

2. For each given pair of numbers, have students draw circles in each column of the base 10 frame to represent the two numbers. The first number of the pair should be drawn in the upper half of the frame and the second number drawn in the lower half of the frame. Here is an example from item #1 on the worksheet, which compares 3,175 to 3,408:

TTH	TH	H	T	O
	○○○	○	○○○○ ○○○	○○○○ ○
	○○○	○○○○		○○○○ ○○○○

3. Starting at the left of the frame, students should find the first column where the amounts of circles drawn for the two numbers differ. Have them draw a ring around the larger amount of circles in that column. The number containing the ring will be the larger of the two numbers. The blank can now be filled with the correct symbol: 3,175 __<__ 3,408.

TTH	TH	H	T	O
	○○○	○	○○○○ ○○○	○○○○ ○
	○○○	(○○○○) [ringed]		○○○○ ○○○○

4. When all students have completed their worksheets, have several students draw their base 10 frames and circles for the different exercises on the chalkboard and explain their results.

NAME ______________________________ DATE ____________________

Worksheet NNR-1.2
Draw to Order

Draw circles on a base 10 frame to show each pair of numbers. Draw the first number (on the left in the pair) in the top half of the given frame and draw the second number in the bottom half of the frame. In the column of the *largest* place value where the two numbers' circles differ in amount, draw a ring around the larger amount. Fill in the blank between the two numbers with the correct symbol: < or >.

1. 3,175 ____ 3,408

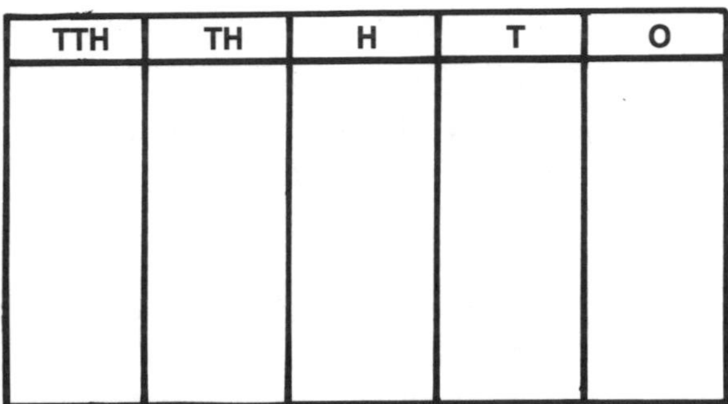

TTH	TH	H	T	O

2. 2,514 ____ 1,963

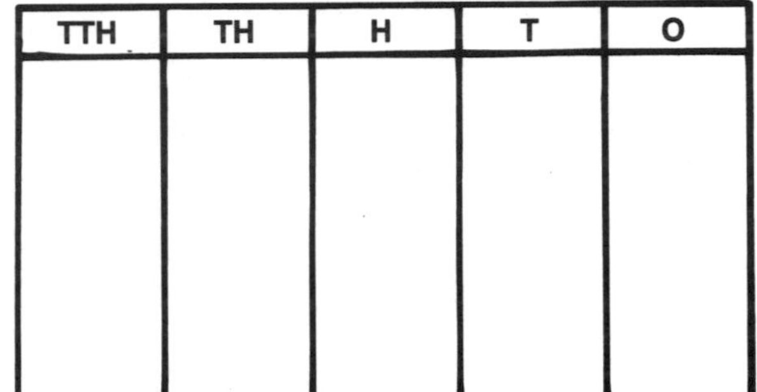

TTH	TH	H	T	O

3. 17,432 ____ 8,941

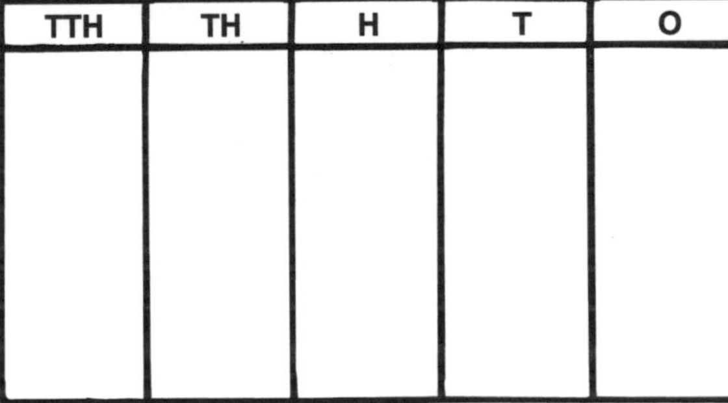

TTH	TH	H	T	O

4. 2,729 ____ 2,750

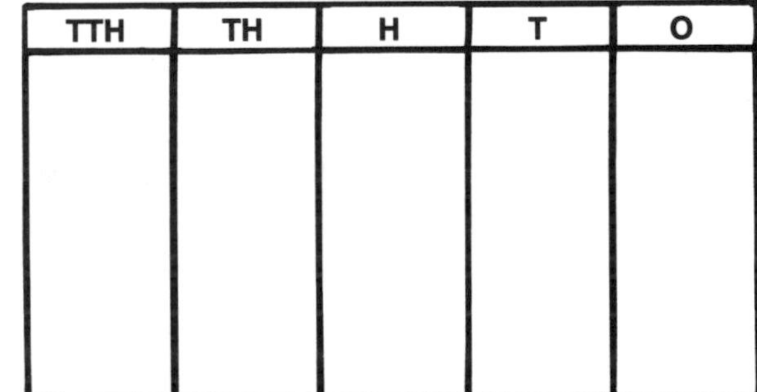

TTH	TH	H	T	O

5. 40,689 ____ 40,095

TTH	TH	H	T	O

6. 29,565 ____ 31,247

TTH	TH	H	T	O

Activity 3: TOTOLOSPI

(Cooperative Groups)

Materials: Small gameboard markers
Gameboards worksheet NNR-1.3a
Spinners worksheet NNR-1.3b with numerals 0–9 with large paper clips
Small Popsicle™ sticks painted on one side
Game Record Sheets NNR-1.3c

Management: Teams of 4 students each (20–30 minutes)

Directions:

1. Background: This game is an adaptation of a Hopi game of chance that was played by both children and adults. The name is pronounced *to-to'-los-pi*. Two or three dice made from pieces of cane were used to tell players how far to move their *animals* (markers), usually kernels of colored corn, across a counting board inscribed on stone. There were several designs used for the counting board: a single ellipse, two ellipses overlapped to form a cross, and a rectangle. Totolospi has been variously described as resembling either Monopoly®, checkers, or Parcheesi®. For more information on this game, please refer to the following sources: Marina C. Krause, *Multicultural Mathematics Materials* (National Council of Teachers of Mathematics, 1906 Association Drive, Reston, VA 22091, 1983); Frances E. Watkins, "Indians at Play: I—Hopi Parcheesi," *Masterkey* 18 (September 1944): 139–41.

2. Give each team of students a gameboard, 2 gameboard markers, a spinner and a large paper clip (for the spinner needle), 2 Popsicle™ sticks (painted on one side), and 2 game record sheets.

3. On each team one pair of students will compete against the other pair. One pair will place their marker (or animal) on the circle at one end of the gameboard and the other pair will place theirs on the circle at the opposite end. Markers will be moved from line segment to line segment, rather than from space to space, until they reach the circle farthest from where they started.

4. On a pair's turn, one of the partners will hold the 2 Popsicle™ sticks in one hand and drop them on end to the playing surface. The pair can advance their marker according to which sides of the sticks land up: 2 painted sides = 3 line segments; 2 plain sides = 2 line segments; 1 plain side and 1 painted side = 1 line segment. The marker can only be moved, however, if the pair of students solves a problem correctly.

5. To determine the problem to be worked, the playing pair must spin the spinner needle (the paper clip held on the spinner with a pencil tip) several times. The numeral digits obtained from the spins are then recorded in the order spun in rows of blanks under columns A and B on the pair's game record sheet. (If four-digit numbers are to be compared, students should spin 8 times; for five-digit numbers, they should spin 10 times. The teacher should assign how many digits to use at the beginning of the game.)

Example of four-digit numbers being compared: 8 digits are spun in the order 3, 5, 2, 7, 1, 0, 9, 3. They are recorded in that same order and the correct symbol drawn in the box:

_ 3 5 2 7 [>] _ 1 0 9 3

6. If the other pair of students agrees with the symbol recorded, the playing pair may move their marker the number of line segments indicated by the Popsicle™ sticks. If the chosen symbol is judged incorrect, a slash should be drawn through it and the playing pair must pass.

7. A pair of students wins if their marker reaches the circle at the opposite end first.

NAME ______________________________ DATE ______________________

WORKSHEET NNR-1.3A
Gameboard Pattern for Totolospi

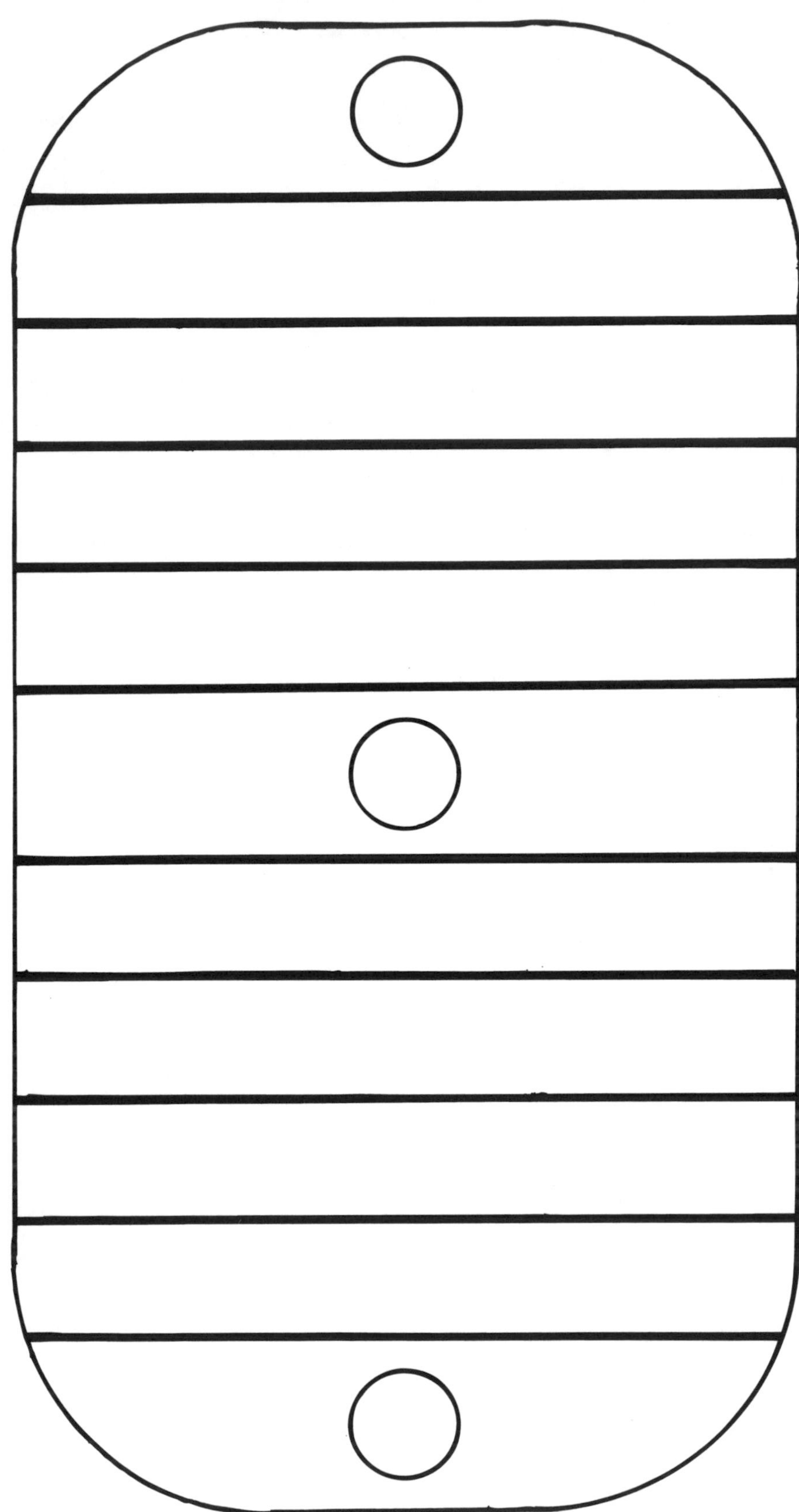

NAME ______________________________ DATE ____________________

WORKSHEET NNR-1.3B
Spinner Pattern for Totolospi

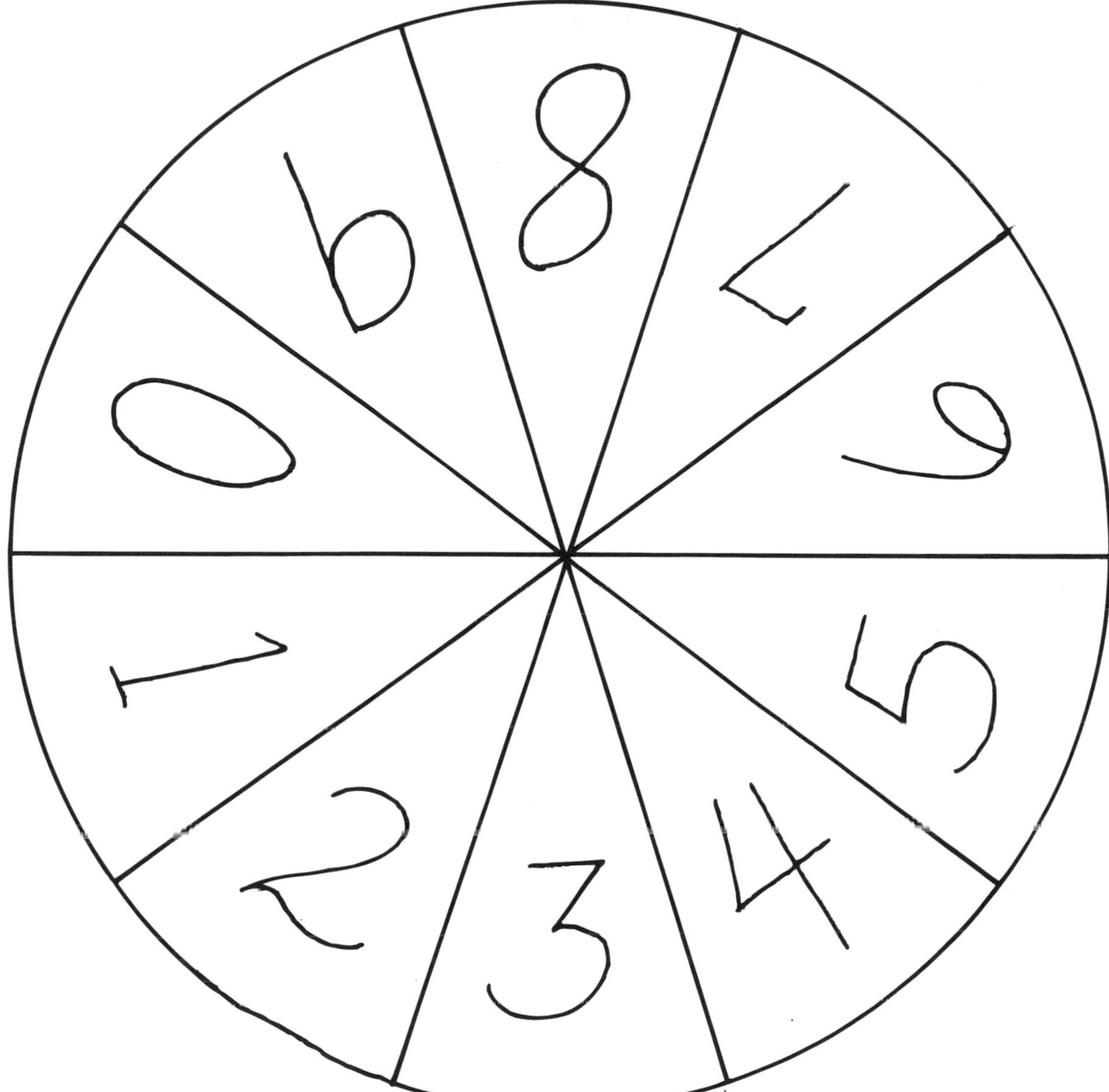

NAME ______________________________ DATE ____________________

WORKSHEET NNR-1.3C
Game Record Sheet for Totolospi

For each exercise below, use a spinner to determine the digits to write in the blanks under column A and column B. Compare the two numbers formed and show their order by writing the correct symbol (< or >) in the box between them.

	A		B
1.	___ ___ ___ ___ ___	☐	___ ___ ___ ___ ___
2.	___ ___ ___ ___ ___	☐	___ ___ ___ ___ ___
3.	___ ___ ___ ___ ___	☐	___ ___ ___ ___ ___
4.	___ ___ ___ ___ ___	☐	___ ___ ___ ___ ___
5.	___ ___ ___ ___ ___	☐	___ ___ ___ ___ ___
6.	___ ___ ___ ___ ___	☐	___ ___ ___ ___ ___
7.	___ ___ ___ ___ ___	☐	___ ___ ___ ___ ___
8.	___ ___ ___ ___ ___	☐	___ ___ ___ ___ ___

OBJECTIVE 2: Round whole numbers to the nearest hundred or thousand.

Activity 1: ENOUGH TO ROUND OFF?
(Concrete Action)

Materials: Small colored counters (4–5 colors)
Pencils
Base 10 frames from Objective 1, Activity 1

Management: Partners (30 minutes)

Directions:

1. Give each pair of students a base 10 frame and 10 counters in each of 4 colors (use 5 colors if working with five-digit numbers). Assign a color to each place value by placing a counter of that color in the heading box of that place value's column.

2. Ask students to place counters in the appropriate columns to show the number: 3,185.

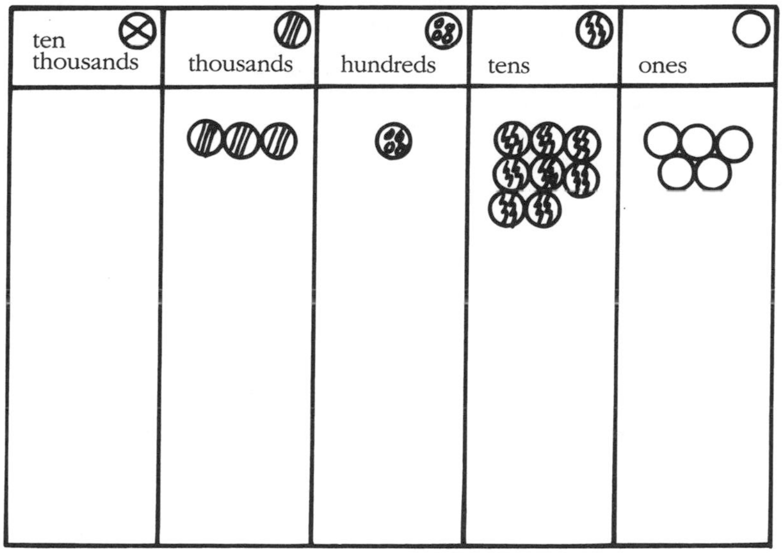

ten thousands	thousands	hundreds	tens	ones

3. Discuss the meaning of *rounding to the nearest hundred*. Have students count the counters in the tens column. We will agree that if there are 5 or more counters there, we have enough to *round off* and trade for another hundred. A new hundred will then be placed on the base 10 frame and the original tens and ones counters will be removed. (There are other ways used in business to round a number, but this method is quite common.) If there are 4 or less tens counters, we will simply keep the hundreds we have and remove any counters of lesser place value from the base 10 frame.

4. Since there are 8 counters in the tens column, they can be rounded off and traded for a new counter in the hundreds column. Any other counters of lesser place value (here, the ones) should be removed along with the tens. When rounding to hundreds, we are only interested in hundreds or greater place values.

5. There are now 3 thousands counters and 2 hundreds counters remaining on the base 10 frame. Have students record on their own papers: *3,185 rounded to the nearest hundred is 3,200.*

6. Repeat the above process to round 5,408 to the nearest thousand. Ask students if there are enough hundreds to *round off* and trade for a new thousand. Since there are only 4 hundreds, we cannot trade, so we must keep the thousands we have and remove the hundreds, tens, and ones counters from the frame.

7. Only 5 thousands counters remain on the base 10 frame. Have students record: *5,408 rounded to the nearest thousand is 5,000.*

8. Now write other four- and five-digit numbers on the board for students to show on their base 10 frames and round to the nearest hundred or thousand. Students should record the results of each rounding in sentence form. Remind students that if rounding off causes a column to have ten counters, the counters must be traded for a new counter in the next column to the left. For example, if we round 1,973 to the nearest hundred, there will be ten counters in the hundreds column. These must be traded for a new thousand. Therefore, 1,973 rounds to 2,000.

Activity 2: DRAW TO ROUND

(Pictorial Action)

Materials: Rounding worksheet NNR-2.2
Regular pencils
Red pencils
Counters base 10 frames from Activity 1 (optional)

Management: Partners (30 minutes)

Directions:

1. Give each pair of students a red pencil and the two-page rounding worksheets (NNR-2.2), which contain several base 10 frames. Small circles can be drawn in the columns of each frame to represent counters. Some students may still need to work with the actual counters and base 10 frames. Allow them to do so, but have them also show their steps on the worksheet.

2. Have students show 23,614 by drawing circles in the appropriate columns of the first frame of the worksheet.

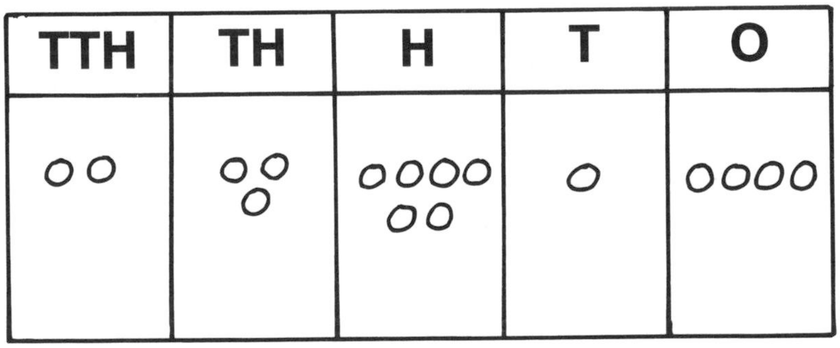

TTH	TH	H	T	O
o o	o o o	o o o o o o	o	o o o o

3. Ask: *If we want to round to the nearest thousand, which counters should we try to round off and trade?* (the hundreds) *Are there enough hundreds to round off and trade for a new thousand?* (yes; there are 5 or more hundreds) Have students use their red pencil to draw a new circle in the thousands column and mark out all the circles in the hundreds, tens, and ones columns.

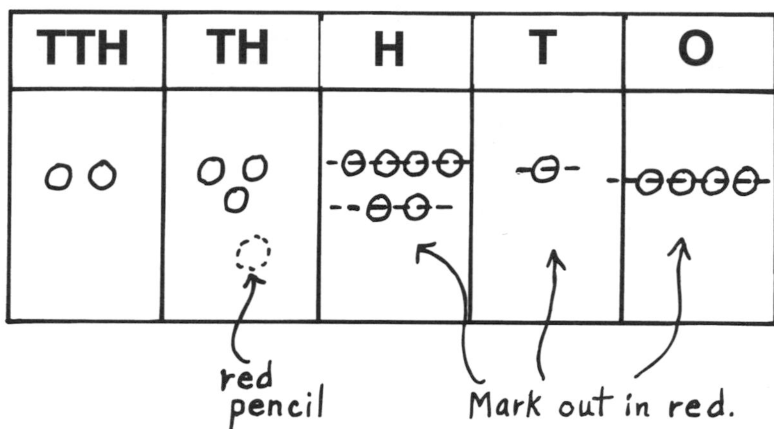

4. Since the 2 ten thousands and 4 thousands have not been marked out on the base 10 frame, the number now showing on the frame is 24,000. Have students record the rounding in the space below the frame as follows:

$$23{,}614 \xrightarrow{1000\text{'s}} 24{,}000$$

5. Repeat the above process to round 35,749 to the nearest hundred. Since there are fewer than 5 tens, they cannot be rounded off to make a new hundred. Thus, students must keep the 7 hundreds and use the red pencil to mark out all the circles in the tens and ones columns.

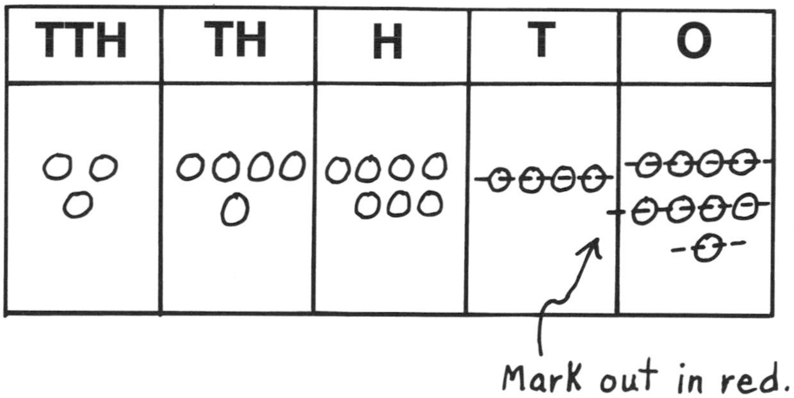

TTH	TH	H	T	O

Mark out in red.

6. Only the original circles remain in the ten thousands, thousands, and hundreds columns. 35,749 is nearer to 35,700 than to 35,800. Have students record the following below their frame:

$$35{,}749 \xrightarrow{100\text{'s}} 35{,}700$$

7. Now write other four- and five-digit numbers on the board for students to draw on their base 10 frames and try to round off, either to hundreds or thousands. Remind students that if rounding off produces ten circles in one column, the ten must be traded for a new circle in the next column to the left. The trade can be shown as follows:

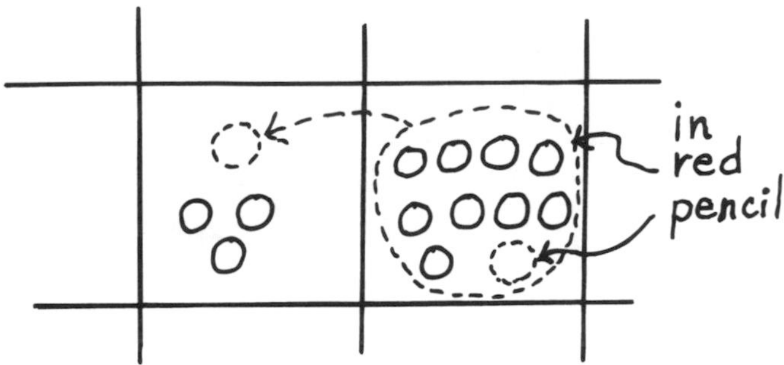

8. When all are finished, have several students describe how they rounded the different numbers.

Activity 3: HOPI RAIN CLOUDS

(Cooperative Groups)

Materials: Unlined paper
Pencils (colored, if preferred),
Problem/Answer Keys (Worksheet NNR-2.3)

Management: Teams of 4 students each (20 minutes)

Directions:

1. Background: Black Mesa in northeastern Arizona is called *Tuuwanasavi* or *Center of the Universe* by the Hopi Indians. This large mesa is where the different Hopi clans met and settled about a thousand years ago. The earlier existence of the Hopi people depended quite heavily on the rainfall, and farming is still important to the Hopi today. Living in an arid region, they grow melons, corn, squash, beans, and cotton. The rain cloud symbol used in this activity is frequently found in Hopi designs placed over altars or on kachina dolls and pottery. For more information on the rain cloud symbol, please refer to the following sources:

- Marina C. Krause, *Multicultural Mathematics Materials* (National Council of Teachers of Mathematics, 1906 Association Drive, Reston, VA 22091, 1983)
- J. Walter Fewkes, “A Few Summer Ceremonials at the Tusayan Pueblos,” *A Journal of American Ethnology and Archaeology,* vol. 2 (edited by J. Walter Fewkes): 1–160. New York: Houghton, Mifflin & Co., 1892.

2. Give each team 2–3 sheets of unlined paper and a problem/answer key that has been cut apart to form separate sheets A and B. Provide colored pencils if students wish to use them to draw their rain clouds.

3. The students on each team will separate into two pairs: A and B. Pair A will read

NAME ____________________ DATE ____________

WORKSHEET NNR-2.2
Draw to Round

Round numbers by drawing circles on the base 10 frames and trading when possible. Record the results below the frames.

1. ____________

TTH	TH	H	T	O

2. ____________

TTH	TH	H	T	O

3. ____________

TTH	TH	H	T	O

4. ____________

TTH	TH	H	T	O

5. ____________

TTH	TH	H	T	O

6. ____________

TTH	TH	H	T	O

NAME ______________________ DATE ______________

WORKSHEET NNR-2.2 (*cont.*)
Draw to Round

7. ____________

TTH	TH	H	T	O

8. ____________

TTH	TH	H	T	O

9. ____________

TTH	TH	H	T	O

10. ____________

TTH	TH	H	T	O

11. ____________

TTH	TH	H	T	O

12. ____________

TTH	TH	H	T	O

problems from sheet A of the problem/answer key and pair B will read from sheet B. The pairs will take turns reading a number and how it is to be rounded from their half of the problem/answer key. The non-reading pair must state what the new number will be after the rounding. If the number given agrees with the answer key, the responding pair may add a new section to the team's *rain cloud* drawing. If the number is incorrect, they must pass on the drawing and become the readers of the next problem.

4. The sections of the rain cloud drawing must be added in the following order:

- 1 long horizontal bar
- 5 short vertical bars for *rain,* only 1 bar added on a turn, starting at left end of horizontal bar
- 3 arcs for *clouds,* only 1 arc added on a turn, starting with either of the two lower arcs
- 2 curves extended above the arcs for *lightning snakes,* only 1 curve added on a turn, starting with either curve
- 2 kites at ends of curves for heads of lightning snakes, only 1 kite added on a turn, starting with either kite

5. The game ends when the *Hopi rain cloud* is finished. A completed drawing is shown below:

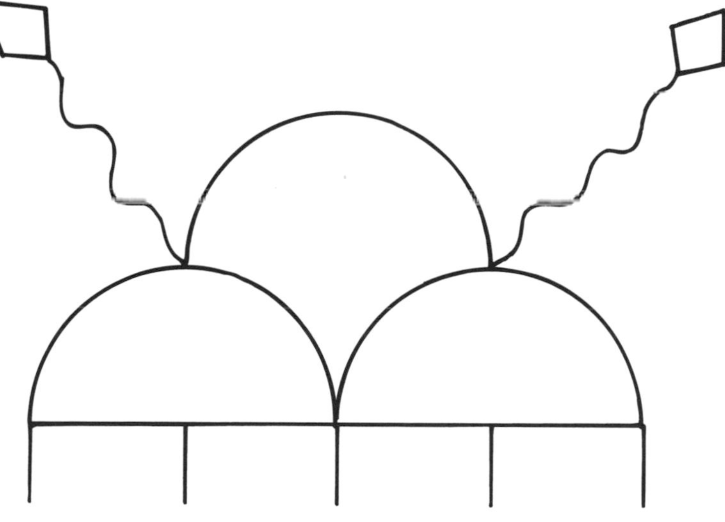

NAME ________________________________ DATE ____________________

WORKSHEET NNR-2.3
Problem/Answer Key for HOPI RAIN CLOUDS

(Cut columns A and B apart; give one to each pair of students on a team.)

A

Number	Rounded To	Answer
1,285	hundreds	1,300
25,306	thousands	25,000
48,075	thousands	48,000
7,545	hundreds	7,500
4,924	thousands	5,000
83,598	hundreds	83,600
37,016	hundreds	37,000
5,527	thousands	6,000
50,985	hundreds	51,000
2,341	thousands	2,000

B

Number	Rounded To	Answer
3,640	thousands	4,000
18,561	hundreds	18,600
59,112	hundreds	59,100
8,094	thousands	8,000
1,750	hundreds	1,800
96,358	thousands	96,000
40,895	thousands	41,000
7,009	hundreds	7,000
37,240	thousands	37,000
3,982	hundreds	4,000

OBJECTIVE 3: Order simple (proper) fractions having like or unlike denominators.

Activity 1: COMPARING FRACTIONS

(Concrete Action)

Materials: Sets of fraction bars (see Patterns/Grids section for pattern)

Management: Partners (40–50 minutes minimum for each denominator type: like and unlike)

Directions:

1. Give each pair of students a set of fraction bars. Each set should contain at least the following: 2 whole units, 4 halves, 6 thirds, 8 fourths, 12 sixths, 16 eighths, and 24 twelfths. It will be assumed in the discussion below that students are familiar with the fraction bars. If not, they need to explore with them to learn the different sizes of parts available, their colors, and their fractional names when compared to the whole unit bar. It is also assumed that students already understand the fraction concept and that, for example, the name *two-thirds* means that we have separated a whole unit into three equal parts called *thirds* and presently have two of those parts. In addition, they should know how to form equivalent fractions using concrete materials. A method for presenting equivalent fractions is discussed in detail in Chapter 2.

2. *For like denominators:* Have each pair of students place 2 whole unit bars on the desktop in front of them. Ask them to place 1-fourth on top of one of the unit bars and 3-fourths on top of the other unit bar.

3. Discuss which amount is greater, i.e., covers more of the unit bar. Have students give reasons for their choices. A common response is that the set of 3 parts is longer than the set of 1 part. Hopefully some will observe that all the part sizes are equal and that since 3 > 1, 3-fourths must be greater than 1-fourth. Record the results by writing the following sentence on the board: *3-fourths of the unit is greater than 1-fourth of the unit.* It is very important to include the phrase *of the unit* with a fraction name as often as possible. Otherwise, the fraction name loses its meaning with the students.

4. Repeat steps 2–3 with other fractions having like denominators. Use only part sizes available in the students' sets of fraction bars. Have students write the resulting sentences on their own paper.

5. *For unlike denominators:* Have partners place 2 unit bars on the desktop in front of them. Ask them to place 1-half on top of one unit bar and 3-fourths on top of the other unit bar. Ask: *Which fractional amount covers more of the unit bar?* Several students will observe that the 3-fourths covers more because its combined parts are longer than the 1-half.

6. Ask: *Can you trade the half or fourths for other part sizes so that you have the same part size on both unit bars?* Several answers are possible. Most students will probably trade 1-half for 2-fourths, then do a one-to-one matching of the two new fourths with the 3-fourths. Other possibilities will be the trading of both the half and fourths for eighths or twelfths. The focus will be on changing both fractions to a common part size, then setting up a one-to-one match to decide which set has the greater number of parts. Do not discuss finding the *least common denominator* at this time. It is a concept that creates confusion for young students when brought in too early in the study of fractions.

7. On the chalkboard record the results with the following sentence: *1-half of the unit is less than 3-fourths of the unit because 2-fourths is less than 3-fourths.* Another possible sentence would be: *3-fourths of the unit is greater than 1-half of the unit because 3-fourths is greater than 2-fourths.* This is a good opportunity for some writing practice.

8. Now write the word names for other pairs of fractions having unlike denominators on the board. Do not use the ratio form, e.g., 2/3, at this time. Have partners build the fractions and do the necessary trading to compare them. They should write sentences on their own paper to record their findings. Use only fractions that can be shown or traded, using the part sizes available in the set of fraction bars. Here are some possible pairs to use:

2-fourths : 3-eighths	1-half : 2-sixths	1-half : 2-thirds
2-thirds : 3-sixths	5-sixths : 9-twelfths	3-fourths : 7-eighths
1-fourth : 3-eighths	1-half : 5-eighths	1-half : 4-sixths
1-third : 3-twelfths	2-sixths : 1-fourth	3-fourths : 8-twelfths
2-thirds : 3-fourths	4-sixths : 7-twelfths	2-fourths : 5-sixths

Activity 2: ORDERING WITH DIAGRAMS

(Pictorial Action)

Materials: Fraction Comparison Worksheets NNR-3.2
Regular pencils
Red pencils

Management: Partners (30–40 minutes minimum for each denominator type: like and unlike)

Directions:

1. Give each pair of students 2–3 copies of the fraction comparison worksheet and a red pencil. Write numbers in the small boxes at the left margin of the worksheet to number the items as needed.

2. Students may need to be trained on how to subdivide the unit bar into different amounts of equal parts. Show them how to use tick marks to estimate where they should draw subdivision bars to form equal parts (or at least *about equal* visually). Since we are drawing without measuring, we will agree to accept parts as equal in size if they *look about the same size.* If two unit bars are *cut* into the same number of equal parts (e.g., each bar shows six equal parts), then we will agree that all the parts shown on both bars must have the same fractional name (e.g., all parts are called sixths).

Examples of how to subdivide a unit bar:

(a) To make fourths, put a tick mark at the midpoint of the bar, then at the midpoint of each half-bar. Draw a vertical bar at each tick mark.

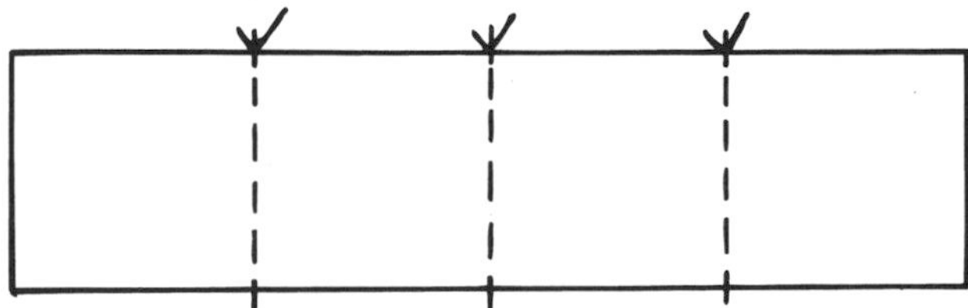

(b) To make thirds, visually locate the midpoint of the unit bar, then place a tick mark a little to each side of that midpoint. Adjust the tick marks, if necessary, to make the three new parts appear equal to the viewer. Draw a vertical bar at each tick mark.

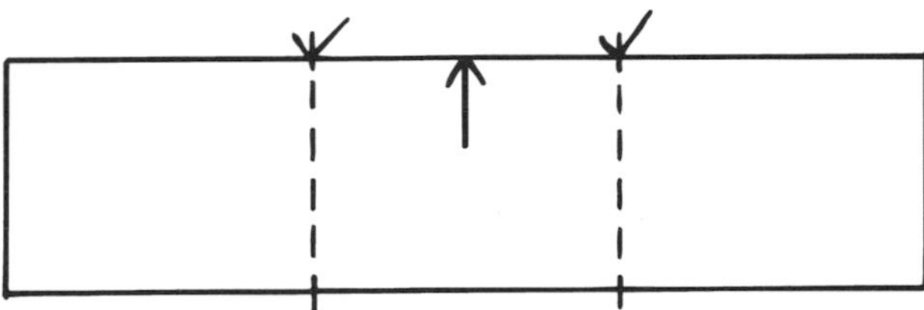

(c) To make sixths, draw thirds on the unit bar first. Mark the midpoint of each third with a tick mark and draw the final vertical bars.

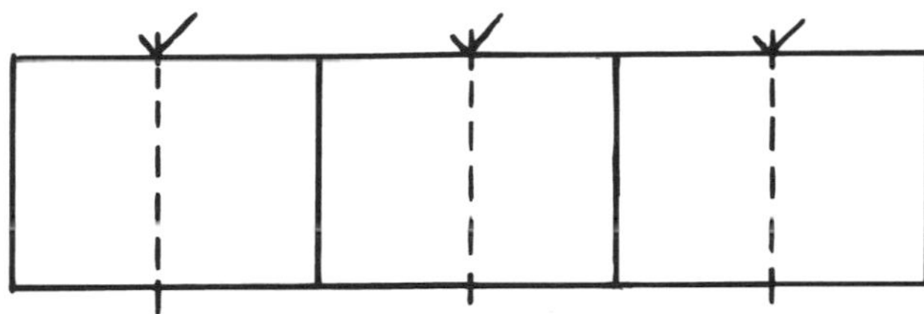

3. *For like denominators:* Have students use their regular pencils to draw and *shade* 3-fourths of the unit on the left unit bar of the first item on their worksheet and 2-fourths on the right unit bar. To shade a part, students should draw diagonal line segments across the part. For adjacent parts, the directions of the diagonal segments should be reversed; this makes it easier to separate the different parts visually and also to make any needed erasures.

4. Have students record the fraction names in the spaces above the unit bars. Since the part sizes are the same and 2 < 3, students should record the following sentence in the space below the two unit bars: *3-fourths > 2-fourths of the unit.*

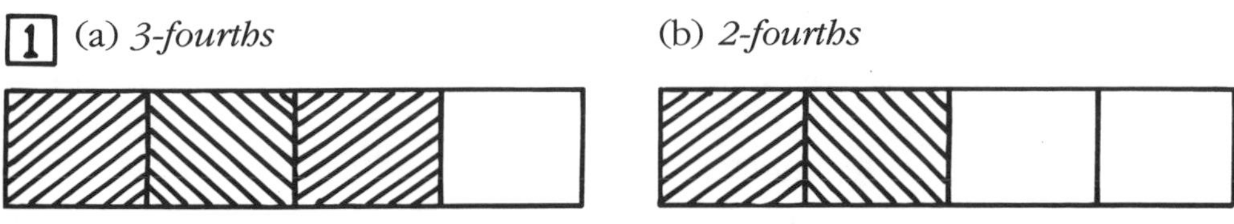

5. Repeat steps 3–4, comparing other pairs of fractions with like denominators. Use 2, 3, 4, 5, 6, 8, 10, and 12 as denominators.

6. *For unlike denominators:* Have students draw and shade 2-thirds of the unit on the left unit bar of an item on the worksheet and 5-sixths of the unit on the right unit bar. Since the two unit bars contain different amounts of parts, we know all the parts are not the same size. Students must now use *trial and error* to find a common part size. First have them try to subdivide all the *larger* parts, the thirds, into two new parts each; this should be done by only placing tick marks initially to see how many new parts will be formed. In this case, six new parts will be formed across the entire unit bar. This agrees with the number of parts on the right unit bar, so new vertical bars can be drawn with a red pencil and students do not have to explore any further. If the amount of parts on the two unit bars had not agreed, students would need to try subdividing the sixths into two new parts each or the thirds into three new parts each, etc., until agreement was finally found. Do not emphasize the *least common denominator* concept at this time.

7. Students can now count the new shaded parts shown on each unit bar and fill in the spaces on the worksheet.

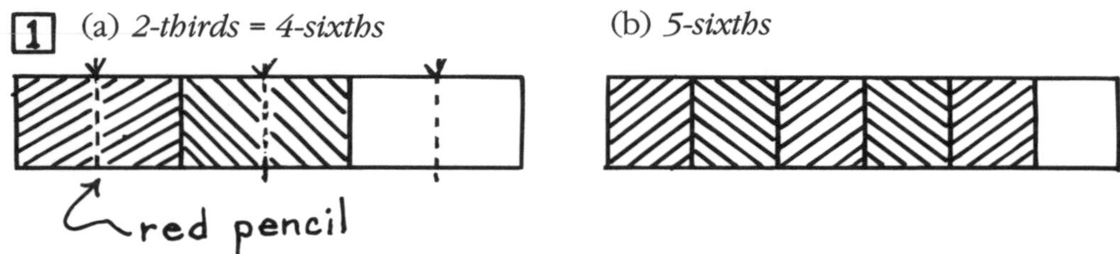

2-thirds < 5-sixths of the unit

8. Repeat steps 6–7 with other pairs of fractions. In addition to the pairs with unlike denominators suggested in Activity 1, use other pairs, such as the following:

3-fifths : 4-tenths 2-fifths : 1-half 1-half : 7-tenths

9. After students have drawn several pairs of fractions to compare them, have them begin to record the final sentence of each exercise with ratio forms instead of word names (e.g., $\frac{2}{3} < \frac{5}{6}$ instead of 2-thirds < 5-sixths).

Draw horizontal bars, not slanted bars, for the ratio forms. This change in notation should be applied in both the like and unlike denominator lessons. Also begin to use the ratio form when recording in the spaces *above* the unit bars on the worksheet. For the unlike denominator lesson, trades should also be recorded symbolically to reflect any changes to equivalent fractions. For example, if 2-thirds and 5-sixths are being compared, each third trades for two new parts and each sixth remains the same. The top spaces would then be completed as follows:

$$\frac{2 \times \textcircled{2}}{3 \times \textcircled{2}} = \frac{4}{6} \qquad \frac{5 \times \textcircled{1}}{6 \times \textcircled{1}} = \frac{5}{6}$$

10. As students move into using this final factored form, ask various students to verbally describe the general process they seem to be following when comparing fractions. Possible responses: *If the denominators of the original fractions are the same, the part sizes are all the same, so we only need to compare the numerators, which tell how many of each part size we have. If the denominators or part sizes are different, we have to change the original fractions to equivalent fractions where the new part sizes are the same and, hence, their denominators are the same. Then we just compare the new numerators.*

NAME ______________________ DATE ______________

WORKSHEET NNR-3.2
Ordering with Diagrams

Show pairs of fractions on the unit bars and compare them. Write a sentence about each fraction pair.

Activity 3: CHECK IT OUT!

(Cooperative Groups)

Materials: Comparison Worksheet NNR-3.3
Sets of fraction bars from Activity 1
Pencils

Management: Teams of 4 students each (20 minutes)

Directions:

1. Give each team a copy of Comparison Worksheet NNR-3.3 and a set of fraction bars.

2. On each team, one pair of students will ask a question from the worksheet about the order of two fractions and the other pair will give the correct order, confirming their answer with the fraction bars. The two pairs of students will take turns asking questions and answering them.

NAME ______________________________ DATE ____________________

WORKSHEET NNR-3.3
Check It Out!

Take turns asking and answering the questions below. Confirm your answers by building each fraction in the given pair with the fraction bars and comparing their amounts.

Sample question: $\frac{2}{3} < \frac{5}{6}$?

How to read the question: "Is two-thirds less than five-sixths of the unit?"

QUESTION:	ANSWER: (circle one choice)
1. $\frac{3}{4} > \frac{1}{2}$?	Yes No
2. $\frac{7}{8} < \frac{3}{4}$?	Yes No
3. $\frac{2}{3} < \frac{3}{6}$?	Yes No
4. $\frac{1}{3} > \frac{1}{4}$?	Yes No
5. $\frac{3}{8} > \frac{2}{4}$?	Yes No
6. $\frac{1}{2} < \frac{5}{6}$?	Yes No
7. $\frac{3}{4} < \frac{2}{3}$?	Yes No
8. $\frac{2}{6} < \frac{3}{12}$?	Yes No

OBJECTIVE 4: Develop the concepts of tenths and hundredths.

Activity 1: BUILDING SPECIAL FRACTIONS

(Concrete Action)

Materials: Base 10 blocks (flats, rods, units)
Paper
Pencils

Management: Partners (30 minutes)

Directions:

1. Give each pair of students a set of base 10 blocks containing one flat, 10 rods, and 100 small cubes.

2. Tell students that the flat will be the whole unit or *one* for this activity. Ask them to find how many rods will cover the whole unit and also how many small cubes will cover the unit.

3. Discuss the idea that since 10 rods cover the whole unit or *one,* each rod equals 1-tenth of the unit and is given the special numeral name of 0.1 (read as *one-tenth of one*). Also, since 100 small cubes cover the whole unit, each cube equals 1-hundredth of the unit and is given the special numeral name of 0.01 (read as *one-hundredth of one*).

4. Now have students show different single-digit amounts of tenths or hundredths by placing the rods or small cubes on top of the flat or whole unit. For example, ask them to show *three-tenths of one.* Students should place three rods on top of their flat. Have a student write the correct numeral name on the board: *0.3 of 1.* To show *eight-hundredths of one,* students should place eight small cubes on top of the flat. The numeral name should be recorded on the board as *0.08 of 1.*

5. After students have built several single-digit amounts of tenths and of hundredths, ask them to build *sixteen-hundredths,* a two-digit amount of hundredths. They should place 16 small cubes on the flat. Now ask: *Can any of the hundredths be traded for tenths?* (yes; 10 cubes can be replaced with 1 rod) *What is another way to describe 16 hundredths?* (1 tenth and 6 hundredths)

6. Write *0.16 of 1* on the chalkboard. Discuss how this numeral name can be interpreted in two ways: 16 hundredths or 1 tenth and 6 hundredths.

7. Now write on the board several other word names for one-digit amounts of rods (tenths) and one- and two-digit amounts of cubes (hundredths) for students to build on their flats. Because of the tedious counting involved, use mostly amounts less than 0.50, but still include a few like 0.65 or 0.73 (Activity 2 will include more of this last type). Students should also record on their own papers the numeral name for each amount they build.

8. Reverse the process by writing several numeral names on the board for students to build. Then have students state or write the word name for each amount they build.

Activity 2: SHADED SQUARES

(Pictorial Action)

Materials: Decimal Worksheet NNR-4.2
Red pencils
Regular pencils

Management: Partners (20–30 minutes)

Directions:

1. Give each pair of students 2–3 copies of a worksheet and a red pencil. Write numbers in the small boxes on the worksheet to number the items as needed. The red pencil will be used for the shading; it allows the black grid marks on the worksheet to be seen easily through the shading.

2. Write several decimal numeral names (tenths or hundredths) on the chalkboard. Use amounts between 0.50 and 0.99 as well as those less than 0.50 at this time. Ask different students to read these numeral names aloud for the whole class.

3. Have students shade the 10 × 10 grids on their worksheets to represent the different amounts on the board. Also, have them record below each shaded grid the numeral name and word name(s) it represents. It might be helpful to students to have a list of the more difficult word names spelled correctly on the board (e.g., twelve, fourteen, fifteen, eighteen, twenty, thirty, forty, . . ., ninety).

Example: 0.46 =forty-six hundredths, or four tenths and six hundredths

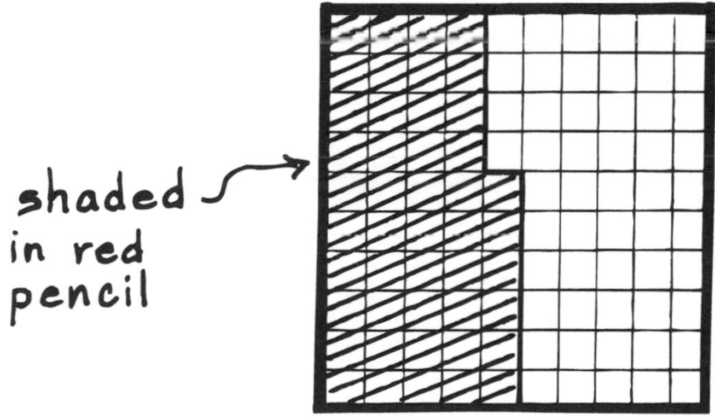

NAME ______________________________ DATE ____________________

WORKSHEET NNR-4.2
Shaded Squares

Show different decimal fractions by shading the unit squares. Write the numeral name and word name for each decimal fraction shown.

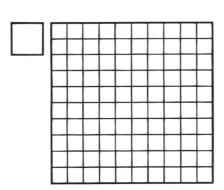

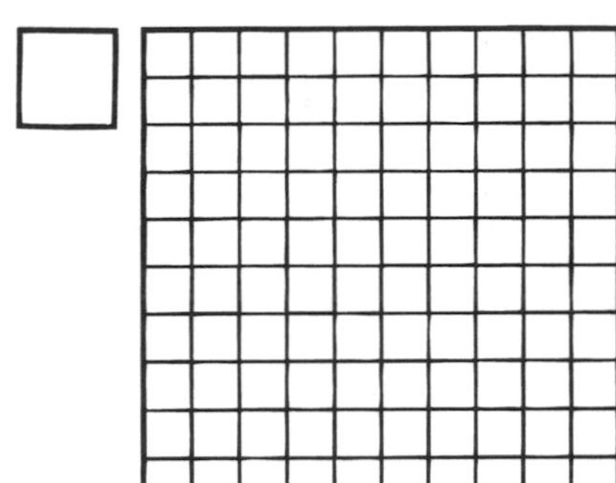

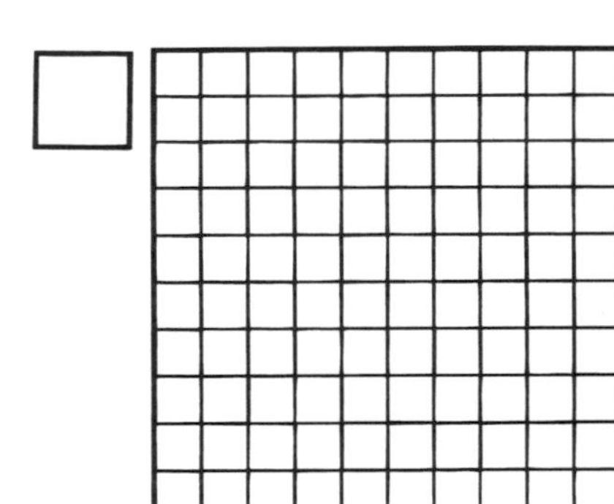

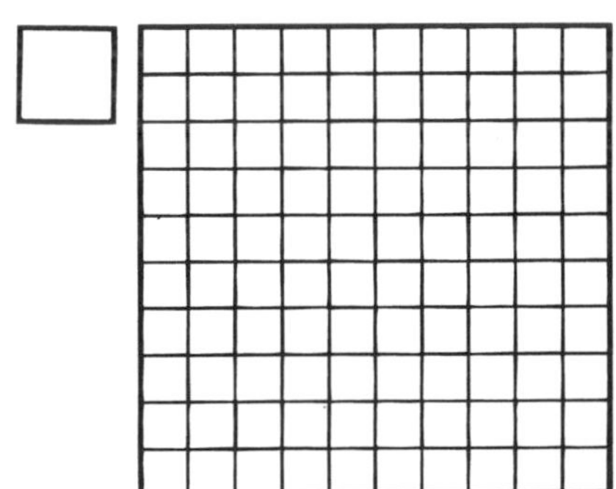

Activity 3: DECI-ROLL

(Cooperative Group)

Materials: Number cubes or dice
Base 10 blocks (flats, rods, small cubes)
Paper
Pencils

Management: Teams of 4 students each (20 minutes)

Directions:

1. Give each team 1 die or number cube (faces show 1–6) and a set of base 10 blocks (1 flat, 10 rods, 70 small cubes). Team members will take turns building and recording the names of decimal numerals.

2. On each turn a player will roll the die twice. The first digit rolled will be the tens digit and the second digit rolled will be the ones digit of the amount of small cubes to be counted out. For example, if a 5 is rolled first, then a 4, the player will count out 54 of the small cubes (hundredths) and place them on top of the flat, which represents the whole unit.

3. The player must now trade every 10 cubes on top of the flat for one rod.

4. Finally, the player should state in words and write the numeral names for the decimal amounts built with the blocks. For example, if 54 cubes have been counted out and traded for 5 rods and 4 cubes, the player will say *54 hundredths is 5 tenths and 4 hundredths,* and write *0.54 = 0.5 + 0.04.*

5. The teams should be monitored carefully to check for correct usage of word names and numeral names.

OBJECTIVE 5: Order decimals (ones, tenths, hundredths).

Activity 1: MATCH-UP!
(Concrete Action)

Materials: Base 10 blocks, paper, pencils

Management: Teams of 4 students (30–40 minutes)

Directions:

1. Give each team of students a set of base 10 blocks (4 flats, 18 rods, 18 small cubes).

2. Write the numeral names, *2.34 and 2.61,* on the chalkboard.

3. Ask each team to build the two numbers with their base 10 blocks. The flats are ones, the rods are tenths, and the cubes are hundredths. Students should show 2 flats, 3 rods, and 4 cubes for the first number and 2 flats, 6 rods, and 1 cube for the second number. A rod should be used in place of 10 cubes whenever possible.

4. To compare the two amounts of blocks, students should compare the largest blocks first. Here both have 2 flats or ones, so the second largest block should be checked. The first number has 3 rods or tenths and the second number has 6 rods or tenths, which is more. Students need to observe that in the second number, the 6 tenths alone are worth more than the 3 tenths and 4 hundredths together in the first number. Therefore, 2.61 is more than 2.34.

5. Write on the chalkboard: *2.34 < 2.61*. State in words: *Two and thirty-four hundredths of one is less than two and sixty-one hundredths of one.* The phrase *of one* should be used often verbally to remind students that the two numbers being compared are both based on the same whole unit or one. Have students record the number sentence on their own papers. Remind students that they may also record the alternative form: *2.61 > 2.34,* but they must always read such sentences from left to right.

6. Now write other pairs of decimal numeral names on the board for the teams to build, compare, and record their final order as a number sentence. Use some combination of ones, tenths, and hundredths, with at most 2 ones in each number (since each set of blocks only contains 4 flats total). Be sure to include pairs such as 1.8 and 1.75, 0.95 and 1.3, and 2.04 and 2.

7. *To compare numbers having more than three place value positions:* To involve numbers having hundreds, tens, ones, tenths, hundredths, and perhaps thousandths, you will need to use counters and a base 10 frame like those described previously in Objective 1. Merely label the column headings for the place values you wish to study. The comparison process still begins with the largest place value found in the numbers being compared.

Activity 2: COUNT TO MATCH
(Pictorial Action)

Materials: Paper
Red pencils
Regular pencils

Management: Partners (30 minutes)

Directions:

1. Give each pair of students a red pencil.

2. Write the decimal numeral names, *4.35* and *4.38,* on the chalkboard.

3. Draw a diagram on the chalkboard for each numeral, using squares for ones, tally marks for tenths, and small circles for hundredths. Have students copy the diagrams on their own paper. A tally mark should equal the side length of a square, and a circle should be considerably smaller than a square, but not necessarily a literal hundredth of the square's area. The pictorial forms used in this activity are only representations of the decimal relationships that students have already discovered and applied in previous activities.

4. Ask students to begin with the largest place value of the two numerals, the ones, and mark out with their red pencil any ones (or squares) that match between the two sets of shapes. If all ones match, have students continue with the next smaller place value, the tenths (or tally marks).

5. Students should continue matching and marking out until they reach the hundredths (or circles). Five circles will match from each diagram, but three circles in 4.38 will remain unmatched. Students should draw a red ring around these three circles. The completed diagrams should look like the following:

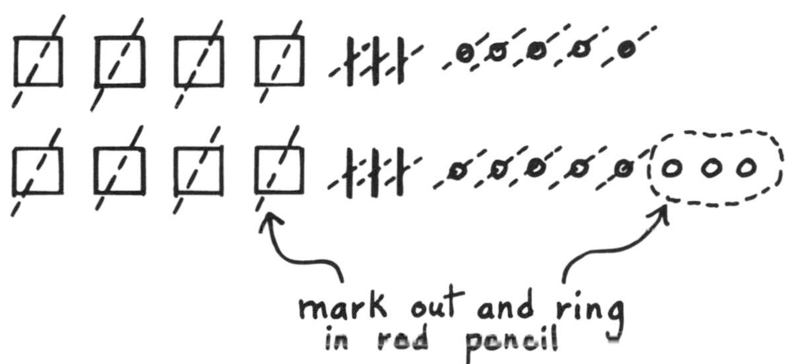

6. Since the ones and the tenths in both numbers match up completely, the hundredths will determine which number is greater. This means that 4.38 is greater than 4.35 because it has more hundredths—as indicated by the red ring around the remaining three circles. In this particular example, there are no other place values less than the hundredths to consider. If there had been (e.g., if we were comparing 4.386 to 4.359 instead), the reasoning would be that 8 hundredths alone is greater than 5 hundredths and 9 thousandths together. On the diagrams for this last pair we would just draw a large X through the thousandths group of each number to show that they were not needed in the comparison.

7. Have the students record the result in numbers and in words: *4.35* < *4.38* (or *4.38* > *4.35*) and *Four and thirty-five hundredths is less than four and thirty-eight hundredths of one* (or *Four and thirty-eight hundredths is more than four and thirty-five hundredths of one*).

8. Now write several other decimal numeral pairs on the board for the students to draw and compare by marking out matching amounts. Use only numbers less than 10 in value. Be sure to include numeral pairs such as 3.8 and 3.75, 0.98 and 1.2, and 5.04 and 5. Also, have students write their results in word sentences and number sentences. Have various students share their sentences with the entire class.

9. *To compare numbers having more than three place value positions:* To involve numbers having hundreds, tens, ones, tenths, hundredths, and perhaps thousandths, you will need to draw circles on a base 10 frame as described previously in Objective 1. Merely label the column headings for the place values you wish to study. The comparison process still begins with the largest place value found in the numbers being compared.

Activity 3: WHO HAS MORE?

(Cooperative Groups)

Materials: Dice or number cubes
Base 10 frames (pattern described in step 1 below)
Sets of base 10 blocks
Record Sheet NNR-5.3

Management: Teams of 4 students each (20 minutes)

Directions:

1. Give each team one die or number cube (faces showing 1–6), two base 10 frames, a record sheet, and a set of base 10 blocks (12 flats, 12 rods, 12 small cubes). The base 10 frame can be made by drawing three columns on 8.5" × 14" paper and labeling them as *ones, tenths,* and *hundredths*. An example of the frame is shown below:

ones	tenths	hundredths
← 6 in. →	← 4 in. →	← 4 in. →

2. Have each team form two pairs of partners for this activity.

3. For each round of play, each pair will roll the die or number cube three times: the first roll for the number of ones (flats), the second for the number of tenths (rods), and the third for the number of hundredths (small cubes). One pair of partners will build a decimal numeral with their rolled amounts of blocks and write its numeral name in column A of the record sheet. The other pair will do the same thing with their rolled amounts of blocks, writing their numeral name in column B of the record sheet and on the same line with the numeral of the other pair.

4. Students on each team will compare their two sets of blocks and numeral names to decide which number is greater. They will then draw a ring around the numeral name on their record sheet that represents the larger value.

Sample recording:

WHO HAS MORE?

	A	B
1.	(3.52)	2.16
2.		

5. Partners should now roll the die again to start the next round.

6. Teams should be monitored closely during the activity to check for correctness of numeral names and comparisons.

7. Play may continue as long as time permits.

NAME ______________________ DATE ______________

RECORD SHEET NNR-5.3
Who Has More?

	A	B
1.		
2.		
3.		
4.		
5.		
6.		
7.		
8.		
9.		
10.		

OBJECTIVE 6: Rename mixed numbers and improper fractions.

Activity 1: TRADING FOR THE WHOLE

(Concrete Action)

Materials: Sets of fraction bars (see Patterns/Grids section for sample pattern)
Paper
Pencils

Management: Partners (30 minutes for each type: mixed to improper and improper to mixed)

Directions:

1. Give each pair of students a set of fraction bars. A set should contain the following: 3 wholes, 6 halves, 9 thirds, 12 fourths, 18 sixths, and 24 eighths. It is assumed that students are familiar with the fraction bars; if not, they need to explore with them before beginning this activity. For this concrete lesson a general knowledge of addition or multiplication of common fractions is not a prerequisite; students only need an understanding of the fraction concept and naming notation (e.g., 3/4 means 3 out of 4 equal parts of the whole unit). A close connection, however, between the actions taken and the written language used must be maintained throughout the lesson.

2. *To change mixed numbers:* Have students place 2 whole bars and 2-thirds of a whole bar on their desktops. Ask them to trade the whole bars for thirds also.

3. Ask: *How many thirds do you have in all now?* (8 of the thirds) Write the steps on the chalkboard. *2 wholes + 2-thirds = 3-thirds + 3-thirds + 2-thirds = 8-thirds of a whole bar.* Have students copy the sentence on their own papers.

4. Repeat steps 2–3, using a variety of mixed numbers (to be determined by the amount and sizes of fraction bars available). Have students build the original whole and common fraction amounts first, then trade the wholes for the same part size as the common fraction. They should carefully follow the writing pattern given in step 3.

5. *To change improper fractions:* Have students place 9-fourths on their desktops. Ask: *Can you do any trading to make some whole unit bars? If so, how can you do it?* Every 4-fourths will trade for 1 whole bar. 2 whole bars can be made this way, leaving 1-fourth by itself.

6. Write the following number sentence on the board to show the steps taken: *9-fourths = 4-fourths + 4-fourths + 1-fourth = 1 whole + 1 whole + 1-fourth = 2 wholes + 1-fourth of a whole bar.* Have students carefully copy the sentence on their own papers. Emphasize how the actual trading steps (i.e., grouping the fourths, then exchanging them for whole bars) are just being recorded in a special number-word sentence.

7. Repeat steps 5–6, using a variety of improper fractions according to the amounts and sizes of fraction bars available. Have students first build the fraction with their fraction bars, then group and trade them for whole unit bars. They should record their steps in a number-word sentence, following the pattern used in step 6.

Activity 2: RENAMING SPECIAL FRACTIONS

(Pictorial Action)

Materials: Special Fraction Worksheet NNR-6.2
Red pencils
Regular pencils

Management: Partners (30 minutes for each type: mixed to improper and improper to mixed)

Directions:

1. Give each pair of students 2–3 copies of the special fraction worksheet and a red pencil. Write numbers in the small boxes at the left margin of the worksheet to number the items as needed.

2. *To change mixed numbers:* Have students show 3 wholes or ones and 1-half of a whole on their worksheets by shading 3 whole bars and a half of another whole bar with regular pencil. The *shading* should be line segments drawn diagonally within each part or whole bar, not *solid* shading, to make erasures easier when needed.

3. Ask students to trade each whole bar for the same part size (here, for halves) as the given fraction. They should do this by using their red pencil to subdivide each whole bar into 2 equal parts. Have them count the total parts they have when finished. Guide them to see 3 groups of 2-halves each or 6-halves plus the extra 1-half for a total of 7-halves of one or a whole bar.

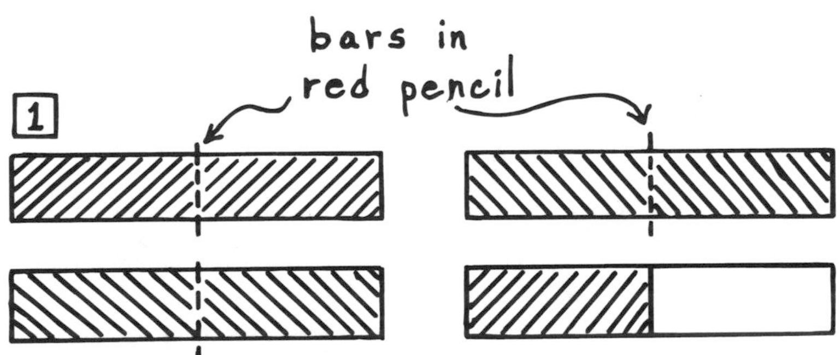

4. Write a number-word sentence on the board that represents the trading and combining steps that were used: *3 ones + 1-half = (3 of 2-halves) + 1 half = 6-halves + 1-half = 7-halves of one.* Have students write the sentence on their worksheets under the bars they have shaded.

5. Repeat steps 2–4, using a variety of mixed numbers. Use 1, 2, or 3 ones or wholes combined with common fractions consisting of halves, thirds, fourths, fifths, or sixths. Students should shade the original mixed number, then subdivide the whole bars into the given fractional part size. They should then write a number-word sentence under their bars similar to the sentence in step 4 to show the steps they used.

6. After students seem comfortable recording with the number-word sentence format, have them begin to record with number sentences that show the fractions in ratio form. For example, instead of the number-word sentence used in step 4, students would write

$3 + \frac{1}{2} = (3 \times \frac{2}{2}) + \frac{1}{2} = \frac{6}{2} + \frac{1}{2} = \frac{7}{2}$ of one. Remember that students are merely using this symbolic notation to record what they have already done pictorially. If they have already mastered fraction addition and multiplication, they should quickly be able to work with this notation at the abstract level.

7. *To change an improper fraction:* Have students show 7-thirds on their worksheet by first subdividing each of the four whole bars into 3 equal parts or thirds, then shading 7 of the new thirds by shading one whole bar completely before going to the next one. This subdivision and shading should be done with a regular pencil. Remember to shade diagonally.

8. Ask: *How many thirds are needed to make a whole unit bar?* (3) Have students draw a ring around each group of 3-thirds with their red pencil. Guide students to observe that there are now 2 groups of 3-thirds and an extra 1-third.

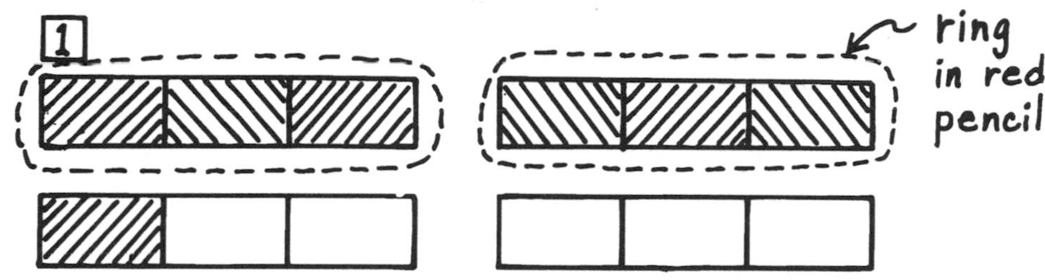

9. Have them record the following number-word sentence below the shaded bars: *7-thirds = (2 of 3-thirds) + 1-third = 2 ones + 1-third.*

10. Repeat steps 7–9, using different amounts of halves, thirds, fourths, fifths, or sixths. Students should first subdivide the four given whole bars into the desired part size and shade the amount of parts needed. Then they should draw red rings around groups of parts that equal whole bars. Finally have them write number-word sentences (as used in step 9) under the shaded bars to record the steps they used.

11. After students have used the number-word sentence format for several improper fractions, have them begin to use a number sentence format that records the fractions in ratio form. For example, instead of the sentence used in step 9, students would write the following:

$$\frac{7}{3} = (2 \times \frac{3}{3}) + \frac{1}{3} = 2 + \frac{1}{3}$$

Again, if students have already mastered the addition and multiplication of common fractions, they should quickly be able to work abstractly with this notation and not merely use it to record their pictorial steps.

NAME ______________________ DATE ______________

FRACTION WORKSHEET NNR-6.2
Renaming Special Fractions

Use the whole bars to change improper fractions to mixed numbers or mixed numbers to improper fractions.

Activity 3: MIXING MAGIC

(Cooperative Groups)

Materials: Sets of 64 cards each (sample set described in step 1)

Management: Teams of 4 students each (20–30 minutes)

Directions:

1. Give each team a set of 64 cards. These cards might be made with small index cards and colored markers. Each card will contain a numerical expression, either a mixed number, an improper fraction, a whole number plus a common fraction, or the sum of two numbers (a mixture of whole or mixed numbers and improper or common fractions). The purpose of this game is to help students become more comfortable with seeing a mixed number in several different equivalent forms, particularly its separation into a whole number added to a common fraction. Younger students seem to be comfortable with the meaning of this latter form, but not with that of the more traditional *mixed number* form. A *book* will consist of one of each type of card where all four expressions are equivalent to each other. There will be 16 books in a set of cards. Here is a suggested list of numbers or expressions to use for the four cards in a book (each row of equivalent expressions represents a book):

$2\frac{1}{2}$; $2 + \frac{1}{2}$; $\frac{4}{2} + \frac{1}{2}$; $\frac{5}{2}$

$3\frac{2}{4}$; $3 + \frac{2}{4}$; $\frac{12}{4} + \frac{2}{4}$; $\frac{14}{4}$

$1\frac{5}{6}$; $\frac{5}{6} + 1$; $\frac{5}{6} + \frac{6}{6}$; $\frac{11}{6}$

$5\frac{2}{3}$; $5 + \frac{2}{3}$; $3\frac{2}{3} + 2$; $\frac{17}{3}$

$4\frac{3}{5}$; $\frac{3}{5} + 4$; $\frac{20}{5} + \frac{3}{5}$; $\frac{23}{5}$

$1\frac{1}{4}$; $1 + \frac{1}{4}$; $\frac{4}{4} + \frac{1}{4}$; $\frac{5}{4}$

$2\frac{1}{3}$; $\frac{1}{3} + 2$; $\frac{1}{3} + \frac{6}{3}$; $\frac{7}{3}$

$3\frac{2}{5}$; $3 + \frac{2}{5}$; $2 + 1\frac{2}{5}$; $\frac{17}{5}$

$4\frac{3}{7}$; $\frac{3}{7} + 4$; $\frac{28}{7} + \frac{3}{7}$; $\frac{31}{7}$

$5\frac{4}{8}$; $5 + \frac{4}{8}$; $\frac{4}{8} + \frac{40}{8}$; $\frac{44}{8}$

$1\frac{4}{5}$; $1 + \frac{4}{5}$; $\frac{5}{5} + \frac{4}{5}$; $\frac{9}{5}$

$2\frac{3}{4}$; $\frac{3}{4} + 2$; $1 + 1\frac{3}{4}$; $\frac{11}{4}$

$3\frac{1}{2}$; $3 + \frac{1}{2}$; $1\frac{1}{2} + 2$; $\frac{7}{2}$

$4\frac{2}{3}$; $\frac{2}{3} + 4$; $1\frac{2}{3} + 3$; $\frac{14}{3}$

$5\frac{1}{4}$; $5 + \frac{1}{4}$; $\frac{20}{4} + \frac{1}{4}$; $\frac{21}{4}$

$1\frac{2}{6}$; $1 + \frac{2}{6}$; $\frac{6}{6} + \frac{2}{6}$; $\frac{8}{6}$

2. Each team should shuffle their set of cards and deal 8 cards to each member. The remaining 32 cards should be turned face down for a drawing pile.

3. Team members should take turns drawing one card from the pile and trying to make books with the cards in their hands.

4. During a turn there are no limits on the number of books a player can make. If the player still has more than four cards in her or his hand after all possible books have been laid down, the player must discard one card to a discard pile. If the player holds four or less cards after drawing a card and possibly laying down a book, she or he will not discard.

5. When necessary, the discard pile should be combined with the drawing pile and all the cards reshuffled to form a new drawing pile.

6. If a player has *no* cards left after all books have been made during a turn and is the first to go out, she or he is declared the "*Mighty Mixer of Math Magic*" of the team, and the game ends.

7. If the drawing pile is exhausted so that every player is unable to lay down a book and must pass, the game must come to an end.

OBJECTIVE 7: Round mixed numbers to whole numbers (mixed numbers may involve common fractions or decimal fractions).

Activity 1: IT'S ROUND-OFF TIME!
(Concrete Action)

Materials: Base 10 blocks (for decimal fractions)
Fraction bars (for common fractions, see Patterns/Grids section for pattern)
Paper
Pencils

Management: Partners (40–50 minutes per mixed number type: decimal fractions and common fractions)

Directions:

1. *To round mixed numbers having decimal fractions:* Give each pair of students a set of base 10 blocks (4 flats, 10 rods, 10 small cubes). It is assumed for this activity that students are already familiar with the blocks and their roles (flats = ones, rods = tenths, cubes = hundredths) and that they realize that a number in hundredths may also be expressed in tenths and hundredths; for example, 36-hundredths is equal to 3-tenths and 6-hundredths. This latter idea minimizes the amount of small cubes needed.

2. Have students show 2.57 with their blocks. They should use 2 ones (flats), 5 tenths (rods), and 7 hundredths (cubes). The rods and cubes should be placed on top of a third flat.

3. Ask: *How many tenths or hundredths are needed to cover half of a one, which is a single flat?* (5 tenths or 50 hundredths) *Do the tenths and hundredths you have in 2.57 cover half or more of your extra one?* (yes) *If so, we can agree to 'round off' the tenths and hundredths to another whole one. We can then state that 2.57 is 'rounded to the nearest whole number', 3.* Have students remove the rods and cubes from the extra flat, leaving only 3 flats on their desktop for the 3 ones. (Other methods of rounding are practiced in the business world, but the method presented here is probably the most common one.)

4. Write on the chalkboard: *2.57 rounds to 3, the nearest whole number.* Have students write the sentence on their own papers as well.

5. Have students now show 1.35 with their blocks. They should show a one with 3-tenths and 5-hundredths placed on top of a second one. Ask: *Do you have enough tenths and hundredths to round off to the next whole one?* (no) *If not, we remove the tenths and hundredths (and the extra one holding them) and work only with the single one. Since we cannot round off to the next whole one, we drop back to the previous amount of ones and say that 1.35 has rounded to the nearest whole number, 1.*

6. Write on the board: *1.35 rounds to 1, the nearest whole number.* Have students write the sentence on their own papers.

7. Repeat steps 2–6, having students build different mixed decimal numbers with their blocks and round them to the nearest whole number. The assigned numbers must involve only the whole number amounts 0–3 because of the amount of flats in each set of blocks. One flat must always be available for showing the tenths and hundredths. Be sure to include numbers that round down as well as those that round up. Students should write a sentence for each rounding they do.

8. *To round mixed numbers having common fractions:* Give each pair of students a set of fraction bars (4 wholes, 2 halves, 3 thirds, 4 fourths, 6 sixths, 8 eighths, 12 twelfths). Ask them to place one whole unit bar on their desktop, then show how a half of the whole bar might look. Students should place the fraction bar, 1-half, on top of the whole bar. Some may place other equivalent amounts like 2-fourths or 3-sixths on the whole bar. Accept this approach, but encourage them to exchange their amounts for the 1-half simply because it will make comparisons easier later on. For rounding purposes, we will agree that if a common fraction covers half or more of a whole bar, we will round off the fraction to the next whole bar. If the fraction covers less than half of a whole bar, we will delete the fraction and work only with any whole bars originally there.

9. Ask students to show 3 and 2-thirds with their fraction bars. There should be 3 whole bars placed on the desktop, followed by 2-thirds placed on top of an extra whole bar. Have students compare their 2-thirds to the 1-half to decide if they have enough to round off to the next whole bar. Since 2-thirds covers more of the whole bar than 1-half does, the 2-thirds can round off to one whole bar. Have students remove the 2-thirds, but keep the extra whole bar. Thus, 3 and 2-thirds can be rounded to 4, the next amount of whole bars.

10. Write on the chalkboard: *3 and 2-thirds rounds to the nearest whole number, 4.* Have students write the sentence on their own papers.

11. Now ask students to show 3-eighths with their fraction bars. The 3-eighths should be placed on top of a whole bar. Ask: *Does 3-eighths cover enough of the whole bar to be rounded off?* (no; 3-eighths covers less than the 1-half covers) Since 3-eighths cannot be rounded off to a whole bar, have students remove the eighths as well as the whole bar holding them. No fraction bars should be left on the desktop. Thus, 3-eighths must round to the nearest amount of whole bars, which in this case is 0 whole bars.

12. Have students write the following sentence: *3-eighths rounds to the nearest whole number, 0.*

13. Repeat steps 9–12, having students build different mixed numbers with their fraction bars, compare the fractional amounts to 1-half of a whole bar, then round the mixed numbers to the nearest whole number. Only the whole numbers 0–3 and the fractional amounts found in the fraction bar set can be assigned. One whole bar must always be available to hold the common fraction to be compared. Students should write a sentence for each rounding they do.

Activity 2: ROUNDING WITH DIAGRAMS

(Pictorial Action)

Materials: Fraction Worksheet NNR-7.2a (for decimal fractions)
Decimal Worksheet NNR-7.2b (for common fractions)
Red pencils
Regular pencils

Management: Partners (30 minutes per type of mixed number: decimal fractions and common fractions)

Directions:

1. *To round mixed numbers having common fractions:* Give each pair of students 2–3 copies of Decimal Worksheet NNR-7.2a and a red pencil. Write numbers in the small boxes at the left margin of the worksheet to number the items as needed. Have students use their regular pencils to shade two whole squares or ones and part of another square on their worksheet to show 2.65. Students should shade 6-tenths of a square, then an additional 5-hundredths, in order to show the 0.65.

2. Have students use a red pencil to vertically subdivide the square shaded for 0.65 into two groups of 5-tenths each. Ask them to look at the partially shaded square that represents 0.65 and decide if the shading covers half or more of the whole square. The red pencil mark will help them compare half of the square to its shaded portion. Since the shaded part extends beyond the red mark or bar, 0.65 must be more than half of a whole square and can therefore be rounded off to a whole square. Have students draw a red ring around the new square that will now be counted with the original two whole squares.

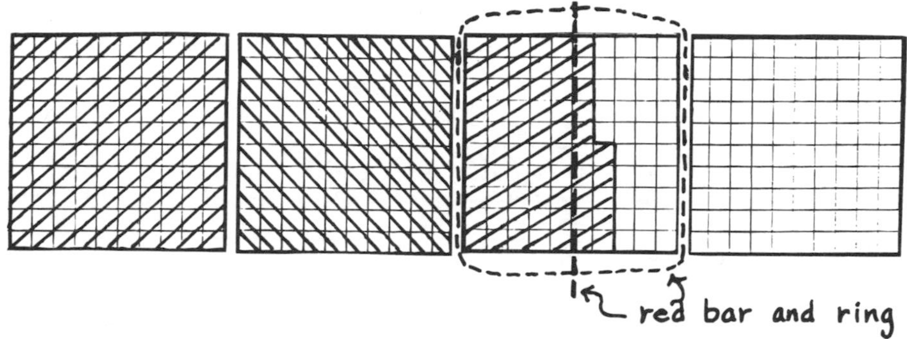

3. Write on the chalkboard: *2.65 rounds to 3, the nearest whole number.* Have students copy the sentence on their worksheet below the shaded squares.

4. Now ask students to show 1.4 by shading another row of squares on the worksheet. One whole square and 4-tenths on a second square should be shaded. Have them draw a red vertical line segment or bar to mark the halfway point on the partially shaded square, then compare half of the square to the shaded portion. Since the shaded 4-tenths covers less than half of the square, it cannot be rounded off to another whole square. The 4 tenths must be removed by marking a large red X across its square. Only the original whole square that was shaded will now be counted.

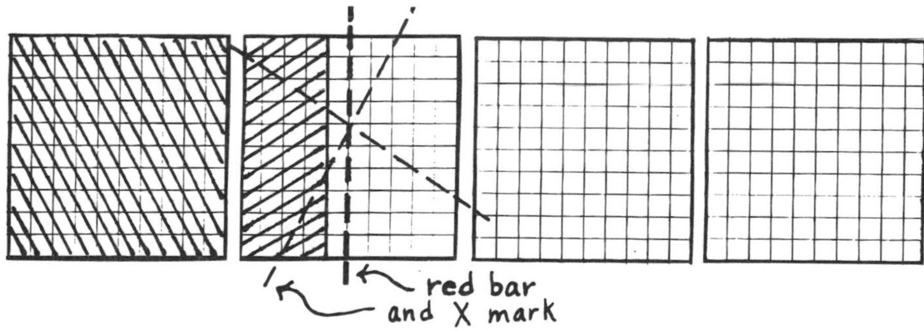

5. Have students write the following sentence below their shaded squares: *1.4 rounds to 1, the nearest whole number.*

6. Repeat steps 1–5 with several other mixed numbers having decimal fractions. The amount of ones used should be limited to 0–3, reserving one extra square for shading the decimal fraction. Be sure to include some numbers that involve only ones and tenths (e.g., 2.6) and others that involve only ones and hundredths (e.g., 1.09). Students should do the necessary shading and comparing for each number, then write a sentence that describes their rounding results.

7. *To round mixed numbers having common fractions:* Give each pair of students 2–3 copies of Fraction Worksheet NNR-7.2b and a red pencil. Write numbers in the small boxes on the worksheet to number the items as needed. Ask students to show 2 and 3-fourths on their worksheet. Have them use their regular pencils to shade two whole unit bars on their worksheet to show the 2 ones. They should then subdivide another whole bar into four equal parts and shade three of the parts to show the 3-fourths of one.

8. Have students use a red pencil to subdivide the whole bar shaded for 3-fourths into 2 halves. Ask them to look at the partially shaded bar and decide if the shading covers half or more of the whole bar. The red pencil mark or bar will help them compare half of the whole bar to its shaded portion. Since the shaded part extends beyond the red mark, 3-fourths must be more than half of a whole bar and can therefore be rounded off to a whole bar. Have students draw a red ring around the new bar that will now be counted with the original two whole bars.

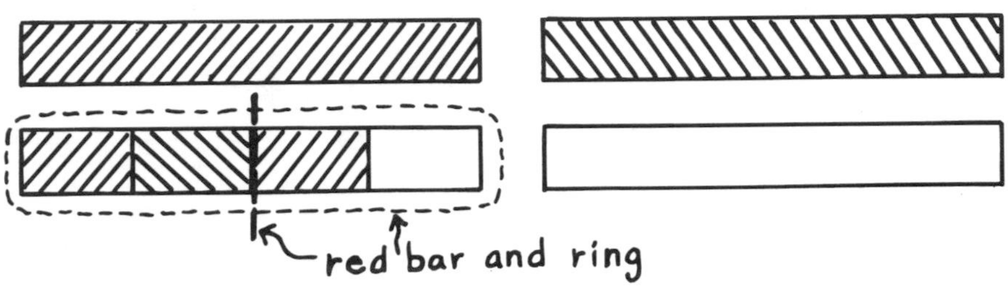

9. Write on the chalkboard: *2 and 3-fourths rounds to 3, the nearest whole number.* Have students copy the sentence on their worksheet below the shaded bars.

10. Now ask students to show 1 and 1-third by shading another set of bars on the worksheet. One whole bar and 1 of 3 equal parts of another bar should be shaded. Have them draw a red vertical line segment or bar to mark the halfway point on the partially shaded bar, then compare half of the bar to the shaded portion. Since the shaded 1-third covers less than half of the whole bar, it cannot be rounded off to another whole bar. The 1-third must be removed by marking a large red X across its bar. Only the original whole bar that was shaded will now be counted.

11. Have students write the following sentence below their shaded bars: *1 and 1/3 rounds to 1, the nearest whole number.*

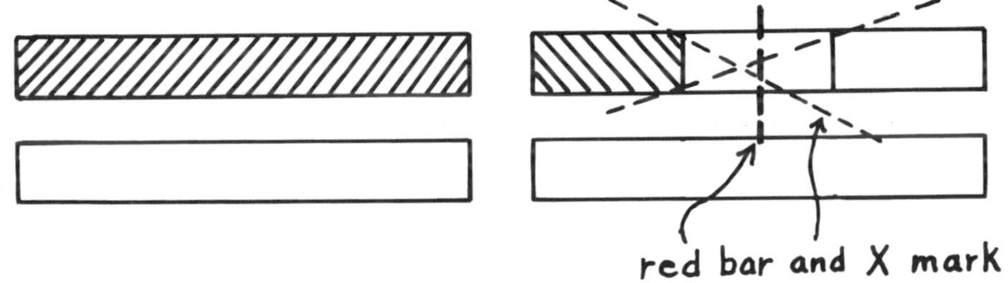

12. Repeat steps 7–11 with several other mixed numbers having common fractions. The amount of ones used should be limited to 0–3, reserving one extra bar for shading the common fraction. Use fractional part sizes such as halves, thirds, fourths, fifths, sixths, and eighths. Students should do the necessary shading and comparing for each number, then write a sentence that describes their rounding results.

NAME ______________________________ DATE ____________________

WORKSHEET NNR-7.2A
Rounding with Diagrams Using Decimal Fractions

Shade the unit squares to show mixed numbers with decimal fractions. Round to the nearest whole number.

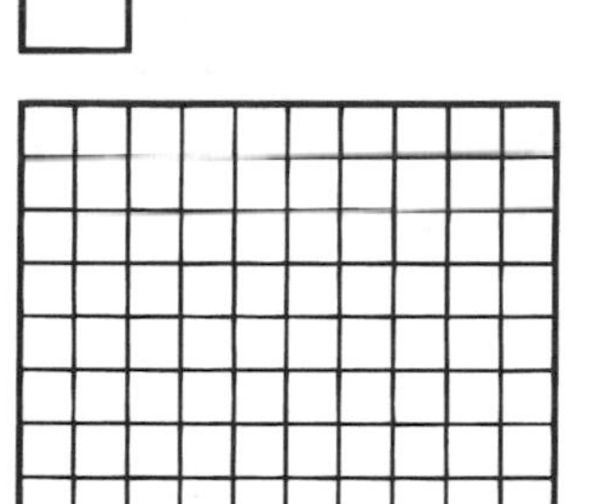
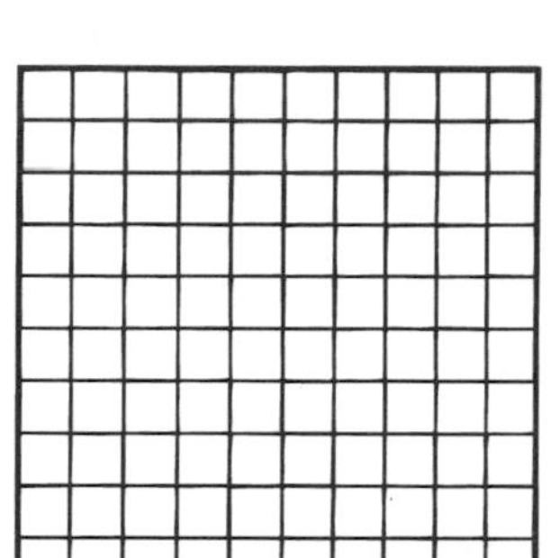
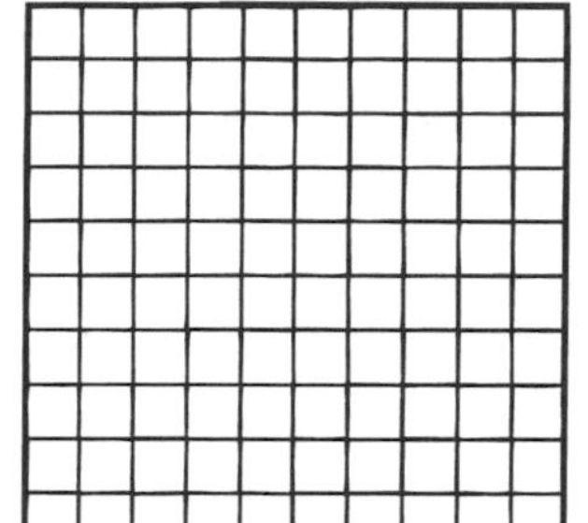
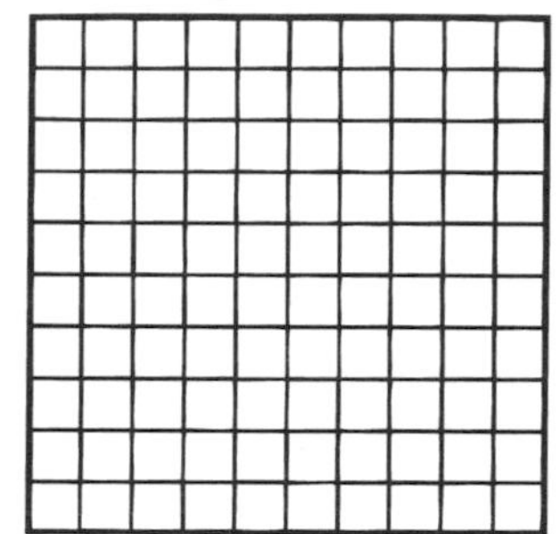

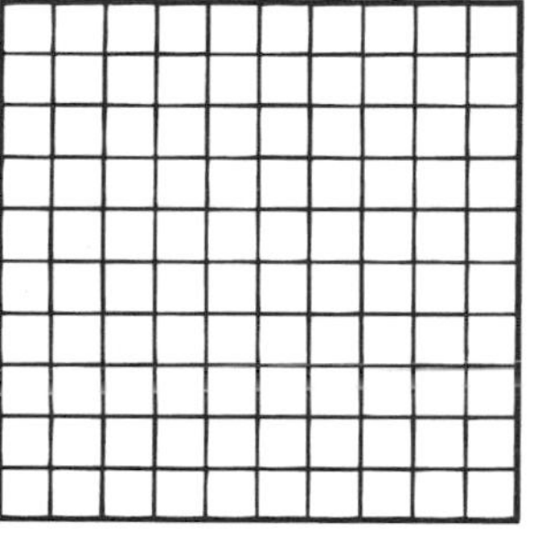
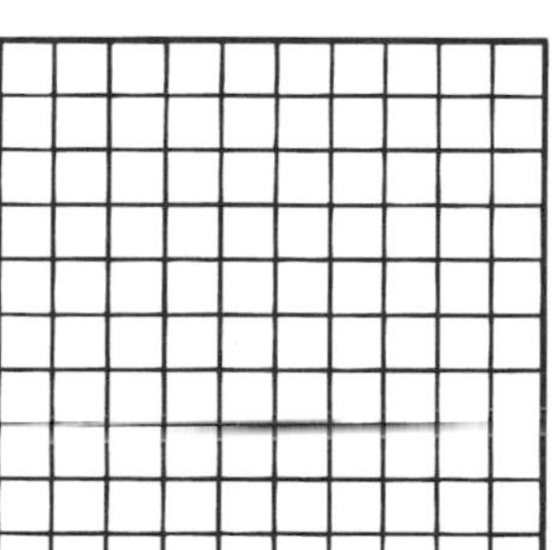
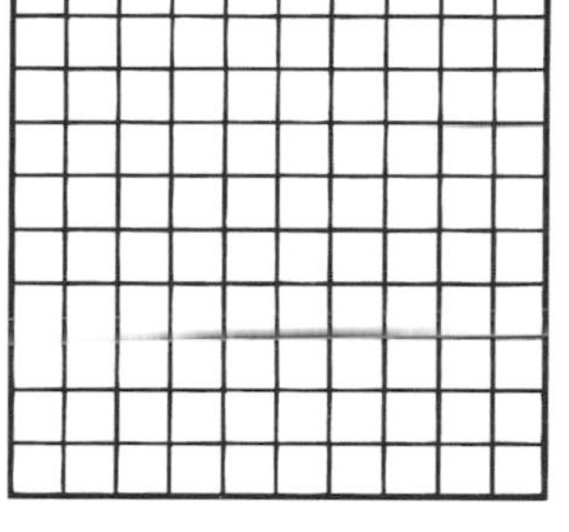
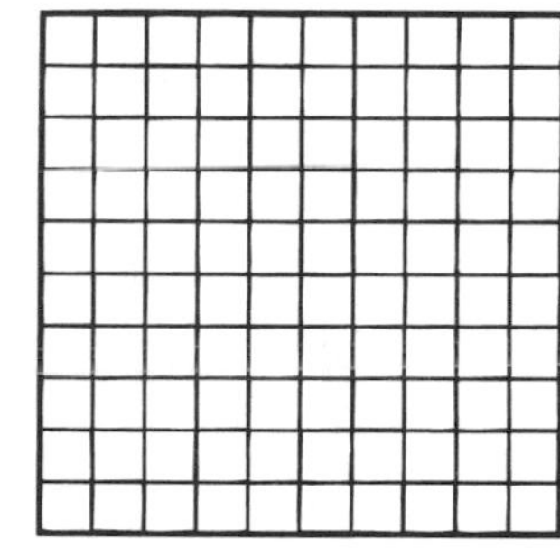

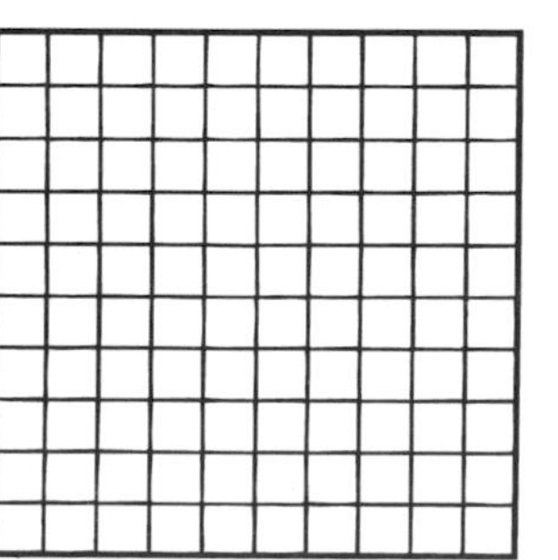
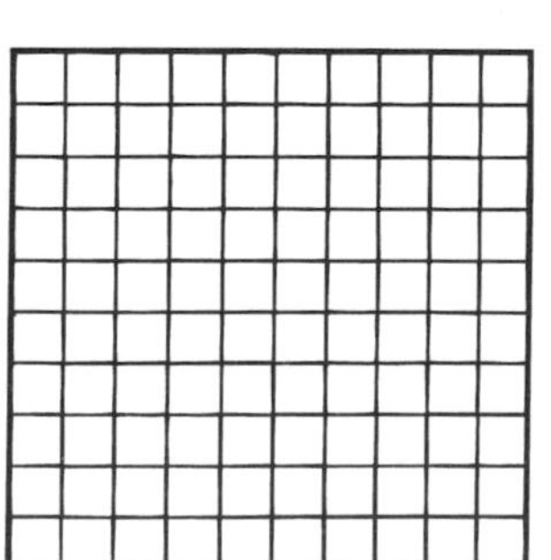

NAME ____________________ DATE ____________

WORKSHEET NNR-7.2B
Rounding with Diagrams Using Common Fractions

Shade the unit bars to show mixed numbers with common fractions. Round to the nearest whole number.

Activity 3: ROUNDO

(Cooperative Groups)

Materials: Sets of 20 playing cards each (described in steps 1–2 below)
Numeral cards for 0–4

Management: Teams of 4 students each (20 minutes)

Directions:

1. Give each team of students a set of 20 playing cards, each containing a mixed number, and four additional cards, each containing one of the whole numbers 0–4. The cards may be made with small index cards and colored markers. Write the whole numbers on the numeral cards in one color of marker and the mixed numbers on the playing cards in another color.

2. The mixed numbers on the playing cards may involve decimal fractions or common/improper fractions, depending on which type is being studied. If students are reviewing both types together, you might wish to combine the two sets into one set of 40 cards. Here are two possible sets of numbers to use, one for decimal fractions and one for common/improper fractions. Some of the numbers will be less than one to provide practice in rounding to 0 or 1.

Numbers with decimal fractions

0.09	0.45	0.3	0.10	0.59	0.9	1.40	1.06	1.8	1.50
2.39	2.08	2.7	2.59	3.20	3.00	3.5	3.99	4.10	4.36

Numbers with common/improper fractions

$\frac{3}{8}$	$\frac{3}{7}$	$\frac{1}{3}$	$\frac{2}{5}$	$1\frac{1}{5}$	$1\frac{5}{12}$	$\frac{7}{8}$
$\frac{3}{4}$	$1\frac{8}{8}$	$2\frac{1}{6}$	$1\frac{14}{10}$	$2\frac{4}{5}$	$2\frac{7}{9}$	$2\frac{5}{4}$
$1\frac{2}{3}$	$3\frac{5}{5}$	$3\frac{8}{11}$	$4\frac{2}{6}$	$4\frac{3}{8}$	$3\frac{3}{10}$	

3. Each team should shuffle, then deal out all of their playing cards. Each person should receive 5 cards (or 10 with the combined sets). The five numeral cards containing 0–4 should be placed on the table in a row with about 2 inches between adjacent cards. These cards will serve as category cards for the playing cards.

4. Students will take turns placing a playing card near the correct numeral or category card. The number on a playing card must be rounded to the nearest whole number, then placed near the numeral card showing that whole number. For example, 1.75 (or 1 and 3/4) rounds to 2, so the 1.75 (or 1 and 3/4) card should be placed near the 2 numeral card.

5. If a player is not sure where to place a card on a particular turn, other students on the team may help, but only by explaining *how* to round the specific number on the card. They should not tell what the final rounded answer will be. The player must make that decision, then place the card correctly. No student should take over another student's playing cards.

6. The game is over when all cards have been placed correctly. The teacher might serve as the *judge of correctness* when needed.

OBJECTIVE 8: Find equivalent fractions by reduction.

Activity 1: BACKWARD TRADES
(Concrete Action)

Materials: Sets of fraction bars (see Patterns/Grids section for pattern)
Building Mat Pattern Worksheet NNR-8.1
Paper
Pencils

Management: Partners (50 minutes)

Directions:

1. Give each pair of students a set of fraction bars (2 wholes, 4 halves, 6 thirds, 8 fourths, 12 sixths, 16 eighths, and 24 twelfths) and a building mat. It is assumed for this activity that students have already worked with fraction bars and have used them to find equivalent fractions where a larger part size (i.e., a smaller denominator) has been traded for two or more equal parts of a smaller size (i.e., a larger denominator). For example, students already know how to trade 2-thirds for 4-sixths or 8-twelfths. This particular *trading forward* skill for finding equivalent fractions is developed in Chapter 2.

2. Have students use the fraction bars to show 4-sixths on the building mat. The 4-sixths should be placed on the whole unit bar that is subdivided into six equal spaces so that all four of the fraction bars touch and begin at the left end of the unit bar. The two spaces at the right end of the unit bar should remain empty, i.e., have no fraction bars covering them.

3. Ask students to find a new single fraction bar that covers the same amount of the unit bar as two of the sixths. After they find the needed third, have them place thirds above the unit bar but next to the 4-sixths already on top of the unit bar. Each third must be matched to two of the sixths. Have students repeat the process, placing thirds below the unit bar so that each third matches to each pair of spaces forming the entire unit bar.

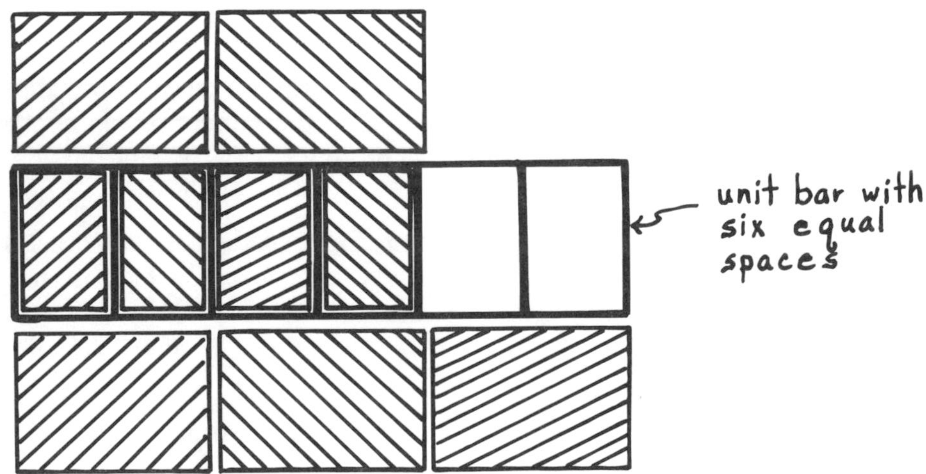

4. Discuss how the lower 3-thirds shows that the unit bar can be resubdivided into 3 equal spaces by regrouping the six original spaces in pairs or by two's. The upper 2-thirds shows that the 4-sixths can also be regrouped in pairs or by two's, so the 4-sixths can be represented by 2 out of the 3 new parts. Thus, a new name for 4-sixths is 2-thirds of the unit bar. This new name requires fewer fraction bars than the original name does. Hence, we have the name for our process: *reduction.*

5. Have students now place 4-eighths on the unit bar that is subdivided into eight equal spaces, placing the four fraction bars together as before at the left end of the unit bar. Ask them to find a new fraction bar that will match to two of the eighths, then place fraction bars of that new part size above and below the unit bar in the same manner as the thirds were placed earlier. The final arrangement of bars should be as follows:

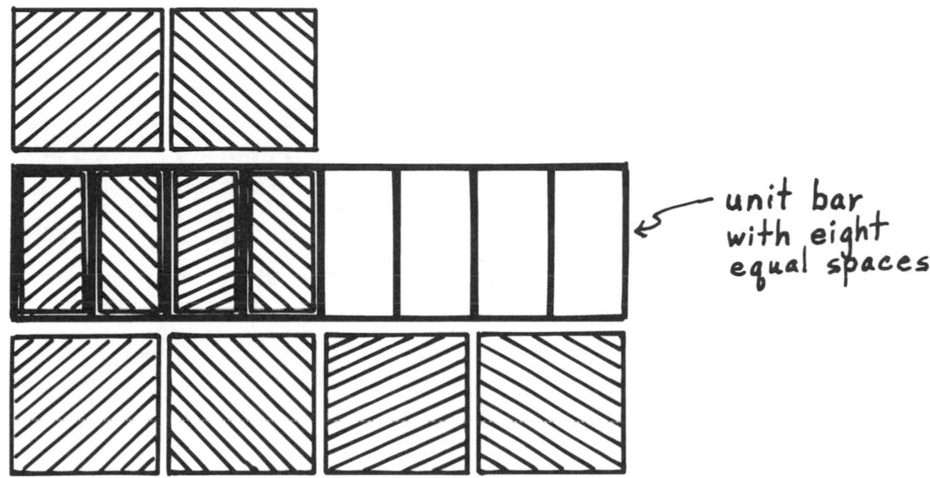

6. Since the 4-eighths can now be represented as 2 new parts out of 4 for the whole bar, a new name for 4-eighths will be 2-fourths of the unit bar. Again, this new name requires fewer parts.

7. Now have the students remove the fourths from the mat but leave the 4-eighths in its original position. Ask students to try to find another new name by matching a new fraction bar to three of the eighths. They must follow the same procedure as before, and they should soon discover that such a matching part cannot be found in their fraction bar set.

8. Have them continue by trying to match a single new fraction bar to four of the eighths. Such a match can be found, using the half fraction bar. Another name for 4-eighths, therefore, is 1-half of the unit bar since 4-eighths can be represented by 1 out of 2 parts for the whole unit bar. The final arrangement will have the following appearance:

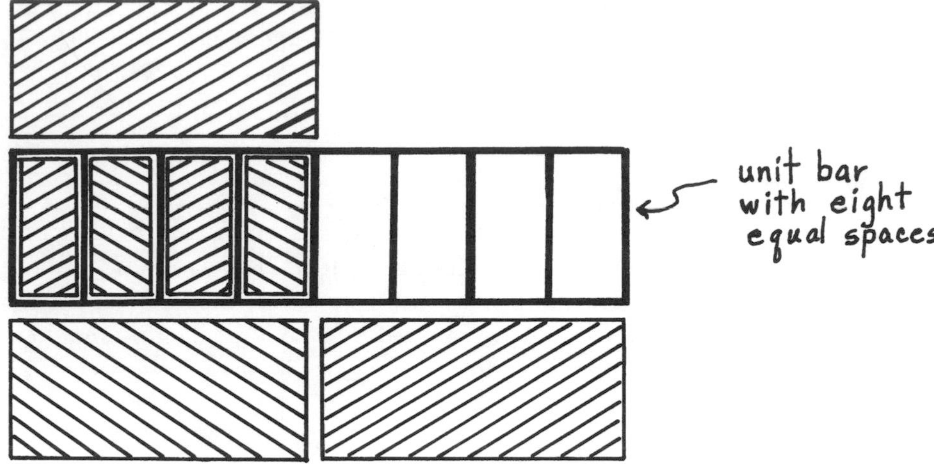

9. Write all the new names for 4-eighths on the chalkboard: *4-eighths = 2-fourths = 1-half of the unit bar.* Have the students write the number sentence on their own papers.

10. Now give students other fractions to try to rename, using the reduction method. Each time they begin with a new fraction, they should explore possible matches by increasing in order the amount of old parts being grouped together: one new part matched to two old parts, then to three old parts, to four old parts, etc., until matches are made that fit the original number of fraction bars as well as the whole unit bar. Encourage students to reduce a fraction to a new form in as many different ways as possible. Have them write number sentences to record their results. Assign reducible common fractions involving fourths, sixths, eighths, or twelfths. Also use a few fractions that cannot be reduced, such as 5-eighths, 3-fourths, and 7-twelfths. Students should explore matches for this type the same way they do for the reducible type.

Activity 2: PICTURING REDUCTION

(Pictorial Action)

Materials: Reduction Worksheet NNR-8.2
Red pencils
Regular pencils

Management: Partners (50 minutes)

Directions:

1. Give each pair of students two copies of Reduction Worksheet NNR-8.2 and a red pencil. Write numbers in the small boxes on the worksheet to number the items as needed.

2. Have students show 3-sixths by subdividing the first unit bar on the worksheet into six equal spaces and shading three of the spaces. The three shaded spaces should be adjacent to each other and begin at the left end of the unit bar. This is done to facilitate later groupings of the shaded spaces.

NAME ______________________________ DATE ____________________

WORKSHEET NNR-8.1
Building Mat Pattern for Backward Trades

3. Tell students to place tick marks along the upper edge of their diagram to show where they wish to separate the spaces in order to form different groups. For example, counting from the left end of the diagram for 3-sixths, students might place a tick mark after the second, fourth, and sixth spaces. Since there is a tick mark at the right end of the unit bar, this tells us that the *whole unit bar* could be resubdivided into three equal parts or grouped by two's. There is no tick mark, however, at the right end of the *shaded* spaces, so we know that the three shaded spaces cannot be grouped by two's.

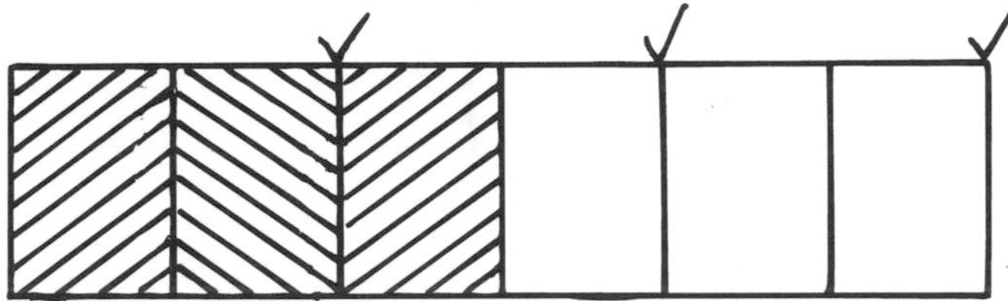

4. Ask students to see if they can group the spaces for 3-sixths by three's. When they discover that such a grouping can be done for the whole bar as well as for the shaded spaces, have students use their red pencil to draw an arc above each group of three spaces, beginning at the left end of the bar. Finally, they should draw a large red check mark over the new group that contains the original shaded spaces. An example of the completed diagram is as follows:

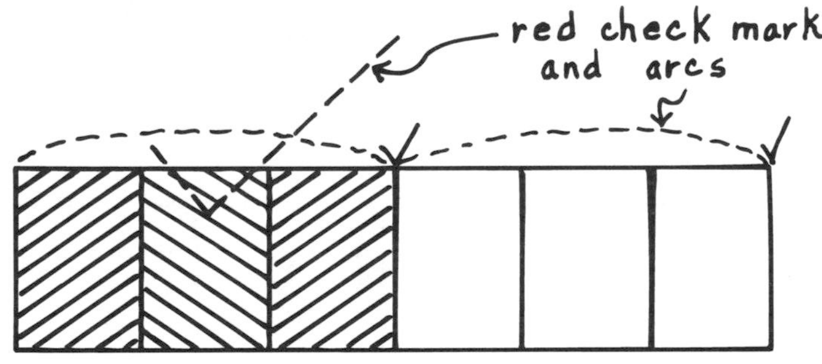

5. Since only one of the two new groups of three spaces each contains all the original shading, the 3-sixths can be renamed as 1-half of the unit bar. Have students write the following sentence under the bar on their worksheet: *3-sixths = 1-half of the unit bar.*

6. Now ask students to show 4-eighths on a new unit bar on their worksheet and to group the spaces by two's. Have them put a red check mark on each new group that is shaded. The new fraction name for 4-eighths becomes 2-fourths, and the finished diagram should appear as follows:

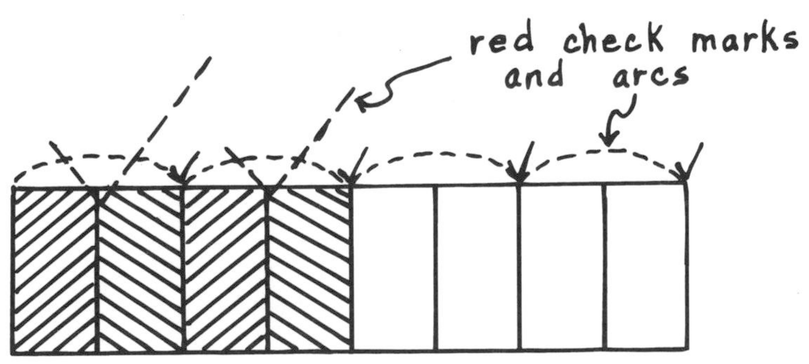

7. Have students repeat the process with 4-eighths, but they should group by four's this time. The new grouping by four's should be done on the same unit bar as the earlier grouping by two's, but the new tick marks and arcs should be drawn at the lower edge of the unit bar.

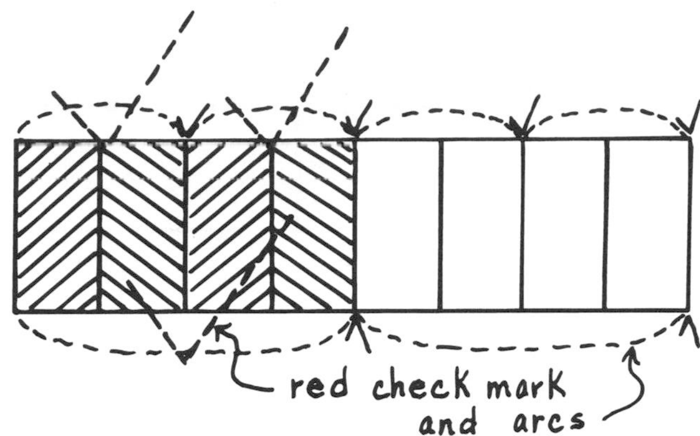

8. This double use of the same unit bar allows students to find more than one new or reduced name for a given fraction without redrawing the original fraction. Have students write the following sentence under their shaded bar to record the reductions: *4-eighths = 2-fourths = 1-half of the unit bar.*

9. Assign other common fractions for students to draw and reduce on the unit bars. Use fractions involving fourths, sixths, eighths, tenths, and twelfths. Include a few that are not reducible (i.e., the tick marks will never come out even for both the shaded spaces and the whole unit bar) like 5-sixths, 3-tenths, and 7-twelfths. Also have students draw and try to reduce some like 2-thirds and 4-fifths. Encourage them to reduce a fraction to more than one new name whenever possible. We are not concerned about finding the *most reduced* name at this time. Activity 3 will emphasize that idea later in a game format. A number sentence stating each reduction shown on a particular bar should be written below that bar on the worksheet. At this stage, you might have the students begin to write their fractions in ratio form, for example, $\frac{3}{6} = \frac{1}{2}$ of 1.

10. After students have drawn diagrams to reduce several different common fractions and have used ratio forms in their number sentences, have them begin to record each reduction in a symbolic notation that shows the type of grouping used. This new number sentence should now be written under the diagram instead of the simpler sentence used previously. As an example, when 4-eighths is grouped by four's, discuss the idea that the shaded spaces form 1 group of 4 spaces and the whole unit bar forms 2 groups of 4 spaces each. The name *4-eighths* describes the shaded *spaces* on the unit bar, whereas the name *1-half* describes the shaded *groups* on the unit bar, but both represent the same shaded amount on the unit bar. The new number sentence for this should be written as follows:

$\frac{4}{8} = \frac{1 \times (4)}{2 \times (4)} = \frac{1}{2}$ of 1.

NAME ______________________________ DATE ____________________

WORKSHEET NNR-8.2
Picturing Reduction

Reduce fractions by shading parts of the unit bars and regrouping the parts.

Activity 3: REDUCTO-MANIA
(Cooperative Groups)

Materials: Worksheet NNR-8.3 for numerator/denominator spinner patterns
Large paper clips for spinner needles
Paper
Pencils

Management: Teams of 4 students each (20 minutes)

Directions:

1. Give each team of students one sheet of spinners (Worksheet NNR-8.3) and one large paper clip. The paper clip serves as a spinner needle when held at the center of the spinner by a pencil point.

2. On each team one pair of students will compete against the other pair. The two pairs will take turns spinning the spinners to get a numerator and a denominator with which to form a fraction. For example, if 4 is spun for the numerator and 20 is spun for the denominator, the playing pair will use the fraction, 4/20. Most fractions formed will be common fractions. Only a few will be improper fractions, but both types can be reduced by the grouping method developed in Activities 1 and 2.

3. On a turn, the playing pair, e.g., pair A, will spin to get the fraction they will use. They must reduce their fraction to a new fraction name that uses smaller numbers and tell their answer to the other pair, e.g., pair B. Pair B will try to reduce the original fraction to lower numbers than pair A did. If they can do so successfully, pair B earns 3 points and pair A earns nothing. If pair B cannot find a more reduced fraction name, pair A will earn 1 point for their original answer. If pair A decides that their fraction *cannot* be reduced and *states that as fact* to pair B, then pair A may earn 5 points if correct. If pair B challenges the statement, however, and is able to reduce the fraction to one with smaller numbers, they will earn the 5 points instead. If pair A is not sure if their fraction will reduce, they may *pass*. Pair B cannot challenge on a pass, so they must now spin to begin their next turn.

4. Players must always be able to explain the steps they use to reduce a fraction. If other team members question the method used by a pair of players, the teacher may serve as judge to determine the method's correctness.

5. The basic strategy of this game is not for a pair to score many points quickly, but to score continuously and to prevent the other pair from scoring higher points on a challenge. Challenges can only be avoided if a pair learns to reduce their fractions to the lowest terms possible!

6. The winning pair is the pair that earns a total of 10 points first.

NAME ______________________ DATE ______________

WORKSHEET NNR-8.3
Spinner Patterns for Reducto-Mania

For Numerators

For Denominators

18
16
15
12
30
24
20

OBJECTIVE 9: Develop the concept of percent.

Activity 1: FINDING PERCENT UNITS

(Concrete Action)

Materials: Base 10 blocks
Paper
Pencils

Management: Partners (40–50 minutes)

Directions:

1. Give each pair of students a set of base 10 blocks (3 flats, 30 rods, 30 small cubes). It will be assumed that students are familiar with the base 10 blocks and already know that ten small cubes make one rod and ten rods make one flat.

2. If students have not done so before, have them discover how many small cubes will cover the flat. Since they only have 30 cubes, they will need to reason out an answer by relating cube to rod and rod to flat. Some commercial base 10 sets have grooves already cut in the flat to show cubes. In that case, have students count to determine that there are 100 cubes forming the flat.

3. Discuss the idea that since the flat contains 100 cubes, each cube can then be considered a hundredth of the flat or one of the 100 cubes. The cube will therefore be given the special numeral name, 1% (read *one percent*) of the flat, which means *one part of each 100 parts.* To show 1% of the flat, we will place one cube on top of the flat to represent one of the possibly *invisible* cubes forming the flat.

4. Ask students to show 40% of their flat. Since one cube is 1% of the flat, they should place 40 cubes on top of their flat to represent 40%. This amount is equivalent to 4 rods placed on the flat.

5. Have students show 76% of their flat. This requires seven rods and six cubes on top of the flat. Remind students that 76% means 76 parts for each 100 parts. Since the flat contains 100 cubes, 76 cubes are needed here. Have students record the following sentence on their own paper: *76% of 100 cubes = 76 cubes.*

6. Repeat the above process with other percents, having students place the required number of cubes or their equivalent in rods and cubes on top of their flat. Students should also write sentences to record what they have built with the blocks.

7. After students have practiced with a *single* flat, have them place two flats together on their desktops. Ask them to now show 20% of the *two* flats, which are equal to 200 cubes when combined. Since 20% means to take 20 for every 100 and each flat is equal to 100 cubes, students need to place 20 cubes (or two rods) on the first flat and another 20 cubes (or two rods) on the second flat. They will then have an amount equal to 40 cubes on the two flats together. Have students record the following sentence on their papers: *20% of 200 = 20 +20 = 40.*

8. Ask students to put 3 flats together to make 300. Have them show 64% of the 300. They should place 64 cubes (or 6 rods and 4 cubes) on each 100 or flat, which yields 3 groups of 64 or 192 cubes total. Students should now record:

64% of 300 = 3 × 64 = 192.

9. Give students other percents to build, using cubes and rods with 1–3 flats. Have them write number sentences to record their results, using either addition as in step 7 or multiplication as in step 8.

10. Challenge: Show 20% of 50 with the blocks. Tell students to cover half of a flat with a sheet of paper. Since a flat is equal to 100 cubes, half of a flat must equal 50 cubes. We want to place some cubes on the exposed half-flat so that we cover a fractional amount of this group of 50 that will be equivalent to the original fractional amount, 20 out of 100, as expressed by 20%. Ask students to find the amount of cubes that needs to be placed on the half-flat in order to meet this condition. Hopefully, students will discover that 10 cubes are needed on the half-flat in order to be equivalent to 20 of the 100 cubes on a full flat. Thus, we can say that 20% of 50 means to find an amount that is the same fractional part of 50 that 20 is of 100. So 20% of 50 must equal 10. Once we know how to find 20% of 50, can we find 20% of 150? Let students explore this idea for a few minutes. They should eventually realize that 20% implies having 20 of the 100 cubes and also 10 of the 50 cubes for a total of 30 cubes. So 20% of 150 equals 30.

Activity 2: PERCENT PICTURES

(Pictorial Action)

Materials: Percent Worksheet NNR-9.2
Red pencils
Regular pencils

Management: Partners (30 minutes)

Directions:

1. Give each pair of students 2–3 copies of Percent Worksheet NNR-9.2. Write numbers in the small boxes at the left margin of the worksheet to number the items as needed.

2. Ask students to lightly shade a large square located on the first row of the worksheet, using a red pencil, to show 50% of that square. Guide students to observe that the square has been marked off in a 10 × 10 grid or 100 small squares. Since 50% means to take 50 of every 100, students only need to shade 50 of the 100 small squares. Students should also record a sentence below the large square that states their results: *50% of 100 = 50 small squares.*

3. Now ask students to show 15% of 400 by shading the necessary large squares on the second row of the worksheet. Translating 15% as 15 of each 100, students should shade with red pencil 15 small squares on each of four large squares. This now forms 4 groups of 15 small squares each. Have students write the following sentence under the row of large squares: *15% of 400 = 4 × 15 = 60 small squares.*

4. Assign several other percents for students to shade in red on their worksheets. Use only whole number amounts for the percents and find the percents with respect to the totals 100, 200, 300, or 400 (1–4 large squares). Have students write number sentences like the one in step 2 or 3 under their shaded squares to record their results.

5. Challenge: Show 80% of 25 by shading part of a large square on the worksheet. To do this problem, students must realize that 80%, or 80 of every 100, can be expressed in smaller, but equivalent amounts. For example, if we split 100 into four equal sets, we must also separate 80 into four equal sets to keep the same relationship. Have students separate a large square on the worksheet into four equal sections by drawing both a vertical and a horizontal red bar through the square. Each red bar separates the square into two equal parts. There are now 25 small squares in each of the four equal sections.

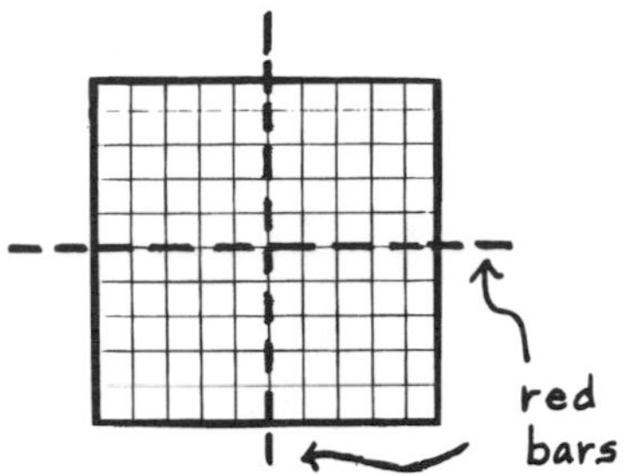

Ask students how many of the small squares must be shaded in each of the four equal sections of the large square so that the fractional part of each *section* that is shaded is equivalent to the fractional part of the *whole square* that is shaded, which is 80 out of 100. Hopefully, they will discover that 20 small squares must be shaded in each section of 25 so that there will be a total of 80 small squares shaded on the whole square. So 80% of 25 equals 20. Now how do we find 80% of 225? Ask students to explore this problem for a few minutes. Eventually they should realize that they need 80 for each of the two 100's and 20 for the 25. Then 80% of 225 will equal 80 + 80 + 20, or 180.

Activity 3: PERCENT ROLL-UP

(Cooperative Groups)

Materials: Dice, Spinner Pattern Worksheet NNR-9.3
Large paper clips as spinner needles
Base 10 blocks

Management: Teams of 4 students each (20 minutes)

Directions:

1. Give each team of students one die, a spinner (Worksheet NNR-9.3) with a large paper clip as the spinner needle, and a set of base 10 blocks (4 flats, 24 rods, 24 cubes).

2. Team members will take turns showing percents of whole numbers with the base 10 blocks. The spinner contains the numerals 1, 2, 3, and 4, and will be used to tell how many flats a player will need. The die will be rolled twice on a turn to indicate the percent assigned to the player; the first roll will tell how many tens and the second roll will tell how many ones to use for the percent number.

3. On a turn a player will spin to find the number of flats to use. For example, if the needle lands on 2, two flats will be placed in front of the player. The die will be rolled twice. If the first roll is 6 and the second roll is 5, the player must show 65% of the two flats with blocks. Since 65% means to find 65 of each 100 and each flat equals 100 cubes, the player will show 65 on each flat, using six rods (tens) and 5 cubes (ones). The total shown on the two flats is 65 + 65, or 130. The player should now state the result in the following way: *65% of 200 is 65 of 100 plus 65 of another 100, or 130 total.*

4. If the other team members agree with this result, the turn passes to the next player. If they do not agree, they must show the player the correct model for the percent before passing to the next player. Play continues as long as time permits.

NAME ________________________________ DATE ______________________

WORKSHEET NNR-9.2
Percent Pictures

Shade the squares to show different percents. Write a sentence below each row of squares to record the results.

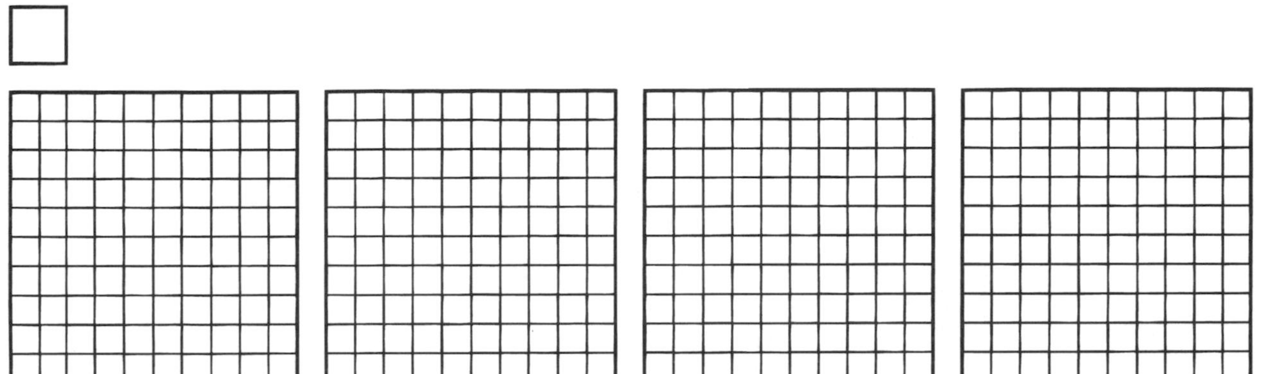

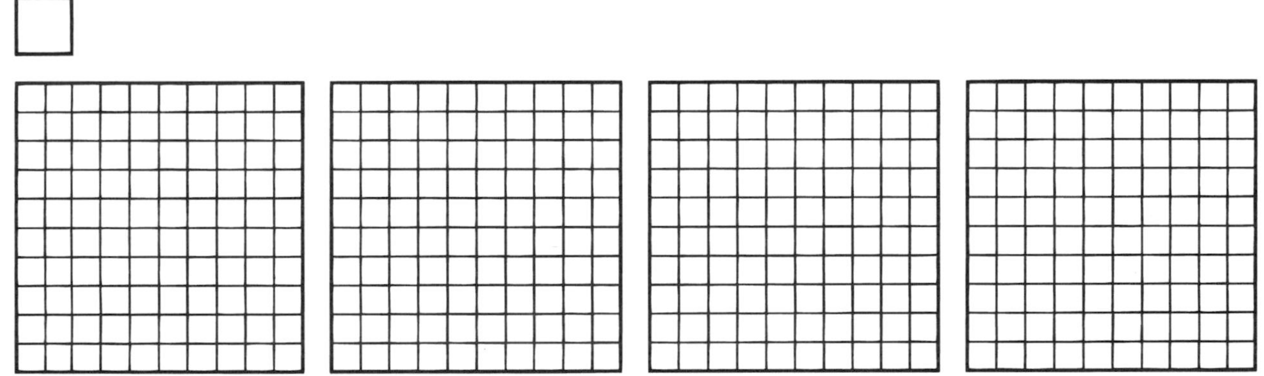

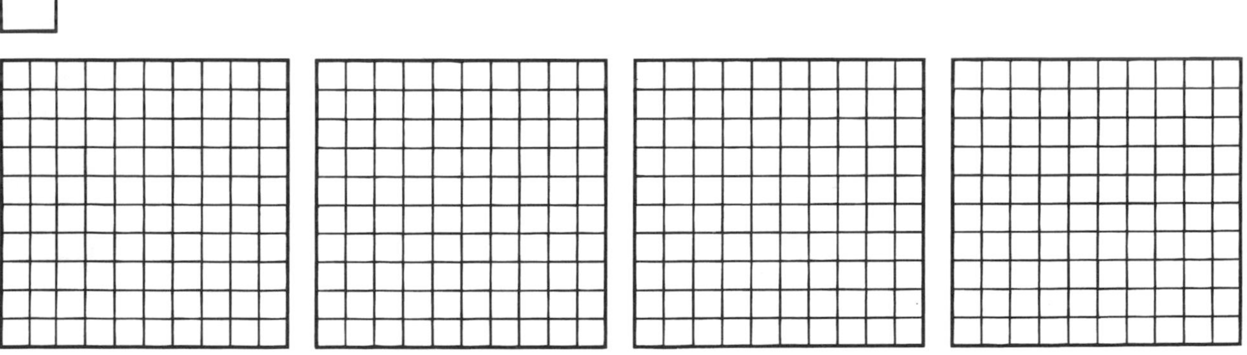

NAME ______________________________ DATE ____________________

WORKSHEET NNR-9.3
Spinner Pattern for Percent Roll-Up

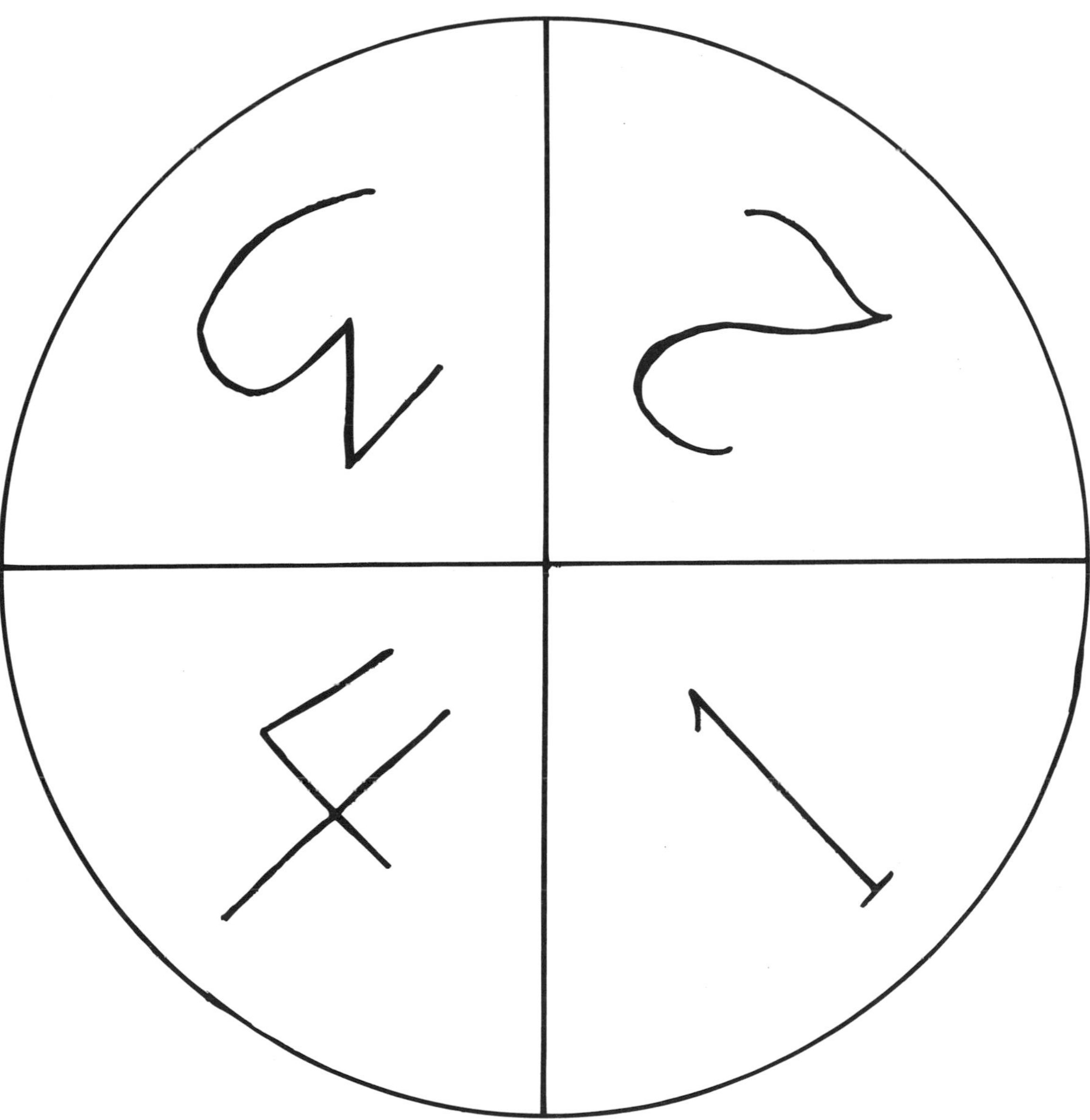

OBJECTIVE 10: Relate fractions, decimals and percents.

Activity 1: RENAMING THE BLOCKS
(Concrete Action)

Materials: Base 10 blocks
Paper
Pencils

Management: Teams of 4 students each (50 minutes)

Directions:

1. Give each team a set of base 10 blocks (1 flat, 20 rods, 100 small cubes). In this activity it is assumed that students understand the concept of a common fraction as relating part to whole and that they are familiar with tenths and hundredths of a unit and their decimal notation.

2. Ask students to find how many small cubes will cover their flat. (100 cubes = 1 flat) Now have students place only a single, small cube on their flat, and ask: *If 100 cubes equal the flat, but you have only one of those cubes, how much of the flat do you have? What is the fractional name for this amount? What is the decimal name for this amount?* The fractional name is written as 1/100 and the decimal name is written as 0.01, both of which are read as *one-hundredth* of the flat. In Objective 9, the term *percent* was defined as *for each 100* and was demonstrated with one cube on the flat also. That is, one cube on the flat shows one cube for each 100 cubes, so the cube is also called *one percent* (1%) of the flat. Thus, a single cube as part of the flat, or 100 cubes, has three different names: 1/100, 0.01, and 1%.

3. Have students place 50 cubes on their flat. Ask them what names the 50 cubes might have when considered part of the flat. Have several students explain their answers. Possible responses: If one cube is 1/100 of the flat, then 50 cubes must be 50/100 of the flat. If one cube is 0.01, then 50 cubes must be 0.50 of the flat. If one cube is 1%, then 50 cubes must be 50% of the flat.

4. Ask if there is another fractional name for the 50 cubes as part of the 100 cubes in the whole flat. Students should be able to suggest several different names. Allow time for exploration. Have them explain each choice, using the blocks. For example, the flat can be separated into two equal groups, each containing 50 cubes. The 50 cubes on top of the flat represent one of those two groups, or one-half of the whole flat. The flat can also be traded for 10 rods or tens, and the 50 cubes can be traded for 5 rods or tens. Then the 50 cubes are shown by 5 of the 10 rods total, or 5-tenths of the flat. The flat can also be separated into four equal groups of 25 cubes, or 2 rods and 5 cubes. The 50 cubes can be shown as two of these four groups, or 2-fourths of the flat. Have students record on their own papers the different names they have found for the 50 cubes as part of the flat: 1/2 of flat; 2/4 of flat; 5/10 of flat; 50/100 of flat; 0.50 of flat; 50% of flat.

5. Now have students explore different names for 20 cubes as part of the flat. They should consider trading the cubes for rods, then grouping the rods as a pair. The names should be recorded on the students' papers. Possible names: 20% of flat; 0.20 of flat; 20/100 of flat; 2/10 of flat; 1/5 of flat. Some students might also form 10 groups of 2 cubes each with the 20 and 50 groups of 2 cubes each with the 100 cubes in the flat. This will give them the name, 10/50 of the flat.

6. Have students continue to search for names for different amounts of cubes placed on their flat. Here are some amounts of cubes to explore and possible names for them when compared to the whole flat. The names in brackets are those less likely to be found through trading or regrouping because of the small group sizes used. Do not expect students to discover all possible names listed below for a particular amount. Just encourage them to look for different groupings using equal set sizes.

25 cubes—25%; 0.25; 25/100; 1/4; [5/20]
30 cubes—30%; 0.30 or 0.3; 30/100; 3/10; [6/20]
5 cubes—5%; 0.05 ; 5/100; [1/20]
75 cubes—75%; 0.75; 75/100; 3/4; [15/20]
15 cubes—15%; 0.15; 15/100; [3/20]
90 cubes—90%; 0.90 or 0.9; 90/100; 9/10
40 cubes—40%; 0.40 or 0.4; 40/100; 4/10; 2/5; [8/20]; [20/50]; [10/25]
60 cubes—60%; 0.60 or 0.6; 60/100; 6/10; 3/5; [12/20]; [30/50]; [15/25]
100 cubes—100%; 1.00 or 1; 100/100; 10/10 ; 2/2; 5/5; [20/20]; [25/25]; [50/50]

Activity 2: PICTURING EQUIVALENT FORMS

(Pictorial Action)

Materials: Equivalence Worksheet NNR-10.2
Colored pencils (red and blue)
Regular pencils

Management: Partners (50 minutes)

Directions:

1. Give each pair of students 2–3 copies of the squares worksheet, a red pencil, and a blue pencil. Write numbers in the small boxes on the worksheet to number the items as needed. Have students observe that each large square is 10 × 10 and thus contains 100 small squares or ones. It is assumed in this activity that students know abstractly how to find equivalent common fractions through reduction.

2. Ask students to shade 35 ones on the first large square on the worksheet. This can be done by shading 3 rows of 10 ones and 5 more ones. Have them list under the large square the more obvious names for the 35 shaded ones when they are compared to the entire large square: 35% or 0.35 or 35/100.

3. Have students shade 60 ones on the next large square. This can be done by shading 6 rows of 10 ones. Ask students to list under the square the three basic names for the 60 ones as part of the total 100. These names are 60%, 0.60, and 60/100.

4. Now ask them to find other fractional names that are equivalent to 60/100, but that use smaller numbers in the numerator and denominator. Some suggestions might be 3/5 and 6/10. Does this mean that 3/5 and 6/10 are also names for the 60 shaded ones on the large square? Have students confirm 3/5 as a new name by using their red pencil to draw red bars across their large square so that the 60 shaded ones are subdivided into three equal groups and the whole square is subdivided into five equal groups. Then have them confirm 6/10 as a new name by drawing blue bars across the same square to form 6 equal, shaded groups out of 10 total groups for the square. Thus, 3/5 and 6/10 must be equivalent to 60%, 0.60, and 60/100, since they all compare the same set of 60 ones to the 100 ones. Have students list the two new names with the others under the square showing the 60 shaded ones.

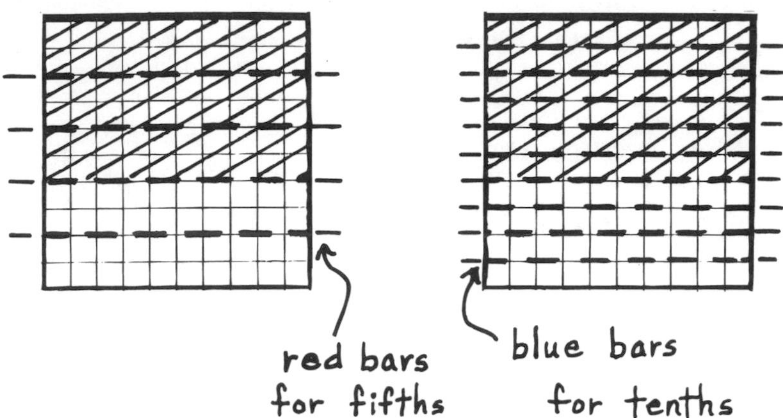

5. Now assign several other amounts of small squares or ones for students to shade on the large squares. For each amount, they should first list the three basic comparison names like those given in step 3. Then they should abstractly find two simpler/reduced names for the common fraction name. They must confirm their two new common fraction names by subdividing the large square and its shaded section with the red pencil to show one of the fractions and with the blue pencil to show the other fraction. All names found should be written under the appropriate square.

6. Here are some possible amounts of ones to be shaded and named by students; typical names are also listed with the amounts:

50 ones—50%; 0.50; 50/100; 1/2; 2/4; 5/10

10 ones—10%; 0.10 or 0.1; 10/100; 1/10; 2/20 (each row of 10 must be split in half in order to have 20 groups)

75 ones—75%; 0.75; 75/100; 3/4; 15/20

80 ones—80%; 0.80; 80/100; 4/5; 8/10; 16/20

100 ones—100%; 1.00 or 1.0 or 1; 100/100; 10/10; 2/2; 5/5

35 ones—35%; 0.35; 35/100; 7/20; no other possible

8 ones—8%; 0.08; 8/100; 2/25 (colored subdivision marks may not be straight or in just one direction for this one); 4/50 is not reasonable to draw on squares of this size

25 ones—25%; 0.25; 25/100; 1/4; 5/20; 2/8 (a special challenge to draw since students must use groups of 12.5 ones each; some ones must be split in half)

NAME ______________________________ DATE ______________________

WORKSHEET NNR-10.2
Picturing Equivalent Forms

Find different names for shaded portions of the large squares.

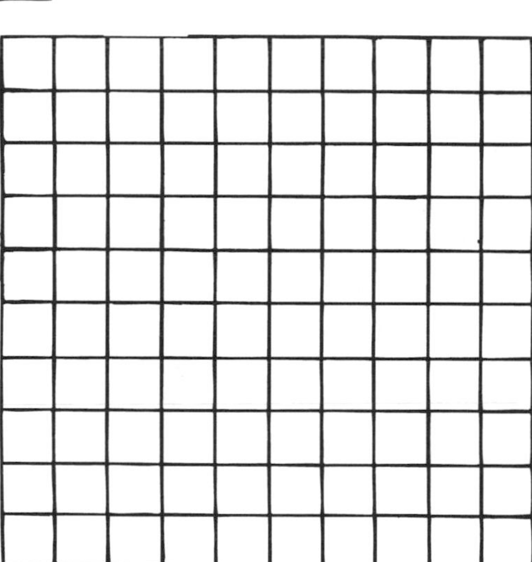

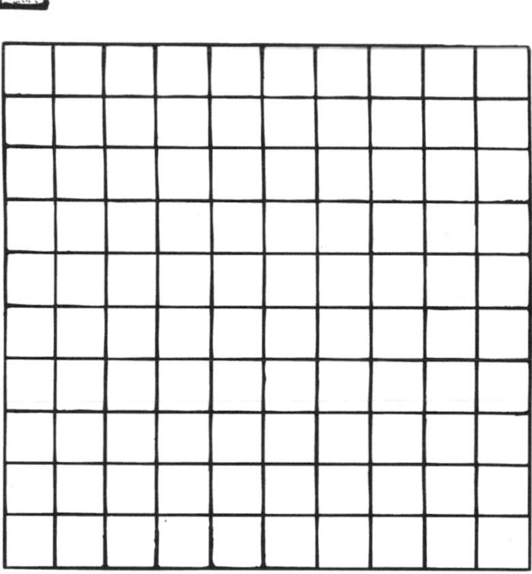

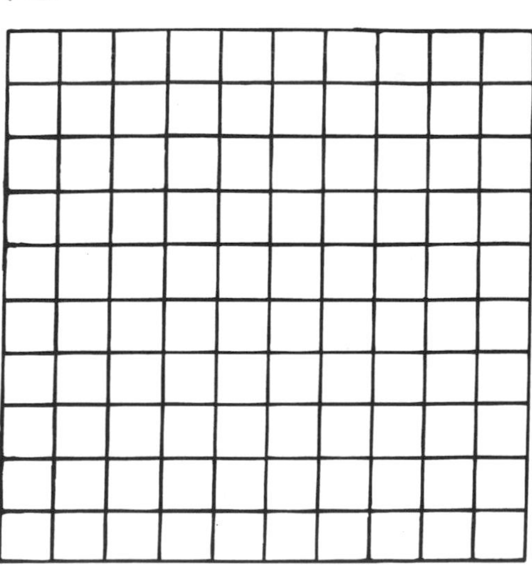

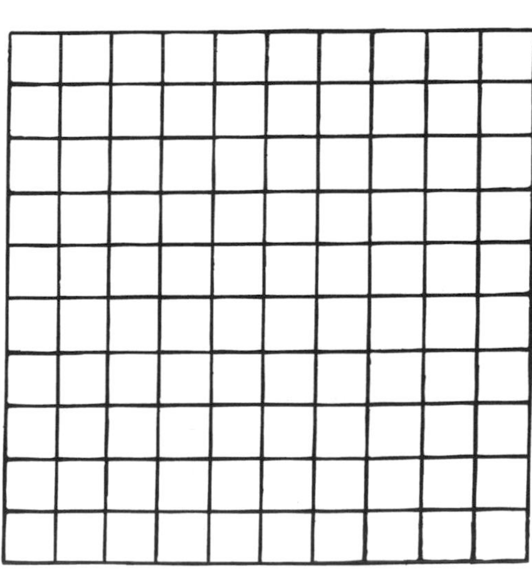

Activity 3: PECULIAR PERCENTS

(Cooperative Groups)

Materials: Bounded Shapes Worksheet NNR-10.3
Pencils

Management: Teams of 4 students each (30 minutes)

Directions:

1. Give each student a copy of Bounded Shapes Worksheet NNR-10.3. The worksheet contains six different shapes drawn in the interiors of large squares, along with a 10 × 10 grid equal in size to a large square. Hints have been provided for some of the shapes in order to help students determine the measurements of those particular shapes. It might also be helpful to know that if the 10 × 10 grid were to be laid over a large square and its shape, no small square units of the grid would be split by the edges of the shape except where the edges slope diagonally. In that case, the square units would be split only along their own diagonals.

2. Team members must work together to compare each shape and its square to the 10 × 10 grid in order to determine the percent of the square that is covered by the shape. The chosen percent must then be expressed as a common fraction in lowest terms. Hopefully students will be able to make only an indirect *visual* comparison and reason through what a shape's measurements might be. If necessary, however, they may actually cut out the grid and place it directly on top of a shape in order to count the percent units or small square units in the grid that are covered by the shape.

3. After all teams have finished the worksheet, have them rate their answers to determine the team's *level of accuracy*. Here is the scoring system to use; P represents the correct percent for a shape as stated in the answer key shown below.

If team percent is within interval:	Team will earn:
P ± 10%	3 points
P ± (11% to 20%)	2 points
P ± (21% to 30%)	1 point

If a shape's *common fraction* is correct and properly reduced, the team will earn an *additional point*. A total score of 24 points for the six shapes on the worksheet will indicate the highest level of accuracy for a team.

ANSWER KEY:

Shape	Part of square covered by shape
#1	75% or 3/4
#2	60% or 3/5
#3	75% or 3/4
#4	25% or 1/4
#5	84% or 21/25
#6	58% or 29/50

NAME ______________________ DATE ______________

WORKSHEET NNR-10.3
Peculiar Percents

1

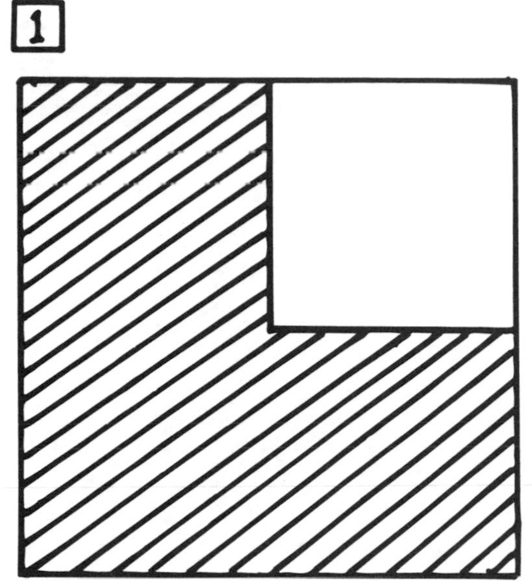

2

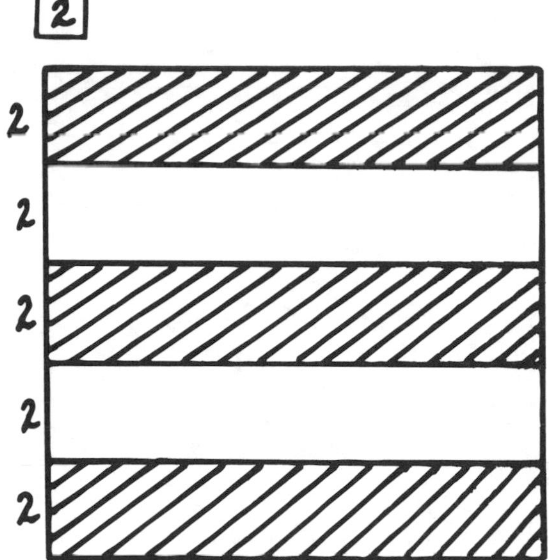

3

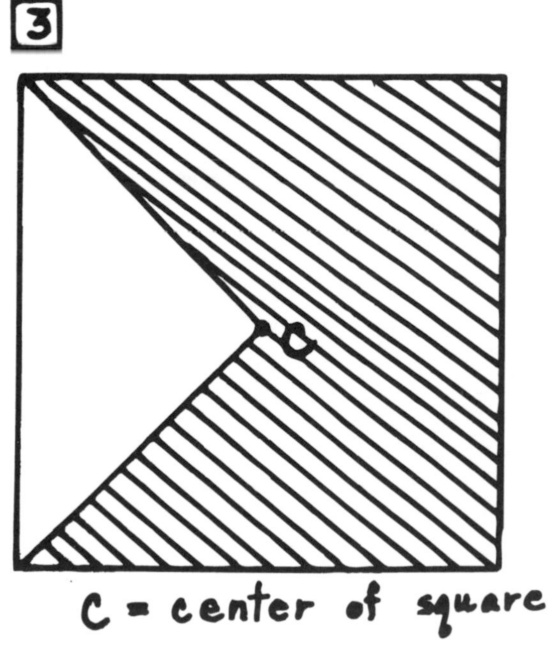

C = center of square

4

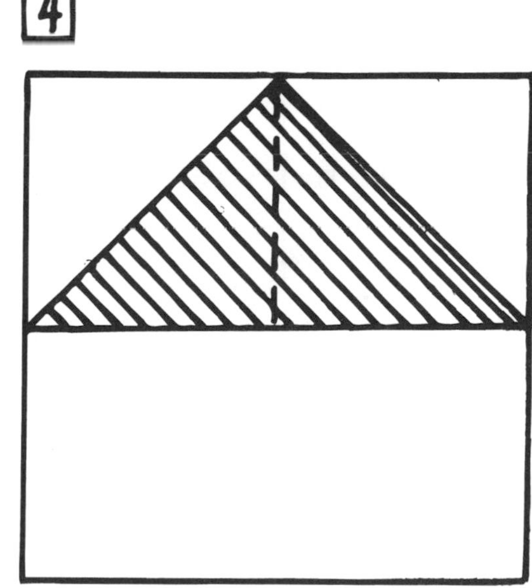

NAME ______________________ DATE ______________

Peculiar Percents (cont.)

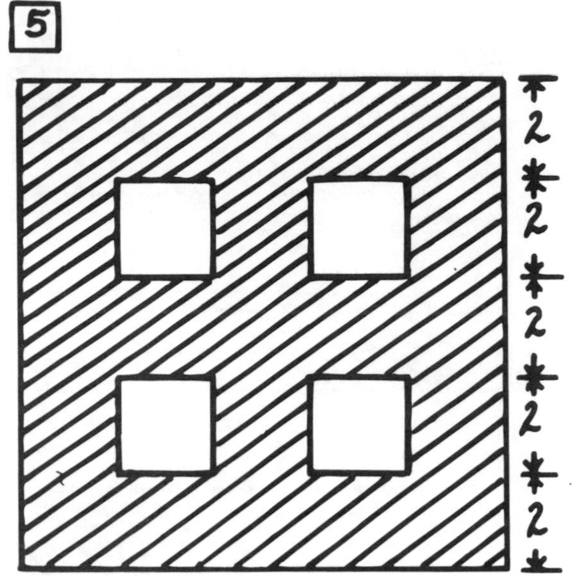

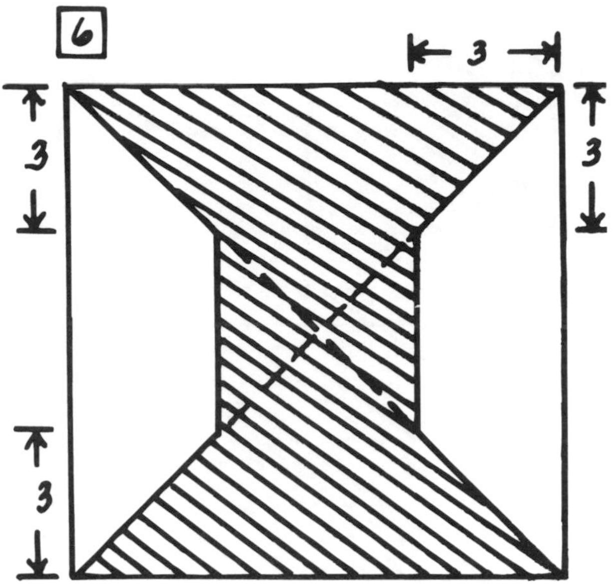

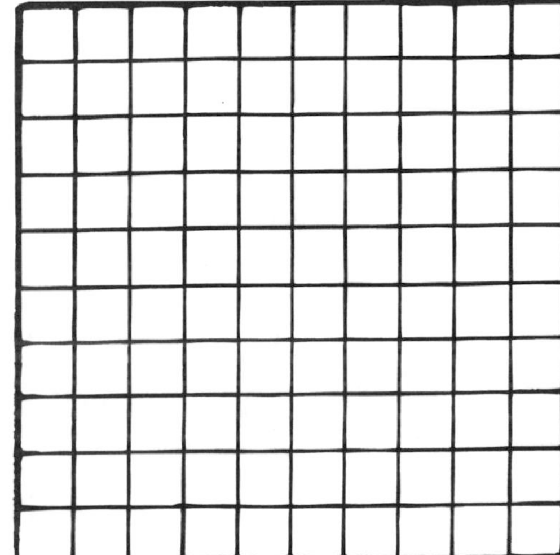

OBJECTIVE 11: Develop the ratio concept and equivalent ratios or proportions.

Activity 1: BUILDING RATIOS
(Concrete Action)

Materials: One-inch paper squares (2 colors)
Ratio building mat (described below in step 1)
Paper
Pencils

Management: Partners (50 minutes)

Directions:

1. Give each pair of students 20 one-inch paper squares in each of two colors and a ratio building mat. The building mat may be made by drawing sections on an 8.5" × 14" sheet of unlined paper and labeling them in the following way:

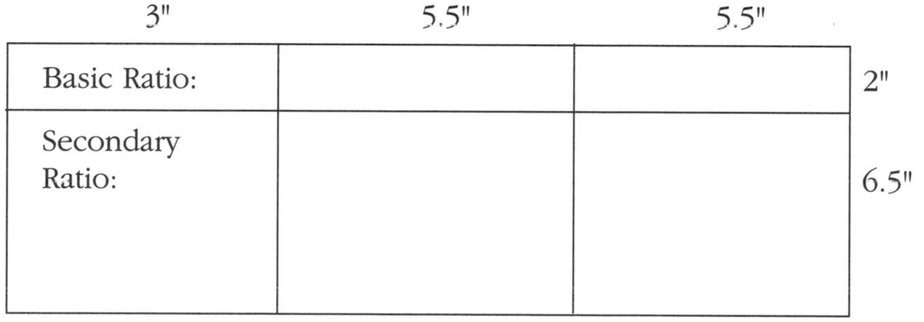

3"	5.5"	5.5"	
Basic Ratio:			2"
Secondary Ratio:			6.5"

2. Different basic or simplified ratios can be shown on the mat by placing one color of paper square in the upper section of the left column and another color of paper square in the upper section of the right column. We will limit the amounts used in the basic ratio to the counting or natural numbers. The two numbers used in a basic ratio will always be relatively prime; that is, they will not have a common divisor greater than one.

3. As an example, have students show the basic ratio of 4 quarters to each dollar by placing 4 paper squares of one color (e.g., blue) in the upper left section of the mat and 1 paper square of the other color (e.g., red) in the upper right section of the mat. For discussion purposes, we will continue to refer to red and blue as our two colors for the paper squares and will choose to place blue squares in the left column and red squares in the right column each time.

4. Discuss how this basic relationship of 4 quarters to one dollar must be maintained, no matter how many dollars or quarters are involved. To show this, have students place two rows of 4 blue squares each in the lower left section of the building mat and two rows of 1 red square each in the lower right section of the mat. Each row across the mat represents 4 quarters being compared to one dollar. The secondary ratio is always built by repeating the basic ratio several times. The building mat should now appear as follows:

Basic Ratio:	□□□□	☒
Secondary Ratio:	□□□□ □□□□	☒ ☒

□ = blue
☒ = red

5. Ask students to find the new secondary ratio for *quarters to dollars* by counting the paper squares in the two lower sections of the mat. Students should have 8 blue squares and 2 red squares. The new ratio is therefore *8 quarters to 2 dollars,* reading from left to right on the mat. The basic ratio and the secondary ratio are placed on the mat in the same order; that is, if we decide to show quarters in the left column and dollars in the right column of the upper level of the mat, then we must keep that order in the lower level also. Have students record the following on their own papers: *4 quarters compare to 1 dollar like 8 quarters compare to 2 dollars.*

6. Assign several other basic ratios for students to show on the upper level of their building mats and then extend to secondary ratios by making two to five rows or copies of the basic ratio on the lower level of the mat. Have them write a sentence like the example in step 5 to describe each result. Use one to five for each number in the basic ratio. The total number of squares used in each column (upper and lower sections combined) is limited to 20, the number of paper squares available in each color. Here are some examples of basic ratios to use: 3 girls to 4 boys; 1 quarter to 5 nickels; 2 pencils to 5 cents; 3 cups to 2 teaspoons; 4 pets to 1 student; 3 stamps to 5 letters.

7. A modified version of the above procedure consists of giving students a basic ratio and one part of a secondary ratio. The missing part of the secondary ratio must then be found. Students would still record their sentences in the same way. As an example, if the basic ratio is *3 girls to 4 boys* and a secondary ratio involves 12 boys, students must discover how many rows of 4 boys each will yield 12 boys total. Since three rows of boys are needed, students must build three rows of 3 girls also to make 9 girls total for the secondary ratio. The final secondary ratio is *9 girls to 12 boys.*

8. After students have had practice with generating a secondary ratio from a given basic ratio, reverse the procedure. Give them a secondary ratio and have them try to find the basic ratio. See step 2 above for the requirements for a basic ratio.

9. As an example, ask students to show *8 cats to 12 dogs* as the secondary ratio on the lower level of their building mat. Since *cats* are mentioned first in the expression, eight blue squares should be placed in the left column. 12 red squares should then be placed in the right column to represent *dogs.*

10. Students must now try to form rows of squares so that the same number of rows is seen in both columns and the number of blue (or red) squares found in one row is also found in each of the other rows. Students might form two rows first, showing 4 blue and 6 red squares in each row. Since the blue squares and red squares in one row can still be regrouped into two groups of 2 blue and two groups of 3 red, that is, 4 and 6 can both be divided by 2, students must separate their blue and red squares into more rows. Hence, the final arrangement for the secondary ratio becomes four rows of 2 blue squares and 3 red squares each.

11. This last combination of 2 blue squares and 3 red squares per row is the basic ratio being sought and should be *copied* by placing 2 new blue squares in the left column and 3 new red squares in the right column of the upper level of the mat. Students should now write the following: *8 cats compare to 12 dogs like 2 cats compare to 3 dogs.*

Basic Ratio:	□ □	☒ ☒ ☒
Secondary Ratio:	□ □ □ □ □ □ □ □	☒ ☒ ☒ ☒ ☒ ☒ ☒ ☒ ☒ ☒ ☒ ☒

□ = blue
☒ = red

12. Have students simplify several other secondary ratios to basic ratios and write sentences for their results like the sentence given in step 11. Here are some possible secondary ratios to try: 12 students to 3 boxes of donuts; 15 guppies to 10 goldfish; 6 wieners to 15 buns; 4 cars to 12 people.

13. A simpler version of this last type of exercise involves giving students a secondary ratio and one part of the basic ratio. Students must then find the missing part of the basic ratio. They would still record their number sentences in the same way. As an example, if a secondary ratio is given as *4 cars to 12 people* and the basic ratio is known to have only one car, students must discover how many rows of cars might be built with the four cars, using one car per row. Since four rows of cars may be built, the 12 people must also be arranged in four rows, which results in 3 people per row. Therefore, the basic ratio is *1 car to 3 people.*

Activity 2: COMPARING CIRCLES TO TRIANGLES

(Pictorial Action)

Materials: Ratio Worksheet NNR-11.2
Pencils

Management: Partners (30–40 minutes)

Directions:

1. Give each pair of students a copy of Ratio Worksheet NNR-11.2. Basic ratios will be shown on special frames on the worksheet. Students are to find the corresponding secondary ratios by drawing the number of rows indicated on each frame. Secondary ratios will also be given on the worksheet. In such cases, students must apply a *trial and error* strategy to find the corresponding basic ratios. Number sentences will be recorded under each frame that compare the two ratios shown there.

2. Have students work item #1 on the worksheet. The basic ratio is given as *3 circles to 4 triangles.* Two rows are indicated for the secondary ratio by dotted line segments on the frame. Students should therefore copy the basic ratio two times on the frame. The secondary ratio is found to be *6 circles to 8 triangles.* Have students write the following number sentence below the frame: *3 to 4 = (2 × 3) to (2 × 4) = 6 to 8.*

Basic Ratio:	O O O	Δ Δ Δ Δ
Secondary Ratio:	O O O O O O	Δ Δ Δ Δ Δ Δ Δ Δ

3. Now have students work the first item on the worksheet that shows the numbers of the secondary ratio, *15 to 6,* in the columns of the lower level of the frame. They should draw the required 15 circles and 6 triangles on the frame, using the greatest number of rows possible. Students may have to find the number of rows needed by first drawing the circles and triangles on scratch paper. All rows must have the same combination of circles and triangles. For this exercise, three rows of 5 circles and 2 triangles each can be drawn. Students should draw the three rows of circles and triangles on the lower level of the frame, then copy one of those rows on the upper level of the frame to show the basic ratio being sought. The following number sentence should be written below the frame: *15 to 6 = (3 × 5) to (3 × 2) = 5 to 2.*

Basic Ratio:	O O O O O	Δ Δ
Secondary Ratio:	15 O O O O O O O O O O O O O O O	6 Δ Δ Δ Δ Δ Δ

4. Also included on the worksheet are some items where the basic ratio and one number of the secondary ratio are given. Students must find the missing part of the secondary ratio by drawing the required rows of circles or triangles. Other items give the numbers for the secondary ratio and one part of the basic ratio. Students must use the given part of the basic ratio to find how many rows to draw for the two parts of the secondary ratio. The required rows then lead to the missing part of the basic ratio.

5. After students have finished their worksheets, have some of them share their number sentences with the class. Guide students to observe that the numbers in the secondary ratio are always multiples of the numbers in the basic ratio. That is, the numbers in the basic ratio are multiplied by the same factor to find their corresponding numbers in the secondary ratio.

6. Discuss the idea that ratio comparisons might also be recorded with *colons.* For example, *3 to 4 = (2 × 3) to (2 × 4) = 6 to 8* might be written as *3 : 4 = 6 : 8.* This sentence may be read as follows: *3 is to 4 as 6 is to 8.* Have students express each number sentence recorded previously on their worksheets in this new format.

NAME ______________________ DATE ______________

WORKSHEET NNR-11.2
Comparing Circles to Triangles

Complete the boxes below to find equivalent ratios. Write number sentences about what you find.

1.

Basic Ratio:	○ ○ ○	△ △ △ △
Secondary Ratio:	___ ___ ___ ___ ___ ___	___ ___ ___ ___ ___ ___

2.

Basic Ratio:	○	△ △ △
Secondary Ratio:	___ ___ ___ ___ ___ ___ ___ ___ ___	___ ___ ___ ___ ___ ___ ___ ___ ___

3.

Basic Ratio:	○ ○	△
Secondary Ratio:		5

4.

Basic Ratio:	○ ○ ○	△ △
Secondary Ratio:		4

5.

Basic	○ ○ ○ ○	
Secondary Ratio:	16	4

6.

Basic		
Secondary Ratio:	15	6

Activity 3: RATIOS IN ADVERTISING

(Cooperative Groups)

Materials: Merchandising ads from such stores as grocery stores, drug stores, or variety stores
Large construction paper or small posterboards
Glue or transparent tape
Colored markers
Scissors
Calculators (optional)

Management: Teams of 4 students each (50 minutes)

Directions:

1. Give each team several pages of advertisements (typically the mailers that are mailed out to homes each week; they have pictures of the items on sale that week along with their prices). Also provide scissors, glue or tape, 1–2 colored markers, and one sheet of small posterboard or large construction paper for mounting the advertisements.

2. This would be an appropriate time to use calculators if they are available. It is assumed that students already have an understanding of both the cents and decimal notation for money and know how to multiply or divide a money amount in dollars and cents by a whole number.

3. Each team should select and cut out eight different advertisements showing quantities of more than one object for a given price, for example, 10 ballpoint pens for $1.99. The listed price should be cut out as well as the picture.

4. The eight advertisements (pictures with prices) should be arranged and mounted in some way on the construction paper or posterboard.

5. Students should find two ratios for each advertisement they have selected: a single object at its *unit price* (e.g., 1 ballpoint pen for $0.199 rounded to $0.20) and the quantity and price for more objects than the quantity given in the advertisement (e.g., 20 ballpoint pens for $3.98). These two new ratios for quantity vs. price should be recorded with colored marker on the advertisement collage or display next to their corresponding picture and listed price.

6. The team collages might then be presented to the entire class and displayed on the classroom wall.

CHAPTER 2

PATTERNS, RELATIONS, AND FUNCTIONS

INTRODUCTION

This chapter shows students how to work with sequences of shapes or numbers by building sequences, and identifying patterns in the number sequences. Ready-to-use games are used to show students how to recognize and compose parts of patterns. Hands-on activities and games also help students explore division and multiplication, and learn how to find equivalent fractions and patterns of divisibility. Students are introduced to exponents and exponential notation, and are shown how to work with the powers of 2, 3, and 10 through various exercises and games.

OBJECTIVE 1: Extend sequences of whole numbers.

Activity 1: TILE BUILDING

(Concrete Action)

Materials: One-inch square tiles (or one-inch paper squares)
Paper
Pencils

Management: Teams of 2–3 students each (40 minutes)

Directions:

1. Give each team a reclosable plastic bag of about 50 square tiles.

2. Have students build "windmills" with their tiles, building them in order of size with the smallest one first. Show them the following shapes already drawn on a transparency; do not draw the shapes in front of the students. They must decide *how* to build each new windmill for themselves.

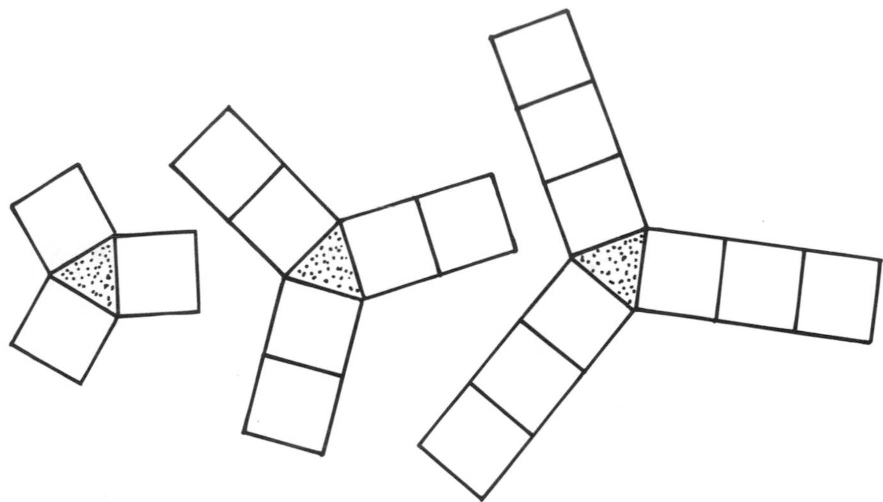

3. Have them make a 2-column table to record their work. Use the headings: *Which Shape* (e.g., write "1" for first shape built) and *Total Tiles in Shape*. The left column for *Which Shape* should show 1, 2, 3, . . . and the right column should show the totals 3, 6, 9, . . .

4. Ask several teams to tell how the first and second shapes are alike and how they are different. (Possible responses: Both shapes have 3 blades; #2 has 1 more tile in each windmill blade than #1 has, or #2 has 2 tiles in each blade instead of 1 tile.) Ask how the second windmill was changed to make the third one. (Responses should be similar to those for #1 and #2.)

5. Ask them to build the fourth windmill (it should have 3 blades with 4 tiles per blade) to the right of the first three.

6. Have some students describe in their own words what each windmill looks like. Encourage the following type of details: *The first shape has 1 tile per blade for 3 blades; #2 has 2 tiles/blade for 3 blades; #3 has 3 tiles/blade for 3 blades; etc.*

7. Now ask the students to predict how the tenth windmill might look, based on their descriptions given in step 6. (Example: *#10 has 10 tiles/blade for 3 blades.*) Have them complete their table through the tenth shape with its total tiles, 3 blades × 10 tiles/blade or 30 tiles. Some students may need to build some of the other windmills (#5– #10) to confirm their predictions of the total tiles needed for each. Discuss how the numbers in the *Total* column change (increase by 3 each time).

8. If appropriate for your class, ask them to try to describe how to find the total tiles needed for making the N-th windmill. The algebraic expression should follow the language pattern used in step 6: *The N-th shape will use N tiles per blade for 3 blades or 3 × N tiles total.*

9. As time permits, lead the class through the building of other sequences of shapes, following the same procedure and questioning used in steps 2–8. Here are some possible sequences to use, along with descriptions of

- how two adjacent shapes are alike/different,
- the type of language needed for step 6, and
- the N-th shape's total tiles.

Example 1: Use as column headings for table: *Which Shape, Red Tiles, Blue Tiles, Total Tiles* (or whatever 2 colors are available in the tiles) [R = red tile; B = blue tile]

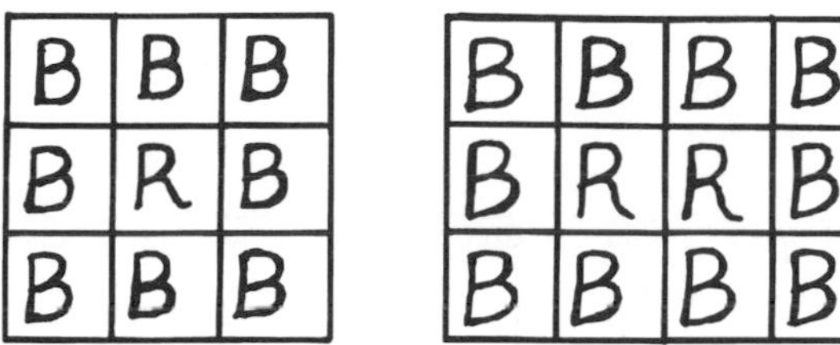

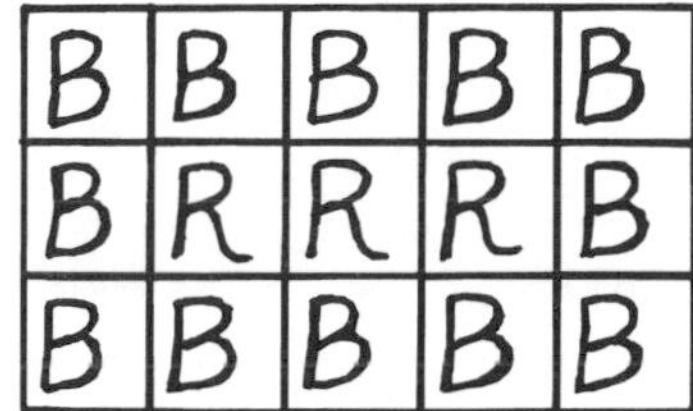

(a) Each new shape to be built uses 1 more red tile and 2 more blue tiles than the previous shape, but all of the shapes have 3 blue tiles on the left end and 3 blue tiles on the right end. (b) Shape #3 has 3 red tiles with 2 blue tiles for each red one plus the 6 blue tiles on the ends. (c) The N-th shape will have N red tiles and 2 blue tiles/red tile plus 6 blue end tiles, or N red + (N × 2 + 6) blue for the total number of tiles. This expression with N should reflect the language used in (b). Do not simplify the expression at this time. Do not write N × 2 as 2N; here N counts the sets of blue tiles, hence should be in the multiplier position. Students need to be able to connect the notation with the process and language as directly as possible.

Example 2: Use as column headings for table: *Which Shape, Towers in Shape, Single Stories, Total Tiles.*

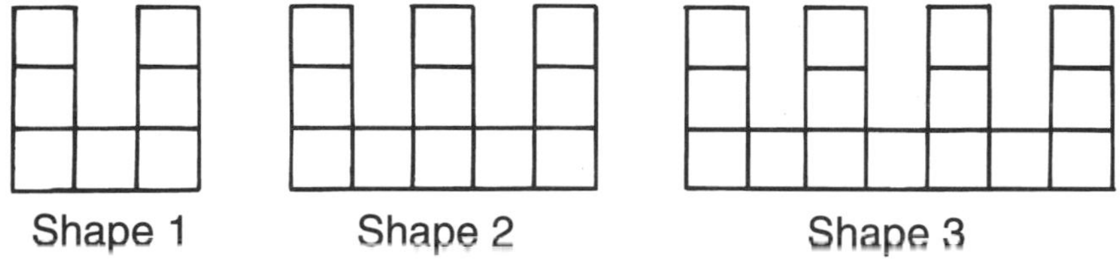

(a) Each new shape has 1 single story and 1 tower of 3 tiles more than the previous shape, but the first shape has 2 towers of 3 tiles and 1 single story between the towers.

(b) Shape #3 has 4 towers of 3 tiles each and 3 single stories.

(c) The N-th shape has N + 1 towers of 3 tiles each and N single stories, or (N + 1) × 3 tiles + N tiles in all.

Activity 2: PATTERN DRAW

(Pictorial Action)

Materials: Paper
Pencils

Management: Partners (30 minutes)

Directions:

1. Follow the procedure used in steps 2–8 of Activity 1 (above), except students will be drawing the shapes rather than building them with tiles.

2. For each sequence discussed, show them the first three shapes of the sequence already drawn on a transparency. Do not allow them to see the shapes being drawn. Deciding how to draw the shapes helps students see the differences in the sequence terms.

3. Show the class the first three shapes of the first sequence. Have the students draw the sequence of shapes on their own paper.

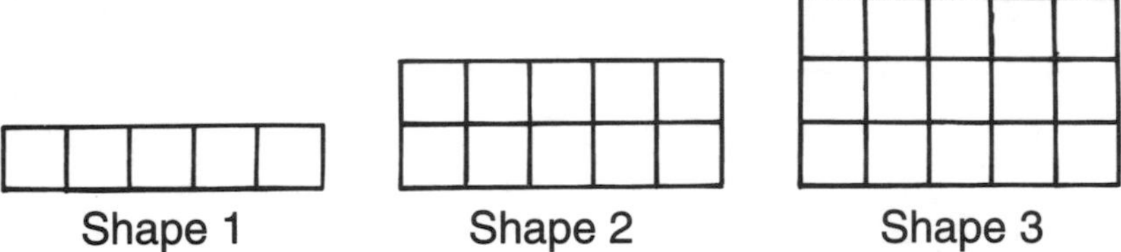

Shape 1 Shape 2 Shape 3

4. Discuss likenesses and differences: *Shape #2 has 1 more row of 5 than #1 has, etc.* Have students describe each shape: *#1 has 1 row of 5 squares; #2 has 2 rows of 5; #3 has 3 rows of 5.*

5. Ask students to draw the fourth shape according to the changes they have seen. (#4 should have 4 rows of 5 squares.) Then have them predict how the tenth shape will look. (#10 should have 10 rows of 5 squares each.)

6. All should now complete a table for the sequence, using column headings (left to right) *Which Shape* and *Total Squares*. The left column will have 1, 2, 3, . . . and the right column will have 5, 10, 15, . . . Students should record information for the first ten shapes of the sequence. Discuss how the numbers in the *Total* column change (increase by 5 each time).

7. If appropriate, ask the students for an algebraic expression that will describe the N-th shape in the sequence. Following the language used for earlier shapes, the N-th shape should have N rows of 5 squares each, or $N \times 5$ squares total. Use $N \times 5$ at first because N is the counter of the rows and hence should be written in the multiplier position.

8. Continue to show sequences to the class, following the procedure and questioning of steps 2–7 of this activity. Here are two possible sequences to discuss, along with descriptions of (a) how two adjacent shapes are alike/different, (b) the type of language needed, and (c) the N-th shape's total tiles. Both require a two-column table with the headings: *Which Shape* and *Total Squares*. Multiple ways to view each sequence are presented for your information. Develop whatever view(s) the students happen to choose.

Example 1:

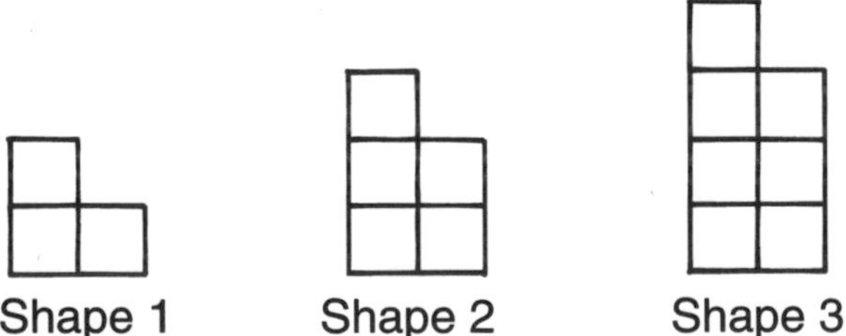

Shape 1 Shape 2 Shape 3

(a) *View 1:* Some students see each new shape as having 1 more row (left to right) of 2 squares than the previous shape with each shape having a single square on top. *View 2:* Others notice that each new shape has 1 more square added to the top of each column of the previous shape and that the first shape starts with one column of 2 squares and another column of 1 square.

(b) *View 1:* Shape #1 has 1 row of 2 squares and a single square on top; #2 has 2 rows of 2 squares each with 1 square on top; #3 has 3 rows of 2 squares each with 1 square extra. *View 2:* Shape #1 has a 2-square column with a 1-square column; #2 has 1 square added to each of #1's columns; #3 has 2 squares added to each of #1's columns.

(c) *View 1:* The N-th shape will have N rows of 2 squares each with 1 extra square, making a total of (N × 2 + 1) squares. *View 2:* The N-th shape will have (N – 1) squares added to #1's 2-square column and (N – 1) squares added to #1's 1-square column, giving (N – 1) + 2 + (N – 1) + 1 for the total number of squares. Again, do not simplify this notation, which is closely related to student perceptions, until students are ready to do so.

Note: Another view that could be developed sees shape #1 as a 2 by 2 with 1 square missing, #2 as a 3 by 2 with 1 missing, and #3 as a 4 by 2 with 1 missing. This is a "subtractive" view, whereas the previous two views are "additive."

Example 2:

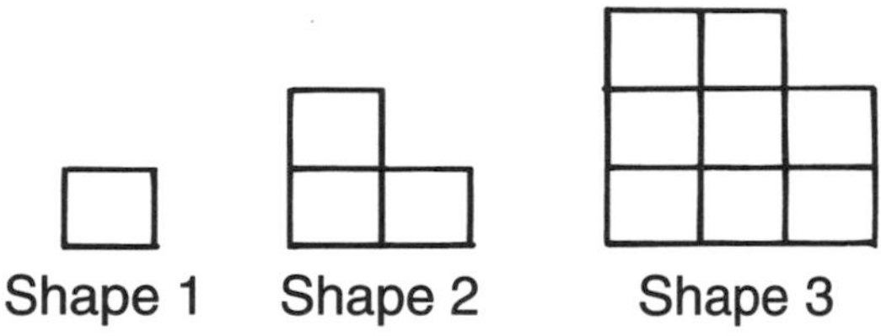

(a) *Additive view:* Each new shape has a strip of squares added along the left and bottom sides of the previous shape; this begins with shape #2. *Subtractive view*: Each new shape has 1 more row and 1 more column than the previous shape and has 1 corner square missing; the shape is a 'perfect square' with a corner missing. Other views are possible.

(b) *Additive view:* #1 has 1 square; #2 has 2 squares on bottom row and 1 square on top at left; #3 is just #2 with 1 stack of 2 squares added on the left and 1 row of 3 squares added at the bottom; #4 will be #2 with 2 stacks of 2 squares added on the left and 2 rows of 4 squares added at the bottom. *Subtractive view:* #1 has 1 square; #2 has 2 rows of 2 squares each with 1 square missing; #3 has 3 rows of 3 squares each with 1 square missing.

(c) *Additive view:* N-th shape has the (2 + 1) squares from #2 with (N – 2) stacks of 2 squares each added on the left and (N – 2) rows of N squares each added at the bottom, making a total of (2 + 1) + (N – 2) × 2 + (N – 2) × N squares. *Subtractive view:* N-th shape has N rows of N squares each with 1 square missing, making a total of (N × N – 1) squares.

Activity 3: BUILD, COUNT, COMPARE

(Cooperative Groups)

Materials: Sequence Worksheet PRF-1.3
Square tiles
Centimeter cubes
Paper
Pencils

Management: Teams of 4 students each (20–30 minutes)

Directions:

1. Give each team Sequence Worksheet PRF-1.3, 50 square tiles, and 50 centimeter cubes.

2. Have each team build three or four terms of each sequence described on the worksheet.

3. For each sequence, students should prepare a table having the column headings: *Which Term* and *Total Tiles* (or *Total Cubes*). They can determine the totals for the first three or four "terms" (shapes) by counting the tiles or cubes actually used in the construction of the terms. At that point they must look at how the shapes are changing and how the numbers in the table are changing, then try to complete the table through the tenth term, using the patterns they see.

4. After all teams have finished or time needs to be called, have students share their results with the entire class. It is possible that two teams could see different patterns in the same set of numbers and therefore generate completely different sequences. If this should happen, allow each team to describe what they saw and what process they used to generate the numbers for their particular table.

NAME ______________________________ DATE ____________________

SEQUENCE WORKSHEET PRF-1.3
Build, Count, Compare

Build the following number sequences with tiles or cubes. For each sequence, record in a table the terms 1 through 10 and the total tiles or cubes needed to build each term. Be ready to describe the pattern you used to extend each sequence.

1. Triangular numbers: 1, 3, 6, 10, . . .
For each total or term in the sequence, arrange rows of tiles in the shape of an equilateral triangle.
Example: 6 total—row 1 = 3 tiles, row 2 = 2 tiles, row 3 = 1 tile

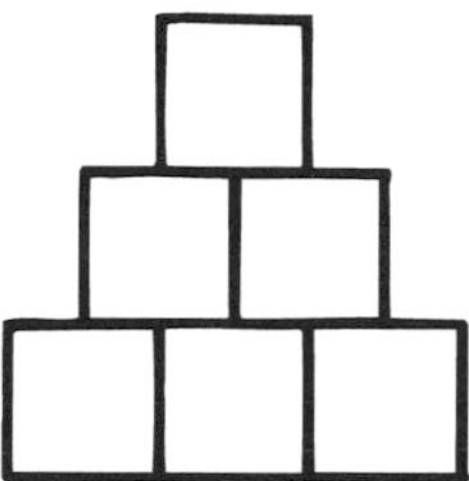

2. Square numbers: 1, 4, 9, 16, . . .
For each total in the sequence, arrange rows of tiles in the shape of a square.
Example: 4 total—2 rows of 2 tiles each

3. Rectangular numbers: 2, 6, 12, 20, . . .
Build tiles in arrays that have one more column than they have rows.
Example: 12 total—3 rows, 4 columns (or 4 tiles per row)

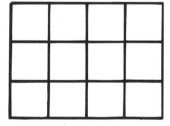

NAME ______________________________ DATE ____________________

SEQUENCE WORKSHEET PRF-1.3 (*cont.*)

4. Tetrahedral numbers: 1, 4, 10, 20, . . .
Stack cubes, making each level in the shape of an equilateral triangle (like a stack of cannonballs).
Example: 10 total—bottom level, 6 cubes; middle level, 3 cubes; top level, 1 cube.

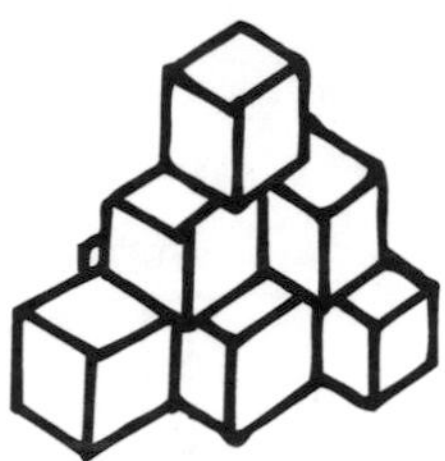

5. Cubic numbers: 1, 8, 27, 64, . . .
Stack cubes to form larger cubes.
Example: 8 total—2 levels of cubes; each level has 2 rows of 2 cubes each.

OBJECTIVE 2: Develop multiplication facts using patterns of rows. Includes extension activities that explore zero as a factor in multiplication.

Activity 1: BUILDING ARRAYS

(Concrete Action)

Materials: Square tiles (or centimeter cubes or 1-inch paper squares)
Large classroom-size hundred chart (10 numbers per row: 1–10, 11–20, . . . , 91–100)
Paper
Pencils

Management: Partners (2 sessions, 30–40 minutes/session)

Directions:

1. Give each pair of students a reclosable plastic bag of 100 tiles or cubes.

2. They are to make arrangements called *arrays* with their tiles (cubes). Arrays are simply row-column arrangements. We will consider a row to be a line-up of objects from left to right in front of the student; a column goes up and down. Students will be asked to build arrays having a given number of rows with a certain number of objects in each row (equal row sizes).

3. For the first session have students build arrays with different row sizes from 2 through 5. For each row size they are to increase the number of rows from 1 to 9 (or 10 if preferred). For example, if working with a row size of 3 tiles, students will first build 1 row of 3 tiles, then 2 rows of 3 tiles each, 3 rows of 3 tiles each, on up to 9 rows of 3 tiles each.

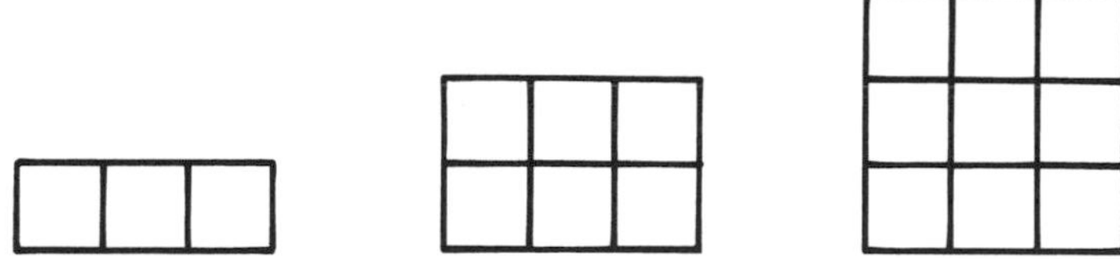

4. Have students write a word-number sentence for each array they build for a given row size and title the list of sentences as *Sets of (row size used)*:

Example: *Sets of 4*

1 row of 4 = 4
2 rows of 4 = 8
etc.

5. As students finish each set of arrays for a particular row size, have them find their totals or products (e.g., 4, 8, 12, 16, 20, . . .) on the classroom hundred chart and look for a pattern in their positions on the chart. Totals can easily be located by a *skip-counting* process.

6. Monitor the activity closely, observing different pairs of students and asking them questions about their work. For example, if a pair is building arrays with a row size of 5, you might ask: *If 3 rows of 5 make 15, how does adding on 1 more row change your total?* (increases total by 5) *Can the total for 8 rows of 5 be found by joining 4 rows with 4 more rows? Could you find the total for 9 rows of 5 by finding 10 rows of 5 and removing 5 tiles?* Similar questions can be asked for any row size being used. Questions involving arrays with two different row sizes might also be used: *Build 2 arrays: 3 rows of 5 and 3 rows of 9. How does one array differ from the other?* (differ by 3 rows of 4) Encourage students to create their own questions, then find answers for them.

7. For the second session, have students build arrays using row sizes of 6 through 9 (or 10 if preferred). Use the same approach (building, questioning, recording) described for the first session. This second group of arrays will have several large arrays in it (e.g., 8×8, 8×9, 9×9). It is very necessary that students struggle through this in order to sense the numerousness of these arrays compared to the earlier ones. Close monitoring will be necessary, however, to help students keep rows and columns properly lined up and to check their counting of the tiles for accuracy. They may even need to build some arrays on the classroom floor. Have them record their arrays as before in Session 1.

8. This is a time for developing *understanding*. Avoid the use of the word "times," e.g. "2 times 3" for 2×3. The meaning of this "condensed" expression is not clear to students. Do not encourage memorization at this time. Comparisons between arrays are much more important here.

Activity 2: FORMING IMAGES

(Pictorial Action)

Materials: Worksheet PRF-2.2 of blank multiplication table
Paper
Pencil

Management: Partners (2 sessions, 30 minutes/session)

Directions:

1. Give each student a copy of Worksheet PRF-2.2.

2. In this activity the focus will be on forming mental images of the different arrays by drawing and on finding ways certain arrays relate to each other.

3. Ask the students to draw 3 rows of 4 small circles each and 4 rows of 3 small circles each on their own paper. Remind them that a row must be drawn left to right on their paper and that several rows must line up and have straight columns up and down. Watch for any papers that are too slanted on the desks. This will interfere with the horizontal-vertical differences students need to see.

4. Have them count the total circles in each array and write the correct number sentence under each array: $3 \times 4 = 12$ for the 3 rows of 4 and $4 \times 3 = 12$ for the 4 rows of 3. Remember that the first factor is the multiplier, which counts the number of rows in the array. We will refer to the numbers of an array, e.g., 3×4, as a factor pair. Also have the students fill in the spaces of the multiplication table to show their totals or "products." The numbers in the left column of the table tell how many rows and the top row of numbers tell the row size.

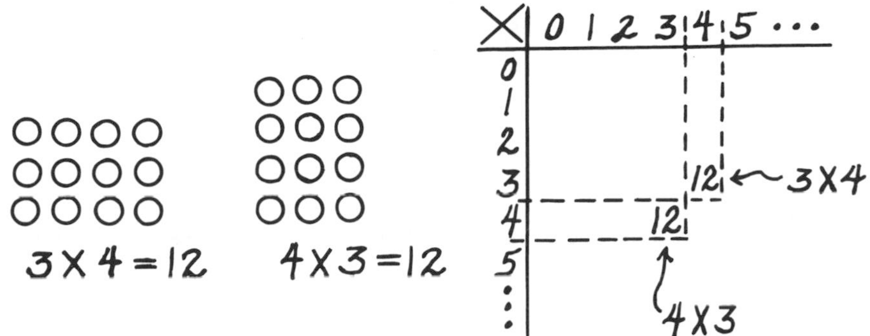

5. Ask students what else they notice about these two arrays besides their having the same product or total. (One array can be rotated to look like the other.) Notice where their products are located on the table also. The number of spaces down from the top for one product equals the number of spaces from the left for the other, and visa versa. These arrays are *rotated* arrays and their factor pairs, 3 × 4 and 4 × 3, are called *commuted pairs.*

6. Now have students draw 1 row of 7 circles, 5 rows of 1 circle each, 1 row of 3 circles, and 4 rows of 1 circle each, and write their number sentences. Ask them to locate each array's numbers on the multiplication table and fill in its product.

1 × 7 = 7 5 × 1 = 5 1 × 3 = 3 4 × 1 = 4

7. Ask them what they notice about the factors (number of rows and row size) and the product each time. (The product and one of the factors have the same number name, even though the *roles* they play are *different;* one factor is always the number 1.) The products lie in either the *1* column or the *1* row of the table. These factor pairs are called *identity pairs.*

8. Have students draw 2 rows of 2 circles each, 4 rows of 4 circles each, and 5 rows of 5 circles each. They should write the number sentences and fill in the products on the table.

9. Ask them what they notice about the shapes of these arrays. (They will look like squares, hopefully.) Also notice that their products lie on the diagonal from upper left to lower right of the multiplication table. The factor pairs of these arrays are called *squared pairs.*

10. Now have students draw the remaining commuted pairs, identity pairs, and squared pairs, writing their number sentences and locating their products on the table each time. They should use 1–9 as the factors (the number of rows and row size) of the arrays they draw. If all pairs have been drawn, all spaces on the table should be completely filled except for the zero-row and zero-column. The factor 0 is developed in the extension objective following Activity 3.

11. It will be helpful if students use a separate sheet of paper to draw the arrays for each type of factor pair (commuted, identity, squared). Such organizing of the pairs by type will be useful as students begin to memorize the pairs with their products.

NAME ______________________ DATE ______________

WORKSHEET PRF-2.2
Forming Images

╳	0	1	2	3	4	5	6	7	8	9
0										
1										
2										
3										
4										
5										
6										
7										
8										
9										

Activity 3: FACTOR CALL

(Cooperative Groups)

Materials: Paper
Pencils

Management: Teams of 4 students each (20 minutes)

Directions:

1. Each team will decide on the order in which their four members will play. Every person will need paper and pencil.

2. For each turn, a member will call out a factor pair to the next person in order. That person must tell what the product is, then draw an array of circles to show that the total is correct. The third person in order must write a complete number sentence, using *another* factor pair that has the same product. The fourth person then starts the process again by calling out a new factor pair.

3. Example of a turn: Player #1 calls out 3×6 (use either *3 times 6* or *3 rows of 6* at this stage); player #2 says *18,* draws 3 rows of 6 circles each on a sheet of paper, and quickly counts the circles (but only if other players demand the count); player #3 might write $6 \times 3 = 18$, $9 \times 2 = 18$, $1 \times 18 = 18$, etc., on his or her sheet of paper with the approval of the other players.

EXTENSION OBJECTIVES: Explore zero as a factor in multiplication.

A. Zero as the multiplicand

(Concrete Action)

Role playing helps students understand this particular concept. Place 3 empty paper cups on a table where all students can see them. Show students that each cup contains 0 counters. Ask a student to pretend to pour counters from each cup, then ask the class how many counters total are now on the table. (0 counters total) Record $3 \times 0 = 0$ on the board. Repeat this process, using different numbers of empty cups, until all students are convinced. Have students also discuss what the total might be if zero empty cups are poured out on the table. (0 counters total; record $0 \times 0 = 0$)

(Pictorial Action)

Ask the students to draw three large squares on their paper. Discuss: *If you were to draw 5 small circles in each square, how many circles would you draw in all?* (15) *But if you draw zero small circles in each square, how many circles will you draw in all?* (0 total; record $3 \times 0 = 0$ on the board) Have them repeat this process, drawing different numbers of squares to fill with 0 circles, until all students are satisfied that $N \times 0 = 0$ for any whole number N given.

Alternative approach: Have students draw 3 large squares as before, but also have them actually draw 5 small circles in each square and find the total. Record $3 \times 5 = 15$. Now have them mark out one circle in each square and find the new total. Record $3 \times 4 = 12$. Continue this marking out process until no circles remain in any square. Then for zero circles in each square, the total will be 0 circles. Write $3 \times 0 = 0$.

B. Zero as the multiplier

(Concrete Action)

This concept is best done by *role playing*. On a table where all students can see them, place 4 paper cups that are each filled with 5 counters of some kind. Ask one student to take 3 of the 4 cups, pour out the counters and count them. Record the number sentence, $3 \times 5 = 15$, on the board. Refill the cups as before and place them on the table again. Ask a second student to take 2 of the 4 cups, pour out the counters, and count their total. Record $2 \times 5 = 10$ on the board. Refill the cups and repeat the process with another student taking 1 of the 4 cups and finding the total. Record $1 \times 5 = 5$. Now ask a student to take 0 of the 4 cups. (Have the student pretend to reach for the cups, but not pick up any, then pretend to pour out counters on the table.) Ask the class how many counters are now on the table. Since they do not see anything, the answer is *zero*. Record $0 \times 5 = 0$.

(Pictorial Action)

List these factor pairs on the chalkboard:

$4 \times 3 =$ _____

$3 \times 3 =$ _____

$2 \times 3 =$ _____

$1 \times 3 =$ _____

Predict: $0 \times 3 =$ _____

Ask the students to draw an array for each of the first four sentences, and write the product in the blank. Discuss how the products decrease by 3 as you go down the list. Ask students how their arrays change as they go in order from 4×3 to 1×3. (A row of 3 is removed each time.) Now have students predict what they think 0×3 should be, based on the patterns of change they have seen. (If the last product 3 is also decreased by 3 and if the last array, 1 row of 3, has a row of 3 removed, the next sentence, 0×3, will have to equal 0. There will be 0 rows of 3 left, an *invisible array*.) Repeat this process, using a row size of 5, etc., as needed. Most students see the patterns quickly and will predict *0* as the product for $0 \times N$ for any whole number N given.

OBJECTIVE 3: Extend sequences of tenths or hundredths.

Activity 1: STICKS AND CUBES
(Concrete Action)

Materials: Base 10 blocks (cubes, longs, flats)
Paper
Pencils

Management: Teams of 2–3 students each (30 minutes)

Directions:

1. Give each team of students the following from a set of base 10 blocks: 5 flats, 30 sticks (longs), and 50 small cubes.

2. A prerequisite for this activity is that students understand that if the flat represents the value *one,* then a stick is a *tenth of one* and a cube is a *hundredth of one.* They must also know the notation: 1 stick has the number name 0.1 (read as *one tenth*) and 1 cube has the number name 0.01 (read as *one hundredth*).

3. Have students place the 5 flats (ones) on the desktop in front of them, lining them up from left to right. Each flat will hold a term of a sequence, with the first term being at the left. (If you do not have enough flats, use 10 cm. by 10 cm. squares cut out of centimeter grid paper.)

4. Ask the students to place 1 tenth on the first flat, 2 tenths on the second flat, and 3 tenths on the third flat. Next, have them decide what amounts need to go on the fourth and fifth flats, based on the increasing pattern seen in the first three flats.

5. Have students draw a picture of the 5 terms built and record the number names under the different terms.

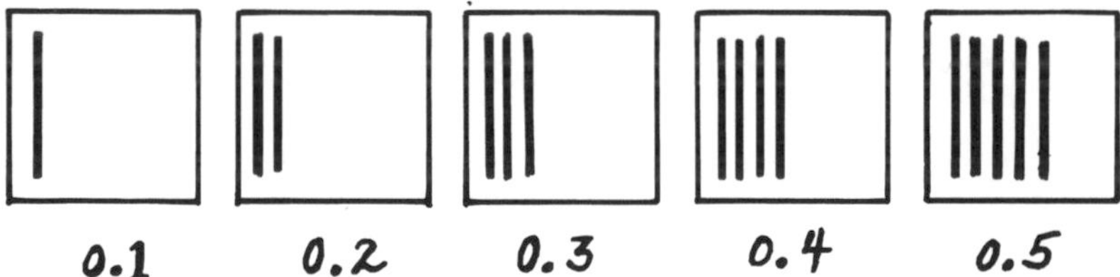

6. Have them build 3 new terms by placing 2 hundredths on the first flat, 4 hundredths on the second, and 6 hundredths on the third. Ask them to decide what amounts should go on the last two flats and build them.

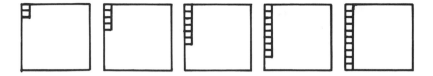

7. Have students draw pictures of the 5 terms and write the numeral names under the terms. For convenience, have them draw circles instead of squares.

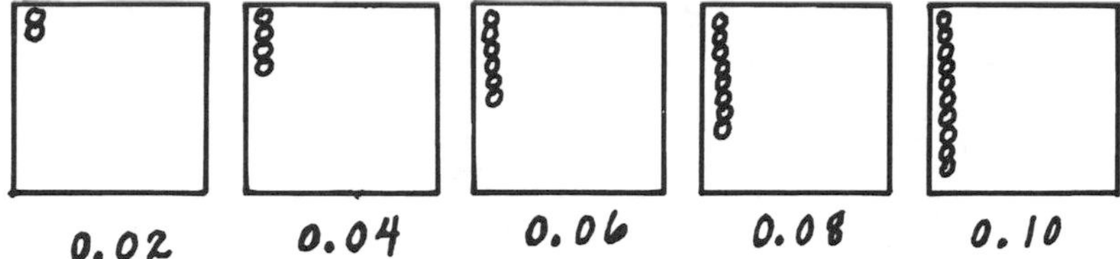

8. Next, have them build several other sequences, following the above procedure (build the first 3 terms as given; predict and build the next two terms; draw a picture of each term; and write number names under the pictures of the terms). Here are some possible sequences to use:

(a) build 5 cubes, 10 cubes, 15 cubes, 20 cubes, 25 cubes; write 0.05, 0.10, 0.15, 0.20, 0.25 (all are read as hundredths)

(b) build 3 cubes, 6 cubes, 9 cubes, 12 cubes, 15 cubes; write 0.03, 0.06, 0.09, 0.12, 0.15 (all are read as hundredths)

(c) build 2 sticks, 4 sticks, 6 sticks, 8 sticks, 10 sticks; write 0.2, 0.4, 0.6, 0.8, 1.0 (since 10 tenths cover a whole flat, the amount is written as 1.0, which is read as *one;* previous terms are read as tenths)

Activity 2: DECIMAL PATTERNS

(Pictorial Action)

Materials: Decimal Sequence Worksheet PRF-3.2
Pencils

Management: Partners (20 minutes)

Directions:

1. Give each student a copy of Decimal Sequence Worksheet PRF-3.2.

2. Have students shade in the first 3 flats to show the terms given in numeral form. They should then shade in the last 2 flats according to the pattern they have seen in the first 3. Ask them to write the numeral names for the last 2 terms in the two blanks of the given sequence.

3. When all have finished, have different students describe what patterns they saw and what notation they finally used to complete the sequences.

NAME ______________________________ DATE ____________________

DECIMAL SEQUENCE WORKSHEET PRF-3.2
Decimal Patterns

Each small square shaded shows a "hundredth" and each strip of 10 small squares shaded shows a "tenth" of the large unit square. Show the terms of each sequence on the unit squares below the numbers. Record the missing numbers in the blanks.

A. 0.1, 0.3, 0.5, ________, ________

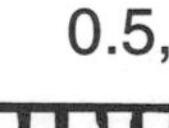

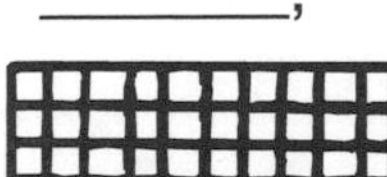

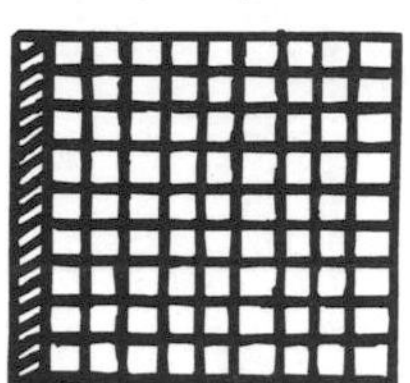

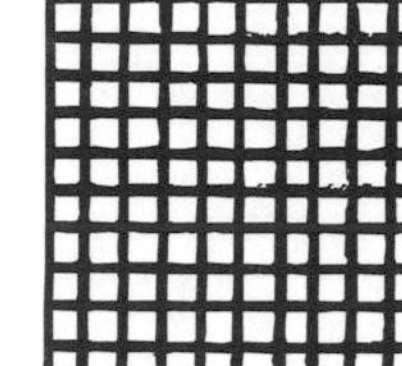

B. 0.06, 0.12, 0.18, ________, ________

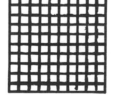

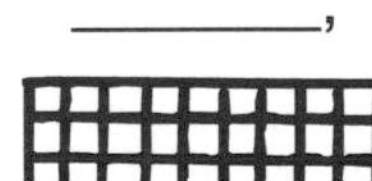

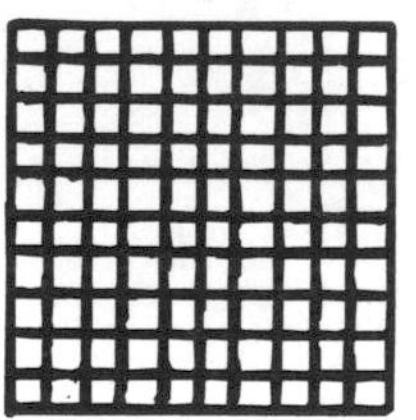

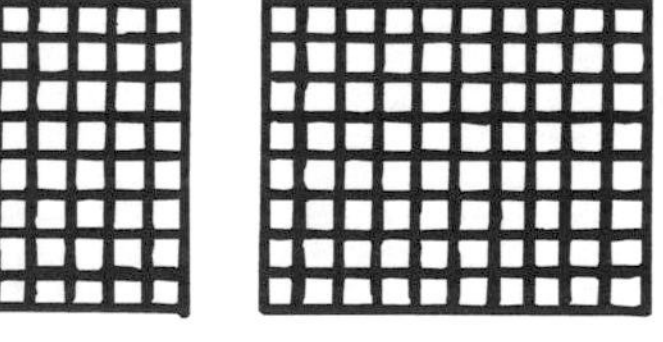

C. 0.8, 0.4, 0.2, ________, ________

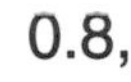

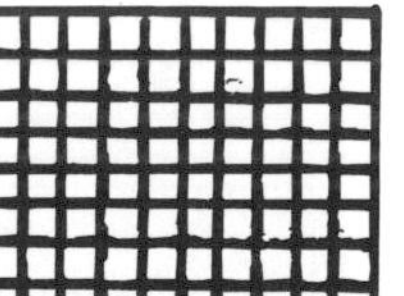

Activity 3: SEQUENCE SCRAMBLE

(Cooperative Groups)

Materials: Card sets of decimal sequences (described in step #1)

Management: Teams of four students each (20 minutes)

Directions:

1. Give each team of students a set of 24 cards containing terms of decimal sequences. The cards can be prepared by writing decimal numerals on small index cards, one numeral per card. There will be 3 different sequences included in the set with each sequence consisting of 8 terms.

2. Here is a possible set of numbers to use for the cards. They are grouped by intended sequence: (a) 0.01, 0.02, 0.04, 0.08, 0.16, 0.32, 0.64, 1.28; pattern used—doubling; (b) 0.5, 1.0, 1.5, 2.0, 2.5, 3.0, 3.5, 4.0; pattern used—add 0.5 each time; (c) 0.03, 0.07, 0.11, 0.15, 0.19, 0.23, 0.27, 0.31; pattern used—add 0.04 each time. Write all numerals in the same style and color; do not provide any hints for the students.

3. Team members should shuffle their set of cards, then deal 6 cards to each person.

4. The team must work together to decide which cards go together to make a sequence. To be in the same sequence, the numbers must be related through some obvious pattern. Some numbers may seem to go to more than one sequence at first, but all cards must be used and there must be 8 numbers in each sequence. It is possible that a team might find different patterns than the ones used to create the cards, but that is acceptable as long as their new sequences follow consistent patterns and there are 8 cards to a sequence.

5. When all teams have finished laying their sequences out on their desktop, have some students share the sequences they found. Discuss any new sequences that differ from the original ones, and check for consistency of pattern in each case.

OBJECTIVE 4: Develop division facts with arrays. Includes extension activities that explore the role of zero in division.

Activity 1: BUILDING FAIR SHARES

(Concrete Action)

Materials: Square tiles (or one-inch paper squares or centimeter cubes)
Paper
Pencils

Management: Partners (2 sessions, 30 minutes per session)

Directions:

1. Give each pair of students a reclosable plastic bag of 100 tiles.

2. In this activity, the *divisor* will indicate *the number of sets to make.* For example, for *6 divided by 3,* three equal shares or sets (the divisor) must be formed from six tiles (the dividend); there will be two tiles (quotient) in each set. The tiles will be arranged as an array (rows left to right and columns up and down) each time where each row is a *fair share.* With the array students and teacher can quickly see that the shares are all equal in size or quantity. Use mathematical terms interchangeably with the objects they name (e.g., total amount of tiles needed = dividend, number of rows used = divisor, and number of tiles per row = quotient).

3. For Session 1, ask students to count out 8 tiles; then separate them one at a time into 2 equal rows from left to right on the desk in front of them.

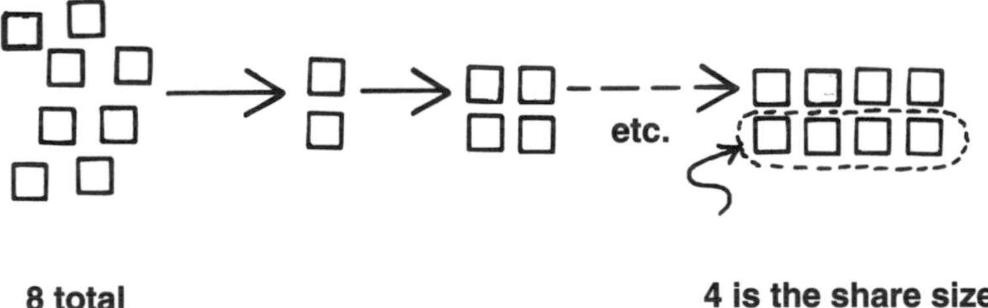

4. Ask how many squares are in the first (top) row, then the second row. Students should say 4 tiles each time. Tell them that each row shows one share, so they have built 2 equal shares.

5. Have students record the word-number sentence: *8 in 2 rows = 4 in a share.* (Here 8 is the *dividend* to be separated into 2 rows, the *divisor,* and the share size, 4, is the *quotient.*)

6. Now have students build different arrays that answer the question: *What amount of tiles can be separated into 2 equal rows? What is the share size?* They should explore by first building 2 rows with 1 tile each and writing *2 in 2 rows = 1 in a share.* Students continue to add 1 more tile to each row to find the total needed and share size formed.

2 in 2 rows = 1 in a share **4 in 2 rows = 2 in a share** **6 in 2 rows = 3 in a share** **8 in 2 rows = 4 in a share**

7. Have students continue the process described in step 6 by building in three rows only, in 4 rows only, and in 5 rows only. For each number of rows being built, the share size should range from 1 tile/row to 9/row (or 10/row). A word-number sentence should be written for each array built.

8. When they are comfortable with building several equal rows, have them build just one row, using a share size from one to nine tiles. Word-number sentences like *5 in 1 row = 5 in a share* will be recorded.

9. For Session 2, students should continue the process from Session 1, but should find the amounts of tiles that separate equally into 6 rows, 7 rows, 8 rows, or 9 rows.

Example:

30 in 6 rows = 5 in a share

10. Monitor the array building carefully to be sure students are making equal rows and are accurately counting the total tiles needed each time. Columns of tiles should also be kept straight.

11. During this activity some students will begin to think in terms of multiplication. They will begin to see the relationship between the number of rows they are using and the share size they must maintain for each row as they build, and they will start to find their *product* instead of just counting the total tiles used each time. This reversal of thinking back and forth between multiplication and division is desirable but should develop naturally within each child.

12. As you observe each pair of students as they build with the tiles, ask questions to help them look for patterns in their word-number sentences. Here are some examples:

- *When you add 1 more tile to each row to increase the share size and you are building 4 rows, how does the total number of tiles needed seem to change?* (Total or dividend increases by 4 each time.)
- *When you separated 10 tiles into 5 rows, you used 2 tiles per row. When you separated 10 tiles into 2 rows, what happened?*
- *As you increase the number of rows you are building, but you keep using the same total amount of tiles, what seems to happen to the number of tiles in each share/row?* (e.g., for 12 tiles, 2 rows will have a share of 6 tiles; 3 rows have a share of 4; 6 rows, a share of 2; as the number of rows increases, the share size decreases)
- *When you build only 1 row with 7 tiles total, what do you notice about the share size?* (amount in share is same as total amount, but roles are different)

Activity 2: SEPARATION PATTERNS

(Pictorial Action)

Materials: Individual Hundred Charts Worksheet PRF-4.2 (10 rows, 10 numerals per row: 1–10, 11–20, . . . , 91–100
Pencils
Paper

Management: Partners (2 sessions, 30 minutes/session)

Directions:

1. Give each pair of students a copy of the individual hundred chart. In this activity the division facts will be grouped according to common characteristics to help students organize the new information they are learning. The chart will help them find the different groups. The natural relationship between multiplication and division will continue to develop. Memorization should not be stressed at this time.

2. Ask students to draw a set of 6 small circles in a single row. Have them observe that the dividend amount (total) to be used all goes into one row, so the share size must be the same number as the total. Have them draw a ring around the entire row and write 6 ÷ 1 = 6 (to be read as *6 divided into 1 share equals 6 per share*). This is called an *identity* pair in division.

3. Have students repeat step 2, using amounts 1–10 for the dividend.

4. Now ask students to start at 2 on their charts and skip count by two's nine times to find the set of 9 numbers: 2, 4, 6, 8, 10, 12, 14, 16, 18. Assign a different number from the set to each pair of students (some numbers will need to be used more than once). They should draw that amount of small circles in a random arrangement on their papers. Then have the students redraw their circles, one at a time, into two separate rows, keeping the rows equal. The original circles should be marked out as they are used. A ring should be drawn around one row when the array is finished to identify the quotient. A number sentence should be written for each separation.

Example:

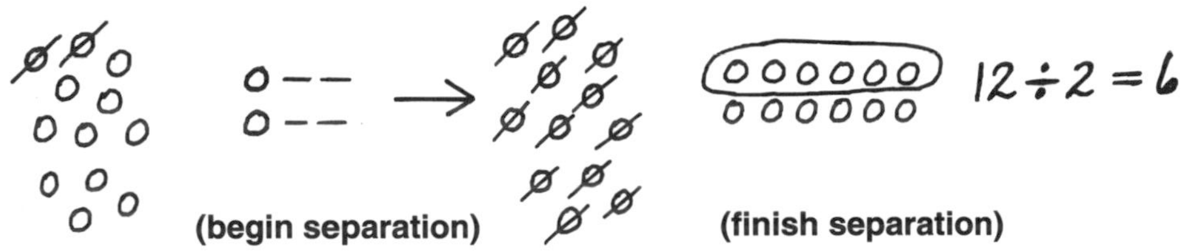

(begin separation)

12 ÷ 2 = 6

(finish separation)

5. Record the number sentences on the chalkboard, ordering them according to the increasing size of the dividend. Ask students what they notice about the quotients (share size) found. (When ordered, they are the counting numbers 1, 2, 3, 4, 5, 6, 7, 8, 9.) Discuss the idea that any dividend, which can be separated into two equal groups to form a share size that is a counting number, is called an *even* number. Any division fact that involves an even number less than 20 being divided by 2 is identified as in the *divisor of 2* family.

6. Now have students repeat the drawing-writing procedure used in steps 4–5 by starting at 3 on the hundred chart and skip counting by three's to find the 9 numbers: 3, 6, 9, 12, 15, 18, 21, 24, 27. The process will involve drawing 3 equal rows of small circles this time and finding the quotients 1, 2, 3, 4, 5, 6, 7, 8, and 9 again. The division facts found will form the family for the *divisor of 3*. Possible patterns in the dividends to notice: the two digits add to 3, 6, or 9, with that order repeating; the ones digits have a decreasing cycle—3, 6, 9–2, 5, 8–1, 4, 7.

7. Continue the skip-counting process to find the division facts for the families of the divisors 4, 5, 6, 7, 8, and 9. Encourage students to look for other patterns in the different division facts they find; e.g., for the divisor 5, each dividend has either a 5 or a 0 in the ones place, and for the divisor 9, the digits in each dividend have a sum of 9.

8. For another way to group division facts, assign different pairs of students a dividend from the set: 1, 4, 9, 16, 25, 36, 49, 64, 81. Some pairs will have the same number. Ask students to try to draw their amount as small circles arranged in an array where the number of rows equals the number of columns (a *square* arrangement), then write a number sentence for the separation process.

Example: 9 ÷ 3 = 3

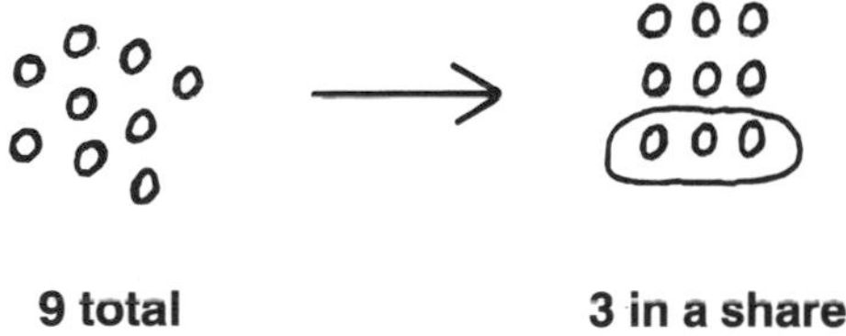

9 total 3 in a share

9. Record the number sentences found in step 8 on the board. Ask students what they notice about the numbers used as divisor and quotient. (They have the same number name but different roles.) Division facts with this property can be called the *perfect square* pairs for division.

10. A final group of facts to explore will be the *related* pairs, e.g., 14 ÷ 2 and 14 ÷ 7. Ask students to draw the diagrams for these two pairs, then compare the arrays. They should notice that one array is a rotation of the other. The quotient (or row size) of one matches the divisor (or column size) of the other. Have students confirm this relationship by drawing diagrams for several other such pairs.

Example:

15 ÷ 3 = 5 15 ÷ 5 = 3

11. Note: As students have more experiences with the separation of a given amount into smaller but equal amounts, they will begin to think of the row size and number of rows as a pair. Hence, although we began the development of division by using the number of rows or sets to be built as the divisor in the written notation, students will eventually begin to think of the row or set size just as easily and be able to use that amount in the divisor position as well. For example, if there are 24 tiles and 8 tiles are needed in each row or set, students will be able to make 3 rows of 8, forming one group of 8 tiles at a time. The number sentence becomes 24 ÷ 8 = 3 in this case, but the array still involves the quantities, 3 and 8, in some way. Activity 3 will develop this pairwise relationship further.

Activity 3: STORYTELLERS

(Cooperative Groups)

Materials: Paper
Pencils
Sets of 36 cards each (described below in steps 1 and 2)

Management: Teams of 4 students each (20 minutes)

Directions:

1. Give each team a set of 36 cards. The cards can be made with small index cards. Each card will have 3 numbers written on it, which are related as divisor, quotient, and dividend. For example, a card might show 27, 3, and 9. The cards represent all the possible division facts (excluding use of 0 or 1).

2. Here is a list of 36 possible triplets of numbers to write on individual cards to form a complete set:

2, 2, 4	6, 2, 3	8, 4, 2	5, 10, 2	2, 6, 12	14, 7, 2
8, 16, 2	18, 9, 2	12, 3, 4	5, 15, 3	6, 3, 18	21, 3, 7
3, 8, 24	9, 3, 3	27, 3, 9	4, 4, 16	5, 20, 4	4, 6, 24
28, 4, 7	8, 32, 4	9, 4, 36	5, 25, 5	30, 6, 5	5, 7, 35
40, 5, 8	9, 45, 5	36, 6, 6	42, 6, 7	48, 6, 8	54, 9, 6
49, 7, 7	8, 56, 7	63, 7, 9	8, 64, 8	72, 8, 9	81, 9, 9

3. Team members should shuffle the cards, then place them face down in a stack in the center of the table. They will take turns drawing a card off the top of the stack.

4. On each turn, a player must create a story problem that will apply the three numbers on the drawn card as quantities in a division or separation situation. For example, if 36, 9, and 4 are on the drawn card, sample story problems might be as follows: *36 cans of tuna are placed in 9 equal stacks on the grocery store shelf. How many cans are in each stack?* (Divisor 9 tells how many sets to make.) *36 children are lined up for a wagontrain ride. Each wagon in the train will hold 9 children. How many wagons are needed to carry all the children at one time?* (Divisor 9 tells the set size.) The second number listed on the card does not have to be used as the divisor each time (as was done in the above examples). In fact, it would be better to vary the ordering of the three numbers on the cards, including having the largest number in the middle on some cards. The largest number will always serve as the given dividend, however.

5. The other three players must decide if the story problem is a correct example of division, then decide what role the divisor plays in the story—set size to use or number of sets to make. If helpful, team members might act out the problem, using objects or counters.

NAME ______________________________ DATE ____________________

HUNDRED CHART WORKSHEET PRF-4.2
Separation Patterns

1	2	3	4	5	6	7	8	9	10
11	12	13	14	15	16	17	18	19	20
21	22	23	24	25	26	27	28	29	30
31	32	33	34	35	36	37	38	39	40
41	42	43	44	45	46	47	48	49	50
51	52	53	54	55	56	57	58	59	60
61	62	63	64	65	66	67	68	69	70
71	72	73	74	75	76	77	78	79	80
81	82	83	84	85	86	87	88	89	90
91	92	93	94	95	96	97	98	99	100

EXTENSION OBJECTIVES: Explore the role of zero in division

A. Zero as the dividend

(Concrete Action)

The concept of zero as the dividend can be easily acted out by the students. Provide a large bucket and 4–5 small buckets. Have one student function as the server. Place 10 objects or counters of some kind in the large bucket and ask the server to share the counters equally among 5 buckets. Have another student count how many objects are in each small bucket. (2 per bucket) Write the number sentence on the board: $10 \div 5 = 2$. Repeat the process, using 8 objects to be shared between 2 small buckets. Finally ask the class how many objects are in the large bucket when it is empty. (They will probably say "nothing" or "none." Guide them to say *zero objects*.)

Ask the server to pretend to share the objects among 3 small buckets, then ask the other students how many objects are now in each small bucket. (Guide them to say *zero objects* are in each bucket.) Write the number sentence on the board: $0 \div 3 = 0$. Repeat this process, sharing the 0 objects in the large bucket among 5 buckets, then writing $0 \div 5 = 0$. Ask the class to compare the roles of the two zeros in the last two number sentences. (The first zero is the dividend and tells how many objects total were in the large bucket to be shared; the last zero is the quotient and tells how many objects were placed in each small bucket.) If necessary, continue the role playing until all students are comfortable with the idea that zero divided by any counting number N (not zero) will equal zero. Do not discuss zero as the divisor at this time; that concept will be developed later.

(Pictorial Action)

Have students work in teams of 3–4 students each. Assign each team a cluster of division problems to draw, using small circles in arrays. Here are some samples of clusters:

Cluster 1:	Cluster 2:	Cluster 3:	Cluster 4:
$8 \div 2 =$ _____	$12 \div 3 =$ _____	$15 \div 5 =$ _____	$16 \div 4 =$ _____
$6 \div 2 =$ _____	$9 \div 3 =$ _____	$10 \div 5 =$ _____	$12 \div 4 =$ _____
$4 \div 2 =$ _____	$6 \div 3 =$ _____	$5 \div 5 =$ _____	$8 \div 4 =$ _____
$2 \div 2 =$ _____	$3 \div 3 =$ _____	Predict:	$4 \div 4 =$ _____
Predict:	Predict:	$0 \div 5 =$ _____	Predict:
$0 \div 2 =$ _____	$0 \div 3 =$ _____		$0 \div 4 =$ _____

Assign one of the clusters to each team. For each number sentence in their cluster, ask students to draw the given number of circles (dividend) in the given number of rows (divisor). Have them draw a ring around one of the rows of circles in the array and record the row size in the blank of the number sentence. The arrays should be drawn in the order given in the cluster. Have them look for patterns in the number sentences of their particular cluster and use those patterns to predict the quotient of the last number sentence where zero is the dividend. After all teams are finished, ask each team to describe the patterns they saw in their clusters, give their choice for the last answer, and tell why they predicted that particular answer. All teams can be expected to predict zero for the last answer and will do so based on the patterns they see.

Here are some possible patterns within a cluster of equations:

- The dividends decrease by the same amount each time, so the final dividend has to be zero.
- The quotients decrease by the same amount each time, so the final quotient has to be zero.
- In the drawn arrays the row size loses one circle each time, so the last array's row size must have zero circles in it.
- The divisor or number of rows drawn stays the same.

Discuss the idea that all teams (hopefully) predicted independently that a zero dividend divided by a counting number (not zero) would yield a quotient of zero. When such agreement occurs based on observed patterns, the predicted answer is considered *logically reasonable.*

B. Zero as the divisor

(Concrete Action)

This concept must *follow* the two previous activities. Students need experience with the easier pattern searches found in those activities before encountering the contradictions that will occur in the next two activities.

Using *role playing* once again, have a student function as the server and hand him or her a large bucket that contains 10 objects or counters of some kind. Place 2 small buckets on the table. Tell the server to share all 10 objects in the large bucket equally between the 2 small buckets. The student will then place 5 objects in each small bucket. Next, return the 10 objects to the large bucket, and remove the small buckets from the table. Tell the server, *You must share all the counters in the large bucket equally among these zero small buckets I have placed on the table.* (There are no small buckets on the table at this time.) *Can you tell me how many counters you will put in each bucket?* Hopefully, the student will realize that the sharing process cannot be completed since there are no small buckets available; that is, there are zero buckets to fill. Hence, we cannot *tell for sure* what the share size or quotient will be.

Write on the board: *10 ÷ 0 = no answer possible.* Do not just leave a blank for the answer. Students must know that this situation is impossible, so there is no number they can use to describe the share size or amount in each small *imaginary* bucket. It also helps to have them draw a large *X* across the incomplete number sentence to strike it out. Repeat this same process, using different amounts of counters in the large bucket and asking the same questions each time. You want them to realize that regardless of the amount or counting number N of objects to be shared, they cannot tell how much is in each share if they cannot even begin to make the *first* share. Thus, the number sentence will always be *N ÷ 0 = impossible.* Students might suggest having 0 objects in the large bucket, but this does not change the reasoning; the sharing process cannot be completed if there are no small buckets. The number sentence for this case is *0 ÷ 0 = impossible.*

(Pictorial Action)

This next activity is quite effective in demonstrating the need for *consistency,* which is basic to all mathematical thought and language. Assign teams of 3–4 students each. Give each team one or two *clusters* of division facts to complete by drawing arrays of small circles *in the order given by the cluster.* The dividend number tells how many total circles to use and the divisor tells how many equal rows of circles to draw. Have students draw a ring around one of the rows in each array to show the quotient. They are to look for patterns in the arrays they draw and in the numbers they see in their completed number sentences, and use these patterns to predict the answer to the final number sentence. Here are some possible clusters to use. (Have several teams work with the same cluster so they can compare their results later.)

Cluster 1:	Cluster 2:	Cluster 3:	Cluster 4:
12 ÷ 4 = _____	8 ÷ 4 = _____	20 ÷ 5 = _____	15 ÷ 5 = _____
12 ÷ 3 = _____	8 ÷ 2 = _____	20 ÷ 4 = _____	15 ÷ 3 = _____
12 ÷ 2 = _____	8 ÷ 1 = _____	20 ÷ 2 = _____	15 ÷ 1 = _____
12 ÷ 1 = _____	Predict:	20 ÷ 1 = _____	Predict:
Predict:	8 ÷ 0 = _____	Predict:	15 ÷ 0 = _____
12 ÷ 0 = _____		20 ÷ 0 = _____	

After all teams have completed their drawings and filled in the blanks (including their prediction), have them describe any patterns they saw and tell what they predicted for the final answer with zero as the divisor. Some possible *patterns* within each cluster that students might mention are the following:

- The dividend stays constant (or the same).
- The divisor decreases, but not by the same amount each time.
- The quotient increases, but not by the same amount each time.
- In the drawings of the arrays, the number of rows decreases, but not by the same amount each time.
- The number of circles per row increases, but not by the same amount each time.

Since these decreases or increases do not occur in a controlled way, the above observations do not really qualify as patterns. Also, even though teams have the same cluster, they will offer different answers for their final equation. For example, using Cluster 1 above, different teams have predicted the final answer for the same cluster to be numbers like 0, 15, 18, and 30, and have given different reasons for their choices. In mathematics we do not want to have an unpredictable variety of answers for the same number sentence because this would be extremely confusing. Therefore, in such cases, we say that the equation has no meaning or is impossible. *Conclusion*: Whenever the divisor is zero, we cannot be certain of the answer, so we write the sentence *N* ÷ *0 = impossible* for any number N, including N = 0. It is helpful to have students actually mark a large X across the expression *N* ÷ *0.*

OBJECTIVE 5: Generate sequences with geometric shapes.

Activity 1: BUILDING GEOMETRIC TRAINS
(Concrete Action)

Materials: Commercial attribute blocks (desktop size preferred) or commercial pattern blocks

Management: Teams of 4 students each (30 minutes)

Directions:

1. Commercial *attribute blocks* contain blocks that vary in size (large, small), thickness (thick, thin), shape (circle, square, triangle, non-square rectangle, hexagon), and color (red, blue, yellow). Commercial *pattern blocks* have blocks that vary only in shape (hexagon, trapezoid, wide parallelogram, triangle, square, narrow parallelogram), but each shape has its own color.

2. Give a set of attribute blocks or pattern blocks to each team of students. Describe 3 or more attribute blocks for them to place on their desktop in the order given. Ask each team to decide which two blocks must go next in the *train* or sequence they have started.

3. Have each team share their two choices and state reasons for those choices. It is possible for teams to select different pairs of blocks and therefore produce different sequences, depending on which pattern they see among the first blocks given.

4. Geometric sequence patterns can be based upon a change in shape, color, thickness, size, quantity, or a combination of any of these. Change is determined as you move in order from one member to the next member in the sequence. There must be a pattern to the changes made. Here are some examples of *change* patterns you might use with your students.

- Color only: (attribute blocks of same size and thickness) yellow circle, blue circle, yellow circle, . . . ; or yellow circle, blue circle, red circle, yellow circle, . . .
- Shape only: (attribute blocks of same size and thickness) red square, red circle, red square, . . . ; or blue circle, blue square, blue triangle, blue circle, . . .
- Size or color: (attribute blocks of same thickness) large red circle, small blue circle, large yellow circle, large red circle, small blue circle, . . .
- Color and shape: (pattern blocks) yellow hexagon, green triangle, yellow hexagon, . . . ; or yellow hexagon, orange square, green triangle, yellow hexagon, . . .
- Quantity, or color and shape: (pattern blocks) orange square, green triangle, green triangle, orange square, green triangle, green triangle, . . . ; or orange square, blue parallelogram, orange square, orange square, blue parallelogram, blue parallelogram, orange square, orange square, orange square, . . .

Note: The more complex the changes within a sequence, the more terms or shapes you will need to provide for the students before asking them to predict the next two terms. When you give fewer terms than needed to establish a certain pattern of changes, students are more likely to predict different sequences from the one you intended to give. If that happens, simply have the team members explain their reasoning, then check for a consistent pattern in their work.

Activity 2: DRAWING GEOMETRIC PATTERNS

(Pictorial Action)

Materials: Geometric Worksheet PRF-5.2
Colored pencils

Management: Partners (20–30 minutes)

Directions:

1. Give each pair of students a copy of Geometric Worksheet PRF-5.2 and a set of colored pencils. The worksheet will contain the first 4–6 members of several sequences. Each of the first few shapes of a sequence will be marked with the first letter of that shape's color name. Have students color the shapes accordingly.

2. Have students draw and color what they believe to be the next three shapes in each sequence.

3. When all have finished, ask different students to describe their sequences, telling what patterns they saw in each one. Accept any reasonable pattern. Be sure to discuss any sequences where students disagree in their choices.

Activity 3: PATOLLI

(Cooperative Groups)

Materials: Patolli Gameboard Worksheet PRF-5.3
Lima beans with a single dot painted on one side of each bean
Small colored markers for playing pieces
Sets of attribute blocks ("individual" or desktop size)

Management: Teams of 4 students each (30 minutes)

Directions:

1. Background: This game is an adaptation of a game played by the Aztecs, an Indian people who dominated central Mexico in the 1500's. A Spanish chronicler, Francisco Lopez de Gomara, recorded in 1552 that Montezuma, emperor of the Aztecs, sometimes watched the game being played. Patolli was played on a mat gameboard in the shape of a cross, which was subdivided into rectangles. The *patolli* were beans that served as one-sided dice. During the game, players would call on Macuilxochitl, the god of dice, and on Ometochtli, the god of gambling, to help them receive good points on the dice. Too few rules of the original game have been preserved; hence, the rules given below are offered as suggestions. For more information on this game, please refer to the following sources:

Marina C. Krause, *Multicultural Mathematics Materials* (National Council of Teachers of Mathematics, 1906 Association Drive, Reston, VA 22091, 1983)

E. G. Tylor, "On the Game of Patolli in Ancient Mexico, and Its Probably Asiatic Origin," *Journal of the Anthropological Institute of Great Britain and Ireland* 8 (1879): 116–31.

NAME ______________________________ DATE ____________________

GEOMETRIC WORKSHEET PRF-5.2
Drawing Geometric Patterns

For each sequence, color the given shapes. Find a pattern to their changes, and draw and color the next 3 shapes.

1. 

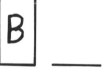

R

R ___ ___ ___

2. 

B

B ___ ___ ___

3. 

P

R

___ ___ ___

4. 

B

___ ___ ___

5. 

P
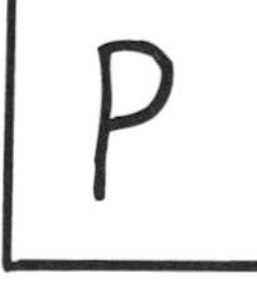

___ ___ ___

6. 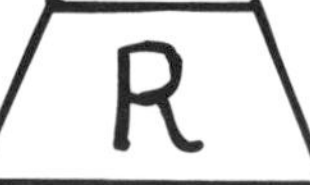

R

___ ___ ___

2. Give each team a patolli gameboard, 3 lima beans (each with one dot painted on one side only), 3 markers or playing pieces of the same color per person (a different color for each player; playing pieces can be 1/2-inch paper squares, small colored stones, small colored buttons, etc.), and a commercial set of attribute blocks. For this game students will randomly generate a sequence of geometric shapes. A sequence pattern may not be obvious among the shapes.

3. Each team member selects a starting place at a different arm of the gameboard—A, B, C, or D. To decide who goes first, each player holds the 3 beans cupped in both hands, then drops the beans onto the mat (or table) near the gameboard cross and counts the dots showing on the beans. If two players tie, they toss again. The player with the highest number of dots tossed goes first. That player then randomly selects an attribute block from the set and places it on the table near the gameboard.

4. On a player's first toss, regardless of the number of dots, his or her first playing piece can be placed on the board in that player's first rectangle. Each of the other two playing pieces can only be brought onto the board later if a 1 is tossed.

5. The number of spaces a playing piece can be moved are as follows: 0 dots = pass, 1 dot = 1 space, 2 dots = 5 spaces, and 3 dots = 10 spaces. A playing piece can only be moved, however, if the player can correctly add a new attribute block to the *attribute train* begun by the first player. Selection of the block to be added is also determined by the bean toss: 1 dot = the new block can only differ from the last block played in one way; 2 dots = the new block must differ from the last one in two ways; and 3 dots = the new block must differ in three ways. The ways in which two blocks might differ are shape, size, color, and thickness. An example of two blocks that differ in two ways might be a yellow, small, thin triangle and a red, large, thin triangle; an example of two blocks that differ in three ways would be a red, large circle with a blue, small square.

6. Players must try to move all their playing pieces completely around and off the patolli gameboard. An example of a complete path for player A is shown below:

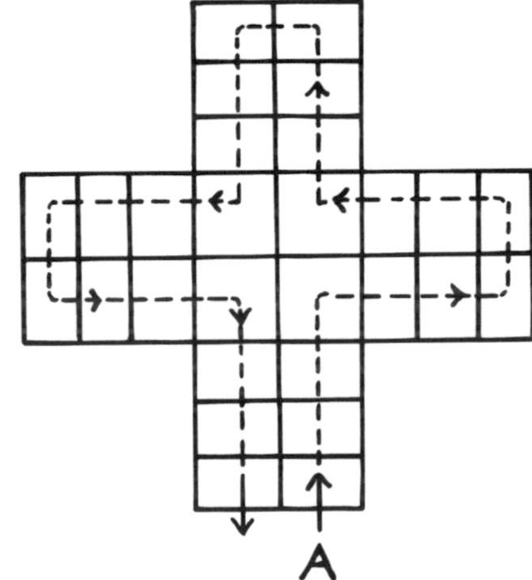

7. A playing piece cannot be removed from the board unless a toss is thrown for the exact number of spaces or more left in its path. The player to remove all three playing pieces from the gameboard first is the winner.

WORKSHEET PRF-5.3
Gameboard for Patolli

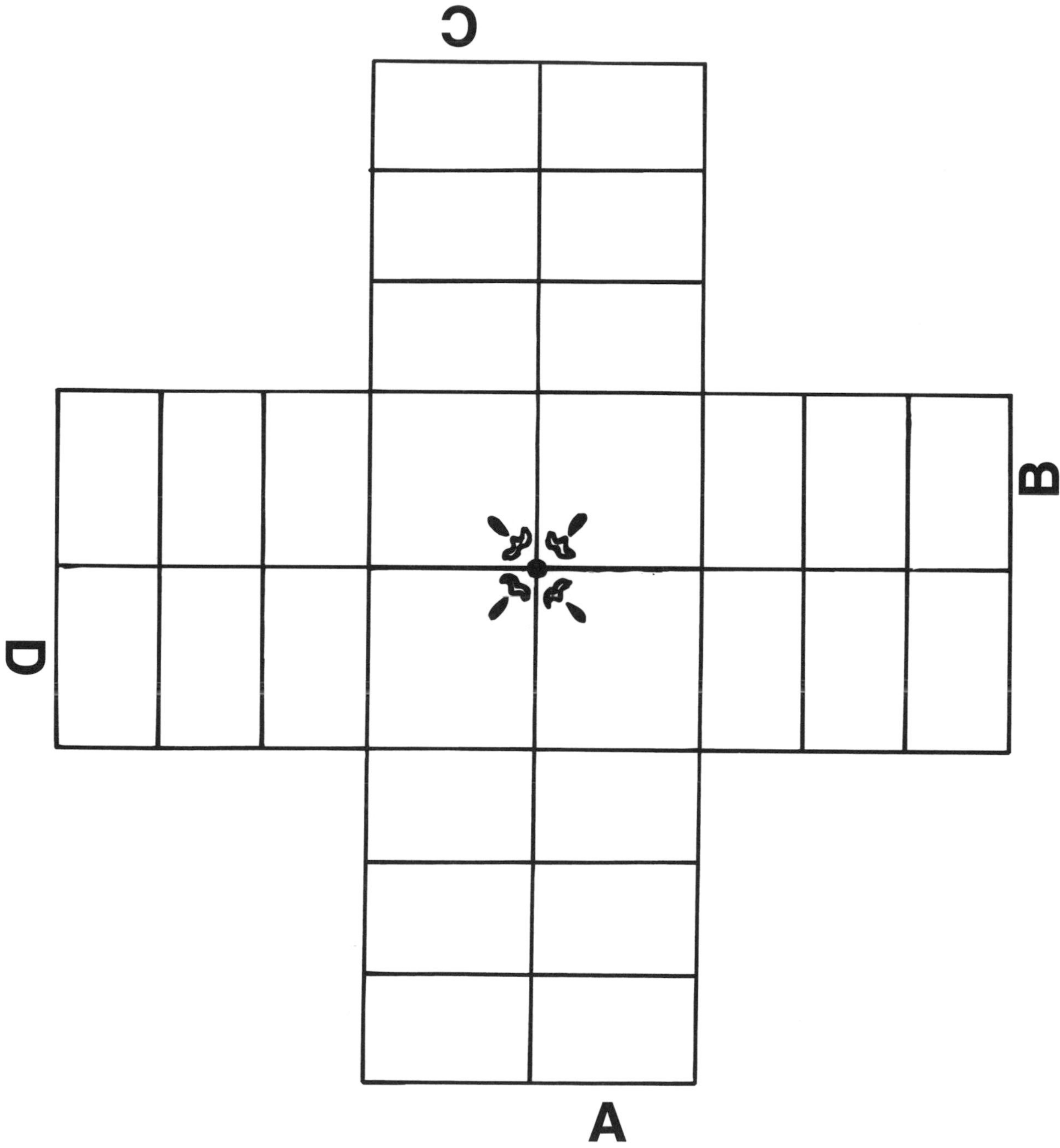

OBJECTIVE 6: Pair quantities of objects from two different sets to build patterns.

Activity 1: CONNECTING COLORED CUBES
(Concrete Action)

Materials: Connectable colored cubes (2 colors)
Paper
Pencils

Management: Partners (30 minutes)

Directions:

1. Give each pair of students a set of cubes (any 2 colors, 40 cubes/color).

2. Have them build straight *trains* by connecting cubes together in the following ways. (For convenience, we will use the colors red and blue; connect cubes as trains in the order given): 1 red, then 2 blue; 2 reds, then 4 blues; 3 reds, then 6 blues.

R	B	B

R	R	B	B	B	B

R	R	R	B	B	B	B	B	B

3. Discuss with students what they think the next two trains should look like. Ask them to build them. (They should build 4 reds with 8 blues, then 5 reds with 10 blues.)

4. Ask how the number of blue cubes seems to relate to the number of red cubes in the same train. (In each train there are twice as many blues as reds.)

5. The trains can now be recorded in a two-column table. The amount of the first color used in each train should be listed in the left column, and the amount of the second color should be listed in the right column.

Example:

Red	Blue
1	2
2	4
3	6
4	8
5	10

6. Repeat steps 2–5 by having students build the first three trains as follows: 1 red, then 2 blues; 2 reds, then 3 blues; 3 reds, then 4 blues. (Students should observe that in each train, there will be 1 more blue than red.)

7. Allow pairs of students to create their own patterns that relate blue cubes to red cubes in trains. Challenge the class to discover and describe the patterns used by some of the partners. When building trains, red cubes should always be used in counting order: 1 red, 2 reds, 3 reds, 4 reds, etc.

Activity 2: COMPARING PARTS
(Pictorial Action)

Materials: Paper
Colored pencils
Pencils

Management: Partners (30 minutes)

Directions:

1. Each pair of students should have a set of colored pencils. Several different sequences that pair two colored geometric shapes in some way as a *design* can be shown on the overhead projector; three such pairings or designs will be given for each sequence. Students are to copy on their own paper the first three designs of a sequence shown on the overhead, then draw the next three and record the sequence as number pairs in a table.

2. For the first example, draw green triangles and red squares on the overhead as follows:

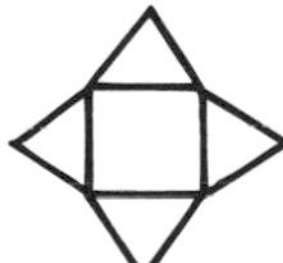

Students should copy these, then draw and color the next three designs, using 4 red squares with 10 green triangles around them, 5 squares with 12 triangles, and 6 squares with 14 triangles.

3. Have students make a recording table to show their results.

Example:

How many squares?	1	2	3	4	5	6
How many triangles?	4	6	8	10	12	14

4. Ask students what they notice about the numbers in the table. Ask: *How does the number of triangles relate to the number of squares used in each design?* Several answers are possible and are acceptable if they seem reasonable and apply to all designs drawn or all pairs of numbers in the table. Some students may note that while the squares are 1, 2, 3, 4, . . . , the triangles are even numbers, beginning with 4. One relationship might be as follows: For N squares in a row together, there are N triangles above and N triangles below the squares with an extra triangle on the left and right ends of the row of squares. Another way to say this is *double the number of squares used and add two more to find the number of triangles needed each time.*

5. Repeat steps 2–4, using the following sequences:

- Red triangles joined together with blue circles touching the exposed edges of the triangles (*Pattern*: There will be 2 more circles than triangles in each design — N + 2 circles for N triangles.)

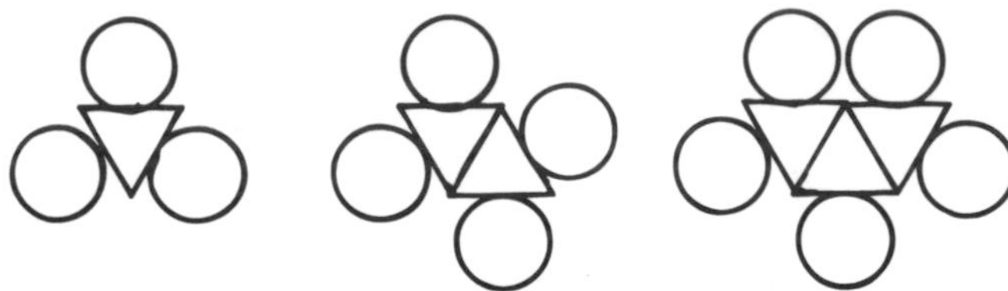

- Green circles joined together in a row, each circle enclosed by a black square, with an extra black square drawn wherever the corners of two *enclosing* squares touch (*Pattern*: For N circles in a design, there will be N squares enclosing the circles plus N – 1 squares above the circle-square row and N – 1 squares below the row. Do not simplify the expression for the total squares unless you are working with an algebra class and want to simplify as an extension of this activity; in that case, the total is N + (N – 1) + (N – 1), or 3N – 2.)

- Long, brown rectangles drawn with long sides touching and with a blue square touching each short side. (*Pattern*: There are twice as many blue squares as brown rectangles in each design—2 × N squares for N rectangles.)

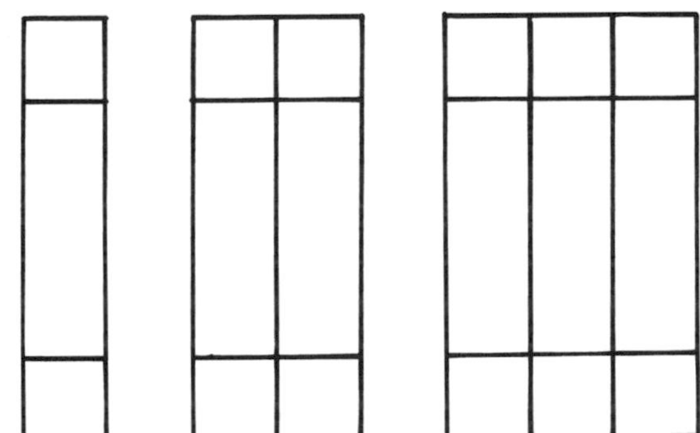

6. If time allows, have different pairs of students create their own sequence and draw its first three designs on the overhead. Other students can then predict the next two or three designs and try to describe the pattern that occurs between the two shapes used.

Activity 3: DARING DESIGNS

(Cooperative Groups)

Materials: Commercial pattern blocks
5- or 10-minute timer
Paper
Pencils

Management: Teams of 4 students each (20 minutes)

Directions:

1. Give each team a set of pattern blocks (squares, triangles, hexagons, parallelograms, trapezoids, narrow diamonds). The quantity of each block needed will depend on the problems or DARES selected for the teams to work.

2. On the chalkboard write three or four DARES for students to try during the allotted time. Sample DARES are provided in step 6.

3. For a given DARE, students are told how many blocks total of each of two different pattern block shapes are to be used to build the first three terms or designs of a mystery sequence. The sequence is being generated according to some specific pattern. Each team must decide how many of each shape belong in each design and build the three designs, using all their blocks. The three designs they build cannot be random, but must be related by a pattern of some kind. Also, one of the blocks, say A, will serve as the *counter* for the sequence: 1 A with ____ B, 2 A with ____ B, 3 A with ____ B. Several patterns and sets of designs may be possible for the same DARE quantities (i.e., patterns other than the one used originally to create the DARE), but students must be able to explain their patterns to the approval of the entire class.

4. Use the timer to limit the amount of time used for one DARE. Five to ten minutes should be all the time allowed for a team's attempt to solve one DARE; that keeps the challenge in the activity and forces students to bring their efforts to an end.

5. After time is called for a given DARE, have 2–3 teams share their results with the entire class and explain the pattern they used to make their three designs (the first three terms of the sequence).

6. Here are some possible DARES to use, along with their original patterns and designs. (For special classes, algebraic extensions are provided.)

- Use 6 trapezoids and 12 squares. (*Pattern*: Trapezoids are joined at their shorter *isosceles* sides to form a row; squares are attached to each short side of every trapezoid that remains exposed in the row. Number pairs are 1 trape-3 sq, 2 trape-4 sq, 3 trape-5 sq. *Algebraic extension*: If N trapezoids are used in a design, N + 2 squares are needed.)

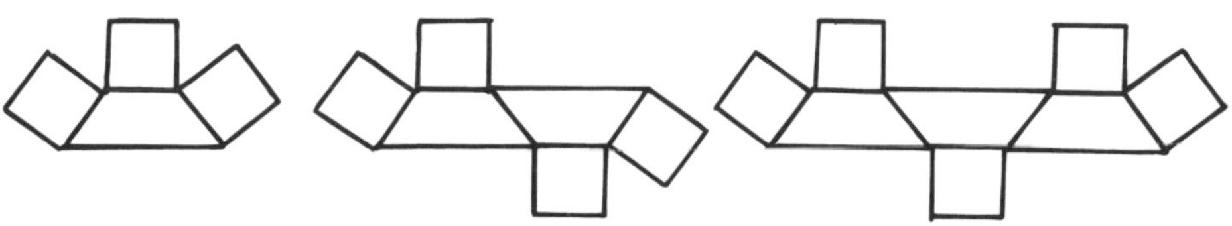

- Use 6 squares and 18 diamonds. (*Pattern*: Squares are placed side by side to form longer rectangles; narrow diamonds are placed around the edges of the rectangle like sections of a pinwheel. Number pairs are 1 sq-4 diam, 2 sq-6 diam, 3 sq-8 diam. *Algebraic extension*: For N squares in a design, N × 2 + 2 diamonds are needed.)

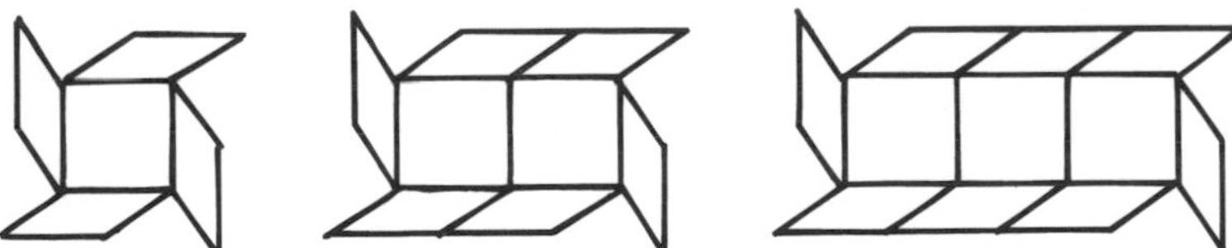

- Use 6 hexagons and 30 triangles. (*Pattern*: Hexagons are joined vertex to vertex to form a row; triangles are placed around the hexagons so that every edge of any hexagon touches a triangle's edge. Number pairs are 1 hex-6 tri, 2 hex-10 tri, 3 hex-14 tri. *Algebraic extension*: For N hexagons in a design, N × 4 + 2 triangles are needed.)

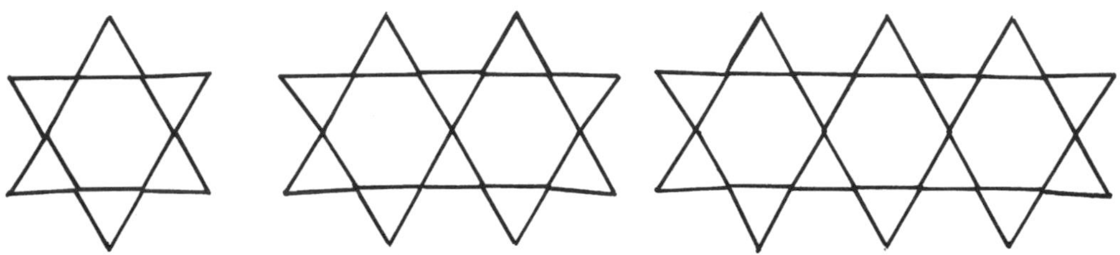

- Use 10 trapezoids and 26 triangles. Build four terms for this DARE. (*Pattern*: Trapezoids are joined together at their parallel edges, putting *longer* edges together first, then *shorter* edges together; triangles are attached to all exposed short edges. Number pairs for the first 4 designs will be 1 trape-3 tri, 2 trape-6 tri, 3 trape-7 tri, 4 trape-10 tri. *Algebraic extension*: This pattern is different from the other three in that the number of triangles needed depends on whether the number N of trapezoids in a design is even or odd. If N is odd, there are N × 2 + 1 triangles; if N is even, there are N × 2 + 2 triangles.) *Note*: A different pattern results if the *shorter* parallel edges are joined first, followed by the *longer* edges.

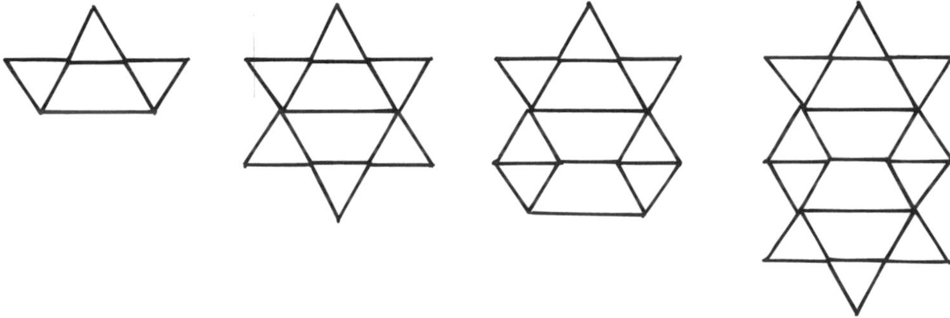

OBJECTIVE 7: Find equivalent fractions, using patterns of change within numerators and denominators.

[**Note:** The activities for this objective will focus only on changing larger part sizes to smaller part sizes to find equivalent forms. Reduction, a more difficult process, is developed in Chapter One.]

Activity 1: WHO GETS TO TRADE?
(Concrete Action)

Materials: Fraction strips (commercial sets available; pattern also included in PATTERNS/GRIDS section)
Building Mat Pattern Worksheet PRF-7.1
Paper
Pencils

Management: Partners (50 minutes)

Directions:

1. Give each pair of students a set of fraction strips (minimal set of individual bars: 1 whole, 2 halves, 3 thirds, 4 fourths, 6 sixths, 8 eighths, 12 twelfths). Do not use materials where nonunit fractions are connected pieces, e.g., where *two-thirds* is a single bar with 2/3 of the bar shaded. Instead, *two-thirds* is shown by two separate *thirds*. Students must be able to move each fractional part individually.

2. For this activity it is assumed that students understand that the fraction name, 2/3, means *2 out of 3 parts of the whole unit.*

3. Have students place the whole unit bar from their set of fraction strips on the middle bar of their building mat, and ask them to trade it for 3 new bars that are equal in size. (They should locate the thirds eventually and exchange 3 of them for the whole bar. Reinforce the idea that the amount they now have on the mat is called *three-thirds of the whole unit.*)

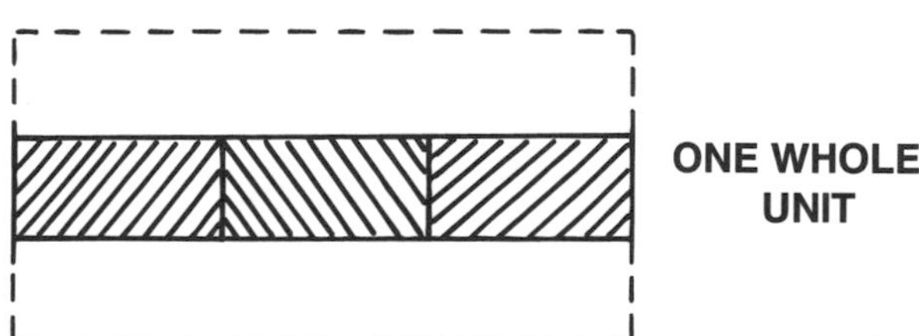

4. Ask students to trade *each* third for 2 new bars that are the *same size,* but to place the new bars on the whole bar space in the lower section of the building mat. (Allow them to search for the proper part size; this is a necessary learning experience. Stress that in a "trade" *each* bar must be exchanged separately. For example, you do not want to trade 2 old bars for 3 new bars just because the two sets have the same total length. Also, in a trade, all new bars used must be the same length. All of these ideas combined together lead to the use of multiplication eventually, but do not mention that at this time.) Discuss how many new bars they now have and how to name the total amount and trade size. (6 new bars cover the whole unit bar, so we have *sixths*.) Have them record the following on their own papers:

3-thirds of whole unit	=	6-sixths of whole unit	[a 2-for-1 trade]

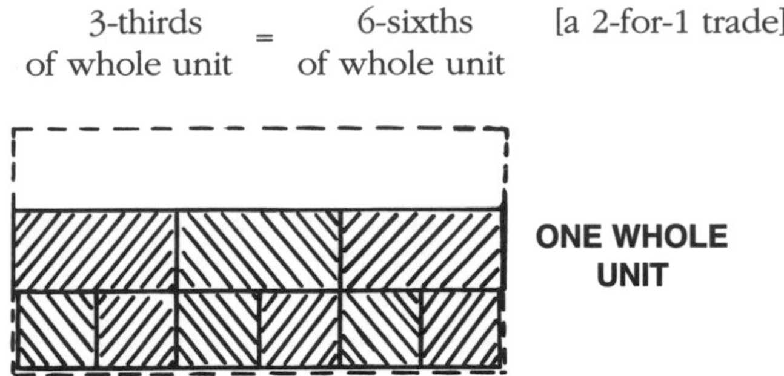

5. From the three-thirds, ask them to remove 1 to show only two-thirds of the whole unit on the mat. We want to rename the two-thirds now, using the same type of trade used for the three-thirds or full unit length. Have students trade each of the two-thirds for two new equal bars again, but show this by placing the new bars on the whole bar space in the upper section of the building mat. Observe that the new bars are sixths also. Since the four-sixths were found only through trading and have the same total length as the two-thirds, the final fractional amount, *four-sixths of the whole unit*, is *equivalent* to the original amount, *two-thirds of the whole unit.* Have students record as follows:

2-thirds of whole unit	=	4-sixths of whole unit	[a 2-for-1 trade]

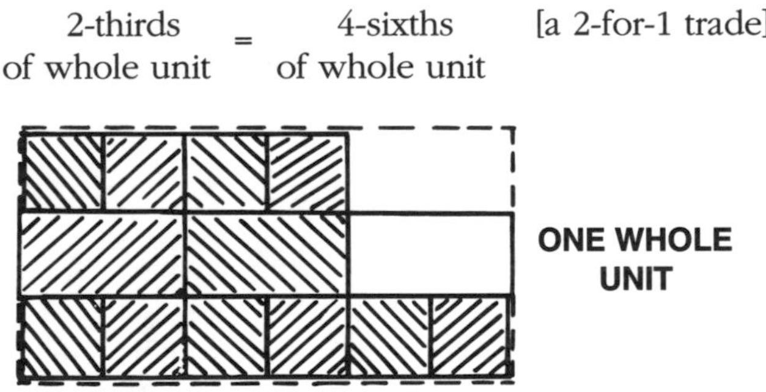

Note: By the same reasoning as given above, we can say that *three-thirds* and *six-sixths* found earlier are *equivalent* amounts.

6. Do not record fraction amounts in ratio form at this time. Use a combination of counting number (for number of parts) and word name (for the part size). The ratio form is very frustrating for students when it is introduced too soon in their fraction experience.

7. Repeat steps 3–5 with a variety of fractions and trades. Students need to build many examples with the fraction strips before they begin to see patterns in the trades for the numerator and denominator. Here are some examples and trades to try:

- Build 1-half—use 4-for-1 trade; record 2-halves = 8-eighths and 1-half = 4-eighths of the whole unit.
- Build 3-fourths—use 2-for-1 trade; record 4-fourths = 8-eighths and 3-fourths = 6-eighths of the whole unit. (similarly for 1-fourth and 2-fourths)
- Build 2-fourths—use 3-for-1 trade; record 4-fourths = 12-twelfths and 2-fourths = 6-twelfths of the whole unit. (similarly for 1-fourth and 3-fourths)

- Build 1-third—use 4-for-1 trade; record 3-thirds = 12-twelfths and 1-third = 4-twelfths of the whole unit.
- Build 1-half—use 3-for-1 trade; record 2-halves = 6-sixths and 1-half = 3-sixths of the whole unit.
- Build 1-half—use 2-for-1 trade; record 2-halves = 4-fourths and 1-half = 2-fourths of the whole unit.
- Build 1-half—use 6-for-1 trade; record 2-halves = 12-twelfths and 1-half = 6-twelfths of the whole unit.
- Build 4-sixths—use 2-for-1 trade; record 6-sixths = 12-twelfths and 4-sixths = 8-twelfths of the whole unit. (similarly for 1-sixth, 2-sixths, etc.)

8. Encourage students to share their observations. Ask: *When you made trades to find a new name for each fraction you built on the mat, how did the trade made for the numerator (upper part of mat) compare with the trade made for the denominator (lower part of mat)?* (Type of trade was the same for both numerator and denominator.) Ask: *After both trades are made, how do the new part sizes counted for the numerator (the portion of the whole bar we actually have on the middle part of the mat) compare to the new part sizes counted for the denominator or whole bar?* (The part sizes are the same.)

Activity 2: PICTURE PATTERNS

(Pictorial Action)

Materials: Fraction Worksheet PRF-7.2
Red pencils
Regular pencils

Management: Partners (50 minutes)

Directions:

1. Give each student a copy of Worksheet PRF-7.2 and a red pencil. Tell the students that each rectangle represents a whole unit and that they will be showing different fractional parts of these whole units.

2. Do not assume that students know how to subdivide rectangles pictorially. Many will not. As a readiness activity show them how to subdivide a rectangle drawn on the chalkboard. An effective way is to use tick marks on the upper edge of the rectangle to show where the new subdivision segments might be located. This allows students to look at their spacing to decide if the new parts will be *about equal;* if not, the tick marks can be erased and redrawn. Once students are satisfied with the positions of the tick marks, they can draw in the subdivision segments. Specifically students need to be shown such skills as:

- finding fourths by placing a tick mark at the midpoint, then one tick halfway between the left end and the midpoint and another tick halfway between the midpoint and right end
- finding sixths by marking the midpoint, then spacing two tick marks equally between the left end and midpoint and two more tick marks equally between the midpoint and right end

NAME ______________________________ DATE ____________________

WORKSHEET PRF-7.1
Building Mat for Who Gets To Trade?

(to be used with FRACTION BAR set; see pattern in PATTERNS/GRIDS section)

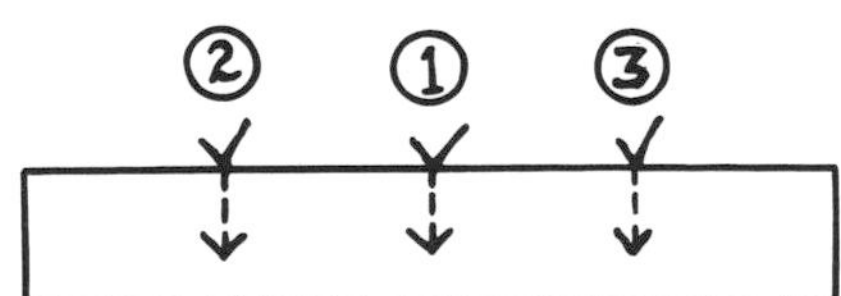

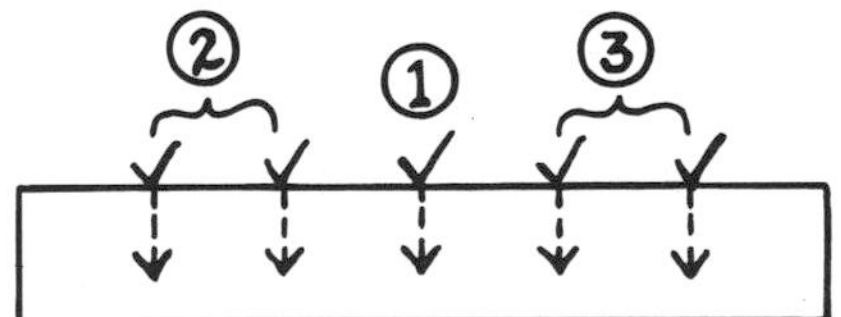

3. Have the students *cut* the first blank rectangle on the worksheet into two *equal* parts by drawing a segment down the middle of the bar (no need to measure; just agree that the two parts *look about equal* to the untrained eye). Ask them to shade one of the two halves they now have for the whole unit bar. To *shade,* have them draw diagonal segments. Full shading takes too long and is difficult to erase when a change is needed.

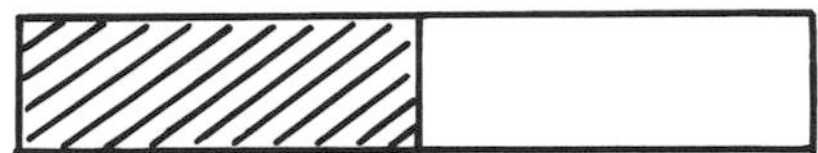

4. Ask the students to show a 2-for-1 trade by cutting each half of the whole unit into two equal parts. Tick marks should be used first, then the final subdivision segments should be drawn in red pencil. Extend the new *cuts* beyond the rectangle itself. This helps to distinguish the new parts from the original ones on the drawing.

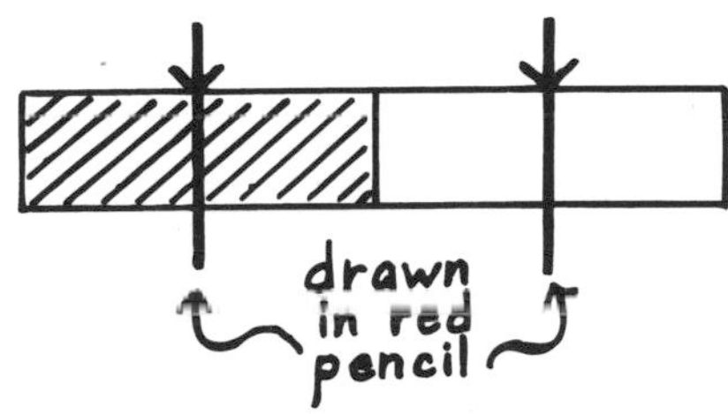

5. Discuss how many new parts are in the whole unit now and what each part should be called. (four; fourths) Discuss how many new parts are now shaded. (two) In the space below the rectangle, have students record *1-half of whole = 2-fourths of whole.*

6. Next, ask: *How many old parts were shaded?* (one of the halves) *How many new parts were traded for 1 old shaded part?* (2 new for 1 old) Write this as *1 × 2 new = 2 new shaded* on the board. Emphasize the language: *1 set of 2 new parts makes 2 new parts shaded in all.*

7. Then ask: *How many old parts were in the whole unit?* (2 of the halves) *How many new parts were traded for each old part in the whole unit?* (2 new for each old) Write this as *2 × 2 new = 4 new total* on the board. Again emphasize the language: *2 sets of 2 new parts each have 4 new parts altogether.*

8. Next, have students record this information under their rectangle as follows: (Continually emphasize that 1/2 or one-half means 1 out of 2 parts, etc.)

$$\frac{1}{2} = \frac{1 \times 2 \text{ new}}{2 \times 2 \text{ new}} = \frac{2 \text{ new shaded}}{4 \text{ new total}} = \frac{2}{4} \text{ of whole unit}$$

9. Repeat steps 3–8, showing 2-fourths and a 3-for-1 trade on the second whole rectangle on the worksheet. Shade the two fourths by drawing diagonals in opposite directions; this makes it easier to *see* the separate parts on the rectangle.

10. Since each shaded fourth will trade for 3 new parts, there will be *2 sets of 3 new parts each* or 6 new shaded parts formed. Since each fourth on the whole unit bar trades for 3 new parts, there will be *4 sets of 3 new parts each* or 12 new parts total for the whole rectangle. Students should have the following shown on their worksheets:

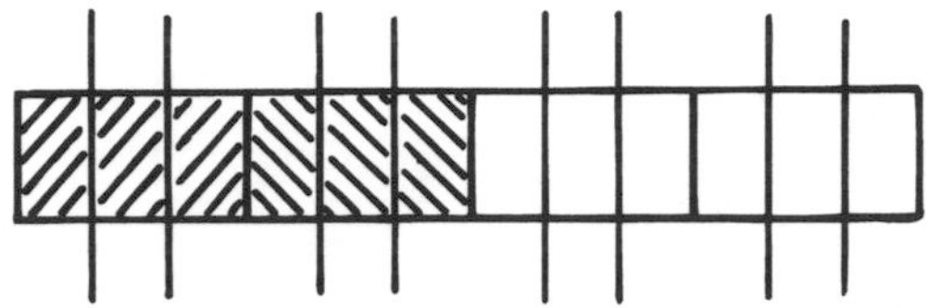

$$\frac{2}{4} = \frac{2 \times 3 \text{ new}}{4 \times 3 \text{ new}} = \frac{6 \text{ new shaded}}{12 \text{ new total}} = \frac{6}{12} \text{ of whole unit}$$

11. Have students draw several other examples. Do not use denominators that are greater than 15 after the trade; the parts become too small to count easily. Here are some possible problems to use:

- 2-thirds—3-for-1 trade to get 6-ninths of the unit (similarly for 1-third)
- 1-fifth—2-for-1 trade to get 2-tenths of the unit (similarly for 2-fifths, etc.)
- 1-half—4-for-1 trade to get 4-eighths of the unit (similarly for 2-halves)
- 3-fifths—3-for-1 trade to get 9-fifteenths of the unit (similarly for 4-fifths, etc.)
- 5-sevenths—2-for-1 trade to get 10-fourteenths of the unit (similarly for 2-sevenths, etc.)

12. Have students share their results; encourage the use of the *set language* (e.g., 2 sets of 3 new parts each makes 6 new parts total) to reinforce the role of multiplication in the trading process.

13. Discuss what happens in the numerator and the denominator when a fraction of a whole unit is renamed through trading. Ask partners to write two or three sentences to describe the change in their own words. Have several students read their paragraphs to the entire class so that they can hear different ways of expressing the same ideas. (The main idea should be that, since both the numerator and the denominator must undergo the same type of trade, the number sentence will show the two original amounts multiplied by the same factor, which is the size of the trade used.)

NAME ______________________________ DATE ____________________

FRACTION WORKSHEET PRF-7.2
Picture Patterns

Each bar below is a whole unit. Your teacher will tell you how to change each bar.

1.

2.

3.

4.

5.

6.

7.

8.

Activity 3: DEMANDO

(Cooperative Groups)

Materials: Paper
Pencils

Management: Teams of 4 students each (20 minutes)

Directions:

1. On each team, one pair of students takes turns challenging the other pair of students.

2. On a turn the challenging pair will call out a common fraction with a denominator less than 10 and tell what the new denominator should be (use numbers less than 40). The new denominator should be a multiple of the old one. The other pair will write the products needed to change the numerator and denominator to the new equivalent form. For example, if 4/5 and the new denominator 20 are called out, the second pair of students must write the following: $\frac{4 \times 4}{5 \times 4} = \frac{16}{20}$

3. At this point the challengers can accept this result as correct or may *demand,* even if the number sentence is correct, that the pair *confirm* their answer by drawing and subdividing a whole unit bar. Students seem to understand the fraction concept better when they draw and subdivide their own unit bars. If a drawing is demanded, a *long* rectangle should be used (approximately as long as the width of the paper and 2–3 writing spaces high) to make the *cutting* easier to see.

4. For a harder challenge, instead of a rectangle for the whole unit, a large circle or square might be *demanded* as the whole unit for the drawing. Care must be taken when making "cuts" to make certain that all new parts can be considered equal in size within reason. Other possible shapes to use (and review some geometry terms as well):

- A regular hexagon (6 equal sides)—for showing halves, thirds, sixths and twelfths only
- A regular octagon (8 equal sides)—for showing halves, fourths, eighths and sixteenths
- A regular decagon (10 equal sides)—for showing halves, fifths, tenths and twentieths.

Whole unit = a regular hexagon

halves

thirds

sixths

twelfths

OBJECTIVE 8: Find patterns in the divisibility of whole numbers.

Activity 1: NUMBER SPLITTING
(Concrete Action)

Materials: Base 10 blocks
Building Mat Worksheet PRF-8.1
Paper
Pencils

Management: Partners (50 minutes)

Directions:

Give each pair of students a set of base 10 blocks (minimum set: 5 tens and 50 ones) and a building mat copied from Worksheet PRF-8.1. In this activity blocks should only be traded when absolutely necessary. In addition, Activities 1 and 2 consist of sections a–c, each for a different divisibility. To focus on only one type, you can do just that section from each activity; for example, to present only divisibility by 5, use section (b) from the two activities.

(a) ***Divisibility by 2***

1. Ask students to find which whole numbers from 1 to 50 can be separated into two equal groups. Each number should be shown with base 10 blocks, then the tens and ones placed on the building mat to form two groups having the same value. Each row on the mat represents a group. For example, for 36, students will begin with 3 tens and 6 ones. A single ten can be placed on each of two rows and a third ten traded for 10 ones. The 10 ones provide 5 ones for each row, and finally the 6 ones are separated, 3 ones per row. Each group (row) now has a value of 18. Hence, 36 is *divisible by 2.*

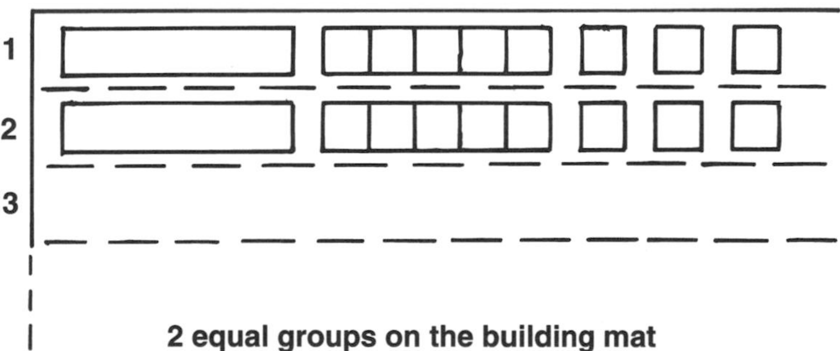

2 equal groups on the building mat

2. After a variety of numbers (not necessarily all 50) have been investigated, have students tell which numbers were divisible by 2; record these numbers on the board. Ask: *What did you notice about the tens and ones as you tried to separate them into two groups? Which combinations of blocks seemed to work and which ones did not?* (All even amounts of tens could be put into two groups. For odd amounts of tens in a number, only 1 ten needed to be traded; yet as 10 ones, it could also be separated into two groups. So any amount of tens worked. Any even amount of ones could also be divided into two equal groups; only odd amounts of the ones could not be used.) Compare the amounts of blocks used to the digits in the number names. Odd amounts of ones are indicated by odd digits 1, 3, 5, 7, or 9 in the ones place of the number names. Thus, of the numbers tested so far (larger numbers will be checked later), those with even digits in the ones place are *divisible by 2.* Students might describe the patterns they find in a *Divisibility Diary* as part of their learning journal.

(b) *Divisibility by 5*

1. Ask students to investigate which numbers 1–50 can be separated into 5 groups of equal value. For example, for 25, the 2 tens cannot be placed on 5 different rows of the mat; however, each ten will trade for 10 ones and then the ones can be separated onto the 5 rows. The original 5 ones can also be put on the 5 rows, 1 one per row. So 25 is *divisible by 5.*

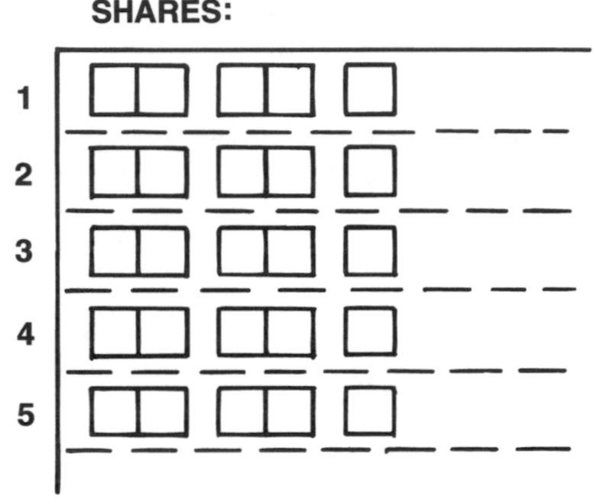

5 equal groups on the building mat

2. After many different numbers have been checked, write the numbers that worked on the board. Ask students to describe which combinations of blocks worked and which did not. (Any amount of tens will work since they can be traded for 10 ones each and 10 ones can always be separated into five equal groups. Only 0 ones or 5 ones can be put into five groups; any other amount of ones cannot.) Compare the amounts of blocks that will work to the digits in the number names. Of the numbers tested so far (larger ones to be checked later), any number that has 0 or 5 in the ones place is divisible by 5. Encourage students to record their discoveries about the block combinations in their notebooks or *diaries.*

(c) *Divisibility by 3*

1. Have students investigate numbers 1–50 that can be separated into three equal groups. For example, for 45, 3 of the tens can be divided and placed onto 3 rows of the mat, 1 ten per row, but the extra ten must be traded for 10 ones. From the 10 ones, 3 ones can be placed on the rows (1 one/row) three different times, leaving 1 extra one. This extra one combines with the original 5 ones and these 6 can then be separated onto the 3 rows. The value of each group is now 15, and 45 is *divisible by 3.*

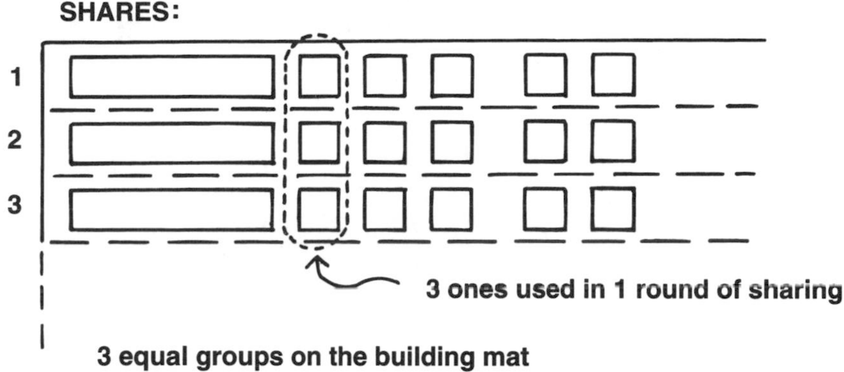

2. After students have tried a variety of numbers, record the numbers that worked on the chalkboard. Ask the class which block combinations seemed to work. (If the amount of blocks could be separated into sets of 3 tens or 3 ones each, then the number was divisible by 3. Each set of three blocks represents one round of sharing, or putting one block on each of three rows. When *each* ten was traded, it provided three rounds of sharing, using 3 ones in each round, and 1 extra one toward another round. These extra ones were then combined with the original amount of ones. Finally, if the total amount of ones was a multiple of 3, the ones could be separated in sets of 3 to go on the 3 rows.) The easiest pattern found so far seems to be for numbers where the amount of tens is a multiple of 3 and the amount of ones is a multiple of 3, e.g., 30, 33, 36, 39, 03, 06, or 09. (*Note*: 00 would be a trivial case; 0 tens and 0 ones would have to be in each of three groups.) Other patterns involve the number of trades made. For example, if *two* tens are traded, we have 9 ones + 9 ones + *two* extra ones. Each set of 9 ones can be separated into 3 sets or rounds of 3 ones each. If the original amount of ones is enough to combine with the extra ones to form another multiple of 3, then our number will work. Again, divisibility seems to depend upon how many ones are left to be separated. We will explore this last pattern more in the next activity.

Activity 2: BLOCKS IN RINGS

(Pictorial Action)

Materials: Paper
Pencils

Management: Partners (50 minutes)

Directions:

This activity will allow students to investigate larger numbers in order to further test the patterns they found with base 10 blocks in Activity 1. They will *draw* blocks for a number, then redraw them 1 block at a time in a required number of rows. Arrangements in rows make the patterns easier to see. Use large squares for hundreds, tally marks for tens, and small circles for ones.

(a) *Divisibility by 2*

1. The pattern for divisibility by 2 predicted earlier with base 10 blocks indicated that if the amount of ones in a number is 0, 2, 4, 6, or 8, then the number is divisible by 2. Ask

NAME ______________________ DATE ______________

WORKSHEET PRF-8.1
Building Mat for Number Splitting

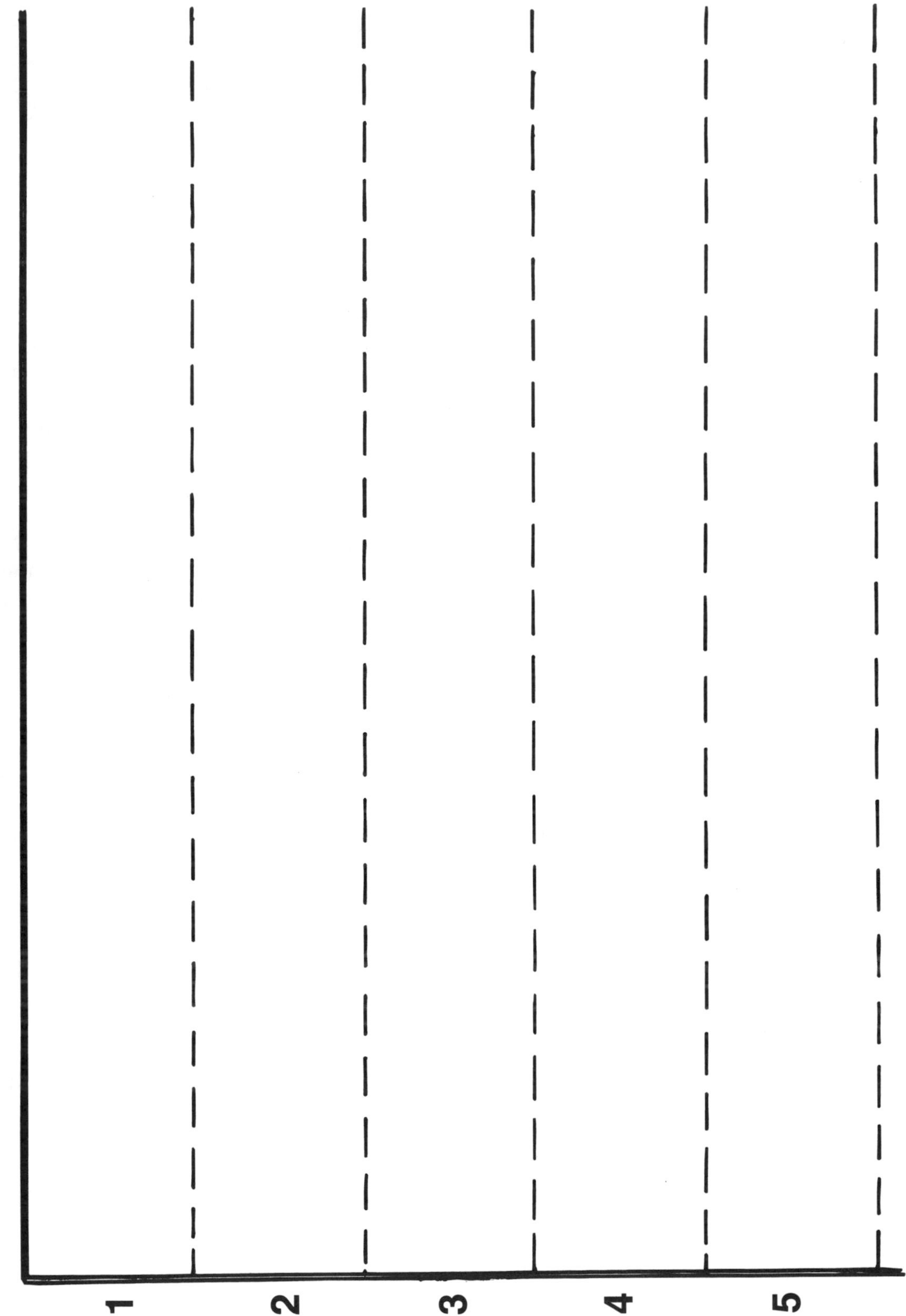

students to test this pattern with the numbers 258, 309, 542, and 175 (two are even and two are odd) by drawing sets of base 10 blocks, then redrawing them in 2 rows, placing 1 block/row at a time. Have students draw on *division frames* similar to the building mat design in Activity 1. Encourage them to draw their shapes large enough to see and count easily.

2. Have them begin with 258 by drawing 2 hundreds, 5 tens, 8 ones, and a division frame on their own paper. You should draw the same blocks on the chalkboard and guide the class through the steps that follow. The 2 hundreds can be redrawn (just mark out the old hundreds) inside the frame, 1 per row. Two sets of 2 tens each can be redrawn inside the frame also.

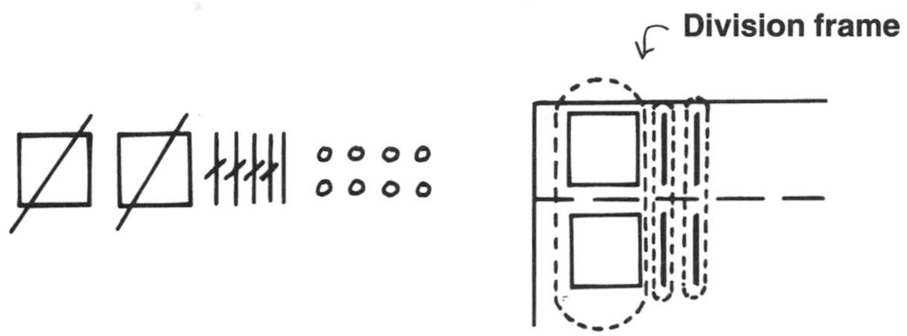

3. The extra ten must be traded for 10 ones, then these ones redrawn inside the frame; five sets of 2 ones each will be used.

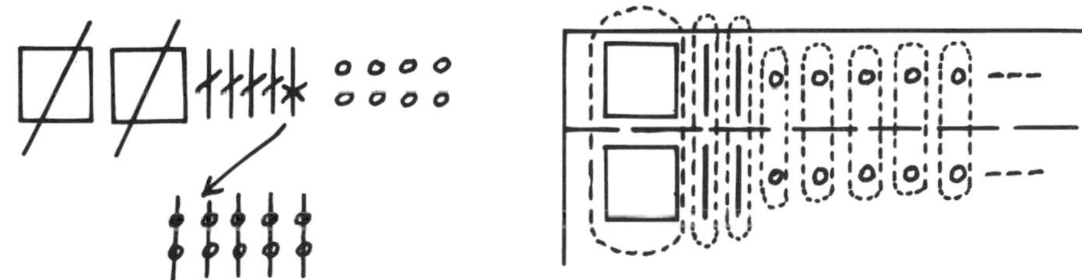

4. Since all blocks, including the ones, can finally be separated into two equal rows (or all blocks ringed in pairs), this shows that the original number, 258, is divisible by 2. Have students draw blocks in division frames for the other three numbers. The odd numbers will each have a single one that cannot be separated into two rows, so they are not divisible by 2. Observe again that each extra hundred or ten can always be traded and redrawn in two equal rows. Divisibility by 2 still depends on the original amount of ones in the number; if the amount is even, pairs of ones can be made with no ones left over and the sharing or division is complete.

(b) ***Divisibility by 5***

1. The earlier pattern found for divisibility by 5 indicated that the amount of ones in a number needs to be either 0 or 5. Have students test this pattern on larger numbers like 130, 327, 245, and 412. Equal sharing now requires sets of 5 like blocks each to be drawn one block at a time in the 5 rows of a division frame.

2. Have students consider the number 327 first. They should draw 3 hundreds, 2 tens, 7 ones, and a division frame on their paper. Since the 3 hundreds cannot be separated into 5 rows, they must be traded for tens. The 30 new tens can be redrawn as sets of 5 tens on the 5 rows of the frame.

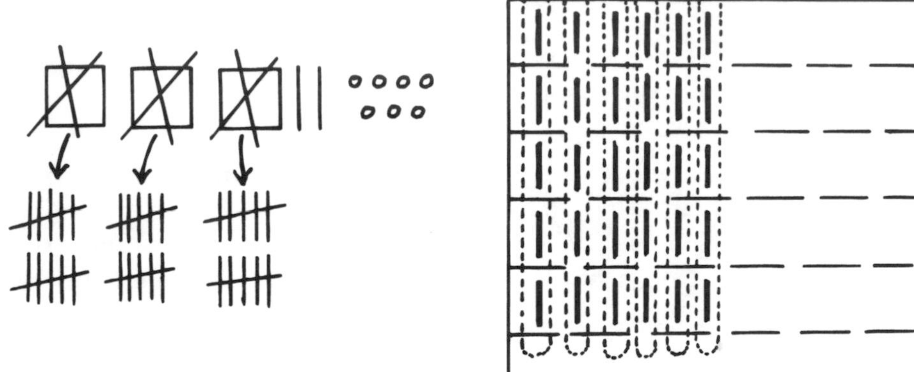

3. The original 2 tens cannot be shared 5 ways either, so they must be traded for ones, which can be redrawn in sets of 5 ones in the frame. Five of the original 7 ones can also be separated onto the 5 rows.

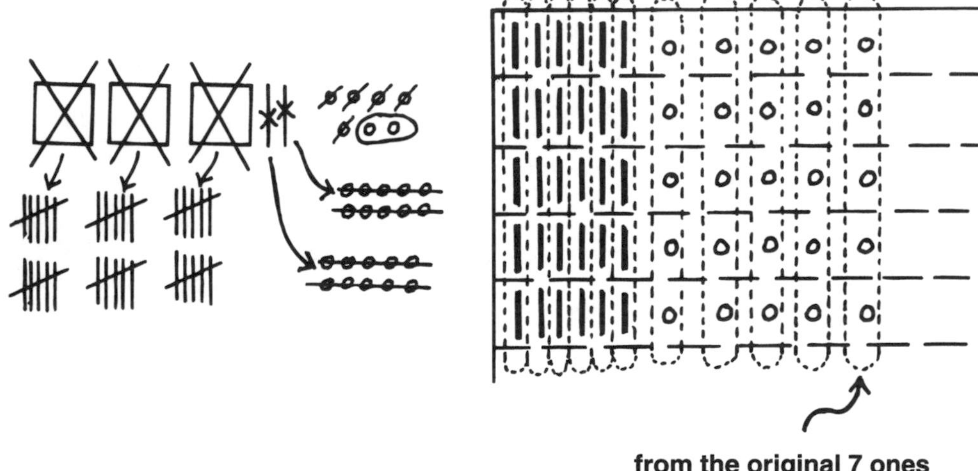

4. Each row in the frame now shows 6 tens and 5 ones, but there are 2 original ones that were not able to be used. This shows that the original number, 327, cannot be separated into 5 equal rows or groups. Therefore, 327 is *not* divisible by 5.

5. Have students draw and separate blocks similarly for the other numbers. When they have completed their drawings, ask if the pattern holds true for the larger numbers. Observe that hundreds and tens, when traded, will always form sets of 5 like blocks, so the divisibility really depends on the original amount of ones. If the ones can be separated into sets of 5 ones each, then the original number will be divisible by 5. Of course, this can only happen if there are 0 or 5 ones in the number.

(c) *Divisibility by 3*

1. Ask students to test their previous *multiples of 3* pattern with the larger numbers 147, 214, 366, and 431. The pattern for 3 is more complex than the previous two, so encourage students to draw their blocks neatly and according to the arrangements shown in the figures below.

2. Have students draw a division frame and the blocks for 147: 1 hundred, 4 tens, and 7 ones. The 1 hundred must be traded for 10 tens, which can be separated into 3 sets of 3 tens each on the frame with 1 ten left over. Since there are other tens still available to help make a set of 3, show this by drawing a box around this extra ten, then redraw it on the top row of the frame and box it again. Mark out any original or traded blocks as they are used or redrawn on the frame.

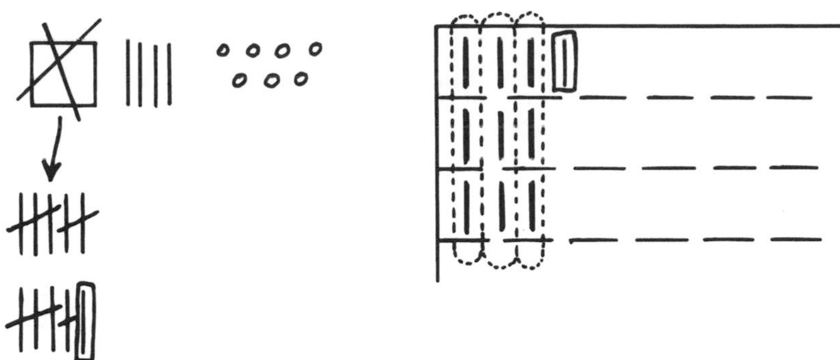

3. Fill in the 2 rows below the extra ten with 2 of the original 4 tens to make another set of 3 tens in the frame; 2 tens will be left over. Do not box these 2 tens since there are no others to complete a set of 3.

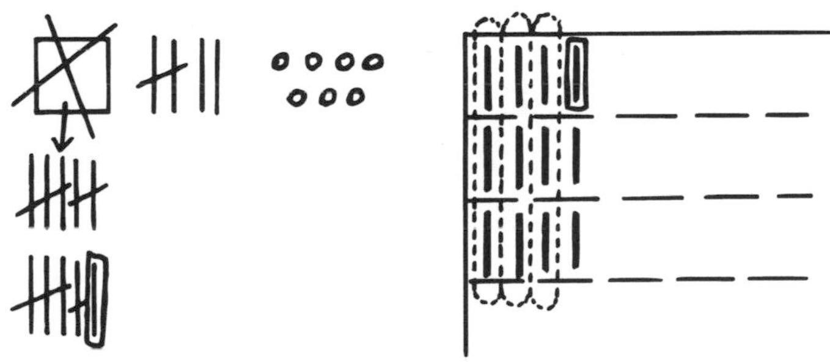

4. Each ten can be traded for 10 ones. Each set of 10 ones should be redrawn as 3 sets of 3 ones each on the frame with the extra one drawn on the top row. Have students draw a box around each extra one to emphasize it. Copy the figure below; do not redraw any of the original 7 ones on the frame yet.

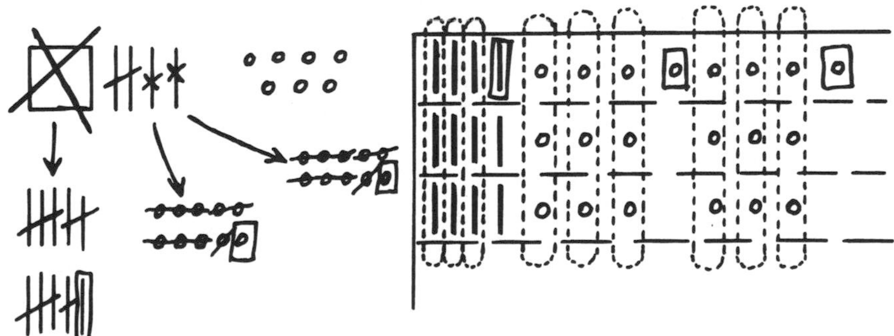

5. Next, ask: *Do we have enough original ones to complete the two sets of 3 ones each that are already started on the frame? If so, how many ones are needed?* (2 ones to go under each boxed one, or 4 ones in all) *Of the 3 original ones still left, can we make another set of 3?* (yes) Have students redraw the rest of the ones on the frame. Since no blocks are left of the original blocks, 147 has been separated into 3 equal groups and thus is divisible by 3.

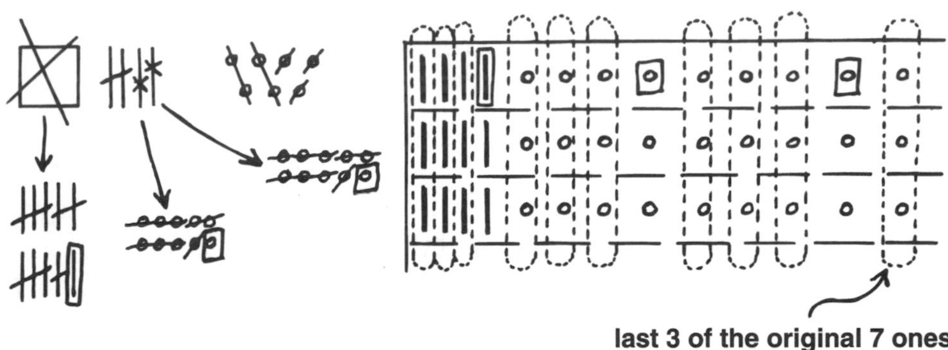

6. Once again the ones determine a number's divisibility. In this case, however, not only must the amount of original ones be considered (shown by the ones digit of the number) but also the extra ones resulting from the trading of larger blocks. The combined ones have to be a multiple of 3. Have students now draw division frames and blocks to test the other three numbers for divisibility by 3.

7. After students have confirmed the effect of the combined ones on the divisibility of their other numbers, guide them through the following exercises to show how this pattern with ones is reflected in *all* the digits of the number. Have them start with a single hundred. They should trade it, trying to form 3 equal groups, until they find how many *ones* are finally contributed from that hundred. (A single *hundred* will provide 1 extra *one* after trading and separating blocks into sets of 3 tens or 3 ones.) Repeat the process with a single ten. (A single *ten* will also provide 1 extra *one* after trading and all possible sets of 3 ones are made.)

8. Ask: *If 1 hundred leaves 1 extra one, then how many will 3 hundreds leave?* (3 ones) *If 1 ten leaves 1 extra one, then how many will 5 tens leave?* (5 ones) Students can confirm their answers with the drawing process, if necessary. Finally, ask: *If our number is 357, how many extra ones will be provided by the 3 hundreds and the 5 tens?* (3 ones + 5 ones) *If these are combined with the original 7 ones, will their total be a multiple of 3; i.e., be able to be separated into 3 equal groups?* (Yes; the total is 3 + 5 + 7 or 15 ones, which is divisible by 3.) Ask students to compare the amounts of *extra* and *original ones* involved to the *digits* of 357. (The amounts and digits match exactly.) Have students write a description of the new pattern they have found for divisibility by 3. **Example:** *If the digits of a number add up to equal a multiple of 3, then the number is divisible by 3.*

Activity 3: DIVIROLL

(Cooperative Groups)

Materials: Dice or number cubes
Paper
Pencils
Calculators (optional)

Management: Teams of 4 students each (20 minutes)

Directions:

1. Give each team a die or number cube.

2. Team members will take turns rolling the die or cube three times; the first number rolled will indicate hundreds; the second, tens; and the third, ones. For example, if 5, 8, and 3 are rolled in that order, the player must use the number 583. The patterns for divisibility discovered in Activities 1 and 2 will be applied to each three-digit number rolled.

3. Using the number obtained from the three rolls, a player must tell if it is divisible by 2, 3, or 5. For each correct divisibility, the player earns that many points; e.g., if the number is correctly identified as divisible by 2 and 5, the player will earn 7 points. For any incorrect answer or lack of a correct answer on a given turn, that answer's points must be subtracted from the earned points accumulated thus far by the player. If the other players need to confirm any given answers as correct, they might use a calculator to divide the number by 2, 3 and 5. If the quotients are whole numbers, then the proposed answers are correct.

4. The player with the highest total points after five rounds will be the winner. *Alternative*: Team members can choose a certain number of points as their goal (e.g., 40 points). The first player to reach that goal wins.

OBJECTIVE 9: Develop positive exponents for whole numbers.

Activity 1: POWER TRAINS
(Concrete Action)

Materials: Cuisenaire® rods
8.5" × 14" paper
Pencils

Management: Teams of 3–4 students (50 minutes)

Directions:

1. Give each team a set of Cuisenaire® rods and a sheet of legal-sized (8.5" × 14") blank paper.

2. Have each team build different *power trains* with the rods. Students should trace each train off on their paper in the order in which it is built and write a number sentence to describe how it was made.

3. For the first sequence of power trains, have students place the red (R) rod on their paper near the upper left corner and trace it onto the paper. Have them measure the red rod's length with white cubes and record this amount (2) below the tracing. This number will now be used to make all the other trains in this particular sequence.

4. Students should now take 2 red rods and place them end to end to make a new train. Ask them to find a single rod equal to this new length (the purple rod, P), exchange it for the 2 red rods, and trace it onto the paper to the right of and in line with the first drawing. The purple rod's length should be found with white cubes and recorded.

R P
2 $2 \times 2 = 4$

5. Students should continue this process by doubling each new rod found. When a single rod that is long enough can no longer be found, have students use orange rods combined with extra white rods, if needed, to show the next new rod. They should find the following: 2 purples = 1 brown (N); 2 browns = 1 orange + 6 white (O + 6W); 2 (orange + 6 white) = 3 orange + 2 white. Students may need to form a second row with their *train* pictures. Each new train's length should be expressed in terms of the previous train's size, using factors of 2. For example, for the train using 2 purple rods, its length (8) comes from 2 × 4, but the purple rod's length (4) comes from (2 × 2). So the number sentence becomes 2 × (2 × 2) = 8. The final sequence of tracings and number sentences should look like the following:

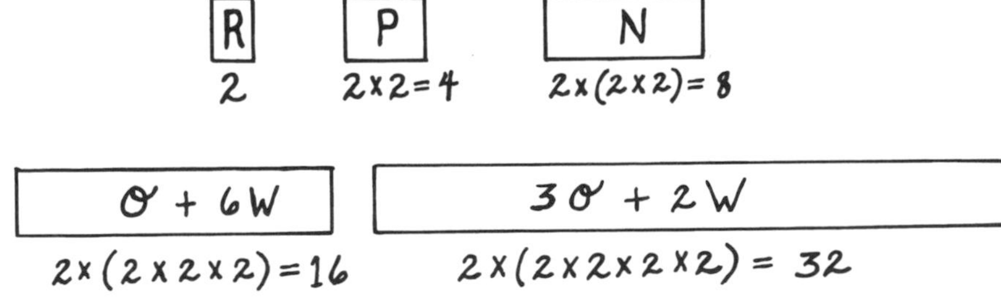

6. When all teams are finished, tell them that *exponents* can be used to show how many factors of 2 are involved without having to write all of them. For example, if only one 2 is used, we write 2^1; in $2 \times (2 \times 2)$, three factors of 2 are used, so we write 2^3. Have students now record exponential sentences under their corresponding factored forms; for example, under $2 \times (2 \times 2 \times 2) = 16$, write the sentence: $2 \times (2 \times 2 \times 2) = 2^4$. They might also title this first sequence as *Powers of 2.*

7. Next, have teams repeat the above process, using the light green rod (G). The length of the light green rod equals 3 white cubes. Therefore, each new train in the sequence will be formed from *three* of the previous train's length. Several *powers of 3* will be produced. Because of the lengths involved, students might only build and label the first three power trains of this sequence. Use the label E for the blue rod, which equals 3 light green rods or 3G.

Activity 2: POWER SLIDES

(Pictorial Action)

Materials: Centimeter grid paper (see pattern in Pattern/Grids section)
Colored markers
Regular paper
Pencils

Management: Partners (30–50 minutes)

Directions:

1. Give each pair of students 2–3 sheets of centimeter grid paper and a colored marker.

2. Have students draw a rectangle by outlining two adjacent squares on the grid paper with a colored marker. The amount of included square units will be 2.

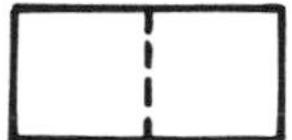

3. Have students begin a chart on their own paper, using the title *Powers of 2.* The first entry will be $2 = 2^1$. The exponent 1 simply tells how many groupings of 2 are there. Students should also write this sentence inside their 1×2 rectangle.

4. Now have students draw another 1×2 rectangle near the first one. Double the new one by mentally *sliding* it *up* and drawing another 1×2 rectangle above it. This forms a 2×2 square that contains 4 square units or 2 of the original 2 square units; write $4 = 2 \times 2 = 2^2$ on the chart and write $4 = 2^2$ inside the new square shape.

$4 = 2^2$

5. Ask students to draw a third shape by first drawing another 2×2 square, then mentally *sliding* it to the *right* and drawing a second 2×2 square. This forms a 2×4 (nonsquare) rectangle that contains 8 square units or 2 of the 2 × 2 shape; write $8 = 2 \times (2 \times 2) = 2^3$ on the chart and $8 = 2^3$ inside the 2 × 4 shape.

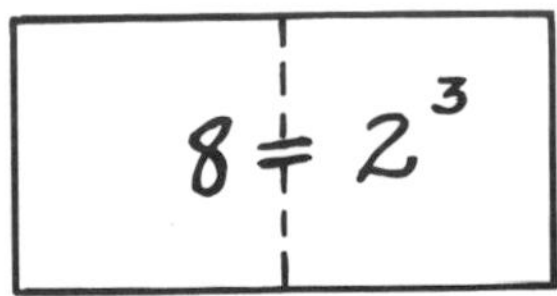

6. Have students continue the procedure to draw two more shapes. The 2 × 4 will *slide up* to double itself; record $16 = 2 \times (2 \times 2 \times 2) = 2^4$. Then this new 4 × 4 will *slide right* to double itself; record $32 = 2 \times (2 \times 2 \times 2 \times 2) = 2^5$.

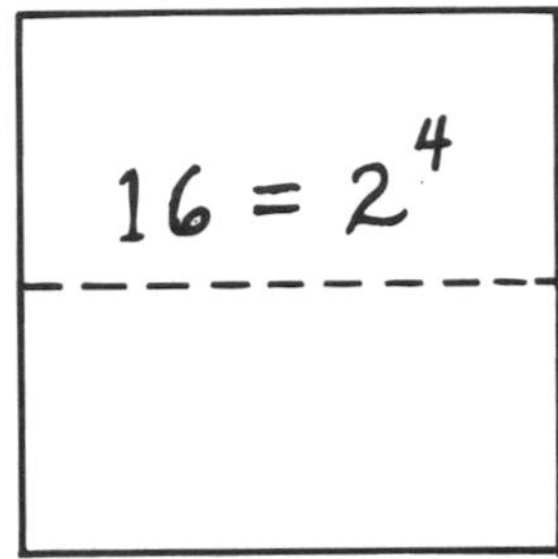

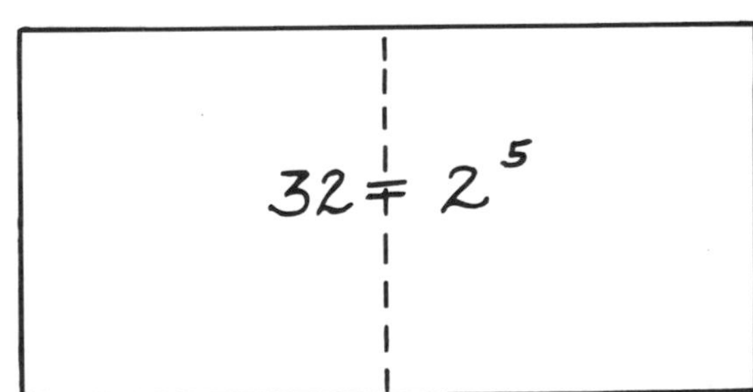

7. Have students write the name of each drawn shape beside its corresponding number sentence on the chart; use *square* or *nonsquare rectangle*. Ask them to compare the types of shapes made to their exponents. (Squares have even exponents; nonsquare rectangles have odd exponents.)

Note: Have students save the *Powers of 2* shapes they have drawn. They will need them for Activity 3.

8. If time allows, have students repeat steps 2–7, using a 1 × 3 rectangle instead of a 1 × 2 rectangle. When sliding a shape up or to the right, the shape will be tripled instead of doubled. *Powers of 3* will be found in 3 × 3, 3 × (3 × 3), 3 × (3 × 3 × 3), etc. Some of these shapes are large and may require two sheets of grid paper to be taped together. For extra credit, students may want to try drawing some powers of 4 or 5.

Activity 3: POWER MATCH

(Cooperative Groups)

Materials: Powers Worksheet PRF-9.3
Powers of 2 shapes from Activity 2
Centimeter grid paper
Pencils

Management: Teams of 4 students each (30 minutes)

Directions:

1. Give each team a set of *Powers of 2* shapes that were drawn in Activity 2, 2–3 sheets of centimeter grid paper, and a powers worksheet.

2. Students are to draw shapes on the grid paper according to the exercises on the worksheet, then try to match these shapes to those in the *Powers of 2* set. In some cases, matches will be made because the shapes look exactly alike; in others, matches will be made simply because the two shapes have the same total number of square units in them. We will be looking for patterns among exponents in this activity.

3. Have each team work the first exercise on the worksheet: $2^1 \times 2^2 = ?$ The first factor is the multiplier and tells how many of the second factor we want. Since the multiplier is a counter, students must translate it as a counting number; in this example, 2^1 becomes the value 2. The second factor represents a shape from the *Powers of 2* set; for 2^2, we select the 2×2 square from the set. The exercise now calls for 2 of the 2×2 shape to be drawn with edges touching on grid paper by team members. The expression *2 of (2 × 2)* should be written in the middle column of the worksheet for Exercise 1.

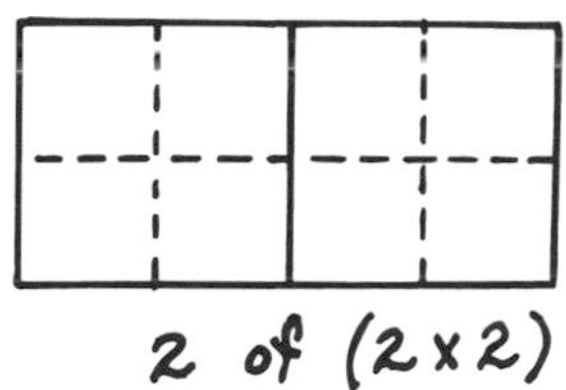

4. The finished drawing is a 2×4 or 4×2 rectangle, depending on how it was drawn. This same rectangle can be found in the *Powers of 2* set; it matches the 2^3 shape. Students should now record 2^3 in the third column of Exercise 1.

5. The second exercise is $2^2 \times 2^3$. This should be translated and written in the *Draw* column of the worksheet as *4 of (2 × 2 × 2)*. Students should now draw 4 of the 2^3 shape on their grid paper, connecting the 4 shapes together in some way. Here are some possible arrangements:

2×2×2	2×2×2
2×2×2	2×2×2

2×2×2	2×2×2	2×2×2	2×2×2

6. The first arrangement in the preceding illustration matches a *power* shape, but the second one does not. Both arrangements, however, contain 32 square units, so they are equivalent. Record 2^5 in the third column of Exercise 2.

7. Have students complete the other exercises on the worksheet. After all teams have finished and shared their results with the class, ask students to compare the exponents of the factors in the *Exercise* column to the matching power shape's exponent found in the third column and to decide if there is a pattern involved. (The sum of the two exponents on the factors equals the matching shape's exponent.) Encourage students to describe the pattern in their own words at the bottom of the worksheet.

NAME ______________________________ DATE ____________________

WORKSHEET PRF-9.3
Power Match

EXERCISE	DRAW	MATCHED POWER SHAPE
1. $2^1 \times 2^2 = ?$		
2. $2^2 \times 2^3 = ?$		
3. $2^1 \times 2^3 = ?$		
4. $2^2 \times 2^2 = ?$		
5. $2^3 \times 2^1 = ?$		
6. $2^3 \times 2^2 = ?$		

Describe any pattern you see in the above problems.

OBJECTIVE 10: Develop expanded notation with exponential form.

Activity 1: BUILDING WITH POWERS OF 10
(Concrete Action)

Materials: Commercial base 10 blocks (thousands, hundreds, tens, ones)
Paper
Pencils

Management: Teams of 3–4 students each (30 minutes)

Directions:

1. Give each team a set of base 10 blocks (minimal set: 2 thousands, 5 hundreds, 9 tens, and 9 ones). For this activity students must know the meaning of positive exponents (e.g., 3^4 means $3 \times 3 \times 3 \times 3$).

2. Ask students to describe each block in terms of the ones or unit blocks, using groupings of size 10. (A ten block is 10 ones; a hundred block is 10 sets of 10 ones; and a thousand block is 10 of 10 sets of 10 ones.) So a number name for the ten block is 10, and a number name for the hundred block is 10×10, which can also be written as 10^2 (read as *10 to the second power* or *10 squared*—like the hundred block *looks*). A number name for the thousand block is $10 \times 10 \times 10$, which can also be written as 10^3 (read as *10 to the third power* or *10 cubed*—like the thousand block *looks*).

3. Write five or six four-digit numbers on the chalkboard for the students to build with their base 10 blocks. The digits selected will be determined by the quantity available for each type of block.

4. As an example, have them build 1,347 with the blocks. They should place 1 thousand block, 3 hundred blocks, 4 ten blocks and 7 unit blocks on their desktop.

5. Starting with the largest blocks, the students should write the following expressions in order on their paper to describe the assigned number with respect to its blocks and the block names:

1,347—1 thousand	+ 3 hundreds	+ 4 tens	+ 7 ones
1 of 10^3	+ 3 of 10^2	+ 4 of 10	+ 7
1×10^3	+ 3×10^2	+ 4×10	+ 7

6. Now have the teams build the other numbers listed on the board and describe each number's blocks in the three different ways given in Step 5. The last way shown is called *exponential notation* for a whole number.

Activity 2: EXPONENT ICONS

(Pictorial Action)

Materials: Notation Worksheet PRF-10.2
Paper
Pencils

Management: Partners (30–40 minutes)

Directions:

1. Guide students in developing special shapes or icons to represent the powers of 10. This activity covers place value up to the ten thousands place. The worksheet can be modified for whatever place values are appropriate for your classes. The construction procedure used will be similar to the method presented previously in Activity 2 of Objective 9. We will use small circles for ones and tally marks for tens. If we imagine that 10 tally marks are laid down parallel to each other and slightly spread out, then their outline might look like a square. Hence, a medium square will represent a hundred or 10 sets of a ten.

o = one **| = ten or 10** **□ = hundred or 10 × 10 or 10^2**

2. Now draw a diagram on the chalkboard that shows a hundred block sliding to the right to mark off 10 of itself (see illustration below). This long rectangle comes from 10 of the hundred block and will be used to show a thousand. Similarly, the thousand block, if it slides up to mark off 10 of itself, creates a large square, which will represent ten thousand.

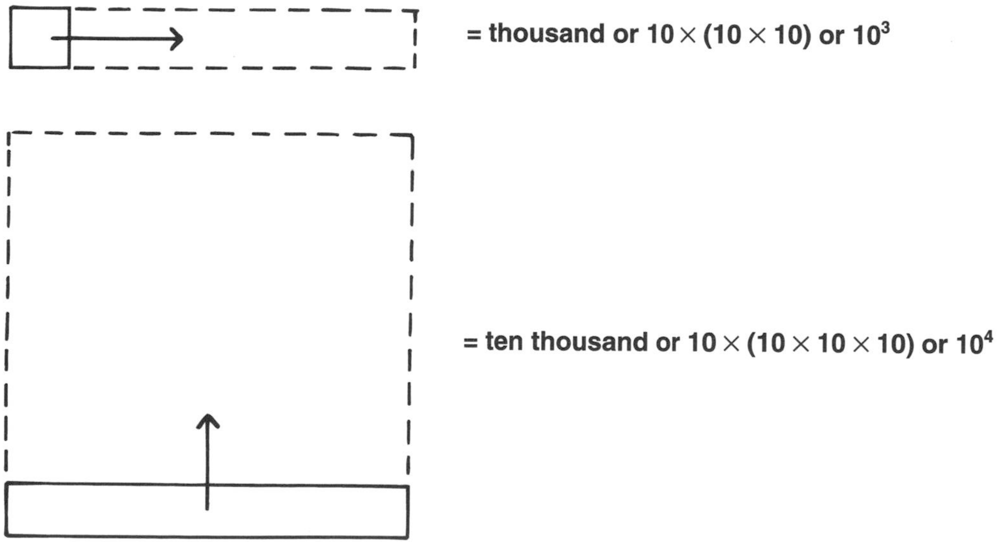

3. Next, give each student a copy of the notation worksheet. We will apply the icons we have just developed for powers of 10. At the top of the worksheet are the icons and what they represent. Do not be concerned about scale when drawing these; *how* they were formed should be emphasized instead (e.g., 10 medium squares made the long rectangle). The two sizes of squares do need to look obviously different, and the long rectangle must not look like a square. Otherwise, exact proportions are not expected.

4. Discuss the first exercise with the class. The following icons are seen: 1 large square, 2 long rectangles, 3 medium squares, 4 tally marks, and 5 small circles. Students are to translate the icons into numerical notation by first labeling each icon with its power, then writing the exponential notation followed by the number name under the shapes.

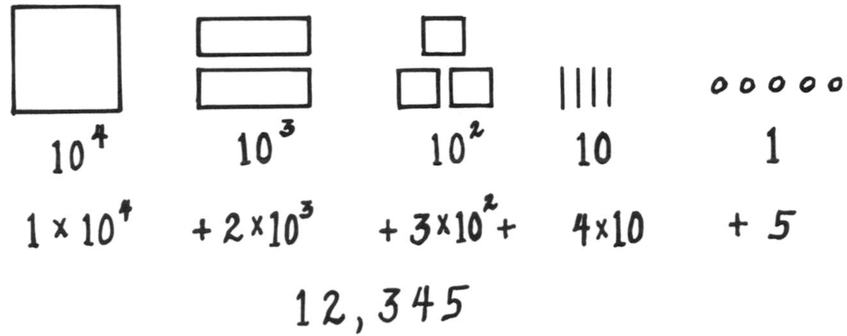

10^4 10^3 10^2 10 1
$1 \times 10^4 + 2 \times 10^3 + 3 \times 10^2 + 4 \times 10 + 5$
12,345

5. Other exercises require students to translate the number name or exponential notation into icons, etc. Have partners work together to complete the worksheet, then let them share their results with the class.

6. As a challenge to find icons for higher powers of 10, start a sequence on the board to establish related sizes: small circle, tally mark, medium square, long rectangle. Ask different students to draw the next icons in the sequence by using the *slide up or right* technique mentally and to tell which powers of 10 they represent. Again, the relationships, not the exact proportions, are the concern here.

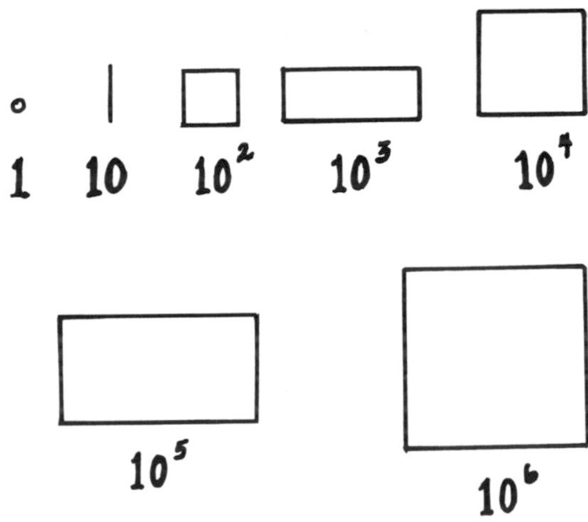

NAME ______________________________ DATE ____________________

WORKSHEET PRF-10.2
Exponent Icons

ICONS

 $= 10^4$ $= 10^3$ $= 10^2$ $= 10$ $= 1$

Write the exponential notation and number name for each:

1. 

2. 

Write the exponential notation and draw icons for each:

3. 5,304

4. 1,653

Draw icons and write the number name for each:

5. $3 \times 10^4 + 1 \times 10^3 + 6 \times 10 + 7$

6. $2 \times 10^4 + 4 \times 10^3 + 1 \times 10^2 + 7 \times 10$

Activity 3: POWER UP!

(Cooperative Groups)

Materials: *Powers of 10* gameboards (Worksheet PRF-10.3)
Sets of clue cards (samples included), counters, paper, pencils

Management: Teams of 4 students each (20 minutes)

Directions:

1. Give each team a *Powers of 10* gameboard, 25 counters, and a set of clue cards. All teams may have the same set or different sets of the cards. Each set has 4 cards, one for each member of the team. (See step 5 on how to make cards.) Players are not allowed to show their cards to each other, and they can only share the information on their own cards by *reading* or *telling* the card's information to the other players. The idea is for all four team members to communicate with each other in order to solve their problem.

2. Students are to place new counters or adjust old counters on their gameboard as each new clue is read. All clues must be satisfied by the positions and amounts of counters on the gameboard before a solution is found.

3. Once a solution is reached, the team members must write the exponential notation and number name for that solution on a sheet of paper, then decide which clue proved most helpful to them, whether in getting started with or in finally solving the problem.

4. After all teams are finished with their problems, have them share their solutions and their *most helpful* clues. Discuss any multiple solutions that might occur for some problems.

5. Here are some possible sets of clues and their solutions. Write each clue (a, b, c, or d) of a given set on a separate index card. The 4 cards will then form a set of clues for a team to use.

Problem 1: (Solution: 3,175 and $3 \times 10^3 + 1 \times 10^2 + 7 \times 10 + 5$)

Clues: (a) There are four more of 10 than of 10^3.

(b) Amounts for 10 and 10^3 are both odd. What is the exponential notation for the number?

(c) 10^2 comes alone with no others of its kind.

(d) There are 5 times as many of 1 as there are of 10^2. What is the number name?

Problem 2: (Solutions: 3,209 or 9,609 with their exponential notations)

Clues: (a) The combined amounts of 10^3 and 10^2 are a multiple of 5 but not of 10.

(b) No 10 can be found. What is the number name?

(c) The amounts of 10^3 and of 1 are each divisible by 3 but not by 2.

(d) If we had one more of 1, we would find a 10. What is the exponential notation of the number?

Problem 3: (Solution: 6,428 and $6 \times 10^3 + 4 \times 10^2 + 2 \times 10 + 8$)

Clues: (a) The amount of 10 is a third of the amount of 10^3. What is the number name?

(b) All amounts are even. What is the exponential notation of the number?

(c) There are twice as many of 1 as there are of 10^2.

(d) When the amounts are taken in pairs, two different pairs each have a sum of ten.

NAME ______________________________ DATE ____________________

WORKSHEET PRF-10.3

Pattern for *Powers of 10* gameboard for *Power Up!*

1	
10	
10^2	
10^3	

CHAPTER 3

DEVELOPMENT OF WRITTEN ALGORITHMS

INTRODUCTION

This chapter helps students learn how to work with larger whole numbers, fractions, and decimals. Through hands-on games and activities, they are shown how to multiply and divide larger numbers (two- to three-digit numbers) by one- and two-digit numbers, as well as acquire the necessary tools to work with fractions. Topics covered include addition, subtraction, multiplication, and division of fractions with like and unlike denominators with special emphasis given to relating fraction multiplication to the division of fractions. Furthermore, students are introduced to decimals, learning how to multiply and divide decimal fractions using ones and tenths.

OBJECTIVE 1: Multiply two- and three-digit whole numbers by one-digit multipliers.

Activity 1: BUILDING IMAGES
(Concrete Action)

Materials: Base 10 blocks
Building mats (described in step 1)
Colored tagboard (described in step 1)
Paper
Pencils

Management: Partners (50 minutes)

Directions:

1. Give each pair of students a set of base 10 blocks and a building mat. The set of blocks should contain 15 rods and 30 small cubes. Also, give each pair of students 15 light tagboard strips. The strips should all be the same color and approximately 1 cm × 12 cm in size, which is as wide as—but just longer than—the base 10 rod. Use a color for the strips that is different from the color of the base 10 rod. Each strip will represent a hundred, even though its length is not proportional to the lengths of the other base 10 blocks. At this point, proportionality is not necessary. The building mat may be drawn on an $8\frac{1}{2}$" × 14" unlined sheet of paper or larger and appears as follows:

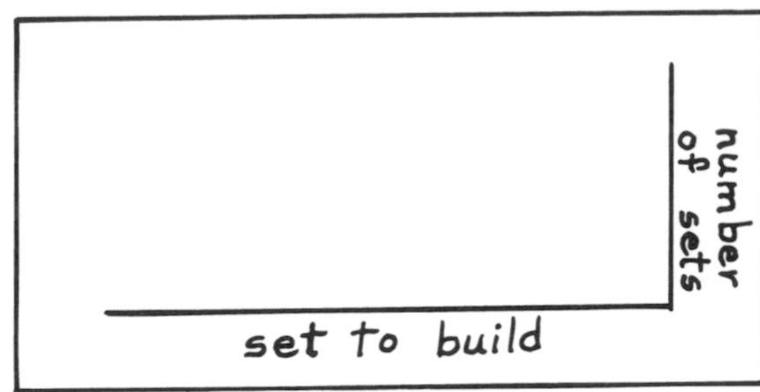

2. It is assumed that students are familiar with the base 10 blocks and know that ten small cubes or ones equal one rod or ten in size. They should already be comfortable with thinking of a whole number in several ways with respect to place value, e.g., 325 as 325 ones, 32 tens and 5 ones, or 3 hundreds, 2 tens, and 5 ones.

3. Have students place three ones along the vertical right edge of the backward L-frame on the building mat and two hundreds, one ten, and four ones below the bottom edge of the L-frame. The blocks should have the following arrangement:

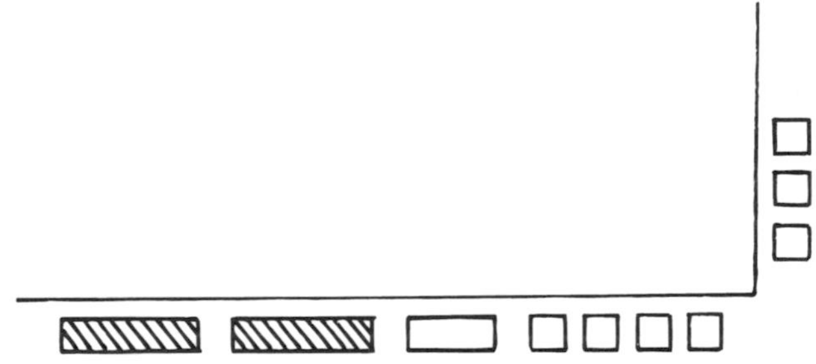

4. Discuss the idea that the 3 ones are the multiplier and tell how many sets to build on the mat. Have students build the set of 2 hundreds, 1 ten, and 4 ones, forming one complete set or row of blocks at a time. The building of the sets should begin with the first row being placed just above the lower edge of the L-frame, then continue upward. A row in an arrangement of blocks will always be considered as left-to-right or horizontal, whereas a column will be up-and-down or vertical. The final arrangement of the blocks should look like the following:

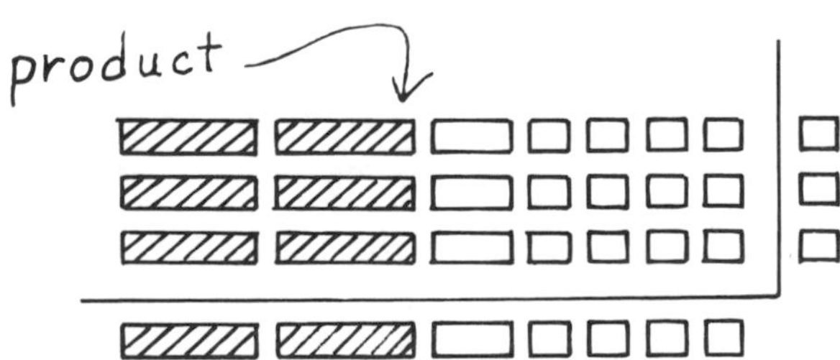

5. Ask students to count and find the value of all the blocks on the mat space to the upper left of the L-frame. There are 6 hundreds, 3 tens and 12 ones, which equal 642. This total value is the product of 3 × 214, or 3 sets of 214.

6. Some students may need to trade 10 of the 12 ones for a new ten in order to agree with the answer of 642. Allow them to make the necessary trade, but then have them rebuild the first arrangement of blocks as found in step 4. Students need to build a mental image of this first arrangement.

7. Have students record their results on their own papers. They should write the following: *3 sets of 214 make 642 in all. 3 × 214 = 642.*

8. Now assign several other exercises for the students to build with their blocks. Write them on the chalkboard in horizontal form like *2 × 143 = ?* The left factor or multiplier should be selected from the counting numbers, 1 to 5. The right factor or multiplicand (the set to build) should have digits chosen from 0 to 3 hundreds, 0 to 3 tens, and 0 to 6 ones. Students should record their results with the two types of sentences shown in step 7.

9. After students have built several products, building one row or set at a time, they may begin to build all the required rows of one type of block together, then all the required rows of another type together. This is quite natural and is merely an application of the distributive property of multiplication over addition.

10. After the students have worked several exercises, have some of them read their sentences and tell how they mentally counted their blocks to find their answers.

Activity 2: PICTURING PRODUCTS

(Pictorial Action)

Materials: Paper
Red pencils
Regular pencils

Management: Partners (two sessions at 50 minutes/session)

Directions:

1. Partners will draw backward L-frames with a regular pencil along the lines on their own paper and use them to show different products. Encourage students to draw large frames so that their final products will be easy to see. A frame having the vertical line segment about $1\frac{1}{2}$ inches long and the horizontal line segment about 3 inches long is a good size. If a frame is drawn across the left half of a sheet of paper, enough space remains on the right half of the paper for the student to record the results in symbolic form.

2. Drawing the products: Have students draw circles for ones, line segments for tens, and narrow rectangles for hundreds to set up the problem, 4 × 132, on an L-frame. When drawing each row or set of 132, they should draw the hundred, tens and ones together, beginning at the bottom. After two or three exercises, allow students to draw all the rows of one shape (e.g., ones) together, then all the rows of another shape (e.g., tens) together, if they prefer. The final drawing for 4 × 132 should appear as follows:

3. Students should count the hundreds, tens, and ones in their product and mentally trade, if necessary, to find their final answer. Have them record their numerical results in vertical form to the right of or under their completed frame:

$$\begin{array}{r} 132 \\ \times 4 \\ \hline 528 \end{array}$$

4. During this first session, write several other exercises like *4 × 132 = ?* on the chalkboard for students to work by drawing them on their own papers. Use the counting numbers 1–8 as multipliers. For the sets, use digits chosen from 0–3 hundreds, 0–4 tens and 0–5 ones. After students have discovered the product of an exercise by counting the total ones, tens, and hundreds they have drawn, they should record their results in vertical form like the example given in step 3. The one-digit multiplier should always be written below the two- or three-digit set or multiplicand.

5. Describing the regions of a product: After students have made any necessary corrections to their drawings from the first session, have them use a red pencil to mark off place value regions within their products and describe these regions through symbolic recordings. For example, for 4 × 132 discussed earlier, the regions should be marked off and numbered as shown in step 6.

6. Show students how to describe the arrangements of the shapes within the three regions. In the example, region 1 contains 4 rows of 2 ones each, so a number sentence that describes this region is *4 of 2 ones = 8 ones.* Region 2 contains 4 rows of 3 tens each, so its number sentence will be *4 of 3 tens = 12 tens.* For region 3, the sentence is *4 of 1 hundred = 4 hundreds.* Do not allow students to reverse the order of their factors. In order for the final algorithm to make sense, for example, they must use *4 of 3 tens* and not *3 of 4 tens.* The multiplier number determines the number of rows each time.

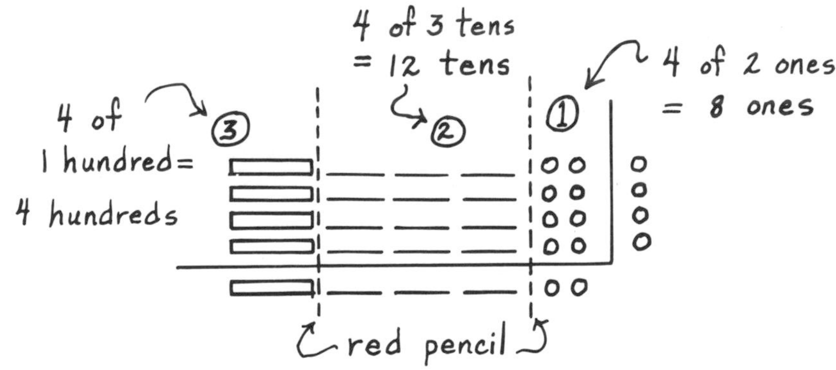

7. Now have students transfer the number sentences they have found to the vertical form. The first step should look like the following:

132
× 4
- - - - - (1) 4 × 2 ones = 8 ones
- - - - - (2) 4 × 3 tens = 12 tens
- - - - - (3) 4 × 1 hundred = 4 hundreds

8. After recording the descriptions of the regions in order as number sentences, students should write their separate amounts in the columns directly under the original factors, 4 and 132. At this point it is helpful to draw vertical line segments to clearly show the place value columns. The ones recording should begin in the ones column, the tens recording should begin in the tens column, etc. For the tens amount, some students find it helpful to write a zero in the ones column. For the hundreds, they need to write zeros in the ones and tens columns. This is acceptable and simply indicates that the tens can be traded for ones; for example, 12 tens equal to 120 ones. The partial products should then be added to find the total or final product of 4 × 132. The completed recording should appear as follows:

1	3	2	
	×	4	
		8	(1) 4 × 2 ones = 8 ones
1	2		(2) 4 × 3 tens = 12 tens
4			(3) 4 × 1 hundred = 4 hundreds
5	2	8	

9. Now ask students to compare the factors used in the regions' number sentences to the digits in the original exercise, i.e., the 4, 1, 3, and 2. The first factor, 4, in the number sentences corresponds to the original multiplier, 4. The second factor from region 1 matches the ones digit in 132, the second factor from region 2 matches the tens digit and the second factor from region 3 matches the hundreds digit. Have students connect the digits 4, 1, 3, and 2 together with arrows and number the arrows according to the regions their digit pairs represent. The final format is as follows:

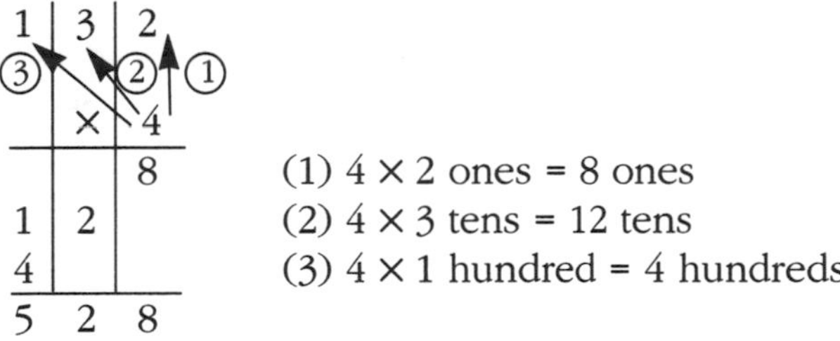

10. If a factor has a zero for a digit, the patterns among the regions are still maintained. Those regions corresponding to the zero digit will simply contain no shapes. An example follows:

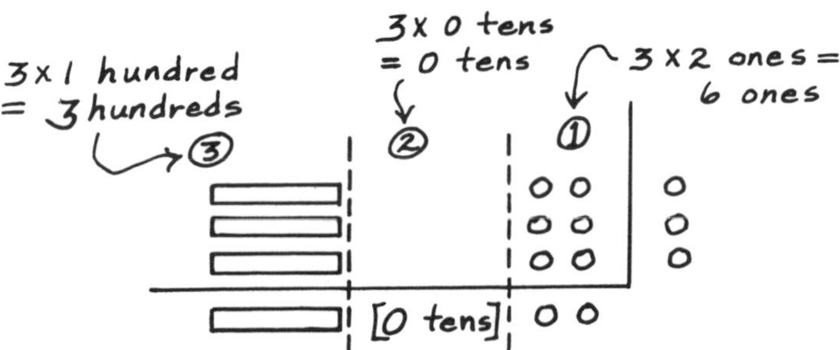

11. The goal is to have students be able to describe the regions of a drawing simply by pairing up the digits in the original exercise. The language should parallel that used with the completed drawing. For example, for 5 × 234, students should be able to give an explanation similar to the following: *When making 5 sets of 234, we will have 5 sets of 4 ones or 20 ones, 5 sets of 3 tens or 15 tens, and 5 sets of 2 hundreds or 10 hundreds. After adding and making place value changes, the sum will be 1,170.*

12. After students have mastered the above procedure of recording each partial product on a separate line, they should be ready to *collapse* the partial products together and record their sum on one line. In examples where no regrouping is needed to find the sum, region 2's partial product will simply be recorded to the left of region 1's partial product and region 3's will be recorded to the left of region 2's. In an exercise like 3 × 145, however, regrouping must occur when finding the sum of the partial products. Students may easily show the regrouping with the following steps:

(1)	**(2)**	**(3)**
145	145	145
× 3	× 3	× 3
1	1~~1~~	~~1~~~~1~~
5	35	435
[15 ones = 5 ones + 1 ten]	[12 tens + 1 ten = 3 tens + 1 hundred]	[3 hundreds + 1 hundred = 4 hundreds]

Recording the regrouped amounts just above their sum seems easier for students than recording them above the multiplicand (here, 145).

Activity 3: BUILDING LARGER PRODUCTS

(Cooperative Groups)

Materials: Light tagboard strips (4 colors; sizes described in step 1 below)
Spinner Pattern Worksheet DWA-1.3
Paper clips for spinner needles
Building mats from Activity 1
Paper
Pencils

Management: Teams of 4 students each (30 minutes)

Directions:

1. Give each team a building mat and a set of light tagboard strips (25 strips of each of four colors). The set should consist of the following: color #1—1" × 1" unmarked strips for ones; color #2—1" × $1\frac{1}{4}$" strips marked with *10;* color #3—1" × $\frac{1}{2}$" strips marked with *100;* color #4—1" × $1\frac{3}{4}$" strips marked with *1000.* Also, provide one Spinner Pattern Worksheet DWA-1.3 and a paper clip for the spinner needle (pencil point holds end of paper clip in place at center of spinner). The spinner pattern contains two spinners in one.

2. Team members take turns spinning the spinner to determine the next product to be built with the paper strips. Students will gain experience with three-digit and four-digit multiplicands in this activity.

3. On a turn one student will spin the spinner several times. The outer ring of the spinner will be read for the first four spins, which taken in order give the number of strips needed to show the thousands, hundreds, tens, and ones in the set to be built. If a 0 has already been spun and is followed by a second 0, the player must respin to replace the second 0. Only one 0 may be assigned as a digit in the four-digit number, even if the first 0 is for the thousands digit. After spinning to find the set to use, the player must spin again, this time reading the inner ring for the number to use as the multiplier.

4. The player now places the strips on the building mat. The multiplier is shown with ones along the right vertical edge of the backward L-frame on the mat. The set or multiplicand is shown with ones, tens, hundreds, and thousands along the bottom edge of the L-frame. As an example, if the first four spins yield the digits 2, 1, 3, and 2, then 2 thousands, 1 hundred, 3 tens, and 2 ones will be placed on the mat for the set to be built. If the fifth spin yields the digit 4 on the inner ring of the spinner, then 4 ones will be placed in the multiplier position along the right side of the mat.

5. The player now builds the product for 4 × 2, 132 on the mat, using the necessary strips. The place value regions should remain intact; no trading should be done. The final product should appear as follows:

1000	1000	100	10	10	10	□	□	□
1000	1000	100	10	10	10	□	□	□
1000	1000	100	10	10	10	□	□	□
1000	1000	100	10	10	10	□	□	□
1000	1000	100	10	10	10	□	□	

6. The other three team members must now record the completed problem in vertical form on their own papers. The building player tells how they are to record the partial products: either summed together and recorded in one line, or separated into several lines first and then summed. Possible examples for recording 4 × 2, 132 are as follows:

(a)

2132
× 4
1 (crossed out)
8528

(b)

2	1	3	2
×			4
			8
	1	2	
	4		
8			
8	5	2	8

7. After the three members have finished their recording, the turn to spin and build passes to the next player. Play continues as long as time allows.

SPINNER PATTERN WORKSHEET DWA-1.3
Building Larger Products

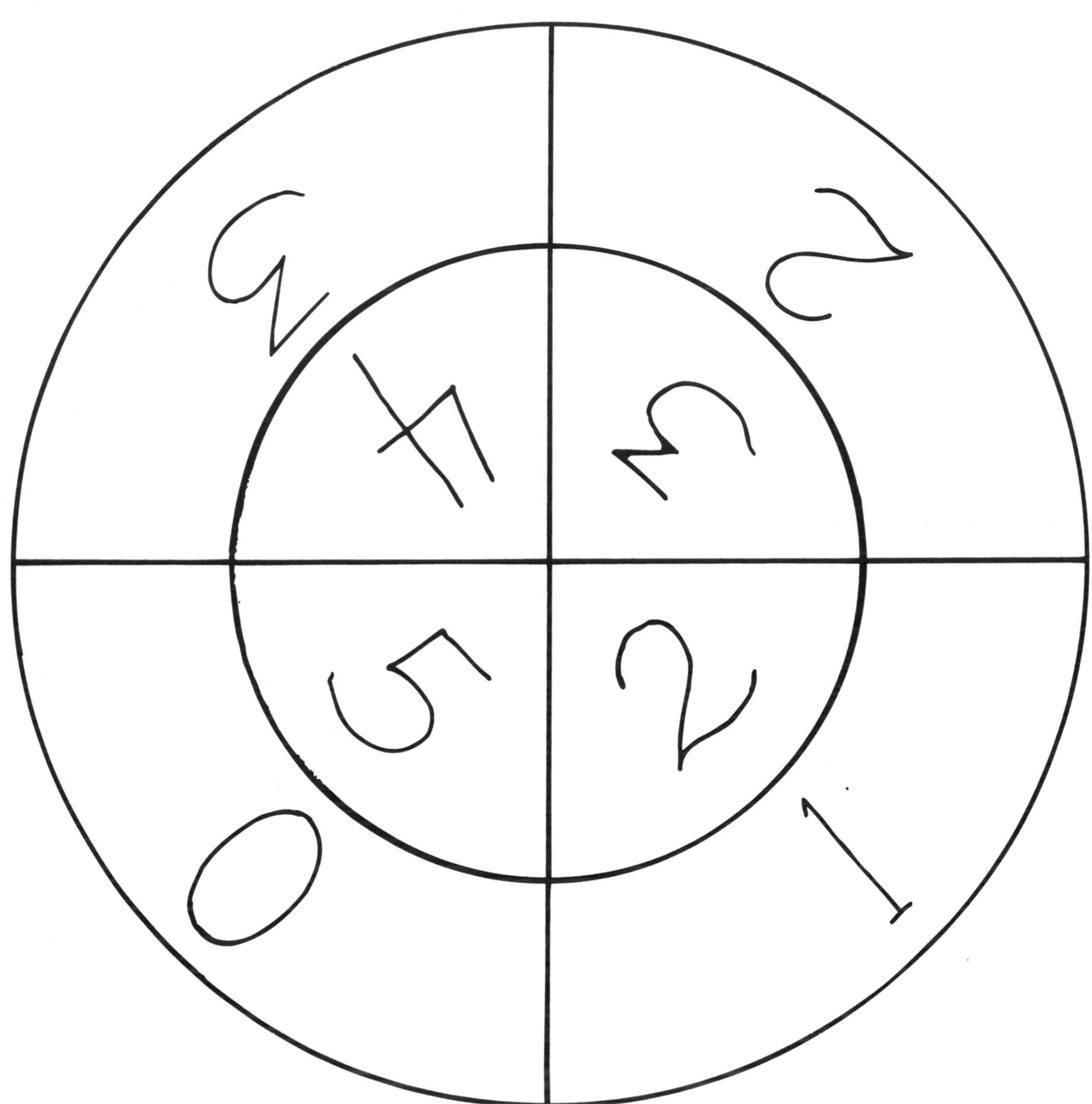

OBJECTIVE 2: Divide two- and three-digit whole numbers by one-digit divisors.

Activity 1: BUILDING EQUAL SHARES WITH BLOCKS

(Concrete Action)

Materials: Base 10 blocks
Building mats (described in step 1 below)
Paper
Pencils

Management: Partners (50 minutes)

Directions:

1. Give each pair of students a set of base 10 blocks and a building mat. The set of blocks should contain 1 flat, 30 rods, and 50 small cubes. The building mat may be drawn on an $8\frac{1}{2}$" × 14" unlined sheet of paper or larger and should appear as follows:

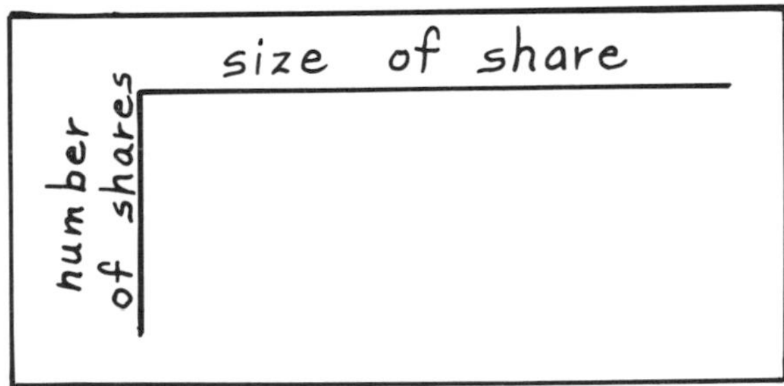

2. It is assumed that students are familiar with the base 10 blocks and know that ten small cubes (ones) equal one rod (ten) in size and that ten rods equal one flat (hundred) in size. They should already be comfortable with thinking of a whole number in several ways with respect to place value, e.g., 325 as 325 ones; 32 tens and 5 ones; 3 hundreds, 2 tens, and 5 ones; or 3 hundreds and 25 ones.

3. Ask students to find the share size when 31 is shared two ways. Have them place 2 ones along the left edge of the L-frame on their building mat to show the number of shares to make, which is the divisor. Students should also place 3 tens and a single one under the L-frame in the lower right corner of the mat. No other blocks should be on the mat.

4. Ask: *Are there enough tens to make 2 shares? Will there be any tens left unshared?* One ten should be lined up with each *share* cube as shown below. There will be one ten left unshared, along with the original unit or one. Place a new ten from the general set of extra blocks above the L-frame to indicate how many tens have been given to each share.

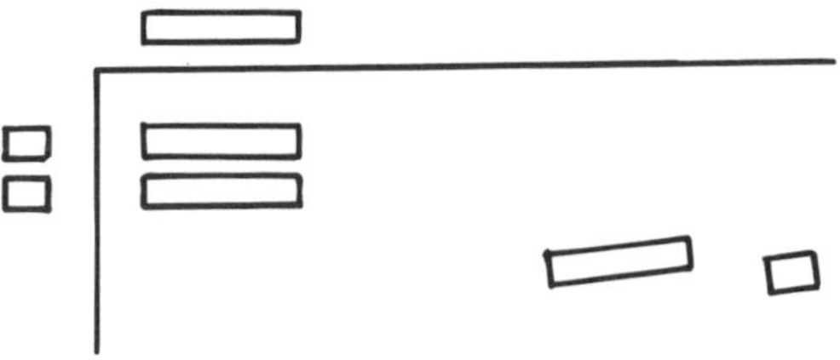

5. Ask: *Since there is one ten left unshared, how can we combine it with the one in order to share the total two ways?* The ten will need to be traded for 10 ones. Then the (10 + 1) or 11 ones should be shared two ways by placing them equally in the two rows beside the tens. There will be 5 ones in each row and 1 one left unshared. Show the 5 ones in each share by placing 5 new ones from the extra blocks above the frame. Leave the unshared one at the lower right corner of the mat.

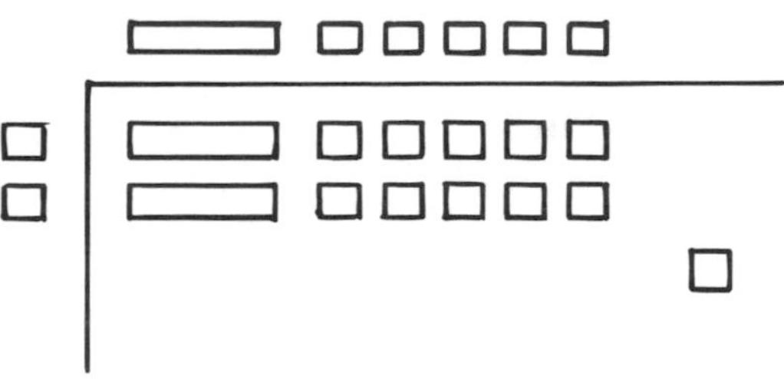

6. Have students record the result on their own papers as follows: *31 shared 2 ways makes 15 per share with 1 left unshared.*

7. Now have students place 1 hundred and 3 tens under the frame of the mat for the dividend and 4 ones along the left edge of the frame for the divisor. The amount, 130, is to be shared four ways.

8. Ask: *Are there enough hundreds to make 4 shares? If not, can the hundreds be traded for tens and then the tens shared?* The single hundred cannot be separated into four equal groups, so students should trade it for 10 tens. The (10 + 3) or 13 tens total can now be shared.

9. Students should realize that 3 tens can be placed in the row of each cube in the divisor to show that each share receives 3 tens. Three new tens from the extra blocks should then be placed above the frame as the quotient to indicate that 3 tens are in each share. There is 1 ten left unshared on the mat.

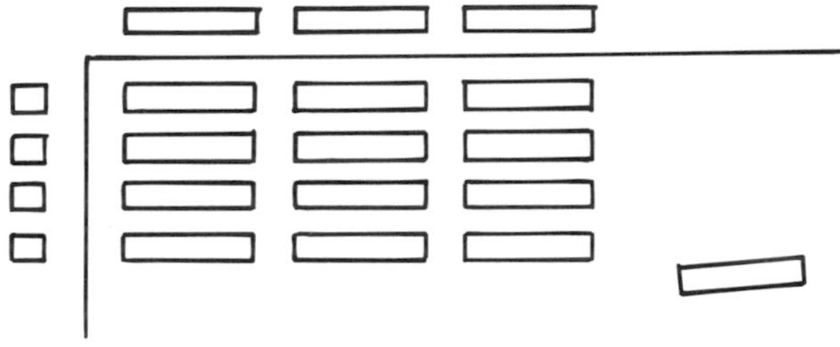

10. Now ask: *Since there is 1 ten left unshared, can we trade it for ones, then try to share the ones four ways?* Students should trade the ten for 10 ones, then separate them equally into the four rows under the frame. Two ones should be placed on each row beside the 3 tens. Two new ones from the extra blocks should be placed above the frame to show the 2 ones in each share. Two ones will be left unshared in the lower right corner of the mat.

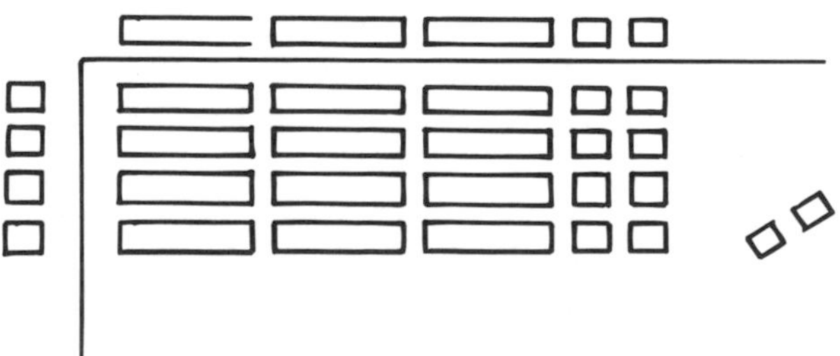

11. Have students record the result on their own papers as follows: *130 shared 4 ways makes 32 per share with 2 left unshared.*

12. Write other division exercises on the chalkboard for students to build with their blocks and record in sentence form as shown in step 11. Remind students to keep their extra blocks away from the building mat, so that the extra blocks do not become mixed with the dividend blocks, thereby causing a building error. Use 2–5 for divisors. For the dividend, choose from 0–1 hundreds, 0–3 tens, and 0–5 ones, but always use a two-digit or three-digit number. This will produce either a one-digit or a two-digit quotient. The dividend number should also be chosen carefully so that for any trade required, at most 3 blocks will need to be traded for the next smaller place value. For example, in 134 divided by 5, there will be 3 tens left unshared after the tens are shared five ways. These 3 tens must be traded for 30 ones before all the ones can be shared. If more than 3 tens have to be traded, the trading becomes too tedious and a rather large amount of ones will be required in the original set of blocks.

Activity 2: DIVISION DRAW

(Pictorial Action)

Materials: Paper
Pencils
Red pencils
Base 10 blocks (optional)
Building mats from Activity 1 (optional)

Management: Partners (2 sessions at 50 minutes/session)

Directions:

1. Each pair of students will need a red pencil. Some students may still prefer to work with the blocks and building mat from Activity 1. Allow them to do so, but have them also draw a diagram on their papers to show what they build with blocks.

2. Have students draw a division L-frame on their own papers, leaving some space to the left of the frame to draw a dividend. The top bar of the frame should be about $2\frac{1}{2}$ inches long and the vertical bar should be about $1\frac{1}{2}$ inches long to allow room to draw rows of easily viewed shapes under the frame. Large squares will be used to represent hundreds. Line segments the same length as the side of the large square will represent tens, and small circles will be used for ones.

3. Drawing equal shares: Have students show 214 divided by 4. They should draw 2 squares, 1 line segment, and 4 circles to the left of the frame on their paper to represent the dividend, 214. Four circles should be drawn in the divisor position on the frame.

4. Have students write the exercise in box format and underline the divisor 4 and the 2 in the dividend box with red pencil. Ask: *Are there enough hundreds to make four shares? If not, can the hundreds be traded for tens and then shared?* Since 2 hundreds cannot be shared four ways, they must be traded for tens. Have students mark out the two squares in the dividend at the left of the frame and draw two new groups of ten line segments each. When possible, each group of ten line segments should be drawn as two rows of five segments each for easy recognition.

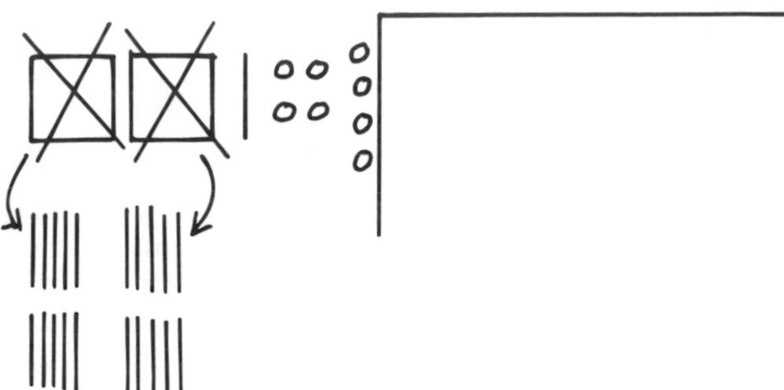

5. Students should now extend the red underlining in the box dividend to the 1 in the tens place, so that 21 tens are indicated. Ask: *Are there enough tens to be shared four ways? If so, can you predict how many tens will be in each of the four shares?* Since $4 \times 5 = 20$, students should predict that there will be 5 tens in each share. Have them draw 5 horizontal line segments in a row with each circle of the divisor, marking out the line segments in the dividend as they are transferred. This will leave one line segment (ten) unused in the dividend, along with the 4 original circles. Students should draw five horizontal line segments above the frame to show the quotient or amount in each share.

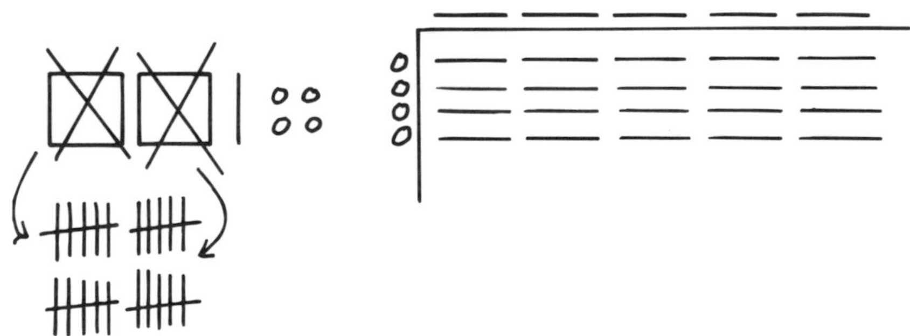

6. Since the single ten cannot be shared four ways, have students mark out the remaining line segment in the dividend and draw ten new circles (ones) in two rows of five circles each. Draw an arrow from the line segment to the new group of circles. Ask: *Can the (10 + 4) or 14 ones be shared four ways? If so, how many ones will be in each share?* Since $4 \times 3 = 12$, students should be able to predict that three ones will be in each share. Have them draw three ones in each row under the frame, marking out the ones or circles in the dividend as they are transferred to the rows. A ring should be drawn around the two remaining ones in the dividend, and three circles should be drawn above the frame as part of the quotient.

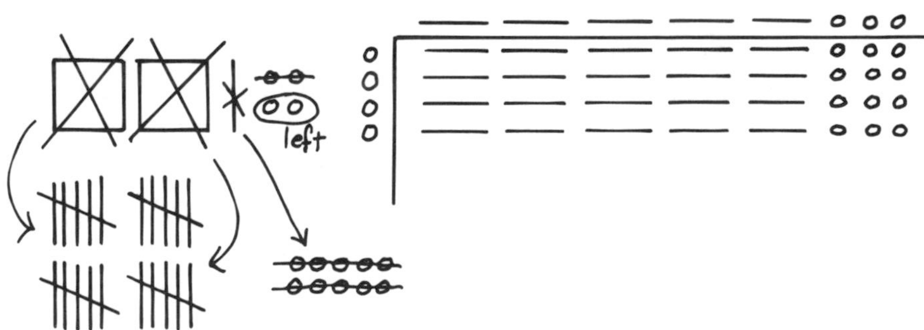

7. Have students record their result above the dividend box, being certain to place the tens digit of the quotient above the tens digit of the dividend number since tens were the first amounts to be shared in the exercise.

```
        5  3    in each share
4  ) 2  1  4
   ==========
           2    ones left unshared
```

8. During this first session, write several other exercises on the chalkboard for students to solve by drawing diagrams. In order to control the number of trades so that too many groups of ten will not need to be drawn, use 2–5 as divisors and the following quantities for digits in the dividend: 0–3 as hundreds, 0–3 as tens, and 0–5 as ones. Other carefully chosen digit combinations are also possible.

9. Describing regions within the dividend: For the second session, after most students are comfortable with the drawing method for showing division, introduce students to a new format for recording their work. Using previously drawn and corrected division diagrams, have students draw vertical line segments in red pencil to separate the tens and ones shown under the L-frame. They should number the regions formed, beginning with the region on the left, and write number sentences that describe the arrangement of the circles or line segments within their own regions. In situations where only a region of ones is involved, i.e., where the quotient is a one-digit number, there will be only one number sentence to write. Remember that rows are left-to-right and the number of rows in a region should correspond to the number used as the divisor. The example discussed earlier would be labeled as follows:

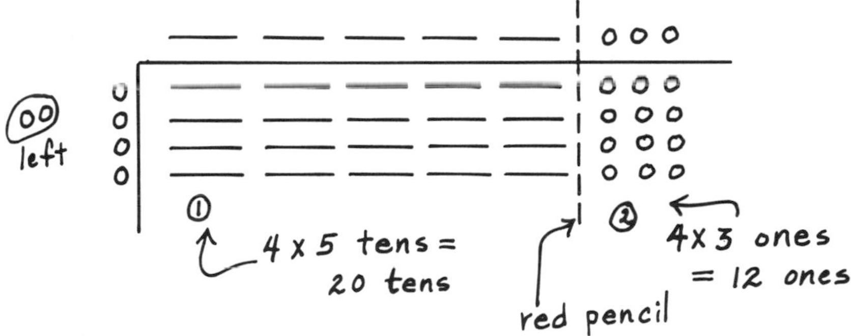

10. After students have numbered each region and written a number sentence for each region of several different division diagrams, including both two-digit and three-digit dividends, have them transfer their number sentences to a box format. This is a very important stage and should not be rushed. As an example, consider the exercise, 214 divided by 4, discussed earlier. Since the quotient has already been found, it should be recorded above the box before any of the number sentences are transferred. Region 1 contains 4 × 5 tens, or 20 tens, which have been removed from the original dividend amount during the sharing process. This should be shown in the box format as 21 tens – 20 tens, which leaves 1 ten unused in the dividend. Students should record the following:

```
        5  3
4  ) 2  1  4
    -2  0        (1) 4 × 5 tens = 20 tens used
        1
```

11. Since the unused ten was traded for ones, which were then combined with the original four ones of the dividend, have students show this by recording and underlining in red the digits 1 and 4 below the line for 20 tens. Region 2 contains four rows of three ones each, which have also been removed from the dividend during the sharing process. This removal should be recorded under the division box as 14 ones – 12 ones, which leaves 2 ones unused or unshared.

		5	3	
4	) 2	1	4	
	–2	0		(1) 4 × 5 tens = 20 tens used
		1	4	
		–1	2	(2) 4 × 3 ones = 12 ones used
			2	ones left

12. After students have transferred number sentences from the division diagram to the box format and have recorded removals for several different exercises, including both two-digit and three-digit dividends, ask them to compare within each recording the factors in the number sentences of the regions to the digits in the divisor and quotient. Since the factors and digits match in each case, the digits can be used to find the number sentences and hence the amounts of tens and ones that will be removed from a dividend during the sharing process. Have students draw arrows on several of their already completed box recordings to connect the digits of the divisor and quotient in the order of the number sentences they represent. The following is an example of arrows applied to the exercise presented in step 11:

(2)				
	(1)	5	3	
4	) 2	1	4	
	–2	0		(1) 4 × 5 tens = 20 tens used
		1	4	
		–1	2	(2) 4 × 3 ones = 12 ones used
			2	ones left

13. The final goal of this activity is to enable students to predict the digits of the quotient, using the dividend and divisor, and then use each of those predicted digits with the digit of the divisor to find the number sentences of the regions involved. Students must connect the symbolic box notation they use for a division exercise with a mental image of the corresponding diagram. For example, here is some of the connecting language that might be used when describing the division of 142 into 4 equal shares: *Since the single hundred in the dividend cannot be equally shared four ways, it must be mentally traded for 10 tens, producing (10 + 4) or 14 tens in the dividend. Since 4 shares of 3 tens each have a total close to the 14 tens, the 3 tens can be used to predict the quotient's first digit and its place value. The new 3 in the quotient and the 4 in the divisor should then indicate that region 1 contains 4 × 3 tens, or 12 tens, which must be subtracted from the 14 tens. The remaining 2 tens cannot be shared 4 ways, so they must be mentally traded for 20 ones and combined with the original 2 ones. Since 4 shares of 5 ones each have a total close to the new 22 ones, the 5 ones should be used to predict the next digit in the quotient. The 5 in the quotient and the 4 in the divisor indicate that region 2 contains 4 × 5 ones, or 20 ones, which must be subtracted from the 22 ones. The remainder will be 2 ones that could not be shared, and the completed quotient will be 35.* Students need much practice in making predictions for quotient digits. They also need practice in finding number sentences for the regions, using the digits in the divisor and in the gradually forming quotient.

Activity 3: SHARING LARGER DIVIDENDS

(Cooperative Groups)

Material: Light tagboard strips (four colors; amounts and sizes described in step 1 below)
Spinner patterns (see Worksheet DWA-1.3 for Activity 3, Objective 1)
Paper clips for spinner needles
Building mats from Activity 1
Paper
Pencils

Management: Teams of 4 students each (30 minutes)

Directions:

1. Give each team a building mat and a set of tagboard strips, 45 strips of each of three colors (for 1's, 10's, and 100's) and 5 strips of a fourth color (for 1000's). The set should consist of the following: color #1—1" × 1" unmarked strips for ones; color #2—1" × $1\frac{1}{4}$" strips marked with *10;* color #3—1" × $1\frac{1}{2}$" strips marked with *100;* color #4—1" × $1\frac{3}{4}$" strips marked with *1000.* Also, provide one Spinner Pattern Worksheet DWA-1.3 with a paper clip as the spinner needle (pencil point holds end of paper clip in place at center of spinner). The spinner pattern contains two spinners in one.

2. Students will gain experience with four-digit dividends during this activity. Team members will take turns showing a division exercise with the tagboard strips on the building mat. One team member will build on the mat, then the other three members will record the completed exercise in box format on their own papers. They will apply and extend the recording method developed for the box format in Activities 1 and 2. This method is the standard algorithm for long division.

3. On each turn a player will spin the spinner four times, reading digits from the outer ring of the spinner. These digits taken in order will determine the dividend's digits for thousands, hundreds, tens, and ones. Only one zero is allowed as a dividend digit. If a second zero is spun, the player must spin again. This guarantees that the dividend will be either a three-digit or a four-digit number. The player will count out the different colored strips according to the digits obtained through spinning. The player will then spin a fifth time, this time reading a digit from the inner ring of the spinner. This final digit (2, 3, 4, or 5) will be the divisor for the exercise.

4. As an example, a player first spins the following digits in order: 3, 1, 0, and 2. The dividend therefore is 3,102. On the fifth spin, the digit 3 is obtained as the divisor. The player places 3 thousands, 1 hundred, and 2 ones on the building mat. Three ones are placed on the mat in the divisor position. The player then separates the different place value strips into three equal shares or rows under the L-frame, beginning with the larger place value and making trades when necessary. The quotient is shown with extra strips above the frame. The final construction might appear as follows:

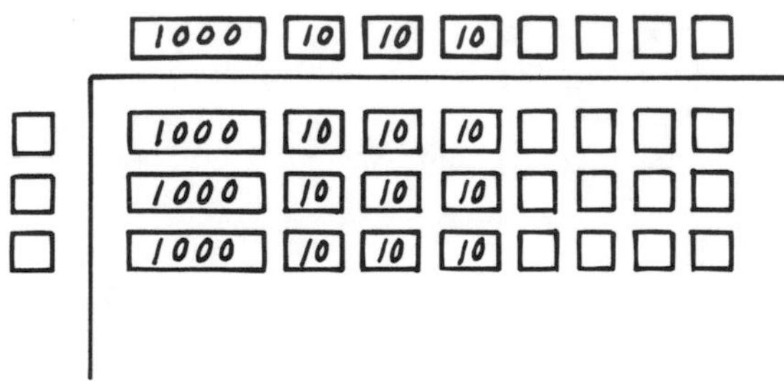

5. The other three team members record one of the following symbolic notations for the completed division exercise:

$$\begin{array}{r|rrrr}
 & 1 & 0 & 3 & 4 \\
\hline
3\,) & 3 & 1 & 0 & 2 \\
 & -3 & & & \\
 & 0 & 1 & 0 & \\
 & & - & 9 & \\
 & & & 1 & 2 \\
 & & - & 1 & 2 \\
\hline
 & & & & 0
\end{array}
\qquad \text{OR} \qquad
\begin{array}{r|rrrr}
 & 1 & 0 & 3 & 4 \\
\hline
3\,) & 3 & 1 & 0 & 2 \\
 & -3 & & & \\
 & 0 & 1 & & \\
 & - & 0 & & \\
 & & 1 & 0 & \\
 & - & & 9 & \\
 & & & 1 & 2 \\
 & - & & 1 & 2 \\
 & & & & 0
\end{array}$$

OBJECTIVE 3: Multiply two- and three-digit whole numbers by two-digit multipliers.

Activity 1: BUILDING PRODUCTS WITH DOUBLE DIGITS
(Concrete Action)

Materials: Base 10 blocks
Building mats (described in step 1 of Activity 1, Objective 1)
Paper
Pencils

Management: Partners (50 minutes)

Directions:

1. This activity develops similarly to and is an extension of Activity 1 of Objective 1. It is assumed that students already know the method presented in Objective 1 for using base 10 blocks to build products with one-digit multipliers. They know that 1 flat (hundred) equals 10 rods (tens) and 1 rod (ten) equals 10 cubes (ones).

2. Give each pair of students a building mat and a set of base 10 blocks. The set of blocks should consist of 3 flats, 40 rods, and 50 small cubes.

3. Have students show 10 × 12 on the building mat by first placing 10 ones in the multiplier position and 1 ten and 2 ones in the set or multiplicand position. Tens in the multiplicand should always be shown with rods, not individual cubes. Students should build the given set one row at a time, beginning at the bottom of the L-frame. The ten individual ones in the multiplier should be pushed together, and the column of tens and each column of ones in the product should also be pushed together vertically. The ten and ones in the same row do not have to be touching. The finished product should appear on the mat as follows:

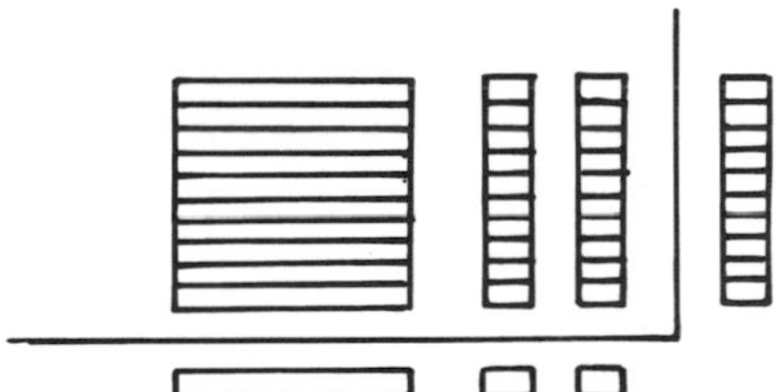

4. Ask students to try to make trades within the product space on the mat while still covering the same amount of mat space and keeping the same rectangular arrangement of the blocks. This can be done by trading each vertical group of 10 ones for 1 ten and the group of 10 tens for 1 hundred. Hence, the product of 10 × 12 becomes 1 hundred and 2 tens, or 120. The blocks now have the following appearance:

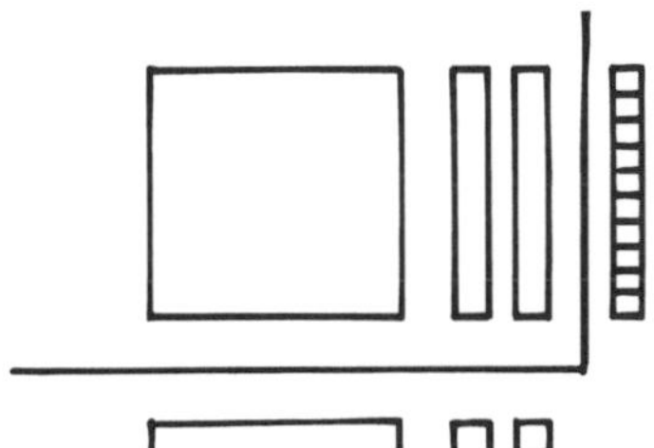

5. Ask students to show 12 sets of 13 or 12 × 13 with their blocks. The multiplier should be shown as 12 individual ones and the set shown as 1 ten and 3 ones on the mat. Again, have students build the set one row at a time. The rows that correspond to the ten group of the multiplier should be touching. Here is the block arrangement:

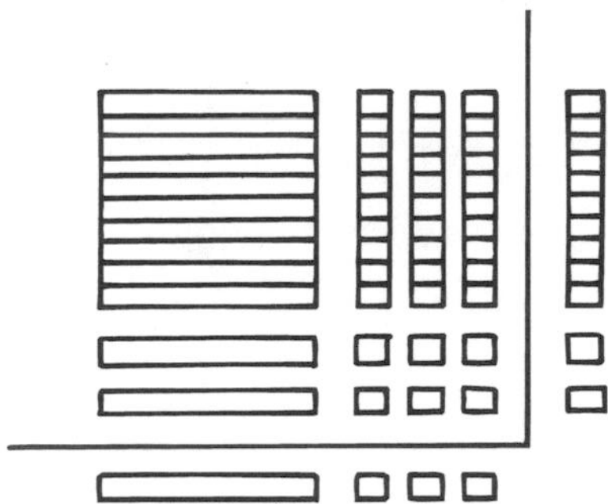

6. Have students make trades within the product without reducing the mat space covered by the blocks. The three vertical columns of 10 ones each can be replaced by 3 tens or rods and the vertical group of 10 tens can be replaced by 1 hundred or flat. The 10 ones that are separate but touching in the multiplier can also be replaced with a ten or rod at this time. Here is the final block arrangement:

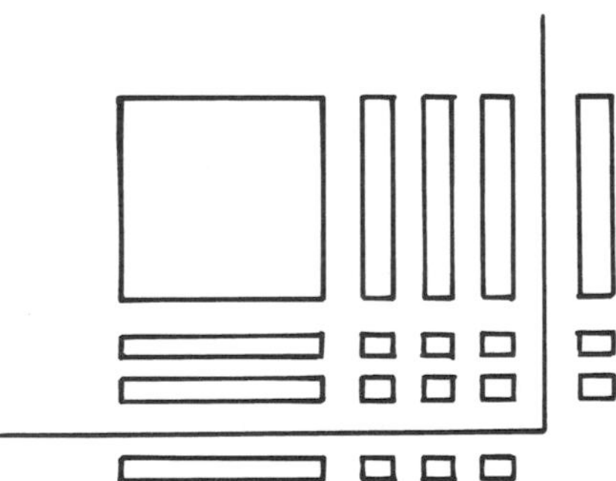

7. Students should now count the blocks shown in the product on the mat. Have them record their result as a number sentence: *12 × 13 = 156.* Remember that the multiplier is always written as the first factor in a number sentence.

8. Write several other multiplication exercises on the chalkboard for the students to build with their blocks. In order to help them see the repetition of sets, they may first build the rows of the product one row at a time, starting at the bottom of the L-frame, and show the multiplier as individual ones, but then they should trade within the product to change the vertical groups of 10 ones to 1 ten and the vertical groups of 10 tens to 1 hundred. This is called *simplifying the blocks*. Eventually, as students are ready to do so, they may build an exercise immediately in its simplified form.

9. Because of the quantities available in the students' sets of blocks, choose multipliers from the numbers 10–15. For the multiplicand, use 1–3 tens and 0–4 ones. After showing each exercise with blocks, students should record a number sentence that expresses the final product.

10. After students have built several exercises, have students explain the steps they took to build some of the products.

Activity 2: PICTURING LARGER PRODUCTS
(Pictorial Action)

Materials: Paper
Pencils
Red pencils
Base 10 blocks and building mats from Activity 1 (optional)

Management: Partners (two sessions at 50 minutes/session)

Directions:

1. Each pair of students will need a red pencil for the second session of this activity. Some students may still prefer to work with the blocks; this is certainly acceptable. After they build each exercise, however, they should also draw a diagram of their product and do whatever recording is required.

2. Students will draw backward L-frames on their own paper like the one drawn on the building mats in Activity 1. The bottom segment of the frame should be about $2\frac{1}{2}$ inches long, and the vertical segment should be about $1\frac{1}{2}$ inches long. Small circles will represent ones, line segments will represent tens, and large squares with sides the same length as the line segments will represent hundreds in the diagrams.

3. Drawing products: Have students show 13 × 24 by drawing 1 ten and 3 ones for the multiplier and 2 tens and 4 ones for the set or multiplicand. Remind students that the multiplier is always the first or left factor when written in horizontal form and is the bottom factor when written in vertical form. Encourage them to use the simplified form when drawing the product. Remind them that ten rows of one can be replaced with a ten and that ten rows of a ten can be replaced with a hundred. Here is the final diagram:

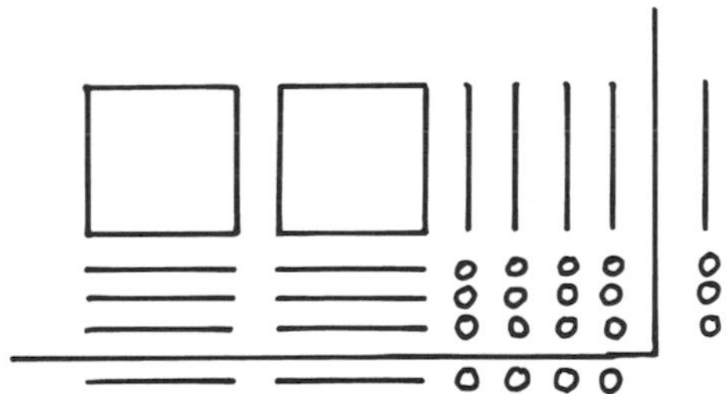

4. Have students record their result in vertical form and label the amounts. There should be room for the recording to the right of the diagram.

24	in a share
×13	shares
312	total

5. During this first session, write several other multiplication exercises on the chalkboard for students to draw on L-frames on their own papers. They should record each result in vertical form as shown in step 4. Use the numbers 10–15 as multipliers. Use 0–5 ones and 1–4 tens for the set or multiplicand.

6. Three-digit multiplicands may be introduced at this time, if preferred. On the diagram, a narrow rectangle a little longer than the line segment or ten may be used to represent a hundred in the original set. Ten of such a hundred in the set would then be represented by a larger rectangle whose length is the same as that of the narrow rectangle, but whose width is the same as the length of the line segment or ten. The diagram of 12 × 113 shown in the illustration below demonstrates these new shapes and their positions within the final product.

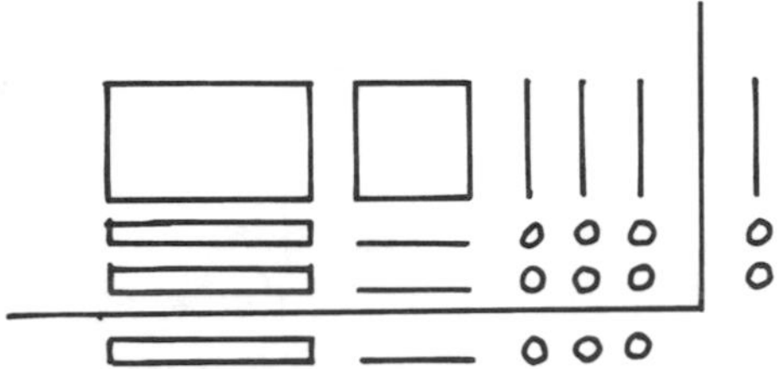

7. Describing the regions of a product: For the second session of this activity, have students correct any errors in the diagrams drawn during the first session. Then have them mark off the different regions of each product with a red pencil. The regions should be numbered, beginning at the lower right of the diagram in order to correspond to the steps of the standard algorithm for multiplication. (See the diagram for 13 × 24 in step 8 as an example.)

8. A number sentence should be written for each region that describes the shape arrangement within the region. Remind students that the number of observable rows within a region must agree with the number of simplified shapes in the multiplier corresponding to the level of the region. Rows are always considered to be formed from left to right. Because of the tall, vertical orientation of the tens arrangement in region 3 of the example of 13 × 24 shown below, some students will try to count the four vertical line segments as individual *rows;* this is a phenomenon of visual rotation. There must be breaks between rows when moving vertically from one row to the next. The tens in region 3 do not have any vertical breaks. Thus, there is only one row (a tall row!) in region 3, and that row contains four tens.

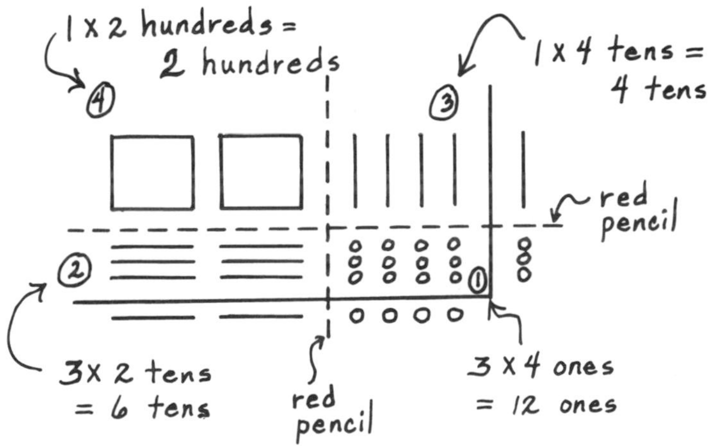

9. The different number sentences for the regions of 13 × 24 must now be transferred to the vertical recording format to show the partial product or amount contained in each of the four regions. The sum of the partial products equals the total product for 13 × 24. The number sentences should be recorded first, then their answers recorded in the columns according to the place value they represent. It is helpful to mark off the columns at this stage. Here is the recording for 13 × 24:

	2	4	
×	1	3	
	1	2	(1) 3 × 4 ones = 12 ones
	6		(2) 3 × 2 tens = 6 tens
	4		(3) 1 × 4 tens = 4 tens
2			(4) 1 × 2 hundreds = 2 hundreds
3	1	2	total used

10. Students should repeat steps 7–9 with several of the diagrams drawn during the first session of this activity. After they are comfortable with the process, discuss the patterns found within the four regions. Observe that the lower level always has ones on the right and tens to the left of the ones. A three-digit multiplicand would show hundreds to the left of the tens. The upper level always has tens on the right and hundreds to the left of the tens. Thousands would be to the left of the hundreds if a three-digit multiplicand were used. The corresponding number sentences reflect the same place value patterns. Also, the first factor in a region's number sentence matches the digit of the multiplier at the same level (lower or upper) as the region. *Note*: Even though a region may contain zero shapes, it must still abide by the arrangement patterns of its adjacent regions.

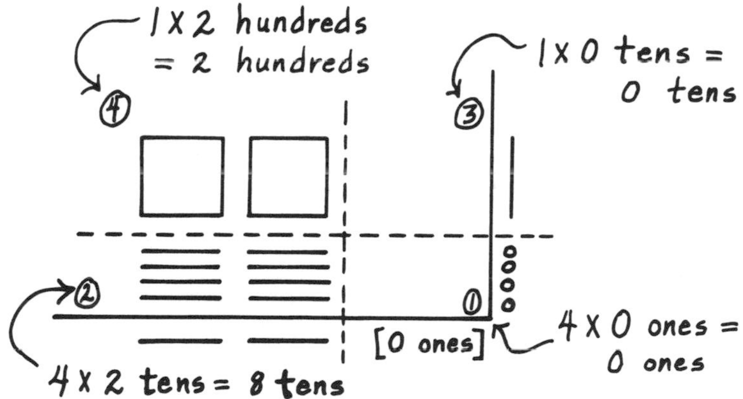

11. After students have recorded the number sentences and partial products for several exercises, ask them to compare the factors in the number sentences of each exercise to the digits in the multiplier and multiplicand of the same exercise. Have students draw and number arrows to connect the digits that correspond to each factor pair in the number sentences. Here are the arrows on 13 × 24 as an example:

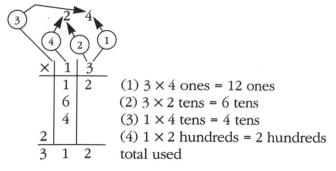

	2	4	
×	1	3	
	1	2	(1) 3 × 4 ones = 12 ones
	6		(2) 3 × 2 tens = 6 tens
	4		(3) 1 × 4 tens = 4 tens
2			(4) 1 × 2 hundreds = 2 hundreds
3	1	2	total used

12. Eventually students should begin to leave off the number sentences and just depend on the observed place value patterns of the four regions and the digits in the multiplier and multiplicand to find the partial products for the different regions. The language used, however, should continue to reflect the arrangements within the regions. For example, to work 23 × 45, students should be able to describe their steps in words similar to the following: *To solve 23 × 45, we will make 3 sets of 5 ones, or 15 ones, and 3 sets of 4 tens, or 12 tens. We will then make 2 sets of 5 tens, or 10 tens, and 2 sets of 4 hundreds, or 8 hundreds. The sum of these four partial products equals 1,035.* Encourage students to describe their steps in such detail until they have mastered the algorithm and are ready to develop their own language "short-cuts."

13. At a future time, after students have thoroughly mastered the recording method that lists each individual partial product, the more traditional, *collapsed* method of recording may be introduced. Students probably were introduced to the technique while working with one-digit multipliers in Objective 1. The collapsed method simply records all the partial products from the same level of the pictorial diagram on the same line in the written algorithm. The trading is noted just above each recording line. This location for showing the trades or regrouping seems easier for students than writing them above the factors. As a traded amount is added to the next partial product, it is marked out. Here are the steps as they would occur for the symbolic recording of 23 × 45. The combining of the newly traded amount with the next partial product is described in brackets at each step.

(a)

  45
× 23
~~1~~
135

[12 tens + 1 new ten = 13 tens]

(b)

  45
× 23
~~1~~
135
~~1~~
 90
1035

[8 hundreds + 1 new hundred = 9 hundreds]

Activity 3: PRODUCT SPIN
(Cooperative Groups)

Materials: Paper
Pencils
Spinner Pattern Worksheet DWA-3.3
Paper clips for spinner needles

Management: Teams of 4 students each (30 minutes)

Directions:

1. This activity provides experience with three-digit multiplicands and two-digit multipliers. It is assumed that students know that 10 sets of 100 equal 1000. In the drawing process, a narrow rectangle will be used in the multiplicand to represent a hundred. The length of the rectangle should be a little longer than the line segment used to show tens and its width should be no greater than the diameter of the circle used to show ones. A large square will be used in the product region of the diagram to represent

10 sets of 10; its side length should equal the length of the line segment being used for tens. A large rectangle (non-square) will be used in the product region to show 10 sets of 100, or 1000. Its length should equal the length of the narrow rectangle and its width should equal the length of the line segment. The shapes will not be proportional. An example of the final diagram for 12 × 113 can be seen in step 6 of the preceding activity.

2. Team members will work in pairs. On a turn, one pair will draw a diagram to show a given product; the other pair will confirm the product, using the symbolic notation developed in Activity 2 and possibly extending it to thousands. The partial product of each region may be recorded separately, or the *collapsed* method may be used.

3. To get the factors to use in the diagram, the drawing pair will spin the spinner five times. The first three spins taken in order will indicate the digits of the multiplicand: first the ones, then the tens and the hundreds. The last two spins will indicate in order the ones and tens digits for the multiplier. As each digit is obtained, that amount of shapes is drawn in the appropriate position on the multiplication L-frame on the pair's paper. The drawing pair will complete the diagram, using the new factors. They will then find the product by counting all the shapes drawn in the product region of the L-frame and adding their values. The other pair will confirm the suggested answer by using the digits of the factors and the appropriate place value patterns to find the product.

4. The drawing and computing may continue as long as time permits.

SPINNER PATTERN WORKSHEET DWA-3.3
Product Spin

2

1

3

OBJECTIVE 4: Divide two- and three-digit whole numbers by two-digit divisors.

Activity 1: BUILDING EQUAL SHARES

(Concrete Action)

Materials: Base 10 blocks
Building mats from Activity 1, Objective 2
Paper
Pencils

Management: Partners (50 minutes)

Directions:

1. Give each pair of students a set of base 10 blocks and a building mat. The set of blocks should contain 3 flats, 40 rods, and 50 small cubes. It is assumed that students have mastered the method of division with one-digit divisors presented in Objective 2. Make sure students are familiar with that material.

2. Have students place 2 hundreds (or flats), 5 tens (or rods), and 4 ones (or cubes) in the lower right corner of the building mat, and place 12 individual ones in the divisor (number of shares) position of the mat. The top 10 ones in the divisor should be touching each other, while the lower 2 ones are left separated from each other and from the other 10. Tell the students that the divisor indicates that 12 equal shares need to be made from the blocks in the dividend, if possible.

3. Have students begin the sharing process with the largest blocks in the dividend, the hundreds. Ask: *Are there enough hundreds to share 12 ways? If not, can the 2 hundreds be traded and the new blocks then shared?* Note that the 2 hundreds cannot be shared 12 ways, so students must trade them for 20 tens.

4. There should now be 25 tens total. Have the students place a ten in line with each of the ones in the divisor; this is one round of sharing. Since there are 13 tens left, have the students repeat the sharing, placing one more ten in the row of each divisor unit. Each share or row now contains two tens. Have students show this by placing two new tens from their general set of blocks, not from the dividend blocks, in the quotient (share size) above the columns of tens.

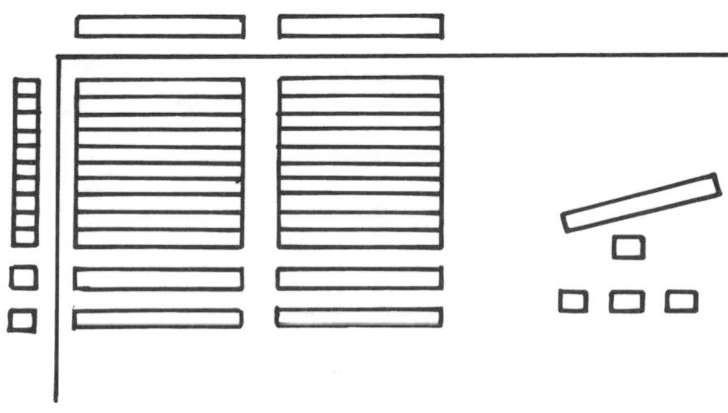

5. Ask: *Since the single ten left in the dividend cannot be shared 12 ways, can it be traded for some new blocks that can then be shared?* The ten should be traded for 10 new ones from the general set of blocks. There are now 14 ones total in the dividend. Have students share them equally by placing one in each row now formed under the L-frame of the mat. There will be 2 ones left unshared in the lower right corner of the mat. Since each row now contains a one, have students show this by placing a new one from the general set of blocks in the quotient above the column of ones.

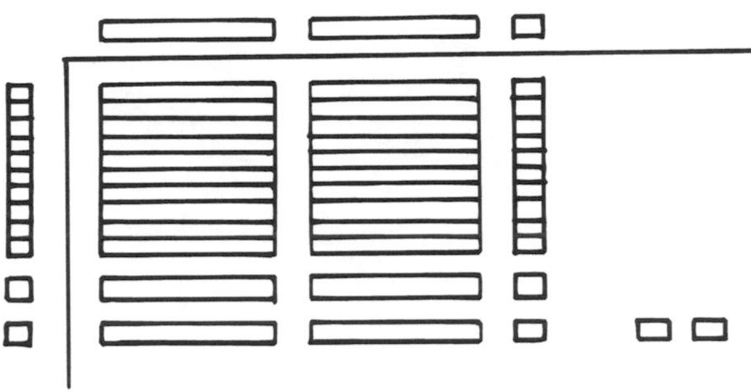

6. Have students record the results on their own paper in the following way:

```
        2  1   in a share
12  ) 2  5  4
    ==========
             2   ones left unshared
```

7. While the above exercise is still shown on the students' building mats, ask students to look at their blocks and see if any of them might be replaced with a single block that would cover the same space on the mat and represent the same value as the blocks being replaced. Several replacements will be possible:

- The upper 10 ones in the divisor can trade for 1 ten.
- The upper 10 tens in the left and middle columns under the L-frame can trade for 1 hundred per column.
- The upper 10 ones in the right column under the L-frame can trade for 1 ten.

This procedure is called *simplifying* the blocks on the mat. Tell students they should simplify their blocks whenever possible to make the building process easier.

8. Now write other exercises on the chalkboard for students to build with their blocks. Each result should be recorded, using the form given in step 6. An exercise may be presented on the chalkboard in either of two possible forms: *254 shared 12 ways = ?* or *254 divided by 12 = ?* Use divisors 10–13 and dividends less than 400. Exercises may be generated by first finding the products of one factor from 10–13 and another factor from 5–24. These products may then be given as the dividend of a division exercise and the first factor given as the divisor. Other exercises may be made by adding 1–5 extra ones to a product, but keeping the same factor as the divisor. This process would produce a remainder. Before assigning an exercise, work through it to be sure that at most three tens will need to be traded for new ones. This guarantees that students will have enough blocks to build the exercise.

9. After students have built several exercises with the blocks, have some of them explain how they built an exercise and write their numerical recording on the board.

Activity 2: DRAWING EQUAL SHARES

(Pictorial Action)

Materials: Paper
Pencils
Red pencils
Base 10 blocks (optional)
Building mats from Activity 1 (optional)

Management: Partners (two sessions at 50 minutes/session)

Directions:

1. Have students work in pairs. Each pair will need a red pencil. Some students may still prefer to build with the blocks; this is quite acceptable. Have them first build an exercise with the blocks, then draw a diagram of their finished arrangement. In the drawings, large squares will be used to represent hundreds, line segments will represent tens, and small circles will represent ones. It is assumed that students are familiar with the drawing technique used in Activity 2, Objective 2.

2. Have students draw a rotated L-frame on their own papers like the one shown on the building mats. The vertical bar should be at least $1\frac{1}{2}$ inches long and the horizontal bar should be at least $2\frac{1}{2}$ inches to make the finished diagrams easy to view.

3. Drawing equal shares: Ask students to show 14 as the divisor by drawing a line segment and 4 small circles to the left of the vertical bar of the L-frame. A dividend of 323 should be shown by drawing 3 large squares, 2 line segments, and 3 small circles to the left of the divisor.

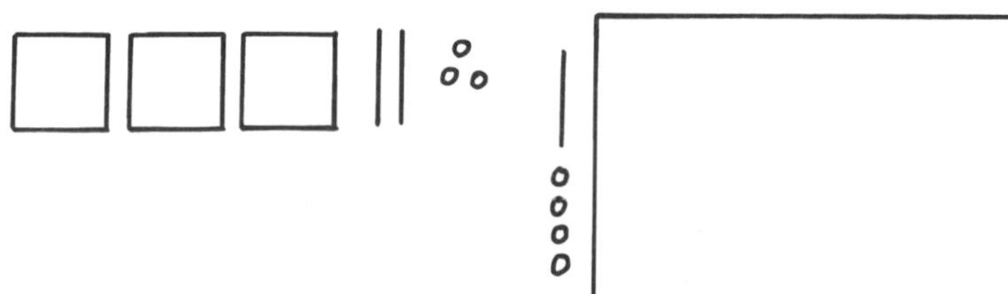

4. Ask if ten equal shares can be made from one of the hundreds in the dividend. From the simplification procedure used in Activity 1, many students will recognize that a hundred represents 10 tens, so each share would receive a ten. Those students may just redraw one of the large squares under the L-frame and to the right of the ten in the divisor, and mark out the used square in the dividend. Other students may need to mark out the square in the dividend, then draw 10 new line segments or tens beside it. They should then redraw the set of 10 tens under the L-frame and to the right of the ten in the divisor, and mark out the 10 used segments in the dividend.

5. Four more tens are needed to complete the first round of sharing, but there are only two tens showing in the dividend. Students must trade one of the hundreds for 10 new tens again. Another square must be marked out, then 10 new line segments drawn beside it. Four of the segments or tens should then be marked out and redrawn under the frame to the right of the 4 ones in the divisor. Now each share contains a ten, so a ten should be drawn in the quotient above the frame. Here are two ways this first round of sharing might be drawn.

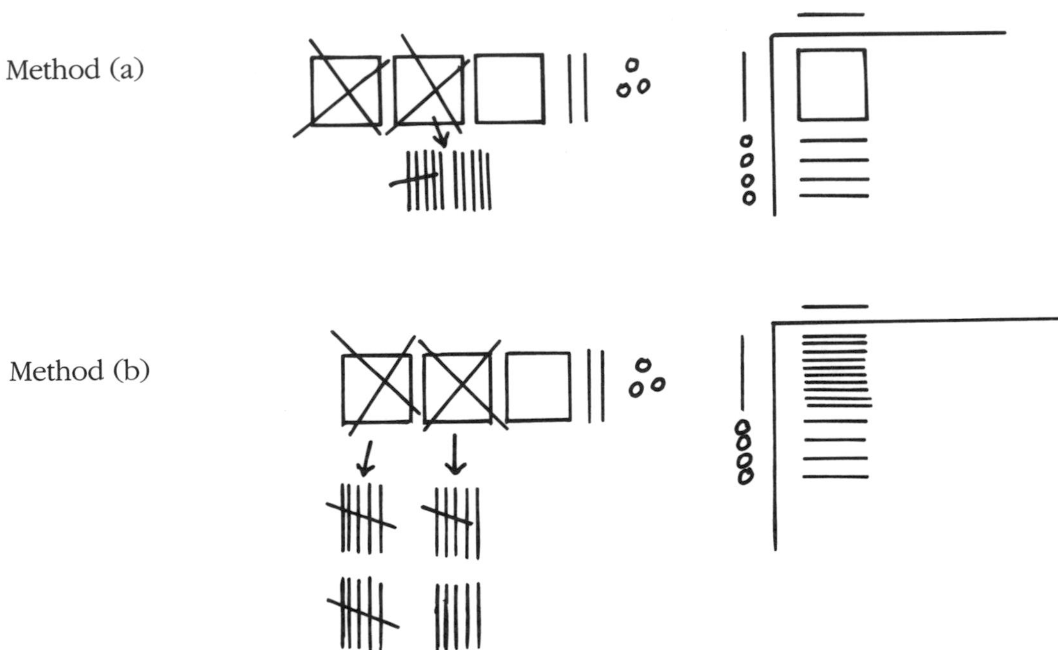

6. Using either method (a) or method (b) from step 5, students should repeat the above process to draw another ten in each row under the frame and in the quotient. The third square and four more line segments should be marked out in the dividend. Four tens (or line segments) and three ones (or circles) remain unmarked in the dividend.

7. Ask students what other sharing might be done. They should decide that only ones can now be shared and that some of the tens may need to be traded for ones. Again, some students will realize that since a ten equals 10 ones, they can draw a segment under the frame beside the large squares to represent placing a one in each of the top ten shares. This is the *simplified* approach. Others will first need to mark out a segment in the dividend and draw 10 new circles or ones beside it before they can transfer the ones to the top ten rows under the frame. Eventually a ten in the dividend must be marked out and 10 new ones drawn in order to have individual ones to redraw in the bottom four rows of the frame. Three ones should finally be placed in each row, causing three ones (not from the dividend) to be drawn in the quotient. All shapes should now be marked out in the dividend except for a single one. Students should draw a ring around that one. Here are two ways the final diagram might be drawn:

Method (a)

Method (b)

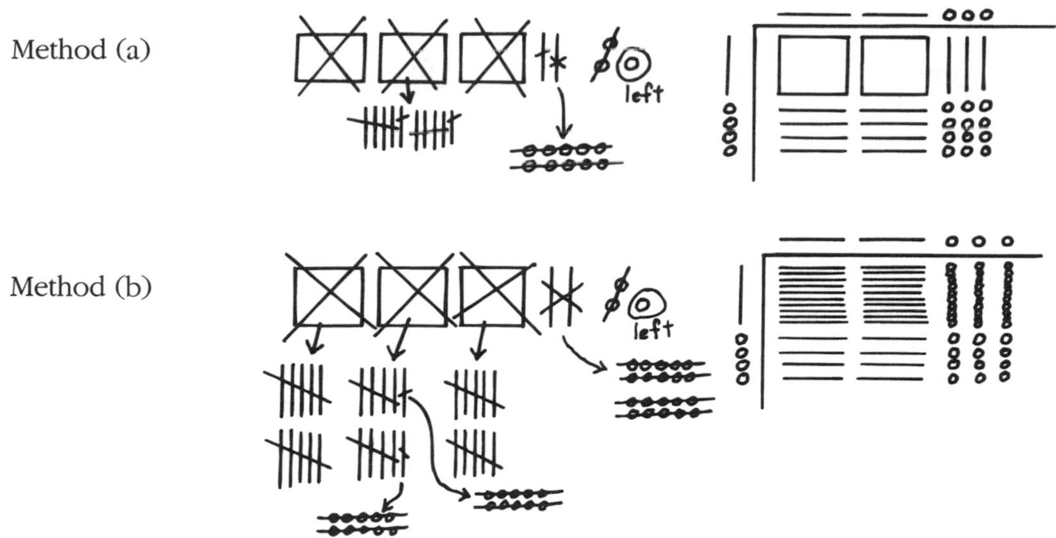

8. Have students record the result on their papers below the finished frame:

```
         2  3   in a share
14  ) 3  2  3
    =========
            1   one left unshared
```

9. Continuing the first session, have students work other division exercises by drawing diagrams on their own paper. Use some of the exercises assigned earlier for Activity 1, or follow the guidelines given in Activity 1 for creating new dividends and their divisors. Encourage students to draw their diagrams in the simplified form, that is, by method (a) in step 7.

10. Describing regions within the dividend: For the second session, have a few students demonstrate to the class how they drew some of their diagrams during the previous session. All diagrams should now be in simplified form. Using the diagrams from the first session and the procedure described for session 2 in Activity 2, Objective 2, have students use a red pencil to mark off the four regions of shapes formed under the L-frame for each exercise. Each region should be numbered and labeled with a number sentence that describes the shape arrangement within that region. The example discussed earlier, 323 divided by 14, would be numbered and labeled as follows:

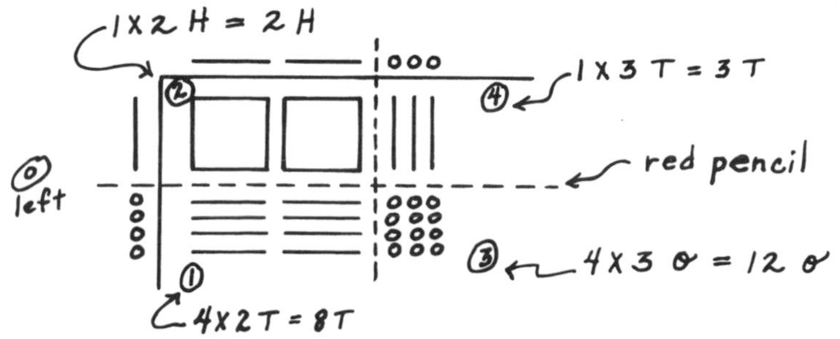

11. After students have numbered and labeled several of their diagrams, guide them to see place value patterns produced by the ordering assigned to the regions. For example, observe that since region 1 contains tens, the quotient begins with tens. Also, when the left-most column under the frame begins with tens in the bottom region, the next column to the right begins with the next smaller value, ones.

12. Students should now transfer the number sentences of each diagram to the symbolic notation for the exercise. They should also draw and number arrows connecting the digits of the quotient with the digits of the divisor to show their relationship to the factors in the regions' number sentences. The example given earlier would be numbered and labeled as follows:

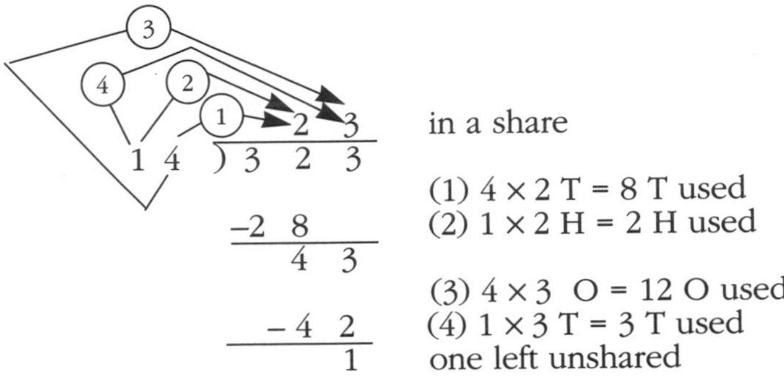

13. After students have developed an understanding of the sharing process and know how to predict regional arrangements by pairing various digits together, they need a strategy for predicting the first digit of the quotient in order to *begin* the pairing of digits. This can be done by underlining digits in the dividend in red pencil to show what trades have been made. For example, in the exercise shown above, if only the symbols are to be used to solve the exercise, students might first underline the 3 in red. This indicates that the 3 hundreds are being considered for sharing 14 ways. Since there are not enough hundreds, they must be traded for 30 tens. Digits 3 and 2 in the dividend are then underlined in red to signify that there are now 32 tens total being considered for sharing 14 ways. Students can estimate that at least 2 tens might be placed in each share, using 32 divided by 14. The 2 tens become the first entry (an estimate that may need to be changed later) in the quotient and provide the first digit to be paired with the digits in the divisor in order to find the first two number sentences to be recorded in the symbolic notation.

Activity 3: CREATING DIVISION RECTANGLES

(Cooperative Groups)

Materials: Base 10 blocks
Dice
Paper
Pencils

Management: Teams of 4 students each (30 minutes)

Directions:

1. Give each team a die and a set of base 10 blocks (6 flats, 6 rods, and 6 small cubes).

2. Students will take turns rolling the die three times to determine how many of each type of block to use. The first number will tell how many flats, the second number will tell how many rods, and the third number will tell how many cubes. The selected blocks must then be used to build a rectangular arrangement containing regions like those used earlier in Activity 1. The builder must write down what division exercises the arrangement represents (no remainders) and will earn points from the number of blocks used in the final arrangement. This is an excellent readiness activity for factoring trinomials later in high school algebra.

3. On a turn, for example, a student might roll in order the numbers 3, 6, and 2. The student then places 3 flats, 6 rods, and 2 cubes on the table and begins to arrange them in a rectangular shape, orienting the blocks as done earlier in Activity 1. The goal is to use as many of the selected blocks as possible. The student might decide on the following arrangement, even though others may be possible.

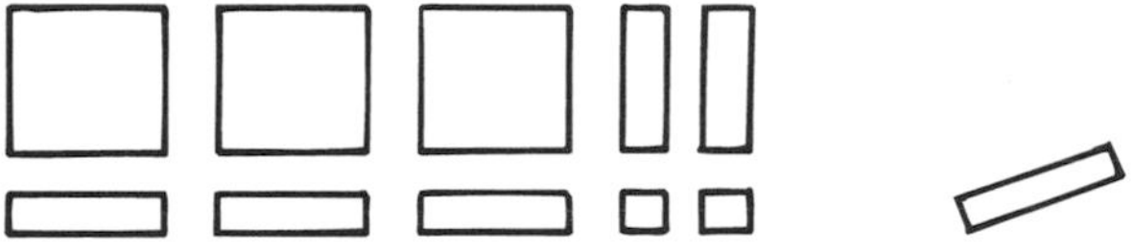

4. The student now writes two exercises on a sheet of paper: *352 divided by 11 = 32* and *352 divided by 32 = 11.*

5. To score, the student *earns* 2 points for each exercise written, if approved by the other team members, and 1 point for each block used in the arrangement. Since one of the selected rods was not used in the final arrangement, the student *loses* 1 point for that block. The total score earned on this turn is therefore (14 − 1), or 13 points.

6. The student to accumulate at least 50 points first is the winner.

OBJECTIVE 5: Add decimals (tens, ones, tenths, hundredths, thousandths).

Activity 1: COUNTING IN TENS
(Concrete Action)

Materials: Small, colored counters (5 colors)
Base 10 building mats (pattern described in step 1 below)
Paper
Pencils

Management: Partners (50 minutes)

Directions:

1. Give each pair of students 20 small counters of each of 5 different colors and a base 10 building mat. The building mat may be made by subdividing an $8\frac{1}{2}$" × 14" sheet of paper into five columns with the headings: *tens, ones, tenths, hundredths,* and *thousandths.* A large decimal point should be drawn on the subdivision bar between the *ones* and *tenths* column headings. A different color of counter should be assigned to each column and a counter placed in its heading on the mat to indicate that column's color. The final mat with counters placed in the headings should appear as shown:

T	O	T-ths	H-ths	TH-ths

2. It is assumed that students understand the 10-to-1 relationships among the place values being studied in this activity. They should already have experienced trading with concrete objects in order to compare values involving thousandths to tens.

3. Have students place counters in the upper portion of their building mats to show *28.045.* Have them also place counters in the lower portion of the mat to show *15.346.*

T	O	T-ths	H-ths	TH-ths

4. Ask students to begin at the right side of the mat and combine the counters within each column. If ten or more counters are found in the same column, they should be traded for a new counter in the next column to the left.

5. Students should find the total counters in each column after all trades have been made. A number sentence showing the addends and sum should be recorded on each student's own paper: *28.045 + 15.346 = 43.391.*

T	O	T-ths	H-ths	TH-ths

6. Now write other pairs of decimal numbers on the chalkboard for students to build on their mats in order to find their sums. They should record a number sentence on their papers for each exercise they build. The addends selected should reflect the place values being studied by the class.

7. After all students have finished, ask several students to explain the various trades they made and tell the final answers for some of the exercises they built on their mats.

Activity 2: DECIMAL DRAW

(Pictorial Action)

Materials: Decimal Addition Worksheet DWA-5.2
Red pencils
Pencils

Management: Partners (50 minutes)

Directions:

1. Have students work together in pairs. Give each student 2–3 copies of the decimal addition worksheet (DWA-5.2) and a red pencil. The worksheet contains several base 10 frames showing thousandths to tens. Have students write numbers in the small boxes to number the frames as needed.

2. Ask students to draw small circles in the upper level of the various columns of the first frame to show *8.52.* Also, have them show *11.604* in the lower level of the columns.

T	O	T-ths	H-ths	TH-ths

3. Have students begin at the right side of the frame counting the circles in each column. As they find a group of ten circles in the same column, they should use the red pencil to draw a ring around the ten circles and mark them out with a large X. An arrow should then be drawn to the next column to the left and a new red circle drawn in that column to show the trade that has occurred.

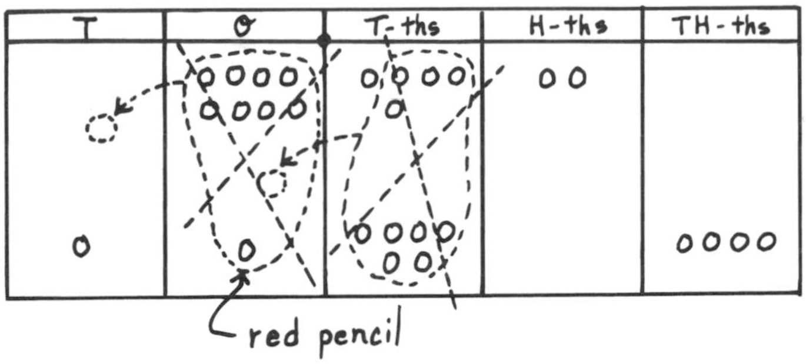

T	O	T-ths	H-ths	TH-ths

red pencil

4. Have students count the circles remaining in each column to find the sum of their two original addends. They should record their result by aligning the columns in vertical format to the right of the base 10 frame:

$$\begin{array}{r} 8.52 \\ +\,11.604 \\ \hline 20.124 \end{array}$$

5. Write other pairs of decimal numbers on the chalkboard for students to draw on their base 10 frames and find the sums. Each number pair should be recorded in vertical format beside its frame to show the result of the addition diagram. Use whatever place values are being studied by the class, but limit the numbers selected to five digits.

6. After all students have finished with their drawings, have several students demonstrate their solutions by drawing some of the exercises on base 10 frames on the chalkboard and explaining their steps.

7. If preferred, after students have drawn several addition exercises on their base 10 frames and seem comfortable with aligning columns in vertical format to record their results, have them also show their trades in the recording notation. Encourage them to use correct mathematical language when describing the trades. For example, for the addition exercise discussed earlier and shown below, the proper description might be as follows: *Initially the adding yields four thousandths and two hundredths. Five-tenths and six-tenths then make eleven-tenths, which equal a new one and one-tenth. Eight ones and a single one combined with the new one make ten ones, which equal a new ten. The new ten finally combines with the other ten to make two tens in all.*

$$\begin{array}{r} 1\,1 \\ 8.52 \\ +\,11.604 \\ \hline 20.124 \end{array}$$

NAME ______________________________ DATE ____________________

DECIMAL ADDITION WORKSHEET DWA-5.2
Decimal Draw

Find sums of decimal numbers by drawing circles on the frames below. Trade when possible.

☐

T	O	T-ths	H-ths	TH-ths

☐

T	O	T-ths	H-ths	TH-ths

☐

T	O	T-ths	H-ths	TH-ths

☐

T	O	T-ths	H-ths	TH-ths

Activity 3: THE GAME OF LU-LU

(Cooperative Groups)

Materials: Playing pieces (described in step 2 below)
Paper
Pencils

Management: Teams of 4 students each (20 minutes)

Directions:

1. Background: The Hawaiian Islands were discovered by the English explorer and navigator Captain James Cook on January 20, 1778. He and his crew landed at Waimea, Kauai, where they found Polynesian settlers. Cook named the islands the Sandwich Islands after John Montagu, the Earl of Sandwich.

The Hawaiians played Lu-Lu with small disks about $2\frac{1}{2}$ cm in diameter. The disks were made of volcanic stone so plentiful in the islands and had red markings painted on them. The game's name, *lu-lu,* means *to shake,* reflecting the use of the disks as dice, which were called *u-lu*. The game was originally a simple game of counting single dots on the disks, but has been modified for this activity to involve decimal numbers. For more information on this game, please refer to the following sources: Marina C. Krause, *Multicultural Mathematics Materials* (National Council of Teachers of Mathematics, 1906 Association Drive, Reston, VA 22091, 1983); and Stewart Culin, "Hawaiian Games," *American Anthropologist,* n.s. 1 (April 1899): 201–247.

2. Each team should have four playing pieces or disks, which might be made from large, flat buttons or flat, wooden disks about two inches in diameter. Balsa wood might be used. Dots should be painted on the disks. Each dot will have the value of 0.1. The disks should be marked or painted on only one side as follows:

 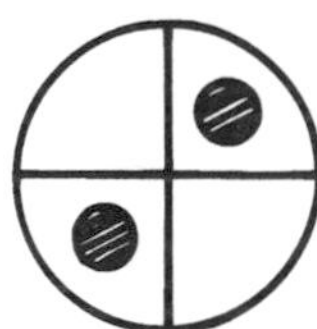  

3. Team members are to take turns shaking the four disks in both hands and tossing them onto the playing surface.

4. On a turn, a player is to toss the set of disks two times. If all four disks fall face up on the first toss, the player scores 1.0, the sum of all the dots' values, and then tosses all the disks a second time. The values of the dots showing on the second toss are then combined with the sum from the first toss. If all four disks do not fall face up on the first toss, the player totals the values of the dots showing on the disks, then tosses *only* the face-down disks a second time to get another sum to add to the first. The two sums combined will be the player's score for that turn.

5. The final sum from each player's turn should be combined with the sums from previous turns of the other players. The team goal is to reach a sum of 10 in as few turns as possible. If each player has had two turns and a team score of 10 has not been reached, the game ends and another game is begun. If a team does reach the goal of 10, a second game may be played to try to reach 10 in even fewer turns than before.

6. Players may wish to record their scores on paper after each turn in order to keep up with the team's accumulated score and the number of turns taken.

7. An alternative form of the game might involve eight disks instead of four. One set of four would be painted in one color and the other set in a second color. Dots in one color would still represent 0.1 each; dots in a second color would represent 0.01 each. Two players would then throw the disks together, one player throwing the disks of the first color and the partner player throwing the disks of the second color. The team goal would still be a score of 10.

OBJECTIVE 6: Subtract decimals (tens, ones, tenths, hundredths, thousandths).

Activity 1: DECIMAL TAKE-AWAY

(Concrete Action)

Materials: Small, colored counters (5 colors)
Building mats from Activity 1, Objective 5
Paper
Pencils

Management: Partners (50 minutes)

Directions:

1. Give each pair of students 20 counters of each of 5 different colors and a building mat from Activity 1, Objective 5.

2. It is assumed that students understand the 10-to-1 relationships among the place values being studied in this activity. They should already have experienced trading or regrouping with concrete objects in order to compare values involving tens to thousandths.

3. Write the following exercise on the chalkboard: *16.504 – 5.628 = ?* Have students place counters in the upper portion of their building mats to show 16.504.

T	O	T-ths	H-ths	TH-ths

4. Ask: *Are there enough thousandths on the mat to remove 8 of them as indicated in the second number of the exercise? If not, can some trades be made to allow the removal?* A trade will be necessary, but since there are no hundredths on the mat at first, a tenth must be exchanged for 10 hundredths. A counter in the hundredths column may then be traded for 10 new counters in the thousandths column. The new column amounts should appear as shown:

T	O	T-ths	H-ths	TH-ths

5. Students should now remove 8 thousandths and 2 hundredths from their respective columns on the mat, leaving 6 thousandths and 7 hundredths in the two columns.

6. At this point ask: *Are there enough tenths on the mat to remove 6 of them? If not, are any trades possible?* There are not enough tenths, so students must exchange a one for 10 new tenths.

T	O	T-ths	H-ths	TH-ths

7. Students should now remove 6 tenths from the tenths column and also remove 5 ones from the ones column. The column amounts remaining after all removals or subtractions will be 1 ten, 8 tenths, 7 hundredths, and 6 thousandths.

8. Have students write a number sentence on their own papers to show their result: *16.504 – 5.628 = 10.876.*

9. Now write other subtraction exercises on the chalkboard for students to solve by placing counters on their mats, making needed trades, then removing the required amounts of counters. A number sentence should be recorded on students' papers for each exercise worked. Use whichever place values are being studied by the class.

10. After all have finished, have several students explain the different steps they used with the counters on the mat in order to find their solutions to some of the exercises.

Activity 2: TAKE-AWAY DIAGRAMS

(Pictorial Action)

Materials: Decimal Subtraction Worksheet DWA-6.2
Red pencils
Pencils

Management: Partners (50 minutes)

Directions:

1. Give each student 2–3 copies of the Decimal Subtraction Worksheet DWA-6.2 and a red pencil. Have students work together as partners. The worksheet will contain several base 10 frames with columns for thousandths to tens. Plain circles will be drawn on the worksheet frames to represent counters in the various place value columns. Have students write numbers in the small boxes on the worksheet to number the frames as needed.

1

T	O	T-ths	H-ths	TH-ths
–	8	2	6	7

2. Have students draw circles in the upper level of the columns of the first frame of the worksheet to show 20.58. Have them write the digits for 8.267 in the proper columns of the subtraction box.

3. Ask: *Are there enough thousandths in the original amount to remove or mark out 7 thousandths? If not, are any trades possible?* Since 7 thousandths cannot be removed from 0 thousandths, one hundredth must be exchanged for 10 new thousandths. This may be shown by marking out one circle in the hundredths column with red pencil and drawing a red arrow from that circle to the thousandths column where 10 new circles should be drawn in red.

red pencil

1

T	O	T-ths	H-ths	TH-ths
—	8	2	6	7

4. To show subtraction, have students mark out 7 circles in the thousandths column, 6 circles in the hundredths column, and 2 circles in the tenths column.

1

T	O	T-ths	H-ths	TH-ths
—	8	2	6	7

5. Now ask: *Are there enough ones to remove 8 of them? If not, will another trade be possible?* Since 8 ones cannot be removed from 0 ones, a single ten must be exchanged for 10 new ones. Students should show the trade with red pencil, then mark out eight of the new ones to complete the subtraction process. They should then count the circles remaining in each column of the frame and record the amounts as digits in the answer box at the bottom of the frame.

1

T	O	T-ths	H-ths	TH-ths
—	8	2	6	7
1	2	3	1	3

6. Also have the students record the results of the exercise by aligning proper columns in vertical format to the right of the base 10 frame.

$$\begin{array}{r} 20.58 \\ -\ \ 8.267 \\ \hline 12.313 \end{array}$$

7. Write other subtraction exercises on the chalkboard for students to solve by drawing circles on the other base 10 frames on the worksheet. The results should be recorded in vertical format to the right of the frames. Use whatever place values are being studied by the class, but limit the numbers selected to five digits.

8. After all students have finished with their drawings, have several students demonstrate their solutions by drawing some of the exercises on base 10 frames on the chalkboard and explaining their steps.

9. If preferred, after students have drawn several subtraction diagrams and seem comfortable with recording their results by aligning columns correctly in vertical format, have them also show their trades in the numerical recording. Be sure to have them use correct mathematical language when describing the trades with the notation. For example, in the exercise discussed earlier and shown below, a proper description might be as follows: *One hundredth trades for 10 new thousandths, leaving 7 hundredths. One ten trades for 10 new ones, leaving 1 ten. Then the subtraction is performed.*

$$\begin{array}{rrcrrr} 1 & 10 & & & 7 & 10 \\ \not{2} & \not{0} & . & 5 & \not{8} & \\ - & 8 & . & 2 & 6 & 7 \\ \hline 1 & 2 & . & 3 & 1 & 3 \end{array}$$

Activity 3: DECIMAL TESSELLATIONS

(Cooperative Groups)

Materials: Decimal Grids Pattern DWA-6.3
Red and blue pencils
Paper
Pencils

Management: Teams of 4 students each (30 minutes)

Directions:

1. Give each team of students a decimal grid (DWA-6.3) and a red and a blue pencil. This activity assumes that students are comfortable with adding and subtracting hundredths and that they have had experience with simple pictorial models for hundredths. It also serves as a readiness activity for future lessons on adding integers.

2. The members of each team will work in pairs, say, pair A and pair B. Pair A will use the red pencil and pair B will use the blue pencil. Students might flip a coin to decide which pair draws first on the decimal grid.

3. On the decimal grid a 10×10 region is shown. This square represents the unit, 1.00, and each small square within the unit represents 0.01. The two pairs of a team will take turns outlining and coloring different whole amounts of small squares adjacent to the

NAME ______________________ DATE ______________

SUBTRACTION WORKSHEET DWA-6.2
Take-Away Diagrams

Find differences between decimal numbers by drawing circles on the frames below. Trade when necessary.

T	O	T-ths	H-ths	TH-ths
—				

T	O	T-ths	H-ths	TH-ths
—				

T	O	T-ths	H-ths	TH-ths
—				

border of the unit. These amounts may be located inside or outside the unit, but whatever the leading pair does, the other pair must reverse it on the opposite side of the unit. A reversal is found by mentally *sliding* a drawn region in a perpendicular path over to the opposite side of the unit until the region's edge that originally touched the unit's border now touches the unit's border on the opposite side. An example of opposite regions is shown in step 4.

4. As an example, suppose pair A is to serve as the leading pair. If they choose to mark off and color a 2 × 3 region inside the unit at the left border, then pair B must mark off and color another 2 × 3 region outside the unit at the right border. Pair A may then decide to mark off an irregularly shaped group of small squares outside the unit at the upper border; pair B must mark off an exact copy of pair A's group inside the unit at the lower border.

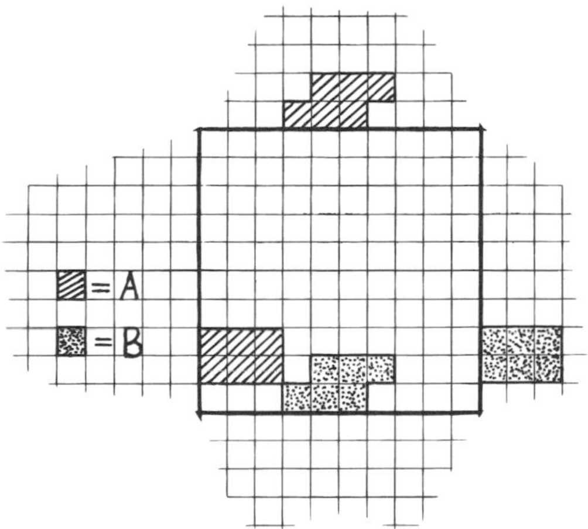

5. When pair A can no longer find a region of small, whole squares to mark off at the border of the unit, whether inside or outside, so that pair B can properly reverse pair A's region, the game is over. Pair A must draw regions that pair B can reverse as long as such regions exist.

6. Once regions can no longer be drawn, each pair must find how many small squares they have colored outside the unit and how many they have colored inside the unit. Then the pair must decide whether they colored more small squares inside or more outside the unit and what the difference was. For example, if pair A colored 32 small squares inside the unit and 27 outside the unit, they colored *5 more* small squares *inside* the unit than outside the unit. If pair B has correctly colored regions that are opposites of pair A's regions, they should find that they have colored *5 more* small squares *outside* the unit than inside the unit.

7. Each pair should also determine how much of the original unit would remain if only their changes were made, and express the result as a decimal. For example, if pair A found that their overall change was to color 5 of the small squares or hundredths *inside* the unit, then they in effect *subtracted* 0.05 from 1.00. So pair A's changes alone would leave (1.00 – 0.05) or 0.95 of the original unit. If pair B found that their overall change was 5 small squares *outside* the unit, then they in effect *added* 0.05 to 1.00. So pair B's changes alone would leave (1.00 + 0.05) or 1.05 of the original unit.

8. If time permits, team members might play another round, using a new decimal grid. The pair that drew second on the previous grid should now draw first.

NAME ______________________________ DATE ____________________

DECIMAL GRID PATTERN DWA-6.3
Decimal Tessellations

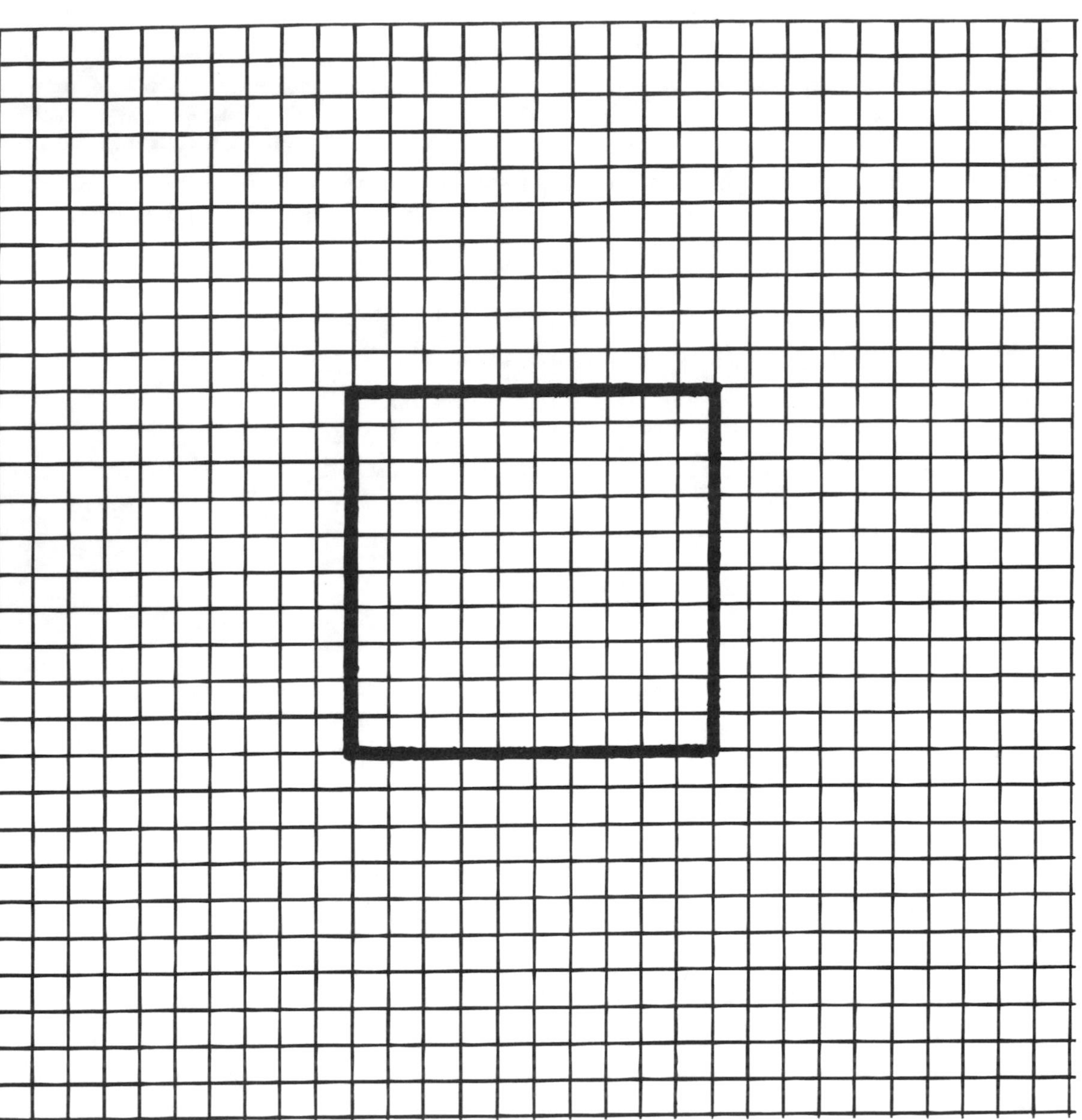

OBJECTIVE 7: Add fractions with like and unlike denominators.

Activity 1: JOINING FRACTIONS
(Concrete Action)

Materials: Sets of fraction bars (see pattern in Patterns/Grids section)
Building mats for addition (pattern described in step 1 below)
Paper
Pencils

Management: Partners (50 minutes for like denominators; two sessions at 50 minutes/session for unlike denominators)

Directions:

1. Give each pair of students a set of fraction bars and a building mat for addition. A set of fraction bars should contain the following: three wholes, six halves, nine thirds, twelve fourths, eighteen sixths, twenty-four eighths, and thirty-six twelfths. The building mat may be drawn on an $8\frac{1}{2}$" × 11" sheet of unlined paper. It should contain four rectangular boxes that are the same size as the whole unit bar in the fraction bar set. It is assumed for this activity that students have had previous experience with the fraction bars and that they have mastered the concept of equivalent fractions and the notation used with such as presented in Chapter 2.

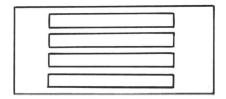

2. For like denominators: Have students place fraction bars on their building mat to show 3-fourths on the first whole bar and 2-fourths on the second whole bar. Placing the two amounts on separate whole bars helps students view them as separate addends when later recording the result.

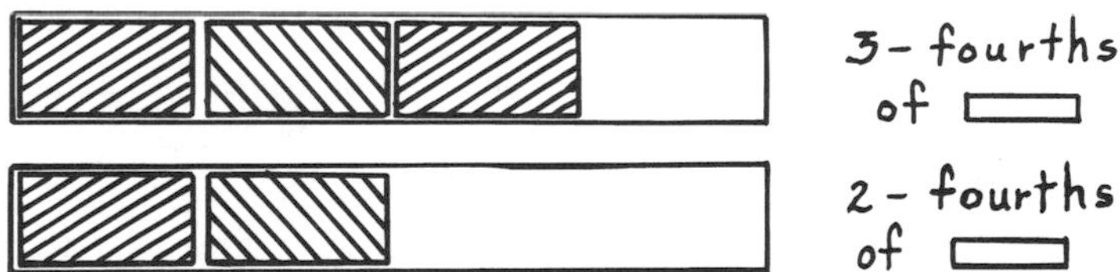

3. Discuss the idea that addition is the joining together of objects that are alike in some way, then the recounting of all the objects to find a total number. Since all the bars on the building mat are already fourths, ask students to recount them for a total number. The answer will be 5-fourths since fourths were being counted. It is not necessary to move one of the fourths on the lower whole bar to the upper bar to complete the set of fourths there. Do not change the 5-fourths to a mixed number at this time. In developing the concept of addition we only want to recount to find a total, not rename the total. Also, in later exercises of this activity where it might be possible to reduce the answer to simpler terms, *do not reduce.* In order to generalize about addition, students must be able to see the same denominator (or part size) in their answer as was used in the recounting process. The concept of reduction presented in Chapter 1 may be combined with fraction addition later *after* the addition concept has been thoroughly mastered by the students.

4. Have students write the following sentence on their own papers to record their result: *3-fourths + 2-fourths = 5-fourths of a whole bar.*

5. Now write other exercises on the chalkboard for students to build with their fraction bars. They should write a sentence for each result they find. Many exercises are possible with the students' set of fraction bars. The part sizes just need to be the same within each exercise. Improper fractions may also be used at this time, if preferred. For example, *8-sixths + 7-sixths* might be built, yielding the answer, 15-sixths. Two whole bars of the mat would be needed to show 8-sixths and another two whole bars needed to show 7-sixths. Keeping the two addends separated on the mat helps students know what amounts to record in their final sentence.

6. After students have built several addition exercises on their mats, have some of them read their sentences to the whole class and explain how they found their answers.

7. For unlike denominators: In this section the emphasis will be on transforming or trading fraction bars to obtain a common part size, which is needed for the recounting stage of addition. The *least common denominator* (LCD) approach will not be applied at this time, even though the trading process used with the fraction bars tends to produce the smallest common denominator possible. The LCD concept, like reduction, is difficult for students and is not a part of the addition concept being developed here.

8. Have students show 3-fourths on the first whole bar and 2-sixths on the second whole bar of the mat.

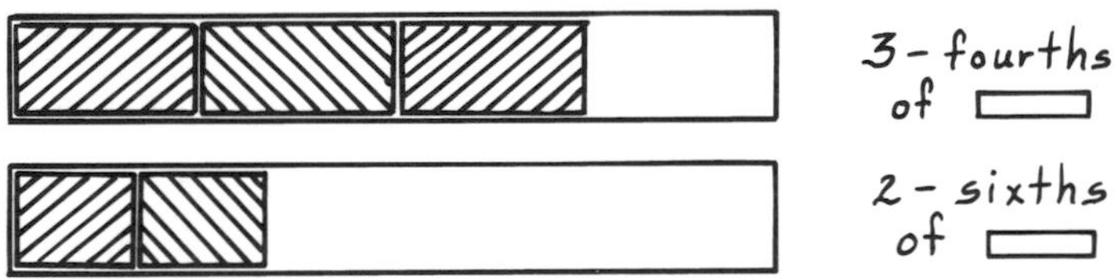

9. Ask: *Can the fourths be traded for sixths? Can the sixths be traded for fourths? If not, is there another part size for which both the fourths and the sixths might be traded?* Allow students time to explore the different fraction bar sizes in their sets of materials. They should eventually discover that each fourth can be exchanged for three of the twelfths (a 3-for-1 trade) and that each sixth can be exchanged for two of the twelfths (a 2-for-1 trade). Some students may suggest that the 2-sixths be changed to 1-third, a *backward trade* to fewer parts or reduction to a simpler name. Accept 1-third as an equivalent name for the 2-sixths, but tell students that in this particular lesson the focus will be on using *forward trades* instead of backward trades. This restriction is necessary in order to develop the addition algorithm for fractions.

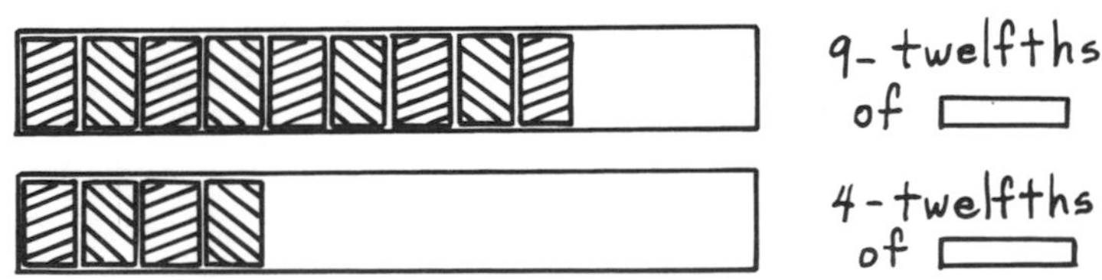

10. Now that all the part sizes are the same (twelfths), students should recount to find the total number of parts on the mat. The following sentence should be recorded on their papers: *3-fourths + 2-sixths = 9-twelfths + 4-twelfths = 13-twelfths of a whole bar.*

11. Using word names to identify the fractions, write other addition exercises on the chalkboard for students to solve by building on their mats. A sentence should be recorded to show the result of each exercise. Include exercises where only one type of trade is needed and where two types of trades are needed. Be sure that the assigned exercises can be worked with the available fraction bar sets.

12. After students have worked quite a few exercises using unlike denominators, have several students explain the steps they used to solve some of the exercises on their mats. Have them identify the different trades they made.

Activity 2: ADDITION DIAGRAMS

(Pictorial Action)

Materials: Fraction Addition Worksheet DWA-7.2
Red pencils
Pencils
Fraction bars and building mats from Activity 1 (optional)

Management: Partners (50 minutes for like denominators; two sessions at 50 minutes/session for unlike denominators)

Directions:

1. Give each student 2–3 copies of Fraction Addition Worksheet DWA-7.2 and a red pencil. Students will work together in pairs to complete the worksheet. Have them number the small boxes on the worksheet to number the items as needed. Some students may still prefer to work with the fraction bars on the building mat; this is acceptable. Allow them to first build an exercise with the fractions bars, then draw a diagram on the worksheet that shows the steps they used with the bars. It is assumed that students have already had experience in subdividing diagrams of whole bars into more than one equal part. If not, training should be provided before beginning this activity (see Activity 2, Objective 3, in Chapter 1, for discussion of this technique).

2. For like denominators: Tell students that each bar on the worksheet represents a whole unit and that all fractions in this lesson will relate to this particular unit. Have students draw and shade 3-sixths of the first whole bar in item #1. Have them draw and shade 2-sixths of the second whole bar of the same item. Diagonal line segments should be used as *shading* to make the fractional parts easy to see.

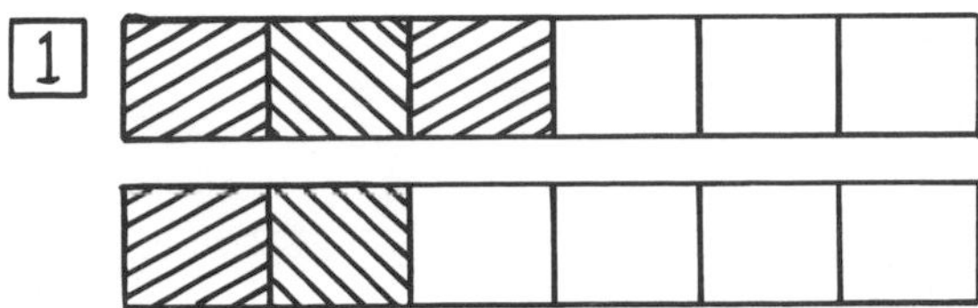

3. Since there are six *equal* parts for each whole bar, the parts of the two bars must be considered the same size (although the free-hand subdividing will not be exact). In order to join these two amounts together, students should recount the shaded parts to find the total number, then write a sentence below the whole bars on the worksheet to record the result: *3-sixths + 2-sixths = 5-sixths of a unit.*

4. Write other exercises on the chalkboard for students to solve by drawing and shading fractional amounts on the whole bars of the worksheet. Select fractions from halves, thirds, fourths, fifths, sixths, eighths, tenths, and twelfths. It should be possible to build most of the assigned exercises on the building mat with fraction bars in case any students are still working with those materials. Avoid larger denominators that would cause the final drawn parts to be too small and difficult to see. Students should write a sentence for each completed exercise below its shaded bars on the worksheet.

5. For unlike denominators: Continue to remind students that a fraction name must always be identified with a specific unit, in this case the whole bar on the worksheet. Have students draw and shade 1-half on the first whole bar and 3-fifths on the second whole bar of a pair of bars on the worksheet.

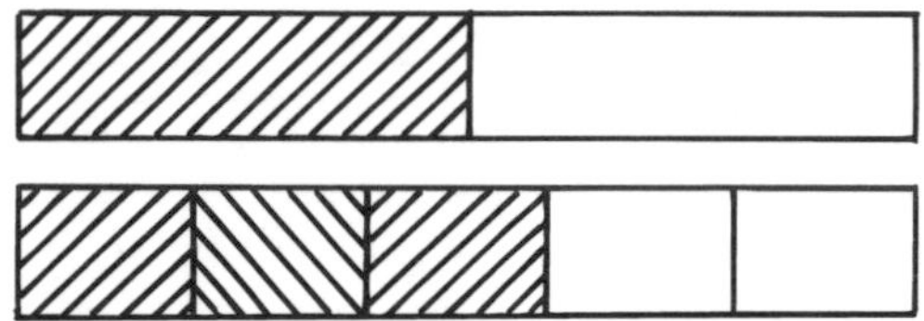

6. Students should use light tick marks to explore how to subdivide both halves to get more parts. Encourage them to start with a 2-for-1 trade. If the tick marks do not indicate a total number of new parts that agrees with the total number on the other whole bar, students should try a 3-for-1 trade, a 4-for-1 trade, etc., until the total number of parts is the same for both whole bars. They should rotate back and forth from one whole bar to the other, trying different trades. For example, a 3-for-1 trade with the halves yields six new parts total, which is more than the five parts shown by the fifths. Students should try a 2-for-1 trade with the fifths, which yields ten new parts total for the second whole bar. This is more than the six new parts proposed via tick marks on the first whole bar, so now students should try a 4-for-1 trade, then a 5-for-1 trade with the halves in order to match the ten new parts proposed for the second whole bar. This testing process is the forerunner of the mental strategy that will be used later at the abstract or symbolic level.

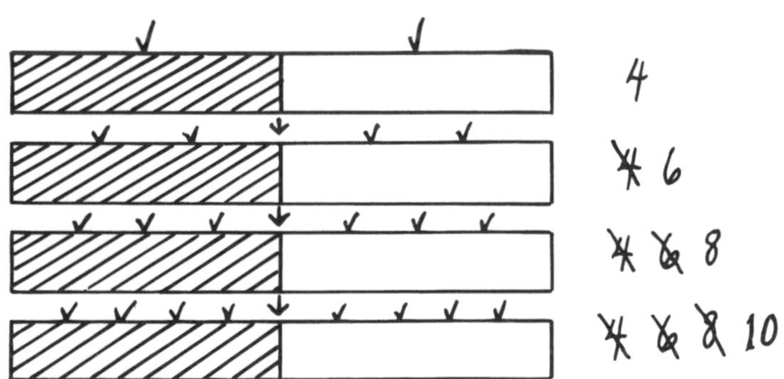

7. Students should use their red pencils to draw new subdivision bars where they have placed the final tick marks on each whole bar.

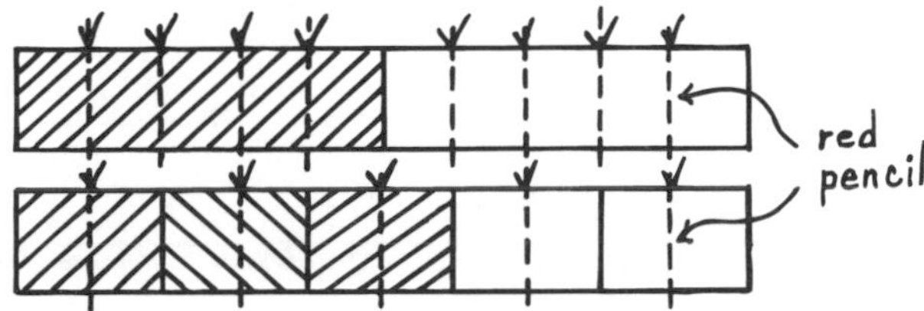

8. The new shaded parts, which are tenths of the whole bar, should now be counted to find the final number of parts total, and a sentence should be written under the pair of bars to record the result: *1-half* + *3-fifths* = *5-tenths* + *6-tenths* = *11-tenths*.

9. Write other exercises on the chalkboard for students to solve by drawing and shading fractional amounts on the whole bars of the worksheet. Occasionally, since a few frames on the worksheet contain three whole bars, one of the addends might be an improper fraction less than two. Select fractions that will trade to fourths, sixths, eighths, tenths, or twelfths. Avoid denominators in the original addends that would cause the new parts after the trade to be too small and difficult to see when drawn. Students should write a sentence for each completed exercise below its shaded bars on the worksheet.

10. Changes in notation: After students have drawn several of either type of exercise, i.e., those with like or unlike denominators, have them begin to use the ratio form to record their sentences. At first, record the new fraction names, but not the trades. The exercise presented in step 5 would then be written as $\frac{1}{2} + \frac{3}{5} = \frac{5}{10} + \frac{6}{10} = \frac{11}{10}$ After students have used this form several times, have them also begin to show the trades that were made. The above exercise then is recorded as follows:

$$\frac{1}{2} + \frac{3}{5} = \frac{1 \times (5)}{2 \times (5)} + \frac{3 \times (2)}{5 \times 2} = \frac{5}{10} + \frac{6}{10} = \frac{11}{10}.$$

11. Throughout the development of the addition of fractions with pictorial models, encourage students to verbally describe the steps they are taking. They should be able to state what trades they have decided to make, what the new equivalent fractions will be, and how they will find the total once the part sizes (or denominators) are the same.

Activity 3: PAIUTE SHELL GAME

(Cooperative Groups)

Materials: Inch grid paper (see pattern in Patterns/Grids section)
Walnut shell halves filled with clay
Pencils
Paper
Small, flat boxes or basket trays

Management: Teams of 4 students each (20–30 minutes)

Directions:

1. Background: The walnut shell game, which has been adapted for this activity,

NAME ______________________ DATE ______________

FRACTION ADDITION WORKSHEET DWA-7.2
Addition Diagrams

originated with the Paiute Indians of Pyramid Lake in northwestern Nevada. These people were considered part of the Northern Paiute, who were scattered over central and eastern California, western Nevada, and eastern Oregon. They lived in cone-shaped houses made of brush, and many earned their livelihood by fishing in nearby lakes and marshes. During the 1800's, the Northern Paiute fought the white settlers who had come to their area. The Indians won an important victory at Pyramid Lake in 1860. Today there are about 4,000 Northern Paiute living on reservations or in communities in the Western United States. For details on the original game, please refer to the following sources:

Stewart Culin, *Games of the North American Indians* (New York: Dover Publications, 1907; reprint, 1975)

Marina C. Krause, *Multicultural Mathematics Materials* (National Council of Teachers of Mathematics, 1906 Association Drive, Reston, VA 22091, 1983)

2. Give each team four strips cut from inch grid paper. Each strip should be one inch wide and at least eight inches long; that is, at least eight square inches should be marked off on the strip. Also give each team six walnut shell halves filled with clay. The clay surface that is exposed should be flat. If preferred, small red and white beads may be pressed down into the clay to decorate the shells. A small, flat box or basket tray will be needed to hold and toss the walnut shell halves during the game.

3. The team members will take turns tossing the six walnut shell halves in the basket or box. They will shade spaces on the grid strips to record their scores. If five of the shells land with the flat (clay) side up, the tossing player may shade in one space on his or her grid strip. If four shells land with the flat side up, one-half of a space may be shaded. If three shells land flat side up, one-fourth of a space may be shaded. No other shell combination will produce a score.

4. The first player to shade in four whole spaces wins. Each player must then write a number sentence that lists all the whole and fractional points earned during the game and the total points accumulated by the end of the game. For example, a player who did not win after five turns might have a grid strip shaded as shown below and would then write the following number sentence on a sheet of paper:

$$\frac{1}{2} + \frac{1}{4} + 1 + \frac{1}{2} + 1 = 3 \text{ and } \frac{1}{4}$$

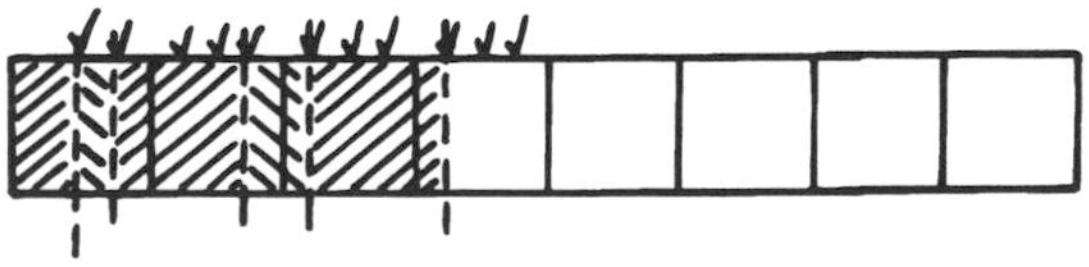

5. The grid strips are long enough to allow for a second game to be played, if time permits.

OBJECTIVE 8: Subtract fractions with like and unlike denominators.

Activity 1: REMOVING FRACTIONAL PARTS
(Concrete Action)

Materials: Sets of fractions bars (use sets from, Objective 7, Activity 1)
Building mats (pattern described in step 1 below)
Paper
Pencils

Management: Partners (50 minutes for like denominators; two sessions at 50 minutes/session for unlike denominators)

Directions:

1. Give each pair of students a set of fraction bars and a building mat for subtraction. A set of fraction bars should contain the following: three wholes, six halves, nine thirds, twelve fourths, eighteen sixths, twenty-four eighths, and thirty-six twelfths. The building mat may be drawn on $8\frac{1}{2}$" × 11" unlined paper. It should contain four rectangular boxes that are the same size as the whole unit bar in the fraction bar set. It is assumed for this activity that students have had previous experience with the fraction bars and that they have mastered the concept of equivalent fractions and the notation used with such as presented in Chapter 2. Hopefully the algorithm for adding proper or improper fractions has been developed with the fraction bars (see Objective 7 of this chapter). The different recording stages used for addition in Objective 7 will be followed for subtraction as well.

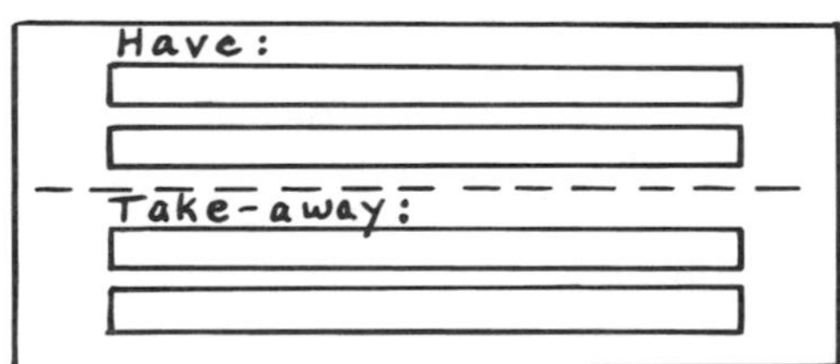

2. In this activity the *take-away* interpretation of subtraction will be used to develop the subtraction algorithm. On the building mat each whole bar will represent the unit to which the fractional parts will be compared. The upper bars will be used to show the original amount or *minuend*, and the bars below the dotted line will be used to show the amount (or *subtrahend*) to be removed or taken away from the minuend.

3. For like denominators: Have students place 3-fourths on the top whole bar of the building mat and 2-fourths on the first whole bar below the dotted line on the mat.

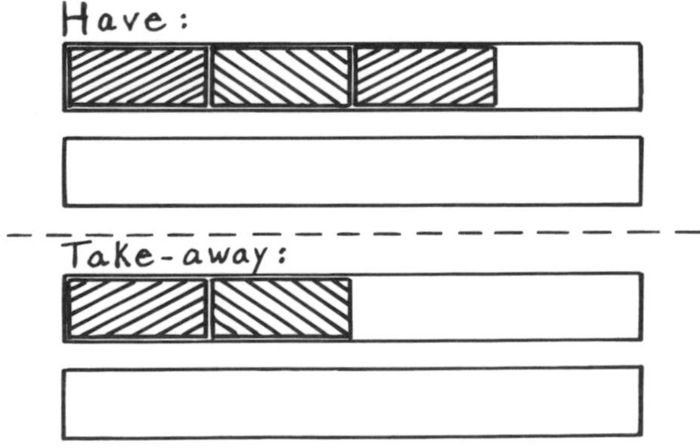

4. Ask: *Are there enough fourths in the first set for 2-fourths to be removed?* Since there are, have students match each part of the 2-fourths to a part of the 3-fourths and remove the matched parts from the building mat. Only 1-fourth will remain on the top whole bar.

5. Have students write on their own papers the following sentence to record their result: *3-fourths – 2-fourths = 1-fourth of a whole bar.*

6. Write other subtraction exercises for like denominators on the chalkboard for students to solve by building with the fraction bars. Use the denominators found in the students' fraction bar sets: halves, thirds, fourths, sixths, eighths, and twelfths. Include improper fractions as in the exercise: *5-thirds – 2-thirds = ?*

7. Have students write a sentence on their own paper for each exercise they build. *Do not* have them *rename or reduce* their answers at this time.

8. For unlike denominators: Have students place fraction bars on the top whole bar of the building mat to show 2-thirds and on the first whole bar of the subtrahend to show 1-sixth.

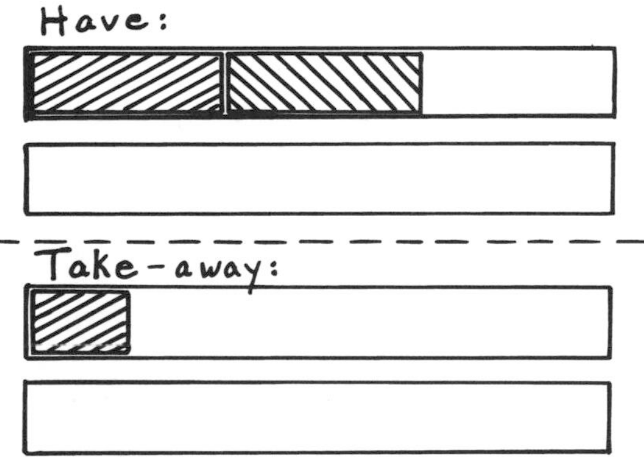

9. Ask: *Is there a sixth in the top set of bars to match the sixth on the lower whole bar and then remove from the mat? If not, can any trades be made so that a matching would be possible?* Some students will simply look at the total bar size of the 2-thirds, conclude that 1-sixth will fit within the thirds, and state that a sixth can be removed from the 2-thirds. They are making a *visual estimate.* Since an algorithm is to be developed, a more exact approach is needed. Tell students that a one-to-one matching of parts that are *known* to be alike must be used. Have them find a *forward trade* (each old part trading for more than one new part) that will make all parts on the building mat the same size. A 2-for-1 trade, or 2 sixths replacing each third, is the most likely. Some students may choose to exchange both the thirds and the sixth for twelfths. This is acceptable since a least common denominator is not being emphasized in the development of the subtraction algorithm.

10. Students should match the sixth below the dotted line to a new sixth on the upper whole bar and remove them both from the mat. If twelfths were used, the lower 2-twelfths should be matched with 2-twelfths on the upper bar and removed from the mat. Have students record the difference or what remains by writing on their own paper the following sentence: *2-thirds – 1-sixth = 4-sixths – 1-sixth = 3-sixths of a whole bar.* For twelfths, use the sentence: *2-thirds – 1-sixth = 8-twelfths – 2 twelfths = 6-twelfths of a whole bar.*

11. Write other subtraction exercises on the chalkboard for students to build on their mats. A number sentence should be written to show the result of each exercise. Select part sizes (or denominators) from the part sizes available in the students' sets of fraction bars. Students must be able to trade the different part sizes used in the original two fractions of an exercise for a common part size also found in their sets of bars.

12. Improper fractions might be included at this time, if preferred. For example, the exercise: *3-halves – 5-fourths = ?* might be assigned. In such cases, fraction bars would be placed on both upper whole bars or both lower whole bars of the building mat if needed. Students should not reduce or rename their answers, however, even though remaining parts for some exercises might cover a whole bar.

Activity 2: DRAWING TO SUBTRACT

(Pictorial Action)

Materials: Fraction Subtraction Worksheet DWA-8.2
Red pencils
Pencils
Fraction bars and building mats from Activity 1 (optional)

Management: Partners (50 minutes for like denominators; two sessions at 50 minutes/session for unlike denominators)

Directions:

1. Give each student 2–3 copies of the Subtraction Worksheet DWA-8.2 and a red pencil. Have students work together in pairs. They should number the small boxes on the worksheet to number the items or frames as needed. Some students may still prefer to build with the fraction bars to find their answers; this is quite acceptable. Allow them to first build an exercise with the fraction bars, then draw a diagram of the steps they used on the worksheet. Exercises should be selected for this activity so that most can also be solved with the available fraction bars. Encourage students to work only with the diagrams as soon as they feel ready. It is assumed that students have already had experience in subdividing diagrams of whole bars into more than one equal part. If not, training should be provided before beginning this activity (see Activity 2, Objective 3, in Chapter 1, for discussion of this technique).

2. For like denominators: Tell students that each whole bar on the worksheet will represent the whole unit to which all fractional names will refer in this activity. Have them draw 5-sixths on the top whole bar of item #1 on the worksheet and 2-sixths on the whole bar below the dotted line. Each part should be "shaded" with parallel line segments drawn diagonally for easier viewing.

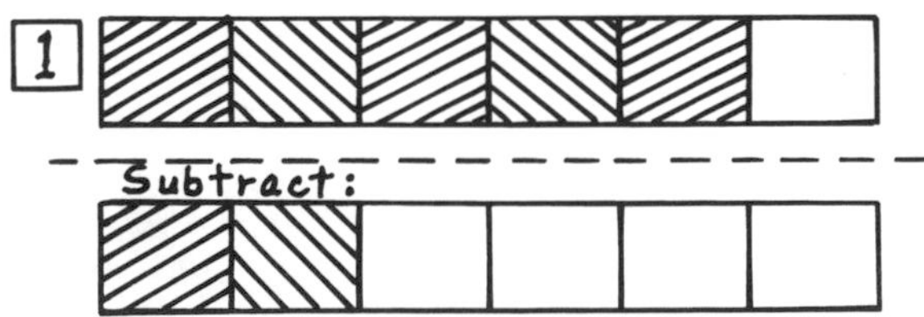

3. Ask: *How can we know if the part sizes are all the same size?* Remind students that if the whole bars are all the same length and each whole bar is subdivided into six equal parts, then the parts on all the whole bars must be the same size.

4. To match the sixths for subtraction, have students use their red pencils to draw an X on each sixth shown on the whole bar below the dotted line. They should then draw a red X on the same number of sixths on the whole bar above the dotted line. Three of the upper sixths should remain after two of them have been *removed* with X's. A red ring should be drawn around the 3-sixths to show the answer.

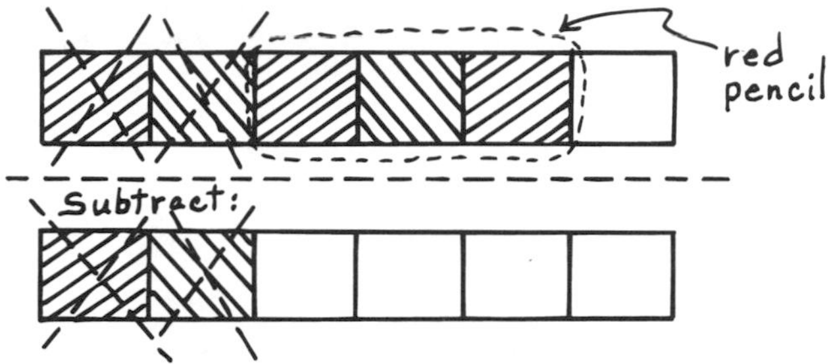

5. Have students write the following sentence below the marked bars on their worksheets: *5-sixths – 2-sixths = 3-sixths of a unit.*

6. Assign other subtraction exercises for students to solve by drawing and shading parts on the whole bars of the worksheet. They should write a sentence below each finished diagram to record its result. Select denominators no larger than 12. A few frames on the worksheet will allow some improper fractions to be used.

7. For unlike denominators: Have students draw and shade 3-fourths as the minuend on the top bar and 4-sixths as the subtrahend on the bar below the dotted line.

8. Ask: *Assuming someone else drew these parts, how might we tell that the parts on the top bar and the parts on the bottom bar are not the same size?* Discuss the idea that the whole bars are the same length, but one is cut into four equal parts and the other is cut into six equal parts. When the number of parts increases, but their total size does not change, the parts themselves must become smaller.

9. Have students explore what trades are needed to have all the parts on the two bars the same size. This should be done using light tick marks in regular pencil. The testing process described here is a forerunner of the mental strategy that students will use later when working at the abstract or symbolic level. If a tick mark is placed above the top bar at the midpoint of each fourth to show a 2-for-1 trade, eight new parts will be possible. Since 8 > 6, the sixths need to be subdivided. By placing tick marks at the midpoint of each sixth on the bottom bar, twelve new parts will be possible. Now 12 > 8, so the fourths need a greater trade than 2-for-1. Two tick marks placed equally within each fourth yield twelve new parts, which is the number of parts last found on the bottom bar, so a 3-for-1 trade will work for the top bar.

10. Now have students use their red pencil to draw vertical line segments across the bars at the points indicated by the final tick marks.

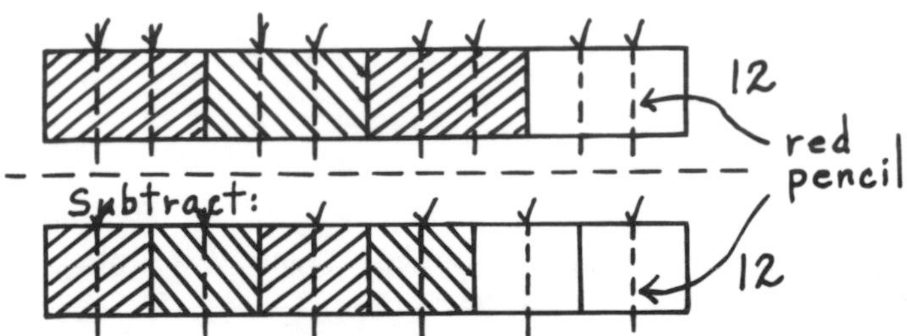

11. Since both whole bars contain twelve equal parts, the parts must be the same size. Students should subtract the lower shaded amount, 8-twelfths, from the upper shaded amount, 9-twelfths, by marking each shaded part on the lower bar with a red X and marking that same number of shaded parts on the upper bar with a red X. There should be one shaded part left unmarked on the upper bar. Have students draw a red ring around this remaining twelfth.

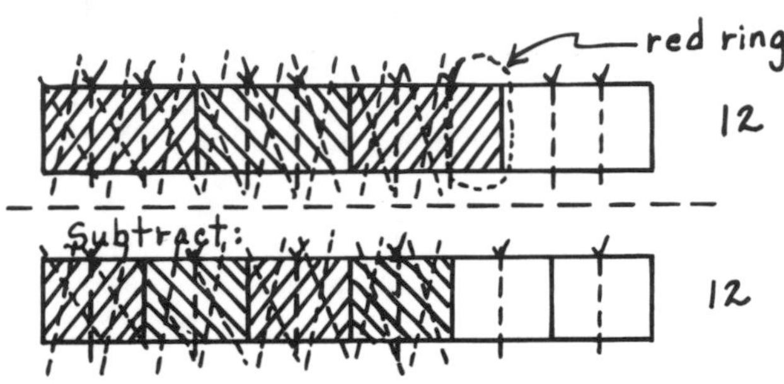

12. Students should write the following sentence below their marked diagram: *3-fourths – 4-sixths = 9-twelfths – 8-twelfths = 1-twelfth of a unit.*

13. Assign other subtraction exercises on the chalkboard for students to solve by drawing on the whole bars of their worksheets. A sentence should be written under each completed diagram to record its result. Improper fractions less than or equal to two may also be used at this time, if preferred. For the exercises, use original denominator pairs that will trade to fourths, sixths, eighths, tenths, or twelfths. Higher amounts yield very small parts on the diagrams, which are difficult to see. It should be possible for most exercises to be built with fraction bars in case any students are still needing to work with those materials.

14. Changes in notation: After students have drawn several of either type of exercise, i.e., those with like or unlike denominators, have them begin to use the ratio form to record their sentences. At first, record the new fraction names, but not the trades. The exercise presented in step 7 would then be written as $\frac{3}{4} - \frac{4}{6} = \frac{9}{12} - \frac{8}{12} = \frac{1}{12}$ of a unit. After students have used this form several times have them also begin to show the trades that were made. The above exercise then is recorded as follows:

$$\frac{3}{4} - \frac{4}{6} = \frac{3 \times \textcircled{3}}{4 \times \textcircled{3}} - \frac{4 \times \textcircled{2}}{6 \times \textcircled{2}} = \frac{9}{12} - \frac{8}{12} = \frac{1}{12} \text{ of a unit.}$$

15. Throughout the development of the subtraction of fractions with pictorial models, encourage students to verbally describe the steps they are taking. They should be able to state what trades they have decided to make, what the new equivalent fractions will be, and how they will find the difference once the part sizes (or denominators) are the same.

NAME ________________________________ DATE ____________________

FRACTION SUBTRACTION WORKSHEET DWA-8.2
Drawing to Subtract

Subtract:

Subtract:

Subtract:

Subtract:

Subtract:

Subtract:

Activity 3: ESTIMATING DIFFERENCES

(Cooperative Groups)

Materials: Sets of fraction subtraction cards and interval cards (described in step 1 below)
Fraction bar sets and subtraction building mats from Activity 1
Paper
Pencils

Management: Teams of four students each (20–30 minutes)

Directions:

1. Give each team a subtraction building mat and one set each of 20 fraction subtraction cards, 4 interval cards, and the fraction bars. The interval cards might be large index cards containing different intervals written with a red marker. The intervals to use are as follows: *includes 0 up to 1/2, includes 1/2 up to 1, includes 1 up to 1 and 1/2,* and *includes 1 and 1/2 up to 2*. For each interval, the larger end value is not included in the interval, but the smaller end value is. The fraction subtraction cards might be small index cards containing different subtraction exercises written with a blue marker. It should be possible to build each subtraction exercise with the set of fraction bars. Improper and proper fractions should be included; if preferred, some improper fractions might be written as mixed numbers. Here are 20 possible exercises to write on the cards, using one exercise per card. The correct interval choice for the exercises in each column is shown at the top of that column.

$(0, \frac{1}{2})$	$(\frac{1}{2}, 1)$	$(1, 1\frac{1}{2})$	$(1\frac{1}{2}, 2)$
$\frac{3}{4} - \frac{1}{2}$	$\frac{5}{4} - \frac{2}{4}$	$\frac{6}{3} - \frac{2}{2}$	$\frac{5}{2} - \frac{2}{3}$
$\frac{1}{3} - \frac{1}{4}$	$\frac{7}{8} - \frac{1}{4}$	$\frac{5}{3} - \frac{2}{4}$	$\frac{7}{4} - \frac{1}{8}$
$\frac{3}{4} - \frac{2}{3}$	$\frac{8}{6} - \frac{3}{6}$	$\frac{3}{2} - \frac{1}{2}$	$\frac{11}{6} - \frac{1}{3}$
$\frac{4}{6} - \frac{1}{4}$	$\frac{5}{6} - \frac{1}{3}$	$\frac{10}{8} - \frac{1}{4}$	$\frac{15}{8} - \frac{2}{8}$
$\frac{7}{8} - \frac{3}{4}$	$\frac{6}{4} - \frac{2}{3}$	$\frac{4}{3} - \frac{1}{4}$	$\frac{4}{2} - \frac{3}{8}$

2. Team members should shuffle the subtraction cards and pass out 5 cards to each person. The four interval cards should be placed side by side and face up on the table. Students will take turns playing a card from their hands.

3. On each turn a player will select a card from his or her hand and mentally estimate what the difference might be for the exercise on the card. The player must then state which of the four intervals will contain this difference.

4. If the other three players do not agree with the interval choice, the estimating player must build the exercise with the fraction bars in order to find the actual difference and determine its proper interval.

5. Once all agree on the interval choice, the estimating player will place the subtraction card next to the appropriate interval card. The turn then passes to the next player, and the game continues until all subtraction cards are placed beside their interval cards.

OBJECTIVE 9: Divide fractions with like and unlike denominators.

Activity 1: COUNTING OUT SHARES
(Concrete Action)

Materials: Sets of fraction bars (see pattern in Patterns/Grids section)
Division building mats (pattern described in step 1 below)
Paper
Pencils

Management: Partners (two sessions at 50 minutes/session)

Directions:

1. Give each pair of students a set of fraction bars and a building mat for division. A set of fraction bars should contain the following: three wholes, six halves, nine thirds, twelve fourths, eighteen sixths, twenty-four eighths, and thirty-six twelfths. The building mat should be drawn on an $8\frac{1}{2}" \times 14"$ sheet of paper or tagboard and labeled as follows:

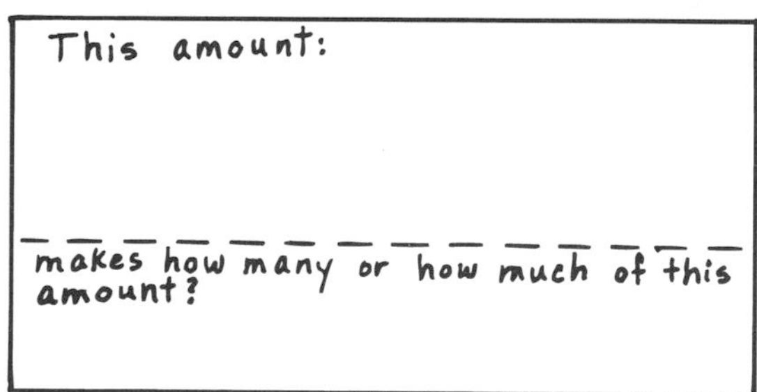

2. In this activity division will be introduced through a *common denominator* approach. Do not discuss the *reciprocal* method at this time. In a later objective, the relationship between division and multiplication will be established. The divisor will be interpreted here as the set size to be made, and the quotient will indicate how many or how much of the set can be made. It is assumed for this activity that students have had previous experience with the fraction bars and that they have mastered the concept of equivalent fractions and the notation used with them as presented in Chapter 2. Hopefully, the algorithms for adding and subtracting proper or improper fractions have been developed with the fraction bars (see Objectives 7 and 8 of this chapter).

3. For whole number quotients: The first group of exercises will answer the question, *How many?* Have students place 2-halves touching end-to-end in the upper region of the division building mat and 1-third in the lower region of the mat. Bars in the upper region will represent the dividend and bars in the lower region will represent the divisor.

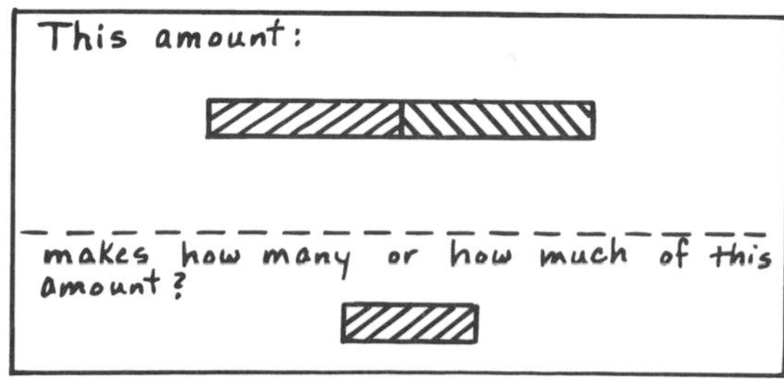

4. Ask: *How many of a set like the 1-third can be made from the 2-halves?* The phrasing ***like*** *the 1-third* is very important. Some students are extremely literal thinkers. If asked "How many of this 1-third can be made?" they will respond with "only this 1 bar that I see." Since the part sizes are not the same, students will only be able to estimate the possible number of sets.

5. Ask: *Can any trades be made so that all the parts on the mat are the same size?* Finding a common part size is the focus of the common denominator method of division. Students should use a 3-for-1 trade to change each half to sixths and a 2-for-1 trade to change the third to sixths. The new sixths in the divisor need to remain connected end-to-end, as though *glued together,* in order to show that they form one set.

6. The connected 2-sixths should be moved to the upper region to match to the other sixths, thereby separating them into three groups of 2-sixths each. Then the divisor set of 2-sixths should be returned to the lower region of the mat.

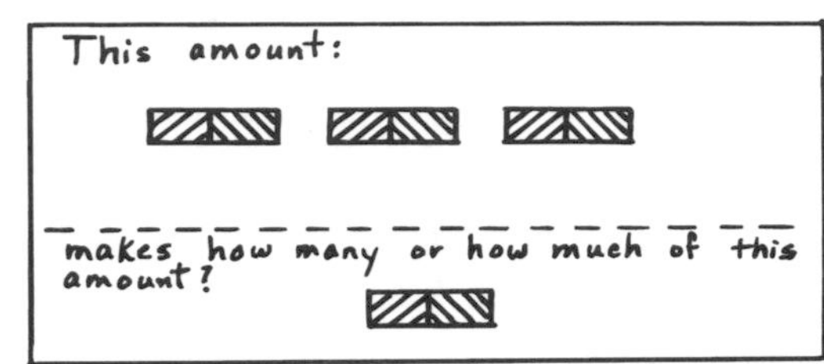

7. Have students write the sentence: *2-halves of a whole bar makes 3 sets of 1-third of a whole bar.*

8. Now assign other division exercises for students to build on their mats. Include whole numbers and improper fractions as dividends and divisors, but be sure each exercise can be built with the available fraction bars. Have them write a sentence for each exercise built to record its result. Here are some possible exercises to use:

Dividend; Divisor	Dividend; Divisor
$2\ ;\ \frac{1}{2}$	$\frac{3}{4}\ ;\ \frac{1}{4}$
$1\ ;\ \frac{2}{4}$	$\frac{2}{3}\ ;\ \frac{2}{3}$
$\frac{1}{2}\ ;\ \frac{1}{6}$	$\frac{4}{6}\ ;\ \frac{2}{6}$

9. For common fraction quotients: The next group of exercises will answer the question, *How much?* Students encounter a quantity of sets made that is less than one, a new idea to their countable world! Have them show 1 whole bar as the dividend and 2 whole bars as the divisor on the building mat. The 2 whole bars should be touching end to end in order to represent a single set.

10. Ask: *Do we have enough in the 1 whole bar to make at least one set of bars* ***like*** *the 2 whole bars? If not,* ***how much*** *of a set can we make?* Have students slide the connected 2 whole bars to the upper region of the mat to match the 1 whole bar, which should be positioned just above the 2 whole bars. Discuss the fact that in the dividend there is only 1 of the 2 parts needed to make a complete set. Some students initially may need to physically stack the 1 whole bar on top of the 2 whole bars in order to see the 1-of-2 relationship. Do not express this relationship as *half of* the 2 whole bars at this time. In this exercise the word *half* has two different meanings and hence tends to confuse young students.

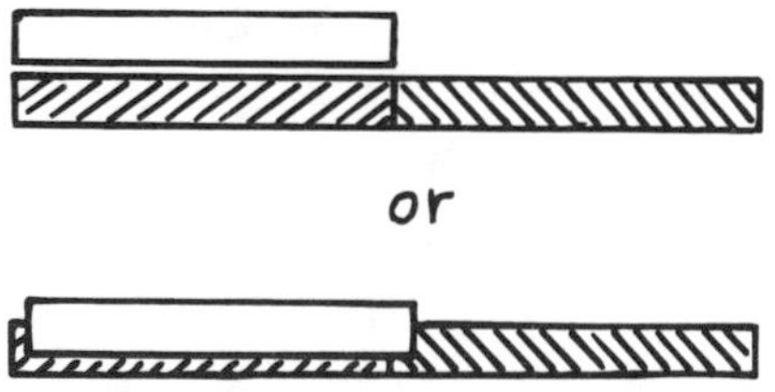

11. Have students write on their own papers: *1 whole bar makes 1 of 2 parts of a set of 2 whole bars.*

12. Have students show 1-half as the dividend and 3-fourths as the divisor on the building mat. Discuss how part sizes must be the same in order to match them for making a set. Ask students to make trades so that all parts on the mat will be the same size. If a 2-for-1 trade is used, 2-fourths will then be in the dividend region with 3-fourths still in the divisor region of the mat.

13. This time there are 2 parts of the 3 parts needed for a complete set of 3-fourths. Have students write the sentence: *1-half makes 2 of 3 parts of a set of 3-fourths of a whole bar.*

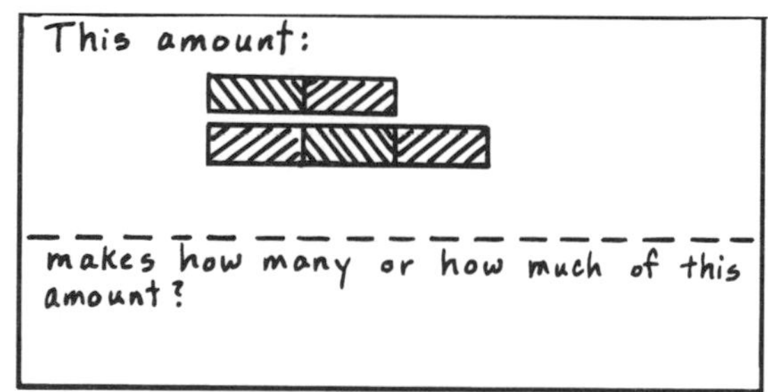

14. Now assign other similar exercises for students to build on their mats. They should write a sentence for each completed exercise to record its result. Here are some possible exercises to use:

Dividend; Divisor	Dividend; Divisor
$\frac{1}{2}$; 2	$\frac{1}{3}$; $\frac{2}{3}$
$\frac{2}{3}$; 1	$\frac{1}{2}$; $\frac{5}{6}$
$\frac{3}{4}$; $\frac{7}{8}$	$\frac{3}{4}$; $\frac{7}{4}$

15. For mixed number quotients: The previous two types of quotients will probably be covered in the same class session; however, do not rush if students seem to need more time to build. This third type of quotient combines the first two into one exercise, so students must be comfortable with the first two before continuing on to this one. Minimal experience with mixed numbers is necessary at this point. Students appear to have the greatest difficulty with the standard notation used for mixed numbers, for example, $2\frac{1}{3}$. It seems more meaningful for them to write in the form, 2 + 1/3. This activity will use the latter form. Activity 2 will attempt to connect the two notations for students.

16. Have students show 4-thirds as the dividend and 1-half as the divisor on the building mat. Ask: *Is 4-thirds enough to make at least one set like the 1-half? Is there enough to make two complete sets? If not, how much of a second set can be made?* This kind of questioning helps students begin to estimate their quotients.

17. Before any matching can be done, trading is needed to change all the bars on the mat to the same part size. Most students will change to sixths, but some may change to twelfths.

18. If sixths are used, the 3-sixths will match twice to the group of 8-sixths in the upper region of the mat. The remaining 2-sixths will form 2 of the 3 parts needed for one more set of 3-sixths. (If twelfths are used instead of sixths, the result will be 2 sets and 4 of 6 parts of one more set. Do not simplify the *4 of 6 parts* to *2 of 3 parts.*) Have students write the sentence: *4-thirds makes 2 sets and 2 of 3 parts of one more set of 1-half of a whole bar.*

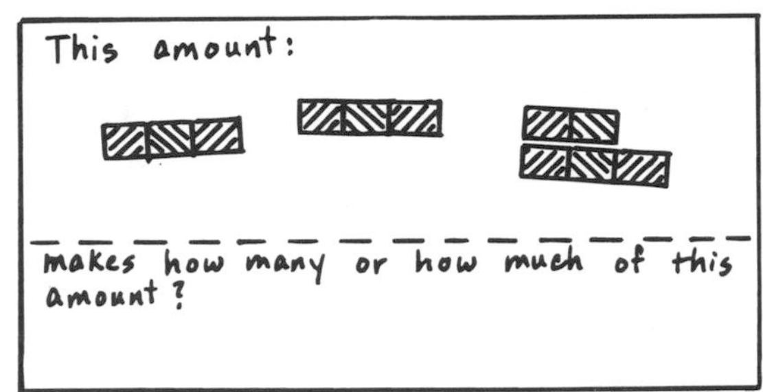

19. Assign other similar exercises for students to build on their mats. A sentence should be written to record the result of each exercise. Whole numbers and improper fractions should be included. Here are some possible exercises to use:

Dividend; Divisor	Dividend; Divisor
$\frac{7}{8}$; $\frac{3}{4}$	$\frac{5}{6}$; $\frac{2}{6}$
1 ; $\frac{3}{4}$	$\frac{4}{3}$; 1
$\frac{7}{3}$; $\frac{2}{3}$	$\frac{4}{2}$; $\frac{3}{4}$

20. For each type of quotient studied, ask different students to verbally explain the steps they used to solve the exercises with the fraction bars. An explanation should include any trades that were needed to have a common part size (the common denominator) on the mat and the way matching was used to find complete or partial sets of the divisor in the dividend.

Activity 2: DIVISORS IN DIAGRAMS

(Pictorial Action)

Materials: Fraction Division Worksheet DWA-9.2
Red pencils
Pencils
Fraction bars and division building mats from Activity 1 (optional)

Management: Partners (one or two sessions at 50 minutes/session)

Directions:

1. Give each student 2–3 copies of Fraction Division Worksheet DWA-9.2 and a red pencil. The small boxes on the worksheet should be numbered to order the exercises as needed. Have students work together in pairs. Some students may still prefer to build with the fraction bars to find their answers; this is quite acceptable. Allow them to first build an exercise with the fraction bars, then draw a diagram of the steps they used on the worksheet. Exercises should be selected for this activity that can also be solved with the available fraction bars. Encourage students to work only with the diagrams as soon as they feel ready. It is assumed that students have already had experience in subdividing diagrams of whole bars into more than one equal part. If not, training should be provided before beginning this activity (see Activity 2, Objective 3, in Chapter 1, for discussion of this technique).

2. Have students draw and shade 3-halves of a whole bar in the upper region and 2-thirds of a whole bar in the lower region of a division frame on the worksheet. Tell students that each whole bar shown on the worksheet will represent a unit. Shading on the bars should be done diagonally so that fractional parts can be easily seen.

3. Students must subdivide each half into sixths and each third into sixths, using tick marks and a red pencil to mark off the new parts. The dividend will then show 9-sixths and the divisor will show 4-sixths.

4. A red ring should be drawn around the 4-sixths in the lower region and labeled as *1 set*. This procedure identifies the divisor set that is to be made in the upper region.

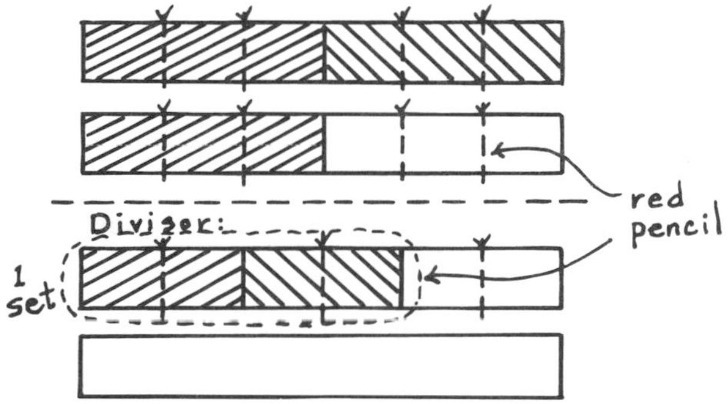

5. A red ring should also be drawn around each group of four sixths in the upper region and each group labeled, beginning with the shaded sixths. In one ringed group, only one sixth will be shaded. This indicates that only a partial set could be made. Students should label the ring as *1 of 4 parts of a set. Note*: If there should ever not be enough parts to complete a ring, one of the whole bars should be extended and extra parts or spaces drawn, using dotted line segments, to make the total parts needed for a full set.

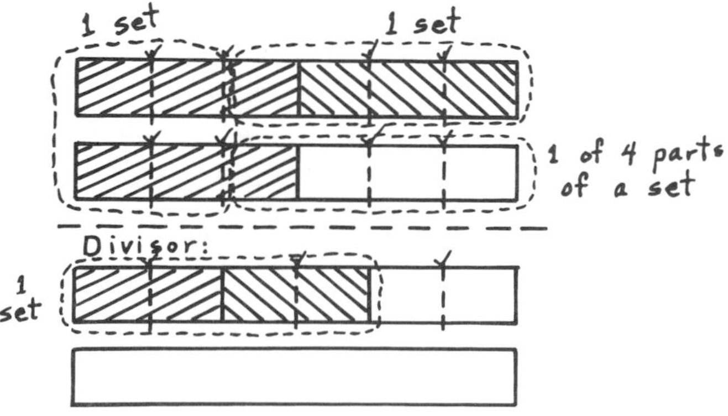

6. Students should write the following sentence under the completed diagram: *3/2 makes 2 sets and 1 of 4 parts of one more set of 2/3 of a unit.*

7. Assign other exercises for students to solve by drawing on their frames. Sentences should be written to record the results. Here are some possible exercises to use:

Dividend; Divisor	Dividend; Divisor
$\frac{5}{8}$; $\frac{6}{8}$	2 ; $\frac{2}{3}$
$\frac{5}{6}$; $\frac{5}{6}$	$\frac{2}{6}$; $\frac{5}{6}$
$\frac{2}{3}$; 1	$\frac{3}{2}$; $\frac{5}{4}$
$\frac{3}{2}$; $\frac{5}{6}$	$\frac{7}{6}$; 1
2 ; $\frac{3}{2}$	$\frac{3}{2}$; $\frac{3}{4}$

8. Occasionally ask different students to verbally explain their steps for some of the exercises. Explanations should include any trading used to change the fractions or whole numbers to a common part size or common denominator. Students should also discuss the process used to find the number of times the set of new parts (or the new numerator) of the divisor could be formed from the new parts (or the new numerator) of the dividend. Partial sets found should not be given simpler names at this time. For example, *4 of 6 parts of a set* should not be changed to *2 of 3 parts of a set.*

9. Changes in notation: After students have worked several exercises for each type of quotient and seem comfortable with the drawing process, have them begin recording their results in number sentences rather than word sentences. The notation used should reflect the changes they made in their diagrams. The notation should gradually evolve through two stages: one where trades are not shown at first and one where they are. For example, the sentences stated in step 6 earlier would first be written as follows:

$$\frac{3}{2} \div \frac{2}{3} = \frac{9}{6} \div \frac{4}{6} = 2 + \frac{1}{4} \text{ or } 2\tfrac{1}{4} \text{ sets of } \tfrac{2}{3} \text{ of a unit}$$

After students have used the above form for a few exercises, they should begin to record the trades or whole number changes used as well. The above number sentence would then appear as follows:

$$\frac{3}{2} \div \frac{2}{3} = \frac{3 \times (3)}{2 \times (3)} \div \frac{2 \times (2)}{3 \times (2)} = \frac{9}{6} \div \frac{4}{6} = 2 + \frac{1}{4} \text{ or } 2\tfrac{1}{4} \text{ sets of } \tfrac{2}{3} \text{ of a unit}$$

Activity 3: ABOUT HOW MANY?

(Cooperative Groups)

Materials: Fraction bars and division building mats from Activity 1
Sets of division cards (described in step 1 below)
Paper
Pencils

Management: Teams of 4 students each (20–30 minutes)

Directions:

1. Give each team a set of fraction bars, a division building mat, and a set of 20 division cards. This activity will provide practice in converting mixed number dividends to improper fractions in order to divide by a common fraction. Until now the mixed number notation has not been used for the dividend; only common or improper fractions or whole numbers have been used.

NAME ______________________ DATE ______________

FRACTION DIVISION WORKSHEET DWA-9.2
Divisors in Diagrams

Divisor:

Divisor:

Divisor:

Divisor:

The division cards might be made with small index cards, each card containing only one division exercise. Here are some possible division exercises to use on the division cards:

$1\frac{1}{2} \div \frac{2}{4} = ?$	$2\frac{1}{4} \div \frac{3}{4} = ?$	$1\frac{1}{3} \div \frac{2}{3} = ?$	$1\frac{1}{2} \div \frac{5}{6} = ?$
$1\frac{1}{2} \div \frac{3}{4} = ?$	$1\frac{1}{2} \div \frac{1}{2} = ?$	$2\frac{1}{2} \div \frac{2}{4} = ?$	$1\frac{1}{8} \div \frac{1}{4} = ?$
$2\frac{1}{3} \div \frac{2}{3} = ?$	$1\frac{1}{2} \div \frac{1}{4} = ?$	$1\frac{1}{2} \div \frac{6}{8} = ?$	$1\frac{3}{4} \div \frac{2}{4} = ?$
$1\frac{3}{4} \div \frac{3}{8} = ?$	$1\frac{3}{4} \div \frac{1}{4} = ?$	$1\frac{1}{2} \div \frac{1}{3} = ?$	$1\frac{1}{2} \div \frac{2}{3} = ?$
$2\frac{1}{4} \div \frac{1}{4} = ?$	$2\frac{1}{4} \div \frac{2}{4} = ?$	$2\frac{1}{8} \div \frac{3}{8} = ?$	$2\frac{1}{8} \div \frac{1}{8} = ?$

2. The members of each team will work in pairs. They will shuffle the set of cards, then place the stack face down on the table. The two pairs will take turns drawing a card from the top of the stack.

3. On a turn, a pair will draw a card and estimate to the nearest whole number *about how many* of the divisor set can be made from the dividend amount. To confirm the estimate, the other pair will build the division exercise with the fraction bars on the building mat, making any necessary trades.

4. If the estimate is confirmed, the estimating pair earns 2 points. If, after building the exercise with the fraction bars, the building pair finds that the estimate is incorrect, they must not give the correct answer, but must allow the estimating pair to look at the full set(s) and/or part of a set displayed on the building mat and to offer a new estimate.

5. If the second estimate is accepted as correct by the building pair, the estimating pair will earn 1 point. If not, 0 points will be earned and the turn passes to the other pair.

6. If the correctness of an estimate is not certain, even after the exercise has been built with the fraction bars, the teacher may be asked to serve as final judge.

7. Each pair must earn a minimum of 10 points to end the game.

OBJECTIVE 10: Multiply fractions with whole numbers or other fractions.

Activity 1: BUILDING WITH PARTS OF SETS

(Concrete Action)

Materials: Sets of fraction bars (see pattern in Patterns/Grids section)
Multiplication building mats (pattern described in step 1 below)
Paper
Pencils

Management: Partners (two sessions at 50 minutes/session)

Directions:

1. Give each pair of students a set of fraction bars and a building mat for multiplication. A set of fraction bars should contain the following: three wholes, six halves, nine thirds, twelve fourths, eighteen sixths, twenty-four eighths, and thirty-six twelfths. The mat should be drawn on $8\frac{1}{2}$" × 14" unlined paper. Each rectangular box on the mat should be the size of the unit bar found in the fraction bar set. The mat should appear as follows:

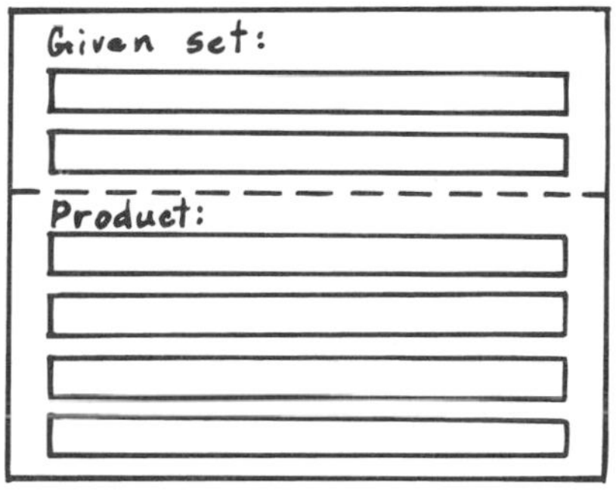

2. It is assumed that students are familiar with the fraction bars and how they relate to each other. As in the case of the common denominator method for division, fractions in multiplication play two roles. The more common role is the fraction used to compare a part to the whole or unit bar. The less familiar and more difficult role for students to comprehend is the fraction used as an operator. In multiplication, the multiplier is the operator because it tells what actions need to be taken on a given set, which is the multiplicand. The idea of an operator needs to be thoroughly presented to students.

3. In this activity one session will be devoted to exercises having a fraction and a whole number as the two factors. The second session will involve two fractions as the factors. It has been found that students who have had no previous instruction in fraction multiplication and have no understanding of the concept tend to multiply numerators for the *upper answer* and multiply denominators for the *lower answer*. This phenomenon is similar to what happens in addition where students add the numerators for the upper answer and add the denominators for the lower answer, with no regard for common denominators, etc. Unfortunately, in multiplication, when the upper and lower answers are combined, they *look* like the correct product. To avoid this phenomenon, whole number factors will be used first to introduce students to the concept of fractions in multiplication.

4. Tell students that each rectangular box on the multiplication building mat will represent a whole bar or unit during the lesson. Remind them that the notation, *3 × 4,* means *3 sets of 4 objects in each set.*

5. Using a whole number as a factor: Have students place 1-half on the top whole bar of the multiplication mat. Ask them to *build a new set that will equal* three of the 1-half. Do not say "show me three of **your** 1-half," because some students (the literal thinkers) will say they do not have enough to meet the request. To show three of the 1-half, students should place 1-half on each of three whole bars below the dotted line on the building mat.

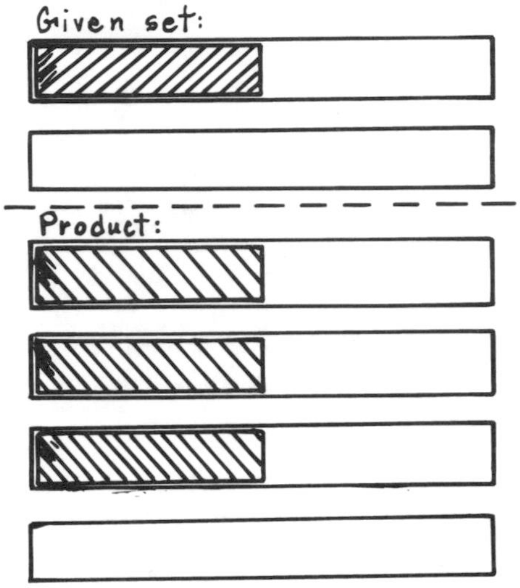

Given set:

Product:

6. Ask students to count the total bars on the lower region (below dotted line) of the mat. They should not simplify or rename their answer, but should only count what they see. The answer or product is 3-halves of a whole bar. Have them write on their own papers the following sentence: *3 of 1-half is 3-halves of a whole bar.*

7. Have students place 2 whole bars on the upper region of the mat. Ask them to build a new set that contains 2 of every 4 equal parts of the 2 whole bars. There are not four obvious parts in the given set. Remind students that new part sizes can only be placed on the mat if they are the result of forward trading; that is, each old part is replaced by two or more of a smaller, new part. Students should replace each whole bar on the mat with 4-fourths. Some may suggest using halves, which would also create four equal parts, but that trade would not lead to the general algorithm. Accept their idea as a correct one for a special case, but tell them to trade *each* bar this time, since such a trade will work for *all* cases.

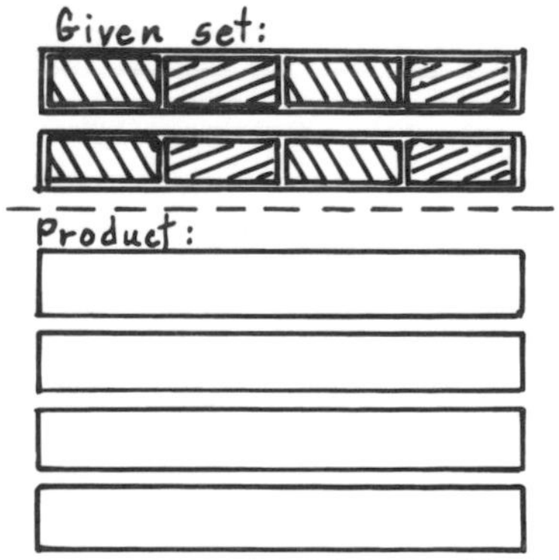

Given set:

Product:

8. Since the new set must contain 2 of every 4 equal parts, whatever the part size may be, have students observe that the top bar of the mat holds four fourths, so they need to put two new fourths on the first bar in the lower region of the mat to start building the new set or product. They should repeat the process for the four fourths on the second bar in the upper region, thus placing two new fourths on the second bar in the lower region.

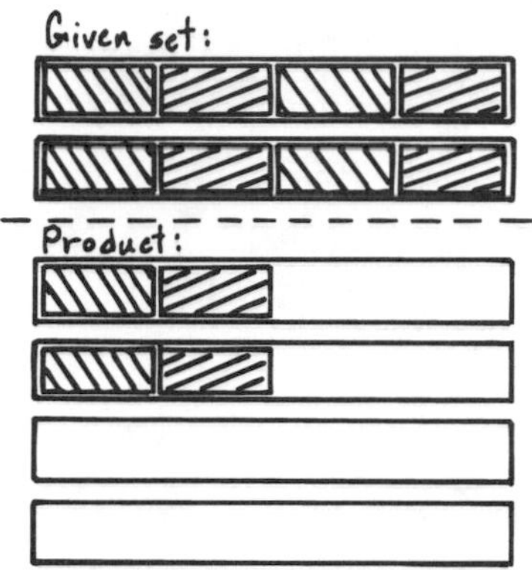

9. Have students count the fourths in the new set, then write the following sentence on their own papers to record the result: *2 of every 4 equal parts of 2 whole bars is 4-fourths of a whole bar.*

10. Assign other exercises on the chalkboard for students to build on the mat. They should write a sentence for the result, using the form demonstrated in step 9 above. The combination of words and numbers in the sentence is important; do not simplify to only numbers at this time. Remind students that *each* fraction bar in the given set of an exercise should be traded when necessary, so that all parts placed later in the new set are the same size and can merely be counted to find the product or answer to the exercise. Answers must not be simplified or reduced at this time so that students might see the patterns forming among the numerators and denominators. Have different students describe their steps for some of the exercises when possible. Here are some possible exercises to use:

- 2 of 5-sixths of a whole bar is ?
- 3 of 2-thirds of a whole bar is ?
- 3 of 2-fourths of a whole bar is ?
- 4 of 3-eighths of a whole bar is ?
- 1 of every 6 equal parts of 1 whole bar is ?
- 3 of every 4 equal parts of 1 whole bar is ?
- 3 of every 8 equal parts of 2 whole bars is ?
- 1 of every 3 equal parts of 2 whole bars is ?

11. Using fractions for both factors: Have students show 1-half of a whole bar in the upper region of the mat. Ask them to build a new set that contains 3 of every 4 equal parts of 1-half of a whole bar. To do this, students must first trade the half for four new, equal parts. Allow them to search to find which part size will work. The fraction bar that is called *1-eighth of a whole bar* should finally be chosen. Some students may want to call the new part *1-fourth* since four of them equal the 1-half. Remind them that the name *1-fourth,* as they are using it, relates the new part *to the 1-half itself,* but *1-eighth,* the name already assigned to this specific piece, relates the new part *to the whole bar,* which is how the answer must be given in fraction multiplication. More specifically, the answer must be compared to the same quantity that the original set or multiplicand is. The realization that a part can have two different relationships simultaneously is logically confusing to young students.

12. Since 3 of the 4 parts of the given set are to be represented in the new set, have students place 3 new eighths on the first bar in the lower region of the mat. They should then write the sentence: *3 of every 4 equal parts of 1-half of a whole bar is 3-eighths of a whole bar.*

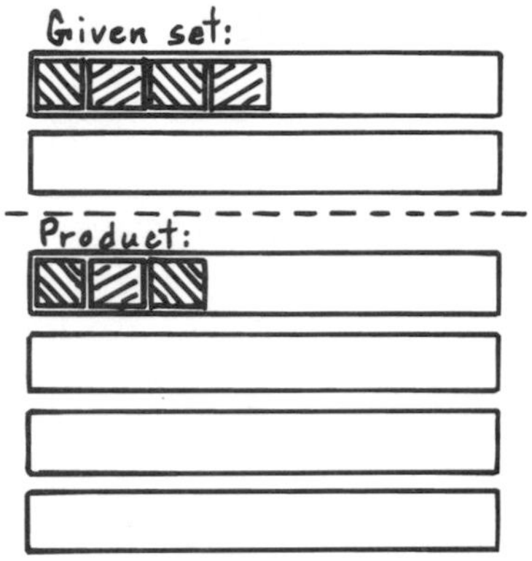

Given set:

Product:

13. Assign other exercises on the chalkboard for students to build on the multiplication mat. Sentences like the example in step 12 should be written to record the results found. Ask various students to describe their steps whenever possible. Here are some exercises to use:

- 1 of every 2 equal parts of 3-fourths of a whole bar is ?
- 2 of every 3 equal parts of 2-fourths of a whole bar is ?
- 5 of every 6 equal parts of 2-halves of a whole bar is ?
- 2 of every 3 equal parts of 1-half of a whole bar is ?
- 1 of every 2 equal parts of 3-thirds of a whole bar is ?
- 3 of every 4 equal parts of 2-thirds of a whole bar is ?

Activity 2: DRAWING PARTIAL SETS

(Pictorial Action)

Materials: Fraction Multiplication Worksheet DWA-10.2
Red pencils
Pencils
Fraction bars and building mats from Activity 1 (optional)

Management: Partners (two sessions at 50 minutes/session)

Directions:

1. Give each student 2–3 copies of the multiplication worksheet and a red pencil. Have students write numbers in the small boxes on the worksheet to number items or frames as needed. Some students may still prefer working with the fraction bars for this activity; this is quite acceptable. Allow them to build each exercise with the fraction bars, but also have them draw a diagram that shows the steps they used to find their answers. Tell students that each bar on the worksheet will represent a whole bar or unit.

2. In this activity one session will be devoted to exercises having a whole number as one of the factors. The second session will involve two fractions as the factors. Some of the exercises will also include an improper fraction as the given set or multiplicand.

3. Using a whole number as a factor: Have students draw and shade 5-fourths on the top two whole bars of a multiplication frame on their worksheet that contains six whole bars. Ask them to *draw a new set that will equal* two of the 5-fourths. To show the new set, students will need to use four whole bars below the dotted line on the building mat.

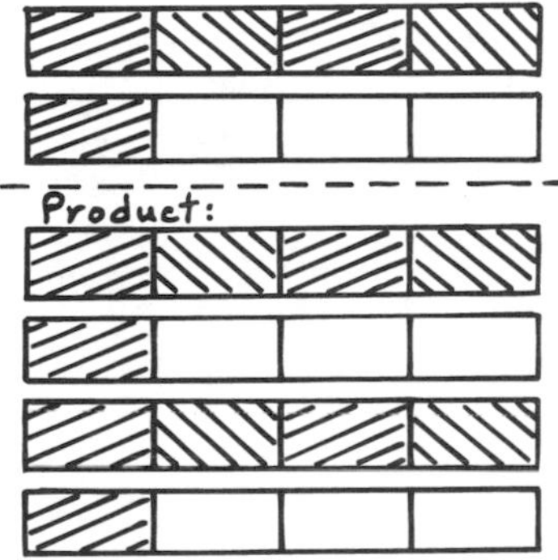

4. Have students count the total number of shaded fourths in the new set and record their result by writing the following number sentence below the frame on their worksheets:

$$2 \times \frac{5}{4} = \frac{10}{4} \text{ of a unit.}$$

Do not have them write the answer as a mixed number at this time, but do allow them to rename it orally if they wish to do so.

5. Have students show a set of 2 ones by shading the top two whole bars on a frame of the worksheet that contains four whole bars. Write *2/3 × 2* on the board and read the exercise as *2 out of every 3 equal parts of 2 ones.* Ask students to find what this amount should be, then draw it on the whole bars below the dotted line of the frame.

6. To do this operation, students must first use a red pencil to divide each shaded whole bar into three equal parts, then draw a red check mark on two of every three parts. A red X may be drawn on each shaded part not needed. The selected parts should be redrawn on one or more of the whole bars below the dotted line.

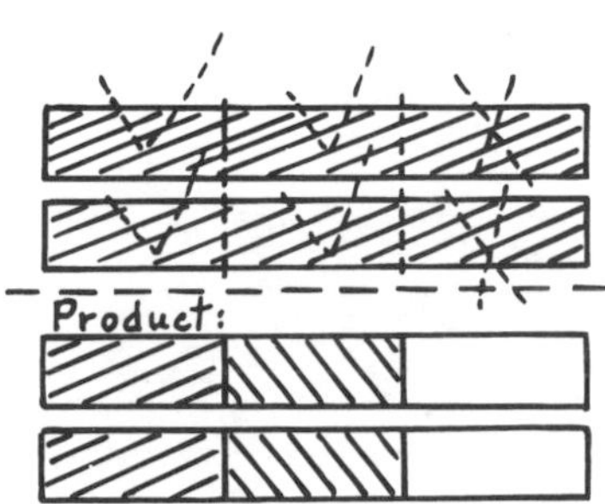

7. Students should count the total shaded parts now in the new set and write the following number sentence below the frame:

$$\frac{2}{3} \times 2 = \frac{4}{3} \text{ of a unit.}$$

Allow students to rename the answer as a mixed number, but do not have them write the mixed number as part of the number sentence at this time.

8. Write several other exercises on the chalkboard for students to draw to solve. They should also write a number sentence to record each exercise worked. The frames on the worksheet that contain six whole bars will be needed when drawing a product of more than one improper fraction. Remind students that *each* initially shaded part must be divided into the required number of equal parts; for example, in *3/8 × 2* suggested below, each shaded whole bar must be divided into eight equal parts, then three of the eight parts marked. This yields two groups of 3/8, or 6/8 total. Some students may try to make eight parts by drawing fourths on each bar and marking three of the fourths. This latter method produces 3/4 as the answer, which is correct but does not reflect the algorithmic pattern being developed in this activity. Here are some possible exercises for students to draw:

$2 \times \frac{2}{4}$ of a unit = ?	$\frac{3}{4} \times 2$ = ?
$1 \times \frac{2}{3}$ of a unit = ?	$2 \times \frac{4}{3}$ of a unit = ?
$2 \times \frac{5}{6}$ of a unit = ?	$3 \times \frac{1}{2}$ of a unit = ?
$\frac{1}{2} \times 1 = ?$	$\frac{3}{8} \times 2 = ?$
$\frac{2}{6} \times 2 = ?$	$\frac{5}{8} \times 1 = ?$

9. After students have completed their drawings, have several share the number sentences they found and redraw some of their models on the chalkboard.

10. Finally write six to eight of the completed number sentences on the board, using a whole number as the first factor in half of the sentences and as the second factor in the other half of the sentences. Ask students to look at the factors and answer or product to see if there is a pattern for finding the numerator and denominator of the answer. Most will easily recognize the pattern: the product of the whole number and the numerator of the only fraction factor equals the new numerator, and the denominator of the fraction factor equals the new denominator.

11. Using fractions for both factors: Write $\frac{2}{4} \times \frac{3}{2}$ on the chalkboard. Have students draw and shade 3/2 on the top two whole bars of a new frame on their worksheet. Ask them to use a red pencil to divide each half of the two whole bars into four equal parts. All parts of a whole bar must be divided in the same way pictorially in order to identify the part size to be counted for the answer. Students should then draw a red check mark on two of every four of the shaded parts only. They may draw a red X on each shaded part not needed. They should redraw the checked parts on the bars below the dotted line of the frame, dividing each whole bar used into the same final number of parts shown on the top bars. All the checked, shaded parts may be combined and redrawn on a single whole bar if possible.

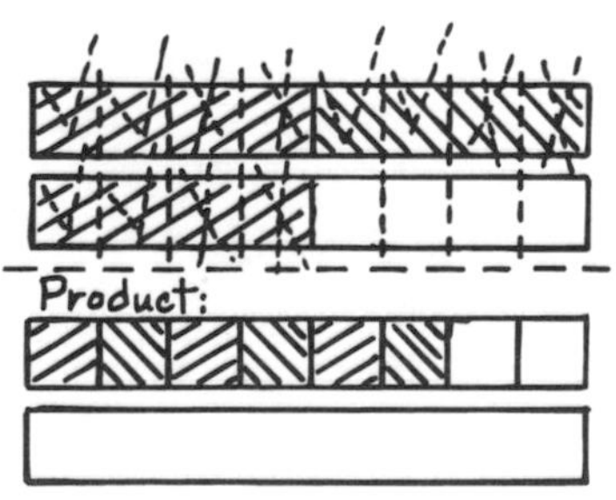

12. The following number sentence should be written below the frame to record the result: $\frac{2}{4} \times \frac{3}{2} = \frac{6}{8}$ of a unit.

13. Write other exercises on the chalkboard for students to draw on their worksheets. Remind them that all parts of a whole bar must be divided, whether shaded or not, in order to know the name of the final part size used in the answer. Here are some possible exercises to assign:

$\frac{1}{3} \times \frac{1}{2}$ of a unit = ?	$\frac{1}{2} \times \frac{3}{4}$ of a unit = ?
$\frac{2}{3} \times \frac{2}{4}$ of a unit = ?	$\frac{4}{6} \times \frac{1}{2}$ of a unit = ?
$\frac{3}{4} \times \frac{2}{3}$ of a unit = ?	$\frac{1}{4} \times \frac{5}{3}$ of a unit = ?
$\frac{2}{6} \times \frac{2}{2}$ of a unit = ?	$\frac{1}{3} \times \frac{3}{2}$ of a unit = ?
$\frac{1}{2} \times \frac{7}{6}$ of a unit = ?	$\frac{2}{3} \times \frac{7}{4}$ of a unit = ?

14. After students have completed their drawings and number sentences, have several share their results by drawing pictorial models on the chalkboard and verbally describing the steps they used.

15. Write five to six number sentences from the worksheet on the chalkboard. Ask students to look at the two factors that are fractions and at the answer or product to see if there is a pattern among the numerators and among the denominators. As discussed in Activity 1, this particular pattern is quite easy for most students to recognize: the new numerator is the product of the initial numerators and the new denominator is the product of the initial denominators.

Activity 3: CRAZY CREATIONS

(Cooperative Groups)

Materials: Cards containing fraction multiplication exercises (described in step 4 below)
Sets of fraction bars and building mats from Activity 1
Paper
Pencils

Management: Teams of 4 students each (30–40 minutes)

Directions:

1. Give each team a set of fraction bars and a building mat. Also give them a large index card containing a fraction multiplication exercise without an answer. In each exercise, the multiplier or first factor may be a common fraction or a mixed number while the multiplicand or second factor will be a mixed number.

2. Each team is to create a crazy story problem to match the team exercise and write the story on the card. For example, if the exercise were *1 1/2 × 1 3/4 = ?* the story might be as follows: *Queen Neon has 1 3/4* ***tons of krypton.*** *She needs 1 1/2 of that amount to defeat Superman's cousin Zadon. How many* ***tons of krypton*** *does she need in all to win?* The unit used in the story (here, a ton of krypton) must be clearly indicated by the team.

3. Each team should exchange cards with another team, then read the story problem on their new card. Team members should use fraction bars on a building mat to build their

NAME ______________________ DATE ______________

MULTIPLICATION WORKSHEET DWA-10.2
Drawing Partial Sets

Product:

Product:

Product:

Product:

new exercise, then express their result in a word sentence, using the unit given in the story. For example, the story given in step 2 might be answered with the solution sentence: *Queen Neon will need 2 5/8 tons of krypton to defeat Zadon.* The fraction bar model can be built in several different ways. Encourage students to find their own method, but require them to simplify their result to a mixed number if possible. For the krypton story, students might first show one full set of 1 unit or ton and 3/4 of a unit or ton. Then they might find 1/2 of the 1 unit and 1/2 of the 3/4 of a unit. Further trading would be needed to get a common part size and finally a mixed number, but the initial stage of building might appear as follows:

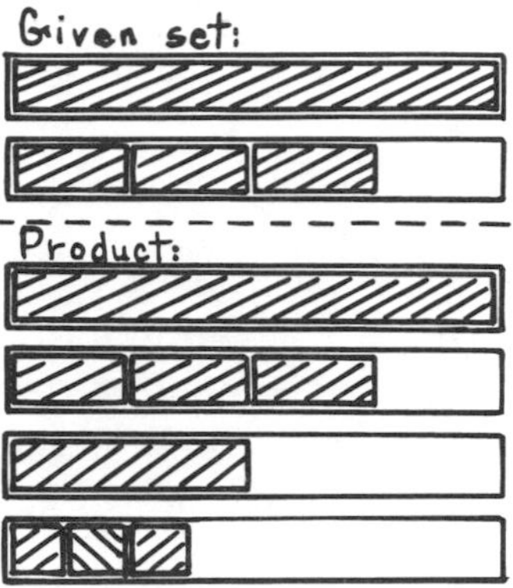

4. Several teams may have the same exercise initially, but their stories should be different. When they exchange cards, however, each team should receive an exercise different from their original one. Here are some suggestions for exercises:

$\frac{2}{3} \times 1\frac{1}{2} = ?$	$1\frac{1}{3} \times 1\frac{1}{4} = ?$
$\frac{1}{2} \times 1\frac{1}{4} = ?$	$1\frac{2}{4} \times 1\frac{1}{2} = ?$
$\frac{3}{4} \times 1\frac{1}{3} = ?$	$1\frac{1}{2} \times 1\frac{2}{3} = ?$

5. If time permits, have different teams read their story and their solution sentence, then describe how they approached the problem with the fraction bars. Some will trade the initial set of bars to get a common part size, then build the amounts they need and simplify. Others will build with the different bar sizes first, then trade for a common part size and simplify. Accept any method as long as it correctly applies the procedures taught in Activity 1 and Activity 2.

OBJECTIVE 11: Relate fraction multiplication to the division of fractions.

Activity 1: BUILDING COMPARISONS
(Concrete Action)

Materials: Sets of fraction bars and division building mats from Objective 9, Activity 1
Paper
Pencils

Management: Partners (50 minutes)

Directions:

1. Give each student a set of fraction bars and a division building mat. Also, give each student three extra whole bars to add to their set of fraction bars, making a total of six whole bars per set. Students will have individual mats, but will work in pairs. It is assumed that students will have successfully completed the activities of Objective 9 (division) and Objective 10 (multiplication) before they are introduced to this activity.

2. Within each pair, one student should be partner A and the other, partner B. Ask partner A of each pair to build *1 divided by 1/3* with fraction bars on the division mat. Ask partner B to build *2 divided by 1/3* on the other mat. Using the common denominator method of Objective 9, the two mats should appear as follows:

Partner A's Mat

This amount:

makes how many or how much of this amount?

Partner B's Mat

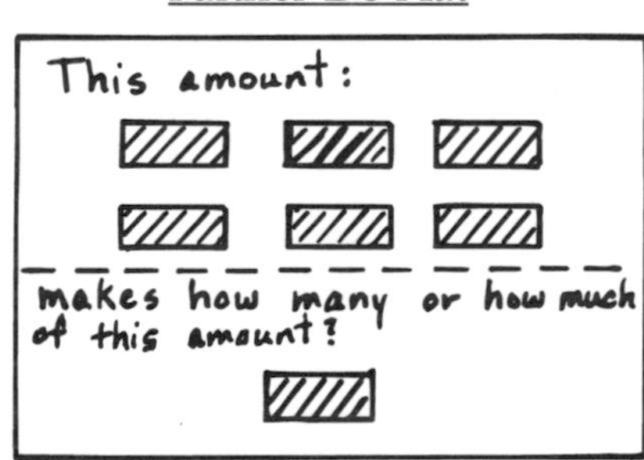

3. Have students look at the amounts in the dividend spaces of the two mats. Ask: *How many of A's answer, 3, are needed to make B's answer, 6?* Students should observe that *2 of the 3 make 6*. They seem to make such a comparison easily as long as the sets of fraction bars are in front of them for a direct, visual comparison.

4. Have students write the following three sentences on their own papers to record what they found:

- *A: 1 divided by 1/3 = 3 sets of 1/3 of a unit.*
- *B: 2 divided by 1/3 = 6 sets of 1/3 of a unit.*
- *2 of the 3 sets = 6 sets.*

5. Have partner A build *1 divided by 3/4* and partner B build *1/2 divided by 3/4* on their mats.

Partner A's Mat

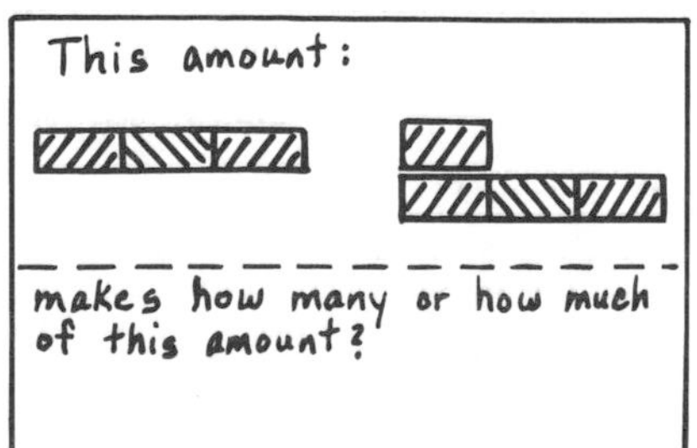

Partner B's Mat

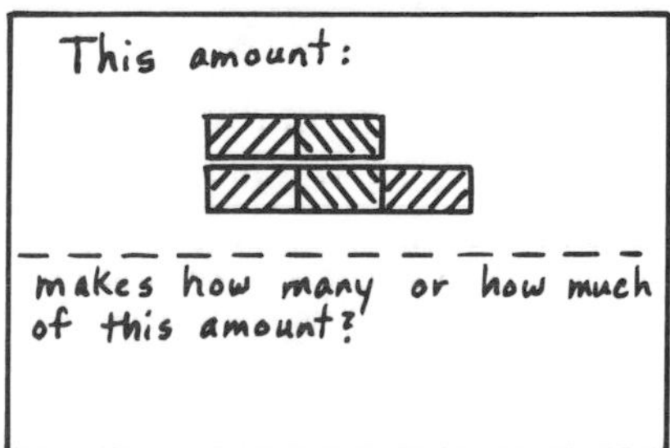

6. Have students compare the two amounts and ask: *How much of A's answer, 1 full set and 1/3 of a set, is needed to make B's answer, 2/3 of a set?* Students should recognize that *1/2 of the 1 1/3 sets will make the 2/3 of a set.* Have students record the following sentences:

- *A: 1 divided by 3/4 = 1 1/3 sets of 3/4 of a unit.*
- *B: 1/2 divided by 3/4 = 2/3 of a set of 3/4 of a unit.*
- *1/2 of the 1 1/3 sets = 2/3 of a set.*

7. Now write other pairs of division exercises on the chalkboard for students to build and compare. Clearly indicate which exercise of a pair is for partner A and for partner B. Three sentences should be written for each pair similar to those given in steps 4 and 6. The comparison sentence should always state how many or how much of A's answer will be needed to make B's answer. It represents the multiplication alternative being developed in this objective. If the roles of the A and B amounts are reversed in the sentence, the desired relationship between multiplication and division will not be shown. Here are some suggested pairs of exercises for students to build:

Partner A		Partner B
1 divided by 1/4	:	3 divided by 1/4
1 divided by 1/2	:	3 divided by 1/2
1 divided by 2/3	:	2 divided by 2/3
1 divided by 5/6	:	2 divided by 5/6
1 divided by 2	:	1/4 divided by 2
1 divided by 2	:	1/3 divided by 2
1 divided by 1/3	:	1/3 divided by 1/3
1 divided by 1/4	:	3/4 divided by 1/4

Activity 2: DRAWING RELATED SENTENCES

(Pictorial Action)

Materials: Activity 2 worksheets from Objective 9 and Objective 10
Red pencils
Pencils
Paper

Management: Partners (50 minutes)

Directions:

1. Give each pair of students Division Worksheet DWA-9.2 (from Activity 2, Objective 9), Multiplication Worksheet DWA-10.2 (from Activity 2, Objective 10), and two red pencils. One student of each pair, partner A, should work with the division worksheet, and the other student, partner B, should work with the multiplication worksheet. It is assumed that all students have successfully completed both Objective 9 and Objective 10 and that they now know how to reduce fractions and rename improper fractions as mixed numbers. Also, reciprocals or multiplicative inverses have already been defined as two numbers whose product can be simplified to equal one. For example, $\frac{1}{3} \times 3 = \frac{3}{3}$ or 1, and $\frac{3}{4} \times \frac{4}{3} = \frac{12}{12}$ or 1, so $\frac{1}{3}$ and 3 are reciprocals of each other and 3/4 and 4/3 are reciprocals of each other.

2. Ask partner A of each pair to draw the exercise *2/3 divided by 5/6* on a frame of the division worksheet, using the common denominator method of division. Ask partner B to draw the exercise *2/3 × 6/5* on a frame of the multiplication worksheet. Each answer should be simplified and renamed as a mixed number if appropriate. Partner A should have the answer, *4/5 of a set of 5/6 of a unit.* Partner B should have the answer, *4/5 of a unit,* after reducing 12/15. Although the division answer is counting portions of the set, 5/6 of a unit, and the multiplication answer is describing a fractional part of the unit itself, the numerals used for both answers are the same.

3. Have students write a *final* number sentence (no steps shown; simplified answers) on their own paper for each exercise. They should write the following:

$$\frac{2}{3} \div \frac{5}{6} = \frac{4}{5} \text{ and } \frac{2}{3} \times \frac{6}{5} = \frac{4}{5}$$

4. Now assign other pairs of exercises for the partners to draw and compare answers. They should record the final number sentences, giving the answers in simplified form for easy comparison. Here are some pairs of exercises to use:

Division	vs.	Multiplication
$2 \div \frac{1}{2} = ?$	and	$2 \times 2 = ?$
$1 \div \frac{3}{4} = ?$	and	$1 \times \frac{4}{3} = ?$
$\frac{3}{4} \div \frac{1}{2} = ?$	and	$\frac{3}{4} \times 2 = ?$
$\frac{1}{3} \div \frac{1}{2} = ?$	and	$\frac{1}{3} \times 2 = ?$
$\frac{1}{2} \div \frac{2}{3} = ?$	and	$\frac{1}{2} \times \frac{3}{2} = ?$
$\frac{3}{4} \div \frac{2}{3} = ?$	and	$\frac{3}{4} \times \frac{3}{2} = ?$
$\frac{1}{4} \div \frac{3}{2} = ?$	and	$\frac{1}{4} \times \frac{2}{3} = ?$

5. After all students have completed their drawings and written their number sentences, write several of the pairs of final number sentences on the chalkboard. Ask students to look at each pair and try to find ways in which they are alike and different. Use colored chalk to highlight their observations. Typical responses might be:

- The first numbers in the division exercise and in the multiplication exercise are the same.
- The two operations are opposites or inverses.
- The second numbers in the two exercises are reciprocals (or opposites) of each other.
- The two answers have the same number name. When these four characteristics are present, the two number sentences are called *related number sentences.* Here is an example of how to highlight the characteristics with colored chalk:

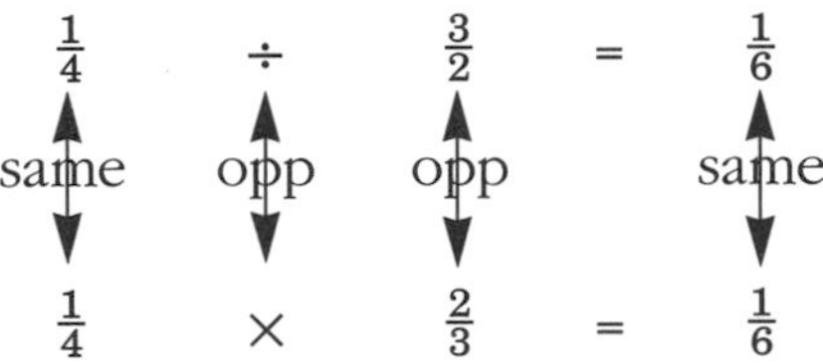

6. Now help students evaluate some of the sentences they recorded in Activity 1. Review the two examples used at the beginning of that activity.

Example 1: 1 divided by 1/3 = 3
2 divided by 1/3 = 6
2 of the 3 = 6

Example 2: 1 divided by 3/4 = 1 1/3
1/2 divided by 3/4 = 2/3
1/2 of the 1 1/3 = 2/3

Guide the students to observe that the last two number sentences in each example form a pair of *related number sentences,* since they have the same characteristics found in the pairs of number sentences drawn earlier in this activity.

7. Discuss the idea that related number sentences may or may not describe the same situation since their numbers have different roles to play. Nevertheless, if two exercises are related in the four ways listed in step 5, their answers are guaranteed to have the same number name. This gives students an alternative. If they want to find the answer to *3/4 × 4/5,* they may choose instead to solve the related division sentence, *3/4 divided by 5/4,* knowing that its answer, *3/5,* will also be the answer to the first exercise. Similarly, if students want to find the answer to *3 divided by 5/7,* they may choose instead to solve the related multiplication sentence, *3 × 7/5,* whose answer of *21/5* also identifies the answer to the division exercise. The goal of this activity has been to introduce students to the relationship between specific division and multiplication number sentences and to make them aware that they have alternatives in computation. That is, if the computation involved in working a given exercise seems complicated, students may choose to work an easier, *related* exercise, knowing that the second exercise will give the same answer they seek for the first exercise.

Activity 3: RELATED SENTENCE CHALLENGE

(Cooperative Groups)

Materials: Paper
Pencils

Management: Teams of 4 students each (30 minutes)

Directions:

1. Have each team form two pairs of students.

2. The two pairs on a team will take turns giving each other a multiplication or division exercise. The other pair must write and solve the related number sentence of the given exercise. Hence, if one pair writes a multiplication exercise, the other pair must write the related division exercise and solve it by the common denominator method. If the first pair writes a division exercise, the other pair must write the related multiplication exercise and solve it by applying the multiplication algorithm.

3. Have students use only fractions whose numerators and denominators are less than nine and only whole numbers less than five when creating their exercises. The two numbers in an exercise may both be fractions or whole numbers, or one number may be a fraction and the other, a whole number. The pair of students solving a related number sentence should express their answer in simplest terms. Improper fractions may be left in that form or changed to mixed numbers.

4. Monitor the teams closely to make certain their computations are correct.

OBJECTIVE 12: Multiply decimal fractions, using factors involving ones and tenths.

Activity 1: BUILDING PRODUCTS WITH DECIMALS

(Concrete Action)

Materials: Base 10 blocks
Building mats (described in step 1 below)
Paper
Pencils

Management: Partners (50 minutes)

Directions:

1. Give each pair of students a set of base 10 blocks and a building mat. The set of blocks should contain the following: 5 flats, 20 rods, and 20 units. The building mat may be made by drawing a backward L on an $8\frac{1}{2}$" × 14" sheet of paper and labeling it in the following way:

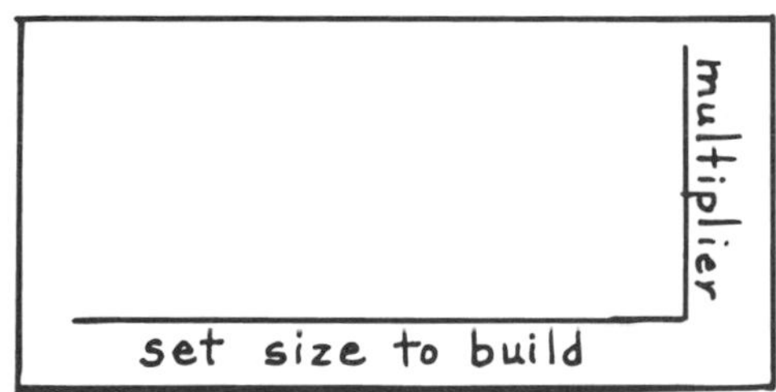

2. It is assumed that students have already been working with the base 10 blocks to identify, add, and subtract decimal numbers. Students should be able to recognize the flats as ones or units, the rods as tenths of a unit, and the small cubes as hundredths of a unit. It would be helpful, but not required, for students to have learned whole number multiplication by the method presented in Objective 1 and Objective 3 of this same chapter. A method similar to that one will be used here in the development of decimal multiplication.

3. Have students place two ones (or flats) in the multiplier position and four tenths (or rods) in the set position of the building mat. The rods must be turned perpendicular to the L-frame.

4. Since the multiplier contains two ones, students should build two rows of the set of four tenths as shown in the diagram below. Have them count the total tenths in the product region and write the following sentence on their own papers: *2 of 0.4 = 0.8 of the whole unit.*

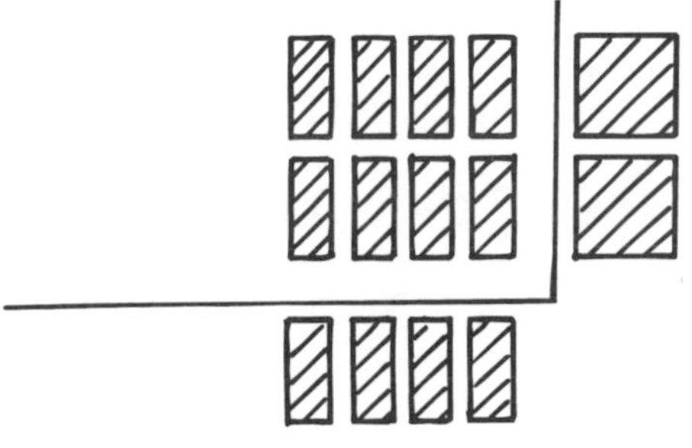

5. Have students place three tenths (or rods) in the multiplier position and a one (or flat) and two tenths (or rods) in the set position of the building mat. A tenth in the multiplier means to find *one-tenth of,* or *one out of ten equal parts of,* each block in the set. One of ten equal parts of a one is a tenth of that one, and one of ten equal parts of a tenth is a hundredth. Therefore, the first or bottom row of the new product should contain a tenth (or rod) and two hundredths (or small cubes), all of which line up with the first tenth in the multiplier. Students should build two more such rows of blocks to match the other two tenths in the multiplier.

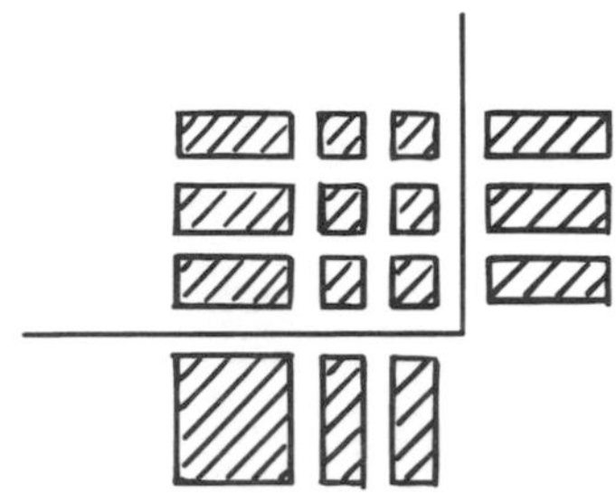

6. Have students count the different blocks in the final product to find their total value, then write the following sentence on their own papers about the result: *0.3 of 1.2 = 0.3 and 0.06, or 0.36, of a whole unit.*

7. Next, write other exercises, such as *1.4 of 2.1 = ?,* on the chalkboard for students to build with their base 10 blocks. For each exercise, they should write a sentence to record their result. For the multiplier, use at most one flat with one to four rods. For the set, use at most two flats with one to four rods.

8. After all students have finished building their exercises, have various students describe how they built some of the products and read the sentences they recorded for those products.

Activity 2: DRAWING DECIMAL PRODUCTS

(Pictorial Action)

Materials: Paper
Pencils
Red pencils
Base 10 blocks (optional)
Building mats from Activity 1 (optional)

Management: Partners (two sessions at 50 minutes/session)

Directions:

1. Have students work in pairs. Each pair should have a red pencil for the second session. Some students may still prefer to build with the blocks; this is acceptable. Have them build an exercise with blocks first, then draw a diagram of the product. It should be possible to build most of the exercises with blocks. For this pictorial activity, squares will represent ones or units, line segments will represent tenths, and small circles will represent hundredths.

2. Drawing diagrams: Have students draw a backward L-frame on their own paper. The vertical bar should be at least $1\frac{1}{2}$ inches long and the horizontal bar should be at least $2\frac{1}{2}$ inches long, so that the drawn shapes in the product will not be too small. Have the students show 1.2 as the multiplier by drawing a square and two line segments to the right of the vertical bar of the frame. Have them also show 1.4 as the set by drawing a square and four line segments below the horizontal bar.

3. Since one of ten equal parts of a tenth is a hundredth and one-tenth of a unit is a tenth, a row of four circles and one line segment should be drawn above the original set and in line with the first tenth or line segment in the multiplier to show 0.1 × 1.4. Another similar row of four circles and a line segment should be drawn for the other tenth in the multiplier. The square in the multiplier indicates that one full set of 1.4 (or the square and four line segments) should be drawn as the top row of the product. Have students count the shapes in the final arrangement to determine the total value of the product. They should then write a number sentence under their completed diagram as follows: *1. 2 × 1. 4 = 1.68 of one.*

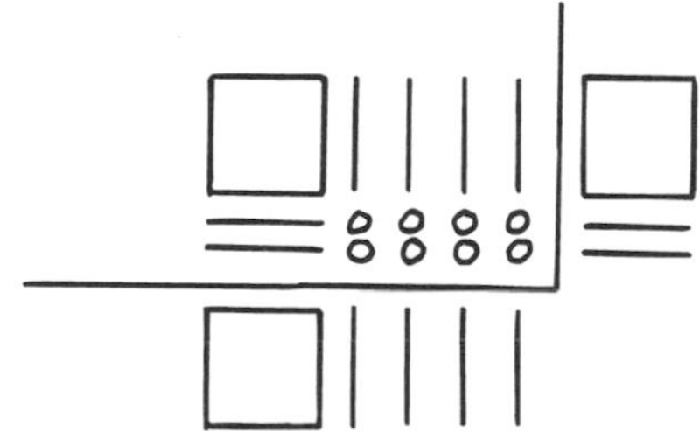

4. Next, write other exercises on the chalkboard for students to draw on their own papers during the first session. At times mental trades may need to be made in order to find the total for a product. For example, if ten line segments are drawn, they may be mentally traded for a square or one whole unit. Students should write a number sentence for each completed exercise. Use at most two squares (ones) and 1–5 line segments (tenths) for each of the factors, the multiplier and the set.

5. Describing the regions within the product: For the second session, have students draw the diagram for 1.3 × 2.4. Show them how to mark off and number in red pencil the four regions formed by the different shapes in the product. Have them also label each region with a pair of factors that describes the arrangement of the shapes within the region (number of rows by number of shapes in each row). The completed diagram should be as follows:

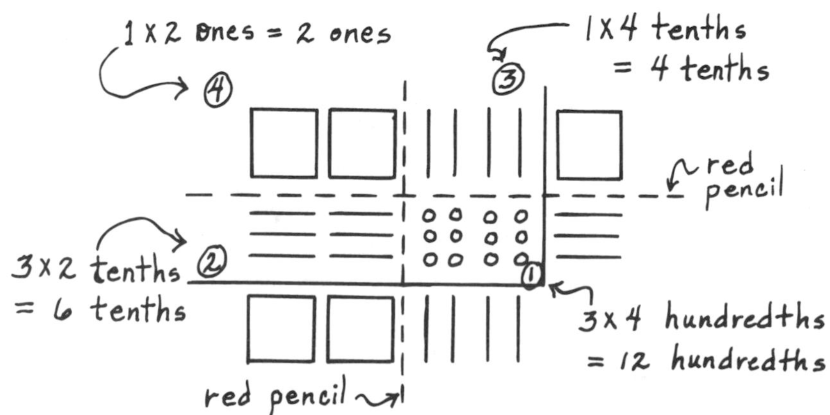

6. Next, have students make any necessary corrections to the diagrams they drew during the first session. Have them repeat the procedure used in step 5, marking off in red pencil the regions contained within each product. Each arrangement of shapes should be described by a pair of factors.

7. Guide students to observe that the regions in the lower level of a diagram always contain hundredths followed by tenths to the left. The upper level has tenths on the right just above the hundredths and has ones on the left. Region 1 will contain shapes of the least value (in the above example, hundredths) in the final product because the drawing process in that region multiplies together the smallest value of each factor in the exercise. In the previous example, a tenth of a tenth was used to get a hundredth.

8. For some diagrams, e.g., the diagram for *1.3 × 2.0 = 2.6,* one or two regions will be empty. These regions should still be described with respect to the shapes that generally would be there, using zeros as factors where appropriate. Here is the labeled diagram for *1.3 × 2.0 = 2.6:*

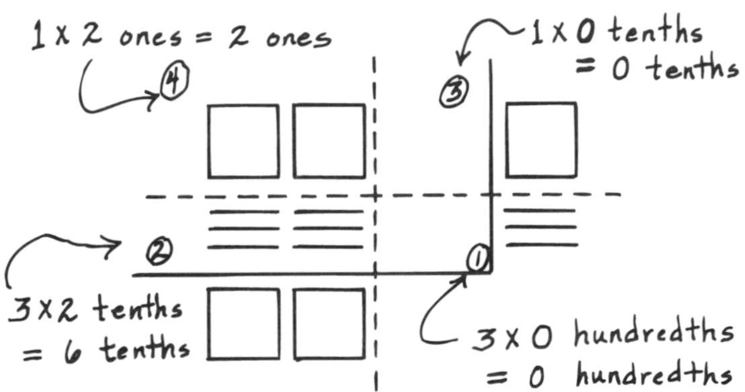

9. Hopefully, the method of identifying regions seems quite familiar to those students who were taught whole number multiplication in earlier grades by the method presented in Objective 3. Students should now transfer the descriptions of the regions of each diagram to the numerical notation for the exercise. *For example,* the regions of *1.3 × 2.4* (shown in step 5) should be recorded as partial products in the following way, beginning with the region of the smallest value and recording the final product in the bottom line of the notation:

2 . 4	
× 1 . 3	
. 1 2	(1) 3 × 4 hundredths = 12 hundredths
. 6	(2) 3 × 2 tenths = 6 tenths
. 4	(3) 1 × 4 tenths = 4 tenths
2 .	(4) 1 × 2 ones = 2 ones
3 . 1 2	

Notice that the decimal points are recorded in the partial products. This emphasizes the place values involved in the different regions and helps students keep the partial products lined up correctly. The right-most digits of the original factors (here, 2.4 and 1.3) should be lined up vertically with the right-most digit of the first partial product; this merely tells students where to start their recording. The decimal points in the two factors of the given example also line up, but this only happens when both factors have the same least place value.

10. After students have recorded the number sentences for the regions of each diagram drawn during the first session, have them look at the notation recorded for *1.3 × 2.4* in step 9. Ask them to compare the factors in the four number sentences to the digits in the multiplier and multiplicand (or set) of the original exercise. The 3 in the multiplier matches the first factors in number sentences (1) and (2) in the recording, and the digits 4 and 2 in the multiplicand match the second factors in (1) and (2). Similarly, the 1 in the multiplier corresponds to the first factors in number sentences (3) and (4), and the 4 and 2 in the multiplicand correspond to the second factors in (3) and (4).

11. Have students check the notations for their other diagrams to confirm that the above observations hold true for them as well. Thus, the digits in the original factors may be used to predict the arrangements of the regions, and the order in which the digits are paired to make partial products, beginning with the digit of least place value in each factor, should reflect the increasing place values of those regions.

12. Assign several exercises for students to try writing only the symbolic notation, including the number sentences describing the regions. They should use the format shown in step 9. If necessary, they may confirm their notation for a given exercise by drawing a diagram.

13. Once students are comfortable with the placement of the decimal points in the partial products, have them *collapse* into one line the partial products that represent regions from the same level on the diagram. This will produce a notation familiar to students from their whole number multiplication experiences. For example, the exercise 1.3 × 2.4 will be written as follows:

```
    2 . 4
  × 1 . 3
  -------
    . 7 2   (regions 1 and 2 combined)
  2 . 4     (regions 3 and 4 combined)
  -------
  3 . 1 2
```

Activity 3: EXTENDING TO THOUSANDTHS

(Cooperative Groups)

Materials: Paper
Pencils
Decks of cards (described in step 2)

Management: Teams of 4 students each (30 minutes)

Directions:

1. This activity will provide students with experience in estimating decimal products and in working with thousandths in products. It is assumed that they are comfortable with the drawing technique used in Activity 2.

2. Give each team of students a deck of 36 cards. The cards may be made with small index cards, using three different colors if possible. Twelve cards will contain multiplication exercises (e.g., *1.2 of 0.8*), one exercise per card; twelve cards will contain upper or lower limits for decimal estimates (e.g., *product* < *1.5*); and twelve cards will contain place value names to be used to identify the smallest place value (*s.p.v.*) expected in an actual product (e.g., *s.p.v.* = *tenths*). Several cards will contain the same place value name. Each set of twelve cards should be made on its own color of index card.

3. The three sets of cards (exercises, estimates, and smallest place values) should be shuffled separately, then three cards from each set given to each member of the team. Members will take turns placing an exercise card face up on the table. They will work together to try to make *books*. Each book consists of an exercise card, an estimate card whose given limit is considered the closest in the set of estimate cards to the actual product, and an s.p.v. card that names the smallest place value expected in the actual product.

4. After one player lays down an exercise card, the other three players must try to complete a book by matching the exercise card with an estimate card and an s.p.v. card from the cards in their hands. No player may put down more than one card during a turn unless no one else has the needed card. If a player does not contribute a card during a turn, that player may lay down the exercise card on the next turn. The goal is to form books, not to run out of cards individually. However, players may not exchange cards or show their cards to each other. The contents of a card may be discussed any time, but the card is not to be laid down on the table until the team members have agreed to select it as part of a book.

5. Students may use several different methods for finding a *best estimate*. For example, to estimate the product for *1.2 of 0.8,* they might reason this way: $1.2 \times 0.8 < 1.2 \times 1 < 1.5$, so 1.5 is a possible close estimate. They might also draw a diagram of the product and quickly count the larger shapes to get an estimate. Students are not allowed to write the different values of the partial products on their papers and add them numerically. All computing must be done mentally with or without use of a diagram, even though students may be finding the exact answer that way. They still gain needed practice with place value when they must select the best estimate to go with their exact answer.

6. To draw diagrams involving thousandths, students will need to modify the shapes used in Activity 2. Discuss the following changes with them before the activity begins. Squares will still be ones, but narrow rectangles will serve as tenths and line segments as hundredths in the factors. In the product itself, a small square will represent the hundredth produced by 0.1×0.1; the original line segment will be used for a hundredth produced by 1×0.01. A short line segment in the product will represent a thousandth produced by 0.1×0.01. Here is a diagram for *1.1* × *1.11* to show how all the shapes fit together:

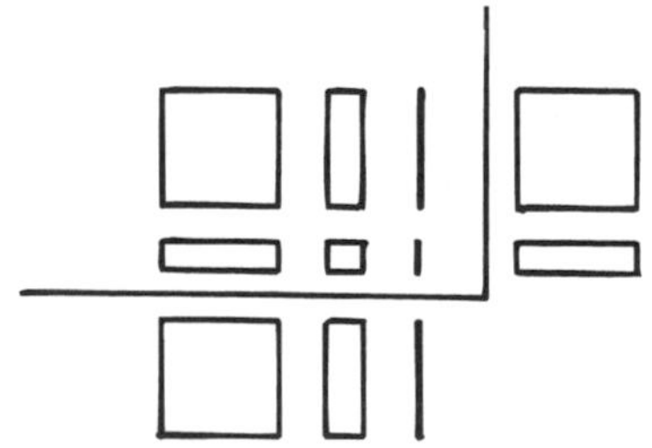

7. Here are some suggestions for the card deck. Since the cards are grouped as books below, this list might also serve as an answer key later to check a team's books for *best* matches.

Exercise Cards	S.P.V. Cards	Estimate Cards
3 of 1.6	tenths	product < 5.0
2 of 2.7	tenths	product > 5.0
1.8 of 2	tenths	product < 4.0
3.1 of 2	tenths	product < 6.4
2 of 0.006	thousandths	product > 0.0
1.3 of 2.02	thousandths	product > 2.5
1.2 of 0.9	hundredths	product > 1.0
2 of 1.52	hundredths	product > 3.0
2 of 3.06	hundredths	product > 6.0
1.5 of 2.9	hundredths	product > 4.0
2.1 of 1.3	hundredths	product < 3.0
0.6 of 3	tenths	product < 2.0

OBJECTIVE 13: Divide decimal fractions, using divisors and quotients containing ones and tenths.

Activity 1: MAKING DECIMAL SHARES

(Concrete Action)

Materials: Base 10 blocks
Building mats (described in step 1)
Paper
Pencils

Management: Partners (50 minutes)

Directions:

1. Give each pair of students a set of base 10 blocks and a building mat. The set of blocks should contain 5 flats, 30 rods, and 30 small cubes. The building mat may be made by drawing a rotated L-frame on an $8\frac{1}{2}$" × 14" sheet of paper and labeling it as follows:

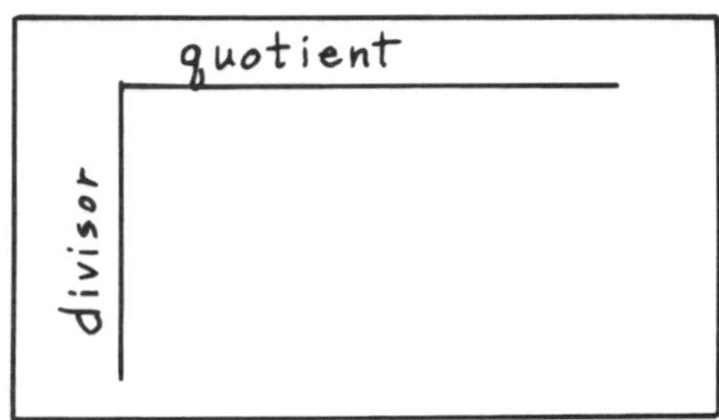

2. It is assumed that students have mastered the content of Objective 12 and that they are familiar with the base 10 blocks and their decimal fraction relationships. That is, they can identify the rod as one-tenth of the flat and the small cube as one-tenth of the rod or one-hundredth of the flat.

3. Have students place a one (or flat), three tenths (or rods), and two hundredths (or cubes) in the lower right corner of the building mat to represent the dividend. Have them also place a one and two tenths on the mat in the divisor position.

4. The divisor in this activity will indicate the set that needs to be formed from the dividend. This is the same interpretation used in Objective 9 for division of fractions. The quotient that results will describe how many full sets and partial sets were finally made from the dividend.

5. Tell students that they must use the dividend blocks to build copies of the set of divisor blocks. The one (or flat) of the dividend blocks can be moved up under the corner of the L-frame and placed in a row adjacent to the one in the divisor. Two tenths (or rods) in the dividend may also be moved up under the L-frame adjacent to the tenths in the divisor.

6. Have students place a new one from their set of extra blocks above the horizontal bar of the frame to show that a full set has been made from the dividend so far. Since there are no other ones in the dividend, another full set cannot be made. The blocks now look like this on the mat:

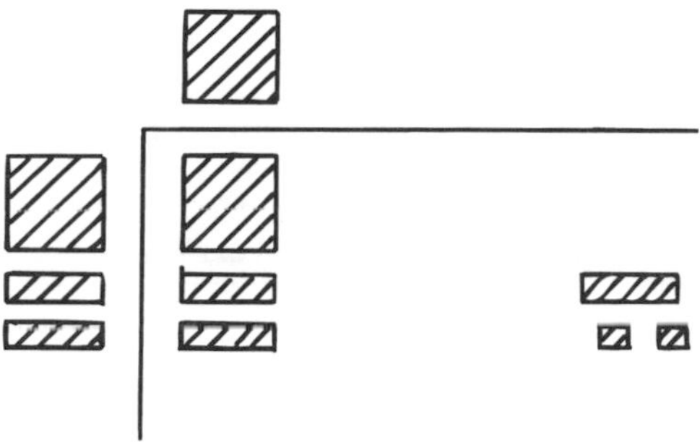

7. The remaining tenth and two hundredths must now be used to make a partial set. Ask: *If the larger block (the tenth) still unused in the dividend is compared to the larger block (the one) in the divisor set, what part of the block from the divisor set does the unused block represent?* The remaining tenth is one-tenth of the one or flat. Ask: *Since the divisor set also contains a tenth to be copied, is there also a block still unused in the dividend that equals one-tenth of a tenth?* Each unused hundredth has this property. Thus, a partial set may be built, using the tenth and two hundredths from the dividend. Since the partial set is one-tenth of the full divisor set, have students show this by placing a new tenth in the quotient above the partial set. The final block arrangement appears as shown below:

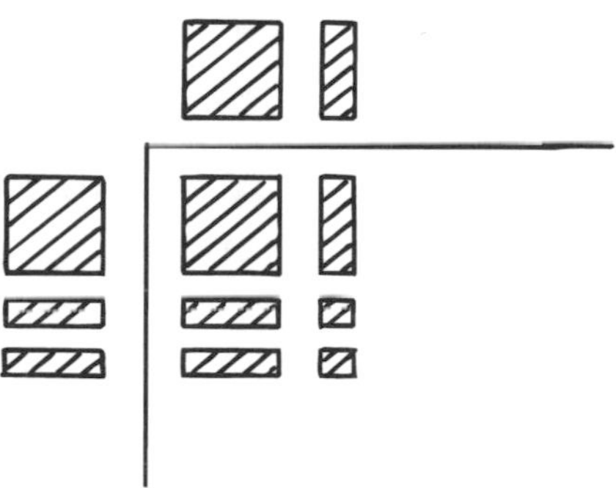

8. Students should record their result on their own paper, using the sentence: *1.32 makes 1.1 sets of 1.2.*

9. Next, have students place four tenths in the divisor position on the mat, and place a one and three hundredths in the lower right corner under the L-frame to show the dividend. Ask: *How might the one be used to build sets of 0.4?* The one must be traded for ten tenths, then the new tenths may be lined up beside the four tenths in the divisor set. A full set of 0.4 can be formed twice, so a one should be placed in the quotient above each full set built to show this. Two tenths and three hundredths remain unused in the lower right corner of the mat.

10. Ask: *Since there are not enough tenths left to form another full set, can a partial set be built?* Have students trade the unused tenths for hundredths and ask: *What part of a tenth in the divisor set does a hundredth in the dividend represent?* Since a hundredth is one-tenth of a tenth, have students distribute the dividend hundredths equally to the four rows under the frame. Five hundredths should be in each row. Have students place a new tenth in the quotient above each column of hundredths to show the partial sets formed. Three hundredths remain unused. The final mat arrangement is as follows:

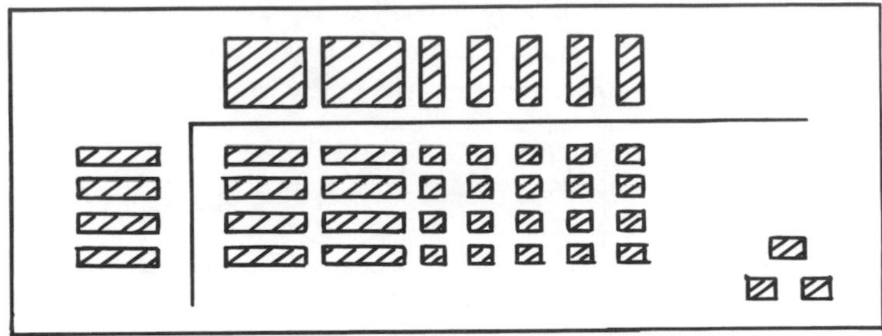

11. Students should write the following sentence on their own paper: *1.03 makes 2.5 sets of 0.4 with .03 left unused.*

12. Now write other division exercises on the chalkboard for students to build with the base 10 blocks. Dividends should be selected by first computing products from factors where the first factor contains 0–1 ones and 1–4 tenths and the second factor contains 0–2 ones and 1–3 tenths. The products obtained may then be used as dividends and their first factors used as divisors. This selection process guarantees that each division exercise can be built with the available quantities of blocks and minimal trading. Two or three extra hundredths might be added to a product in order to yield a dividend that will have a remainder. Students should also write a sentence describing the result of each exercise.

13. As time permits, have different students explain how they built some of the exercises and read the sentences they wrote about the results.

Activity 2: DRAWING FULL OR PARTIAL SETS

(Pictorial Action)

Materials: Paper
Pencils
Red pencils
Base 10 blocks (optional)
Building mats from Activity 1 (optional)

Management: Partners (two sessions at 50 minutes/session)

Directions:

1. Have students work in pairs. Each pair should have a red pencil. Some students may still prefer to work with the base 10 blocks; this is quite acceptable. Have them first build each exercise with blocks, then draw a diagram of the final block arrangement. In the diagrams, large squares will represent ones, line segments will represent tenths, and small circles will represent hundredths. During the first session students will learn to work division exercises with diagrams. In the second session they will connect symbolic notation with their diagrams.

2. Drawing diagrams: Have students draw a rotated L-frame on their own paper similar to the one on the division mats in Activity 1. The vertical bar should be at least $1\frac{1}{2}$ inches long and the horizontal bar should be at least $2\frac{1}{2}$ inches long in order for the shapes in the diagram to be large enough to see easily.

3. Have them show 1.3 as the divisor by drawing a square and three line segments to the left of the vertical bar, and show 2.78 as the dividend by drawing two squares, seven line segments, and eight small circles to the left of the divisor.

4. Ask students to transfer the dividend shapes to the L-frame in order to make copies of the divisor set. They should mark out the original dividend shapes as they are redrawn under the frame. Two full copies of the divisor set can be made this way, which is shown by two ones or squares drawn in the quotient, thereby producing the following diagram.

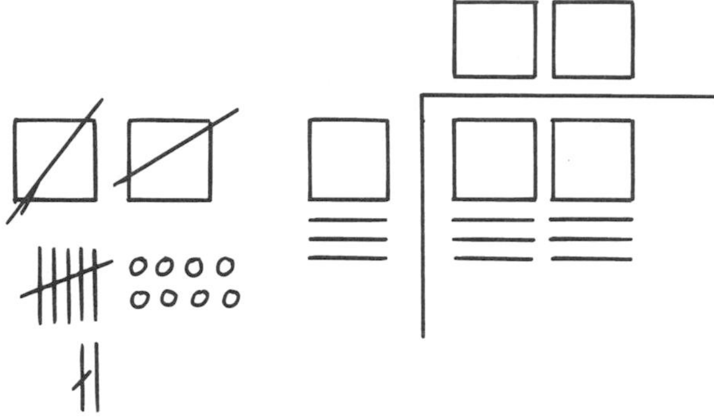

5. Since there are no more ones in the dividend, students must try to make a partial copy of the divisor set from the amounts left. Have them compare the tenth, the largest place value remaining in the dividend, to the one, the larger place value in the divisor. The tenth will make one-tenth of the one. Ask: *Are there shapes left in the dividend that might represent one-tenth of each tenth in the divisor?* Each hundredth (or circle) represents one-tenth of a tenth (or line segment), so a partial set can be drawn, using the tenth and three hundredths from the dividend. Students should mark out the original tenth and three hundredths to show they have been used to make a partial set.

6. Since the partial set is one tenth of the divisor set, a new tenth should be drawn in the quotient above the partial set to show this. Five hundredths should be left in the dividend unused. Have students draw a ring around the remaining five circles or hundredths. Here is the final diagram:

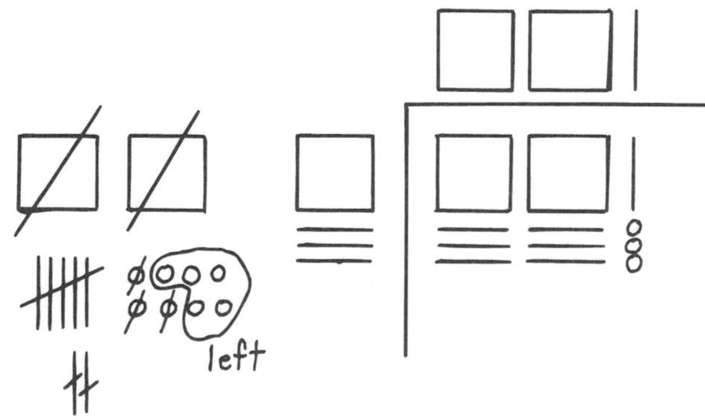

7. Have students record the result in division box format. Since tenths from the dividend were involved in the first copies of the divisor set, students should draw a red, dotted bar vertically between the tenths and hundredths digits in the dividend. The number of full sets made should be written in the quotient to the left of the red bar. The number of partial sets made should be written to the right of the bar. The final recording should appear as follows:

```
              2 . | 1      = 2.1 sets built with 0.05 left
1 . 3 ) 2 . 7     | 8
```

8. Now write other division exercises on the chalkboard for students to draw to find the quotients. Use some of the exercises from Activity 1. The result of each diagram should be recorded in box format like the example in step 7.

9. Describing regions with notation: For the second session, have students draw horizontal and vertical bars in red pencil on their completed diagrams to mark off the different regions of shapes. As done in Objective 4 for the division of whole numbers, the regions should be numbered in the order required by the algorithm and labeled with number sentences that describe the arrangement of the blocks within each region. The diagram shown in step 6 should be marked and labeled as follows:

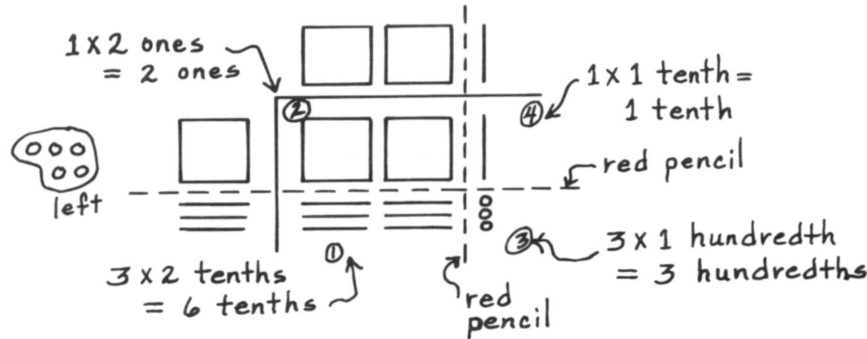

10. After students have labeled all their diagrams, have them transfer the number sentence of each region of an exercise to the box format. Decimals are shown throughout the notation to emphasize the role of place value in the entire division process. The completed box format for the example given in step 9 will appear as follows:

```
              2 . | 1      = 2.1 sets built
1 . 3 ) 2 . 7     | 8
                           (1) 3 × 2 tenths = 6 tenths used
       −2 . 6              (2) 1 × 2 ones = 2 ones used
          . 1   8
                           (3) 3 × 1 hundredth = 3 hundredths used
       −  . 1   3          (4) 1 × 1 tenth = 1 tenth used
          . 0   5          left unused
```

11. As students record their new notation, guide them to observe the ordering of the place values used in the number sentences and in the diagrams. *For example,* if the first group [(1) and (2)] of number sentences begins with tenths, then the next group [(3) and (4)] will begin with the next lower place value, hundredths. Students should also notice the patterns in the factors of the number sentences from the regions. In each pair of number sentences recorded together as a product in the notation, the first factors match the digits of the divisor and the second factor matches the digit in the quotient that is written directly above the right digit of the product being formed by the two sentences. Students should recognize that the patterns found in the decimal notation correspond to those found for whole number division in Objective 4.

12. Once students are comfortable with how the different digits of the divisor and quotient are used to find the products of the regions, encourage them to work some of the exercises, using only the symbolic notation.

Activity 3: HOW MANY WILL THIS MUCH BUY?

(Cooperative Groups)

Materials: Play money (dollars, dimes, pennies)
Sets of problem cards (described in step 1 below)
Paper
Pencils

Management: Teams of 4 students each (30 minutes)

Directions:

1. Give each team a set of 20 problem cards and a set of play money. Each problem card will contain a brief question. For example, a card might have the following: *$2.25 makes how many $0.79?* The set of play money should contain 5 one-dollar bills, 30 dimes, and 30 pennies.

2. Team members should take turns drawing a card from their stack of cards and estimating the answer to the nearest whole number without going over the given total. *For example,* a member might estimate that only two sets of coins worth $0.79 each can be made from $2.25.

3. The next member in order of play then confirms or corrects the suggested estimate by trading and separating $2.25 worth of play money into sets of coins worth $0.79 each. The original total must first be made with the *least* number of coins and bills possible before any trading begins. For example, $2.25 must first be counted out with 2 one-dollar bills, 2 dimes, and 5 pennies. Remember—there are no nickels available in the set of play money!

4. After an estimate has been confirmed, the student who did the checking with the money should draw the next problem card and make an estimate. Another member then confirms the new estimate with the paper money. The cycle continues until time is called.

5. Here are twenty possible problems to write on the cards so that minimal trades with the paper money will be needed:

$4.10 makes how many $1.35?	$5.00 makes how many $2.50?
$2.15 makes how many $0.90?	$1.78 makes how many $0.50?
$4.60 makes how many $2.25?	$4.00 makes how many $3.75?
$0.75 makes how many $0.24?	$4.60 makes how many $1.50?
$4.00 makes how many $1.50?	$0.80 makes how many $0.25?
$2.55 makes how many $0.85?	$5.40 makes how many $2.65?
$0.60 makes how many $0.12?	$5.00 makes how many $2.45?
$0.84 makes how many $0.25?	$2.29 makes how many $0.55?
$3.85 makes how many $1.20?	$2.10 makes how many $0.65?
$3.00 makes how many $0.75?	$1.75 makes how many $0.25?

CHAPTER 4

GEOMETRY AND SPATIAL SENSE

INTRODUCTION

This chapter uses games and simple activities to help students develop an understanding of geometric shapes and angles. In each activity, students physically handle items (e.g., shapes), create their own tools (e.g., a protractor), or play simple games. They learn how to tell the difference between types of the same shape (e.g., triangles), including similarities and congruencies. They also learn perspective by using building blocks and by determining the views when looking at solids from different sides. Through activities that build on each other, students gain familiarity with simple geometric tools and learn how to measure angles.

OBJECTIVE 1: Identify two-dimensional figures by their characteristics.

Activity 1: SHAPE CLUES
(Concrete Action)

Materials: Sets of cardboard shapes (polygons, circles)

Management: Teams of 3–4 students each (20 minutes)

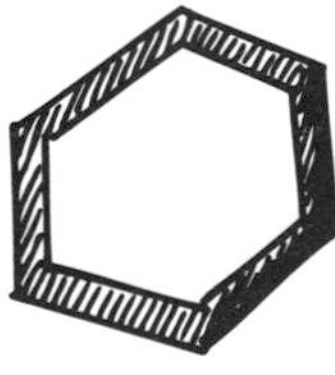 

Directions:

1. Give each team a set of 4–5 polygons and circles cut out of cardboard. The edges of the shapes should be outlined with a wide marker to clearly show that the edges, not the interior, form the shape. Use whatever shapes are being studied at the time.

2. Have each team feel around the edges and then write down what they notice about each shape (number of sides, corners, curves). They should include ways their various shapes are alike and ways they are different.

3. After all teams are finished, have each team select a reporter to share their observations with the rest of the class.

Activity 2: SHAPE TRACE

(Pictorial Action)

Materials: Cardboard shapes
Large sheets of paper

Management: Partners (15 minutes)

Directions:

1. Give each pair of students two different shapes from the previous activity.

2. They are to trace around each shape on a large piece of paper, then write beside each outline the name of the shape and two or three complete sentences describing it. These papers can then be displayed on the classroom wall.

Activity 3: SIDE TALK

(Cooperative Groups)

Materials: Planar Shapes Worksheet G-1.3
Index cards labeled "more than 1 interior," "rounded," "more than 4 segments,"and "4 segments or fewer"

Management: Teams of 4 students each (15 minutes)

Directions:

1. Prepare a deck of 20 cards from tagboard or construction paper for each team. Each card will have a different shape drawn on it. The shapes will be of the types being studied. Additional shapes that might be included are shown on Worksheet G-1.3.

2. Give 4 index cards to each team. The index cards will be labeled as "more than 1 interior," "rounded," "more than 4 segments," and "4 segments or fewer," using one label per card. The index cards are to be spread apart in the center of the team members.

3. The team deals out 5 shape cards per person. The members take turns naming a shape in their hands, then placing that shape's card next to an index card whose label matches a characteristic of that particular shape. Some cards may be able to be placed with more than one labeled card; the choice is then left to the player. The activity is over when all shape cards have been played.

4. This activity can be repeated with different sets of shapes and different labels on the index cards, such as "right angles," "4 or more angles or corners," "opposite sides parallel," etc., depending on the geometric vocabulary of the students.

WORKSHEET G-1.3
Sample Planar Shapes for Side Talk

Cut apart and glue on cards, if desired.

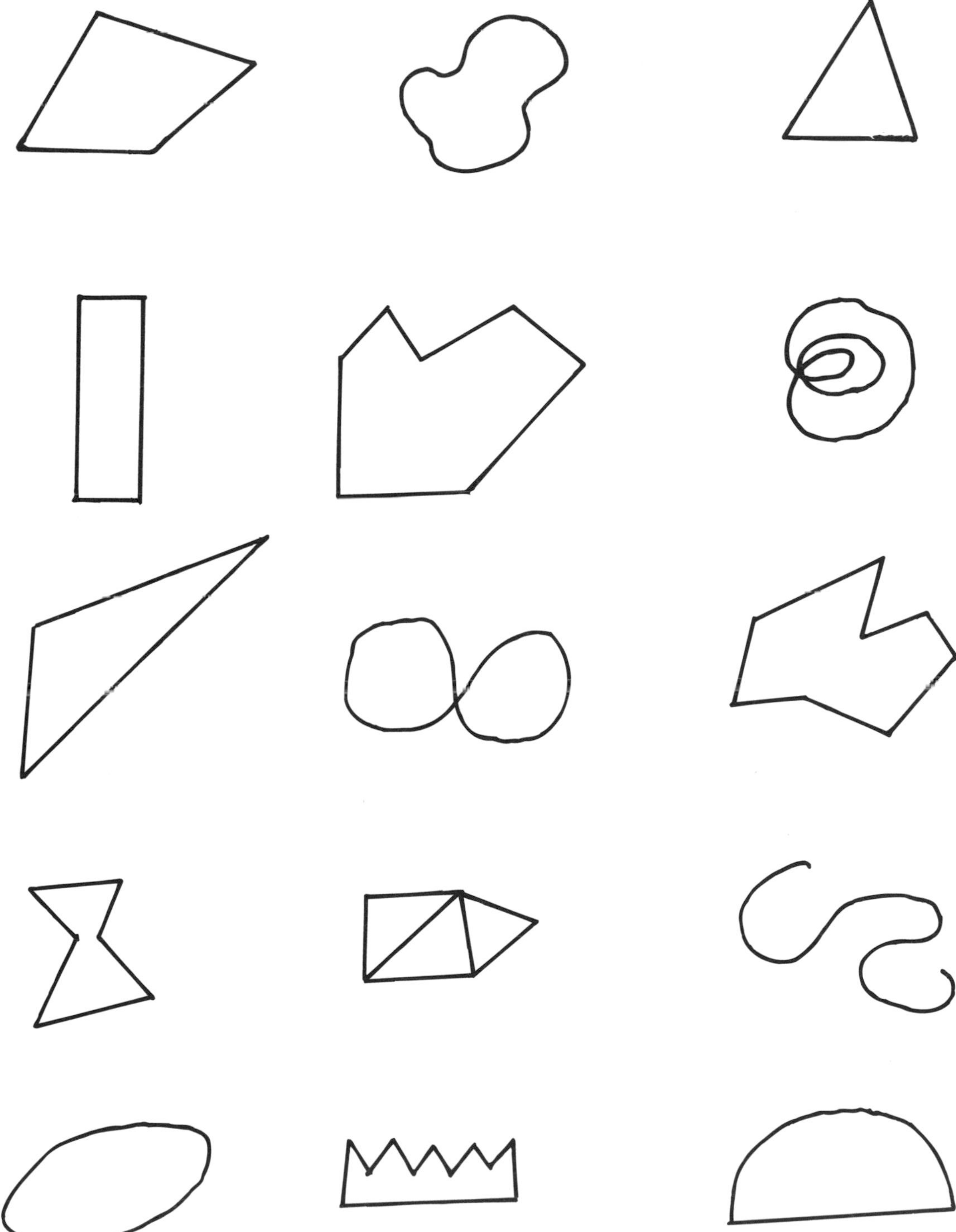

OBJECTIVE 2: Determine symmetry for two-dimensional figures.

Activity 1: FOLDING SHAPES
(Concrete Action)

Materials: Simple, closed curves drawn from Worksheet G-2.1
4 scissors
Red marking pen
Large sheets of paper for mounting shapes
Glue

Management: Teams of 3–4 students each (20 minutes)

Directions:

1. Using Worksheet G-2.1, give each team of students a set of 4–6 different geometric designs (simple, closed curves or polygons, both standard and nonstandard) drawn on 2–3 sheets of paper. No design should contain any line segments or curves that cross each other. Most designs should be symmetrical. Do not make the designs any smaller than 4" × 4" in area; otherwise, they will be difficult to fold and mark.

2. The students should cut out their shapes, then try to fold them so that one half of the design fits exactly on top of the other half. The crease where the successful fold has been made is then drawn over with a red marking pen. Some teams should have a design that has more than one line of symmetry (e.g., circle, diamond). Others should have a design that has no line of symmetry.

3. Each team will make three columns on a large piece of paper, labeling the columns as "one line of symmetry," "no line of symmetry," and "more than one line of symmetry." Each cutout design is to be glued in its correct column.

4. Each team will then share their findings with the entire class. They should tell how many lines of symmetry each design actually has. The circle may be described as having "a lot" or "an infinite number," depending upon the ages of the students.

Activity 2: STAINED-GLASS WINDOWS
(Pictorial Action)

Materials: Centimeter grid paper
Large construction paper
Small mirror (optional)
Glue or tape
Colored marking pens

Management: Partners (15 minutes)

Directions:

1. Give each pair of students a sheet of centimeter grid paper. Have them draw a bold red line segment down the middle-most vertical segment of the grid.

WORKSHEET G-2.1
Sample Shapes for Folding Shapes

Enlarge for student use. The correct number of lines is indicated below each shape for answer key.

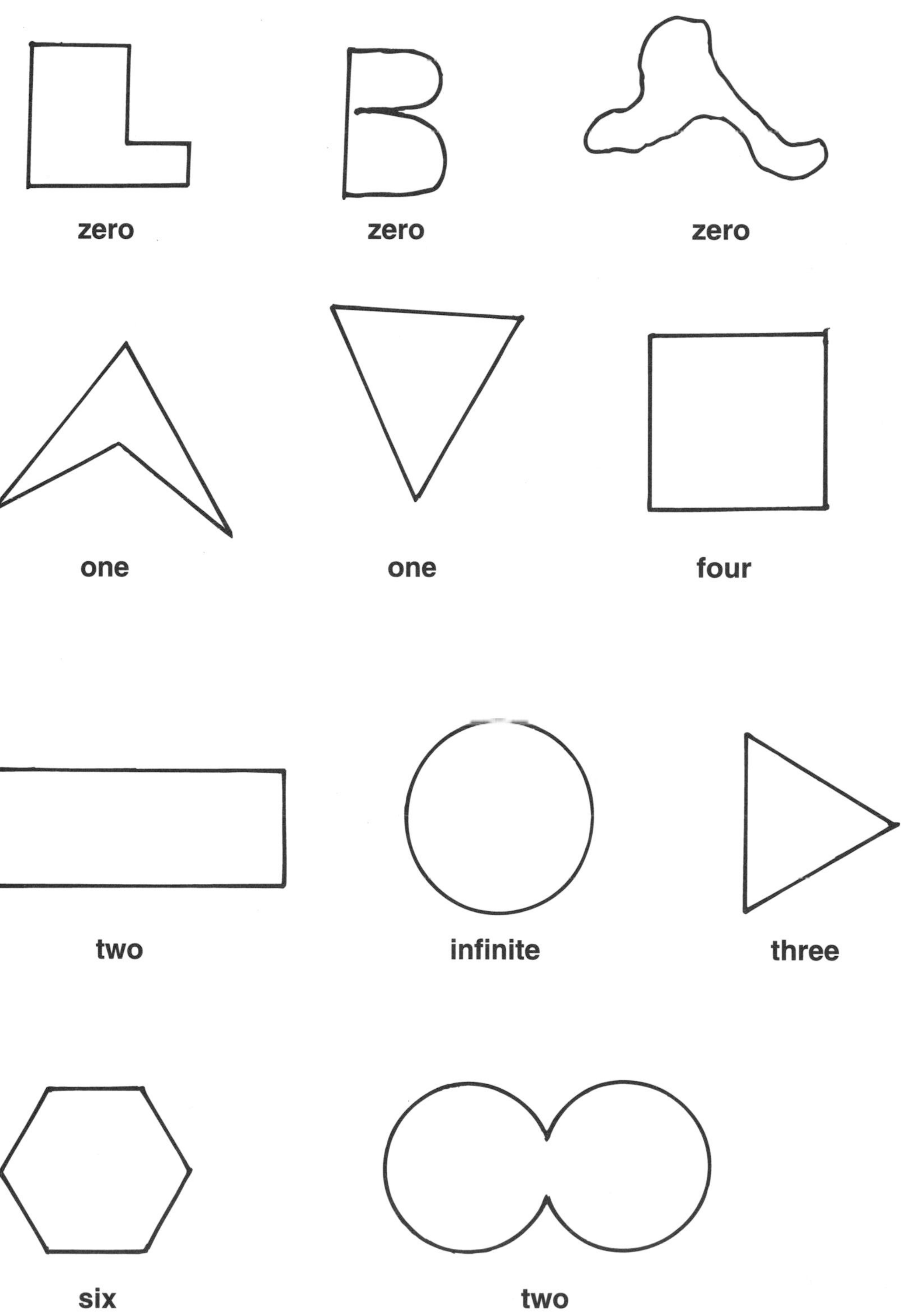

2. They are to color in various squares on the left side of the red bar, using different colors to form a pattern, then copy their coloring pattern on the right side of the red bar in order to create a symmetrical design.

3. They can test their design for correctness by folding it along the red bar to see if the two halves match. A small mirror may also be used to see if the reflection of the first half looks like the second half of the design.

4. As an extra challenge give students another grid sheet. Have them draw a horizontal red bar halfway down the paper in addition to drawing the vertical bar again. Have them color a design that will have both red bars as lines of symmetry. This is more difficult to do; trial and error will be the main strategy used by the students. Encourage students to fold their new design both ways to test for symmetry, or place a small mirror on each bar to compare the different reflections with the drawn design.

5. Have the students cut out their grid designs and mount them on colored construction paper, perhaps with the title "Our Symmetrical Design: A Stained Glass Window" (or some other such title of their own choosing). The designs can then be displayed on a wall in the classroom or hallway.

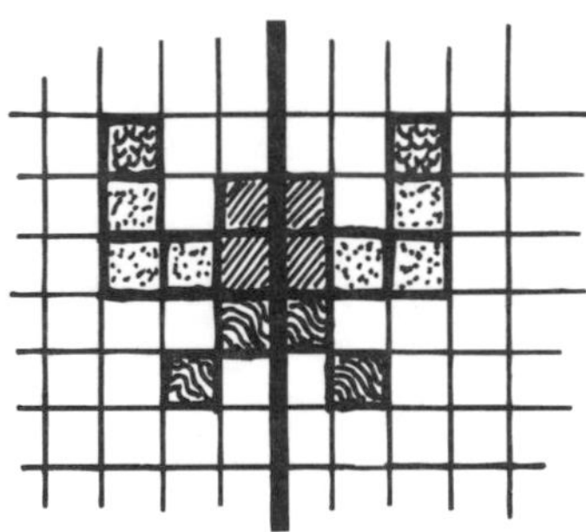

Activity 3: SYMMETRY DOMINOES

(Cooperative Groups)

Materials: Sets of symmetry dominoes (see Worksheet G-2.3 for sample)

Management: Teams of 4 students each (15 minutes)

Directions:

1. Prepare a set of symmetry dominoes for each team by drawing a grid on a large piece of tagboard where each grid cell is approximately 2" × 3". There should be 20 or 24 such cells or dominoes in the total grid before the dominoes are cut apart. While the grid is still whole, draw a different symmetric design across each line segment of the grid. (A line segment is the line of symmetry for its particular design.) Color the designs so that their symmetry is still preserved. The grid can now be laminated, if desired, and the dominoes cut apart at the lines of symmetry, making 20 to 24 dominoes.

2. A team of students shuffles their set of dominoes and distributes them equally. The first player will place a domino in the center of the table.

3. On each turn, a player will try to match edges with other dominoes already played in order to form symmetric designs. If a match cannot be made, the player must pass. The winner is the one who goes out first. Example of domino grid design being constructed:

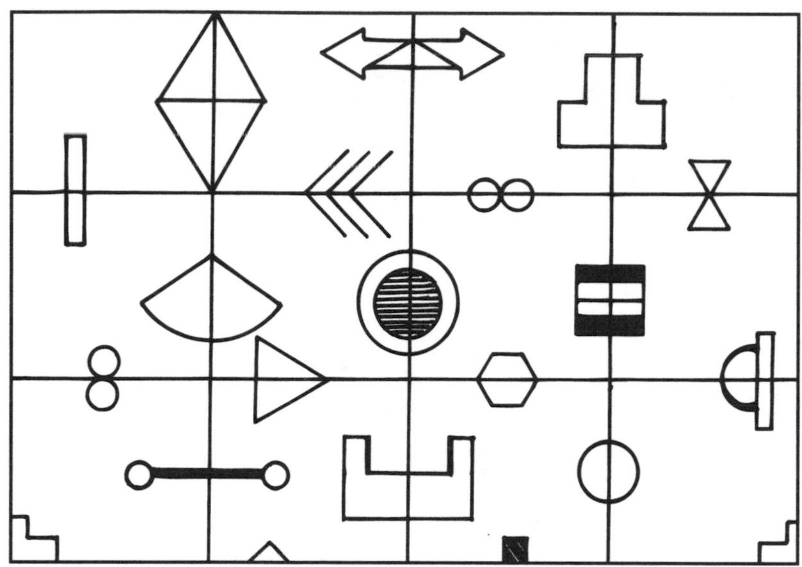

WORKSHEET G-2.3
Sample Set for Symmetry Dominoes

Enlarge, then mount on tagboard and cut apart.

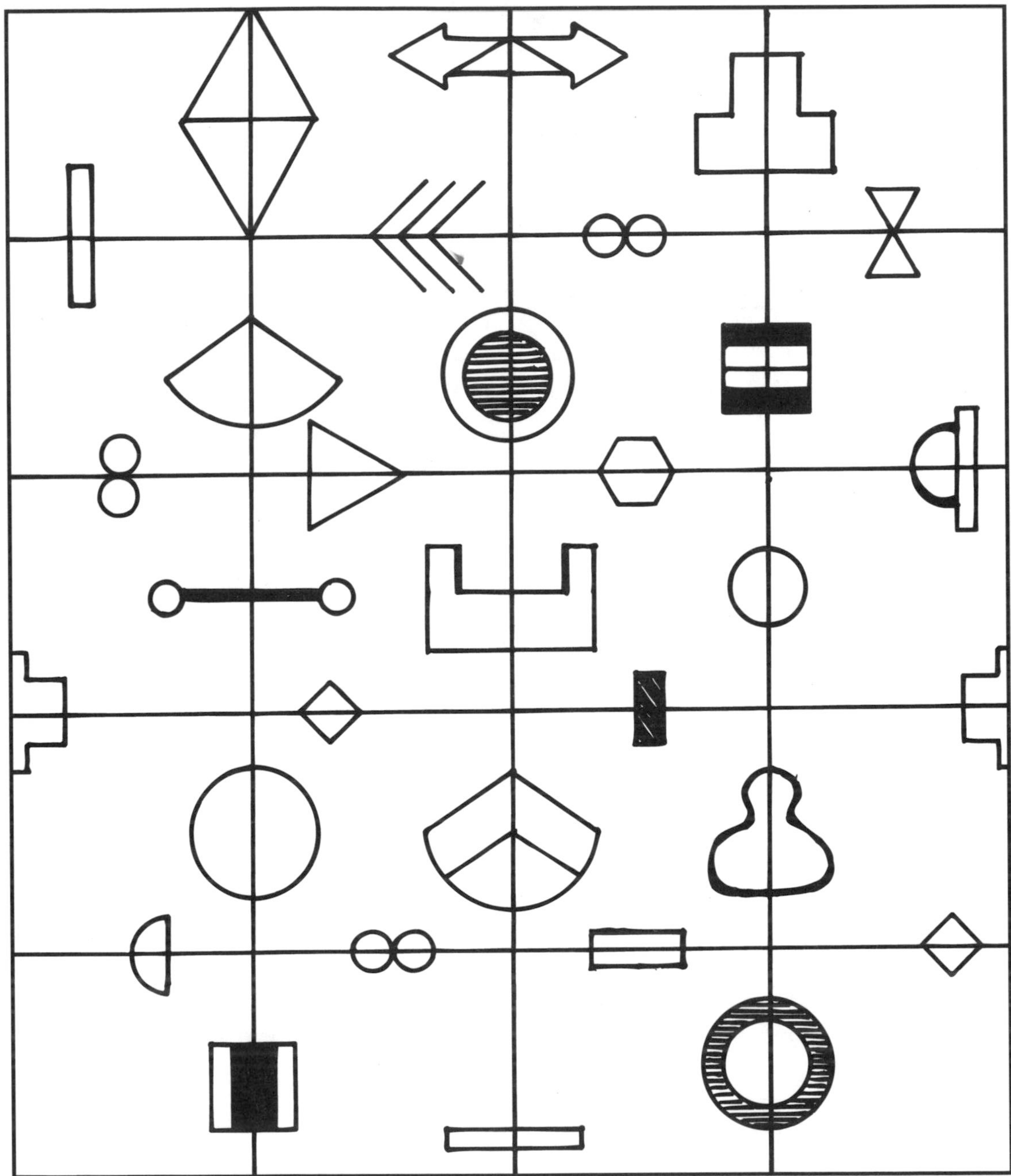

OBJECTIVE 3: Build or select a set of cubes that is a copy of a given solid shape made from cubes also.

Activity 1: BLOCK STRUCTURES
(Concrete Action)

Materials: Building mats
One-inch cubes
(similar materials for teacher)

Management: Teams of 2–4 students each (20 minutes)

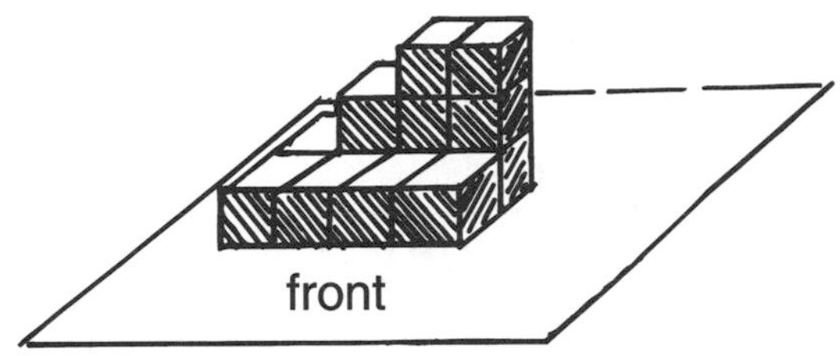

Directions:

1. Give each team of students 15 cubes and a large sheet of plain paper with FRONT labeled along one of the longer edges. The students should place this mat on the desk so that the labeled edge is closest to them (assuming team members can sit beside each other).

2. On a table surface high enough for all students to see easily, tape a similar sheet of paper so that the paper's edge labeled FRONT is toward the students. This helps the students to orient their work with the display surface.

3. Build a multileveled configuration of blocks (make solid with no hidden holes) while the students watch. Ask the students to make an arrangement just like yours with their blocks. The students may need to come closer to look at the stack of blocks from different sides. If the display surface is moveable, it might be slowly rotated so that the students can view the different sides from their desks.

4. As each team finishes, check their work to make sure their copy is accurate. Repeat this process several times as time permits. Build simple stacks at first.

Activity 2: CHANGING THE PERSPECTIVE
(Pictorial Action)

Materials: Worksheet G-3.2
One-inch cubes
Building mats (from Activity 1, Objective 3)

Management: Partners (15 minutes)

Directions:

1. Distribute Worksheet G-3.2 to pairs of students. On each row, there will be 4 figures, each representing a three-dimensional or perspective (corner) view of a stack of blocks. The students are to look at the left-most figure on each row and try to match it to another figure on the same row that is just a different view or rotation of the same stack.

2. If students have difficulty matching a given figure, encourage them to build a copy of the figure on their mat with their blocks. They can then move around or turn their mat to see different views of the stack and try to match to one of the pictures.

Note: There are several resource books available from which to get pictures for this worksheet. (Check commercial catalogs for math works.) Some involve colored rods, while others use stackable cubes.

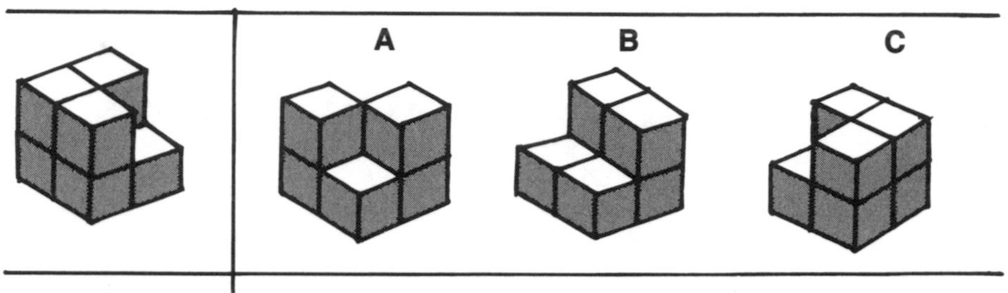

Example of row of choices on worksheet: (C is correct response)

Activity 3: MATCHING STACKS

(Cooperative Groups)

Materials: Sets of 10 cards each (sets described below) made from Worksheet G-3.3
15 one-inch cubes
Building mat and one-inch cubes from Activty 1

Management: Teams of 4 students each (15 minutes)

Directions:

1. Prepare two sets of cards from Worksheet G-3.3 for each team, giving one set to each pair of students on the team. The two sets will be identical and contain 10 cards each. Each card will show a different three-dimensional drawing (corner view) of a stack of blocks similar to those used on the previous worksheet. Give each team cubes and a mat.

2. For each turn, a pair of students will select a card from their set (unknown to the other two students) and build the pictured stack with blocks in the center of the table. The other two students have to decide which card in their own stack was being copied; they should not search through their cards for a match until the builders have completed the new stack.

3. Once the correct card is found, the two matching cards are set aside, and the next pair of students takes its turn at building. The play continues until all cards have been used.

NAME ______________________________ DATE ____________________

WORKSHEET G-3.2
Changing the Perspective

Find the stack of blocks at the right (A, B or C) that is a different view of the stack shown at the far left. Circle the letter of the stack you choose.

	A	B	C
1. 	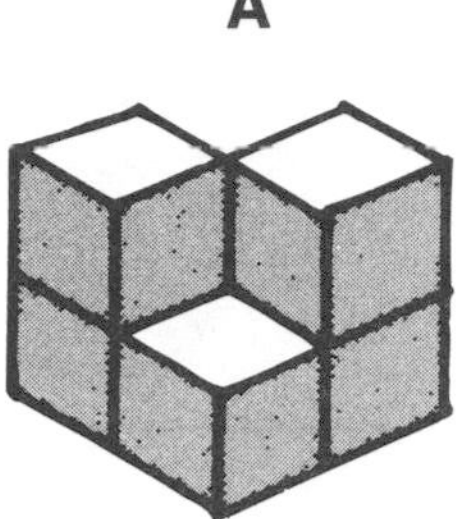		
2. 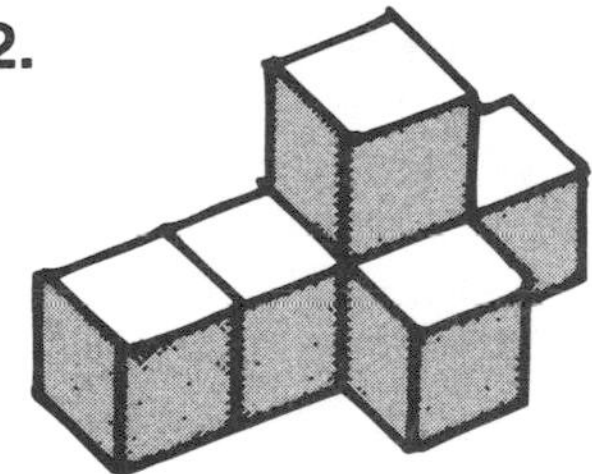	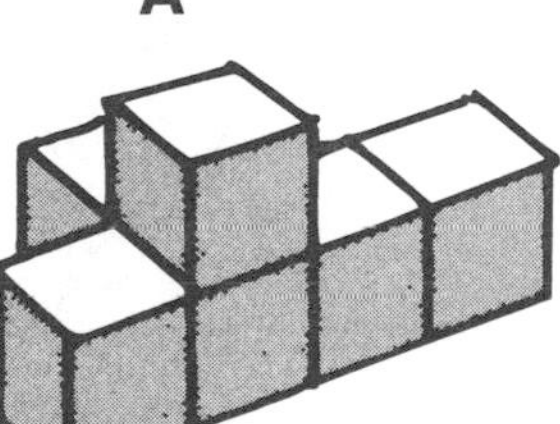	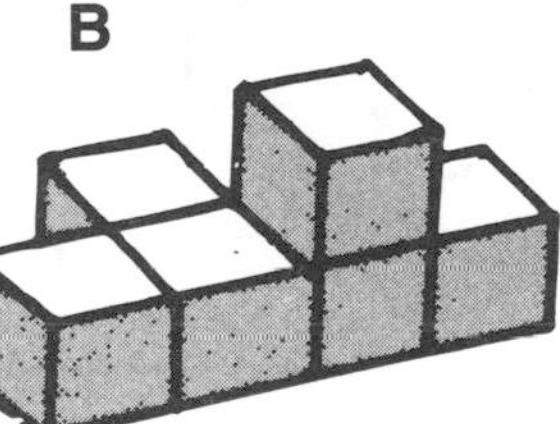	
3. 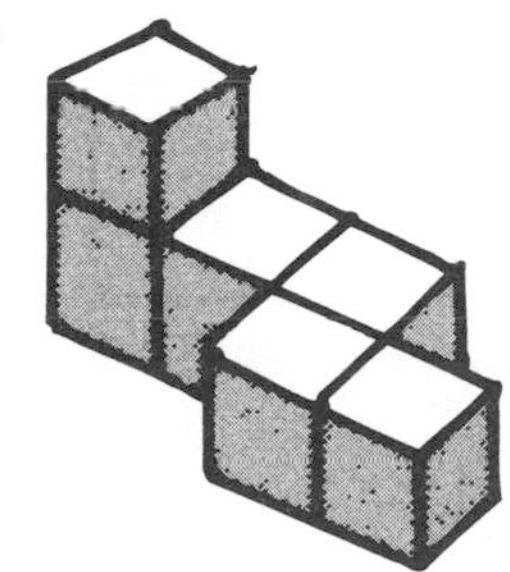		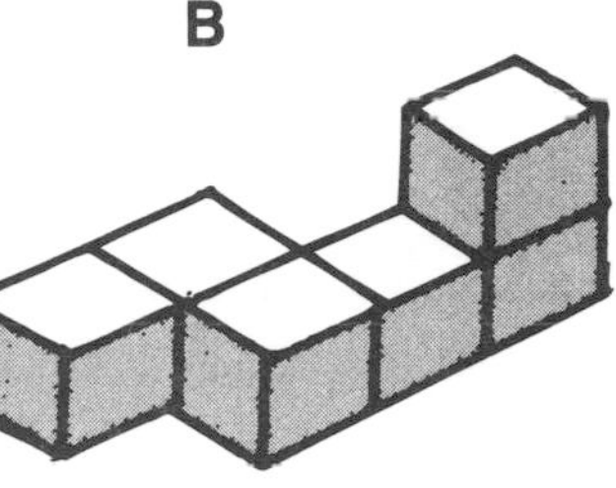	
4. 	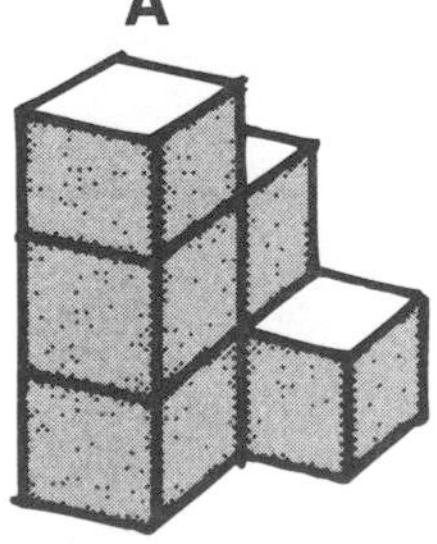		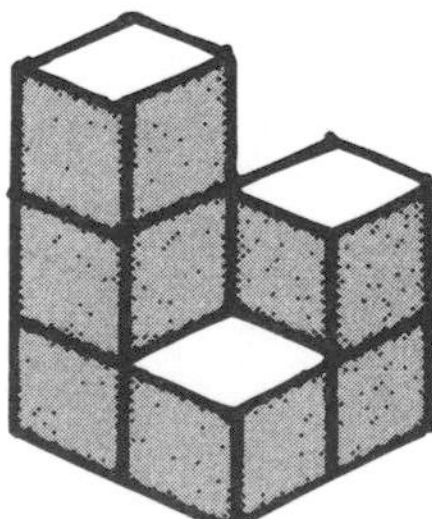

WORKSHEET G-3.3
Sample Cards for Matching Stacks

Enlarge, then mount on tagboard and cut apart.

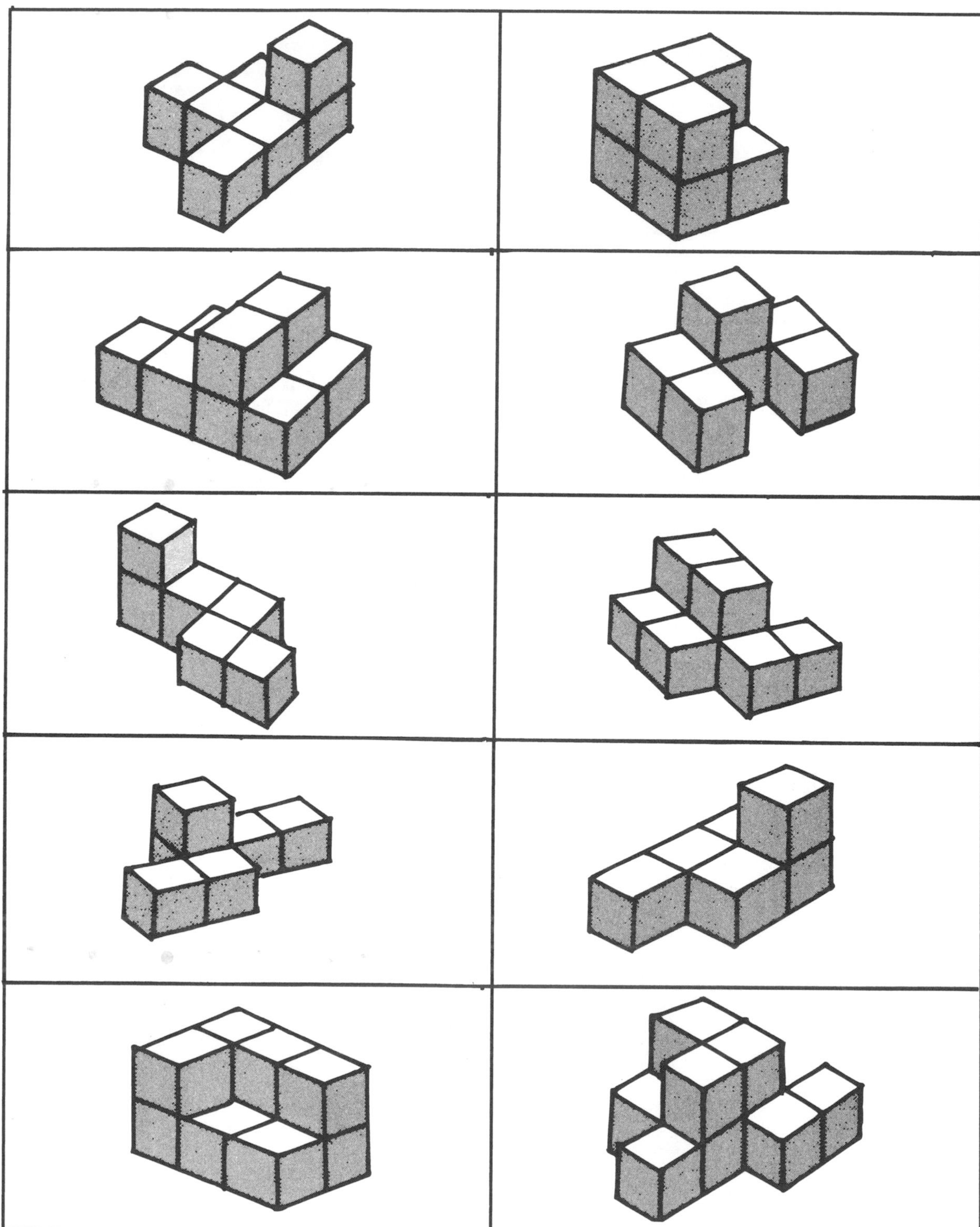

OBJECTIVE 4: Make (a) reflections of a given planar shape, or (b) rotations of a given planar shape

Part (a): Reflections

Activity 1: PAINT REFLECTIONS

(Concrete Action)

Materials: Paint
Large sheets of paper
String (optional)
Black marker

Management: Partners (20 minutes)

Directions:

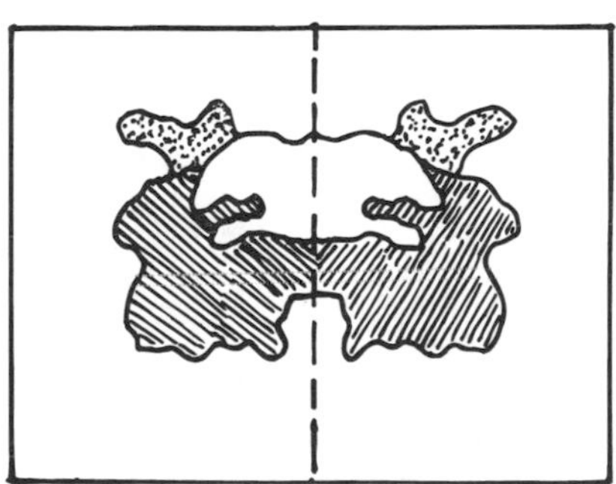

1. Give each pair of students a large sheet of paper folded in half vertically.

2. Have them paint a simple design on the left (or right) half of the paper, using watercolors, tempera, or poster paint. They may want to use several colors in their design.

3. Before the paint dries, have the students fold the other half of the paper over on top of the painted design. This will produce the "reflection" of the design on the other half of the paper.

4. Have the students draw a line segment along the fold line with a black marker or crayon and label the segment as the "reflection line."

5. Let each pair of students show their design and its reflection to the entire class, then display the papers on the classroom wall.

6. Optional: Have students lay a piece of string on the wet paint with one end hanging off the paper. They then hold the other half of the paper down on the paint and string and slowly pull out the string. A beautiful wavy design will be created.

Activity 2: DRAWING MIRROR IMAGES

(Pictorial Action)

Materials: A small mirror
Paper
Pencil

Management: Partners (20 minutes)

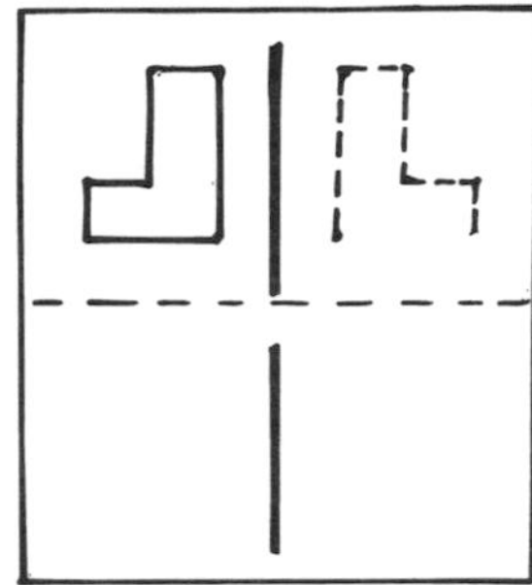

Directions:

1. Give each pair of students a small mirror (at least 3" × 4" in size) or a plastic Mira® (commercially available).

2. Have them fold a blank sheet of paper in half horizontally, then draw a vertical 4-inch line segment (or *bar*) in the middle of the upper half of the paper and again in the lower half. These will serve as the reflection lines.

3. Have students draw a simple shape on one side of the bar on the top half of the paper. The shape does not have to touch the bar. They should then place the mirror on the bar so that they see the reflection of their shape.

4. While looking in the mirror as needed, they should try to draw the mirror image onto the paper behind the mirror. The mirror image should be the same distance from the bar as the original shape is.

5. To check their work, students can fold their paper along the bar to see if the two shapes match completely. Since the drawing is done free-hand, the students may have to adjust their first draft of the mirror image after they check their work by folding.

6. Once students have completed the first image, have them draw another shape on the lower half of the paper and find its mirror image or reflection across the given line segment.

7. Note that the original shape combined with its reflection forms an overall design that is symmetrical.

Activity 3: BUILD-REFLECT
(Cooperative Groups)

Materials: Centimeter grid paper
Colored centimeter cubes
Red marker
Small mirrors (optional)

Management: Teams of 4 students each (20 minutes)

Directions:

1. Give each team 40–50 colored centimeter cubes and a piece of centimeter grid paper with a red bar drawn horizontally across the middle of the grid.

2. Two of the students will arrange colored centimeter cubes on the grid spaces in some way on one side of the red bar. The cubes may or may not touch the red bar.

3. The other two students will try to build the reflection of the arrangement on the other side of the red bar (the "reflection line"). The correctness of the "reflection" can be checked visually or by placing a small mirror on the red bar to see if the mirror image matches the colored cube design behind it.

4. The two pairs continue playing, rotating who "builds" and who "reflects."

Part (b): Rotations

Activity 1: ROTATING DESIGNS
(Concrete Action)

Materials: Paper (approximately 12" × 12")
Colored markers
Scissors
3" × 3" tagboard pieces
Coffee stirrers
Thumbtacks
Large cardboard mat (approx. 15" × 15")
Tape

Management: Partners (20 minutes)

Directions:

1. Have each pair of students cut a small, irregular shape (about 2" × 2" in size) out of tagboard.

2. A plastic coffee stirrer (about 5" long) should then be taped across the middle of the cutout so that the stirrer extends only off one side of the shape. (See figure.)

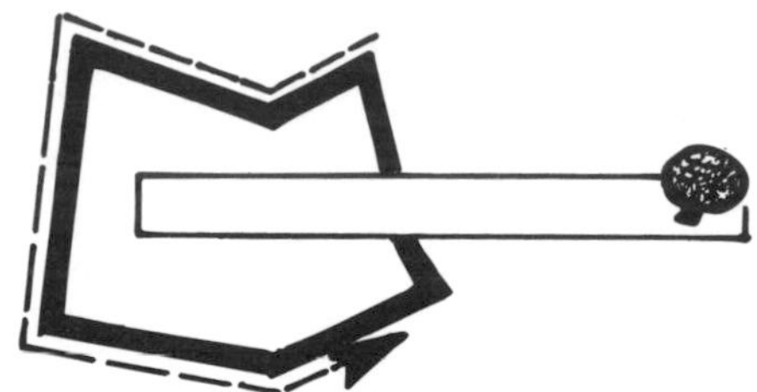

3. Give each team a large square sheet of paper (12" × 12"). Have them fold it in half three times, *lightly* crease the folds, then unfold the paper. The creases will subdivide the paper into 8 sectors measuring 45 degrees each.

4. Have the students tape down the paper onto a large piece of cardboard and mark the point in the center of the paper where all the creases meet. Pin the extended end of the stirrer to the center point on the paper with a straight pin or thumbtack. The cutout should be under the stirrer next to the paper. Position the coffee stirrer on top of a crease.

5. Have the students trace around their cutout, then rotate the stirrer clockwise to the next crease (the stirrer controls the rotation) and trace again. The students should keep turning the shape to the next crease and tracing until the shape reaches its original position.

6. The cutout and stirrer can now be removed and all the drawn shapes colored in some way. Using rotations of the same shape, the students have now created a design that has 45-degree rotational or turn symmetry. The center point is the turn center of rotation.

Example of design made with coffee stirrer:

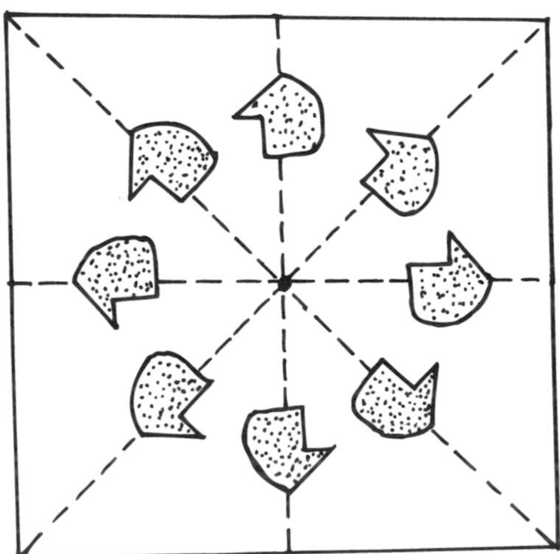

7. Let each team show their design to the class. Discuss how the rotations of the same shape differ from each other within the final design. Ask: *If you flipped your shape over and traced again to make another design, would your new design look like your first one?* (probably not unless shape being traced has a line of symmetry)

Activity 2: TRACE-AND-TURN

(Pictorial Action)

Materials: Rotation Worksheet G-4.2
Tracing paper
Pencil

Management: Partners (20 minutes)

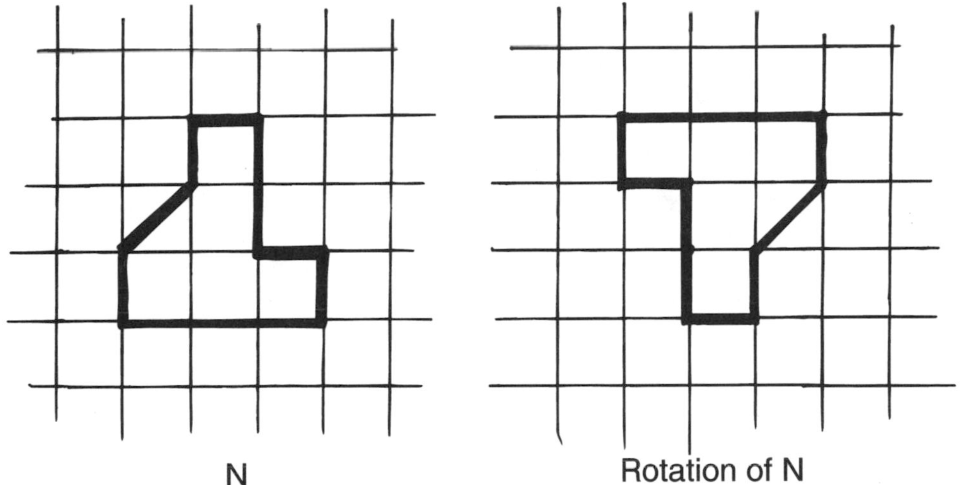

Directions:

1. Give each pair of students a copy of Worksheet G-4.2 that has three different shapes drawn in the left half of the paper, one shape above the other with space between each two shapes, (and the shapes are labeled as A, B, and C).

2. For shape A, have the students turn their worksheet upside down and study A in this new "upside down" position.

3. Students should then turn the worksheet upright again and try to draw A on the grid at the right in its "upside down" position. They may need to turn the worksheet several times while they draw.

4. Have students check their new drawing by tracing the original shape onto tracing paper, then carefully *rotating* the tracing paper clockwise about 180 degrees to see if the traced shape will fit on top of the new shape drawn on the grid. They can make corrections as needed.

5. Have the students label the new drawing as "the rotation of A."

6. Repeat the procedure for shapes B and C.

NAME ______________________________ DATE ____________________

WORKSHEET G-4.2
Trace-and-Turn

Draw an "upside-down" (rotated) image of each shape.

A.

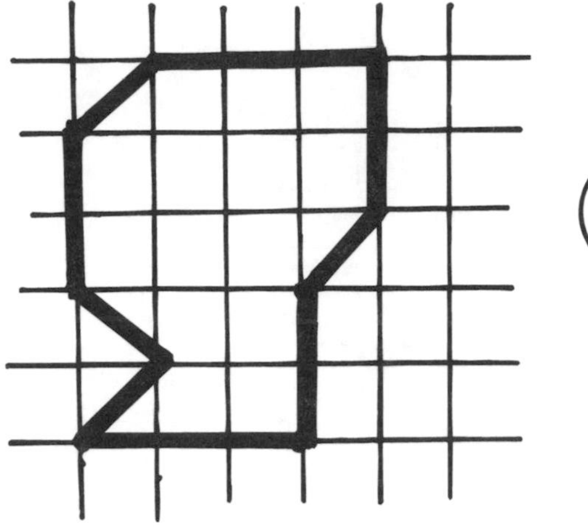

B.

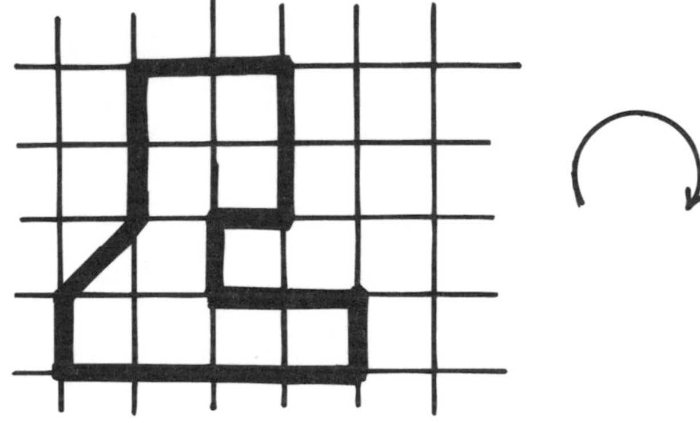

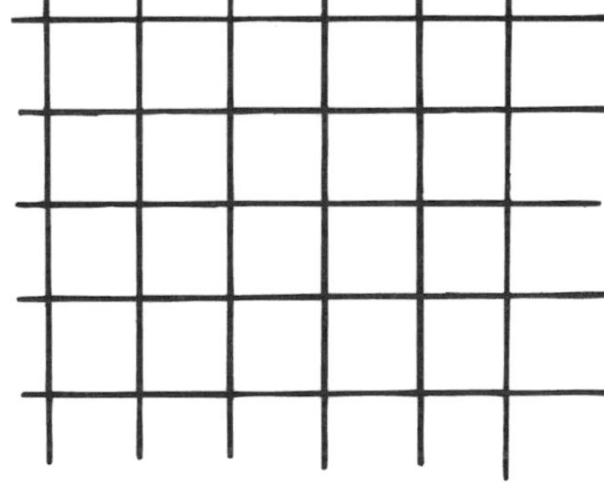

C.

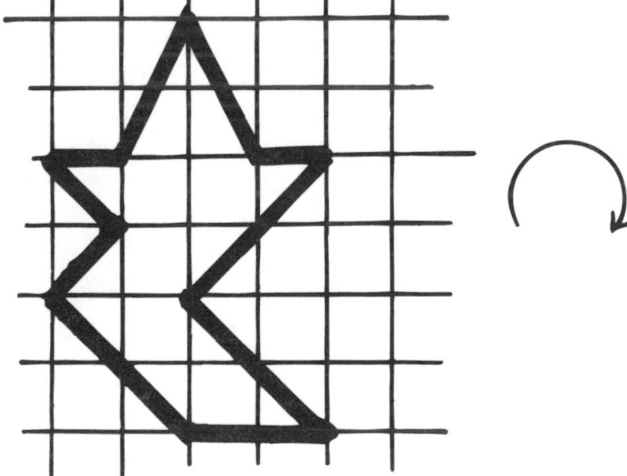

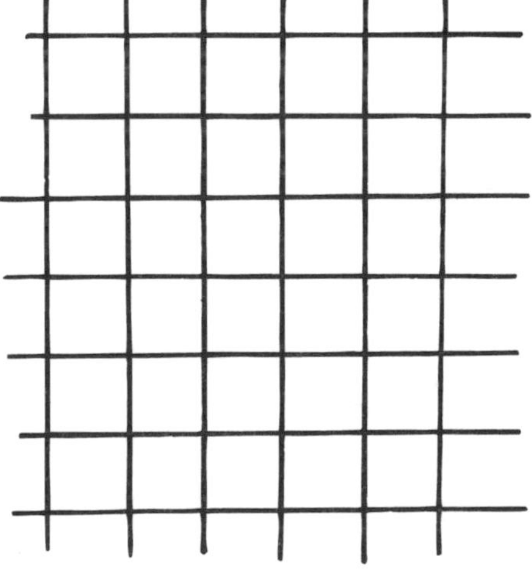

Activity 3: ROTATION CONCENTRATION

(Cooperative Groups)

Materials: Sets of "Concentration" cards (described below; see Worksheet G-4.3 for samples)

Management: Teams of 4 students each (20 minutes)

Directions:

1. For each team prepare a set of "Concentration" cards (an even number; approximately 40 cards per set) using Worksheet G-4.3. Four, six, or eight cards can have the same shape drawn on them, but in different rotated positions. Thus, it is possible to have several pairs of cards involving the same shape. To help with the proper recognition of rotations, draw a bar across the top edge of each card.

2. During the playing of the game, students are not allowed to turn the cards in an effort to match the shapes in the same orientation. All cards must be placed with their marked "tops" in the same direction on the table.

3. A team will shuffle their cards, then place them face down on the table in rows and columns.

4. They will take turns turning two cards face up to see if their shapes are rotated forms of each other (tops of cards must remain oriented in same direction). If they are, the player keeps the pair of cards. If not, the cards are turned over in their original locations, and another player gets a turn. Once a player states that he or she has a match, the other players are allowed to rotate the two cards to see if it is a true match. A card can *only* be *rotated, not flipped over,* to make it match another card. The player with the most pairs at the end is the winner.

WORKSHEET G-4.3
Sample Cards for Rotation Concentration

Enlarge, then mount on tagboard and cut apart.

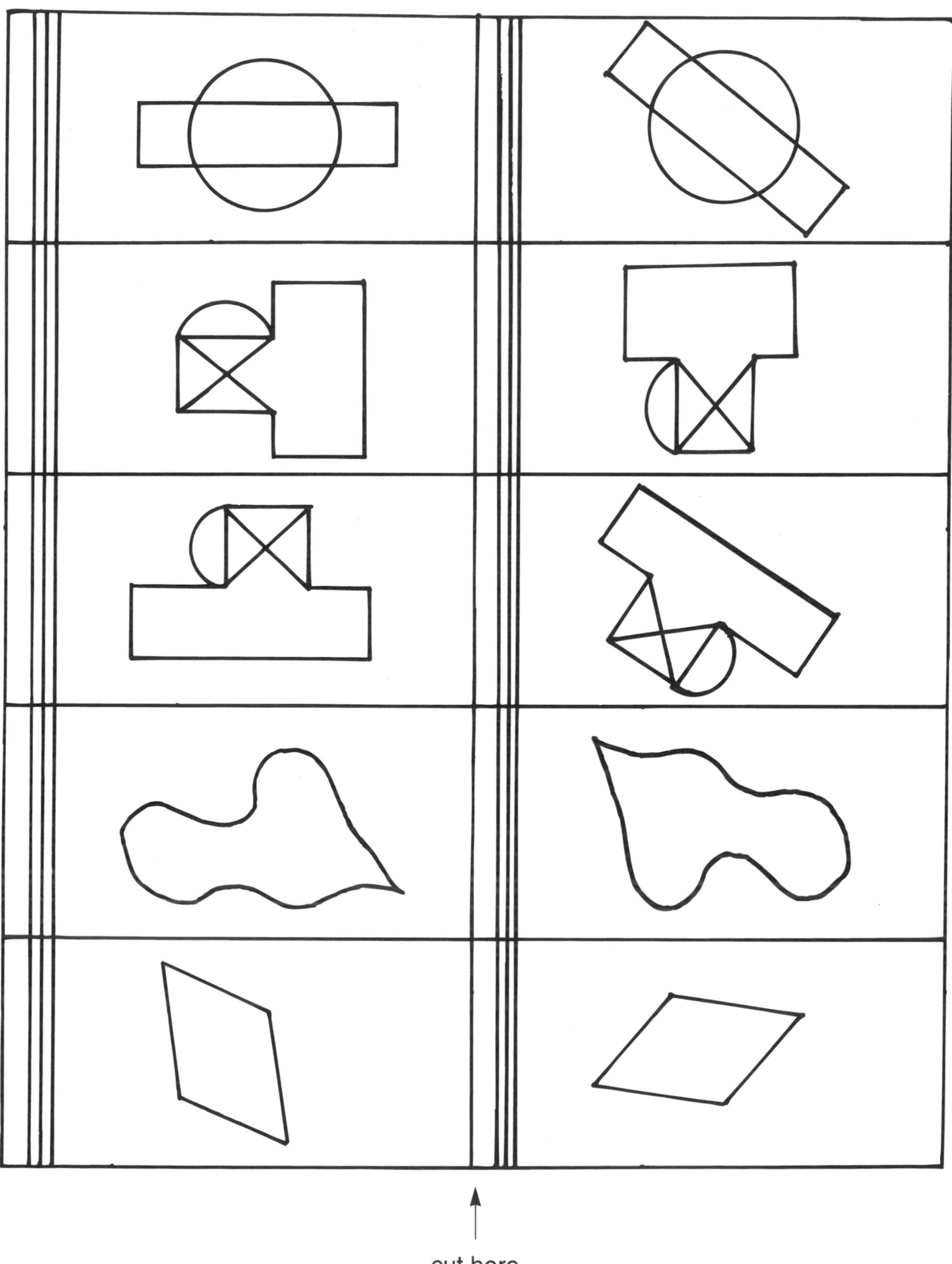

OBJECTIVE 5: Classify angles as right, acute, or obtuse angles.

Activity 1: ANGLE SEARCH

(Concrete Action)

Materials: Flexible drinking straws
3" × 5" index cards
Red pencils
Paper
Pencils

Management: Partners (20 minutes)

Directions:

1. Give each pair of students a 3" × 5" index card and a bendable or flexible plastic drinking straw with a paper "arrowhead" taped at each end. Tell them to bend the straw until it fits around one of the corners of the index card. The straw now forms a "right angle."

(bent straw)

2. Have partners go around the classroom quietly and locate corners of objects or furniture whose edges may or may not fit or line up to the bent straw. In order to test for a fit, the vertex of the corner must fit into the vertex of the straw and one edge of the corner must line up with one part of the straw. If the other edge of a corner lies inside the straw's outline, the angle of the corner is "acute." If the edge lies outside the straw's outline (but does not form a straight angle), the angle of the corner will be "obtuse." The students should try to find two or three examples of each type of angle. (*Note*: A "flattened corner" or an angle measuring 0 degrees is not "acute.")

3. Have the students draw a sketch of each object found, outline its angle in red pencil, and write the name of the angle under the drawing. Each angle should have arrowheads drawn on its rays. An object should be drawn from a viewpoint that uses the surface of the paper as the plane of the object's angle. That is, the drawing should not distort the angle.

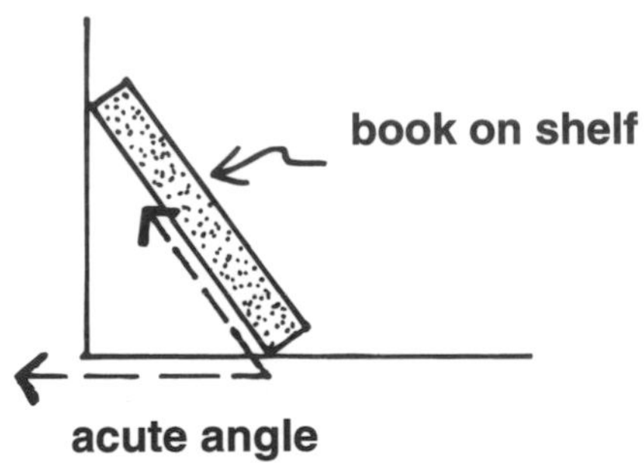

4. As students work, it may be necessary to compare their straw with the index card once in a while to make certain the straw is still in a 90-degree position.

5. If time permits, have some of the students share their findings with the class.

Activity 2: ANGLE CHECK

(Pictorial Action)

Materials: Worksheet G-5.2
Flexible straws or index cards

Management: Partners (10 minutes)

Directions:

1. Give each pair of students Worksheet G-5.2 with a variety of angles drawn on it.

2. Have the students use either an index card or a bendable straw positioned at 90 degrees to place on each drawn angle to compare the angle to a right angle. The vertex of the bent straw or corner of the index card must match the drawn angle's vertex, and at least one side length of the card or straw "angle" must align with a ray of the drawn angle. The other side length should be near or at the drawn angle's other ray. If the other ray of the drawn angle lies inside the straw or card angle, the drawn angle is acute; if outside, it is obtuse. A "perfect fit" indicates a right angle.

Example of obtuse angle measured with 90-degree straws:

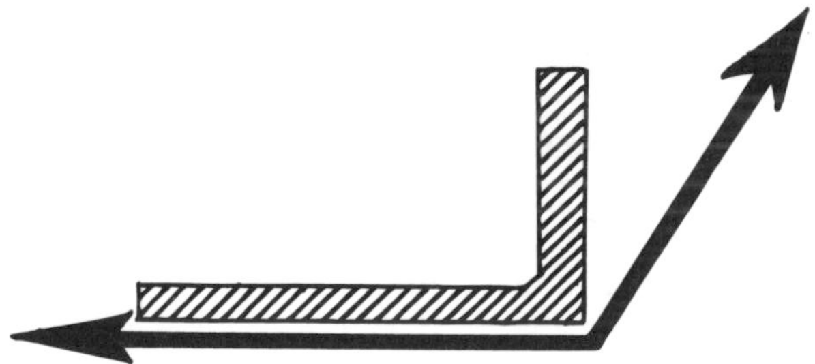

3. Have the students write the correct angle name (right, acute, or obtuse) on the worksheet under each angle tested.

Note: In preparing worksheets, draw acute and obtuse angles so that their measures differ from 90 degrees by 10 degrees or more. This will make the comparing process easier for the students. Be sure to draw arrowheads on the rays of the angles.

NAME ______________________________ DATE ____________________

WORKSHEET G-5.2
Angle Check

Identify each angle below as **right, acute,** or **obtuse**.

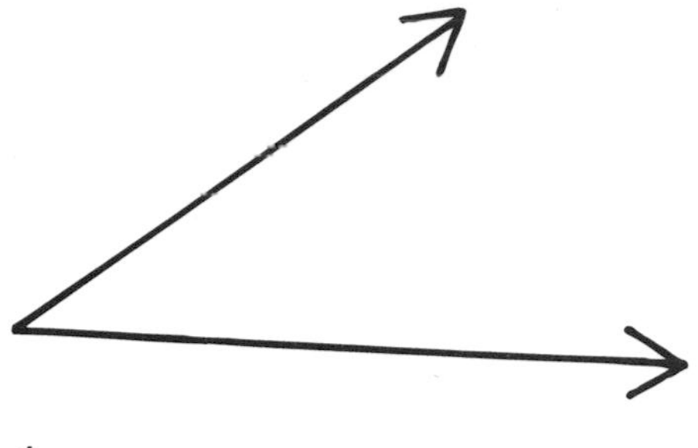

1. ____________

2. ____________

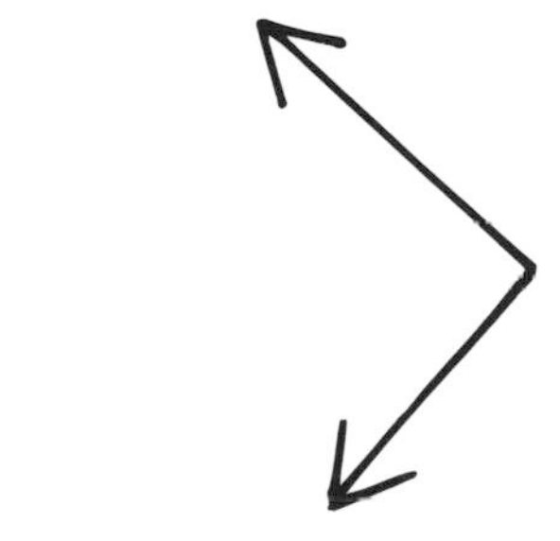

3. ____________

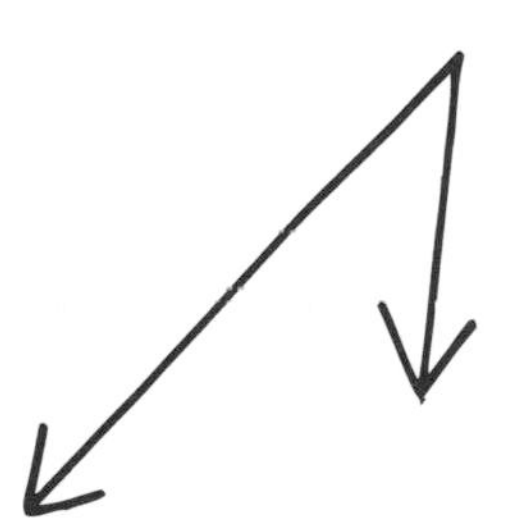

4. ____________

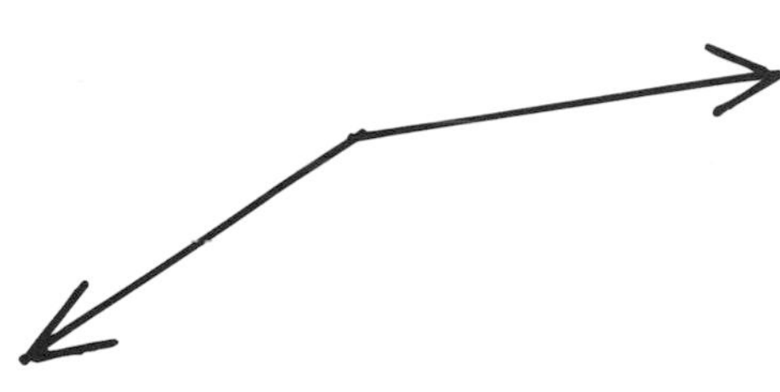

5. ____________

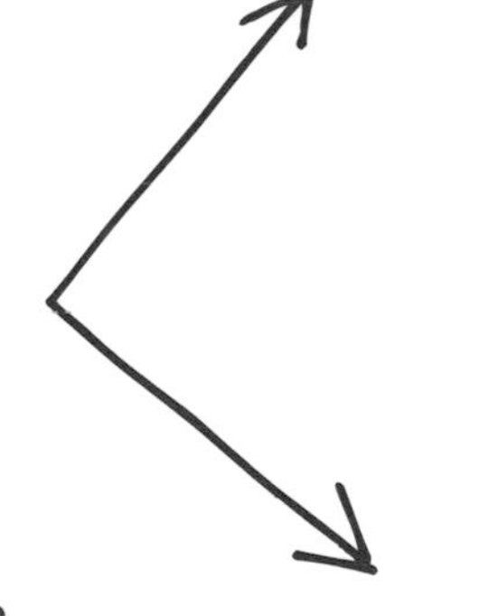

6. ____________

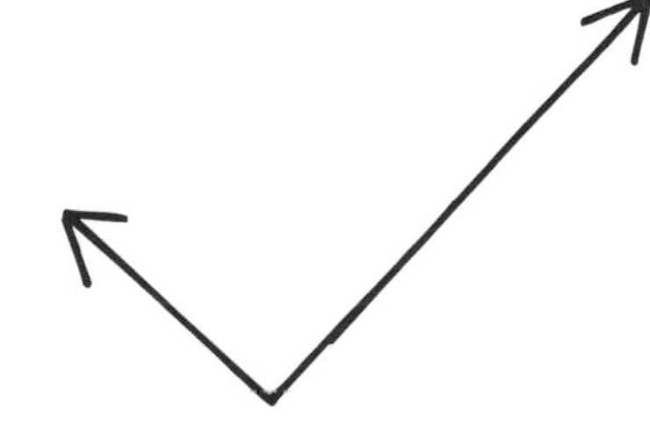

7. ____________

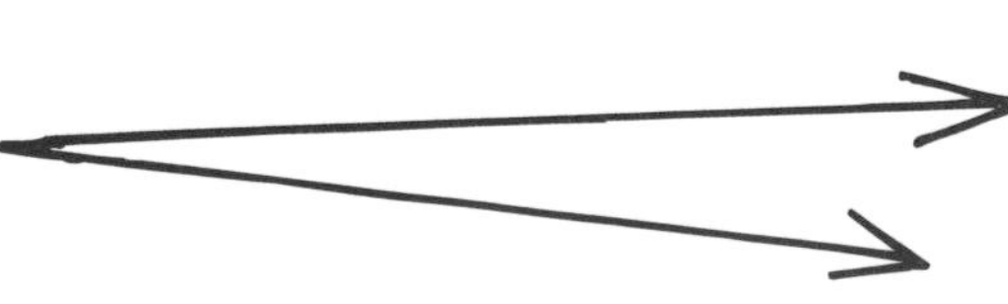

8. ____________

Activity 3: ANGLE SORT

(Cooperative Groups)

Materials: Decks of cards (described below; see Worksheet G-5.3 for samples)
Index cards labeled "right angle," "acute angle," "obtuse angle," and "neither"

Management: Teams of 4 students each (15 minutes)

Directions:

1. Using Worksheet G-5.3, each team prepares a deck of 36 cards: 10 containing acute angles, 8 with right angles, 11 with obtuse angles, and 7 with lines, single rays, simple curves, or two line segments joined at their endpoints. Have only one angle or figure per card. Remember to draw arrowheads on all rays and lines. Vary the measures and orientations of the angles on the cards. Give each team 4 index cards labeled "right angle," "acute angle," "obtuse angle," and "neither."

2. Team members will shuffle and hand out all cards, and spread the 4 name cards apart in the center of the table.

3. For each turn, a player will place a figure card in a stack next to its correct name card; for example, an acute angle will be stacked next to the "acute angle" card, but a line will be stacked next to the "neither" card. If a player does not select the correct name card for a certain angle, other players may assist, but they must give reasons for their choice. The game is over when the players have placed all their cards.

WORKSHEET G-5.3
Sample Cards for Angle Sort

Enlarge, cut apart and glue on cards, if desired.

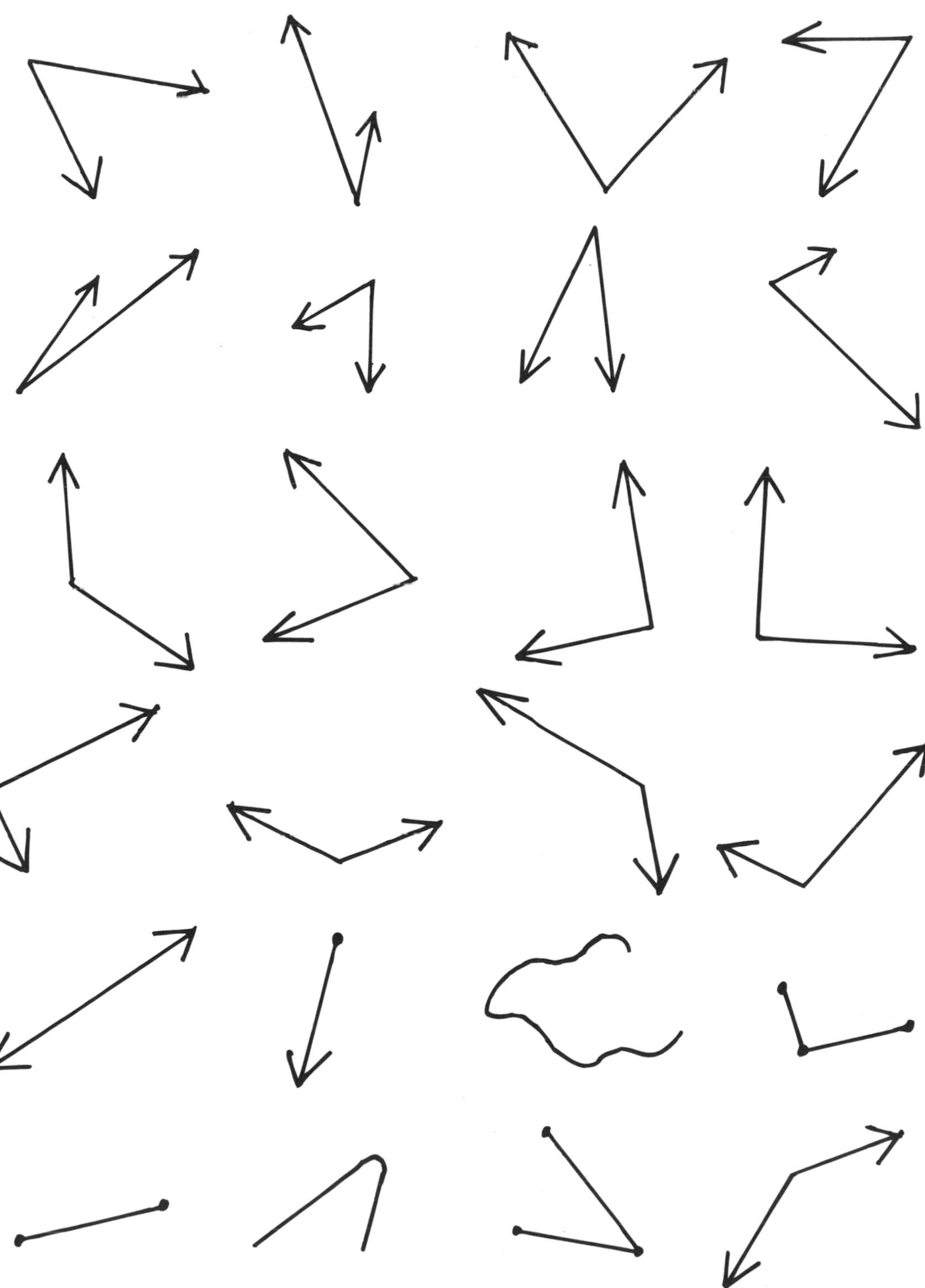

OBJECTIVE 6: Classify pairs of lines as intersecting, parallel, or perpendicular lines.

Activity 1: BUILDING LINES
(Concrete Action)

Materials: Tinkertoy™ rods and connectors (or Play-doh® with small straws or coffee stirrers)
Tagboard arrowheads
Small index cards
Tape

Management: Teams of 3–4 students each (20 minutes)

Directions:

1. Give each team a bag of construction materials. (Several different types of construction materials are available commercially.)

2. *For intersecting lines:* Have students assemble the materials to make models of intersecting lines, varying the lengths of the different line models (to reinforce the idea of infinite length for a line) and their angles of intersection. Lengths can be varied by attaching several straws or sticks together end-to-end. Tape tagboard arrowheads to the ends of straws or sticks to indicate the ends of lines or rays.

3. *For parallel lines:* Have each team place or tape several 3" × 5" index cards end to end on their desk and build line models to fit along each of the two long sides of the "rectangle" made of cards. Discuss how the shortest (perpendicular) distance between the two lines always remains the same (here, the width of one index card), no matter where on the two lines this distance is measured. Repeat this construction, using a width of 2 index cards for the new "rectangle."

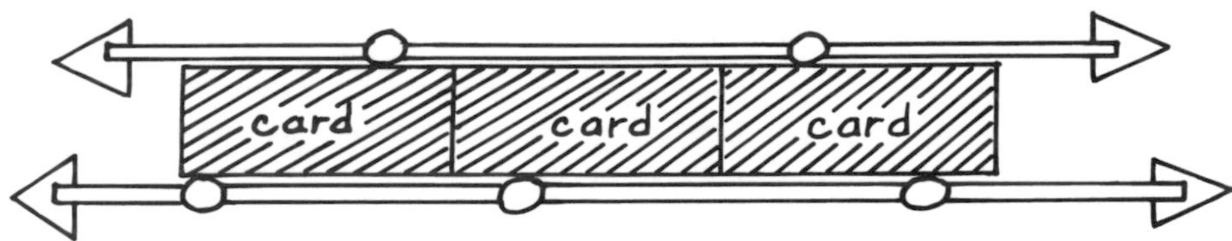

4. *For perpendicular lines:* Have each team build models of intersecting lines so that an index card will fit in the space or "corner" formed by each adjacent pair of rays; that is, 90-degree angles have been formed by the intersecting lines.

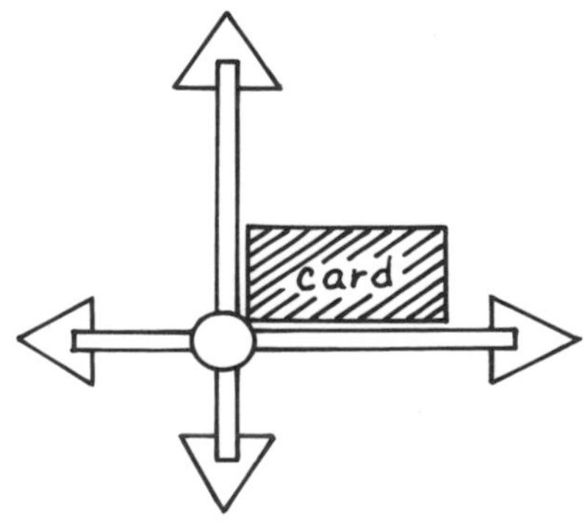

5. After each team has built one or more models of each type of line pair, have the students draw a diagram of each type and write a description of a real-world example of each. For example, intersecting lines might be represented by two straight roads that cross each other at any angle. Parallel lines might be represented by railroad tracks or horizontal fence railings. Perpendicular lines could be represented by the two main cross pieces of a kite's frame or fencing wire attached horizontally to a vertical fence pole in the ground.

6. Have each team share its examples with the class. Accept any example that generally appears to have the characteristics with which it is being associated.

Activity 2: FINDING LINES IN THE REAL WORLD

(Pictorial Action)

Materials: Old magazines
Scissors
Glue
Colored markers
Posterboard or large construction paper

Management: Partners (15 minutes)

Directions:

1. Give each pair of students an old magazine that contains a large variety of pictures.

2. For each type of lines, have the students find two pictures in which that particular pair (or more) of lines is present in some way. They should outline the "lines" directly on the pictures, using a brightly colored, wide marking pen. The pictures should be cut out, mounted on posterboard or large sheet of construction paper, and labeled for the type of lines identified in each picture.

3. Each poster can then be displayed in the classroom.

Activity 3: BUILD-DRAW-TELL

(Cooperative Groups)

Materials: For each team:
A pair of dice
A list of numbered instructions (step 1 below)
6–8 sheets of unlined paper
Ruler
Pencil
Tinkertoy™ rods and connectors with paper arrowheads (or similar construction materials)

Management: Teams of 4 students each (15 minutes)

Directions:

1. Prepare a list of special numbered instructions for each team. Here is a possible list:

1) Draw a pair of intersecting lines. [or use parallel or perpendicular]
2) Build a pair of perpendicular lines. [or use parallel or intersecting]
3) Build 3 lines that intersect at the same point.
4) Draw 3 lines intersecting at the same point.
5) Tell in words what parallel lines are.
6) Name this figure or set of points. (Show diagram of 2 parallel lines.)
7) Draw 4 lines parallel to each other.
8) Build 3 lines parallel to each other where the distance between one pair of adjacent lines is greater than the distance between the other pair of adjacent lines.
9) Build 2 lines that are each perpendicular to a third line.
10) Draw 2 lines that are each perpendicular to a third line.
11) Name this set of lines. (Show diagram of 3 lines intersecting at same point.)
12) Tell in words what perpendicular lines are.

2. Each student will take turns rolling the dice and finding the sum of the two numbers rolled. The player will then find the numbered item on the list of instructions that matches the sum and follow those particular instructions. The other team members will judge the correctness of the player's response. (A definition sheet with sample diagrams of the different types of lines might also be provided for each team to help them check their answers, but it should be used only as a last resort.)

3. Be available to settle any disputes that might occur within a team!

OBJECTIVE 7: Identify congruent figures.

Activity 1: GEOBOARD MATCH
(Concrete Action)

Materials: Geoboards with rubber bands

Management: Partners (20 minutes)

Directions:

1. Have each pair of students work together with their geoboards. One student will make a 2-dimensional shape on his or her geoboard with a rubber band(s), and the partner will try to make an exact copy on the other geoboard.

2. During the activity select various pairs of students to show their congruent shapes to the whole class and tell why they are congruent (i.e., look alike in shape, one is an exact copy of the other, etc.).

3. If the geoboard is too difficult for some students to manipulate, give the students several 2-dimensional shapes cut from tagboard and have them find pairs that match or fit each other in shape and size. Include some irregular shapes; for example, concave polygons.

Activity 2: DOT DRAW
(Pictorial Action)

Materials: Rectangular or hexagonal dot paper
Pencils

Management: Partners (15 minutes)

Directions:

1. Have pairs of students take turns with one person drawing a 2-dimensional shape on rectangular (or hexagonal) dot paper and the other making a congruent copy of it on the same sheet of paper.

2. Monitor the students as they work in order to check their drawings for correctness. Encourage them to draw some irregular shapes.

3. If some students have difficulty judging or copying shapes on dot paper, give them cutout patterns of shapes to trace onto a sheet of paper, positioning their tracings in different orientations. Have each pair of students work with 3–4 different patterns.

Activity 3: FINDING CONGRUENT SHAPES

(Cooperative Groups)

Materials: Centimeter grid paper
Colored markers

Management: Teams of 4 students each (20 minutes)

Directions:

1. Give each pair of students a sheet of centimeter grid paper. Have them draw 4–5 different shapes and also draw a congruent copy of each shape somewhere else on the grid paper, but in a different orientation from its original. Have them color the interiors of their shapes. Congruent shapes may or may not be the same color.

2. When all grid papers are full of pairs of scattered congruent shapes, have students trade papers with other students. Then partners can try to find pairs of congruent shapes on the new paper, labeling each two shapes that match with the same letter of the alphabet. For example, the first congruent pair found will be labeled with the letter A.

3. When all students are finished, have them return the papers to their original owners, who will check for correctness.

OBJECTIVE 8: Identify similar figures.

Activity 1: ENLARGING SHAPES
(Concrete Action)

Materials: Sets of commercial pattern blocks (minimum amounts needed per set: 10 green triangles, 10 orange squares, 2 yellow hexagons, 2 blue parallelograms, 6 red trapezoids)
Record sheets (Worksheet G-8.1)
Pencils

Management: Teams of 3–4 students each (30 minutes)

Directions:

1. Give each team a set of pattern blocks and Worksheet G-8.1 that contains four recording tables.

2. Ask each team to take out a triangle, a square, a trapezoid, and a hexagon from their set of blocks. Have them find the recording table for each shape on their worksheet.

3. Using the edge length of a single green triangle as 1 unit, the students should now count the number of units along each side of the triangle and record these numbers in the small shape column of the triangle's table as sides 1, 2, and 3. (All 3 sides should have a length of 1 unit each.)

4. Students should repeat this process for the square, trapezoid, and hexagon. (square's 4 sides, 1 unit each; trapezoid, 1 unit each for 3 sides, 2 units for fourth side; hexagon's 6 sides, 1 unit each)

5. Now ask the students to build onto their one triangle, enlarging it until *at least* one side of the new triangle is 3 units long. Different shapes may be used as needed. (The words "at least" should be used to prevent telling students what *all* the final dimensions will be.) The larger triangle should have the same shape as the single triangle. Students must decide when their new triangle meets this condition. To help them with this, have the teams locate the corresponding sides and angles of the small and large triangles, then compare them by placing the single triangle on top of the larger one and rotating it until it has the same orientation as the larger one.

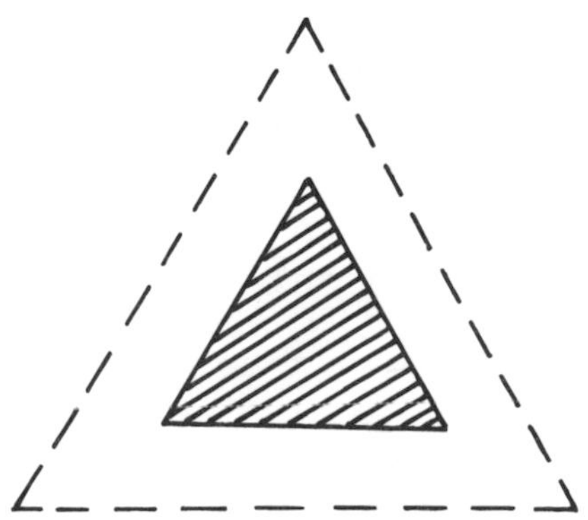

6. The side lengths of the enlarged triangle should now be recorded in the large shape column of the table. (3 units per side)

7. Have students count around the two triangles to find the number of units in their perimeters, then record these amounts on the table.

8. Have each team repeat the above enlarging process with the other three shapes (a square, a trapezoid, and a hexagon) and find their perimeters, recording all the data on their respective tables. For variety in the total data, enlarge the shapes as follows:

(a) the large square has *at least* one side 3 units long;

(b) the large hexagon has *at least* one side 2 units long; and

(c) the large trapezoid has *at least* one *shorter* side 2 units long. *Note*: Longest side must equal twice a shorter side in length to be similar to the small trapezoid.

9. Once all enlarged shapes have been built and the tables completed, ask the teams to compare the numbers in the small shape column with the numbers in the large shape column. Do this for both the side lengths and the perimeters.

10. Have each team write 2–3 sentences about what they have noticed about the original small shape and its enlargement. The two shapes are said to be similar to each other. What conditions exist for two shapes to be similar?

11. Have one person from each team share their sentences with the whole class. [Possible observations: (a) Each side of the large shape is a multiple of its corresponding side of the small shape, and all sides of the same small shape have been multiplied by the same number (factor) to equal the sides of the large shape, e.g., all have been doubled or all have been tripled. (b) Corresponding angles of the two shapes have the same measure. (c) The perimeter of the large shape is a multiple of the perimeter of the small shape, or the small shape's perimeter has been multiplied by the same number (factor) as its sides. (a) and (b) are the major conditions for two shapes to be similar.]

12. To finalize the definition, ask each team to build two rectangles that do not have the same shape, but where one is seemingly larger than the other. For example, the angles will be equal in measure but the large rectangle's width might be twice that of the smaller one and its length three times that of the smaller.

13. Have the teams determine whether these two new shapes have the same angle and side relationships found in the previous pairs they built. They will not have; therefore, they are not *similar* to each other. *Note*: For older students, this activity can be extended to include a comparison of area for the triangle, trapezoid, and hexagon. Find out how many green triangles (the non-standard unit of area) will fill each small shape and its enlarged shape. Compare the area factor to the side length factor for the same pair of shapes. (Example: Using the orange square as the unit of area for the pair of squares built, the side length factor is three, but the area factor is nine.)

NAME ______________________ DATE ______________

WORKSHEET G-8.1
Record Sheet for Enlarging Shapes

Write about what happens when two shapes have the same shape but one is larger than the other.

(triangle)	Small shape	Large shape
Side 1	1 unit	
Side 2		
Side 3		
Perimeter		

(square)	Small shape	Large shape
Side 1		
Side 2		
Side 3		
Side 4		
Perimeter		

(hexagon)	Small shape	Large shape
Side 1		
Side 2		
Side 3		
Side 4		
Side 5		
Side 6		
Perimeter		

(trapezoid)	Small shape	Large shape
Side 1		
Side 2		
Side 3		
Side 4		
Perimeter		

Activity 2: COMPARING AREAS OF SIMILAR SHAPES

(Pictorial Action)

Materials: Worksheet G-8.2
Pencils
For demonstration: a transparency of rectangular dot paper and transparency pen

Management: Partners (30 minutes)

Directions:

1. Give each pair of students a copy of Worksheet G-8.2 of rectangular dot paper marked off into four quarters by a vertical bar down the middle of the sheet and a horizontal bar drawn midway down the sheet. Each quarter of the sheet has a small, simple, closed polygon drawn (mostly with right angles) at the top of it. This shape is to be enlarged (side lengths doubled, tripled, or quadrupled) to another similar shape. For example, if the given shape is a 1×2 rectangle, one might double the width and double the length to draw a 2×4 rectangle. Demonstrate this procedure, using a transparency grid on an overhead projector.

2. Have all students enlarge the first shape by *doubling* each of its side lengths. Ask them to see how many of the smaller shape can be drawn inside the larger shape (for the doubled sides, four smaller shapes will fit inside the larger one). The positioning of copies of the smaller shape within the larger one will vary. Encourage students to share their different arrangements.

3. Repeat the enlarging and comparing processes with the other three shapes on the worksheet. Sometimes the smaller shape may have to be dissected or rearranged in order to fill the larger space completely.

Example of one shape with its sides tripled to make the larger shape (9 of the small shapes fit inside the large one):

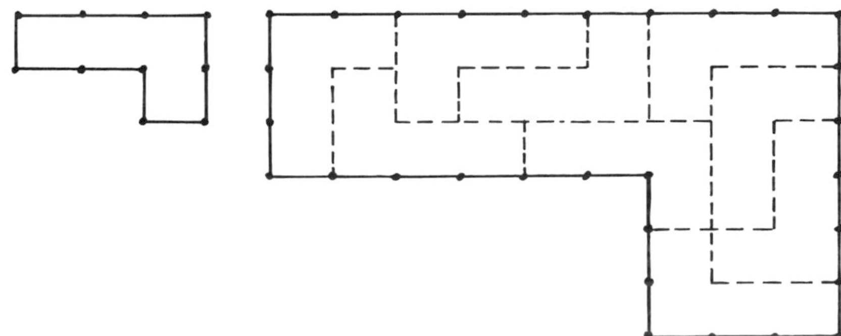

4. Discuss the results with the students. What happens with shapes whose sides have been tripled (quadrupled)? How many of the smaller shape will then fit inside the larger one? (nine of them if sides are tripled; sixteen, if sides are quadrupled) Ask different students to work on the overhead projector to show the class how they made their enlarged shapes and how they placed their smaller shapes. Techniques will vary. (Some students may need to trace and cut out several paper copies of a smaller shape to place on top of the enlarged shape before *drawing* the final arrangement.)

NAME ______________________________ DATE ____________________

WORKSHEET G-8.2
Comparing Areas of Similar Shapes

A. Enlarge by doubling.

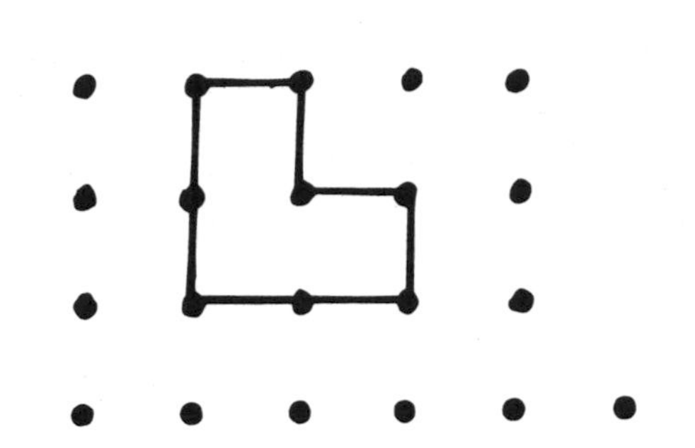

B. Enlarge by doubling.

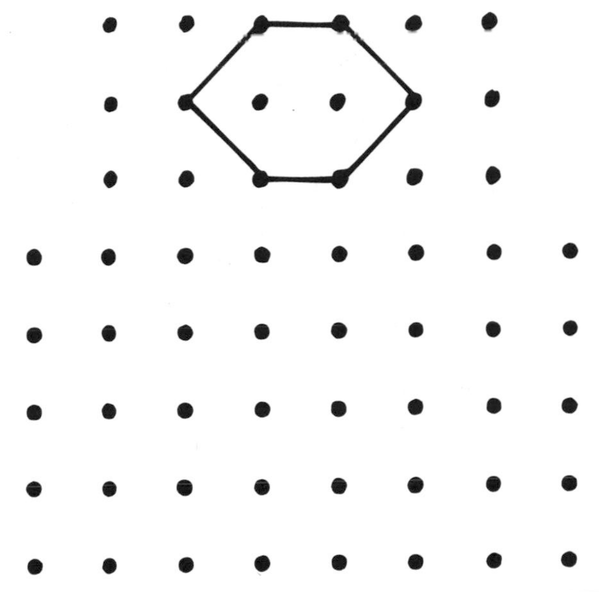

C. Enlarge by tripling.

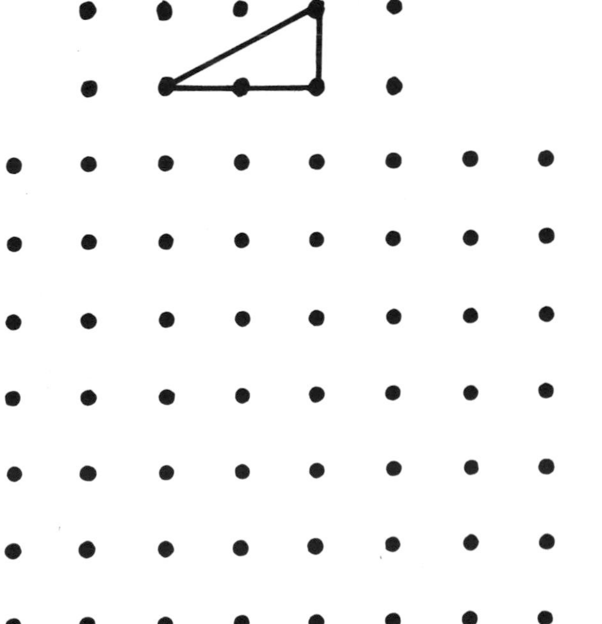

D. Enlarge by quadrupling.

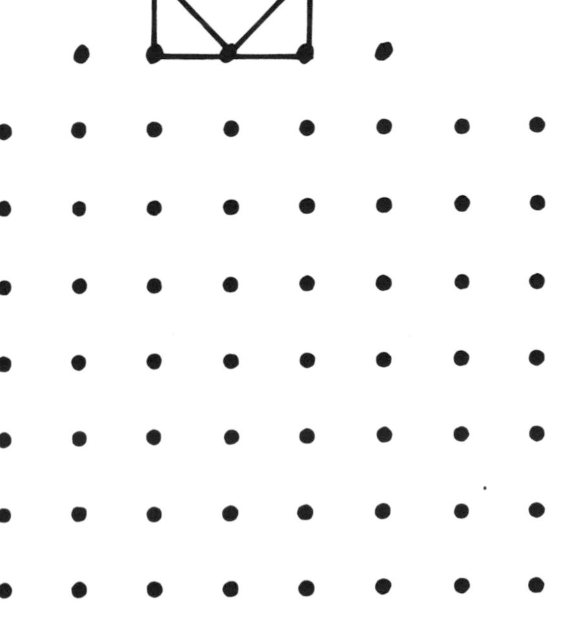

Activity 3: SIMILARITY SEARCH

(Cooperative Groups)

Materials: Decks of cards (described below)
Worksheet G-8.3

Management: Teams of 4 students each (20 minutes)

Directions:

1. Give each team a deck of 20 cards made from Worksheet G-8.3: 5 triangles, 5 rectangles, 5 (nonrectangular) parallelograms, and 5 simple concave hexagons. Each shape can be drawn on millimeter or $\frac{1}{2}$ centimeter grid paper, then cut out and glued on a tagboard game card. For each type of shape, 3 of the shapes will be similar to each other but will vary in size, and the other 2 shapes will not be similar but will have an appearance close to that of the first 3. Also for each type of shape, label each card with an identifying letter A–E for ease of discussion.

2. Each team will work together to decide for each set of 5 shapes which ones are similar and which ones are not. Students will be able to use the grid markings to compare the corresponding lengths of the different shapes.

3. If desired, each team might write a summary of their findings and explain why certain shapes were similar while others were not. (If some students have difficulty *visually* comparing angle measures and side lengths, allow them to make tracings of the shapes, which can then be moved from card to card as needed.)

Worksheet G-8.3.
Sample Set for Similarity Search

Enlarge, cut apart, and glue on cards, if desired.

[Matches—triangles A, C, E; rectangles A, B, D; parallelograms B, C, E; hexagons A, D, E]

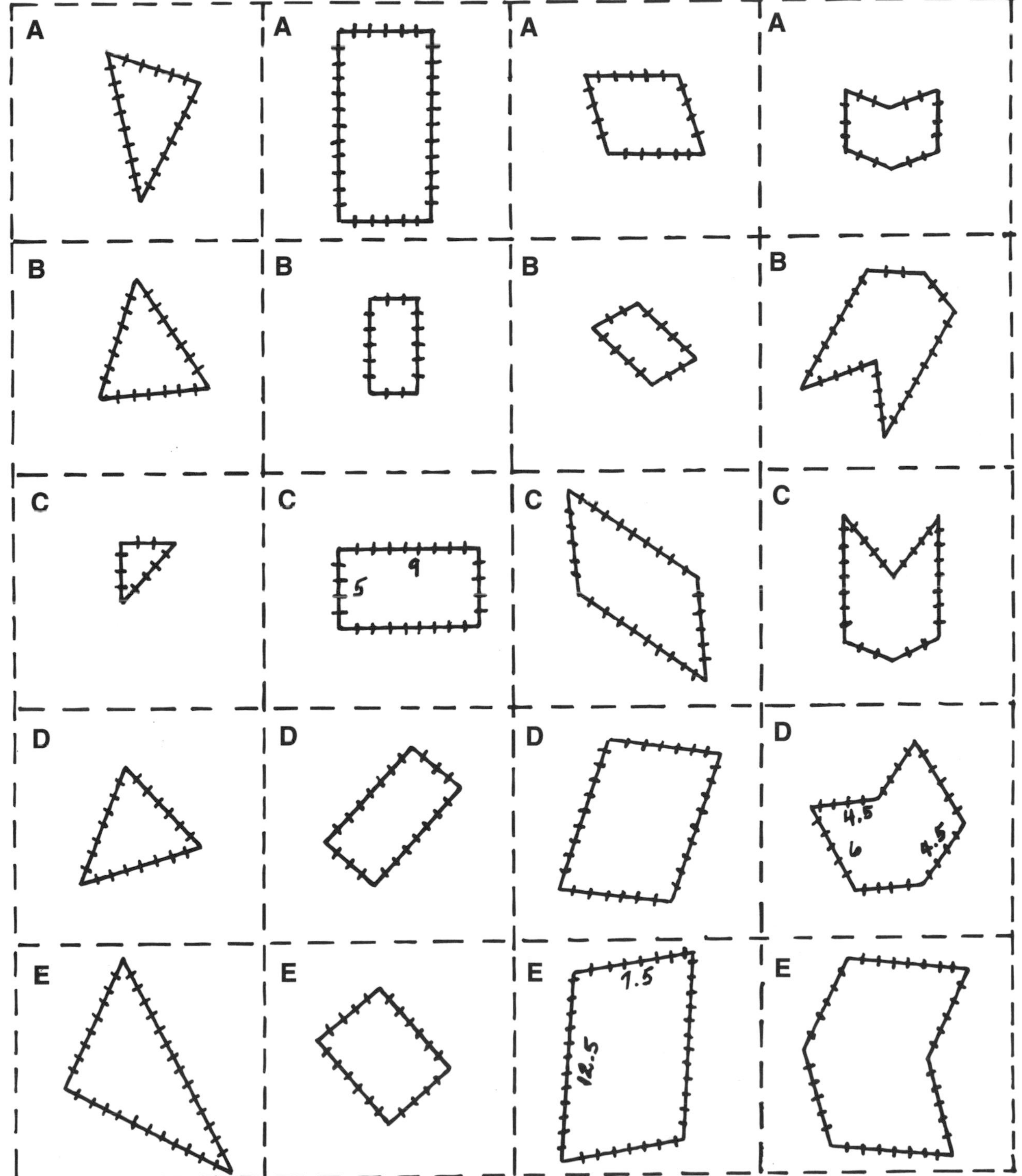

OBJECTIVE 9: Analyze three-dimensional models from different viewpoints.

Activity 1: VIEWPOINTS
(Concrete Action)

Materials: One-inch stackable cubes and building mats

Management: Teams of 3–4 students each (30 minutes)

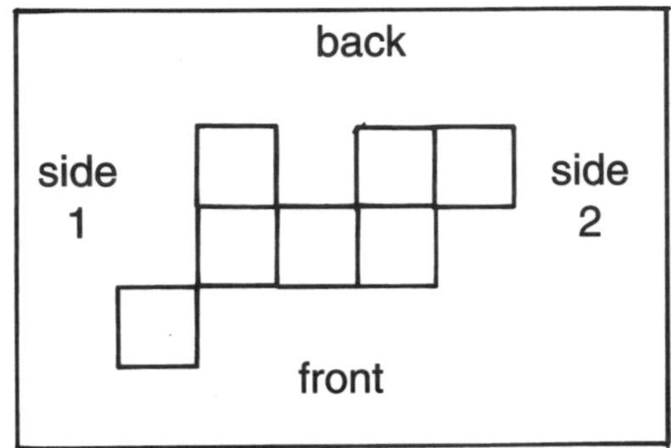

Directions:

1. Give each team of students approximately 15 stackable cubes (preferably inch cubes or larger).

2. Have them build different stack arrangements with various amounts of cubes on a building mat with labeled edges: *front, back, side 1,* and *side 2.* The cube edges should be aligned with the building mat edges. One cube's face cannot touch only part of another cube's face; it must touch the *entire* face. Two cubes may also touch at only a *corner edge.*

3. Have the students make two-dimensional drawings of each side view (front, back, side 1, and side 2) and the top view of each block arrangement they create. These will not be perspective drawings, so should not reflect distance between stacks in that one stack appears farther back on the mat than another stack. No shadows will be shown. To draw a side view, a student's eye level should be about 1 inch above the surface of the mat.

4. Monitor the teams closely to be sure they are drawing their side views correctly.

5. *Alternative materials:* Cuisenaire™ rods or geotubes, which are simply toilet paper cores sprayed lightly with paint. The geotubes can be laid on their sides without rolling and look like rectangles from the side view but like circles from the end view.

Activity 2: STACKS IN PERSPECTIVE

(Pictorial Action)

Materials: Copies of Worksheet G-9.2
One-inch cubes
Building mats
Pencils

Management: Partners (20 minutes)

Directions:

1. Give each pair of students 1–2 copies of Worksheet G-9.2 containing 4–6 items in all. Each item will consist of four side or top views for some block arrangement. Three different perspective drawings of stacks of blocks will also be given.

2. The students must decide which perspective drawing belongs to the four views given.

Example of item that matches side views to a perspective drawing:

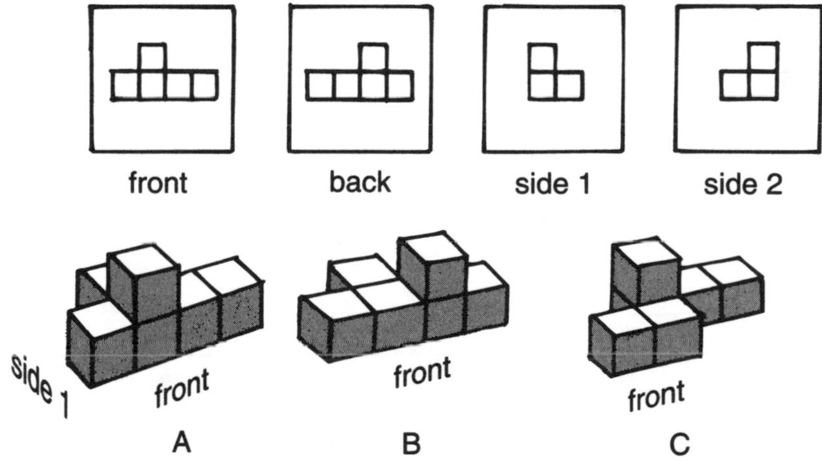

3. If necessary, the students may build on a building mat each block arrangement shown in perspective and compare its actual side or top views with the four given views in order to make a match.

4. Answers to Worksheet G-9.2:

1. C
2. A
3. A
4. B

NAME ________________________________ DATE ____________________

WORKSHEET G-9.2
Stacks in Perspective

Match each set of side or top views to the correct stack of blocks (A, B or C). Circle the letter of the chosen stack.

1.

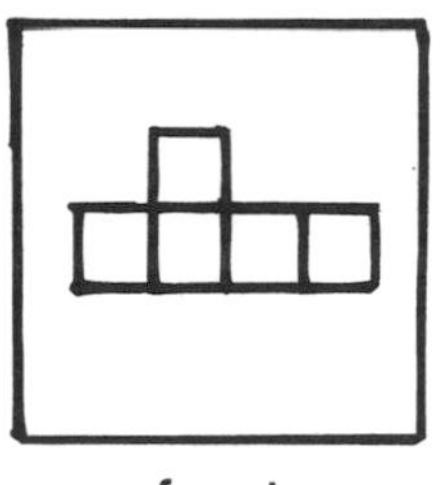
front

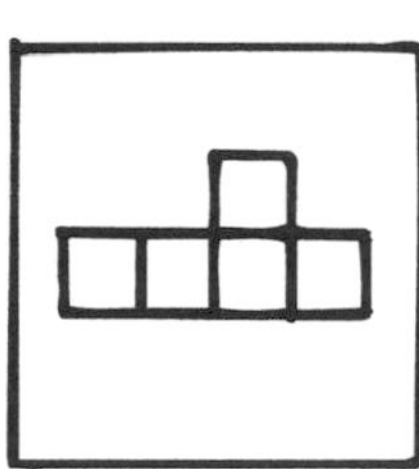
back

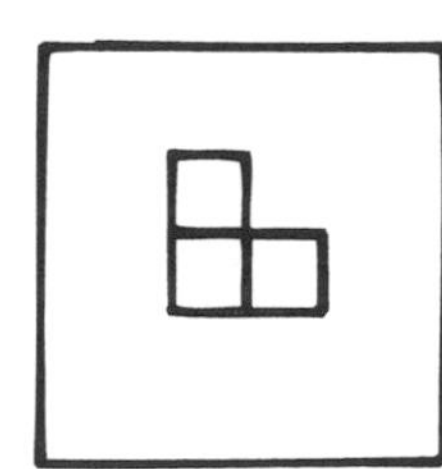
side 1

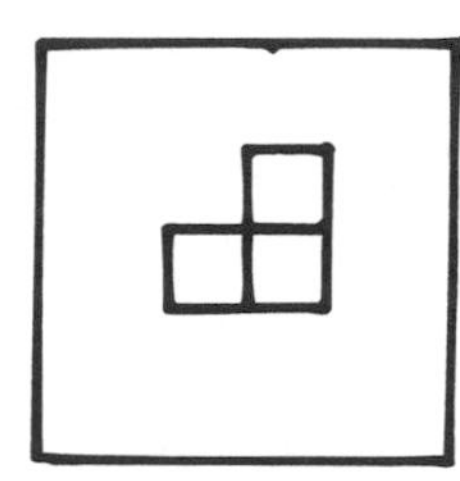
side 2

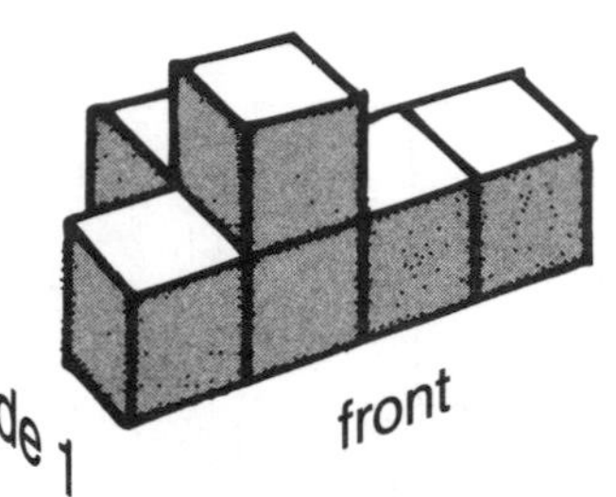

A

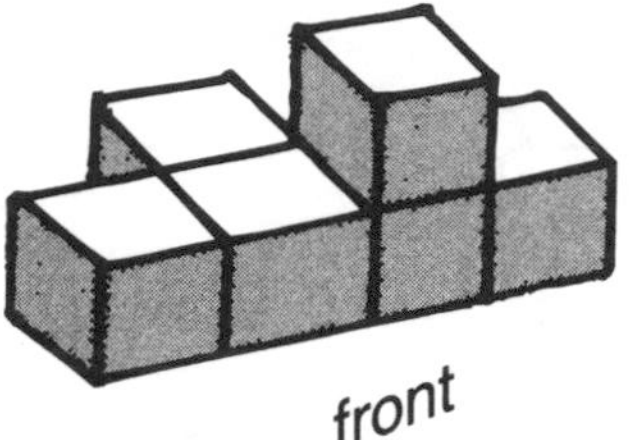

B

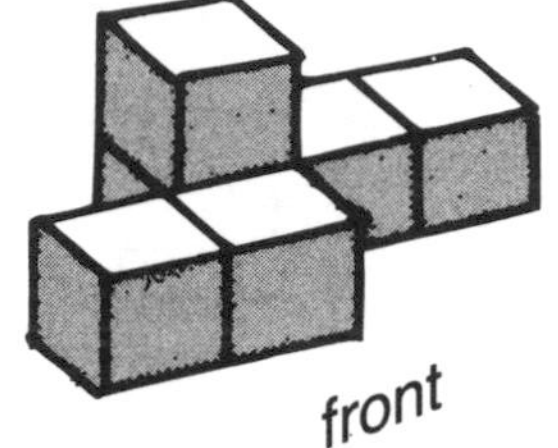

C

2.

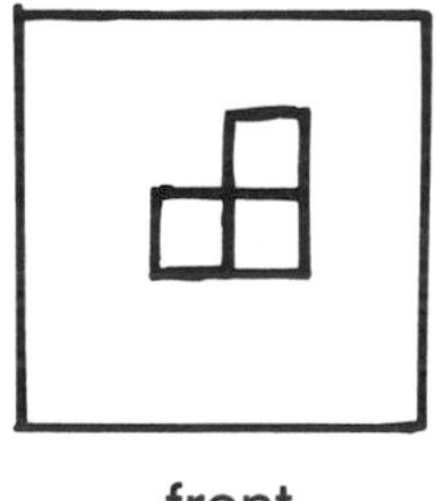
front

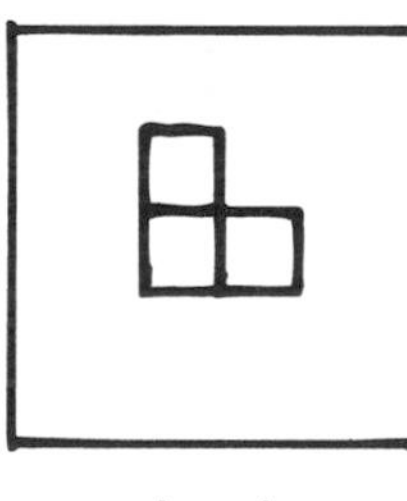
back

side 1

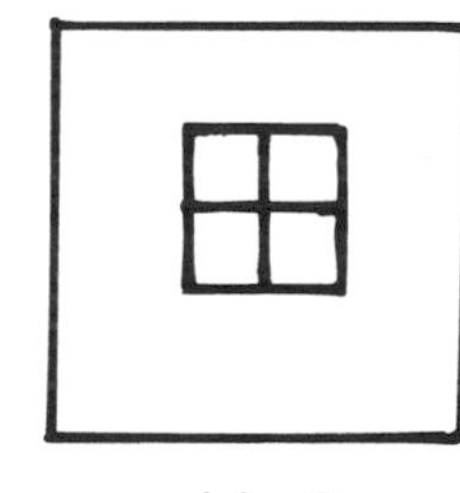
side 2

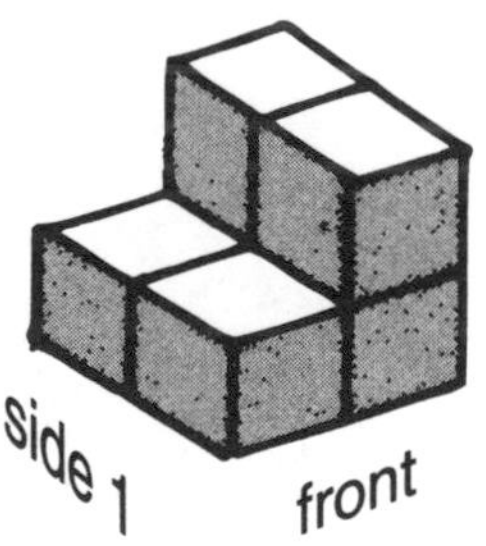

A

B

C

NAME ______________________________ DATE ____________________

WORKSHEET G-9.2 (cont.)

3.

front

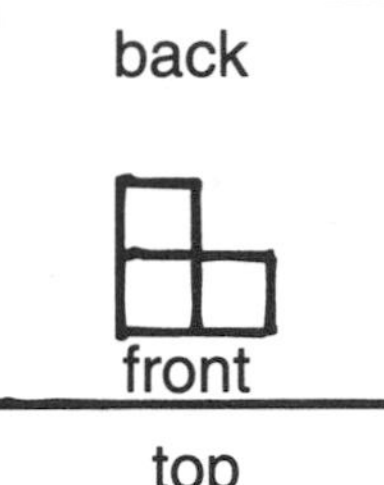

top

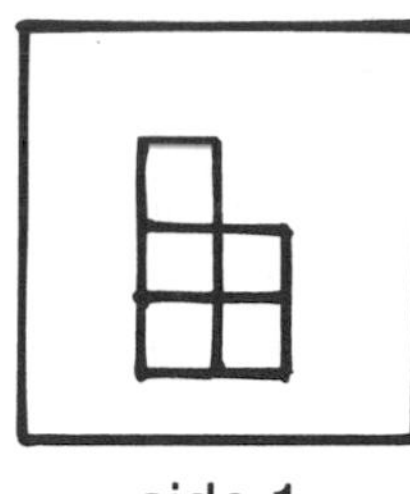

side 1

side 2

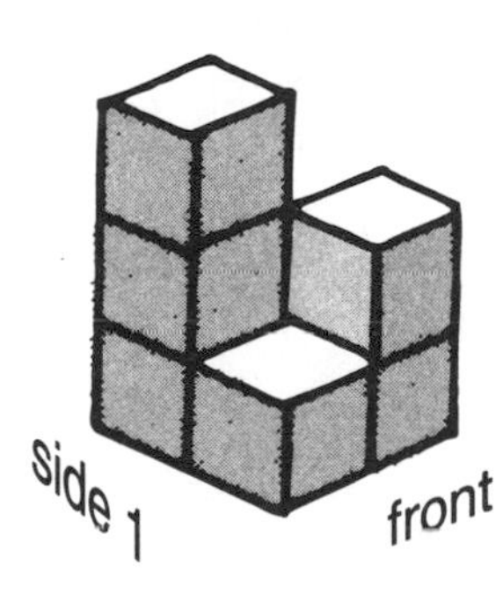

A

B

C

4.

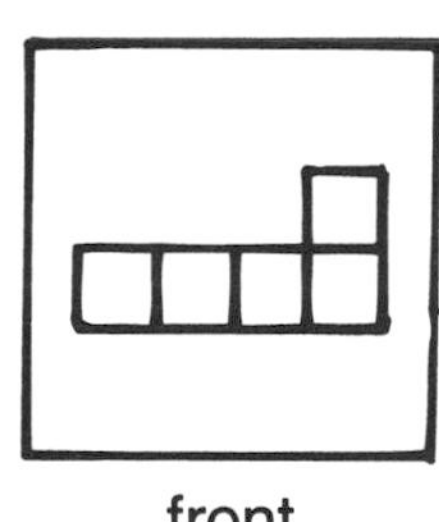

front

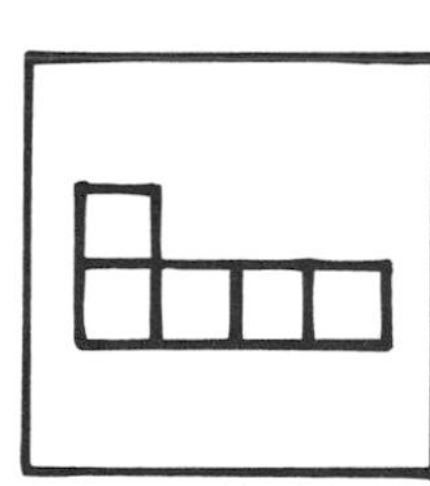

back

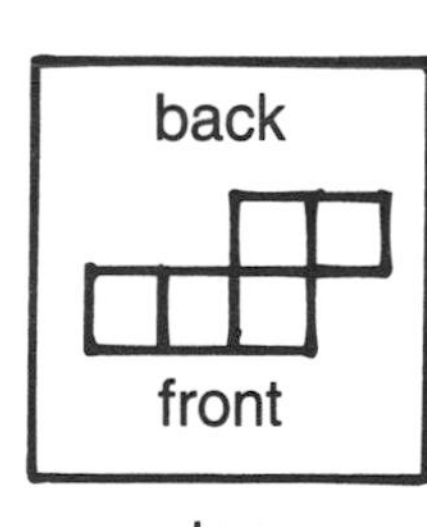

top

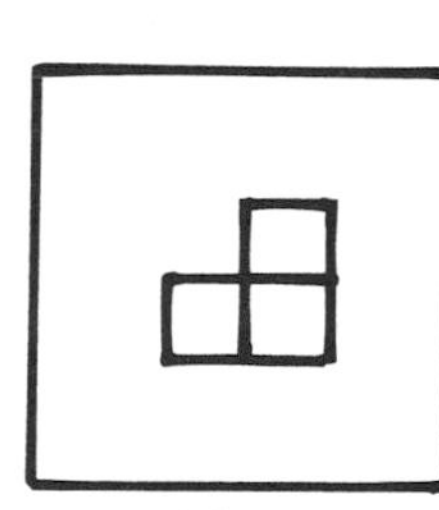

side 2

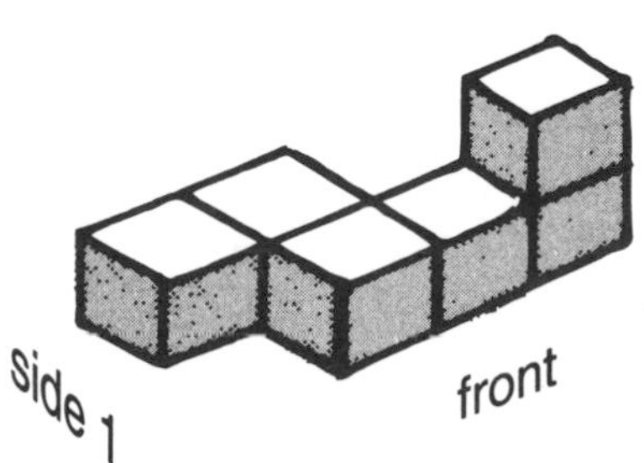

A

B

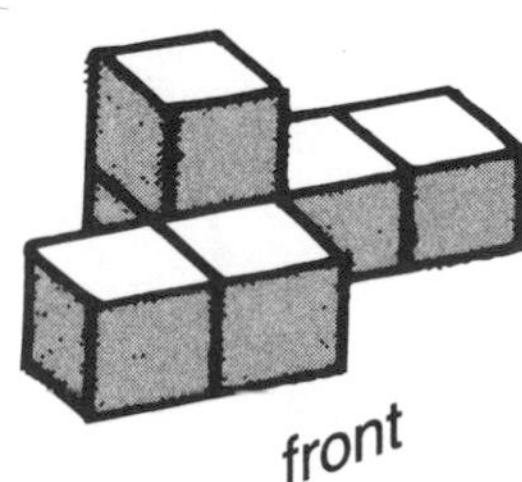

C

Activity 3: MYSTERY STACKS

(Cooperative Groups)

Materials: One-inch cubes
Building mats

Management: Teams of 4 students each (30 minutes)

Directions:

1. Have each team build its own block arrangement on a building mat, then draw only three *side* views (3 views selected from front, back, side 1, and side 2) on one sheet of paper and the *top* view on another sheet of paper.

2. Each team then trades its paper of *side* views with another team. Students are to try to replicate another team's original arrangement by using only the views given them.

3. Once a potential arrangement has been built, the original designers will compare the top view of this new stack with their sketch of the original top view. In many cases the top views will not agree. There will often be several different arrangements possible that satisfy the side views given, yet have different top views.

4. Have each team explore to find all the different solutions or block arrangements that could belong to the side views that they sketched originally.

OBJECTIVE 10: Construct and measure angles with a protractor.

Activity 1: CONSTRUCTING WITH PAPER ANGLES
(Concrete Action)

Materials: Paper angles (described below in step 1)
Paper
Pencil
Colored markers
Circle pattern (Worksheet G-10.1)
Scissors

Management: Partners (30 minutes)

Directions:

1. Give each pair of students a *paper angle* (made of two 1" × 5" tagboard strips fastened together at one end with a brad). Also give each pair the Worksheet G-10.1 with a circle drawn on it (circle radius is $2\frac{1}{2}$").

2. Have the students cut out the circular piece, then fold it in half and cut it apart to form half-disks (now called *protractors*). Mark a dot on each new protractor to show where the center of the original circle was.

3. Have students fold one of the protractors in half twice to make four equal sectors. Draw along each crease with a colored marker, then label in order each edge and crease as 0, 45, 90, 135, and 180 to show degree markings. This is the 45-degree protractor.

4. Now have them fold the other half-disk in half, then in thirds to make six equal sectors. Draw along each crease with a colored marker, then label in order the edges and creases as 0, 30, 60, 90, 120, 150, and 180 to show degree markings. This is the 30-degree protractor.

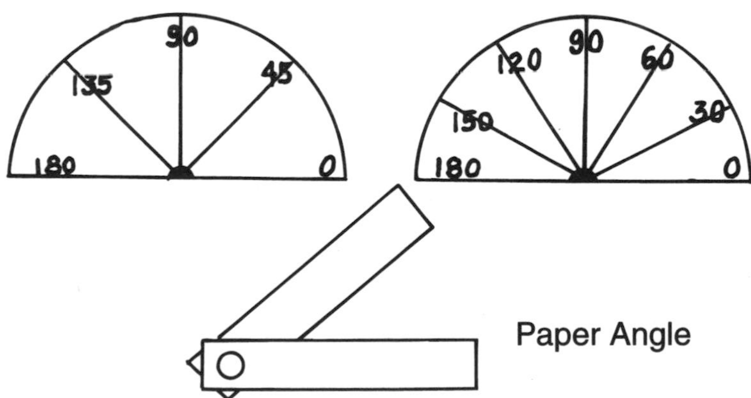

5. Now have the students use their paper angle and 45-degree protractor to draw a 135-degree angle on a sheet of paper.

6. Have the students place their paper angle on the 45-degree protractor so that the inside edge of one strip lines up below the protractor's bottom straight edge. The other strip can now be rotated over the protractor until its inside edge lines up with the 135-degree marking. At the same time, the point of the V-shape formed by the inside edges must coincide with the center dot on the protractor. Students should lightly mark the point on the strips where their inside edges touch. This will preserve the correct opening for the angle being formed. The paper angle can then be moved onto a sheet of paper where the inside edges can be traced off to form an angle of the desired size.

7. Have students measure, then draw several different angles with this method, practicing with both paper protractors.

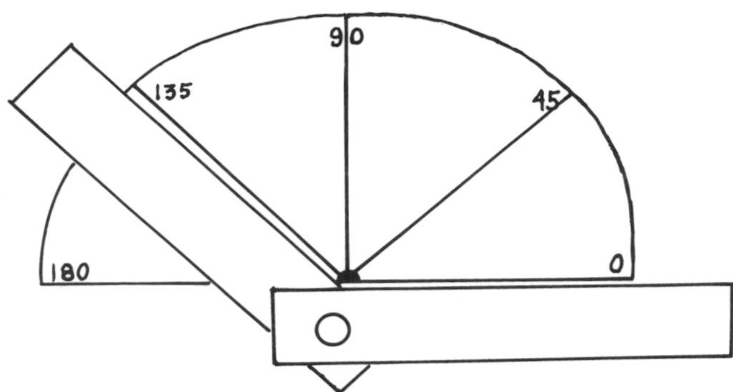

Measuring a 135-degree angle

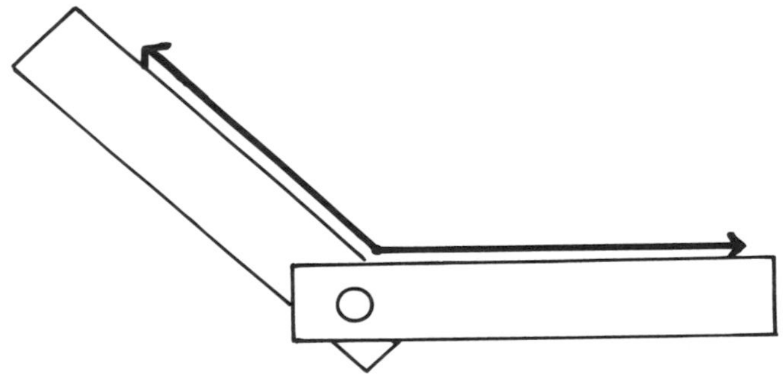

Drawing a 135-degree angle

Activity 2: MEASURING AND DRAWING ANGLES

(Pictorial Action)

Materials: Paper Patterns Worksheet G-10.2a for 10-degree protractors
Scissors
Rulers
Angle Worksheet G-10.2b

Management: Partners (20 minutes)

Directions:

1. Give each pair of students Angle Worksheet G-10.2b and the Patterns Worksheet G-10.2a for two paper protractors where markings are in 10-degree intervals. One

WORKSHEET G-10.1
Protractors Pattern for Constructing with Paper Angles

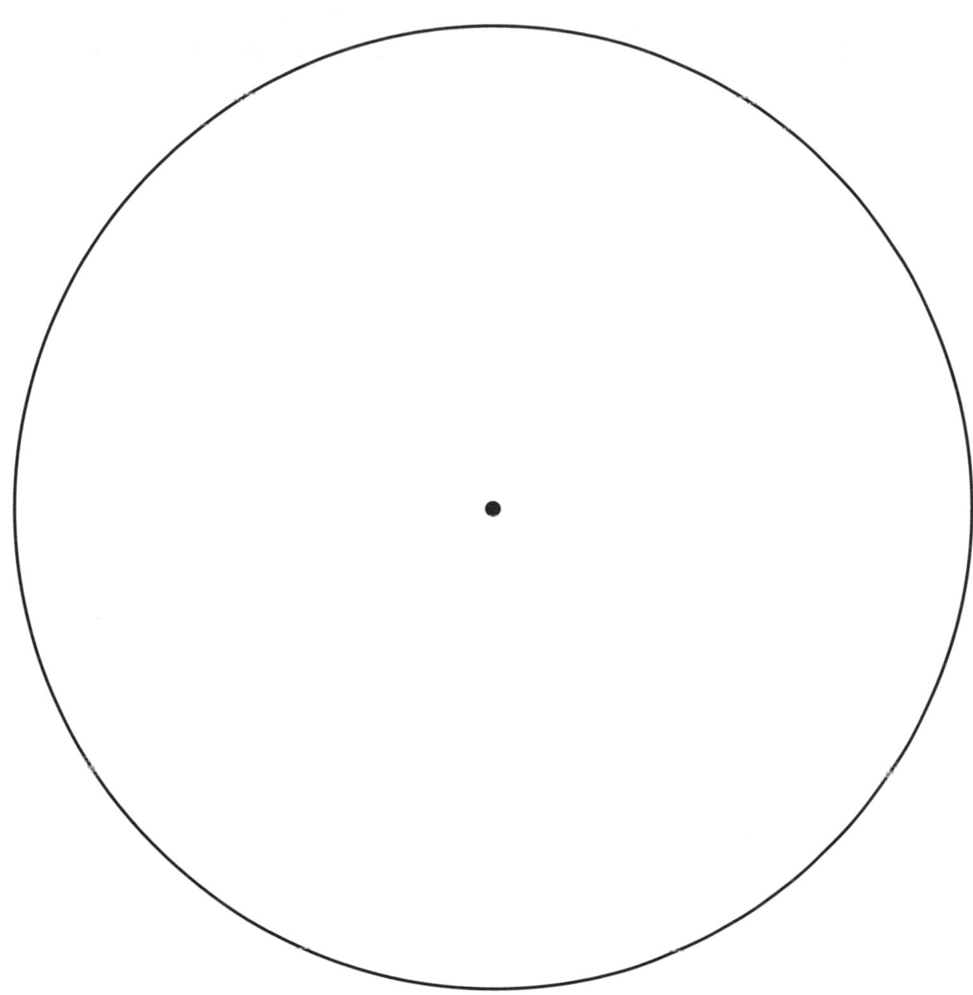

protractor pattern should have 0 on the left with numbers increasing clockwise. The other should have 0 on the right with numbers increasing counter-clockwise. These will provide practice with both left- and right-hand scales.

2. Have the students cut out the protractors and use them to measure off and complete several different angles whose initial rays are given on the worksheet.

3. Also have the students use the protractors to measure angles already drawn on the worksheet. All angles should be drawn or measured to the nearest ten degrees.

4. Supervise the students carefully, making sure before they measure that they line up one ray or side of the angle with the 0-edge of the protractor and the vertex of the angle with the center point of the protractor.

Activity 3: ANGLE CHALLENGE

(Cooperative Groups)

Materials: Commercial protractors
Pencils
Paper

Management: Teams of 4 students each (20 minutes)

Directions:

1. Have 2 members of each team state an angle measure. The other two members of the team are to construct an angle having that measure by using a commercial protractor (to the nearest degree). The first pair of students will then use the protractor to check the drawn angle for correctness.

2. The two pairs on each team should reverse roles and repeat the process.

3. Have students do this procedure several times, using right, acute, and obtuse angles. Remind students that they must view a point on a protractor from *directly above* the degree marking sought, not from a side view.

WORKSHEET G-10.2A
Patterns for 10-Degree Protractors for Measuring and Drawing Angles

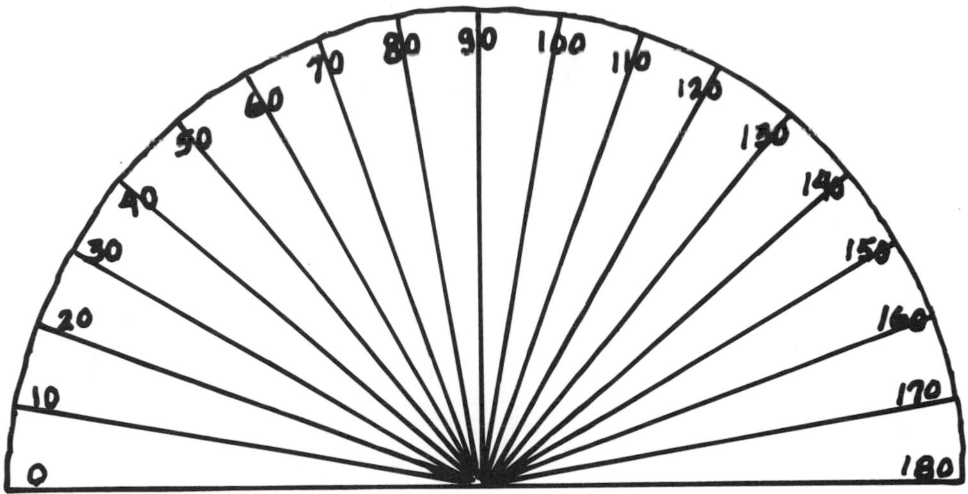

Left-Hand Scale

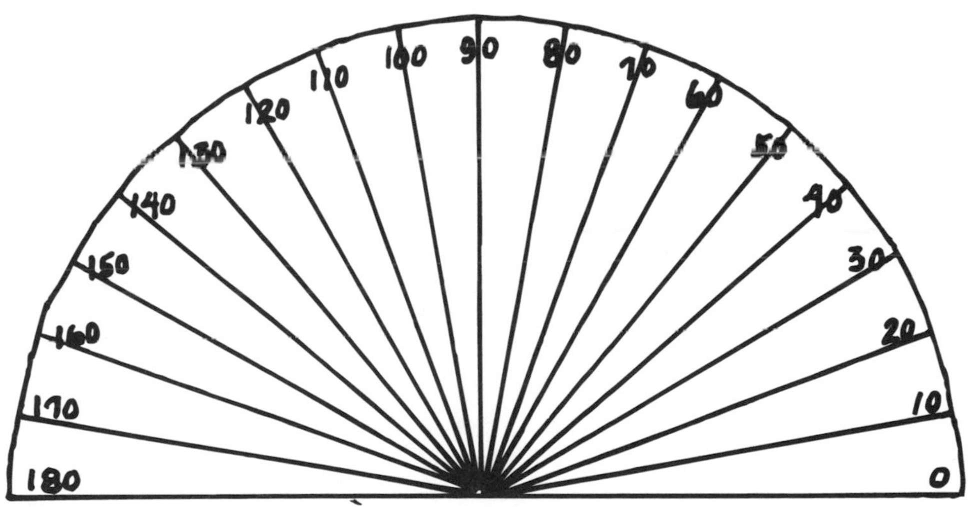

Right-Hand Scale

NAME ______________________________ DATE ____________________

WORKSHEET G-10.2B
Measuring and Drawing Angles

Use the 10-degree protractors to measure or draw angles to the nearest 10 degrees. Select whichever scale (left- or right-hand) is appropriate for a given angle. Extend rays when necessary to see them beyond the protractor's edge.

Measure.

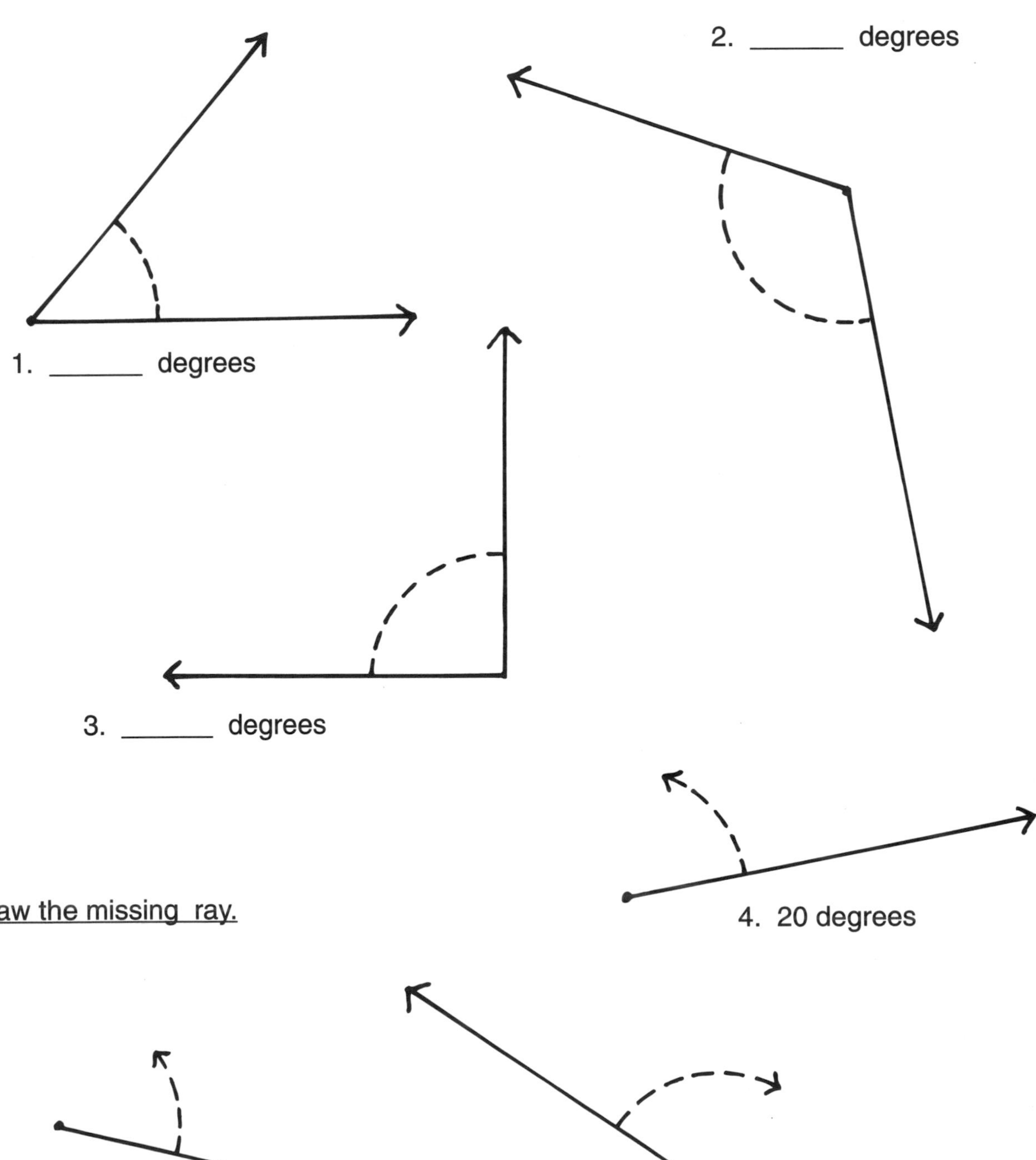

OBJECTIVE 11: Find the sum of the angle measures of a triangle.

Activity 1: FINDING THE ANGLE SUM

(Concrete Action)

Materials: Large triangle patterns
Glue
Paper
Colored markers
Straightedges

Management: Partners (20 minutes)

Directions:

1. Give each pair of students a sheet of paper with a large triangle drawn on it. The triangle should fill most of the page. Use a variety of triangles (acute, obtuse, right, isosceles, equilateral, scalene) throughout the class.

2. Have the students make a copy of their particular triangle and put a large dot in the interior of the copy near each vertex. They should then cut out their copy of the triangle.

3. On another blank sheet of paper, the students should draw a straight angle by drawing a horizontal line about midway down the paper and showing the vertex of the angle as a large dot at the midpoint of the line.

4. Each pair of students should now tear off the corners of the copy of their triangle and place them on their straight angle, matching all vertex dots to the vertex of the straight angle and placing the torn corners so that they do not overlap. Once the pieces are properly placed, have the students glue them down.

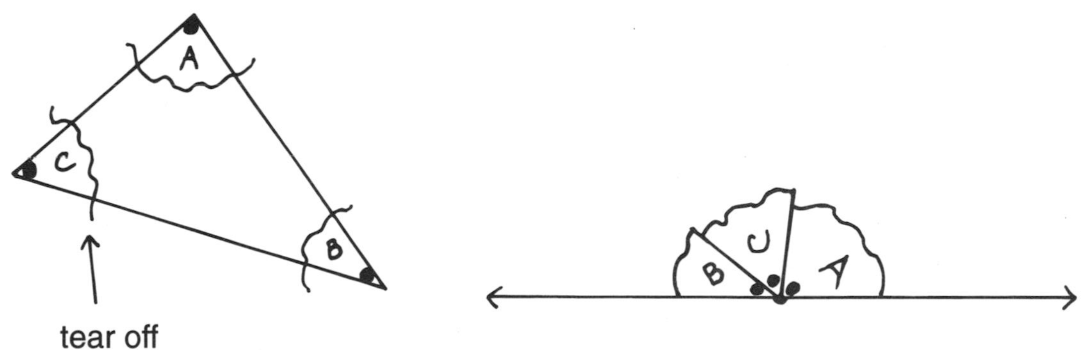

5. Each pair of students should now write a sentence or two below their *paper sum,* answering the question: *How are the angles of a ______ triangle related to a straight angle?* They should fill in the blank with the type of triangle they have used.

6. When all students are finished, have them share their original triangle, paper sum, and sentences with the whole class. The final observation should be that the angles of any triangle, regardless of its type, will have the same total measure as that of a straight angle (180 degrees).

Activity 2: COMBINING ANGLE MEASURES

(Pictorial Action)

Materials: Angle Worksheet G-11.2
Paper angles (shown below in step 2)

Management: Partners (20 minutes)

Directions:

1. Give each pair of students a copy of Worksheet G-11.2 with an acute triangle drawn in the upper left corner and an obtuse triangle drawn in the lower left corner. A straight angle is drawn to the right of each triangle.

2. Have students label the angle vertices of each triangle with capital letters. For each triangle, they are to use a *paper angle* to transfer each angle over to the straight angle, matching the angle's vertex to the vertex of the straight angle and positioning the three angles so that their interiors do not overlap. (See Activity 1 of Objective 10 for details on how to use the *paper angle*.)

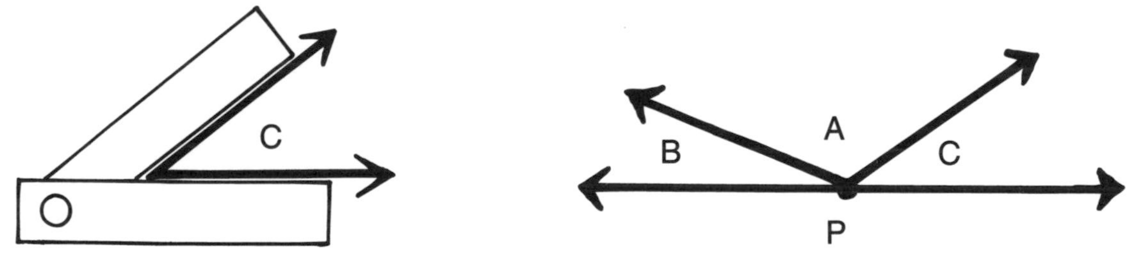

3. Have the students write one or two sentences describing the relationship they have found concerning the angles of a triangle. (*Relationship:* Regardless of the type of triangle used, the three angles, when joined together, have a total measure equal to the measure of a straight angle—180 degrees.)

Activity 3: ANGLE SPIN

(Cooperative Groups)

Materials: Spinners Pattern Worksheet G-11.3
Large paper clips
Calculators
Paper
Pencils

Management: Teams of 4 students each (20 minutes)

NAME ______________________ DATE ______________

WORKSHEET G-11.2
Combining Angle Measures

Copy each triangle's angles onto the straight angle at the right, using point P for the vertex of each angle's copy. Do not overlap the angles being drawn, but make them adjacent to each other.

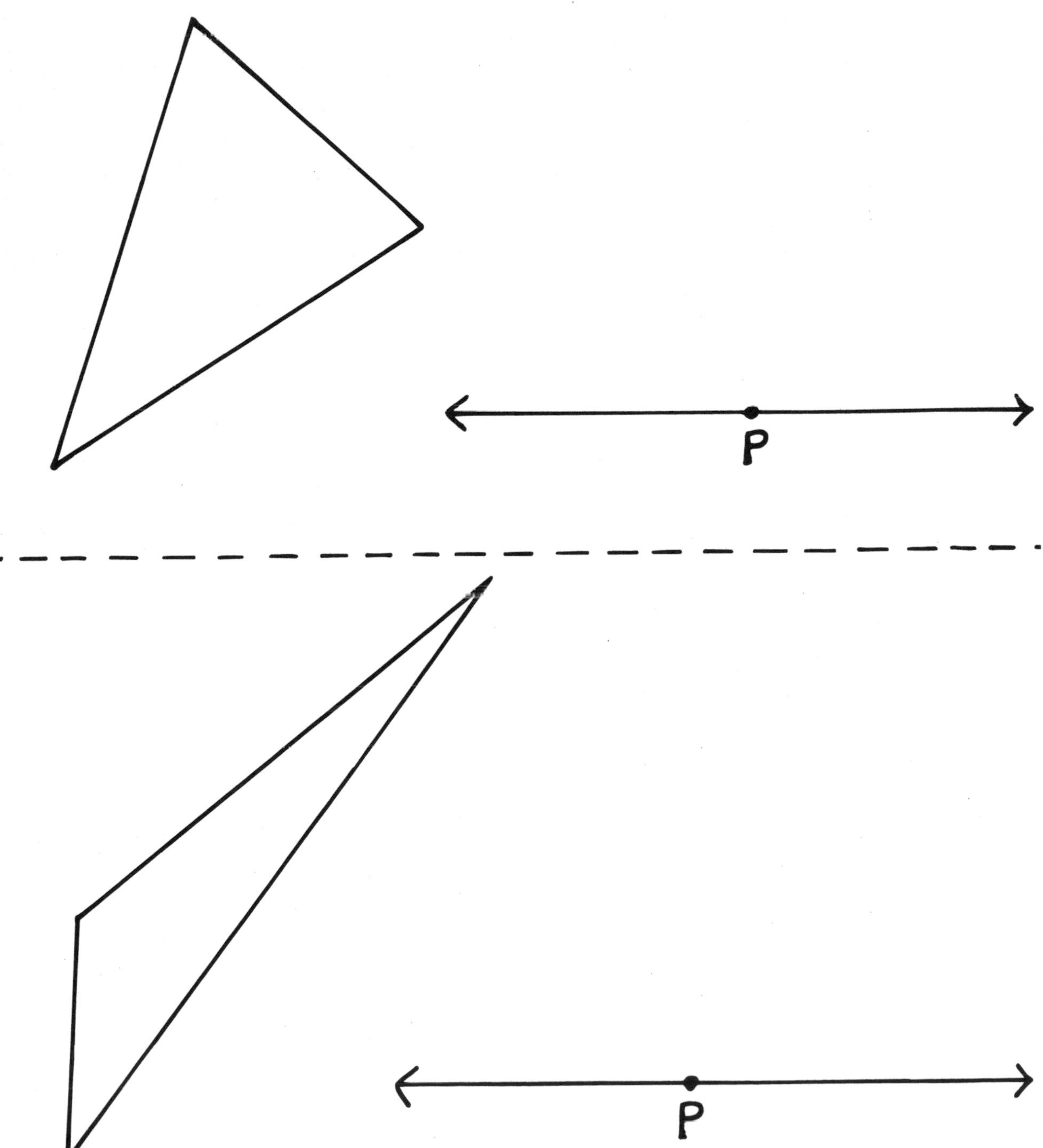

Directions:

1. Give each team Worksheet G-11.3 with two spinners drawn on it. Each spinner has 8 equal sectors, each sector containing a degree measure less than 90 degrees. Each of the 16 sectors contains a different amount from all the others. For a spinner needle, students can hold a large paper clip in place with the tip of a pencil at the center of the spinner and spin the paper clip around the pencil.

2. Taking turns, each student on a team spins each spinner once, obtaining two degree measures. These values represent two angle measures for a triangle. The player must compute to find what the third angle measure will be for that particular triangle. The other team members can use a calculator to check the correctness of the third angle measure found by the player.

3. The game continues until each player has had four turns or time is called.

WORKSHEET G-11.3
Spinners Pattern for Angle Spin

Spinner A
(in degrees)

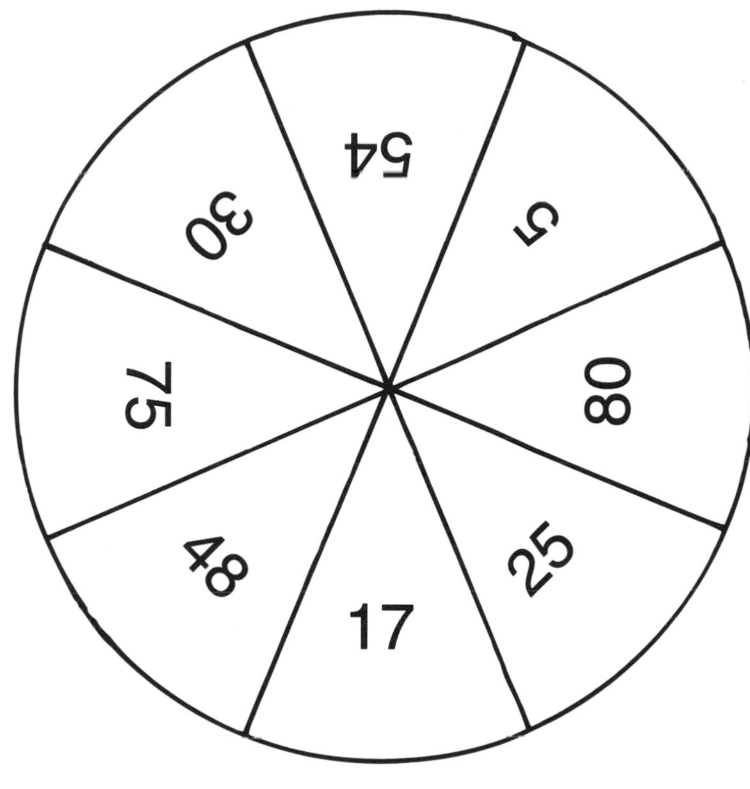

Spinner B
(in degrees)

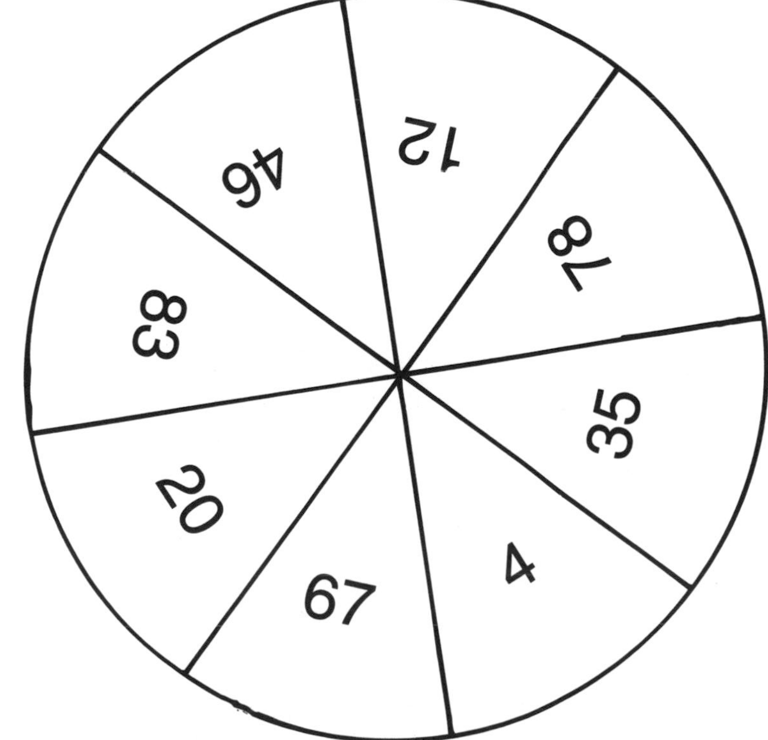

OBJECTIVE 12: Classify polygons by their number of sides.

Activity 1: GEOBOARD POLYGONS

(Concrete Action)

Materials: Geoboards with rubber bands
Colored markers
Rectangular dot paper
Pencils

Management: Partners (20 minutes)

Directions:

1. Give each pair of students a geoboard.

2. On their geoboard have the students build examples of the different polygons being studied (list them on the chalkboard), then draw each polygon they make on a sheet of rectangular dot paper. Beside the drawing they should also write the name of the polygon according to its number of sides (triangle, quadrilateral, pentagon, etc.).

3. Each polygon drawing can then be colored by *outlining* its sides with a wide marker. Do not color the interiors of the polygons.

4. Record sheets can be displayed in the classroom in order to show the variety of polygons possible.

Activity 2: POLYGON DRAW

(Pictorial Action)

Materials: Labeled slips of paper placed in a box or small container
Blank transparencies
Transparency pens (optional)

Management: Partners (15 minutes)

Directions:

1. Have each pair of students draw a slip of paper out of a box. Each slip has a number (from 3 to 10 if appropriate) written on it that represents the number of sides of a polygon. Depending on the grade level of the students, *convex* or *concave* and *regular* or *not regular* could also be written with the number on some of the slips.

2. Allow the students a few minutes for planning.

3. When called upon, each pair of students should go to the chalkboard or overhead projector and draw an example of a polygon having the number of sides and any other characteristics listed on their slip of paper. They are to write the general family name (e.g., quadrilateral, hexagon) as well as any specific name they might know (e.g., square, regular concave hexagon) for the polygon they draw.

Activity 3: POLYGON SHUFFLE

(Cooperative Groups)

Materials: Sets of 20 tagboard polygon cutouts and labeled index cards (described below in step 2)

Management: Teams of 4 students each (15 minutes)

Directions:

1. Give each team a set of about 20 tagboard cutouts of assorted polygons with 3 to 10 sides, depending on which polygons are being studied at the time. Include a variety of concave and convex polygons, whether or not the students have studied these terms, and some regular polygons as well as those with uneven side lengths. Have at least 3 polygons for each number of sides being studied. Make each polygon approximately 3 inches across. Be sure to outline each cutout with a bold marker to indicate clearly that the polygon is the edge and not the interior of the cutout.

2. Give each team a labeled index card for each family of polygons in their set (e.g., triangle, quadrilateral, pentagon, hexagon, heptagon, etc.).

3. The students are to separate the polygons into their correct categories according to their number of sides by placing the cutouts next to the appropriate index cards.

4. Monitor the teams closely to make sure they are separating their polygons correctly.

Example of polygon cutout (bold outline; interior is left plain):

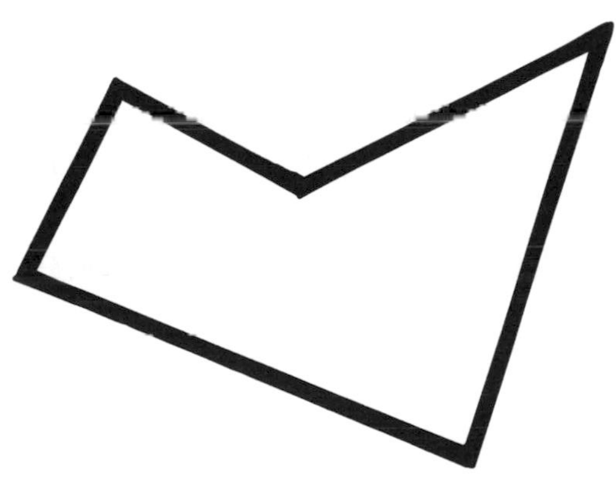

A Concave Pentagon

OBJECTIVE 13: Classify triangles by their sides—scalene, isosceles, equilateral.

Activity 1: BUILDING SIDE BY SIDE
(Concrete Action)

Materials: Plastic bags of 20–25 small paper clips (or flat coffee stirrers cut into *one-inch* lengths)
Felt building mats (approximately 10" × 12")
Paper
Pencils

Management: Teams of 2–4 students each (20 minutes)

Directions:

1. Give each team 20–25 small paper clips in a bag and a piece of colored felt (approx. 10" × 12") to use as a building mat. One paper clip will be one unit of length.

2. Have students build the different types of triangles by varying the number of paper clips used to make each side. The paper clips do not have to be connected, but their ends must touch. The felt building mats are used to keep the paper clips from sliding around too much.

3. Also have students make freehand drawings of the triangles they build, labeling each side with the number of paper clips used to make it and writing the type of each triangle below its picture. The sides of the triangles can be drawn to look like paper clips or like line segments.

4. Discuss how an equilateral triangle is just a special member of the isosceles triangle family. (*Isosceles* requires 2 *or* 3 congruent sides; *equilateral* has 3.)

Activity 2: COUNTING OFF SIDES
(Pictorial Action)

Materials: Worksheet G-13.2
Pencils

Management: Partners (15 minutes)

Directions:

1. Give each pair of students Worksheet G-13.2 with a variety of triangles (scalene, isosceles, equilateral) drawn on it. The unit lengths need to be marked off on each side of every triangle.

2. The students are to count the units of length forming each side of a given triangle and label this side's length on the drawing.

3. Then they are to write on the drawing the correct name of that triangle according to its sides. *Remember:* An equilateral triangle may also be called an isosceles triangle, but an isosceles triangle is not always equilateral.

Example of unit lengths marked on a triangle:

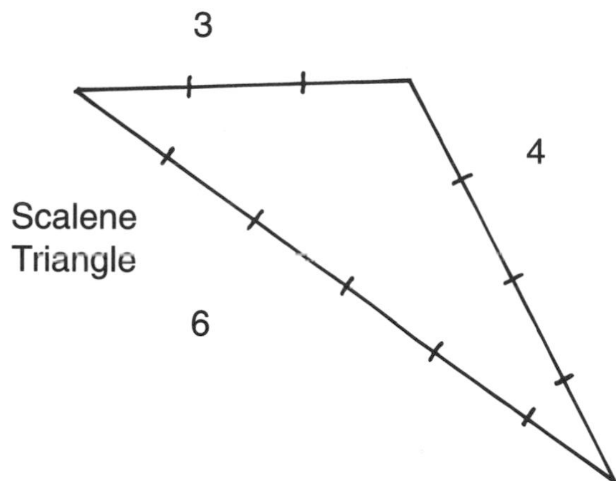

Activity 3: TRIANGLE JOURNALS

(Cooperative Groups)

Materials: Centimeter rulers
Old magazines
Colored markers
Pencils
Paper
Scissors
Glue
Posterboard (optional)

Management: Teams of 4 students each (30–50 minutes)

Directions:

1. Each team is to prepare *information sheets* on the scalene, isosceles, and equilateral triangles.

2. Students are to draw a sample diagram for each type of triangle and then write a short paragraph describing its characteristics. A magazine picture with an example of this triangle type outlined with a bold marker should also be included. A colored design composed of several different examples or repeated copies of this triangle type might also be made.

3. The completed information sheets can then be mounted on posterboard or bound together as a small book to be read by other students.

NAME ______________________________ DATE ____________________

WORKSHEET G-13.2
Counting Off Sides

Label each side of a triangle with its number of marked-off units of length. Identify each triangle as *scalene, isosceles,* or *equilateral*.

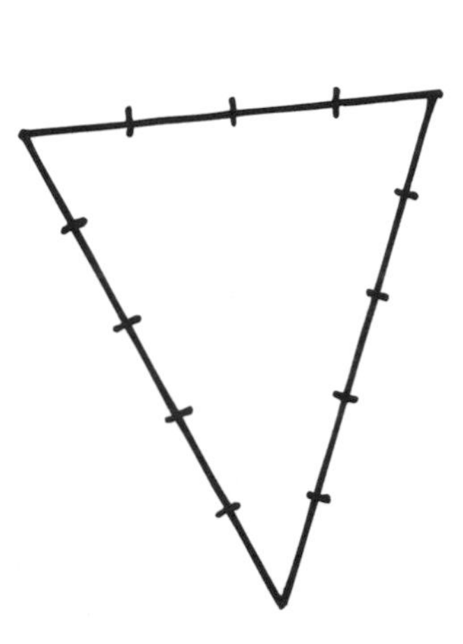

1. ____________

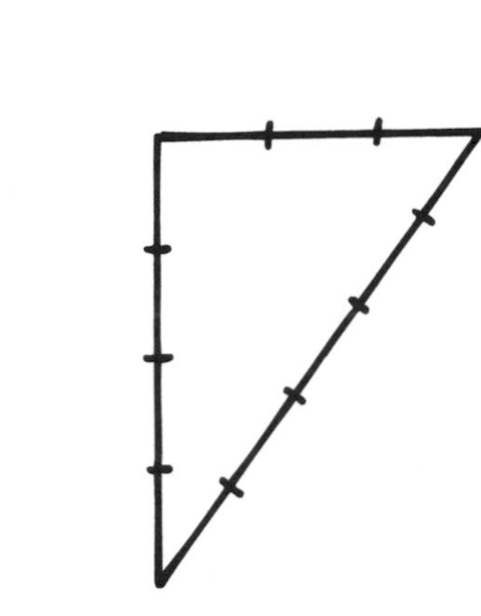

2. ____________

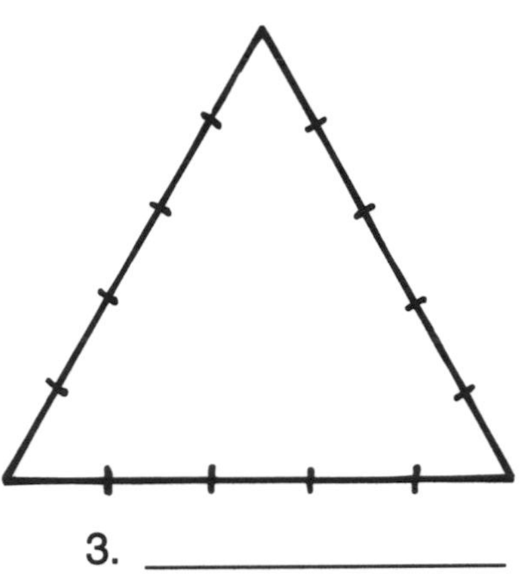

3. ____________

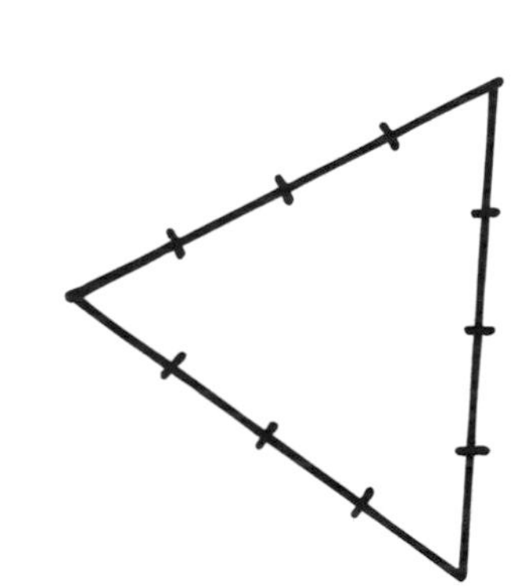

4. ____________

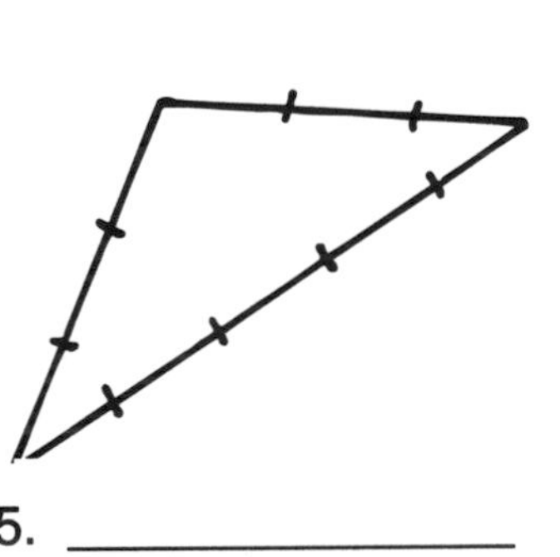

5. ____________

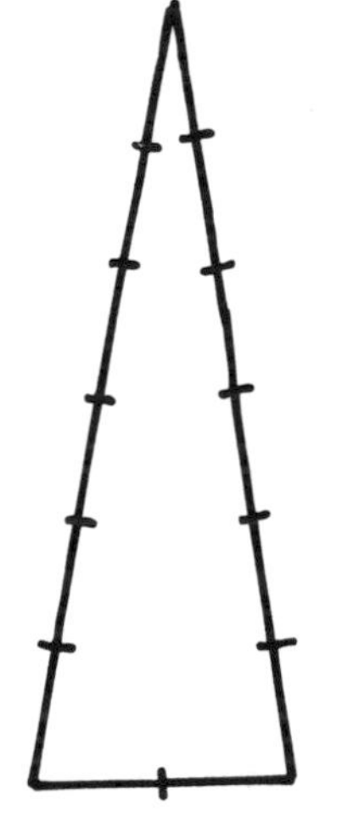

6. ____________

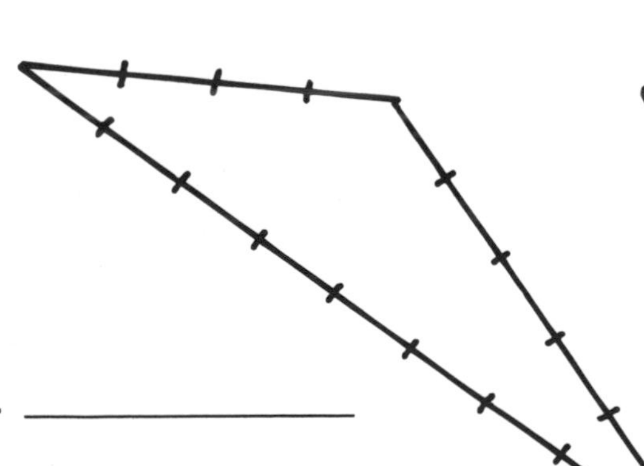

7. ____________

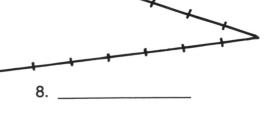

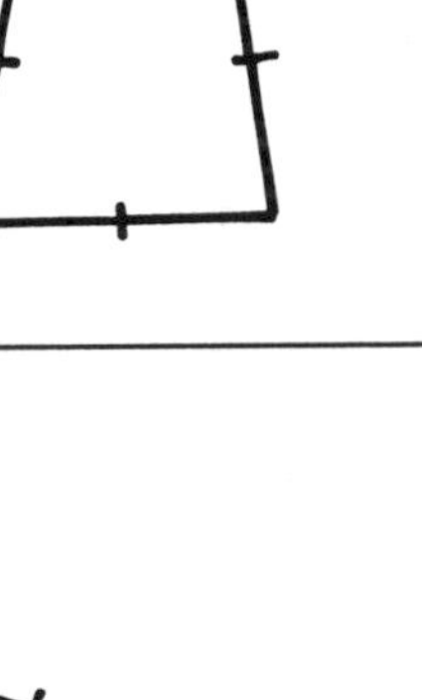

8. ____________

OBJECTIVE 14: Classify triangles by their angles—acute, obtuse, and right.

Activity 1: BUILDING WITH ANGLES
(Concrete Action)

Materials: Geoboards with rubber bands
Rectangular dot paper
Pencils

Management: Partners (20 minutes)

Directions:

1. Give each pair of students a geoboard and have them build various examples of acute, obtuse, and right triangles with the rubber bands.

2. Challenge them with questions like *How many obtuse angles can an obtuse triangle have?* or *Can a right triangle have two right angles?* Have the students try to build a triangle with two obtuse angles or with two right angles.

3. Have them draw pictures of the geoboard triangles on rectangular dot paper and label each picture with its correct name according to its angles.

Activity 2: TRACKING ANGLES
(Pictorial Action)

Materials: Triangle Worksheet G-14.2
Pencils
Red, yellow, and blue markers
Index cards

Management: Partners (15 minutes)

Directions:

1. Give each pair of students a worksheet with a variety of triangles (acute, right, and obtuse) drawn on it.

2. Have students outline each triangle's angles according to their type. Acute angles should be colored blue; all obtuse angles, yellow; and all right angles, red. Some students may need to compare their angles to the corner edges of an index card (a right angle) to help determine the types of angles they have.

3. By looking at the number of angles outlined in each color, and hence, the number of each type of angle present in a triangle, students will label each triangle with its correct name according to its angles.

NAME ______________________ DATE ______________

WORKSHEET G-14.2
Tracking Angles

Outline each angle of a triangle with a colored marker. Use blue for *acute* angles, yellow for *obtuse* angles, and red for *right* angles. Identify each triangle as *obtuse, acute,* or *right*.

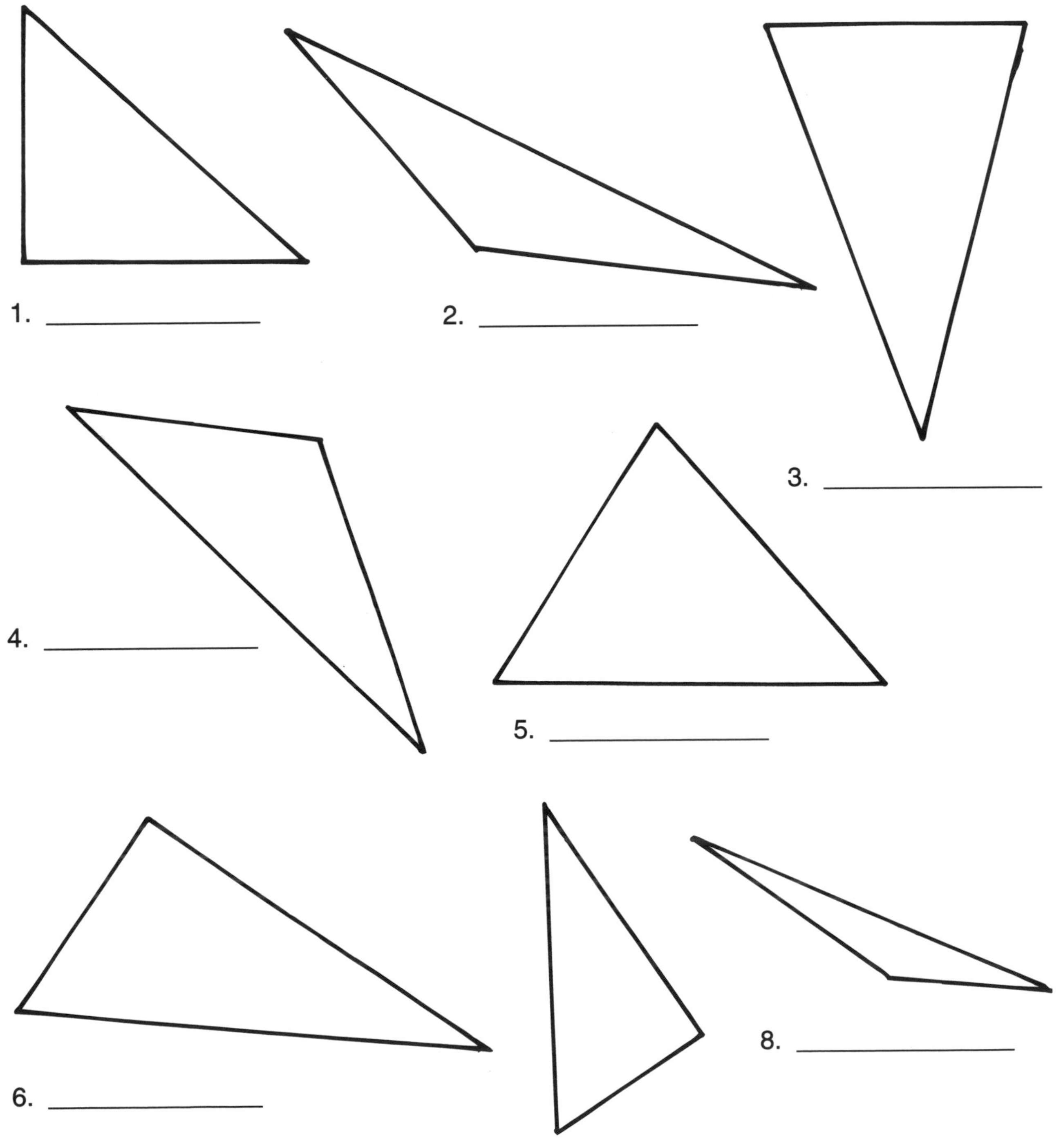

Activity 3: TRIANGLE CONCENTRATION

(Cooperative Groups)

Materials: Decks of 36 cards (described below in step 1)
Worksheet G-14.3
An index cards (optional)

Management: Teams of 4 students each (20 minutes)

Directions:

1. Give each team of students a deck of 36 cards made from Worksheet G-14.3 (6 with pictures of acute triangles, 6 with the words "acute triangle," 6 with pictures of obtuse triangles, 6 with "obtuse triangle," 6 with pictures of right triangles, and 6 with "right triangle"). Shapes drawn on the cards should be randomly oriented. Indicate a right angle inside a triangle with a "box."

2. The students should shuffle the cards, then arrange them face down in rows and columns. They should play according to the basic rules for "Concentration."

3. Taking turns, the players will try to find two cards that match, that is, a triangle shape matched to its angle-related name. A player can make at most two matches on a turn, however, in order to keep all students alert and involved. Unmatched cards must be returned face down to their original positions. Some students may occasionally need to *test* an angle with an index card (90-degree corners) to see if the angle is acute or obtuse.

4. The game is over when all matches have been made or time is called.

WORKSHEET G-14.3
Sample Cards for Triangle Concentration

Enlarge, cut apart and glue triangles on cards, if desired. See Activity 3 for additional instructions on how to make a complete card set.

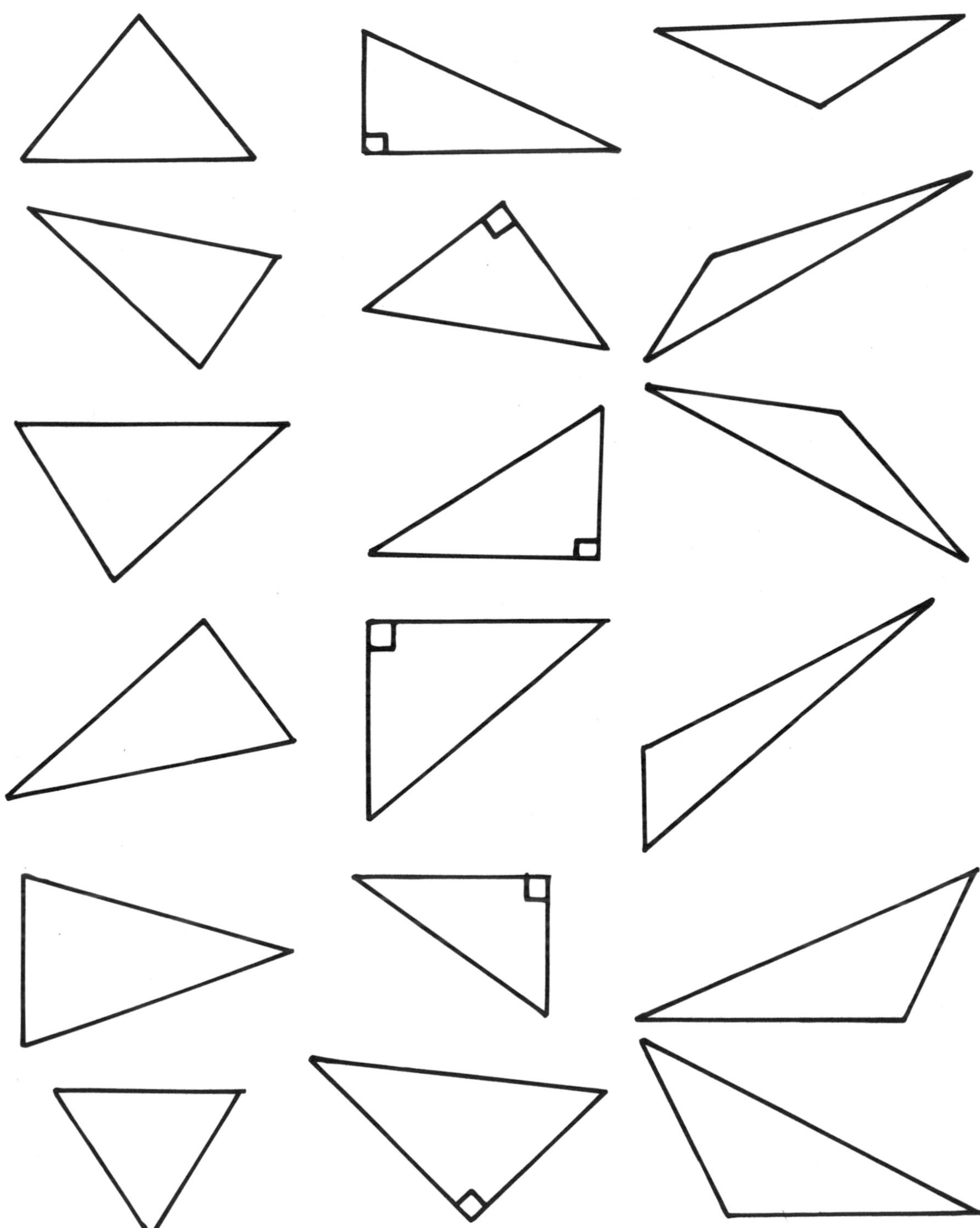

OBJECTIVE 15: Identify three-dimensional figures by their characteristics (cones, pyramids, prisms, spheres, cylinders, etc.).

Activity 1: DESCRIBING SOLIDS
(Concrete Action)

Materials: Three-dimensional shapes
Pencils
Paper

Management: Teams of 2–4 students each (30 minutes)

Directions:

1. Give each team one of the three-dimensional figures to be studied. These figures or solids are commercially available in plastic or wood or can be found as everyday containers. If necessary, some of them can be constructed from paper or tagboard patterns or from Play-doh®.

2. Ask students to notice all the different features of their particular figure by touching and looking at it, then write a paragraph that describes their shape.

3. When all students are finished, have them read their paragraphs while they show their three-dimensional figures to the entire class.

4. *Alternative:* Place three figures where all the class can see them. Have a team read their description of one of the three figures without naming their figure. Ask the class to identify the figure being described.

Activity 2: A SHAPE COLLAGE
(Pictorial Action)

Materials: Old magazines
Scissors
Glue
Construction paper
Colored markers

Management: Partners (20 minutes)

Directions:

1. Have pairs of students cut out magazine pictures of the three-dimensional shapes being studied, then glue the pictures onto a large sheet of construction paper to create a collage.

2. Have them paste on name labels in some way to identify the different shapes in their collage.

3. They should also create an interesting name for their collage. These collages can then be displayed in the classroom or hallway.

4. *Alternative:* Have each pair of students make a collage using only one kind of three-dimensional shape. Then the title for the collage can be the name of the shape used.

Activity 3: 3-D FISH

(Cooperative Groups)

Materials: Decks of cards (described below in step 1)

Management: Teams of 4 students each (20 minutes)

Directions:

1. Prepare a deck of 36 (or 48) cards for each team. (Blank playing cards are available commercially.) A *book* will consist of three cards: a shape card (shows picture of a 3-D shape, but no shape name or definition), a name card (shows name of the 3-D shape, but no picture or definition of the shape), and a definition card (lists different characteristics of the 3-D shape, but gives no name or picture of the shape). The 12 (or 16) 3-card sets needed for a full deck should represent an assortment of the shapes being studied. The orientation of like shapes on the shape cards should vary, and the wording on the definition cards should vary a little even though shapes may be of the same type. Students can help you make the decks by collecting magazine pictures of the 3-dimensional shapes to be studied in class. These pictures may be glued on tagboard, laminated, and cut apart to form *shape* cards. Photographs of real objects are preferred, but 2-D drawings of the 3-D shapes may also be used. A possible list of shape names and definitions are given at the end of this section.

2. The game rules are similar to the rules of "Go Fish." Seven cards are dealt to each player, and the remaining cards placed face down in the center of the table. A student must find a shape card, name card, and definition card that describe the same shape in order to form a *book*.

3. The first player examines his or her own cards and forms whatever books are possible, placing them on the table face up so the other players can check them for correctness. Player 1 then asks any other player for a specific card (e.g., the definition card for a *cone*). Player 1 must be able to describe the card needed well enough for the other player to recognize it. If the other player has the requested card, it must be given to Player 1. If the requested card is received, Player 1 may also ask that same player for the other card pertaining to the first card's shape. If not, Player 1 must draw or "fish" a card from the deck in the center.

4. The turn now passes to the next player in order, even though Player 1 may be able to form another book after drawing from the deck. This helps keep all the players more alert and involved. Also, by not having the shape name on all cards, the students are more challenged when trying to make matches.

5. The game ends when all 12 (or 16) books have been formed by the players. (Note: During the game, check each team's books occasionally to make certain that correct matches have been made.)

Suggested 3-D shape names and various definitions for them (shape names can be repeated and matched with different forms of the definitions):

Shape Name	**Possible Definitions**
Pyramid with rectangular base	1) Four lateral faces are triangular. 2) Faces use 4 triangles, 1 rectangle.
Pyramid with triangular base (or tetrahedron)	1) All faces are triangular. 2) There are 4 faces total.
Rectangular prism that is not a cube	1) Faces use 2 different-sized rectangles. 2) At least 4 faces are rectangular (but not square).
Cube (a special prism)	1) All 6 faces are congruent. 2) All faces are square.
Triangular prism	1) Only 3 lateral faces are rectangular. 2) Two parallel faces are triangular.
Sphere	1) Total surface is curved. 2) No faces have planar shapes.
Cylinder with circular base	*1) Lateral surface is curved; and 2 flat bases. 2) Two parallel faces are circular.
Cylinder with elliptical (oval) base	1) Two bases are oval. *2) There are 1 lateral surface and 2 bases.
Cone with circular base	*1) There is only 1 vertex. 2) Only 1 face is circular.
Cone with oval base	1) Only 1 face is oval-shaped. *2) Lateral surface is curved; 1 flat base.

Note: The (*) definitions listed for cylinders will match to either cylinder. Those starred (*) for cones will match to either cone. All other definitions are unique to their specific shapes listed above.

OBJECTIVE 16: Find angle bisectors.

Activity 1: BISECTING BY FOLDING
(Concrete Action)

Materials: Angle Worksheet G-16.1
Colored markers
Paper straightedges
Pencils

Management: Partners (20 minutes)

Directions:

1. Give each pair of students two half-sheets of paper, each with an angle drawn on it, made from Worksheet G-16.1. For convenience, use a 60-degree angle for one and a 140-degree angle for the other. The rays of each angle should be extended 4–5 inches from the vertex.

2. Have the students fold the smaller angle through its vertex so that one ray lies on the other ray. Students should then draw along the crease with a marker and label the crease as *angle bisector.*

3. Ask them what they know about the two new angles formed by the bisector with each original ray. The two angle measures should be the same because of the folding, so have students show this property by drawing a single arc of the same color across each interior of the two angles. (Do not measure the new angles with a protractor at this time. That will be done later.)

4. The students should now label the vertex as point C and move along one of the rays about 2–3 inches from C and mark a new point A. Have them refold along the bisector crease to find the image of A on the other ray. The image point should be marked A'.

5. Have students also mark a point P on the bisector about 4 inches away from C.

6. Ask students to make observations about the distances from C to A, C to A', A to P, and A' to P. Measuring can be done by just marking off distances on a paper straightedge. Distances might also be compared by once again folding along the bisector to see which line segments match completely.

Example of completed angle bisection by folding:

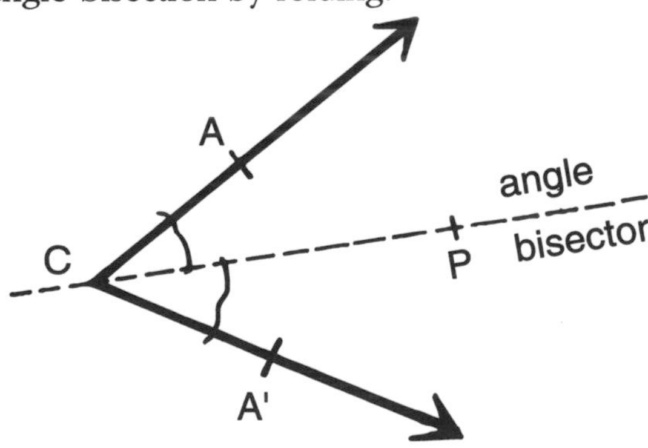

7. Now have students repeat the above process with the larger angle provided.

8. Have students share their findings. They should notice that the bisector forms two new angles of equal measure. Also, the gross measuring with the paper straightedge should show that lengths CA and CA' are equal and that lengths PA and PA' are equal. Some students may notice that the bisector behaves like a line of reflection, reflecting one ray of the angle onto the other ray. A line segment and its image will have the same length as a result of the reflection.

Activity 2: DRAWING BISECTORS

(Pictorial Action)

Materials: Angle Worksheet G-16.2
Index cards
Centimeter-inch rulers
Commercial protractors
Pencils

Management: Partners (20 minutes)

Directions:

1. Give each pair of students a worksheet with an 80-degree angle drawn in the upper half of the paper and a 130-degree angle drawn in the lower half. Extend the angle rays several inches.

2. For the smaller angle, tell the students to mark a point on each ray (use points A and B) so that the point is 2 inches from the vertex C. The edge of an index card can now be lined up with ray CA with its corner at A.

3. A line segment 2–3 inches long can be drawn along the adjacent card edge from point A into the angle's interior. The segment will be perpendicular to the ray CA at point A. Repeat this process to draw a line segment from point B on ray CB. The two line segments should intersect each other; if not, have students extend them until they cross.

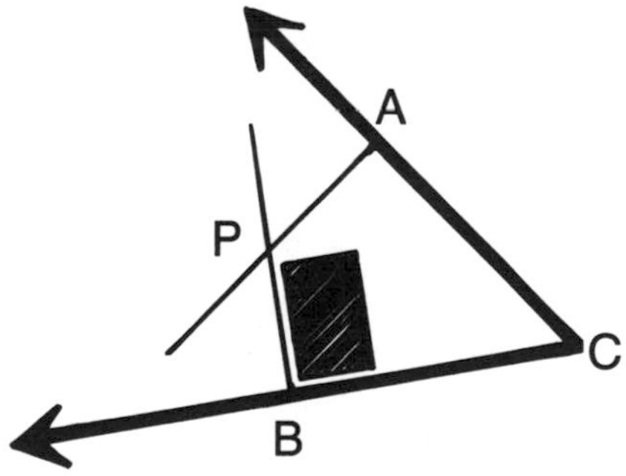

4. The point of intersection should now be labeled as point P. A line should be drawn from C through P.

5. Ask students to measure the lengths AP and BP to the nearest centimeter (they should be equal) and also use a protractor to measure the two new angles formed to the nearest 5 degrees (they should be equal). (Students should already know how to use a protractor for this activity.)

NAME ______________________ DATE ______________

WORKSHEET G-16.1
Angle Patterns for Bisecting by Folding

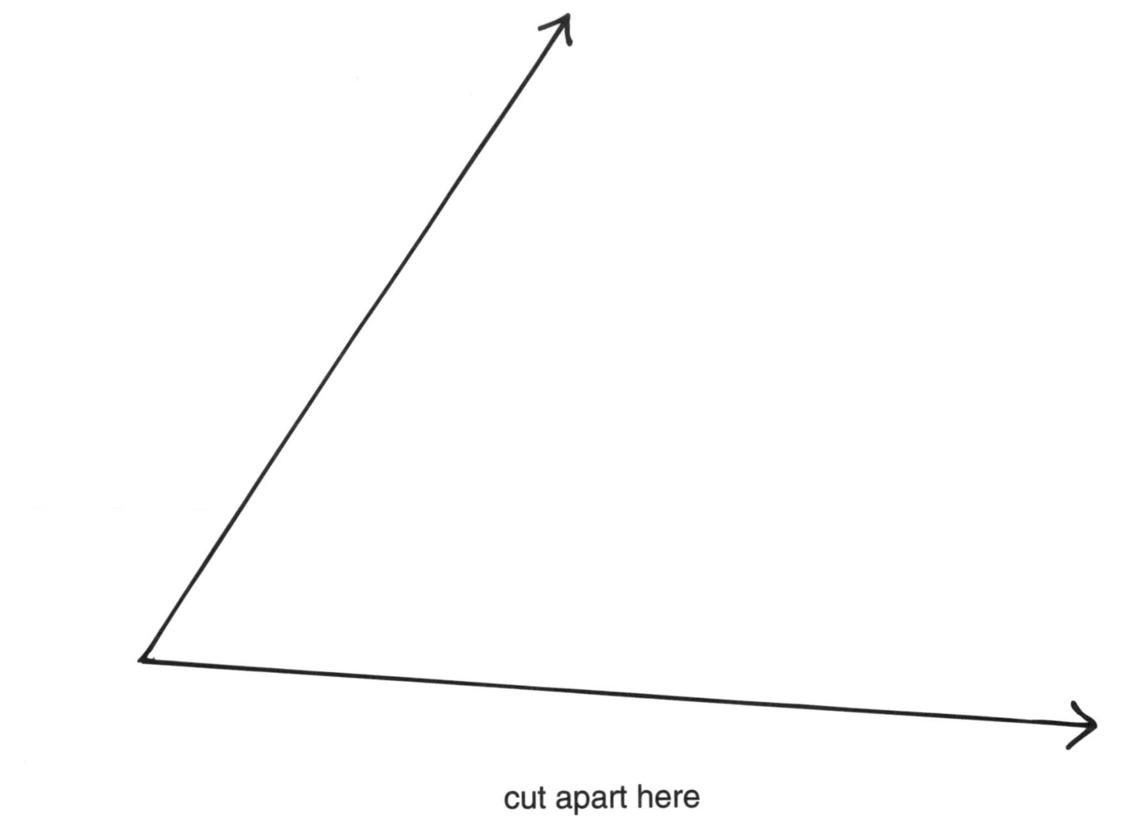

cut apart here

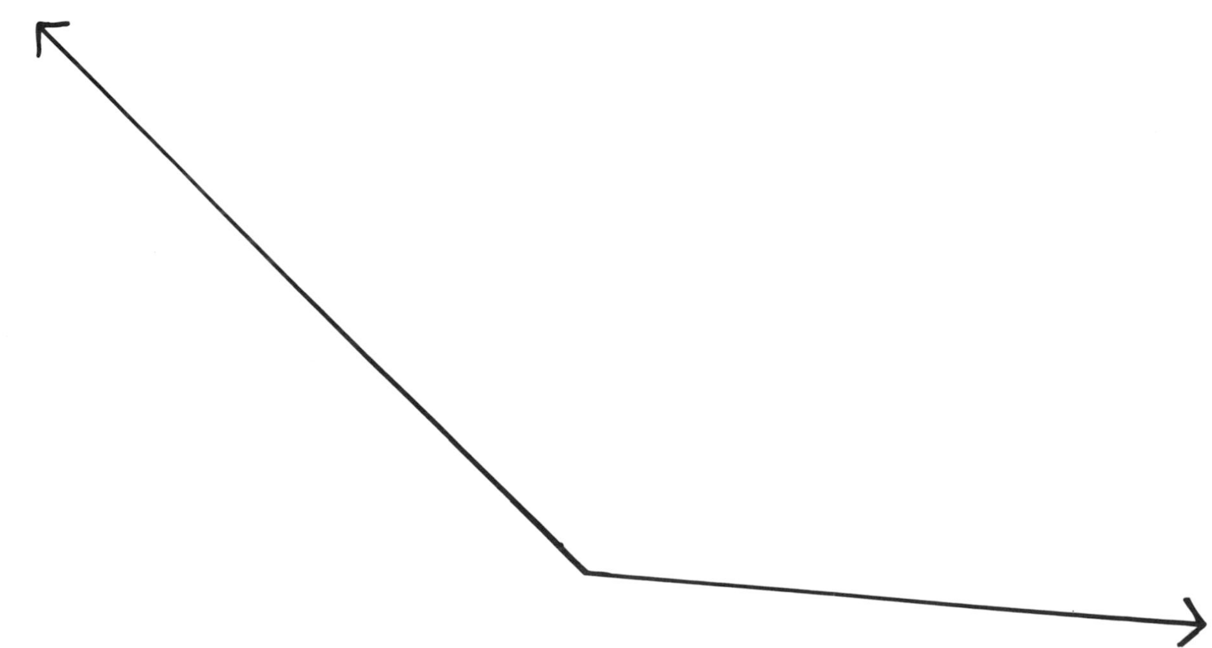

NAME ________________________________ DATE ____________________

WORKSHEET G-16.2
Drawing Bisectors

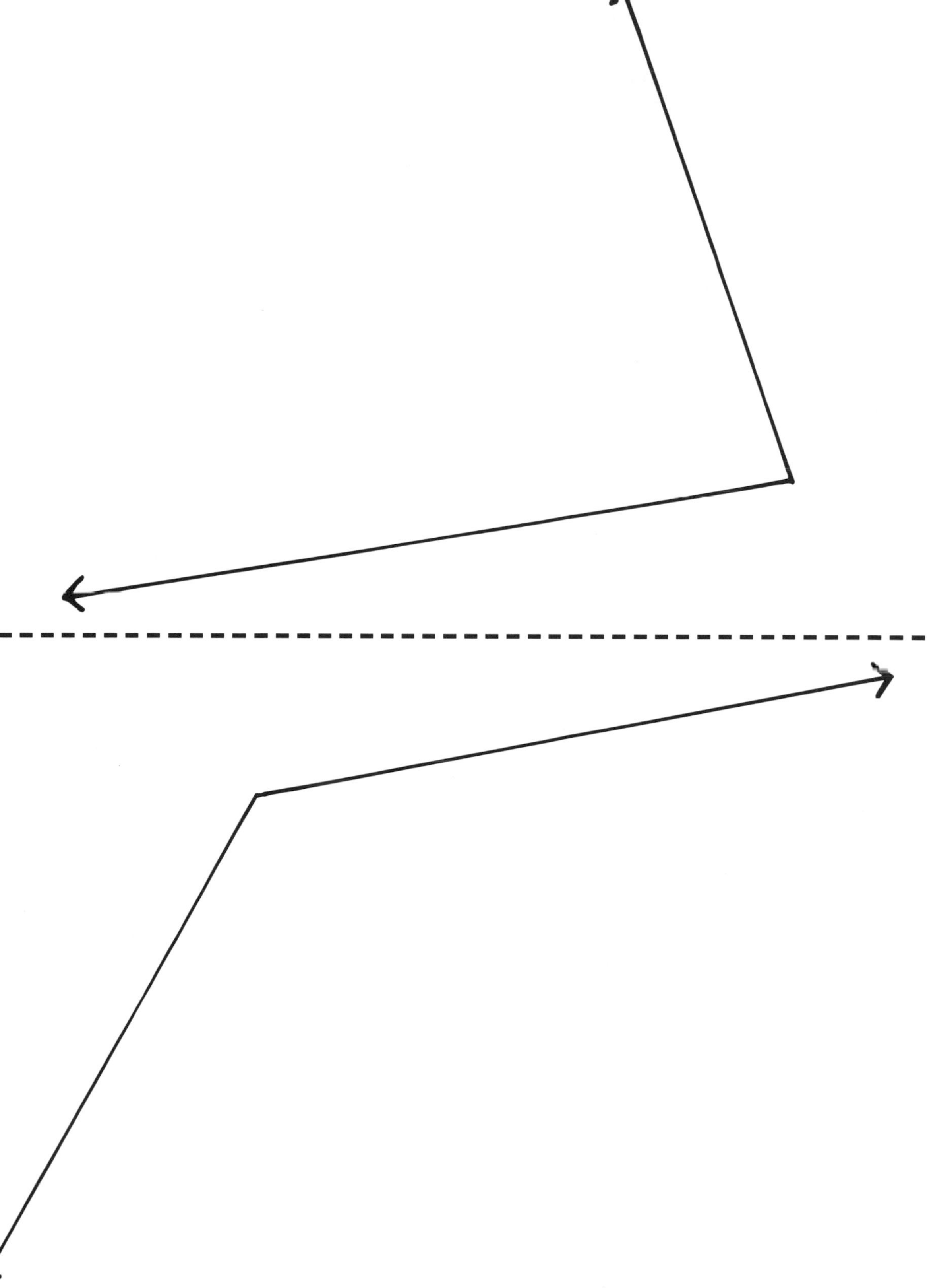

6. Have students label line CP as the *angle bisector.*

7. Now have students repeat the above process with the larger angle provided.

8. Ask students to share what they have learned about an angle bisector and some of its properties. Observations will be similar to those made previously in Activity 1.

Activity 3: CHECKING OUT BISECTORS

(Cooperative Groups)

Materials: For each team:
Protractor
Centimeter ruler
Index card
Pencils
Paper

Management: Teams of 4 students each (20 minutes)

Directions:

1. On each team, two members will construct an angle (up to 180 degrees in size) and the other two members will try to construct its bisector. They may use one of the measuring methods developed in the previous activity. Applying one method, they might mark off equal distances along the rays, then use an index card or a protractor to construct a line segment perpendicular to each ray at its newly marked point. The intersection point of the two drawn segments, when connected to the vertex of the original angle, will locate the angle bisector. Using the second method, they might measure the original angle, then construct an angle half its size on top of it. The new angle will share one of the original rays. The new ray needed for the new angle will be the bisector.

2. The two students who drew the original angle should now check the correctness of the bisector's position by folding along the bisector to see if the angle's rays match. If not, the bisector must be redrawn.

3. Student roles can be reversed several times until the students have worked with several different sizes of angles.

OBJECTIVE 17: Identify skew lines.

Activity 1: SKEW LINES IN THE CLASSROOM

(Concrete Action)

Materials: Pencils
Paper
Colored markers

Management: Partners (20–30 minutes)

Directions:

1. Have each pair of students move around the classroom until they locate two examples of pairs of skew lines (lines that are in two different planes and never meet).

2. Have them make a realistic or perspective sketch of each scene they find and boldly outline the locations of the skew lines on the sketch. The drawings can be displayed on the classroom wall.

3. Have other students look at a pair's sketch, then try to find the actual skew lines somewhere in the classroom.

Note: Perspective drawings are difficult to make, so encourage students to clarify their drawings with word descriptions when necessary.

Activity 2: HUNTING FOR SKEW LINES

(Pictorial Action)

Materials: Colored markers
Worksheet of different room scenes (described below in step 1)

Management: Partners (15 minutes)

Directions:

1. Give each pair of students a worksheet containing 1–2 pictures of room scenes. The pictures may be large, bright photographs cut from magazines or catalogs or perspective drawings of various room settings (living room, kitchen, classroom, etc.). Such pictures can easily be photocopied for classroom use. Each view should be a close-up where edges of furniture and corners of walls can be easily seen. Do not use flat floor plans.

2. Have students locate three to four examples of skew lines in each scene and outline the skew lines with a colored marker. Use a different color of marker for each *pair* of skew lines.

Example of a pair of skew lines: The imaginary line that runs along a horizontal, top edge (not top "face") of an *open* door and the imaginary line that runs along an outside vertical edge of the door frame in the wall from the ceiling to the floor. These two lines will never intersect each other, nor are they parallel to each other. They cannot lie in the same plane.

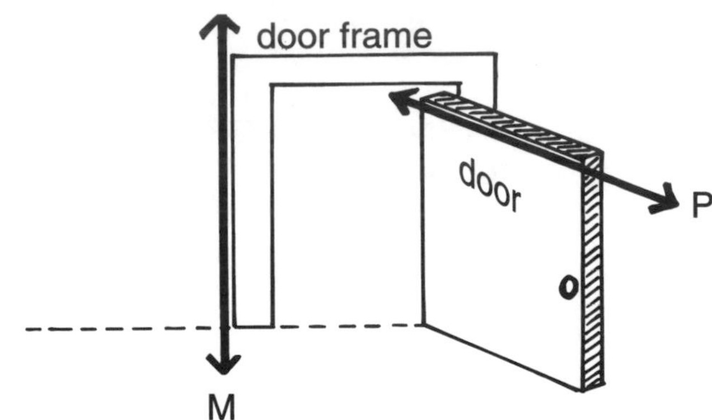

Lines M and P will not intersect...or lie in the same plane.

Activity 3: BUILDING BATTLE

(Cooperative Groups)

Materials: For each team:
A deck of cards and racetrack made from Worksheets G-17.3a and G-17.3b
2 game markers
Attachable tagboard arrowheads
Approximately 8 Tinkertoy™ rods and 6 connectors (or other similar construction materials)

Management: Teams of 4 students each (20 minutes)

Directions:

1. Use this activity to review several kinds of lines (parallel, intersecting, skew), as well as other geometric concepts (angles, rays, line segments). Using Worksheets G-17.3a and G-17.3b, give each team a deck of 12 cards and a sheet of paper with a short, curved racetrack drawn on it (show *Start* in one end space and *Finish* in the other end space with approximately 8 spaces drawn between them). Prepare the deck as follows:

- 2 cards contain the words "2 skew lines";
- 1 has "3 skew lines";
- 1 has "2 parallel lines";
- 1 has "3 parallel lines";
- 1 has "3 lines intersecting at one point";
- 1, "acute angle";
- 1, "obtuse angle";
- 1, "ray";
- 1, "line segment";
- and the 2 remaining cards might say "Go forward 1 space" and "Go back 1 space."

2. The deck is shuffled and placed face down in the center of the table. On each team, one pair of students will play against the other pair of students.

3. Each pair of partners places a game marker on Start, then the pairs take turns drawing a card off the deck.

4. Each pair of players must build a model of whatever the card names or move their marker the indicated number of spaces on the gameboard. (Tinkertoys™, straws with Play-doh®, or other similar materials are very good for building geometric models.) If the other players agree with the model, the pair may move their marker one space forward on the gameboard. They then place their used card in the Discard Stack.

5. If the drawing deck is depleted before the game is over, players should reshuffle all the cards and begin a new deck. Play continues until a marker reaches Finish.

WORKSHEET G-17.3A
Sample Cards for Building Battle

Enlarge, glue on tagboard, laminate, then cut apart, if preferred.

2 skew lines	2 skew lines	3 skew lines
2 parallel lines	3 parallel lines	3 lines intersecting at one point
acute angle	obtuse angle	ray
line segment	Go forward 1 space.	Go back 1 space.

WORKSHEET G-17.3B
Sample Racetrack for Building Battle

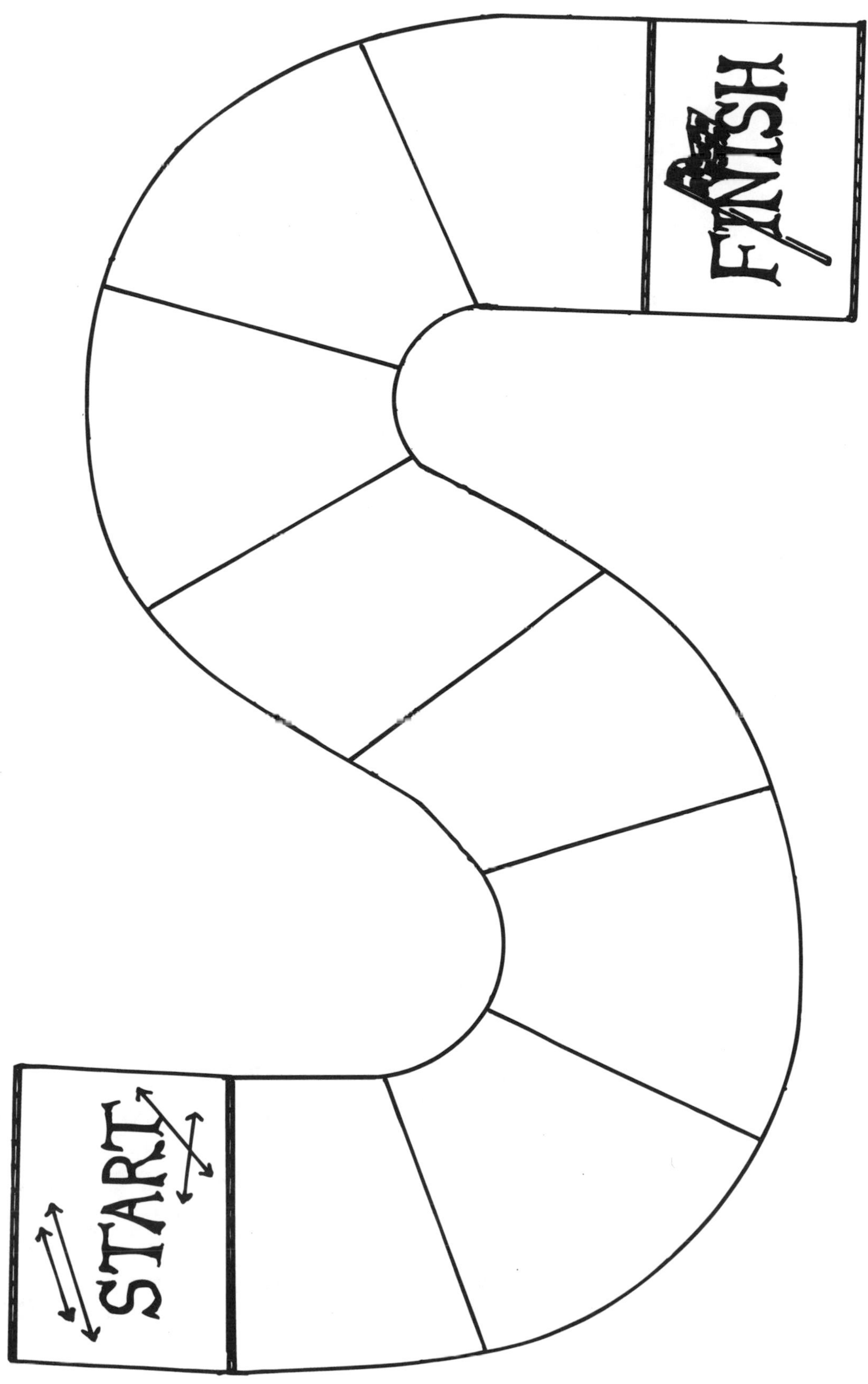

OBJECTIVE 18: Recognize transformations of two-dimensional figures.

Activity 1: TANGRAM DESIGNS
(Concrete Action)

Materials: 7-piece tangram sets (Worksheet G-18.1)
Large sheets of paper
Pencil
Colored markers

Management: Partners (20 minutes)

Directions:

1. Give each pair of students a 7-piece tangram set (commercial or teacher-made using Worksheet G-18.1).

2. Have them make different designs (boat, animal, house, etc.), using all 7 pieces of their tangram set. They should trace around each design on a large sheet of paper, then color and name the design in some creative way. They may show the outline of each individual piece in the drawn copy if they prefer.

3. Have the students show their designs to the entire class. Discuss how all the different designs are made from the same 7 tangram pieces, but the pieces have just been arranged differently.

Activity 2: MISSING PARTS
(Pictorial Action)

Materials: Worksheet G-18.2
Scissors
Tracing paper
Pencils

Management: Partners (15 minutes)

Directions:

1. Give each pair of students a copy of Worksheet G-18.2 that contains four to five rows of figures. Each row shows a design at the far left, then four design *parts,* three of which will combine like puzzle pieces to make the design given at the left.

2. The students must ring the parts that will make the total figure without any overlapping or gaps.

3. If they have difficulty with a particular design, have them trace the parts onto another sheet of paper and cut out the traced pieces. They can then physically rearrange the cut-out pieces to find which ones make the total figure.

Note: To prepare an additional worksheet, draw 4–5 irregular polygons on a sheet of paper. Trace these onto the worksheet to serve as the original designs. Then cut each initially drawn

WORKSHEET G-18.1
Pattern for Tangram Designs

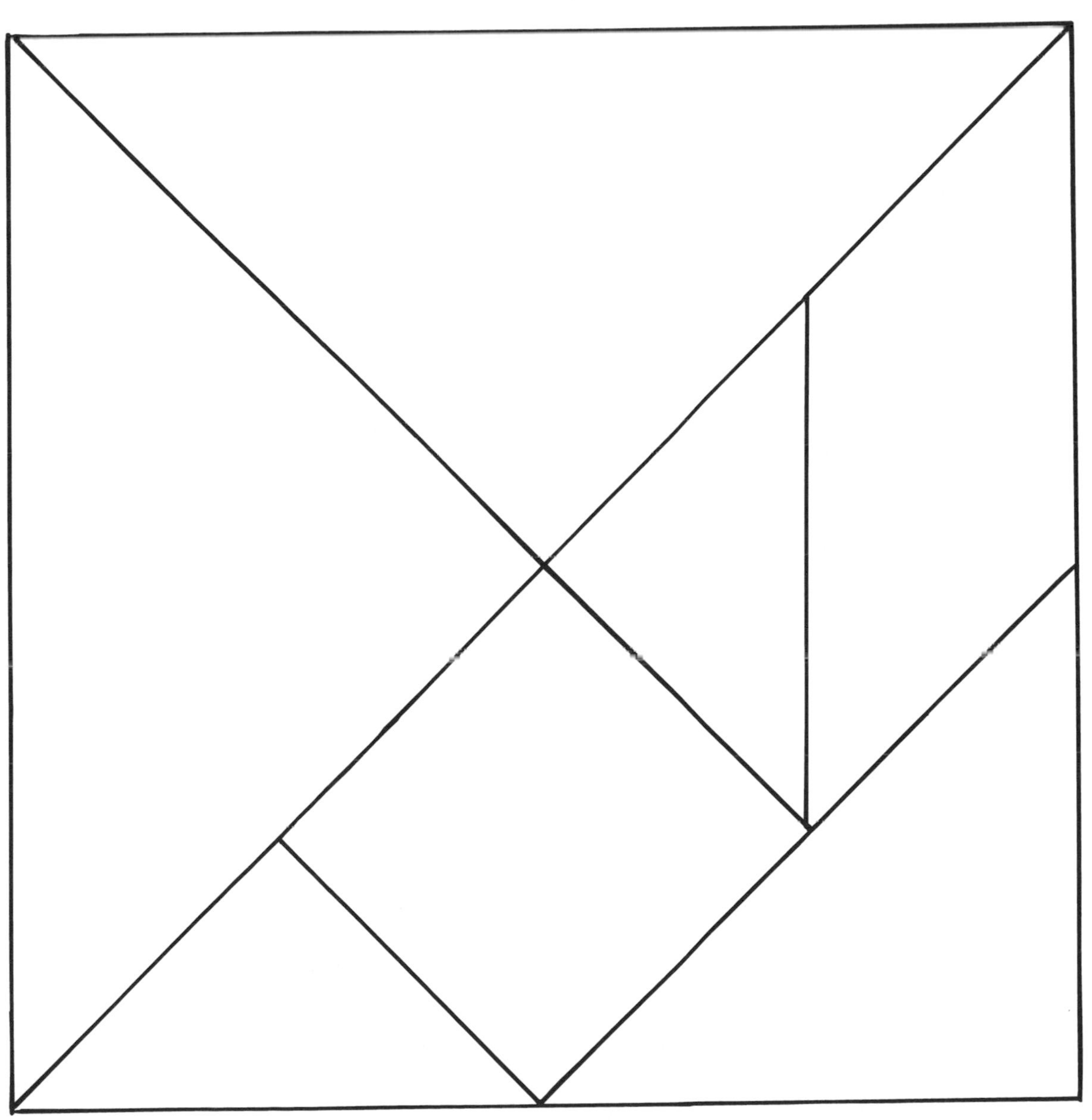

polygon into 3 pieces and trace these pieces onto the worksheet as the design parts according to their initial or slightly rotated positions in the original figure. Add another unrelated part to the row to serve as a distractor. Vary the distractor's location from row to row.

Example of a row on the worksheet (starred parts form original design):

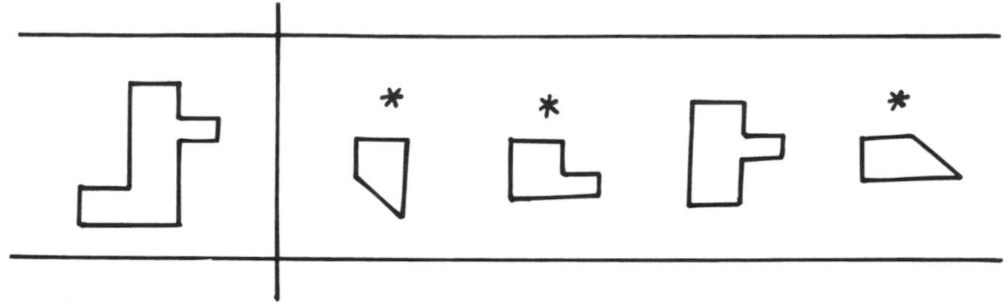

4. Answer key for Worksheet G-18.2:

1. A C D
2. A B D
3. B C D
4. A B C
5. A B D

Activity 3: PUZZLING POLYGONS

(Cooperative Groups)

Materials: Polygon Worksheets G-18.3a and G-18.3b (a set of cut-out polygon parts)

Management: Teams of 4 students each (20 minutes)

Directions:

1. Give each team a copy of Worksheet G-18.3a with 5 large irregular polygons drawn on it and labeled A, B, C, D, and E. There are two pairs of polygons on this worksheet where, within each pair, the two polygons are transformations of each other or rearrangements of the same set of parts.

2. Also give the students 4 cut-out parts from Worksheet G-18.3b that, when put together in certain ways like a puzzle, will match (i.e., be similar but not necessarily congruent to) a pair of related polygons on Worksheet G-18.3a. (For younger students, these parts might be congruent quadrilaterals; for older students, the parts might have various polygonal shapes.) Make the parts no smaller than about 3 inches across for ease of handling.

3. Each team member is responsible for maneuvering one of the parts. No one person should be holding or moving all the parts; this must be a cooperative effort. The students must work together to arrange the four parts to determine which of the original polygons (A, B, C, D or E) they can match in form.

4. Once they have matched to one polygon, they must try to match their set of parts to another polygon on the same worksheet.

5. Extension Activity: To convert the sample materials to a higher level of difficulty, simply divide each of the four cut-out polygon parts into two new parts. Students must then work with *eight* parts instead of *four*.

NAME ______________________________ DATE ____________________

WORKSHEET G-18.2
Missing Parts

For each item below, draw rings around the parts on the right that will combine (without overlapping or gaps) to make the shape shown on the left. Some parts may be rotated, but sizes will not change.

1. 

A  B C  D

2. 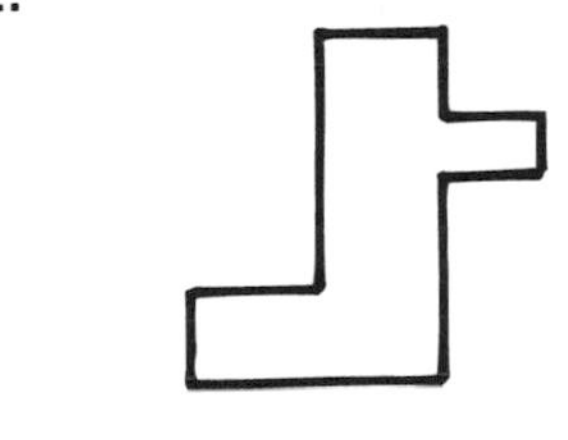

A 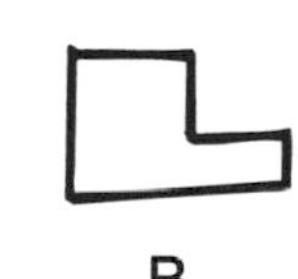 B 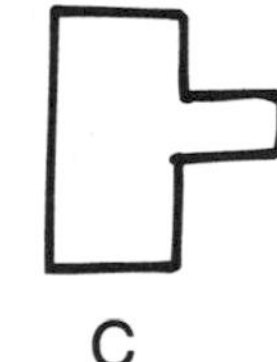 C  D

3. 

A 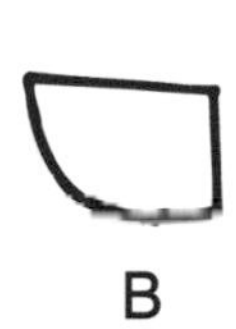 B  C  D

4. 

A  B C  D

5. 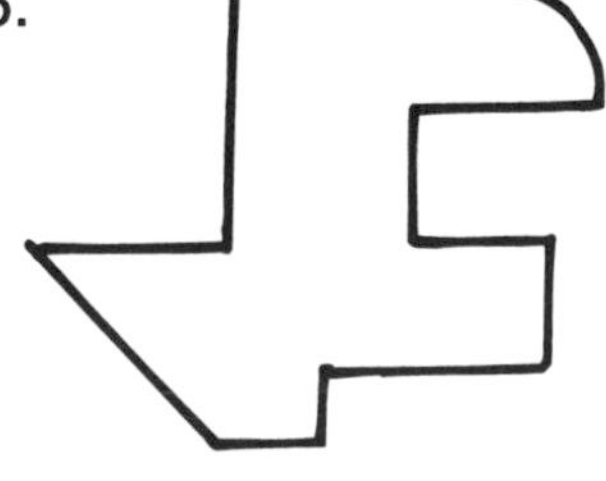

A B C  D

NAME ______________________ DATE ______________

WORKSHEET G-18.3A
Puzzling Polygons

Find two polygons where one is a *transformation* of the other, that is, where both can be made from the same set of parts.

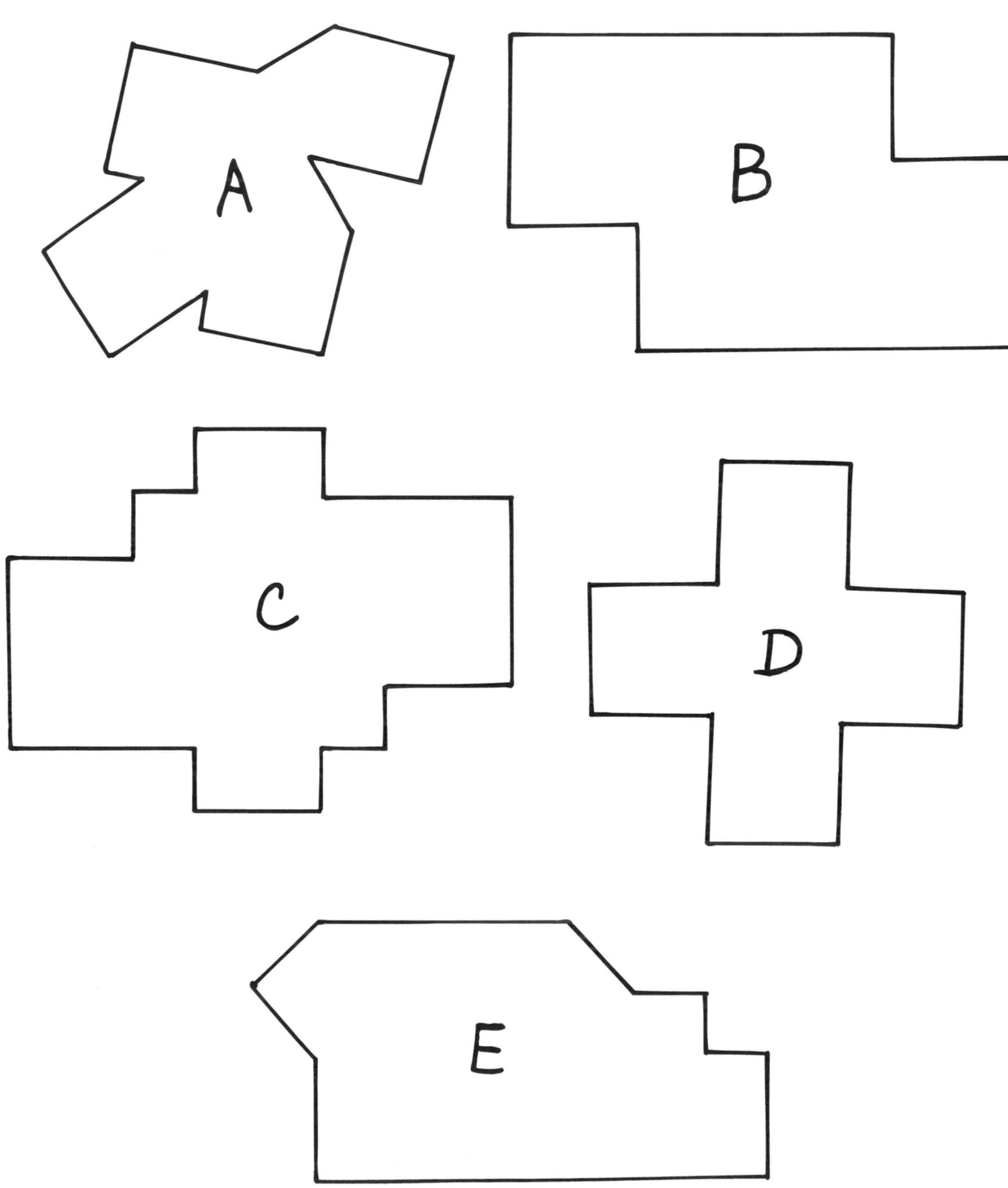

WORKSHEET G-18.3B
Patterns for Puzzling Polygons

Enlarge, then remove the solution information from the sets below. Give each team one of the sets to cut out and use for Activity 3.

Set of parts for matching polygons A and D:

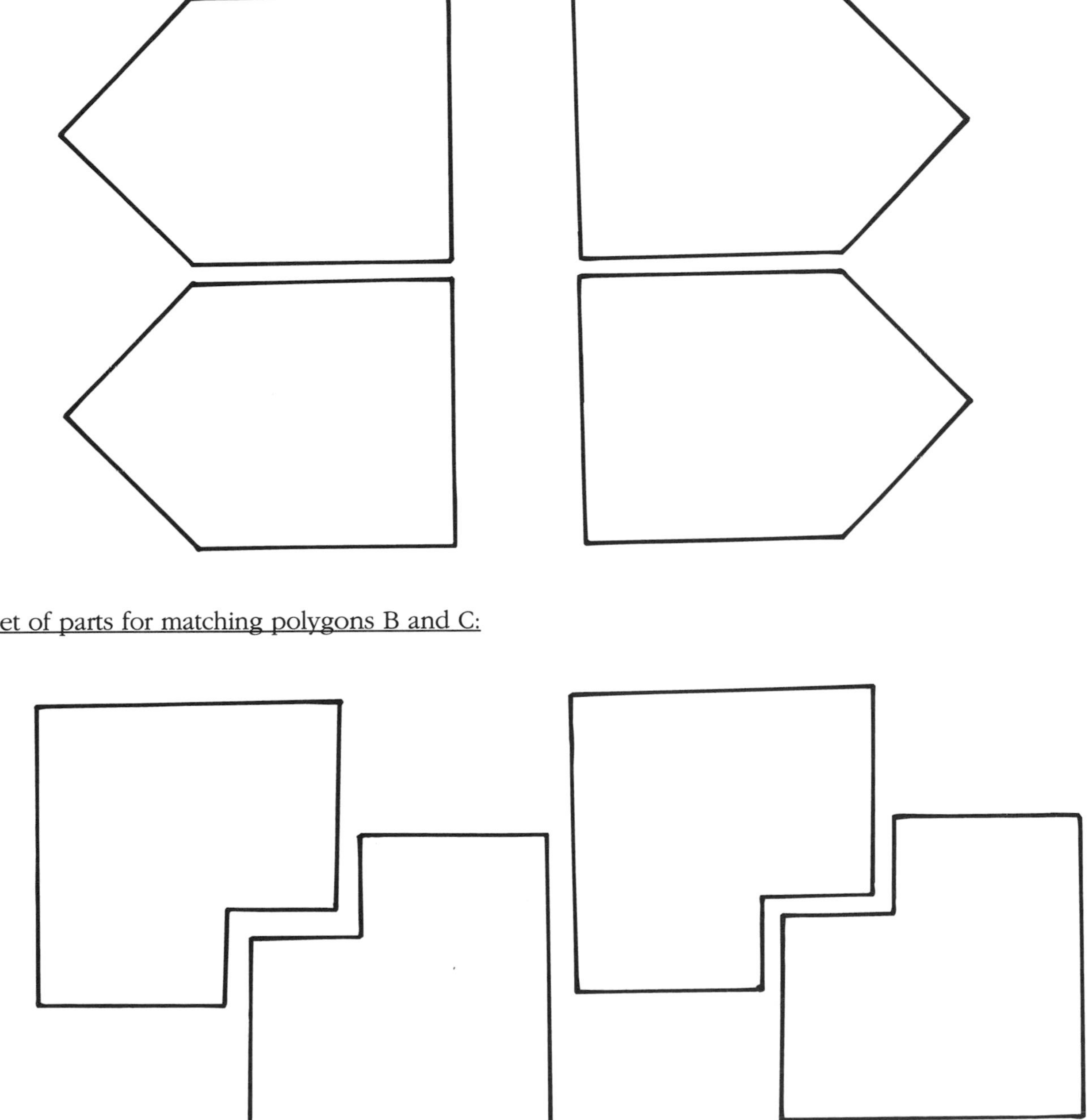

Set of parts for matching polygons B and C:

CHAPTER 5

MEASUREMENT

INTRODUCTION

This chapter introduces students to the concept of measurement, including the simple measurement of perimeters of various shapes to the circumferences of circles. It also provides fun activities that help students understand the concepts of area, volume, and dimension. Students are shown how to use simple tools, such as scales, through game activities emphasizing various measurement methods. The concept of the constant, pi, is also introduced with special procedures for students to learn how to measure this constant. The measurement of the areas of triangles, rectangles, parallelograms, trapezoids, circles, squares, and irregular shapes is also covered for class use.

OBJECTIVE 1: Find the perimeters of irregular polygons.

Activity 1: BUILDING FENCES

(Concrete Action)

Materials: Bags of 30–40 flat-sided toothpicks each (or medium-sized paper clips or flat coffee stirrers cut in one-inch strips)
Paper
Pencils

Management: Partners (20 minutes)

Directions:

1. Give each pair of students a bag of toothpicks. Have them build various polygons having different numbers of sides and different lengths of sides. Some should be concave, others convex. Toothpicks should be placed end to end to form the sides. Each toothpick represents one unit of length.

2. Have the students draw pictures (freehand, not to scale) of the polygons they build, marking off the toothpicks on their drawings and recording the number used to make each side.

3. Ask them to find out how many toothpicks were used to make each polygon, then write this amount beside its picture and label the amount as *perimeter.* If they already know the general polygon names (e.g., quadrilateral, pentagon, or hexagon), they might also write a polygon's name beside its picture. If a polygon has more than 10 sides, numerical names like *15-gon* or *20-gon* may be used where the number indicates the number of sides.

4. Have each pair of students write two or three sentences about how they found the perimeters of their polygons. This will vary from directly counting one by one to adding the different side lengths in some way. If there is sufficient time, have them read their sentences to the rest of the class.

Activity 2: PERIMETER CHECK

(Pictorial Action)

Materials: Centimeter or half-inch grid paper
Colored markers

Management: Partners (15 minutes)

Directions:

1. Give each pair of students a sheet of grid paper and a colored marker.

2. Have the students take turns drawing an irregular polygon on the grid paper, following only the segments on the grid (no diagonals). After one student draws a polygon, the other should count the unit segments used to make the shape and write the total below the polygon, using the form "perimeter = _______ units." The first person then recounts the segments to check the amount given.

3. Allow students to continue taking turns as long as time permits.

Activity 3: ROLL 'N DRAW

(Cooperative Groups)

Materials: For each team:
2 dice
1-minute egg-timer
4 sheets of half-inch or centimeter grid paper
2 colored markers

Management: Teams of 4 students each (20 minutes)

Directions:

1. On each team, one pair of students will roll the dice and multiply the two numbers rolled. The other pair has to draw as many polygons having a perimeter equal to the given product as they can on their grid paper, using only grid segments and no diagonals.

2. After one minute, the drawing must stop and the pair that rolled the dice will check the perimeters of the new polygons. For each correct polygon, the pair doing the drawing will earn 2 points; for each incorrect one, they will lose 1 point.

3. The turn to draw now goes to the pair who rolled the dice on the previous turn and the game continues.

4. If after one minute a pair cannot think of any polygons to draw, the turn passes back to the other pair.

Note: If 1-minute egg-timers are not available, the teacher or a student might serve as a timer for the entire class. All pairs involved in drawing during a particular turn would then do it at the same time.

5. The pair on each team having the most points when the game is called will be the winners. An alternative might be to have the pair win who reaches a chosen total first, say, 15 points. The number selected for the points limit would depend on the abilities of the students to quickly think of and draw polygons of the desired perimeters.

OBJECTIVE 2: Find the perimeters of parallelograms.

Activity 1: BUILDING PERIMETER LOOPS
(Concrete Action)

Materials: Bags of 25–30 large paper clips or commercial multilinks
Paper and pencils

Management: Partners (20 minutes)

Directions:

1. Have students discuss the characteristics of parallelograms (four sides, opposite sides parallel and congruent).

2. Give each pair of students a Bag of paper clips (or multilinks). Ask them to make a chain loop by connecting 12 of the paper clips together end to end.

3. Have the students shape the loop into different parallelograms, both rectangular and nonrectangular. For each shape made, have them record the lengths of the four sides and write a number sentence for finding the perimeter.

For example, for the loop with a perimeter of 12 paper clip units, a parallelogram with 1 unit and 5 units for its adjacent sides might be formed. Then students might write 1 + 5 + 1 + 5 = 12 units or 2(5) + 2(1) = 12 units or 2(1 + 5) = 12 units. Commuted forms are also acceptable, such as 2(5 + 1) = 12 or 2(1) + 2(5) = 12. Other possible parallelograms would use 2 and 4 or 3 and 3 for the adjacent side lengths.

4. Encourage students to write as many different number sentences as they can for the perimeter of each shape they form. Other perimeter values for chain loops that will allow several parallelograms to be formed are 16, 18, and 20. Have students try these perimeters, as well as others.

5. After several perimeter values have been explored, ask students to try to make a parallelogram with 17 paper clips (or any other odd number less than 30). They will not be able to do this. Have students share their ideas about why they think the task is impossible (e.g., 17 cannot be separated into two equal groups of adjacent side lengths) or what might be needed to make it work (e.g., cut some paper clips in half).

6. Guide students to observe that the number sentences for rectangular and nonrectangular parallelograms having the same side lengths will look the same. Right angles do not affect the perimeter value.

Activity 2: SUMMING THE SIDES
(Pictorial Action)

Materials: Parallelogram Worksheet M-2.2 for each pair of students
Pencils

Management: Partners (25 minutes)

Directions:

1. Give each pair of students a copy of Worksheet M-2.2 containing several parallelograms (rectangular and nonrectangular) with unit lengths marked off on their sides. Shapes with four equal side lengths should also be included.

2. For each shape ask the students to find the lengths of the four sides and the perimeter and to write a number sentence that uses the side lengths to find that perimeter. Number sentences will vary.

3. Students should now write two or three sentences, telling in their own words how the perimeters of such shapes can be found. Sample ideas to be expanded:

Add the two adjacent sides, then double their sum.

Double one side, double the other side; add the two new amounts together.

4. Have each pair of students exchange paragraphs with another pair, then edit the paragraphs for clarity of meaning. These *perimeter* paragraphs can then be revised, rewritten, and displayed on a classroom bulletin board or perhaps placed in a special student booklet describing the properties of parallelograms.

5. *Extension:* Once students have expressed the perimeter process in sentences, have them try to create their own *formulas* using words or symbols of their choosing.

Examples: (2x side 1) + (2x side 2) = perimeter where side 1 and side 2 are adjacent side lengths, or 2(a + b) = p where a and b are adjacent side lengths and p is the perimeter.

After they have shared their creations with the class, introduce them to whatever form their textbook may use. Acknowledge that the book's formula is simply *another* way to find perimeter (if different).

Activity 3: PERIMETER CHALLENGE

(Cooperative Groups)

Materials: Bags of 30 flat-sided toothpicks

Management: Teams of 4 students each (15 minutes)

Directions:

1. Give each team a Bag of toothpicks.

2. Two students on each team will call out two numbers for the side lengths of a parallelogram (any two numbers whose sum is 15 or less; the two numbers can be the same). The other two members of the team must build a rectangular parallelogram with the toothpicks, using the given lengths, then transform it to a nonrectangular parallelogram of the same dimensions. The builders must also tell the other pair what the perimeter is in toothpick units and how they computed it, using the side lengths. Methods of computation will vary.

3. If a pair's explanation is satisfactory to their teammates, they may then call out two numbers for the other two to use to build new parallelograms.

4. The pairs continue to take turns until time is called.

NAME ______________________ DATE ______________

WORKSHEET M-2.2
Summing the Sides

For each parallelogram, find the length of each side and the perimeter. Write a number sentence that shows how you found the perimeter.

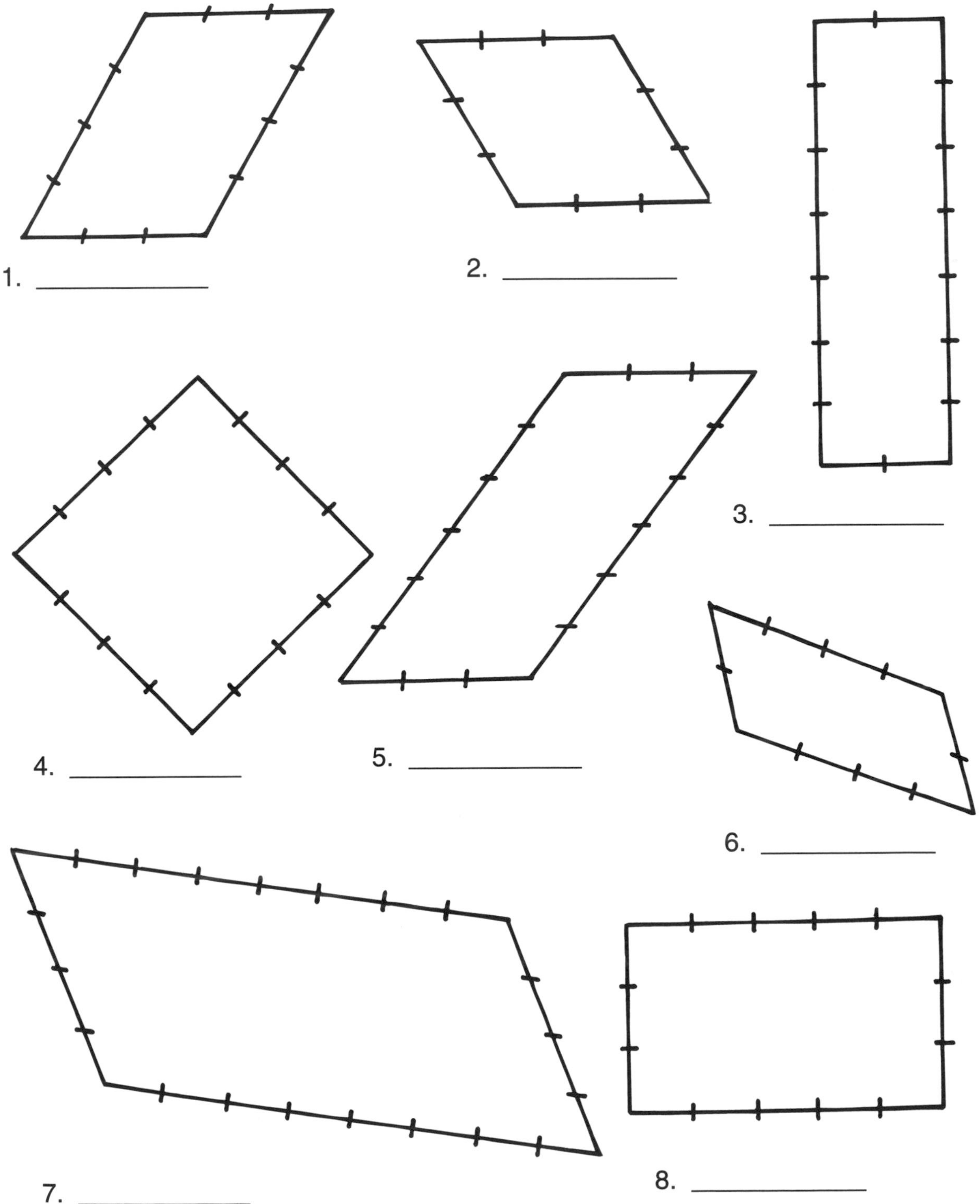

OBJECTIVE 3: Measure the mass (weight) of small objects.

Activity 1: WEIGHING IN
(Concrete Action)

Materials: Two-pan balances
Assorted small objects (crayons, coins, keys, jar lids, erasers, small plastic scissors, etc.)
Selected materials to serve as the counters or units for measuring weight

Management: Teams of 4 students (30 minutes)

Directions:

1. There are a variety of materials that can serve as the measuring units for this activity. For older students, commercial mass sets in grams might be used. For younger students, objects that are uniform in weight and size and are available in large quantities can be used: buttons, wooden centimeter cubes, medium paper clips, checkers, large dried beans, etc. The name of the material is then used as the name of the measuring unit. For example, an eraser may weigh 4 wooden checkers' worth.

2. Give each team a bag of the chosen measuring units (enough to weigh any of the selected small objects) and a two-pan balance. Also provide the team with 5–6 small objects to weigh, or have them find their own objects in the classroom.

Note: If commercial two-pan balances are not available, you can make your own with coat hangers and paper cups. The point where the wire is twisted together serves as the fulcrum. Add weights to the appropriate side if the hanger is not balanced when the cups are empty. A second coat hanger held by a student can provide the hook for holding up the balance.

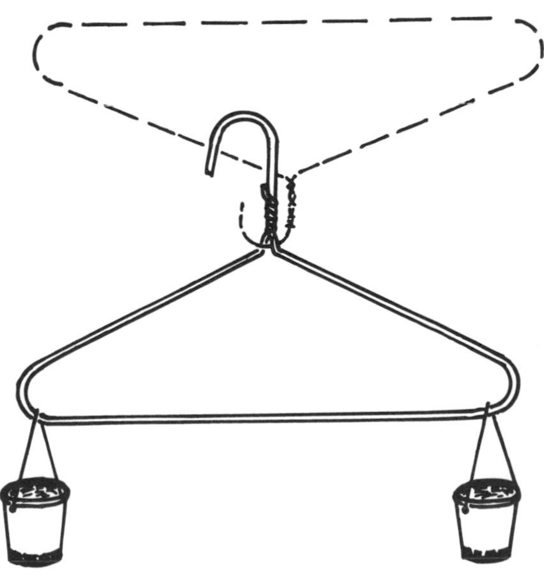

3. Each object will be placed in one pan of the scale and the measuring units added to the other pan until the two pans are balanced. The amount of units that balances the object will be the weight of that object in that particular unit of measure.

4. Students should record the name of each object weighed and the number of units that balance it.

5. Encourage students to hold one object in each hand and try to feel the difference in their weights. Have them repeat the process with various pairs of objects. (This practice will prepare them for future weight judgments needed in Activity 3.)

6. If there is time, give each team a second type of measuring unit and ask them to reweigh their objects, using the new units. Have them compare the two weights found for the same object. Ask the students to explain why the two amounts are the same or different, especially since the two measuring units used do not look alike physically.

Activity 2: SELF-CHECK

(Pictorial Action)

Materials: Small objects used in Activity 1
Two-pan balance for demonstration only
Worksheets listing pairs of objects from Activity 1

Management: Partners (15 minutes)

Directions:

1. Prepare a worksheet that lists the small objects from Activity 1 in *pairs*. The objects in a pair may weigh about the same or may be noticeably different. Display the objects in the classroom where all students can see them.

2. Ask pairs of students to estimate which object in each pair is *heavier* or if they weigh the *same*. They should complete their worksheets without holding the objects themselves; they may, however, look at the objects on display in the room.

3. After all students have finished their estimates, have various students test their answers by holding one object of a pair in each hand. Also have others share their results from Activity 1 in order to determine correct answers to the worksheet.

4. If some do not agree with a suggested answer or if two objects being compared in the list were not weighed with the same type of measuring unit in Activity 1, compare their weights by having two students place the objects in separate pans of the balance scale.

5. When two objects are *nearly* the same in weight, accept any answer, but require students to explain why they think the objects are the same or different (e.g., one balanced with more paper clips than the other did; the two differed only by one bean, which the balance scale cannot detect very easily). Comparing the weights of extremely small objects is quite difficult to do, especially for the young and inexperienced.

Activity 3: CAN YOU GUESS HOW MUCH?

(Cooperative Groups)

Materials: Assorted small objects
Two-pan balances
Bags of 75–80 medium paper clips, or gram mass sets

Management: Teams of 4 students each (20 minutes)

Directions:

1. Give each team a pan balance and a bag of medium paper clips or a gram mass set. Two medium-sized paper clips (approximately $1\frac{1}{4}$ inches long) weigh about 1 gram and can therefore be used to estimate an object's weight in grams if actual gram units are not available.

2. Give each team 6–8 small objects. Have the students practice holding then weighing two or three of their objects in grams (or in paper clips, which they should convert to grams). At this point it may be helpful to students to know that a nickel weighs about 5 grams. Weights of objects should *not* be written down at this point.

3. Two students on a team will then choose an object from their set and ask the other two to hold then estimate its weight in grams. After a value is given, the first pair will weigh the object to check the estimate. An estimate within 3 grams of the actual weight is acceptable.

4. The other two students now take their turn by choosing a new object for the first two to hold and estimate its weight. Then the object is weighed.

5. The pairs continue to take turns until time is called or all their objects have been weighed.

OBJECTIVE 4: Compare and measure the capacities of assorted containers.

Activity 1: FILL IT UP!

(Concrete Action)

Materials: Assorted watertight containers of different sizes, shapes, and heights
Pitchers of water
Small plastic dishpans for catch basins
Paper towels
Measuring cups or graduated cylinders

Management: Teams of 4 students each (20 minutes)

Directions:

1. For younger students, have team members practice filling one container with water, then pouring its water into other containers in order to learn which container holds more. Include containers found at school, such as cold drink cans, juice or milk cartons, ice cream cups, or gallon cans used in the cafeteria, all with their tops cut off for easy pouring. Also have some unusually shaped containers.

2. All pouring should be done over the plastic dishpan in order to catch *most* spills. The spilled water can later be poured back into the pitcher. (Alternatives to water: rice, salt, sand, or beans)

3. For older students, if preferred, have team members fill each container with water, then pour the water into measuring cups or graduated cylinders (milliliters) to learn how much the container will hold. It is also helpful to have the older students pour directly from one container into another. This strengthens their ability to visually compare the capacities of different containers.

Activity 2: WHICH HOLDS MORE?

(Pictorial Action)

Materials: Worksheet M-4.2
Pencils

Management: Partners (15 minutes)

Directions:

1. Give each pair of students a copy of Worksheet M-4.2 containing pictures of familiar containers grouped in pairs. Magazines are a good source for such pictures.

2. Ask the students to decide which container in each pair holds more.

3. Have real samples of the pictured containers available, if possible, but do not show them to the students at first. After they have completed their worksheets, discuss their answers. If there is disagreement, show the students the actual containers. If necessary, pour water or rice from one container into the other or, if possible, physically place one inside the other to convince the doubters!

NAME ______________________________ DATE ____________________

WORKSHEET M-4.2
Which Holds More?

For each pair of containers, circle the one you think holds *more*. The pictures are not drawn according to their real sizes.

1.

half-pint

12-oz. can

2.

mug of hot chocolate

pudding cup

3.

school box

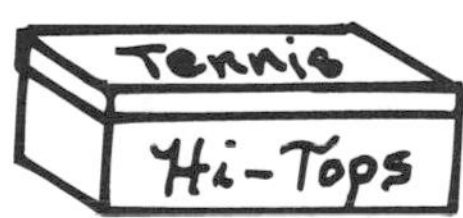

shoe box

4.

medium balloon

car tire's innertube

5.

school trash barrel

book bag

6.

box of crayons

30 1" x 3" strips

7.

salt shaker

jar of peanut butter

8.

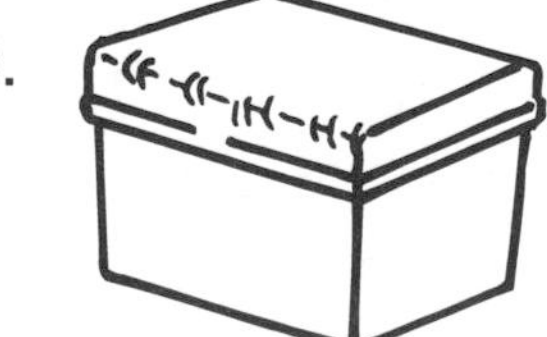

index card box

mustard jar

4. Accept any logical reason for an answer. For example, a child may be familiar with mustard only in a jumbo-sized jar, whereas others may be thinking of smaller sizes based on their own personal experiences.

Activity 3: MYSTERY CONTAINERS

(Cooperative Groups)

Materials: 6 different containers labeled A through F (include 2–3 with unusual shapes; certain vases are good choices)
Paper
Pencils

Management: Teams of 4 students each (30 minutes)

Directions:

1. Place the 6 empty containers beside each other in random order where all students can see them easily.

2. Ask each team to study the containers carefully and try to order them by capacity from *least* to *most*. Do not allow them to actually measure the mystery containers. They can only compare them visually.

3. Students should record their reasons for placing each container ahead of another in the ordering. They should write down the six letters A–F in the order they have selected for the containers.

4. After all teams have completed their ordering, have each team present its solution and reasons. List all the different orderings on the chalkboard.

5. Finally pour water from one container to another to demonstrate what the actual capacity ordering should be for the 6 containers. Prizes for the winning teams perhaps?

OBJECTIVE 5: Determine the amount of time elapsed in a given situation.

Activity 1: HOW LONG DOES IT TAKE?

(Concrete Action)

Materials: Clocks or watches with second hands (alternative: digital watches)
Paper
Pencils

Management: Whole class or teams of 4 students each (30 minutes)

Directions:

1. This activity can be done with the entire class, using the teacher or a student as timekeeper. If teams are used, the members will need their own watch and can take turns being timekeeper.

2. In any case, it might be more effective (and less disturbing to other classes) to take the class outside or to the school gym or cafeteria where there is room to spread out.

3. Select a variety of actions for the students to perform and time, the sillier the better. Either ask them to count how many times they can do a certain thing in 1 minute or ask them to time how long in minutes or seconds it takes them to do a given number of movements. Have the class suggest some activities themselves, but here are some ideas to try:

- *How many times in 1 minute can you:*

  jump on just one foot?

  say "Mary Had a Little Lamb"?

  blink your eyes (or just your right eye)?

  say the whole alphabet out loud?

  touch your toes?

  write "I'm Number One"?

  blow a soap bubble with a wand or straw?

  move a marble from one bowl to another, using a plastic teaspoon (place several marbles in one bowl, then transfer them one at a time to a nearby bowl)?

  step on a different floor tile in the classroom or hallway (must step on a minimum of 6 different tiles; a tile may be stepped on more than once as long as consecutive steps are on different tiles)?

  stack and unstack 6 paper cups (a stacking and unstacking counts as one time)?

  stack one checker or wooden cube or jumbo marshmallow on top of another (i.e., how tall a stack can you make before the stack falls)?

  move a paper square (approximately 2" × 2") from one location on the table to another location 12 inches away by sucking on it through a drinking straw (prepare a pile of 20 paper squares, then move the pile one square at a time)? [Hint: Place straw near corner of paper, not its center.]

- *How long in minutes or seconds will it take you to:*
  hold your breath?
  blow one sustained whistling sound?
  turn around 20 times?
  drink a small cup of water?
  run around the baseball diamond (or football field or gym floor)?
  count to 100 out loud?
  balance only on one hand and one foot?
  balance a long pencil on the tip of your finger?
  empty water from a full eyedropper one drop at a time?
  melt down a burning birthday candle?
  watch an ice cube melt completely?
  keep a bubble-gum bubble inflated without its popping or collapsing?

Activity 2: TIMING YOURSELF
(Pictorial Action)

Materials: Worksheet M-5.2
Pencils

Management: Partners (15 minutes)

Directions:

1. Give each pair of students a worksheet that lists different events that occur daily in their lives.

2. Ask them to estimate in minutes how long it takes each event to occur. Answers will vary.

3. When all students have completed their worksheets, have them share their time estimates with the class. If the times offered for the same event differ too much, discuss with the class what might be the more appropriate amount of time. *Example:* 60 minutes to eat lunch in the school cafeteria is too much time and 5 minutes to eat is too little; 20 minutes is probably more reasonable.

Activity 3: TIME PREDICTING
(Cooperative Groups)

Materials: For each team:
List of simple tasks
Objects needed for the tasks
Watch with second hand (or digital watch)

Management: Teams of 4 students (20 minutes)

Directions:

1. Two members of a team predict how many *seconds* are needed to complete the first task on the list. The other two then time them as they actually perform the task.

NAME ______________________________ DATE ____________________

WORKSHEET M-5.2
Timing Yourself

Estimate how many minutes it takes for each event to occur.

Event	*Time (in minutes)*
1. Brush your teeth	
2. Fasten your shoes	
3. Travel to school in the morning	
4. Read one page of your history book	
5. Eat lunch at school	
6. Walk around your school building	
7. Comb your hair	
8. Drink one can of soda	
9. Eat a single-dip ice cream cone	
10. Sharpen a pencil in the pencil sharpener	

2. The second pair of students now predicts the time for the next task on the list and performs the task while the others time them.

3. Have the teams continue this process until they finish the list or time is called.

4. Before assigning this activity, ask students for their ideas on some tasks to include on the list. Select tasks that require less than $1\frac{1}{2}$ minutes. Here are some suggestions you might want to consider: link 10 paper clips together to form a chain; turn 4 paper cups upside down, then right side up, turning one cup at a time; place 6 mixed-up pencils parallel to each other with their erasers at the same end, then reverse their direction, one pencil at a time, to place the erasers at the other end; place 10 separated checkers into one stack; for 15 times, toss a small ball about 1–2 feet into the air and catch it when it comes down; open the rings of a notebook, place 5 sheets of paper one at a time onto the rings, and close the rings.

OBJECTIVE 6: Find the area of a rectangle.

Activity 1: COUNTING SQUARES

(Concrete Action)

Materials: One-inch paper squares
Record sheet (Worksheet M-6.1)
Pencils

Management: Partners (20 minutes)

Directions:

1. Give each pair of students a bag of 40–50 one-inch paper squares. Construction paper or lightweight tagboard may be laminated, then cut into one-inch squares. These will be called *square units,* our measures for area.

2. Have students build a rectangular region with the paper squares by placing 5 squares with edges touching in a "row" (left to right) in front of them on their desktop, then place a second row lengthwise beside the first row. Explain that this is *2 rows of 5 square units per row.* The number of square units used is the *area* of the rectangular region or the rectangle, which is the region's boundary.

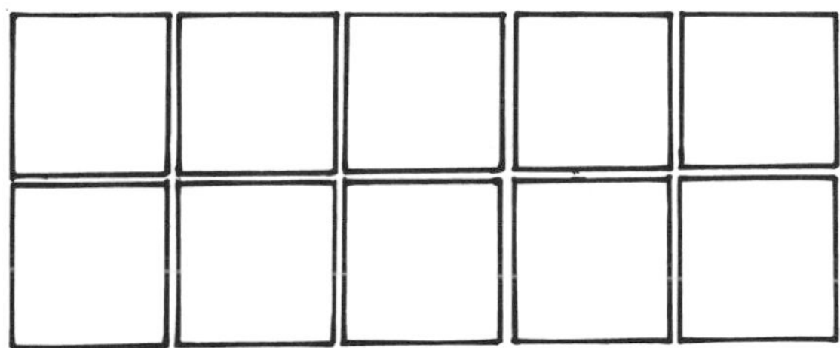

2 rows of 5 square units per row

3. Ask them to build several different regions, using the row-row size language of step 2 above. Include some square regions as well, such as 4 rows of 4 square units per row.

4. Have them record their results on the record sheet. Do not talk about the edge lengths of the rectangles at this time.

5. Once students are easily building the required regions, as well as some of their own, ask them to share their methods of finding the amount for the area. Do not try to lead them to a formula at this time. Possible methods:

- count each square one by one;
- add the number of squares in one row to the amount in the next row, etc.;
- multiply the number of rows by the number of squares in each row.

NAME ______________________________ DATE ____________________

WORKSHEET M-6.1
Counting Squares

Build different rectangular regions with the paper squares. Record your results in the table below.

Number of rows	Squares in a row	Total squares or area
2	5 sq. units	______ sq. units

Activity 2: HOW MANY DO YOU SEE?

(Pictorial Action)

Materials: Area Worksheet M-6.2
Pencils

Management: Partners (20 minutes)

Directions:

1. Have students count the square units inside each rectangle and complete the table on the worksheet.

2. At this point they should also record the length in units of each side of the rectangle. Use "side 1" and "side 2" for the adjacent edges here, not "length" and "width." Allow students to decide which edge is to be side 1 and which is to be side 2. It does not matter.

3. Have some students describe the rectangles they drew for the given area in the last item. Two sizes will be possible (2 × 12 or 3 × 8).

4. Then ask them to look at their completed tables and compare the number of rows and row size used for each rectangle to its two side lengths. This is a relationship that most students recognize quickly—the numbers in the two situations are *equal in value,* but they play *different roles* in the rectangle.

5. Have them write one or two sentences that tell how they can find the area of a rectangle, (a) using the number of rows and row size, and (b) using the two side lengths of the rectangle. Ask several students to read their sentences to the entire class.

Activity 3: AREA ROLL

(Cooperative Groups)

Materials: For each team: 2 dice and 40 one-inch paper squares

Management: Teams of 4 students each (15 minutes)

Directions:

1. Students on a team take turns rolling the 2 dice and building a rectangle whose side lengths equal the two numbers rolled.

2. After a region is complete, the builder tells the others what the area for the rectangle will be in square units. The other members must agree with the answer before the next person gets a turn.

3. Do not require a specific method for finding area during this activity. At first the builder may just count the squares one by one. Eventually he or she will simply state the product of the two numbers rolled rather than do the counting.

NAME ______________________ DATE ______________

AREA WORKSHEET M-6.2
How Many Do You See?

Find the area in square units of each rectangle. Complete the table below.

1. 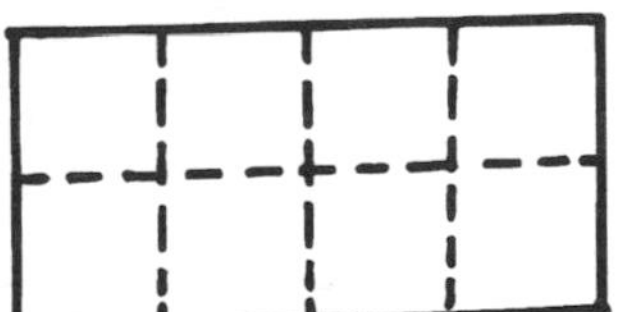

2. 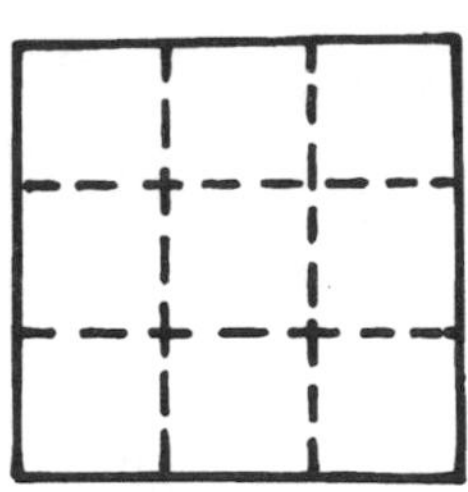

3.

4. 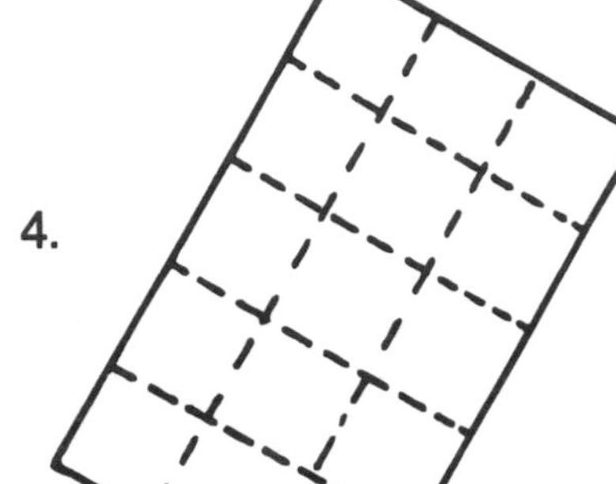

5. 6. 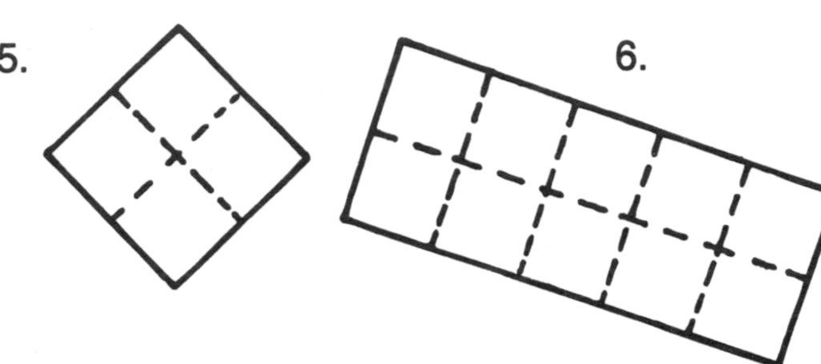

7. On the grid below, draw a rectangle whose area is 24 square units.

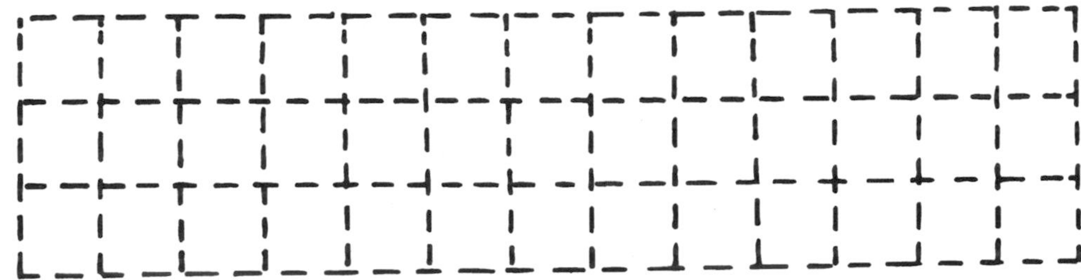

Rectangle	Number of rows	Squares in a row (or row size)	Area in sq. units	Length in units	
				Side 1	Side 2
1					
2					
3					
4					
5					
6					
7					

OBJECTIVE 7: Find the area of a parallelogram.

Activity 1: TRANSFORMERS
(Concrete Action)

Materials: Parallelogram grid patterns (Worksheet M-7.1)
Scissors
Red and blue markers (or any two colors; not black)
Paper and pencils
Transparent tape

Management: Teams of 4 students each (30 minutes)

Directions:

1. Give each team several patterns for parallelograms (use nonrectangles) drawn on grids, scissors, and red and blue markers.

2. Ask them to cut out the first parallelogram and trace around it on a plain sheet of paper. Now they are to try to find a *simple* way to rearrange the shape into a rectangle without losing any of the original area. This can be done by cutting the grid shape apart, making the least number of cuts possible. To prevent possible confusion, all cuts should be made along grid segments that are perpendicular to one of the longer sides of the parallelogram. Examples of possible cuts in the *same direction* and *perpendicular to* a pair of parallel sides:

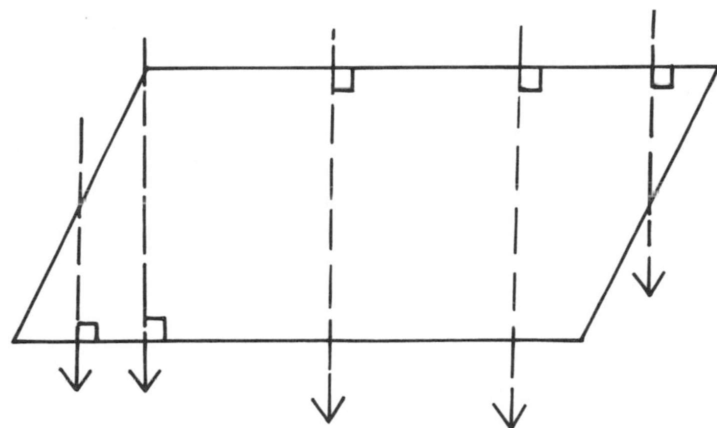

3. Encourage teams to explore different ways, but tell them not to do any actual cutting until they feel confident that their new way will work. For example, cutting the shape completely into individual centimeter squares is not an acceptable solution. One major strategy is to try to rearrange the more obvious triangular sections of the parallelogram.

4. Once students have converted their grid shape into a rectangle, have them temporarily tape the parts together and mark off a line segment in red along the rectangle's length. Have them also mark off another segment in blue along its width, and find the rectangle's area, using the grid units to measure the red and blue segments.

5. Now have the students untape and move the parts back into their original positions to reform the parallelogram by placing the parts on the shape's outline traced earlier. The parts can now be taped down on this tracing of the original parallelogram.

6. Ask them what they notice about the locations of the colored line segments on the reformed shape. The segments may appear fragmented at this time, depending on how the students cut the original shape apart. Even though segments in the *same color* may not be completely aligned, they should be oriented in the *same direction*. One set of colored segments should be in a perpendicular direction to the second set of colored segments.

7. Guide students to see that the combined length of segments in one color equals the length of one edge of the parallelogram. The segments in the other color should be perpendicular to that same edge, and when combined, their total length should extend to the edge of the parallelogram that is opposite to the first one.

Some ways to rearrange and mark a parallelogram (symbols a, b, and c are used in the examples to show change in location of the different parts):

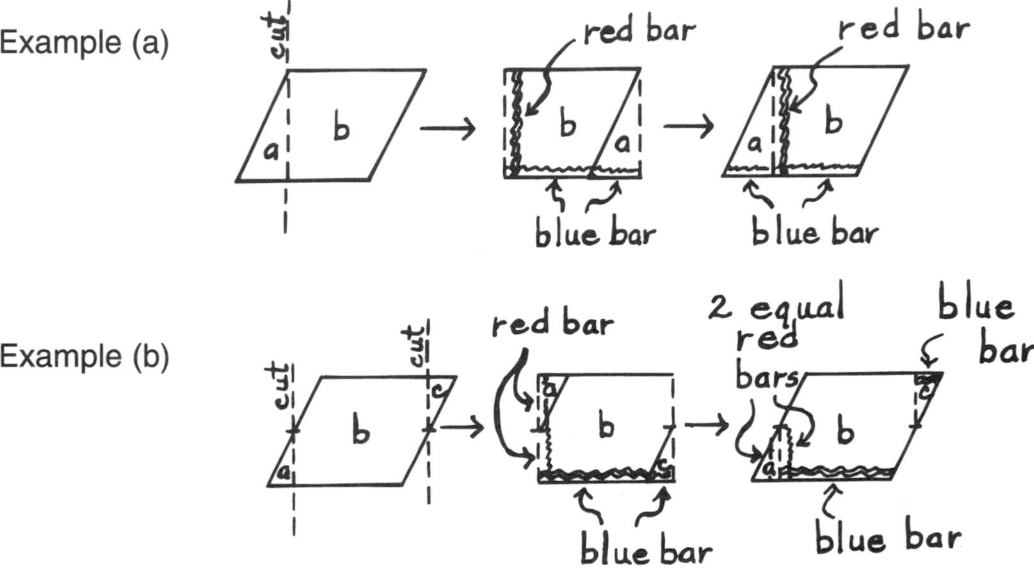

8. See the following illustration for a simple way to transform the original shape. Show this procedure to students whose first efforts prove too complicated.

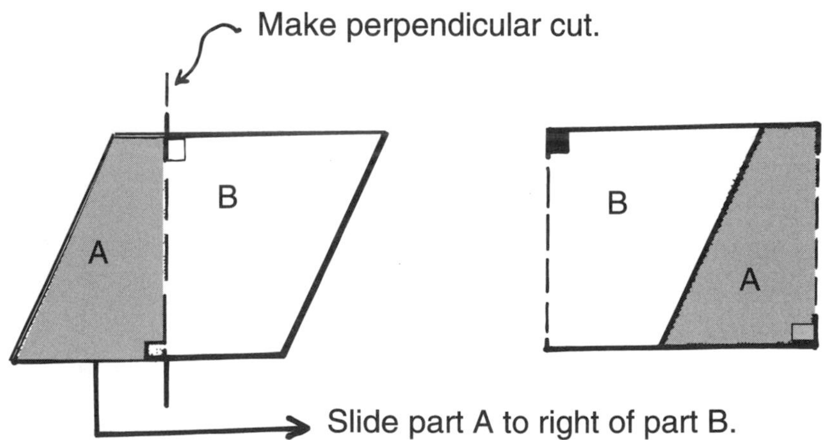

9. Now have students apply the procedure in step 8 to their remaining patterns. The lengths of each rectangle's adjacent edges should be marked as before and the area computed, then the rectangle transformed to the original parallelogram again. The number sentence used to find the area can be written below the tracing of the parallelogram.

10. Ask students what they have learned about the area of any parallelogram and the area of its transformed shape, a rectangle. (Since the area of the first shape has only been rearranged to form the second, the two areas must be equal. Make certain that all students intuitively accept this.)

Activity 2: FINDING DIMENSIONS

(Pictorial Action)

Materials: Area Worksheet M-7.2
Pencils
Centimeter rulers
Small index cards
Red and blue markers (or any two colors; not black)
Calculators (optional)

Management: Partners (30 minutes)

Directions:

1. Give each pair of students an area worksheet, a red and a blue marker, small index card, and a centimeter ruler.

2. For the first items students are to decide where to vertically "cut" each parallelogram, then mentally "slide" the left part to the right end and redraw it. The method to use is shown in the illustration below.

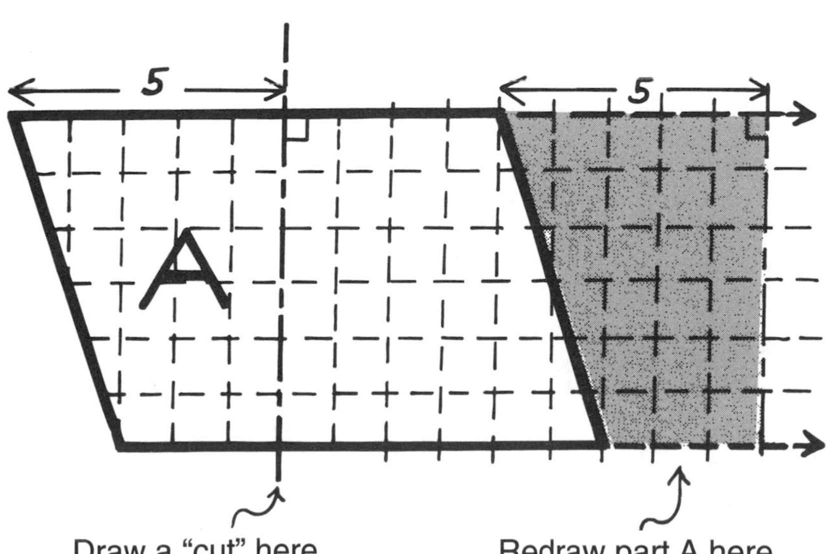

WORKSHEET M-7.1
Sample Parallelograms for Transformers

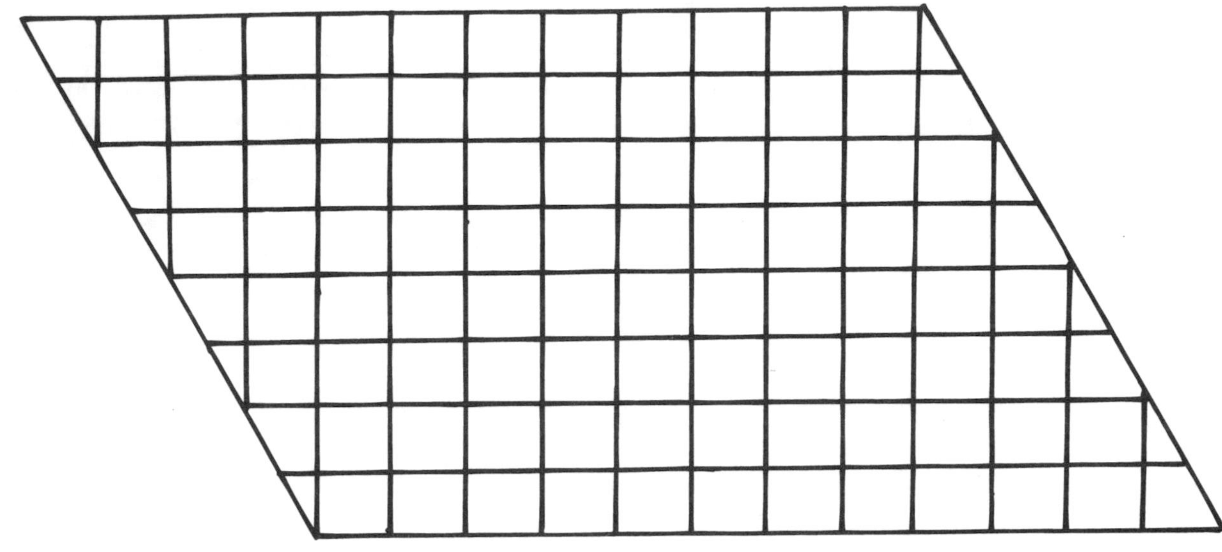

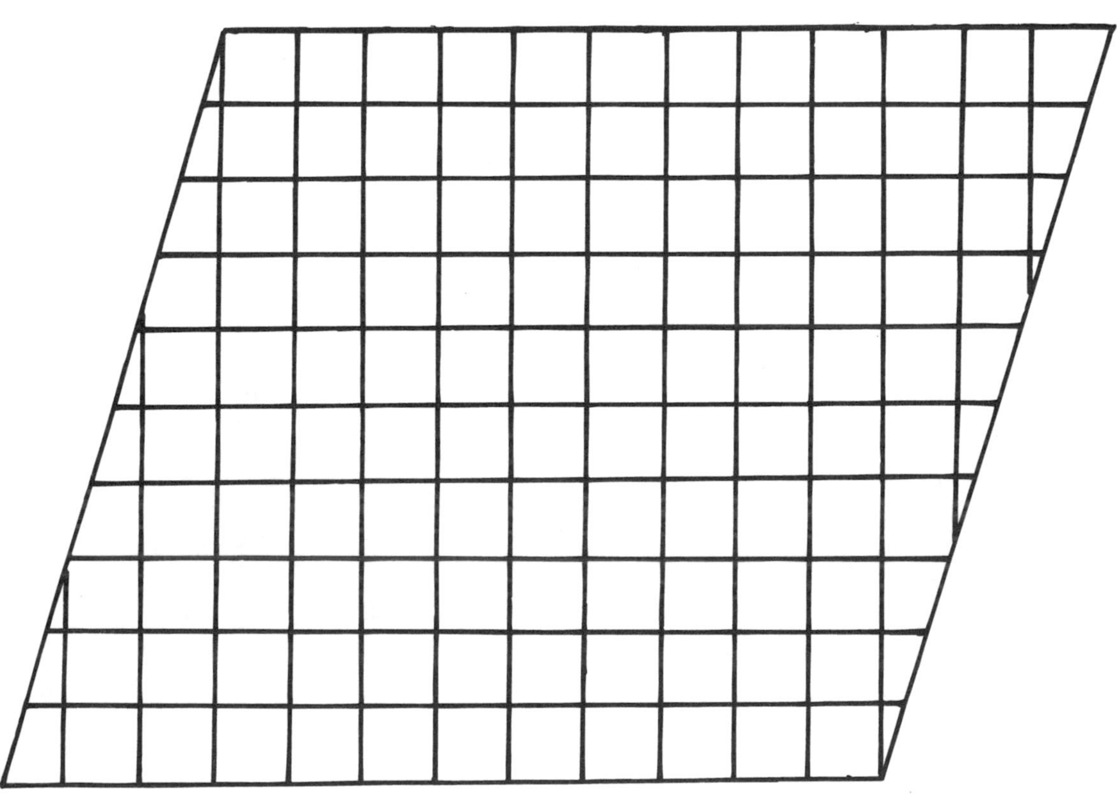

WORKSHEET M-7.1 (*cont.*)

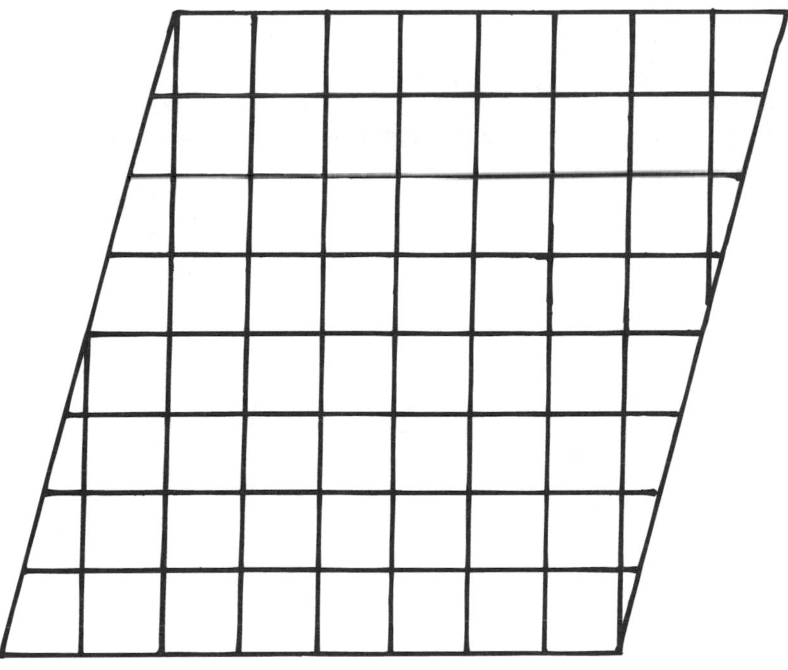

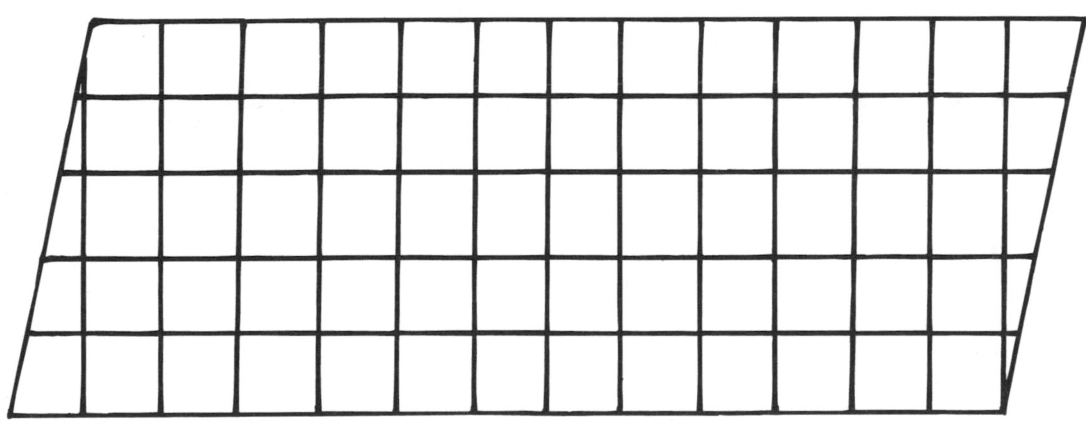

3. They will mark off the new rectangle's adjacent sides, one in red and one in blue, then find their values from the grid and compute the area in square units for the rectangle and hence for the parallelogram.

4. For the second group of items students are to select one side of each parallelogram and color it red. They should then place an edge of the index card against the red line segment or bar and use the card's adjacent edge to draw a blue line segment that connects perpendicularly from the red segment over to the opposite side of the shape.

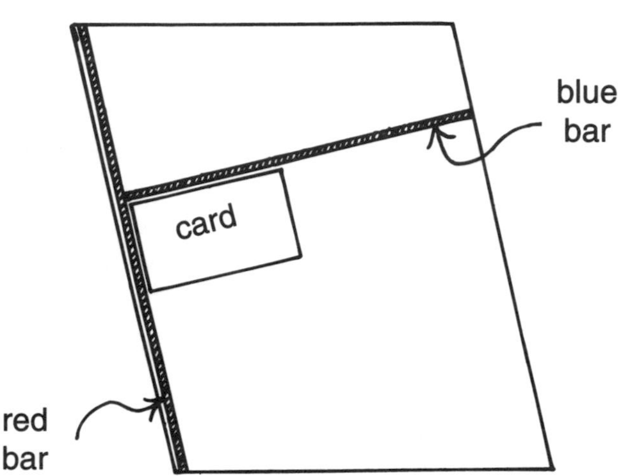

5. The red and blue segments now need to be measured in centimeters. These values (dimensions for area) are to be multiplied to find the area of the parallelogram.

6. For this last group, ask students to find another red-blue pair of perpendicular segments for each shape. They may have to extend one of the sides to do this. Have them measure to find the two new lengths and compute the area again.

7. Have students compare the two area values they have found (they should be equal). Discuss: *If both red-blue pairs produce the same area, does it matter which pair you use? What determines which pair you use?* (It does not matter. In reality you use the pair whose measurements you know.)

NAME ______________________________ DATE ____________________

AREA WORKSHEET M-7.2
Finding Dimensions

Follow the teacher's instructions to change the parallelograms to rectangles. Compute their areas.

1.

Dimensions used: _____ units and _____ units Area = _______square units

2.

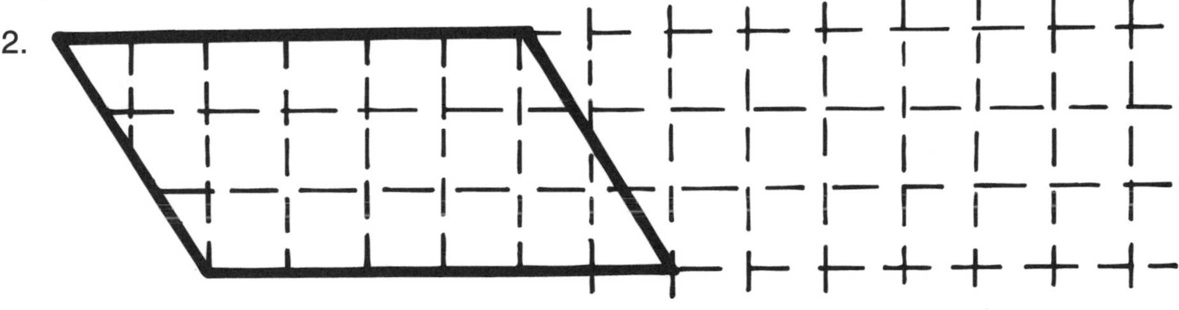

Dimensions used: _____ units and _____ units Area = _______square units

3.

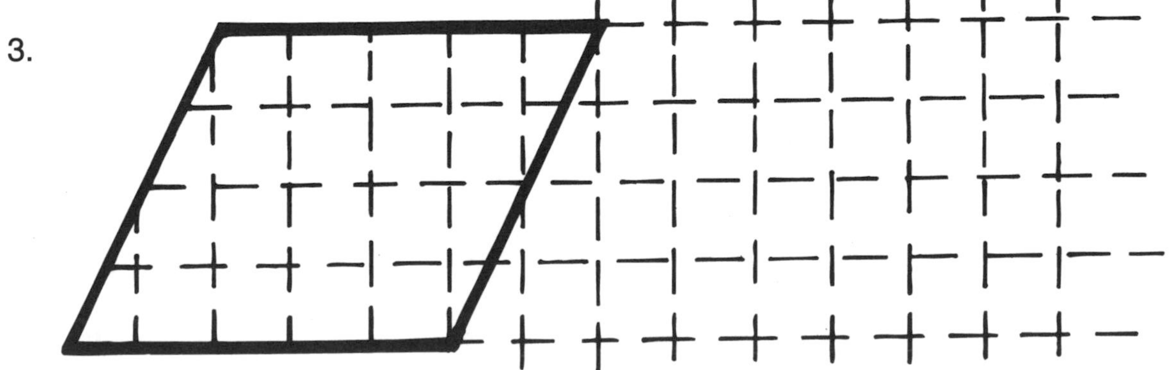

Dimensions used: _____ units and _____ units Area = _______square units

NAME ______________________________ DATE ____________________

AREA WORKSHEET M-7.2 (*cont.*)

On each parallelogram, mark and measure in centimeters the dimensions needed to find the area. Compute the area. Repeat with a different set of dimensions.

4.

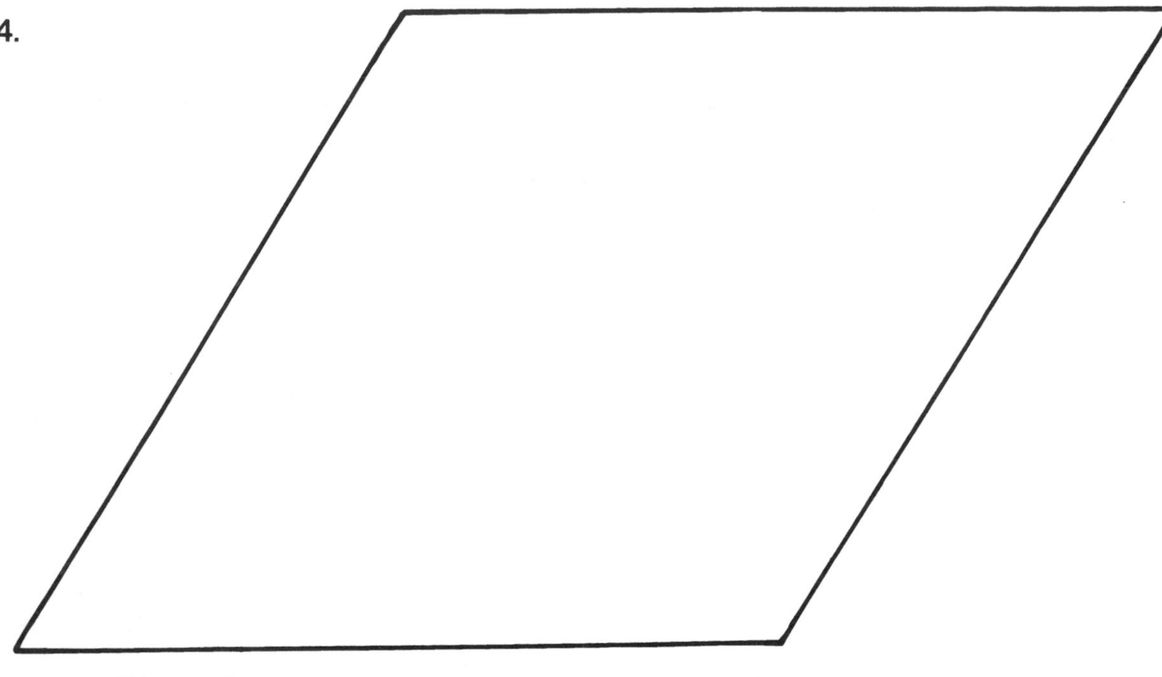

a. Dimensions used: ____ cm and ____ cm Area = ________ sq. cm

b. Dimensions used: ____ cm and ____ cm Area = ________ sq. cm

5.

a. Dimensions used: ____ cm and ____ cm Area = ________ sq. cm

b. Dimensions used: ____ cm and ____ cm Area = ________ sq. cm

Activity 3: TELL-OGRAM

(Cooperative Groups)

Materials: Sets of 20 cards (Worksheet M-7.3)
Calculators (optional)

Management: Teams of 4 students each (15 minutes)

Directions:

1. Team members place their set of cards in a stack face down and take turns drawing a card from the top of the stack.

2. There is a parallelogram pictured on each card. Upon drawing a card, each student must decide which measurements shown on the parallelogram are the correct ones to use to find its area and tell the other team members. In some cases, there will be more than one possible pair of numbers.

3. If they agree with the choices, the student holding the card then computes the area for the shape and tells the others. (Computation may be done mentally, with paper and pencil, or with a calculator, depending on the needs of the student.)

WORKSHEET M-7.3
Sample Card Set for Tell-ogram

Enlarge, cut out, and glue on tagboard cards. Orient the shapes on the cards as shown below. [shapes not drawn to scale]

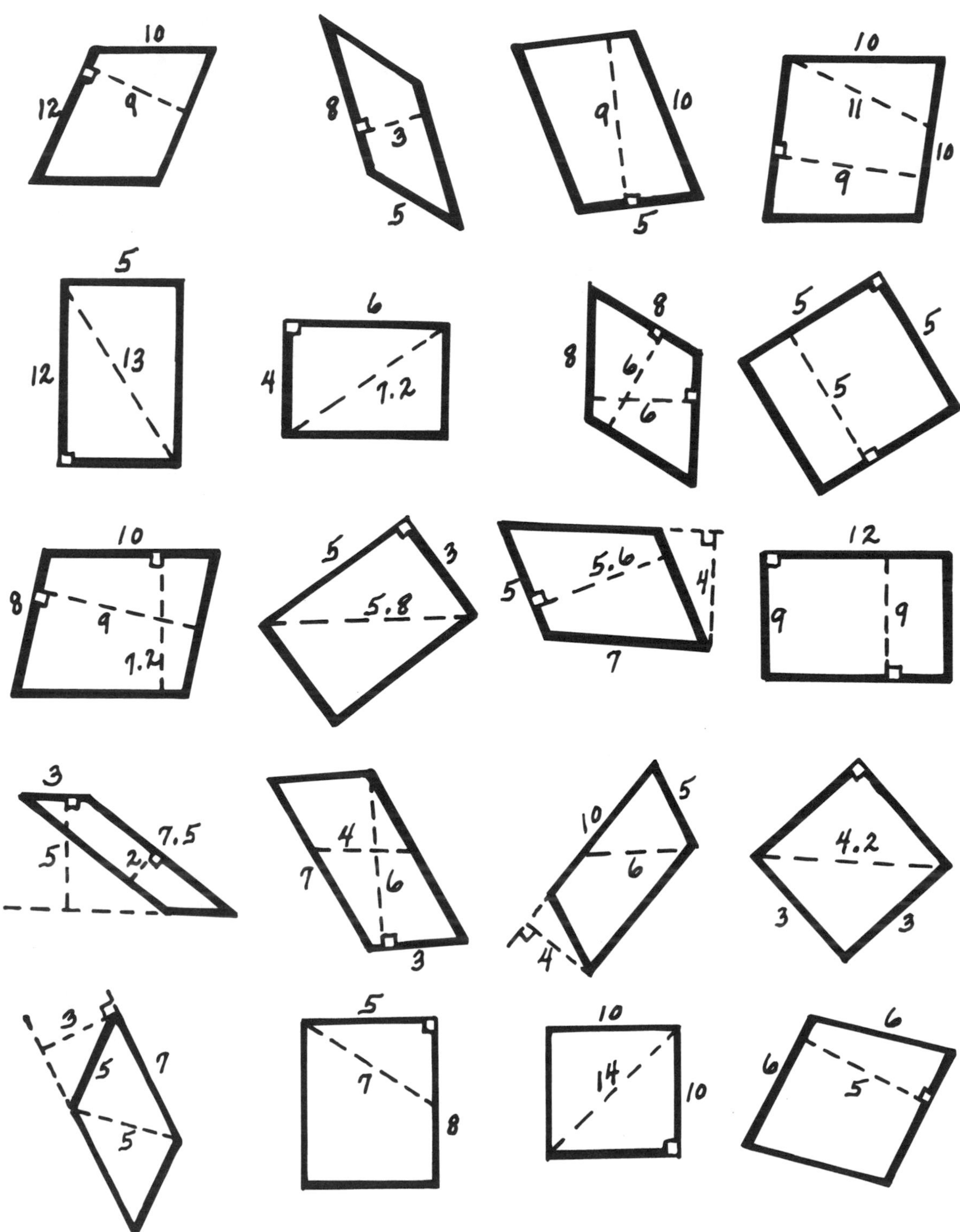

OBJECTIVE 8: Determine the volume of a right rectangular prism.

Activity 1: BUILDING PRISMS

(Concrete Action)

Materials: Cubes (2-cm or 1-inch preferred; connectable cubes optional)
Building mats
Record sheets (Worksheet M-8.1)
Paper
Pencils

Management: Teams of 2–3 students each (30 minutes)

Directions:

1. Give each team about 75 cubes, a record sheet, and a building mat. The mat is a sheet of paper with *front* written along a longer edge of the paper and *side* written along a shorter edge. This will enable students to clearly describe the prisms they build. Ask them to turn the mat so that the front edge is directly in front of them on the desktop.

2. Have students build the first level of a *solid box,* using 4 cubes across the front and 3 cubes along the side. There are to be no holes in any level built. When they are finished, ask them how many cubes they used to make the level. (12 cubes—from their front viewpoint, 3 rows of 4 cubes each)

3. Have them build another level of the "box" or prism by placing more cubes on top of the first level. Ask them how many cubes are in the second level alone (12—3 rows of 4 cubes each) and then how many are in the entire prism. (24 cubes—2 levels of 12 cubes each)

4. Do not stress the description of each level as three rows of four at this time. A pattern will be discovered later.

5. Students should now complete the record sheet for this first prism.

6. Have them build other prisms, following this same procedure and recording the information on the record sheet. You may tell them the number of levels, front cubes, and side cubes to use each time, or just let them create their own prisms, as long as each is a solid box.

7. After the teams have built 8–10 prisms, ask them to look at the numbers for each prism on their record sheet. Do they see a relationship between the numbers in the first three columns and the number in the *total cubes* column? This pattern is usually very easy for them to see.

8. Ask them to write their discovery in one or two word sentences. Have some read theirs to the entire class. *Sample response:* If you multiply the numbers that tell how many levels and how many front and side cubes, you will get a product that equals the number of cubes used in all.

NAME ______________________ DATE ______________

WORKSHEET M-8.1
Building Prisms

On the table below, record the data for each "solid box" or prism you build with cubes.

Number of front cubes	Number of side cubes	Number of levels	Total cubes (volume)

What have you discovered about the volume of a prism so far?

Activity 2: DRAWING BOXES

(Pictorial Action)

Materials: Volume Worksheet M-8.2
Red and blue pencils
Regular pencils

Management: Partners (30 minutes)

Directions:

1. Give each pair of students a worksheet. For the first prism, show them how to mark off the top level according to the number of cubes needed along the front (3) and the side (2). Color the lateral faces blue.

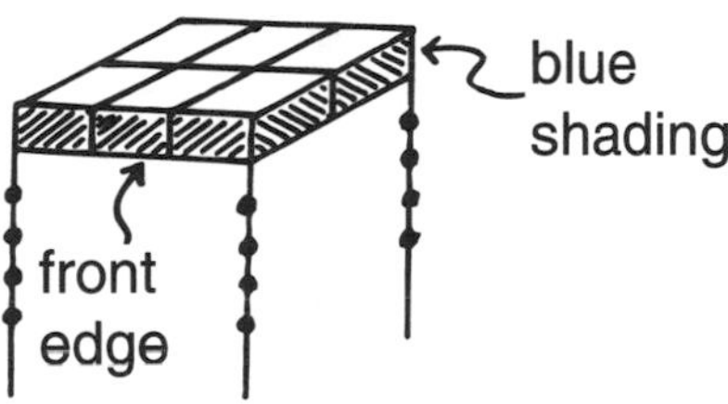

2. Use the dots on the vertical posts as guides. Show how to add on the second level by drawing a line segment parallel to the front lower edge of the top level and another parallel to the side lower edge, then extending the division marks down to show the cubes. Color the new lateral faces red.

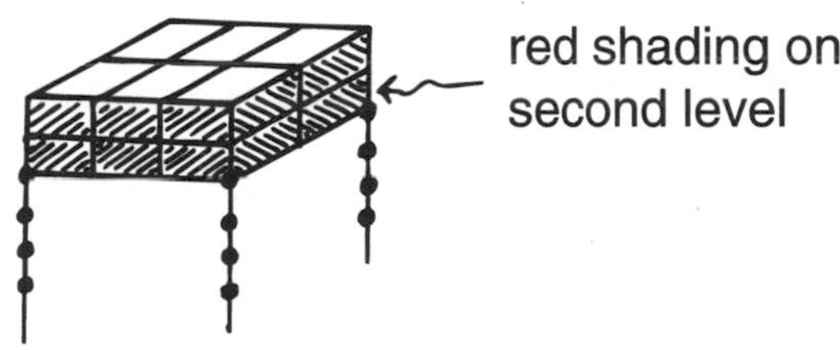

3. Have the students complete the blanks of the first item after they have drawn all the required levels on the diagram, alternating the red and blue shading.

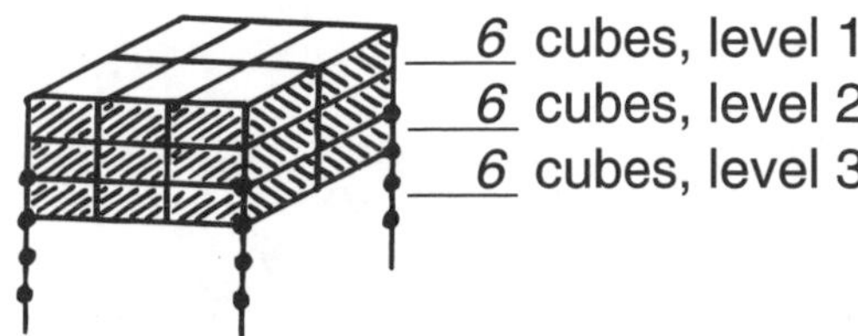

4. Ask them to follow the same process to complete the other prisms on the worksheet. Monitor their work carefully to be sure they are drawing the levels correctly and recording the number of cubes at each level.

5. After all have written two or three sentences about what they need to know to find the volume of a prism, ask them to create a *formula* that others might follow to find a prism's volume.

Sample: levels X (front length) × (side length) = total cubes or volume (in cubic units) or $L \times F \times S = V$

6. When several students have shared their creations, tell them about the other formula that people sometimes use: length × width × height = volume. Discuss how it is equivalent to all of theirs. (It just uses different terms for the same measures.)

Activity 3: VOLUME VICTORIES
(Cooperative Groups)

Materials: Cubes
Paper
Pencils
Dice

Management: Teams of 4 students each (20 minutes)

Directions:

1. Give each team 75 cubes and 1 die.

2. Taking turns, each pair of students on a team will roll the die twice (first roll=tens digit; second roll=ones digit) to find the number of cubes to use for their volume. The pair will count out that amount of cubes.

3. They will then arrange all their cubes, say, 24 cubes, into a solid prism. They must write a number sentence that relates the prism's dimensions to the volume, for example, $2 \times 4 \times 3 = 24$ cubes. Order the dimensions in the following manner: The first two factors show the level size, and the third factor shows the height or number of levels. For example, $2 \times 4 \times 3$ means a level size of 2×4 was used and 3 levels were built. Consider a 2×4 level the same as a 4×2 level, but $2 \times 4 \times 3$ and $3 \times 4 \times 2$ will be counted as different prisms. In other words, a prism just turned around on the table is still the same; a prism that is "tipped over" becomes a new prism to be counted. For the sake of time, use only single-digit numbers as factors. Examples of different prisms using 24 cubes: $2 \times 6 \times 2$, $4 \times 3 \times 2$, $4 \times 6 \times 1$, $3 \times 8 \times 1$, $1 \times 8 \times 3$, $2 \times 4 \times 3$.

4. The purpose is to build *more than one* prism that requires the rolled amount of cubes for its volume. For two different prisms and their correct number sentences, the builders will earn 1 point; for three different prisms and their number sentences, they will earn 3 points.

5. Pairs take turns until time is called.

NAME ______________________________ DATE ____________________

VOLUME WORKSHEET M-8.2
Drawing Boxes

Follow your teacher's instructions to complete the prisms or boxes below. Find the volume.

1.

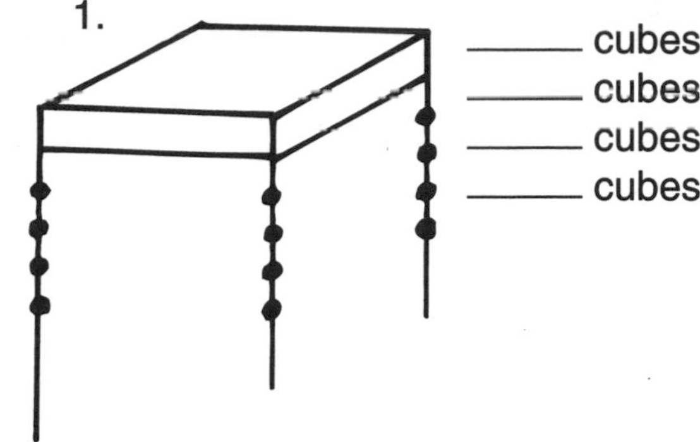

Level:
3 front x 2 side = _____ cu. un.
Volume:
_____ cu. un. x 3 levels =
_____ cu. un. total

2.

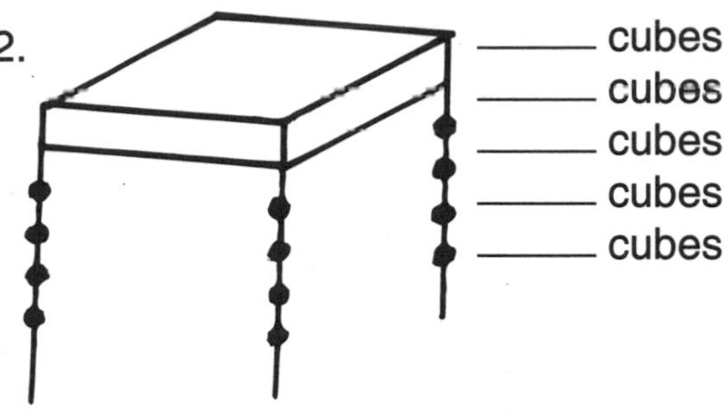

Level:
4 front x 3 side = _____ cu. un.
Volume:
_____ cu. un. x 4 levels =
_____ cu. un. total

3.

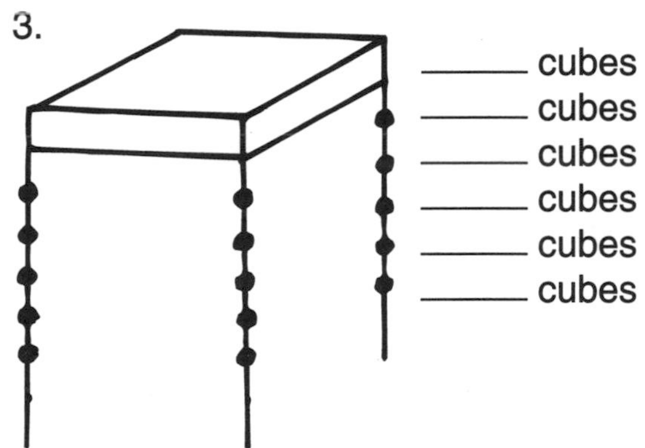

Level:
3 front x 3 side = _____ cu. un.
Volume:
_____ cu. un. x 5 levels =
_____ cu. un. total

4.

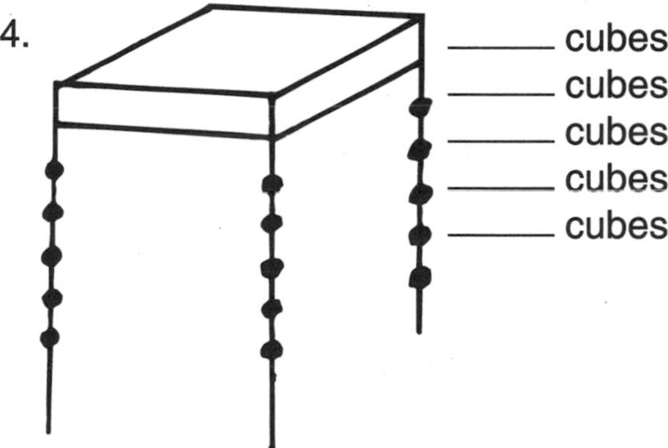

Level:
2 front x 2 side = _____ cu. un.
Volume:
_____ cu. un. x 4 levels =
_____ cu. un. total

NAME ______________________________ DATE ____________________

VOLUME WORKSHEET M-8.2 (*cont.*)

5.

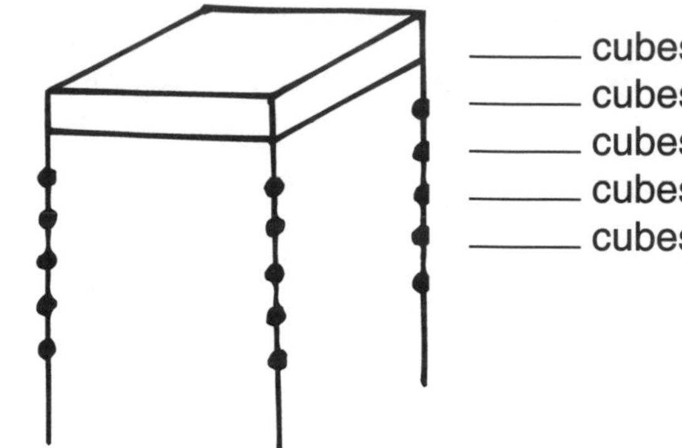

_____ cubes
_____ cubes
_____ cubes
_____ cubes
_____ cubes

Level:
3 front x 4 side = _____ cu.un.
Volume:
_____ cu. un. x 2 levels =
_____ cu. un. total

6.

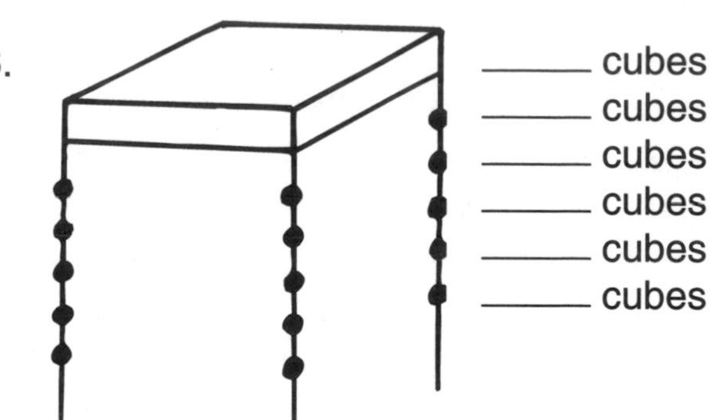

_____ cubes
_____ cubes
_____ cubes
_____ cubes
_____ cubes
_____ cubes

Level:
2 front x 3 side = _____ cu.un.
Volume:
_____ cu. un. x 5 levels =
_____ cu. un. total

7. Write complete sentences to tell what you need to know to find the volume of a prism.

OBJECTIVE 9: Find the circumference of a circle.

Activity 1: ALL WRAPPED UP

(Concrete Action)

Materials: Assorted plastic lids
Cotton string (nonstretchable)
Scissors
Paper
Pencils

Management: Teams of 4 students each (30 minutes)

Directions:

1. Give each team 4–5 plastic lids with diameters of different sizes and a piece of string long enough to easily wrap around the largest lid.

2. The students are to use the string to wrap around each lid's outer edge to find the size of its circumference. It will be helpful to mark off the string to show where the wrapping stops for a particular lid.

3. They should then place the marked-off length of string across the lid top through the lid's center point to find how many diameters this length will make. If students have been careful wrapping the string, they should get 3 diameters out of the string length with a little string left over, regardless of the lid size used.

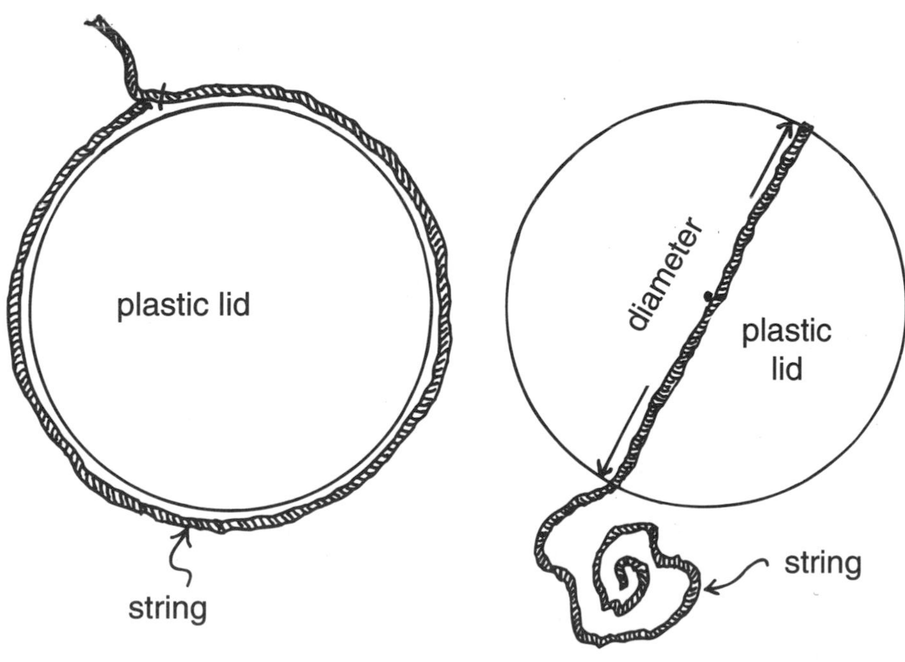

4. Have students write one or two sentences about what they have discovered about the diameter and circumference of any circular (flat) object. (*Sample:* A circumference makes about 3 diameters.) Ask them to draw diagrams showing what they did with the lids.

Activity 2: AROUND AND ACROSS

(Pictorial Action)

Materials: Circle Worksheet M-9.2 with recording table
Adding machine tape
Scissors
Centimeter rulers
Calculators
Pencils

Management: Partners (20 minutes)

Directions:

1. Give each pair of students a worksheet, calculator, centimeter ruler, and a strip of adding machine paper about 18 inches long.

2. The students are to use the paper strip to form a "collar" around each circle to find its circumference. It will be helpful to mark off the paper to show where the wrapping stops. This marked-off distance should then be measured with the centimeter ruler in order to find the circumference in centimeters to the nearest tenth.

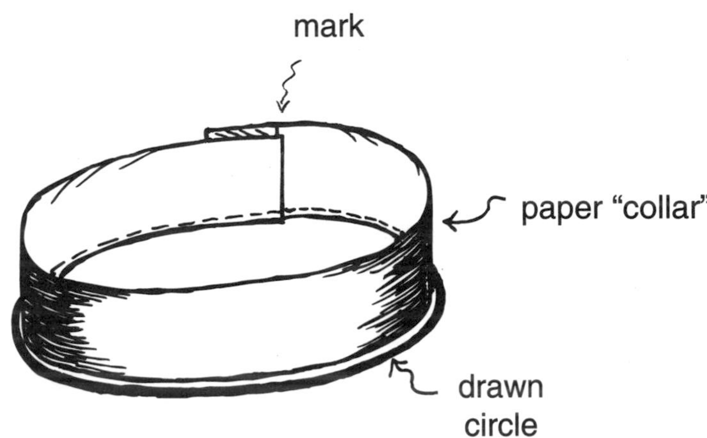

3. The diameter should also be measured to the nearest tenth of a centimeter. Students need to make certain that they measure across the circle *through the center point* to find this particular measure.

4. Both measures for each circle should be recorded on the table on the worksheet. Then the ratio for the two measures can be computed in decimal form to the nearest hundredth. Calculators are useful at this stage to avoid tedious calculations.

5. After all partners have measured and calculated for all their circles, write all the ratios (circumference/diameter) in decimal form that they have found on the chalkboard. Include any that may be repeats. Ask the students to find the average (mean) of all the ratios found.

6. When students have measured carefully and 20 or more ratios are averaged together, the mean is usually quite close to 3.14. Ask students to write a sentence that describes a diameter's relationship to its circumference. (*Sample:* A circumference equals about 3.14 of the diameter.)

7. Discuss the meaning of pi (π) with the class. Emphasize that we do not know what all the decimal places are for its numerical value, but computers have been used to calculate it to over a thousand decimal places so far. Because of this, students will only use an estimate for its value, which will often be 3.14. Some students may enjoy making a report to the class on the history and uses of pi (π).

Activity 3: CIRCLESPIN

(Cooperative Groups)

Materials: Spinners Pattern (Worksheet M-9.3)
Calculators
Large paper clips
Paper
Pencils

Management: Teams of 4 students each (20 minutes)

Directions:

1. Give each team a worksheet of spinners and a calculator. To use the spinners, one end of a large paper clip should be held at the center of the spinner by a pencil point while the free end is spun around.

2. Each person takes a turn first spinning the NAME Spinner, then the NUMBER Spinner. The *number* that is spun becomes the value of the circle's part whose *name* is spun. The other two parts must then be calculated, using this value for the chosen part. For example, if *diameter* and *3* are both spun, the student playing must find the radius and circumference for a circle having a diameter of 3 units. The estimate of 3.14 will be used for pi. The other three team members must approve of the playing student's procedures and results.

3. The students continue to take turns until time is called.

NAME ______________________________ DATE ____________________

WORKSHEET M-9.2
Around and Across

Find the circumference and diameter of each circle. Complete the table.

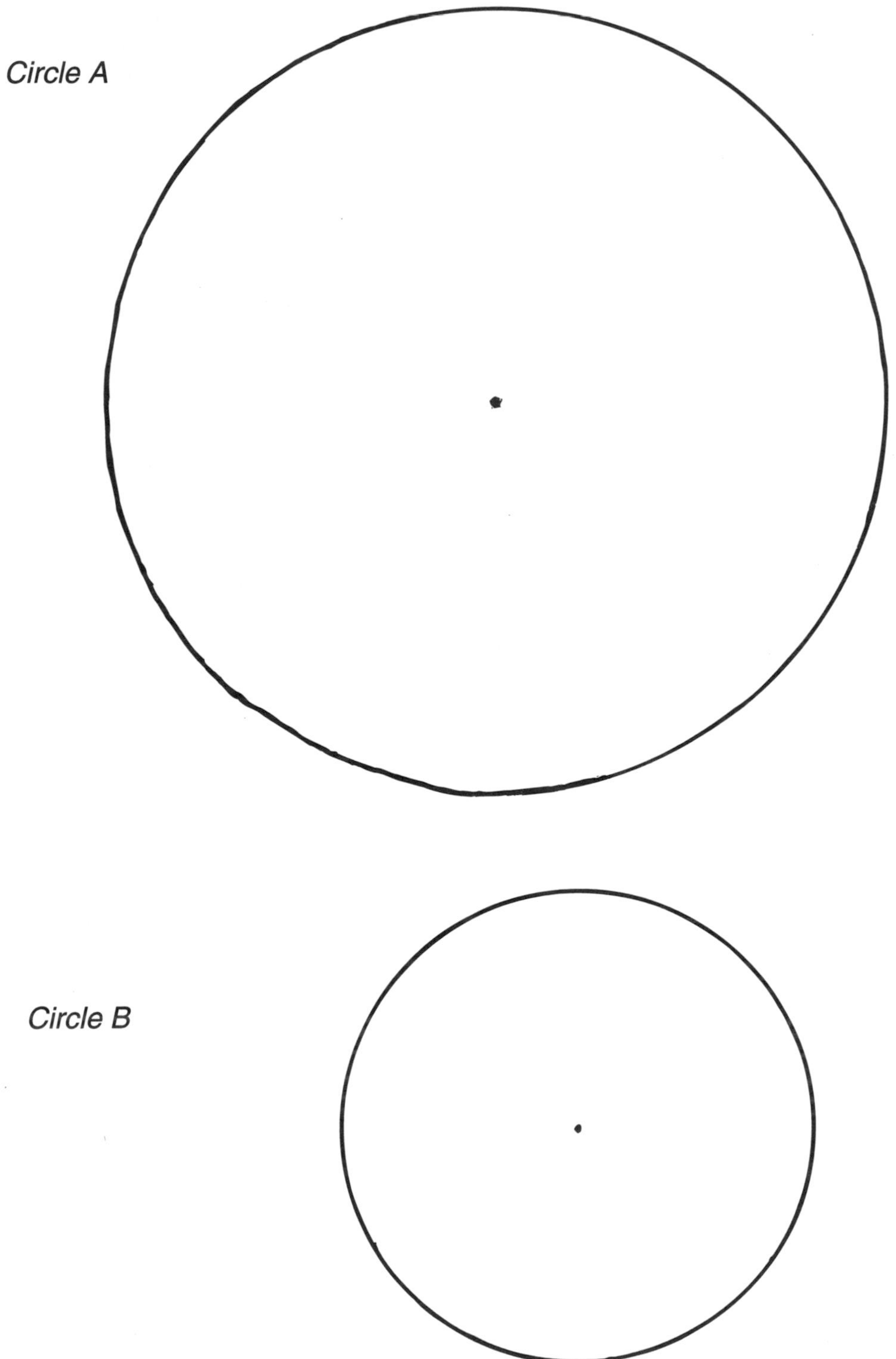

NAME ______________________________ DATE ______________________

WORKSHEET M-9.2 (*cont.*)

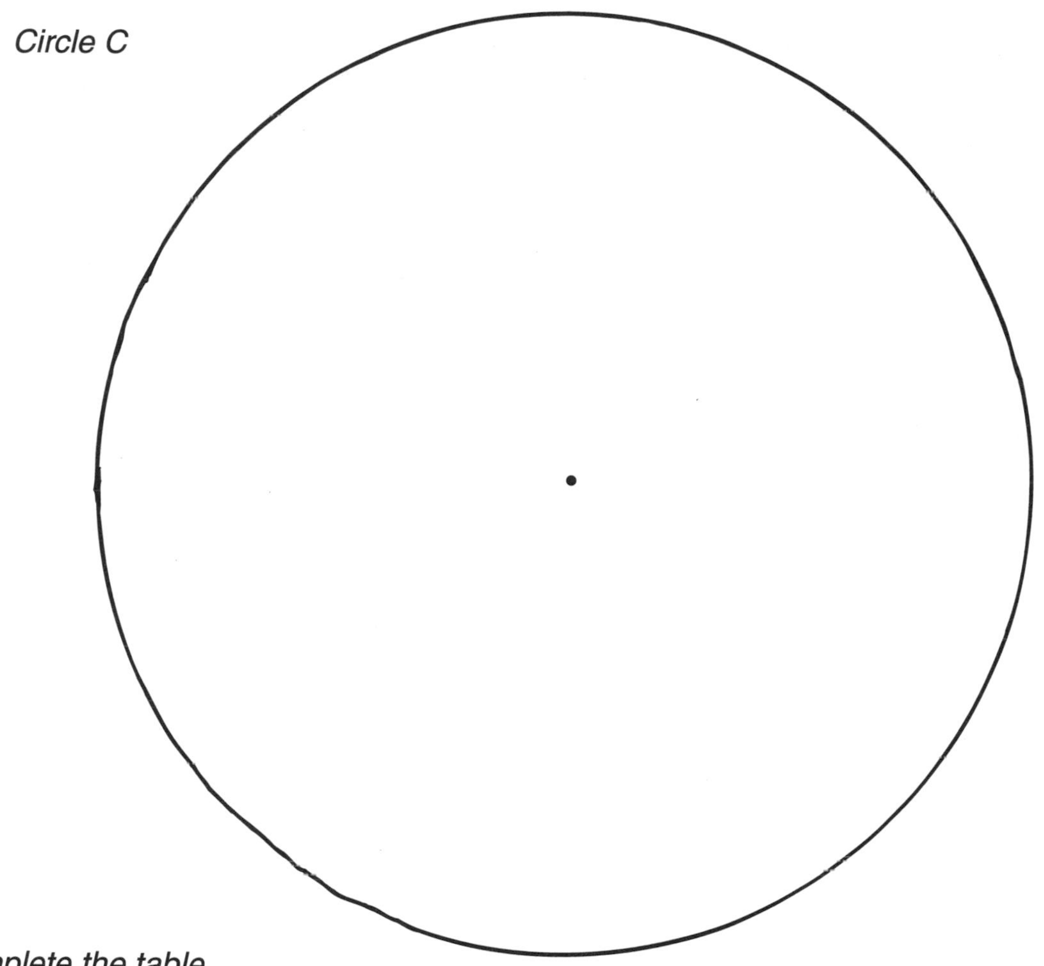

Complete the table.

Circle	Circumference	Diameter	Circumf./Diam.
A			
B			
C			

Class mean for C/D = ______

Write a sentence about the relationship between a circle's diameter and circumference.

WORKSHEET M-9.3
Spinner Patterns for Circlespin

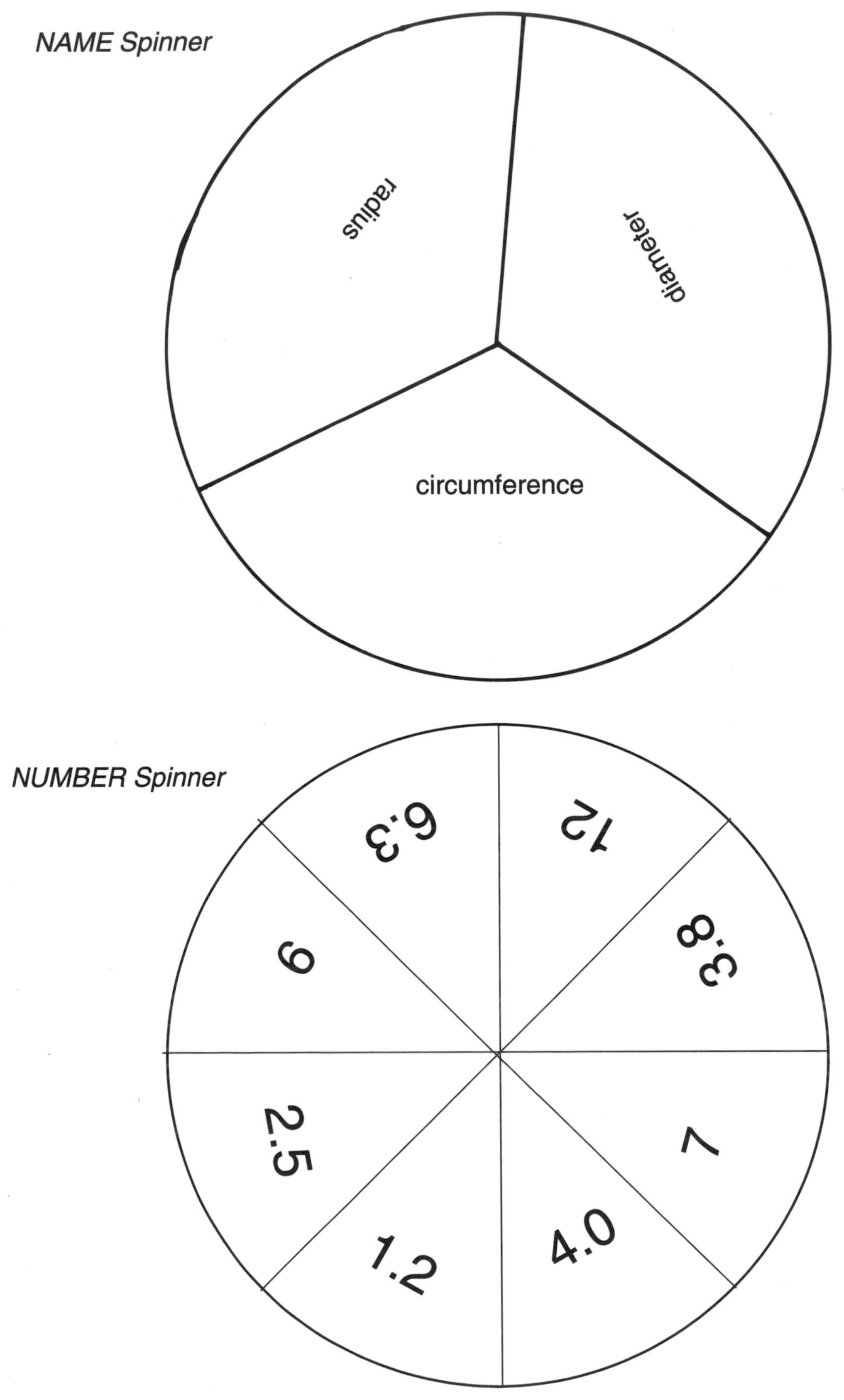

OBJECTIVE 10: Find the area of a triangle.

Activity 1: ENCLOSING TRIANGLES
(Concrete Action)

Materials: Geoboards with rubber bands (2 colors, if possible)
Geoboard record sheets (Worksheet M-10.1)
Overhead geoboard
Red pencils
Regular pencils

Management: Partners (20 minutes)

Directions:

1. Give each pair of students a geoboard with rubber bands (2 colors), a red pencil, and a geoboard record sheet.

2. On the overhead geoboard, show students different right triangles and acute triangles where at least one side coincides with a row of pegs on the geoboard. A *row* of pegs runs parallel to an edge of the geoboard; it does not run diagonally. An obtuse triangle may also be used as long as its longest side coincides with a row of pegs. (See step 8 for the excluded case.)

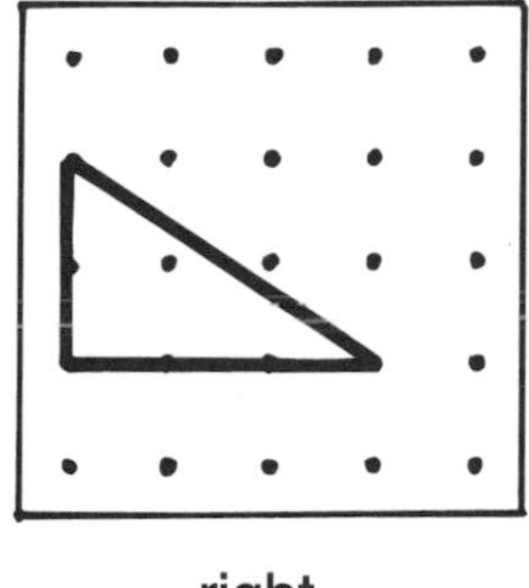
right

acute

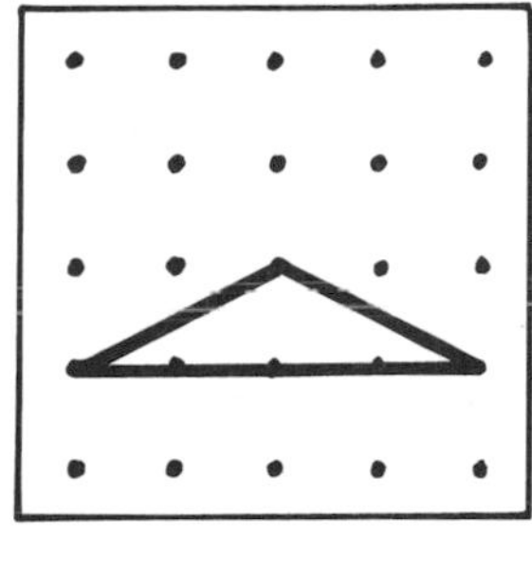
obtuse

3. Have the students build the same triangles on their geoboards, using one color of rubber band.

4. For each triangle, ask them to find a rectangle on the geoboard that encloses the triangle so that at least one side of the rectangle coincides with and is congruent to a side of the triangle (preferably the side along the row of pegs). Each vertex of the triangle should lie on a side or vertex of the rectangle. The rectangle should be built with a color of rubber band different from the color used for the triangle, if possible. This helps students visually separate the rectangle from the triangle on the geoboard.

5. Students should draw the triangle-rectangle pairs they find on their geoboard record sheet, drawing the triangle in regular pencil and the rectangle in red pencil. They should draw only one pair of shapes per frame.

6. Ask students to compare the size of each triangle to the size of its related rectangle on the geoboard. Have them find the area of the rectangle, then use that amount to find the area of the enclosed triangle. Area will be measured in geoboard square units and should be recorded on the geoboard record sheet. (The area of the triangle should equal half the area of its related rectangle.)

7. Have students share some of their strategies for finding the areas of the different triangles. Different ways are possible, depending on the shape of the original triangle and which side of the triangle coincides with a side of the rectangle.

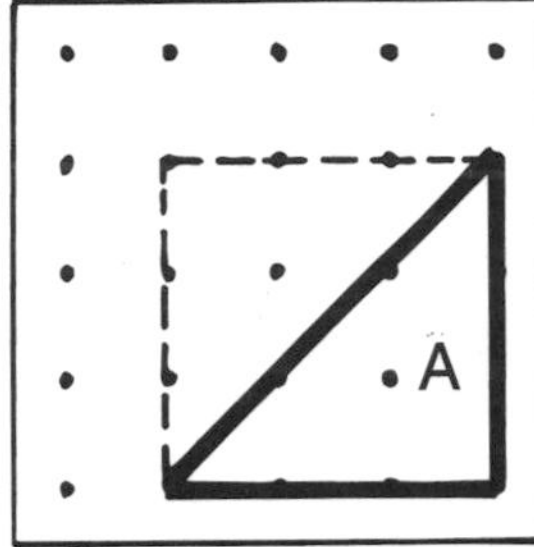

rectangle: 3 x 3 = 9 sq. un.
triangle A: (3 x 3)/2 = 4.5 sq. un.

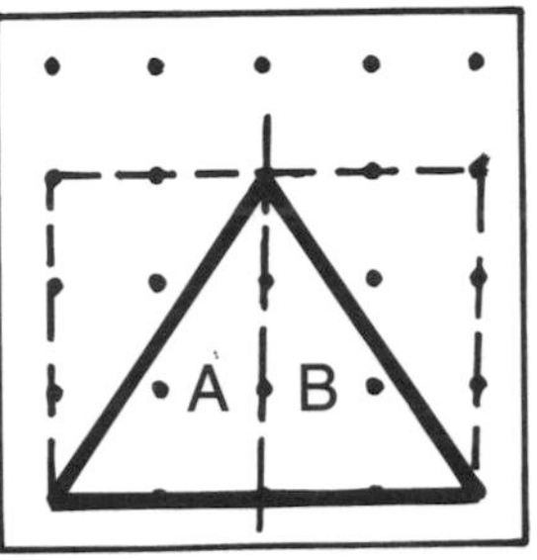

large 3 x 4 rectangle viewed as two 3 x 2 rectangles
triangle (A + B): (3 x 2)/2 + (3 x 2)/2 = 3 + 3 = 6 sq. un.

8. *Challenge:* Have students build an obtuse triangle like the one following (i.e., one of the two shorter sides coincides with a row of pegs). This type requires them to subtract instead of add area in order to find the triangle's actual area. The visual discrimination needed to separate or subtract parts is often more difficult for students than the visual combining or adding of parts seems to be.

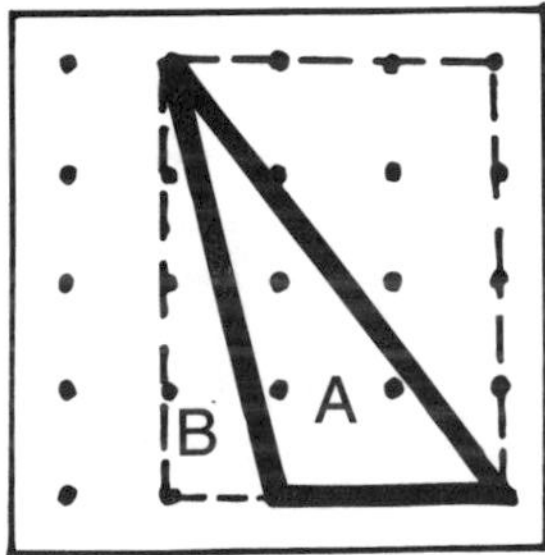

triangle (A + B): (4 x 3)/2 = 6 sq. un.

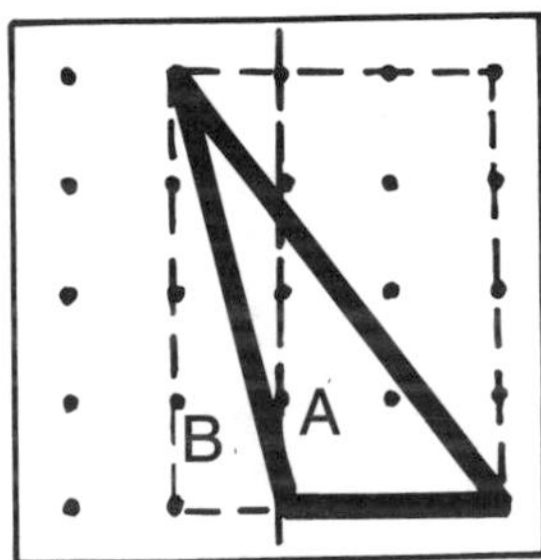

triangle B: (4 x 1)/2 = 2 sq. un.
triangle A or (A + B) – B: 6 – 2 = 4 sq. un.

NAME ______________________________ DATE ____________________

WORKSHEET M-10.1
Enclosing Triangles

Build on a geoboard. Draw what you build on this record sheet.

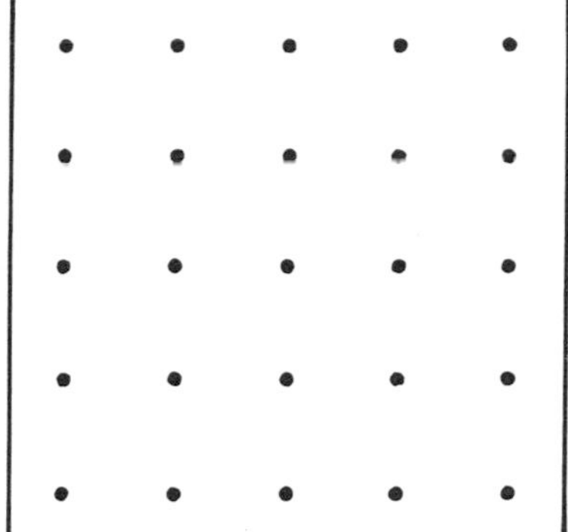

1. Area = ______

2. Area = ______

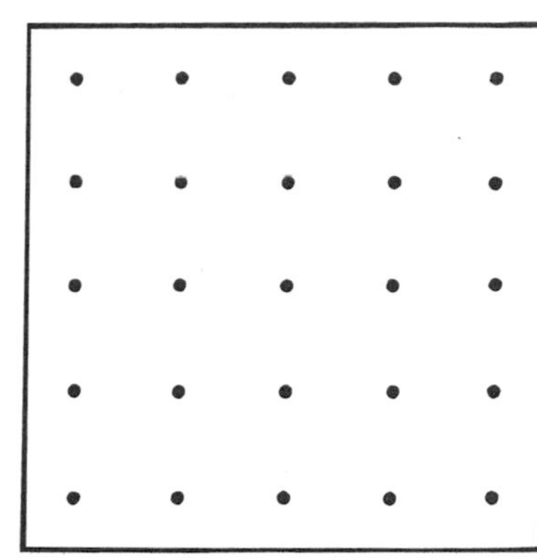

3. Area = ______

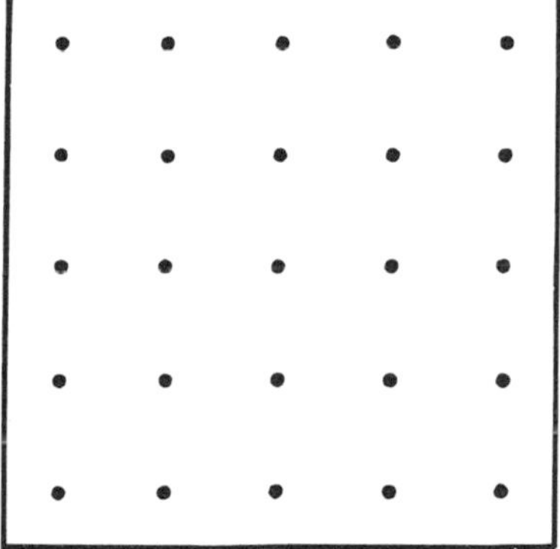

4. Area = ______

5. Area = ______

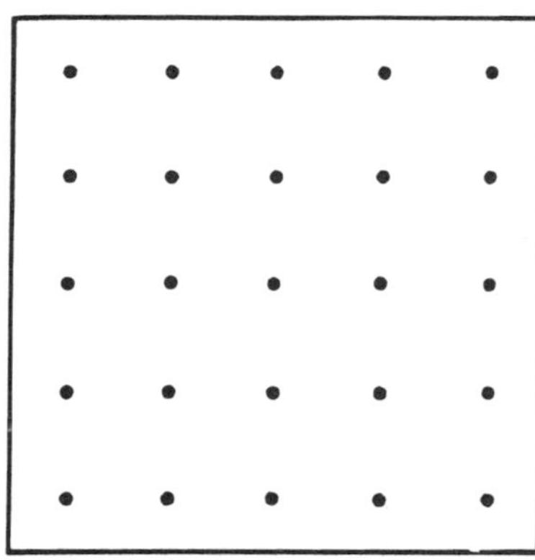

6. Area = ______

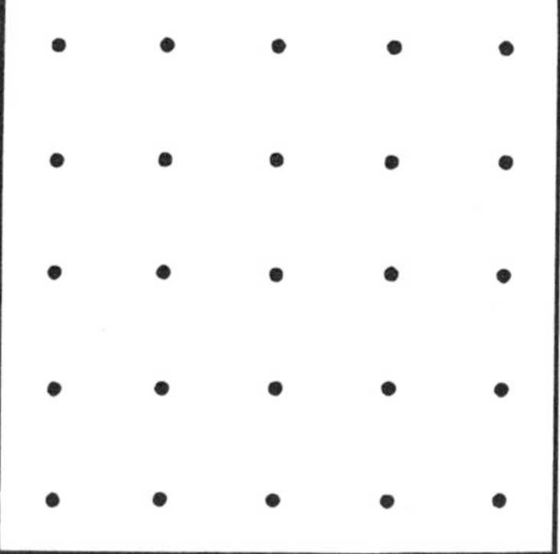

7. Area = ______

8. Area = ______

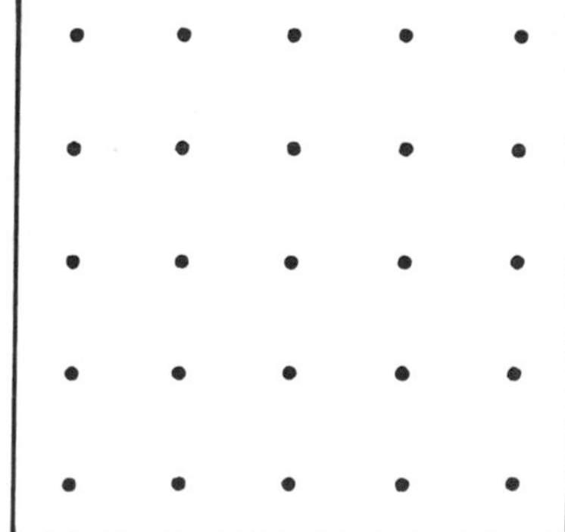

9. Area = ______

Activity 2: TRIANGLE TWINS

(Pictorial Action)

Materials: Triangle Worksheet M-10.2
Scissors
Unlined paper
Red markers
Pencils

Management: Teams of 4 students each (30 minutes)

Directions:

1. Give each team a worksheet of triangles drawn on grids, two scissors, a red marker, and two sheets of unlined paper. Obtuse, acute, and right triangles should be included on the worksheet.

2. Ask students to estimate the area of each triangle by counting the square units of the grid in its interior and writing the amount on the triangle.

3. Have students trace each triangle onto unlined paper and cut out the tracing.

4. The tracing should be rotated over the original shape on the worksheet until a parallelogram is formed. Since some right triangles will be used, rectangles will be formed as special parallelograms in this activity.

5. Have students hold the tracing in its new position and draw around it in order to record the complete parallelogram on the worksheet.

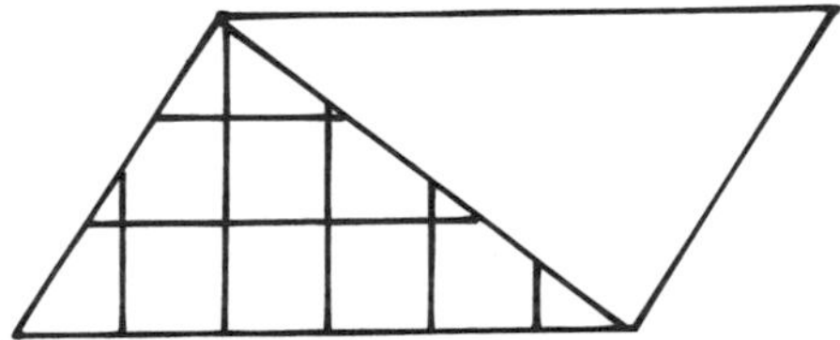

6. Using the red marker and the partial grid on the original triangle, they can now locate and mark off two segments on the parallelogram whose measures can be used to compute the area of the parallelogram.

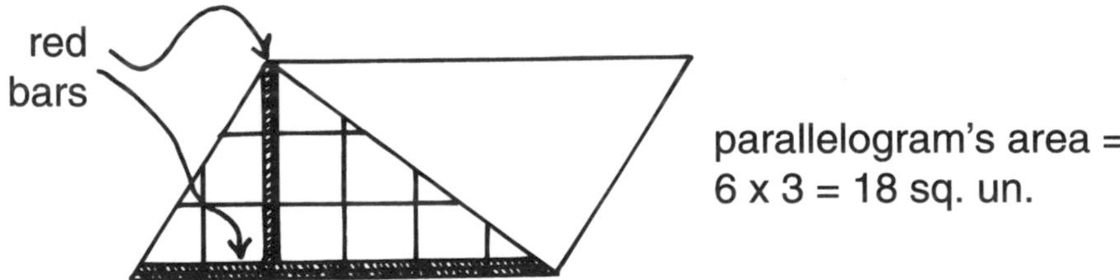

7. Often these measures or dimensions for area will coincide with actual grid segments. For some obtuse triangles, however, the grid does not *appear* to extend all the way across the parallelogram so that the measure of the height is not immediately apparent. Ask students how they might find such a measure. The *interior* height can still be found by extending the grid and determining a parallel grid distance elsewhere on the shape. This distance sometimes appears to be measured *outside* the triangle and its related parallelogram.

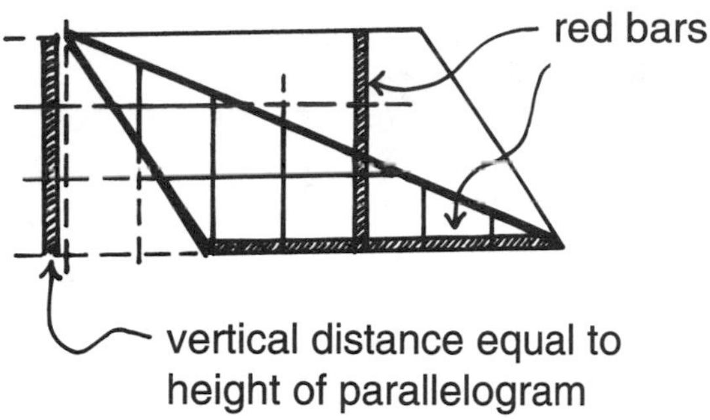

8. Ask students how they might find the area of the original triangle now that they know the parallelogram's area. (*Sample response:* Take half of the parallelogram's area.) Have them compute each triangle's area.

9. Ask them to write on the worksheet the number sentence used to compute each triangle's area, then compare the computed area of the triangle to their original estimate found by counting grid squares. If they estimated carefully, the two values should be relatively close.

10. Ask students what distances they might measure *on the triangle itself* in order to find its area if they do not want to draw the parallelogram every time. Help students see that the perpendicular distance from a side shared by both the triangle and the parallelogram to the *triangle's* opposite *vertex* will be the same as the desired distance to the *parallelogram's* opposite *side*.

Activity 3: DIMENSION DETECTIVES

(Cooperative Groups)

Materials: Triangle Worksheet M-10.3
Small index cards
Red and blue markers (or two other colors)
Centimeter rulers
Calculator
Pencils

Management: Teams of 4 students each (30 minutes)

Directions:

1. Give each team a worksheet containing triangles with grid interiors, an index card, centimeter ruler, red and blue markers, and a calculator.

2. For the first triangle on the worksheet, one pair on each team will count the square units inside the triangle to estimate its area in square centimeters.

NAME ______________________ DATE ______________

TRIANGLE WORKSHEET M-10.2
Triangle Twins

Follow your teacher's instructions to make parallelograms from the given triangles.

1.

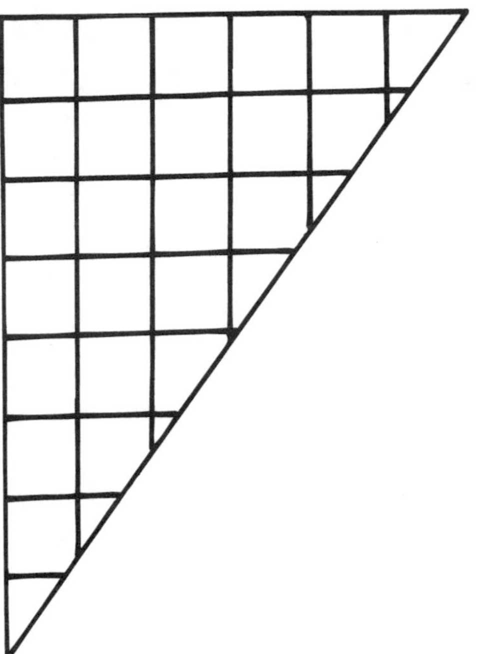

2.

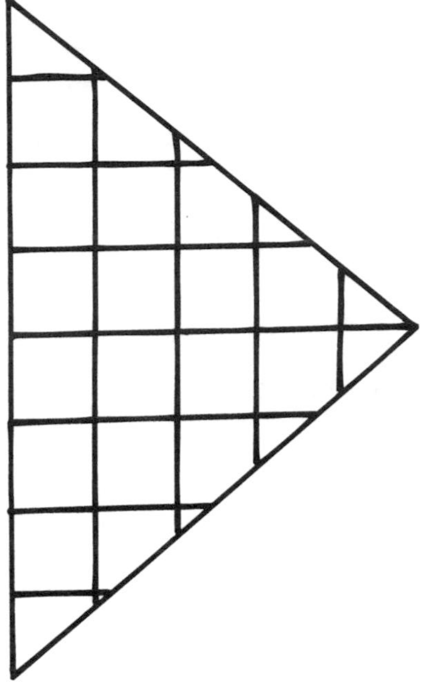

3.

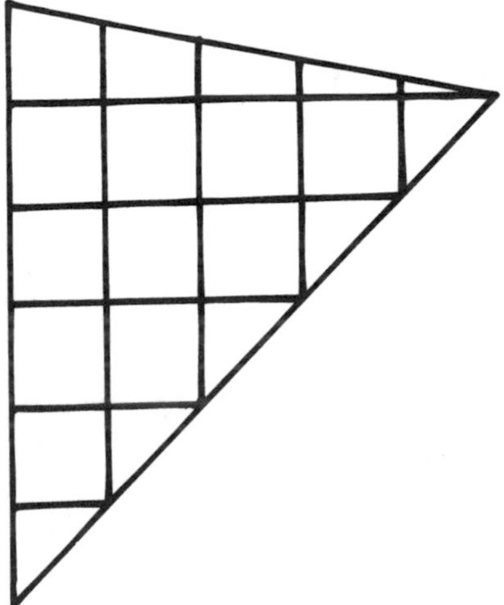

4.

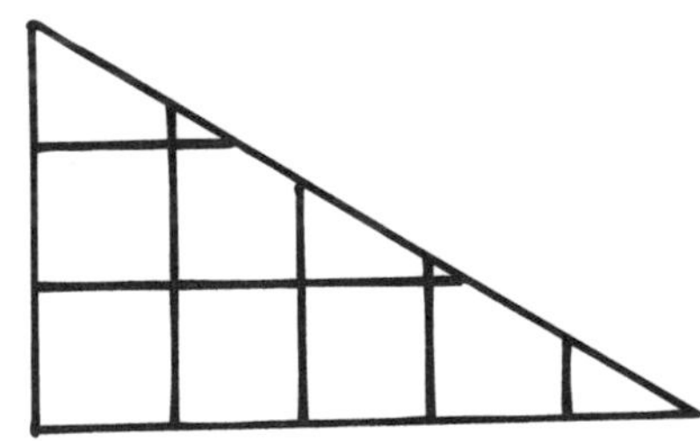

NAME ______________________ DATE ______________

WORKSHEET M-10.2 (*cont.*)

5.

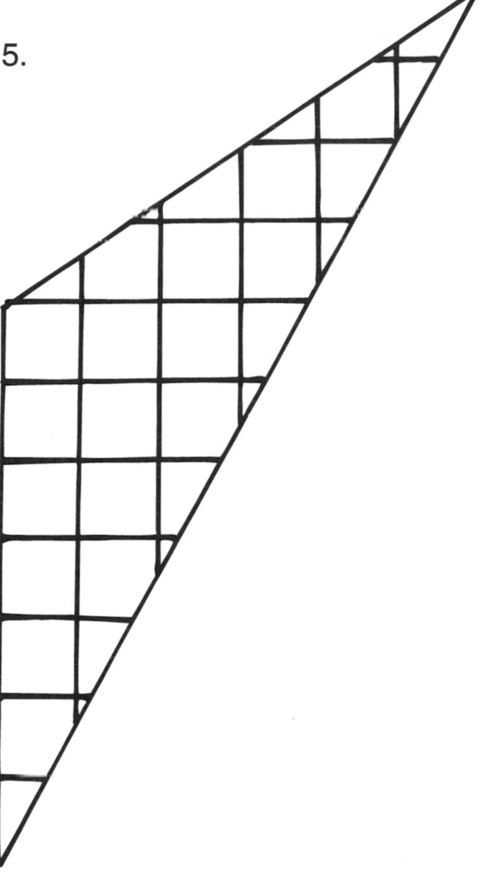

6.

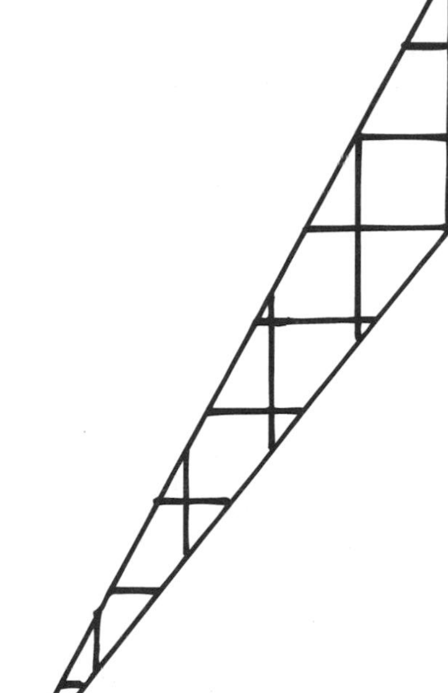

7.

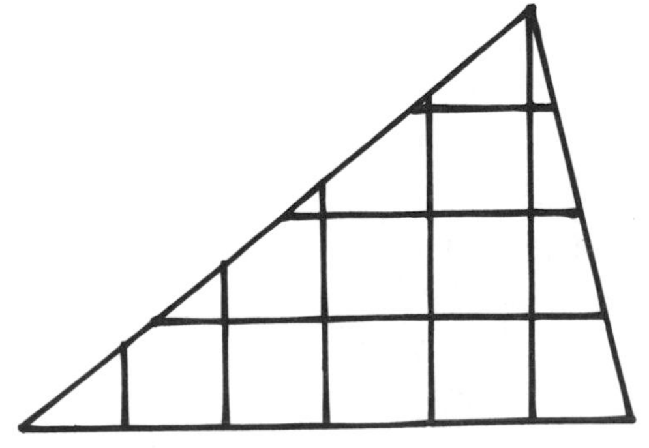

8.

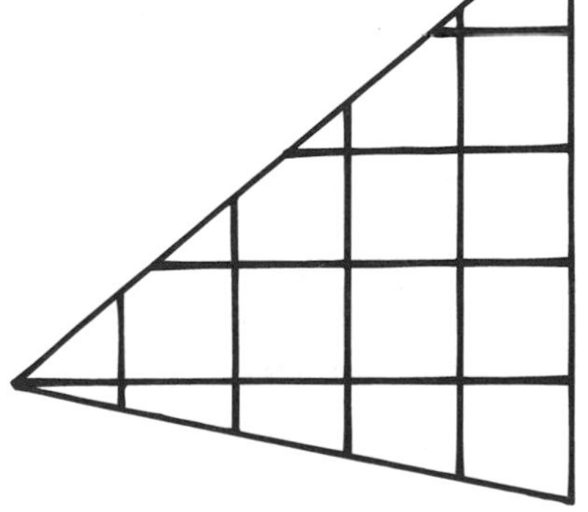

3. The other pair on the team will find the side of the triangle that aligns with a grid segment, then draw that side in red. They will also draw a red line segment that connects perpendicularly from the red side to the opposite vertex. (For some obtuse triangles, the red side may need to be *extended,* then the perpendicular segment drawn from this *extension* to the opposite vertex.) This pair of students can determine the measures of the two red segments by counting grid units. With these centimeter lengths they should compute the area of the triangle.

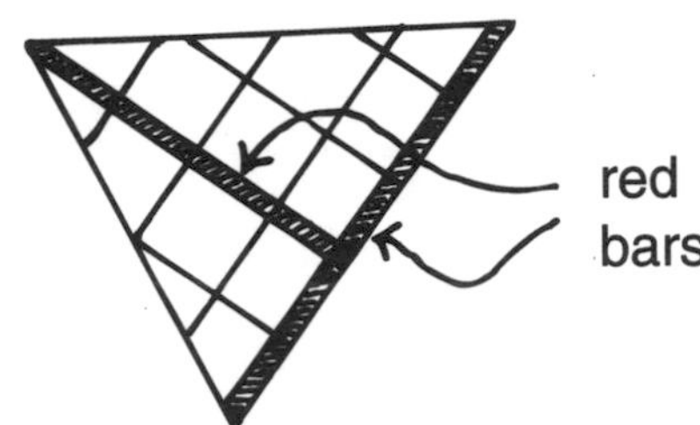

triangle's area = (5 x 4)/2 = 10 sq. units

4. The first pair who estimated now draws another side of the same triangle in blue. This side probably will not be aligned with any grid segment, so the students must align one edge of the index card with the blue side and trace along its adjacent edge to the opposite vertex with the blue marker. The two students must now use the centimeter ruler to measure the two blue segments to the nearest tenth of a centimeter and use these two values to compute the area of the triangle.

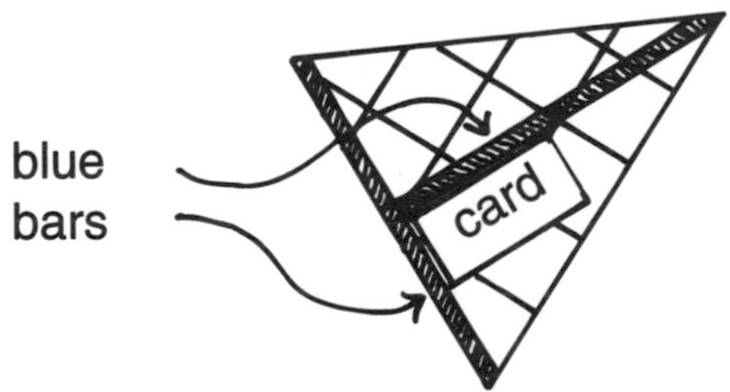

5. Ask students to record their *red* and *blue* area computations as number sentences on the worksheet by the triangle and compare their two computed results with their original estimate of the area. The computed answers should be approximately the same (or within a few tenths) when rounded to the nearest tenth. If any of the three values differ greatly, ask students to recheck their counting or measuring in order to improve their accuracy.

6. Have teams repeat the process of steps 2–5 for the other triangles on the worksheet, rotating which pair begins first with the estimation of the area.

7. After all teams have finished the worksheet, have students tell what they have learned about the red pair of dimensions and the blue pair of dimensions for the same triangle. (*Sample response:* It does not matter which pair of dimensions you use; you will be able to find the area of the triangle with either pair.)

NAME ______________________________ DATE ____________________

TRIANGLE WORKSHEET M-10.3
Dimension Detectives

On each triangle, mark off two different pairs of measures that can be used to compute the area of the triangle. Find the area with each pair.

1.

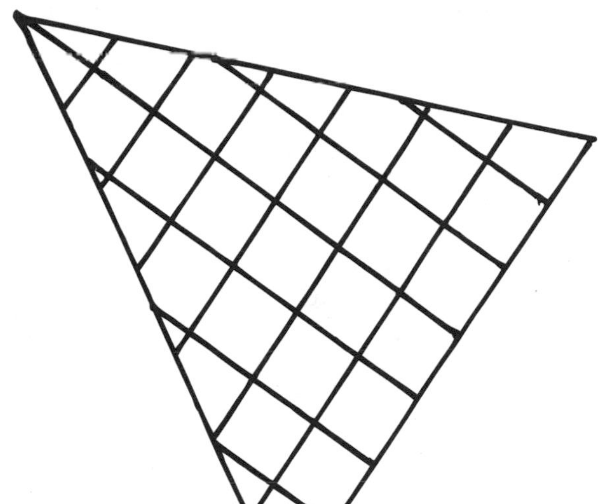

Estimated area:

____

2.

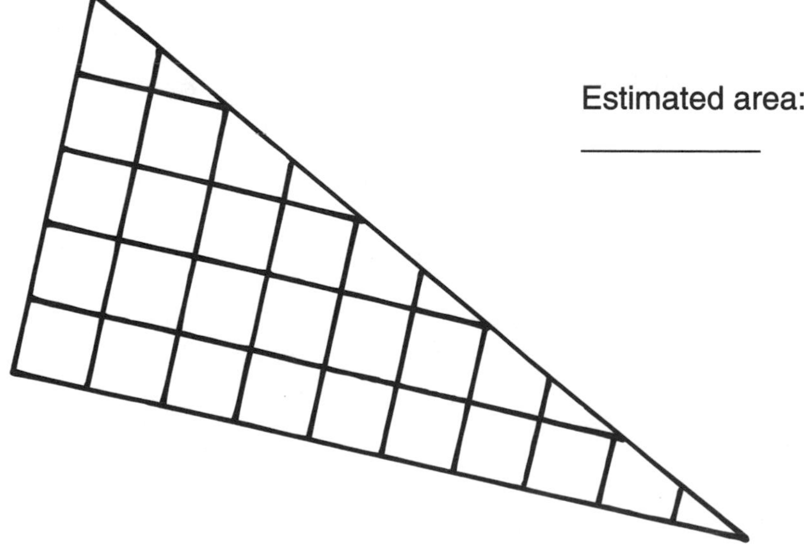

Estimated area:

____

NAME ______________________________ DATE ____________________

TRIANGLE WORKSHEET M-10.3 (*cont.*)

3.

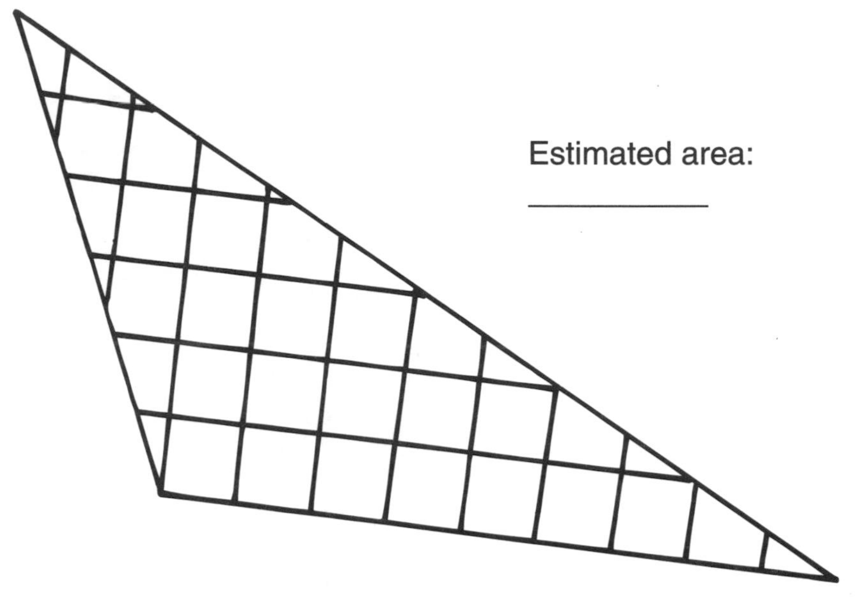

Estimated area:

____

4.

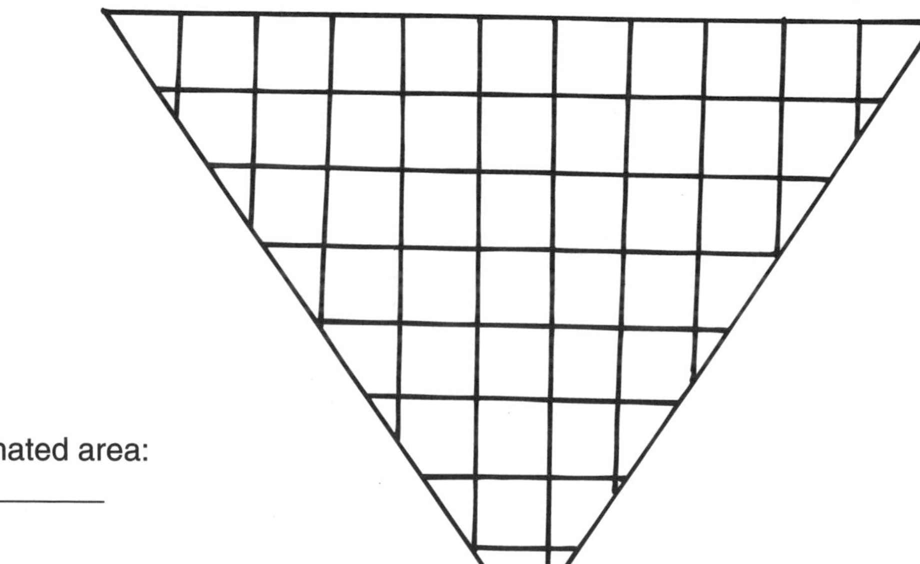

Estimated area:

____

OBJECTIVE 11: Find the area of a trapezoid.

Note: For the following activities, the trapezoid is considered to have exactly one pair of parallel sides.

Activity 1: DIVIDE AND CONQUER

(Concrete Action)

Materials: Trapezoid grid patterns (Worksheet M-11.1)
Scissors
Red and blue markers (or any two colors; not black)
Transparent tape (optional)
Paper
Pencils

Management: Teams of 4 students each (30 minutes)

Directions:

1. Give each team several patterns for trapezoids drawn on grids, scissors, and a red and a blue marker.

2. Ask them to cut out the first trapezoid and try to find its area by subdividing it with pencil markings into more familiar shapes and finding their separate areas. Use the grid to find the necessary measurements. (It is assumed that students know how to find the area of a parallelogram, a rectangle, and a triangle at this time.)

3. Many ways are possible. Have different teams share their methods of subdividing the trapezoid with the whole class. Their values for the total area may vary a little, especially if they are counting partial square units on the grid.

Examples of subdivisions of the same trapezoid:

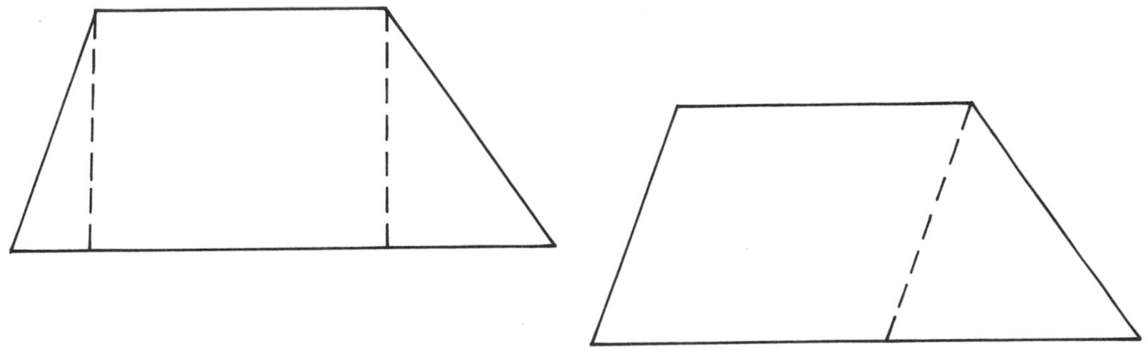

4. Now have them use the same trapezoid, fold one of the parallel sides over to touch its opposite side, and crease the fold. Students should cut along the crease line to separate the trapezoid into two parts. Show them how to rotate one part clockwise and place it next to the other part to form a parallelogram.

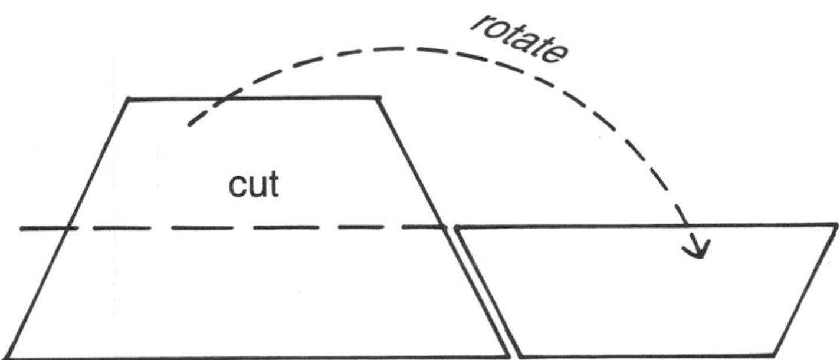

5. Ask them to color one longer side of the parallelogram red, then color in blue another segment that is the perpendicular distance from the red side to its opposite side. Have students use the grid to find the lengths of the red and blue segments, then use these two values to find the parallelogram's area.

6. Now have the students move the parts back into their original positions to form the trapezoid again. If preferred, the two parts may be taped back together. Ask them what they notice about the locations of the colored line segments on the trapezoid.

7. If necessary, guide students to see that the red side of the parallelogram has been broken into two parts: the two parallel sides of the trapezoid. The blue segment, the parallelogram's *height,* should now be perpendicular to the red segments, but only extend half the distance between the two parallel sides of the trapezoid.

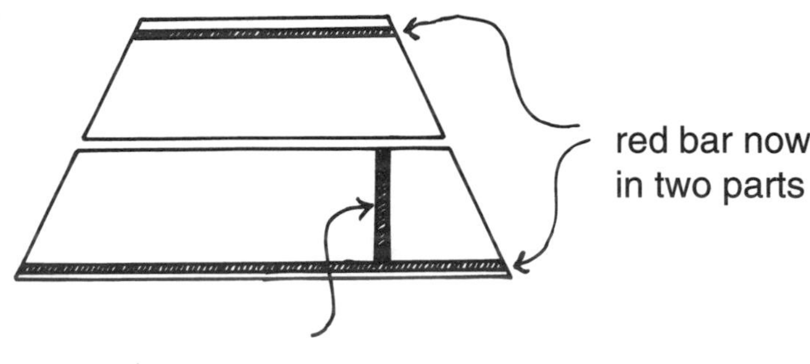

8. Ask the class to compare the area of the trapezoid found in step 2 to the area of the parallelogram found in step 5. Ask them why the two values are approximately the same. (The interior region of the trapezoid has just been rearranged to form the parallelogram. Therefore, their area values should be equal.)

9. Now have students apply the procedure used in steps 4–7 to their remaining patterns. The needed dimensions on the parallelogram should be marked as before and the area computed, then the parallelogram transformed to the trapezoid again. Ask students if the red and blue segments drawn on the parallelograms always end up in the same locations on their related trapezoids. (They should; the blue segment may appear, however, in either half-section between the trapezoid's two parallel sides, depending on where it was drawn on the parallelogram.)

10. Ask students to write two or three word sentences that describe how they might find the lengths of the red and blue segments on the parallelogram by using the red and blue segments shown on the trapezoid. Have them share their ideas with the rest of the class. (*Sample response:* The lengths of the two red sides on the trapezoid need to be added together, and half the distance between the two red sides can be found as the length of the blue segment. These two new lengths can then be multiplied to find the area of the parallelogram.)

Activity 2: ROTATING TOPS

(Pictorial Action)

Materials: Area Worksheet M-11.2
Red and blue markers (or 2 different colors; not black)
Calculators (optional)
Pencils

Management: Partners (20 minutes)

Directions:

1. Give each pair of students a worksheet with trapezoids drawn on centimeter grid paper, a red and a blue marker, and a calculator (optional).

2. Ask the students to transform each trapezoid to its related parallelogram according to the diagrams below:

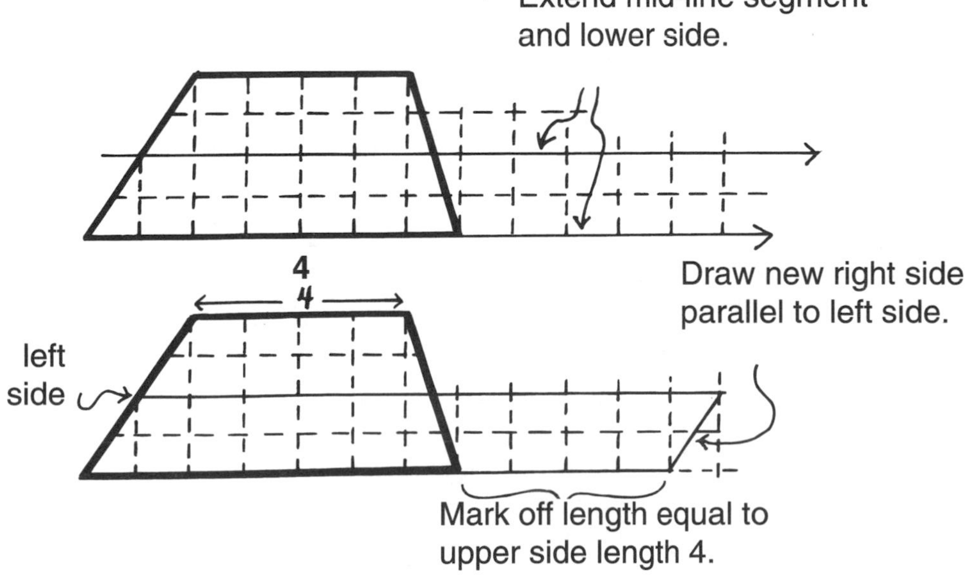
Extend mid-line segment
and lower side.
4
4
Draw new right side
parallel to left side.
left
side
Mark off length equal to
upper side length 4.

WORKSHEET M-11.1
Trapezoid Patterns for Divide and Conquer

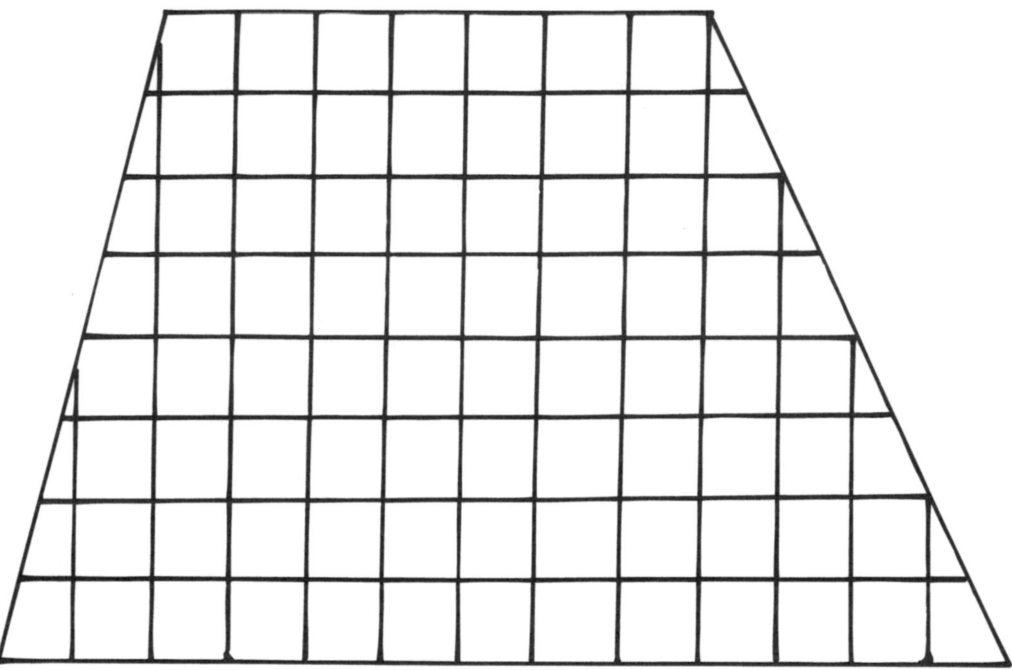

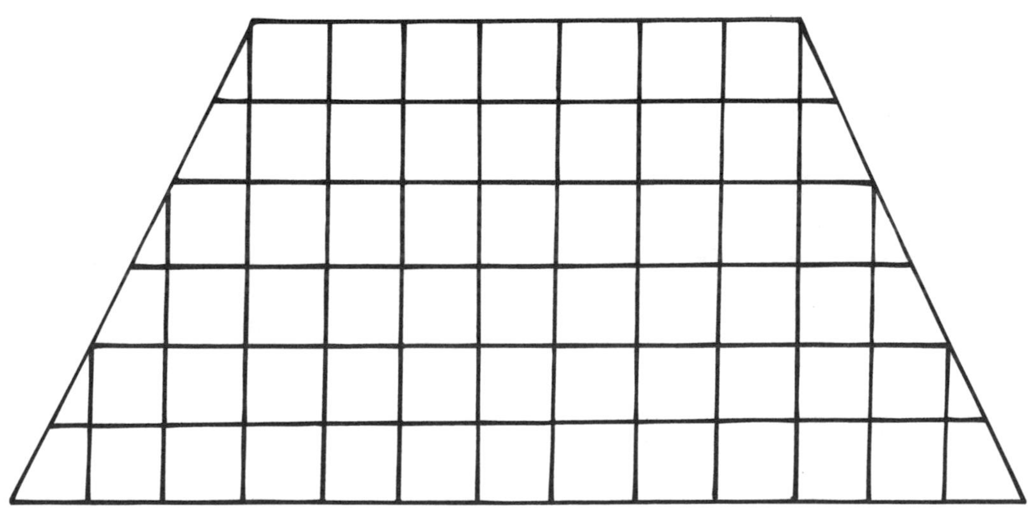

WORKSHEET M-11.1 (*cont.*)

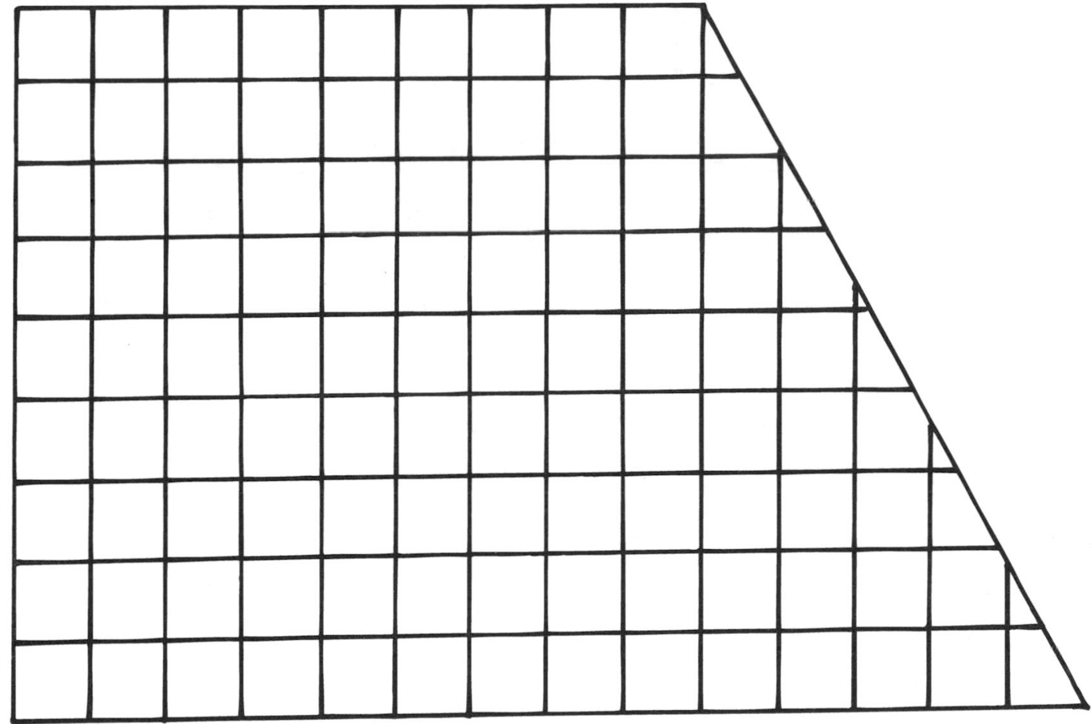

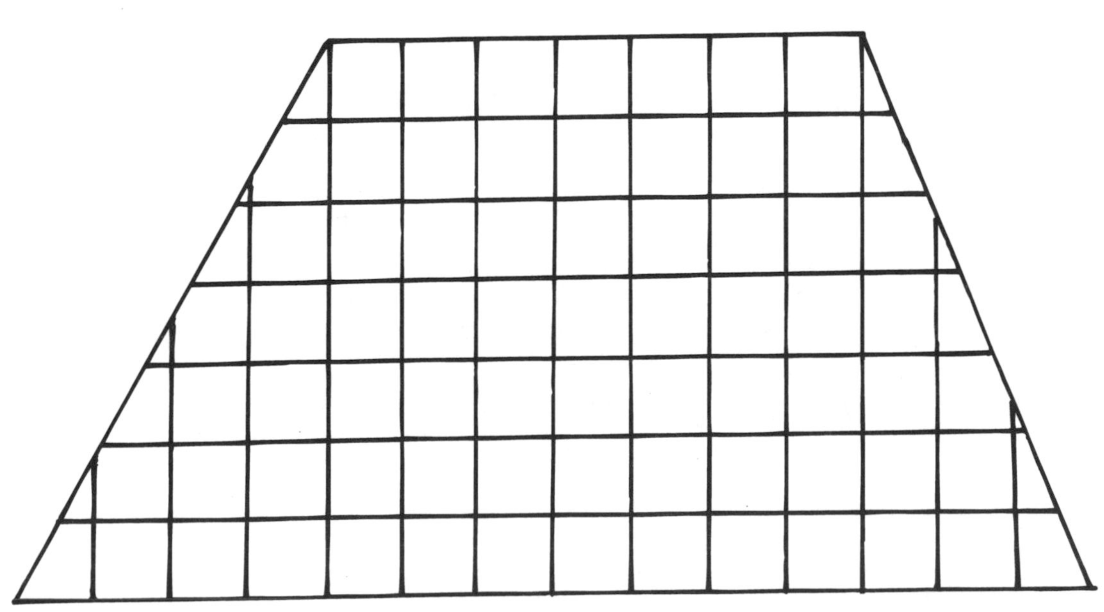

3. Have them draw the bottom side of the parallelogram in red and its height in blue, then find the lengths of the two segments by using the grid.

4. The students should then write on the worksheet below the transformed trapezoid a number sentence that relates the *red* and *blue* measures of the parallelogram to the measures of the trapezoid and thus gives the area of the trapezoid, as well as the parallelogram.

Sample number sentence:

$$(4 + 7) \times (4/2) = 11 \times 2 = 22 \text{ sq. units, the area of the trapezoid}$$

5. For the last item on the worksheet, have the students try to create a formula in words that shows how to find the area of a trapezoid if you know the lengths of the two parallel sides and the perpendicular distance between them. *Sample response:* (sum of lengths of 2 parallel sides) × (half of distance between these 2 sides) = trapezoid's area

6. After students share their own formulas, discuss the formulas presented in their textbooks as alternative forms.

Activity 3: TRAPEZOIDAL TRADERS

(Cooperative Groups)

Materials: Rectangular strips of paper (24" × 5")
Scissors
Centimeter rulers
Paper
Pencils
Calculators
Index cards

Management: Teams of 4 students each (20 minutes)

Directions:

1. Give each team two strips of paper, one pair of scissors, one centimeter ruler, an index card, and a calculator.

2. On each team one pair of students will cut a trapezoid from their strip of paper and give it to the other pair to measure and compute its area. The edges of the paper can be used for the two parallel sides, thereby making the width of the strip serve as the height of the trapezoid. Students may also cut off some of the paper's width to create a shorter height, but they must be careful to cut parallel to the paper's edge.

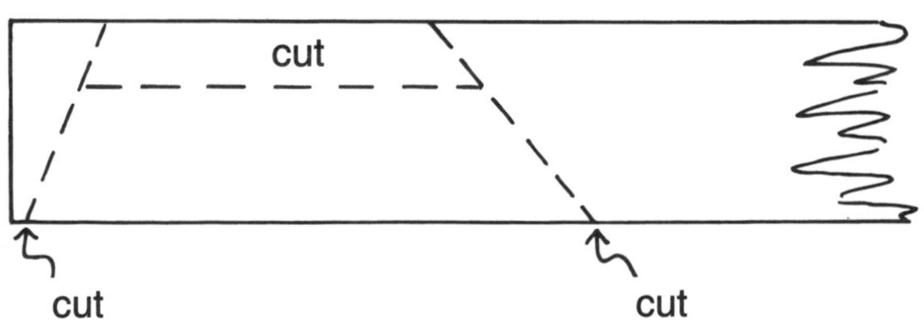

NAME ______________________________ DATE ____________________

AREA WORKSHEET M-11.2
Rotating Tops

Change each trapezoid into a parallelogram. Find the area of each trapezoid.

1.

2.

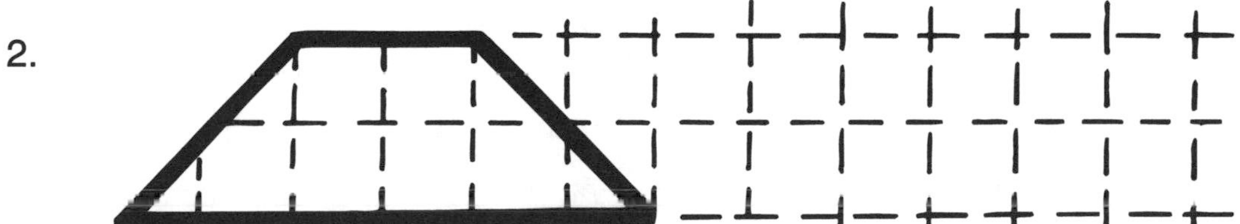

3.

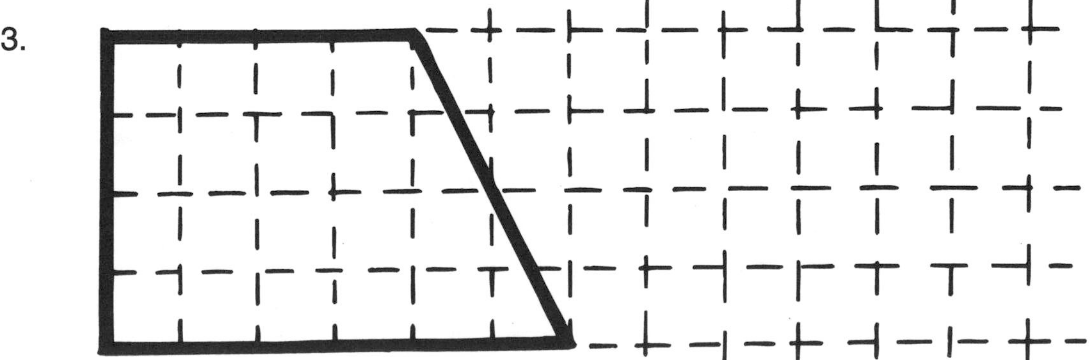

NAME ______________________ DATE ______________

WORKSHEET M-11.2 (*cont.*)

4.

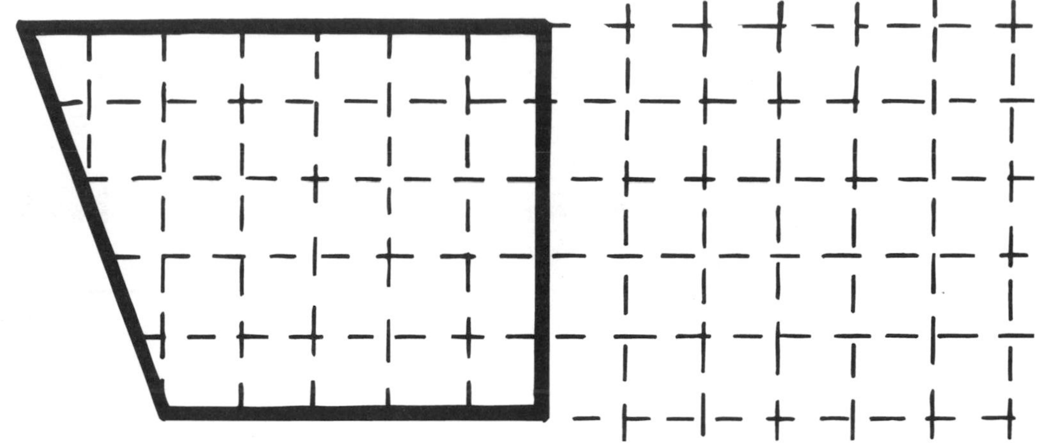

5.

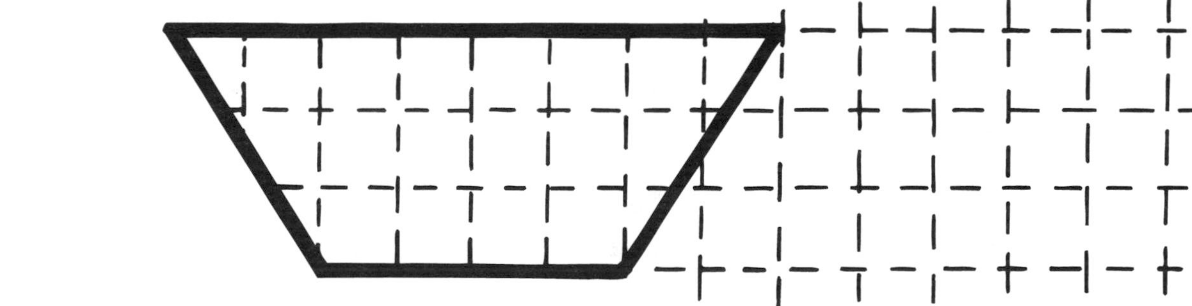

6. Write a formula in your own words that describes how to find the area of a trapezoid.

3. The measuring pair will use the index card to draw the perpendicular distance between the two parallel sides of their trapezoid. They will measure this distance and the lengths of the two parallel sides to the nearest tenth of a centimeter. These values will then be used to compute the shape's area.

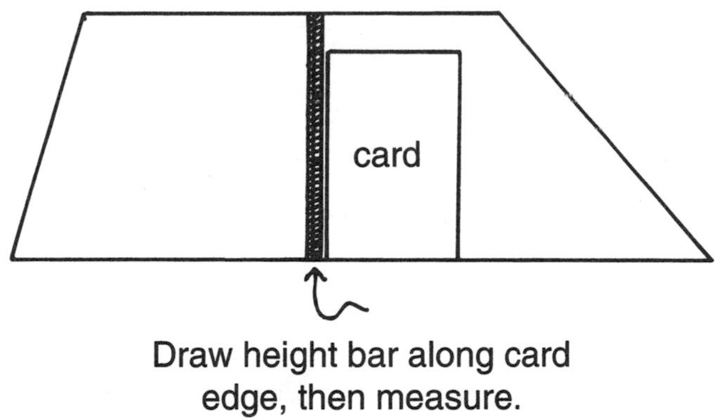

Draw height bar along card edge, then measure.

4. The two pairs of students on each team will rotate which pair cuts off the trapezoid and which pair measures and computes the area. The process will continue until time is called.

OBJECTIVE 12: Find the area of a circle.

Activity 1: CIRCLE COVER-UP
(Concrete Action)

Materials: Circle patterns (Worksheet M-12.1)
Centimeter grid paper
Scissors
Tape or glue (optional)
[Note: Copy centimeter grid paper on colored paper and circle patterns on white paper to make cut pieces of the squares easier to see.]

Management: Teams of 3 students each (30 minutes)

Directions:

1. Give each team of students a sheet of circles and a colored sheet of centimeter grid paper, scissors, and tape or glue.

2. Ask students to cut 3–4 squares out of the grid paper, using a side length equal to the radius measure of the first circle.

3. Ask them to predict how many of these large squares will be needed to completely cover the interior of the circle. Record their predictions on the chalkboard.

4. Students should now gradually cut one square apart and place the pieces inside the circle, then repeat the process with a second and a third square. The pieces must not overlap and gaps should be avoided as much as possible. Encourage students not to rush; this can be a tedious task for some people. Once students are satisfied with their positioning of all the pieces, they might want to tape or glue them onto the circle to hold them in place.

5. After students have finished, have them compare the number of squares they actually used to the number they predicted earlier. (The actual covering should use 3 whole squares plus part of a fourth square.)

6. Now have the students repeat the cutting and covering process for the other circle. Discuss their results. The actual covering should again take 3 and a little more squares, even though the second circle is different in size from the first one.

7. Ask students: *If you know the area of a square, can you figure out the area of its related circle (i.e., radius equals side length of square) from what you have learned from this activity?* (Yes; area of circle will equal a little more than three times the area of the square.)

WORKSHEET M-12.1
Circle Patterns for Circle Cover-Up

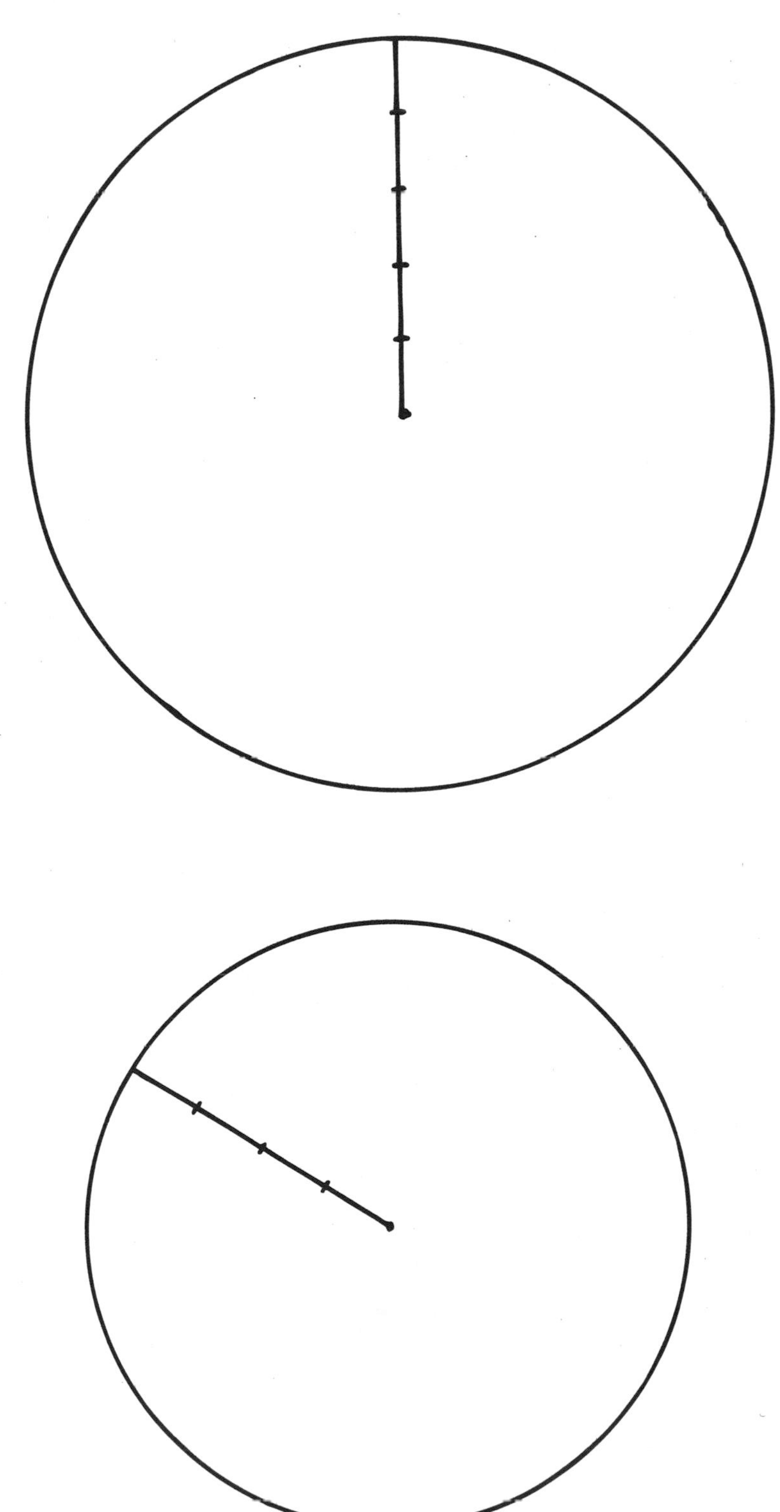

Activity 2: CIRCLE VS. SQUARE

(Pictorial Action)

Materials: Circle Worksheet M-12.2
Red markers
Calculators
Paper
Pencils

Management: Partners (20 minutes)

Directions:

1. Give each pair of students a circle worksheet, red marker, and a calculator.

2. Tell students to estimate the area of the first circle by counting whole square units and parts of square units of the grid inside the circle.

3. Ask them to draw a vertical and a horizontal diameter on the circle with the red marker. They should then draw other segments to form large squares, as shown in the following diagram:

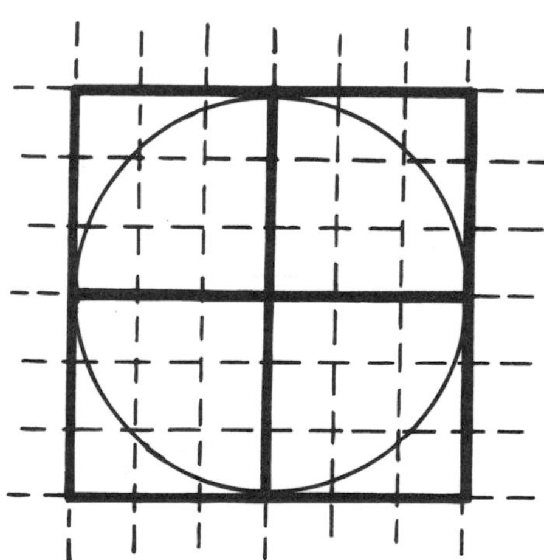

4. Students should now count the square units of the grid that are inside one of the large squares they have drawn. Have them compare this amount to the circle's area found earlier. The square's area will be less, so have them add on areas of the other squares, one at a time, to the first square's area and compare each new sum to the circle's area. The areas of 3 squares should be just less than the counted area of the circle (if students estimated carefully), and 4 areas will be too much.

5. Ask students to figure out how much more in area they need to add to the areas of the 3 squares to equal the circle's area. Have them express this difference as a decimal fraction of the area of another whole square. (Answers will probably be about 0.1 or 0.2 of a square's area.)

Example: Estimate of circle's area—28 sq. units
Circle's estimate – 3 squares' areas = 28 – (3 × 9) = 1 sq. unit
Difference/a square's area = 1 sq. units/9 sq. unit = 0.1 of another square's area

6. Have students write a number sentence that uses the squares to find the circle's area near the circle on the worksheet.

Example: 3.1 × 9 sq. units = 27.9 sq. units for the circle's area

7. Have the students repeat the above procedure with the other circle on their worksheet. Results should be similar to those for the first circle, even though the circles are of different size.

8. Write on the chalkboard all the decimal fractions found in step 5 by students and ask the class to find the average (mean) fraction to the nearest hundredth. This fraction can now be added to 3, the number of whole squares needed, to find the *amount of squares* (not amount of area) needed total, whose areas together will equal the area of the circle. (This number should be quite close to 3.14, the value of pi.)

9. Have students write two or three word sentences to describe this newly found relationship between the area of a circle and the area of a square whose side length equals the radius of the circle. (*Sample response:* It takes about 3.14 of the area of the square to equal the area of the related circle. The area of the square is found by computing side length × side length, which is the same as radius × radius. So another way to find a circle's area is to take 3.14 of radius × radius.)

Activity 3: CIRCLE ATTACK

(Cooperative Groups)

Materials: Compasses
Centimeter rulers
Calculators
Paper
Pencils

Management: Teams of 4 students each (20 minutes)

Directions:

1. Give each team a compass, centimeter ruler, and calculator. (*Note:* Flat, plastic safety compasses are now available commercially.)

2. Two students on each team use the compass to draw a circle on a sheet of paper. The other two members of the team measure to find the circle's radius to the nearest tenth of a centimeter and *mentally* estimate what the circle's area might be in square centimeters. The drawing pair then calculates the circle's area to see how close the estimate is to the computed amount.

3. The two pairs of students take turns with the two roles, drawing-calculating or measuring-estimating, until time is called.

4. If a team wishes to keep score during this activity, the difference between the estimate and computed amount for area can be recorded for the estimating pair each time. After each pair has estimated with 3–4 circles, the average of the recorded differences can be found for each pair. The pair with the lowest average then earns the title, "Knights of the Round," or another of their own choosing.

NAME ______________________ DATE ______________

WORKSHEET M-12.2
Circle vs. Square

Cover each circle with its "related" squares. How many squares will be needed? Find the area of each circle.

1.

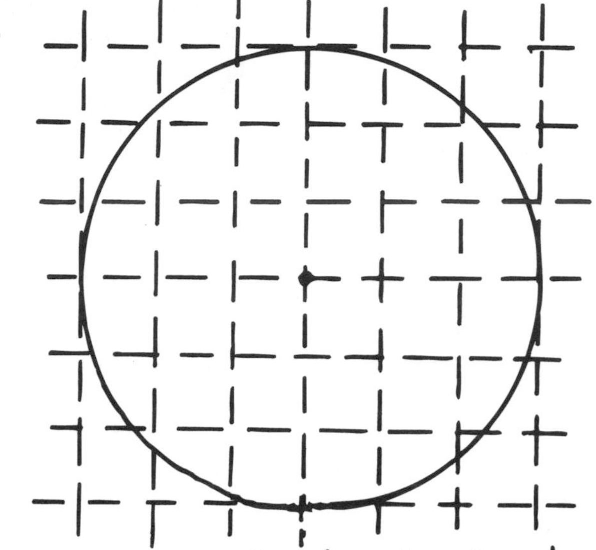

2.

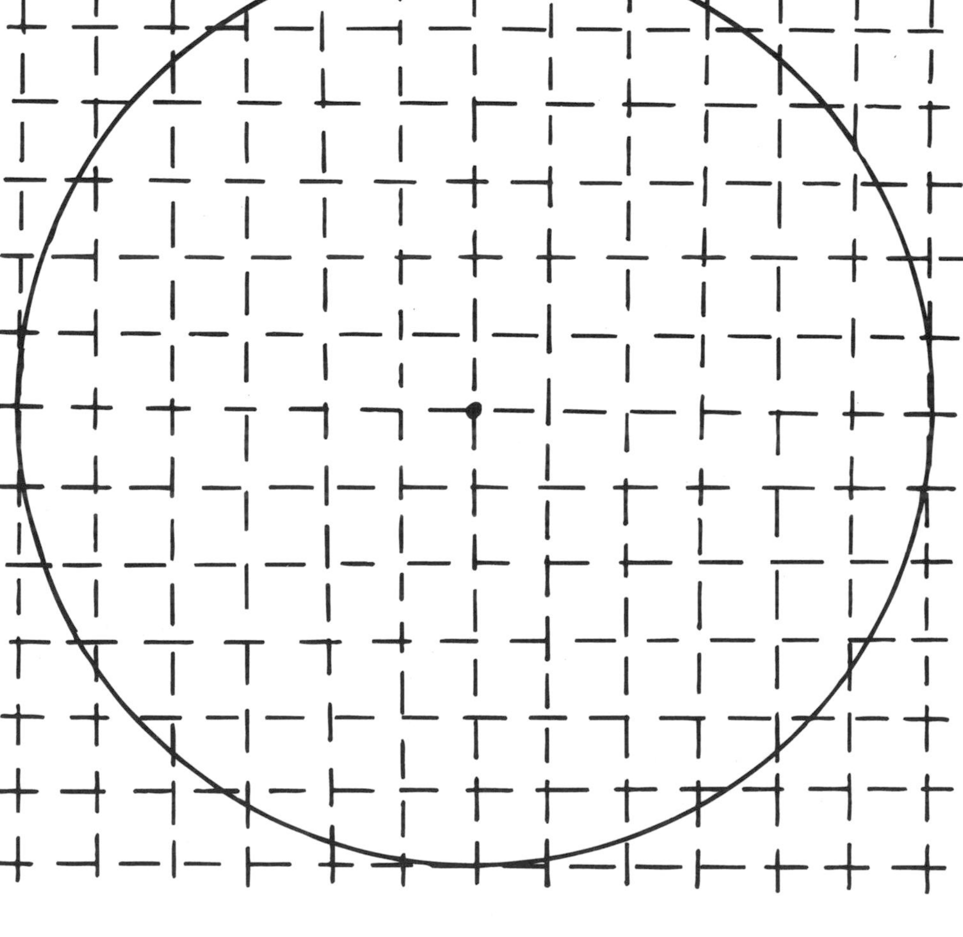

OBJECTIVE 13: Use the relationship between units to convert measures within the same measurement system.

Note: For convenience, the activities described below will pertain to the linear measures, the foot and the yard. The methods used, however, can be applied to any two measures (length, capacity/volume, area, mass/weight, or time) whose relationship students have already discovered through concrete experiences. A two-or three-column building mat similar to a base ten frame can be made from tagboard and laminated with blank heading boxes for the columns. Then headings can be taped on or written with washable transparency pens according to whichever units are being studied at the time.

Activity 1: MAKING TRADES

(Concrete Action)

Materials: Building mats
Counters (2 colors)
Paper
Pencils

Management: Partners (15 minutes per trading procedure)

Directions:

1. Give each pair of students about 5 counters of color #1 and about 15 of color #2. Color #1 represents the larger unit and color #2, the smaller unit. The amount of color #2 will vary, depending on the trading ratio of the two unit sizes involved in the activity. Our example involves feet and yards, so the ratio is 3 to 1. Hence, we need the color #2 amount (feet) to equal 3 times the color #1 (yards) amount in order to have enough to trade.

2. Review with the students that 3 feet are equal in length to 1 yard. Show this with a yardstick and 3 foot-long rulers placed on top of the yardstick.

Procedure A: Trading smaller units for larger units

3. Ask students to place 6 of the color #2 counters on the building mat in the right column, whose heading is *feet.* Have them count and pick up 3 #2 counters and remove them from the mat, then place 1 of the color #1 counters in the left column, whose heading is *yards.* Repeat this process for the remaining 3 counters in the feet column. Students may record their result by writing the number sentence: 6 feet = 2 yards.

4. Give students a variety of exercises like the one above. Also give some where there will be feet left over, e.g., of 5 feet, 3 feet will trade to 1 yard in the left column and 2 feet will remain in the right column. Another type to include begins with both yards and feet on the mat. For example, 2 yards and 4 feet may be on the mat at first. 3 feet trade for 1 new yard, leaving 3 yards and 1 foot on the mat. The number sentence is as follows: 2 yards 4 feet = 3 yards 1 foot. Use the full names of the units for a while before changing to their abbreviated forms.

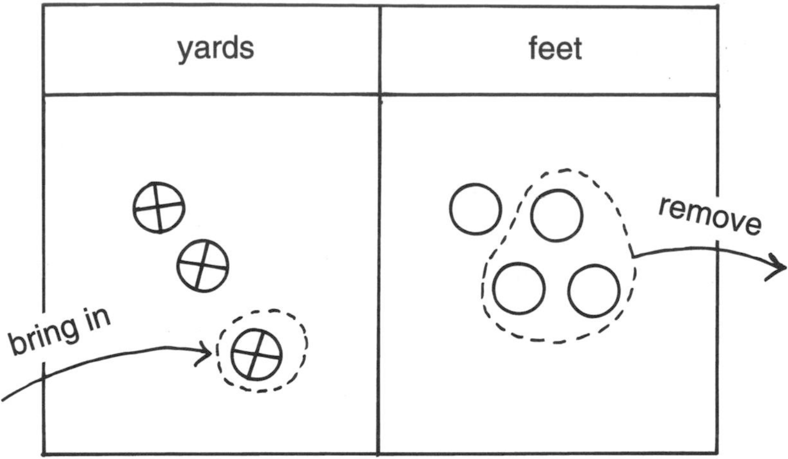

Procedure B: Trading larger units for smaller units

5. Have students place 2 of the color #1 counters on the mat in the left column (yards). Since 1 yard equals 3 feet, 1 counter in the yards column can be removed from the mat and 3 of the color #2 counters placed in the right column (feet). Repeat this process for the other counter in the yards column. Students may now record their result by writing the number sentence: 2 yards = 6 feet.

6. Give students a variety of exercises like the one above. Also include some where both yards and feet are present at first. For example, for 1 yard and 2 feet placed on the mat, the yard will trade for 3 new feet, leaving 5 feet total on the mat. The number sentence will be as follows: 1 yard 2 feet = 5 feet.

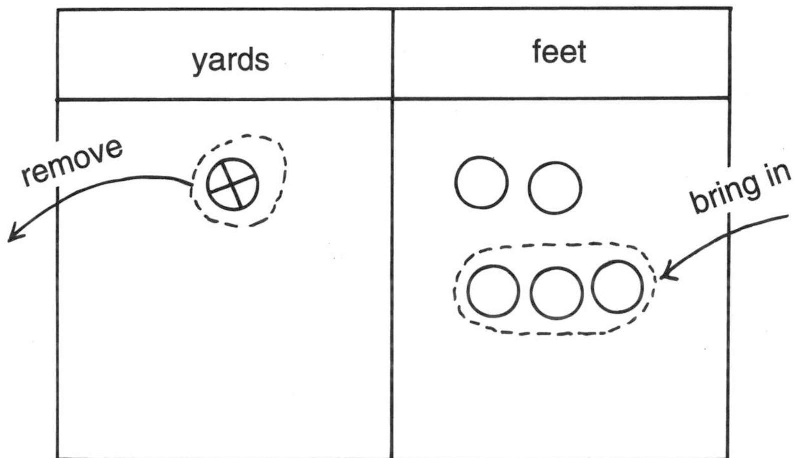

7. Let students make up their own exercises for others to work.

Activity 2: DRAWING TO TRADE

(Pictorial Action)

Materials: Building Frame Worksheet M-13.2
Red pencils or pens
Regular pencils

Management: Partners (15 minutes per procedure)

Directions:

1. Give each pair of students a worksheet and a red pencil.

Procedure A: Trading smaller units for larger units

2. Ask students to draw 4 small circles in the right column of the first building frame shown on the worksheet. These represent 4 feet. Have the students count and draw a red curve around 3 of the circles. They should put a red *X* over the 3 circles, then draw a red arrow from them to the left column. Near the arrowhead in the left column, they should draw a small square in regular pencil to show 1 yard. If there were 3 or more circles still unused in the right column, students would repeat the trading process. For the given example, there is only 1 circle remaining in the feet column, so they may record the final result as *4 feet = 1 yard 1 foot.*

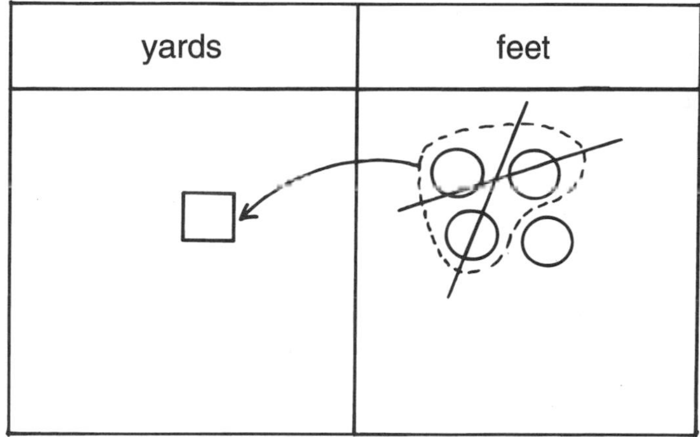

3. Give students additional exercises similar to those discussed in Activity 1 under Procedure A.

4. Ask students to describe in words how they change feet to yards.

Sample response: To find the number of yards, find out how many groups of 3 feet each can be removed from the given number of feet.

NAME ______________________ DATE ______________

BUILDING FRAME WORKSHEET M-13.2
Drawing to Trade

Make trades by drawing on the given frames. Write a number sentence below each frame to describe the trade shown on the frame.

1.

yards	feet

2.

yards	feet

3.

yards	feet

4.

yards	feet

5.

yards	feet

6.

yards	feet

Procedure B: Trading larger units for smaller units

5. Have students draw 2 small squares in the left column of a building frame on the worksheet to show 2 yards. They should draw a red *X* on one of the squares, then draw a red arrow from the square over to the right column, where 3 new circles are now drawn with a regular pencil. This process is repeated for each square in the left column. Students count the total circles now shown in the feet column. The result may be recorded as *2 yards = 6 feet.*

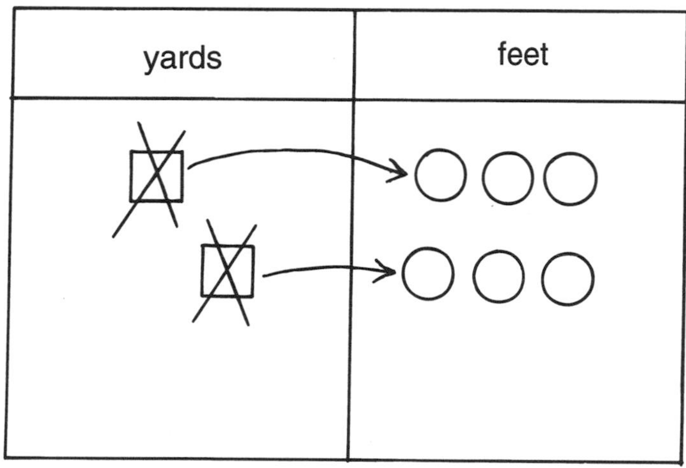

6. Give students additional exercises similar to those discussed in Activity 1 under Procedure B.

7. Ask students to describe in words how they change yards to feet.

Sample response: To find the number of feet, find out how many times a group of 3 feet can be formed from a yard, using the given number of yards.

Activity 3: SPIN 'N TRADE

(Cooperative Groups)

Materials: Spinner patterns (Worksheet M-13.3)
Building mats
Counters (2 colors)
Paper clips
Paper
Pencils

Management: Teams of 4 students each (20 minutes)

Directions:

1. Give each team a sheet of spinners, a paper clip, a building mat, 5 counters of color #1 (yards), and 18 counters of color #2 (feet). Team members will rotate having the following tasks: (a) spin the 2 spinners, (b) place counters on the building mat according to the amounts shown on the spinners, (c) make any trades necessary to simplify the number of all counters placed on the mat, and (d) record the results as a number sentence.

2. For example, player 1 will hold the paper clip on each spinner and spin it. If the paper clip lands on 2 on Spinner A (shows 0, 1, 2, 3), player 2 places 2 counters of color #1 in the *yards* column on the mat. If the paper clip lands on 7 on Spinner B (shows 3, 4, 5, 6, 7, 8), player 2 places 7 counters of color #2 in the *feet* column on the mat. Then player 3 trades 3 of the feet counters twice for one of the yards counters to leave 2 original + 2 new counters in the yards column and 1 counter in the feet column, the least number of counters possible to leave on the mat. Player 4 records the result as "2 yards 7 feet = 4 yards 1 foot."

3. Player 1 now rotates to task 4, player 2 rotates to task 1, etc., and the play continues.

4. A *two-way trading* alternative to the *simplification* game: On each turn, a player will toss a coin. HEADS will mean to trade larger units for smaller units; TAILS will mean to trade smaller units for larger units. The spinner instructions remain the same. Instead of only simplifying feet to yards each time, students will now trade either way, depending on the coin toss. This is good practice for future measurement problems requiring subtraction.

5. When other trade ratios besides the 3 to 1 trade (the one used for feet and yards) are used, the amount of color #2 counters needed for the smaller unit and the numbers on the second spinner (B) will have to change. Here are some sample trade ratios and the quantities/spinner numbers they will require:

- 10 to 1 (milliliter to centiliter or decigram to gram):
  25 counters (75 for 2-way trades); Spinner B—12, 15, 16, 19, 20, 22
- 12 to 1 (inch to foot):
  30 counters (75 for 2-way trades); Spinner B—14, 15, 17, 20, 24, 25
- 16 to 1 (ounce to pound):
  35 counters (115 for 2-way trades); Spinner B—17, 18, 21, 25, 32, 33
- 7 to 1 (day to week):
  15 counters (40 for 2-way trades); Spinner B—8, 9, 11, 12, 14, 15
- 4 to 1 (quart to gallon):
  10 counters (30 for 2-way trades); Spinner B—5, 6, 7, 8, 9, 10

WORKSHEET M-13.3
Spinner Patterns for Spin 'n Trade

Spinner A for larger units (yards).

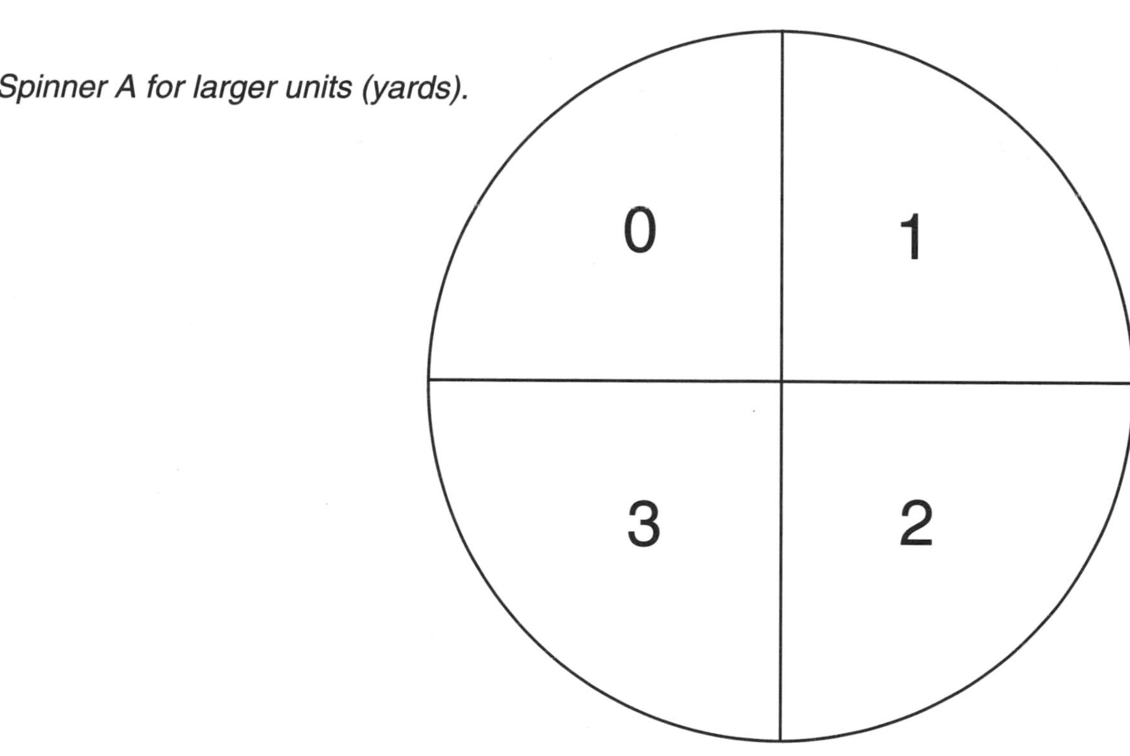

Spinner B for smaller units (feet).

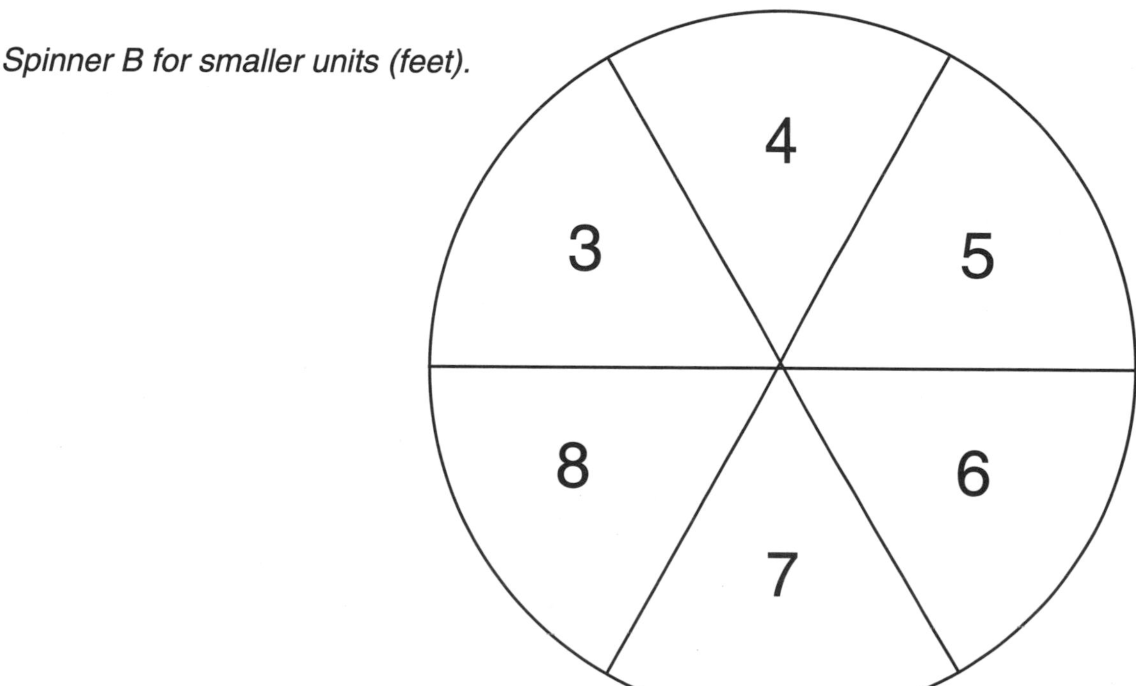

OBJECTIVE 14: Determine the areas of irregular figures.

Activity 1: CREATIVE SPACES
(Concrete Action)

Materials: Centimeter grid paper
Scissors
Calculators
Tape
Compasses
Construction paper
Paper
Pencils

Management: Teams of 4 students each (30 minutes)

Directions:

1. Give each team 2 sheets of centimeter grid paper, 2 pairs of scissors, tape, 1 sheet of construction paper, a calculator, and a compass (if you want them to draw circles).

2. Ask students to design an unusual room by cutting and taping regular or standard shapes together to create an irregular floor plan. Some standard shapes to consider are rectangles, circles, triangles, parallelograms, and trapezoids.

3. The standard shapes should be cut out of the centimeter grid paper and taped edge to edge with no overlapping or gaps. Students must use the square unit or the unit segment of the grid to help them compute the areas of the different shapes they will be using.

4. Encourage them to use semicircles (half circles) and a variety of triangles in their designs to give them more practice with the different area formulas. It might be helpful to write the area of a new shape directly on the shape as soon as it is drawn on the grid before it is cut out and taped to other parts of the floor plan.

5. When the floor plan is complete, it should be taped onto the construction paper for display. The total area in square centimeters of the floor should be written on the construction paper also.

Sample floor plan:

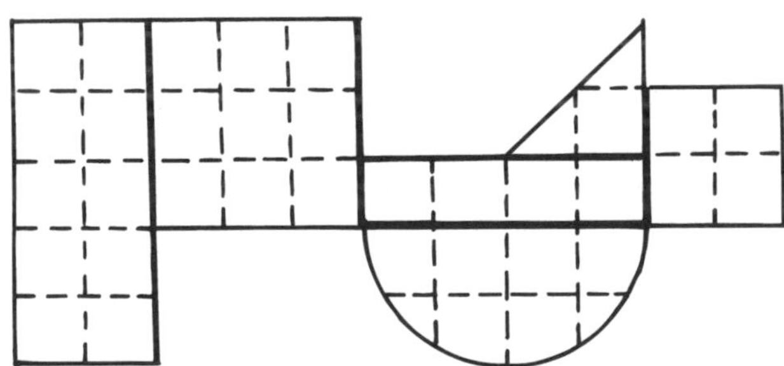

Activity 2: SEARCH FOR FAMILIAR SHAPES

(Pictorial Action)

Materials: Worksheet M-14.2 of irregular shapes
Red markers
Rulers
Calculators
Pencils

Management: Partners (20 minutes)

Directions:

1. Give each pair of students a copy of Worksheet M-14.2 containing irregular shapes with grid interiors, a red marker, a calculator, and a ruler.

2. The students are to find a way to subdivide each irregular shape into several standard shapes. The red marker and ruler can be used to show the boundaries of the newly found shapes.

3. The area of each standard shape must be computed, then all of the separate areas combined to find the total area of the irregular shape. The grid markings will help students find the various measurements needed to calculate the areas in square centimeters.

4. If possible, make a transparency of the worksheet. Have different students draw the subdivisions they used on the transparency shapes (or on their projections on the chalkboard) in order to share various approaches with the entire class. Most irregular shapes will have more than one way to be subdivided into standard shapes, and students need to be made aware of these alternatives.

Example of two different subdivisions for the same irregular shape:

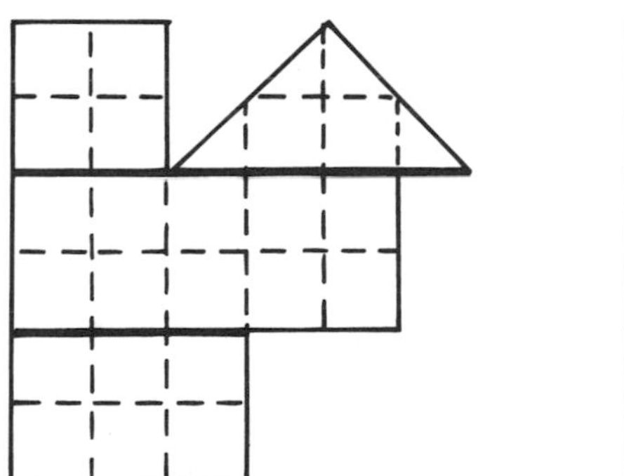

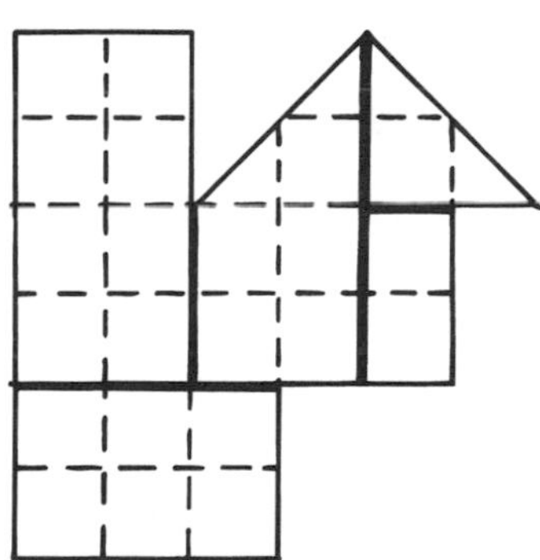

5. Have the different pairs also share the areas they have found for the different irregular shapes. The amounts for the same shape should be equal, regardless of how they subdivided the shape. Answers may differ a little if students have rounded off their numbers at different stages of their calculations.

NAME ______________________________ DATE ____________________

WORKSHEET M-14.2
Search for Familiar Shapes

Find the area of each irregular shape by subdividing it into several more familiar shapes.

1.

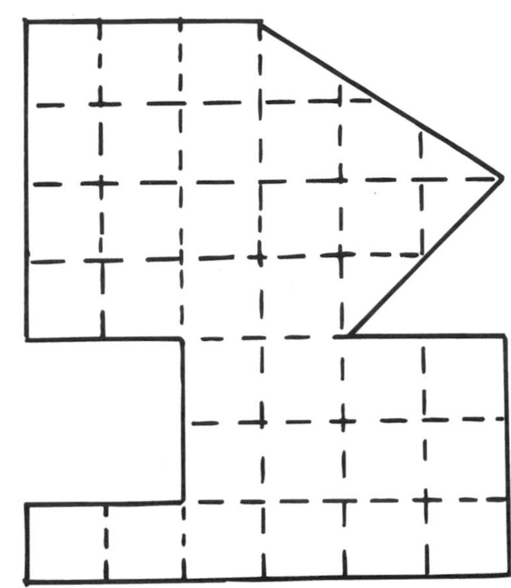

2.

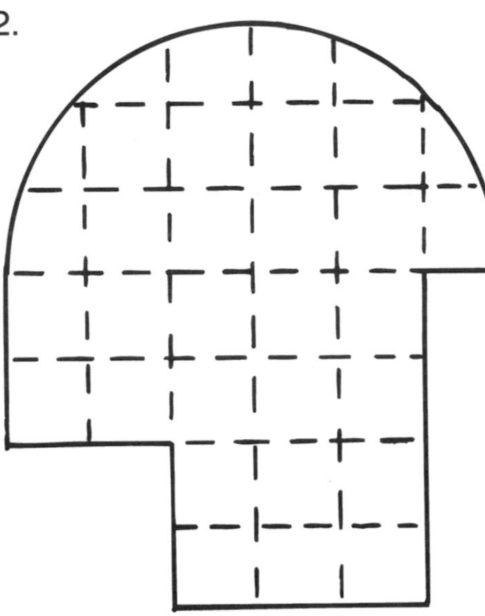

3.

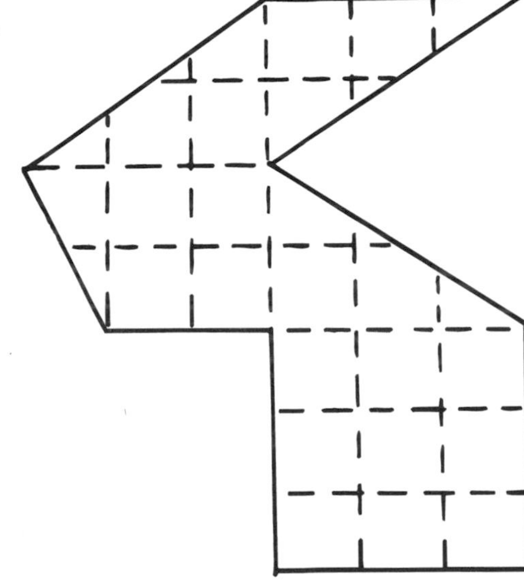

4.

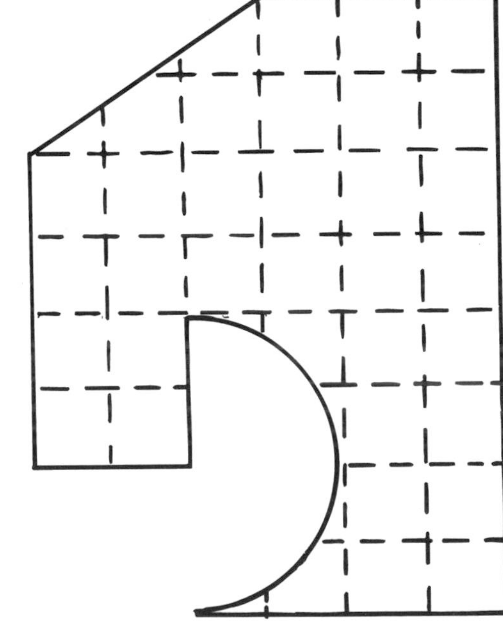

Activity 3: HIDDEN BOUNDARIES

(Cooperative Groups)

Materials: Worksheet M-14.3 of irregular shapes
Index cards
Centimeter rulers
Calculators
Paper
Pencils

Management: Teams of 4 students each (20 minutes)

Directions:

1. Give each team a worksheet containing one or two irregular shapes, an index card, a centimeter ruler, and a calculator.

2. The shapes were drawn originally on a centimeter grid, but the grid markings are no longer showing. The students must measure to the nearest centimeter with their rulers to decide where to draw off boundaries to form standard shapes within the irregular one. Measuring will also help them to draw *parallel* boundaries where needed. The index card may be used to make sure certain angles are *right angles.*

3. Once team members have all the extra boundaries drawn and measured that they need, they should find all the separate areas involved and combine them to get the total area of their irregular shape. Have them record the number sentences they use.

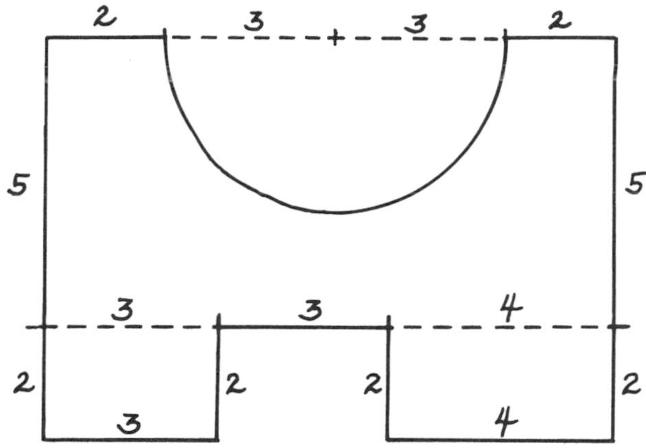

4. If time permits, teams can repeat the above process and find the total area of a second irregular shape.

5. The various team drawings and area results may be shared with the entire class by displaying the papers and calculations on the classroom bulletin board.

NAME ______________________ DATE ______________

WORKSHEET M-14.3
Hidden Boundaries

Find the total area of each irregular shape by subdividing it into familiar shapes and measuring their sides in centimeters.

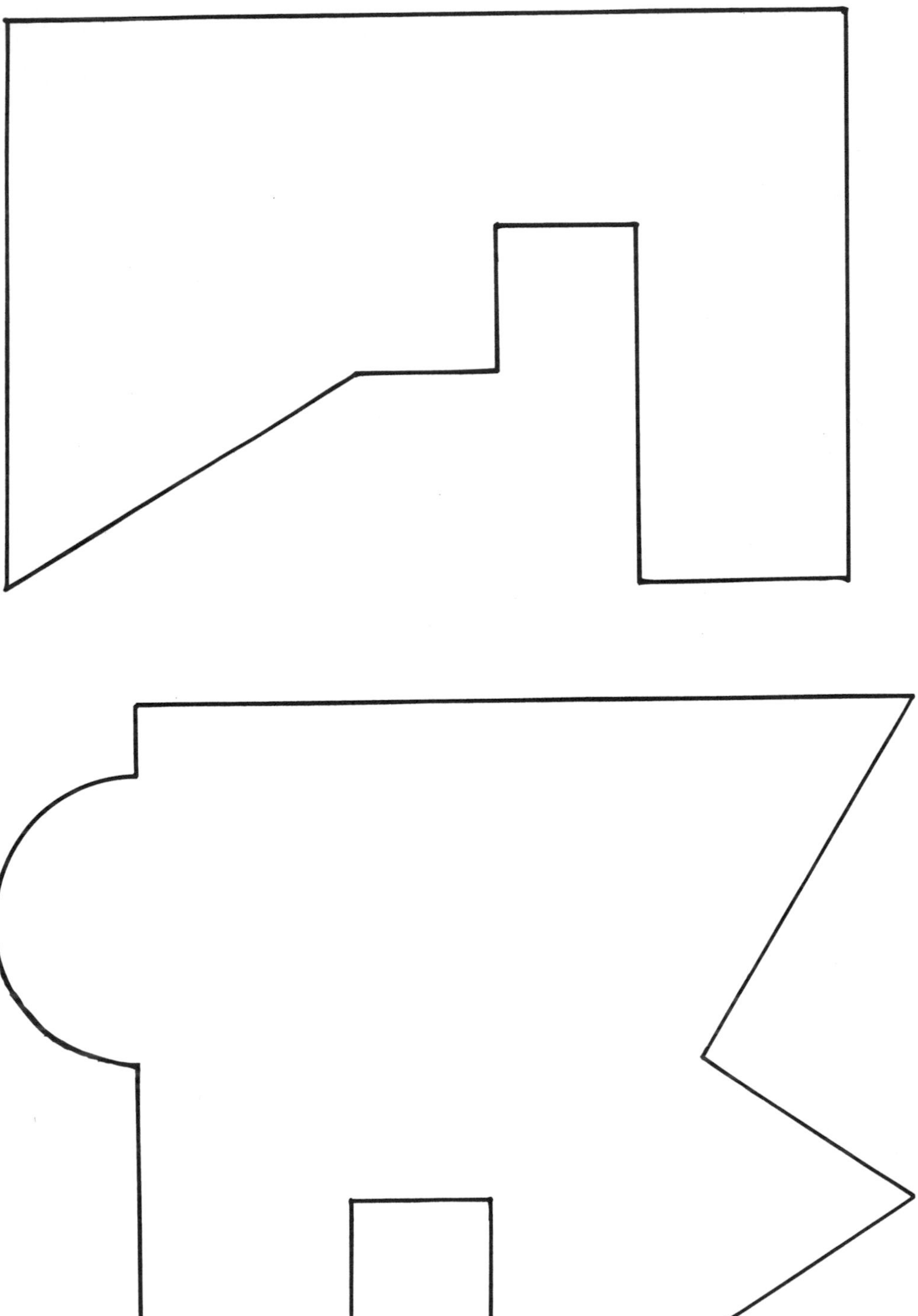

CHAPTER 6

STATISTICS AND PROBABILITY

INTRODUCTION

This chapter introduces the concepts of statistics and probability using common objects and simple activities. Students are shown how fractions can be used to describe probabilities. Through step-by-step exercises, students learn to work with number scales and to draw bar graphs, line graphs, and circle graphs. Students learn how to determine all possible outcomes and arrangements for a set of data. In addition, students find three basic statistics for a set of data: the mean, median, and mode.

OBJECTIVE 1: Explore proportions through reductions and enlargements.

Activity 1: LOOK-ALIKES

(Concrete Action)

Materials: Centimeter cubes
Inch cubes (alternative: 1-inch paper squares and 2-inch paper squares)

Management: Partners (30 minutes)

Directions:

1. Give each pair of students 30 cubes each of the centimeter and inch cubes.

2. Have students build simple designs with one size of cube, then copy that design with the other size of cube. The two designs should look exactly alike except for their size. That is, the designs will be similar. When a design has been copied with the larger cubes, it has been *enlarged.* When it has been copied with the smaller cubes, the design has been *reduced.*

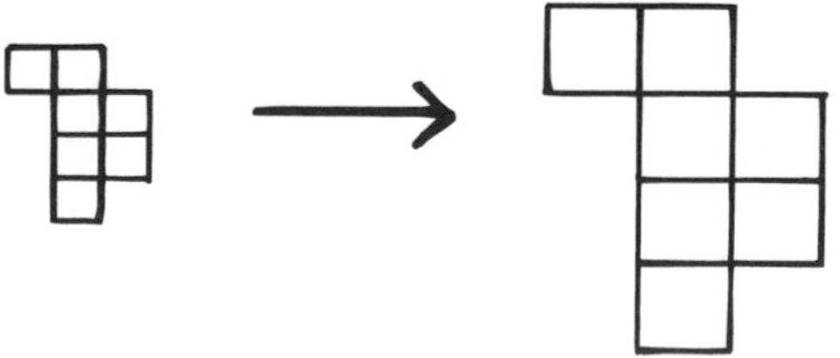

3. Partners should take turns building with the two sizes of cubes and also take turns being the one to make the initial design for the other to copy. Each student needs experience in creating a design with each cube size, as well as in copying a design with each cube size.

Activity 2: INCA BIRD DESIGNS

(Pictorial Action)

Materials: Inca Bird Patterns (Worksheet SP-1.2)
Inch grid patterns (see PATTERNS/GRIDS section)
Colored pencils or markers
Inch rulers
Paper
Regular pencils

Management: Partners (30–40 minutes)

Directions:

1. Background: The Inca were a South American Indian people who ruled one of the largest and richest empires in the Americas. They founded Cusco (in Peru), the center of their empire, during the eleventh century and expanded their empire along the western coast of South America. Their lands included areas known today as Colombia, Ecuador, Peru, Bolivia, Chile, and Argentina. The empire fell about 1532, when the Inca were conquered by the Spaniards.

The Inca were skilled in engineering and architectural construction and built a network of roads that linked all the provinces of the empire together. They also produced many fine articles made of gold, silver, tin, and other materials. The Inca Bird used in this activity is similar to designs found in their weaving or pottery.

Sources for more information on Inca Bird designs:

Glubok, Shirley. *The Art of Ancient Peru.* New York: Harper & Row, 1966.

Krause, Marina C. *Multicultural Mathematics Materials.* Reston, VA: National Council of Teachers of Mathematics, Inc., 1983.

2. Give each pair of students an Inca Bird pattern, a sheet of inch grid paper, an inch ruler, and a set of assorted colored pencils or markers.

3. Students are to *enlarge* their bird design by transferring the design from its smaller grid to the larger grid. This is to be done by copying one square of the design at a time. That is, whatever segment or curve is drawn across a single square in the original design will be redrawn the same way in the corresponding square on the larger grid.

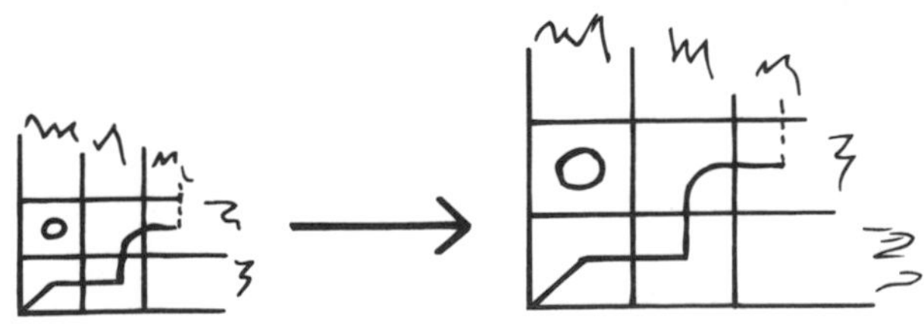

4. After the copy is completed, students should color their bird design according to their own preference.

5. Have students use their rulers to measure the original bird design and their copy at the tallest point and widest point. Tell them to measure to the nearest half inch each time; this will simplify later computations. Have them record the measurements in inches in the following way on their own paper and compute the quotients for the ratios formed. (Each unit segment on the larger grid is twice the length of the unit segment on the smaller grid, so quotients found below should both equal 2; therefore, the scale for smaller to larger must be 1 to 2.)

a. $\dfrac{\text{maximum width of copy}}{\text{maximum width of original}} = \dfrac{?}{?} = ?$

b. $\dfrac{\text{maximum height of copy}}{\text{maximum height of original}} = \dfrac{?}{?} = ?$

6. Additional activity: As a pictorial experience in *reducing* a design, students might transfer their original design from its half-inch grid to a centimeter grid (see PATTERNS/GRIDS section). If any comparisons of measurements are to be done, have students measure to the nearest tenth of a centimeter with centimeter rulers and use calculators so that they can compute easily with the tenths.

Activity 3: MYSTERY KINGDOMS

(Cooperative Groups)

Materials: Large butcher paper (or its equivalent)
Inch grid patterns (see PATTERNS/GRIDS section)
Colored pencils or markers
Inch rulers or yardsticks
Paper
Regular pencils
Large index cards

Management: Teams of 4 students each (50 minutes)

Directions:

1. Give each team a large sheet of butcher paper (approximately 3' × 4'), a sheet of inch grid paper, assorted colored pencils or markers, an inch ruler or a yardstick, and a large index card (for making right angles when drawing perpendicular lines for a grid).

2. Each team is to create a map of its own mystery kingdom. Have students first draw the kingdom's boundaries on the inch grid paper and mark where they want rivers, roads, and mountains to be located.

3. They are to use a scale of 1 to 4 to copy their initial map of their kingdom onto the larger sheet of butcher paper. Have students use their ruler or yardstick and their index card to draw a new grid on their butcher paper, making each pair of parallel grid lines 4 inches apart instead of 1 inch. Hence, each inch of length on the smaller grid will correspond to 4 inches of actual length on the larger grid.

WORKSHEET SP-1.2
Inca Bird Pattern for Inca Bird Designs

Enlarge this design by drawing it on the larger grid.
Key: 1 small unit → 1 large unit

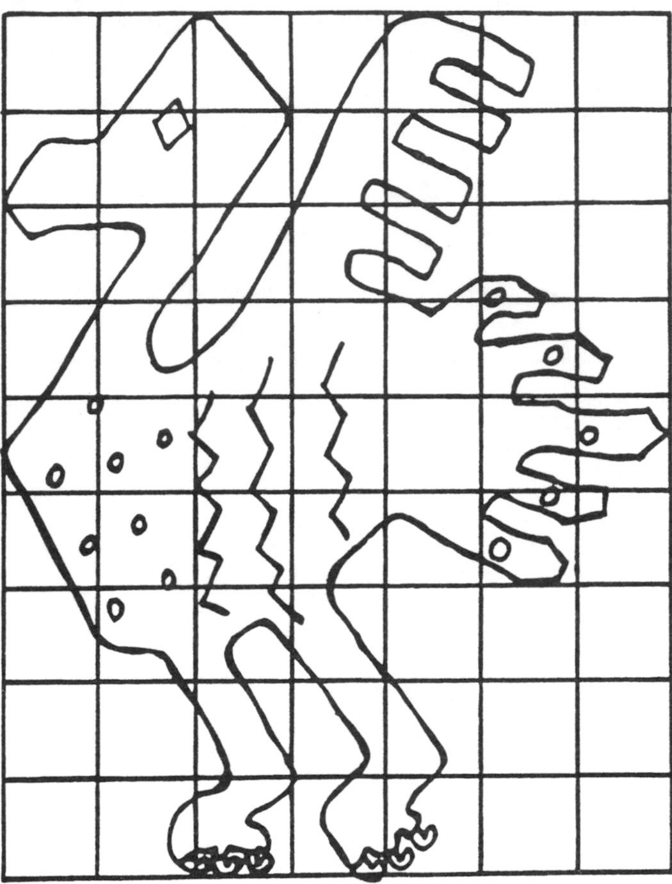

4. The initial map, including all rivers, roads, and mountains, should now be transferred to the new grid. Students should color the larger map according to their original plans and give names to any important geographic features. All maps can then be displayed on the classroom walls.

5. Have students measure various line segments or curves to the nearest inch on their original map and measure those same segments or curves on their new map. The length on the new map should be about 4 times as long as the corresponding length on the smaller map. To say it another way, the shorter length should be about 1/4 of the longer length.

6. For older students, you might also want to give them a scale for their new map; for example, 1 inch on the map might represent 10 kilometers of distance in the actual kingdom. Have students then measure different segments to the nearest inch on their new map and convert those lengths to kilometers.

7. Extension activity: Students might also write a description of their kingdom, including its form of government, characteristics of its inhabitants, and any unusual conditions that might exist in the kingdom. They could then present their report and map to the entire class.

OBJECTIVE 2: Locate points on a grid.

Activity 1: PUSHING PEGS
(Concrete Action)

Materials: Large pegboard (approximately 20 holes × 20 holes)
10 pegs or golf tees
36-inch piece of colored yarn
Masking tape

Management: Whole group (30 minutes)

Directions:

1. Tape a strip of masking tape along the left edge of the pegboard just to the left of and touching the first column of holes. Tape another strip of masking tape along the lower edge of the board just under but touching the bottom row of holes. The strips of tape will serve as the vertical and horizontal axes for the grid, and the vertical or horizontal distance between two adjacent holes will be the counting unit or step used to locate points.

2. Place the pegboard on the chalkboard tray or an easel, or hang it on a bulletin board. Glue one peg in the bottom left hole to mark the origin, (0,0). Tie one end of the colored yarn to this fixed peg.

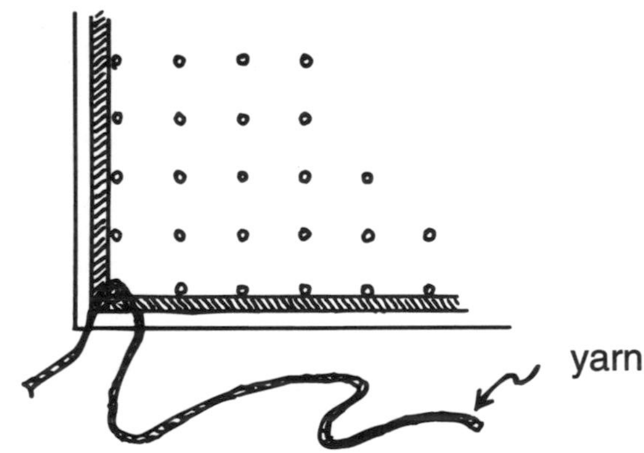

3. Explain to the students that they will be locating points according to your directions. They will stretch the yarn to the right so many steps, hold the yarn at that point, and stretch the rest of the yarn upward so many steps. A peg will then be placed where the yarn path finally stops.

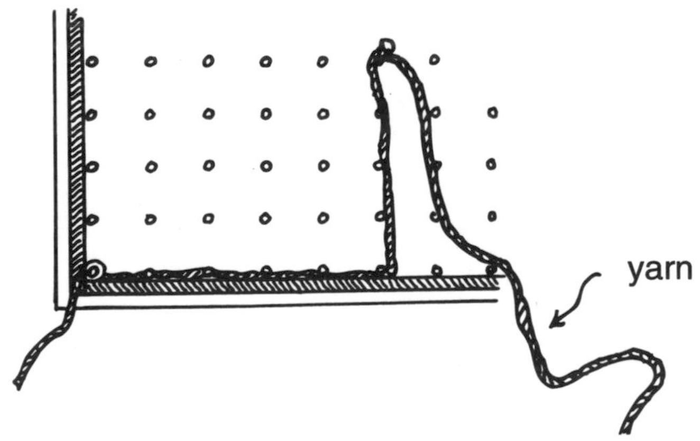

4. Have a pair of students come to the pegboard. Ask the students to stretch the yarn 3 steps to the right along the bottom row of holes. While one partner holds the yarn in place at (3,0) with his/her finger, ask the other one to stretch the rest of the yarn upward 5 steps and hold the yarn at that point or hole. Place a peg in the hole indicated by the second student. Have the two students continue to hold the yarn in place while you explain to the class that the horizontal yarn segment was made by *counting across 3 steps* from the bottom left or *zero* corner and the vertical yarn segment was made by *counting up 5 steps* from where the horizontal piece stopped and the yarn turned. You will continue to use this language to give directions for locating peg holes throughout this activity.

5. Now have three students come to the pegboard together. Call out different directions for them to follow to lay out the yarn and locate a new hole on the board. The first student will follow the *count across* directions and hold the yarn at that point or hole. The second student will follow the *count up* directions and hold the yarn at that point or hole. The third student will place a peg in the hole being marked by the second student.

6. Continue to give directions to three different students each time to find various holes on the board until all students have participated.

Activity 2: MARKING POINTS

(Pictorial Action)

Materials: 1-cm rectangular dot paper (see PATTERNS/GRIDS section)
Colored pencils
Pencils
Record Sheet (SP-2.2)
Sticky dot labels
Large pegboard and pegs from Activity 1

Management: Partners (30 minutes)

Directions:

1. Before the lesson, place 10 pegs in various holes of the large pegboard used in Activity 1. Use sticky dot labels to number each peg on the board from 1 to 10.

2. Give each pair of students one sheet of the rectangular dot paper, a record sheet, and at least five different colors of colored pencils. The dot paper should already have a vertical axis drawn up the left column of dots and a horizontal axis drawn along the bottom row of dots. The lower left corner will be the origin or zero corner.

3. Ask students to record the location of each peg on the pegboard by drawing it as a large point with a regular pencil on their dot paper. A *colored yarn* path should also be drawn to each point, using a colored pencil. If two points are close together, different colors should be used to draw their overlapping yarn paths. The distances needed to find each point should be recorded on the record sheet beside the number that corresponds to the number of the matching peg. For example, for peg #1 the colored path might be drawn across 7 steps and up 5 steps. On the record sheet beside #1, students would write

7 in the "across" column and 5 in the "up" column. Make them aware that the two numbers are also being recorded in the form: (7,5).

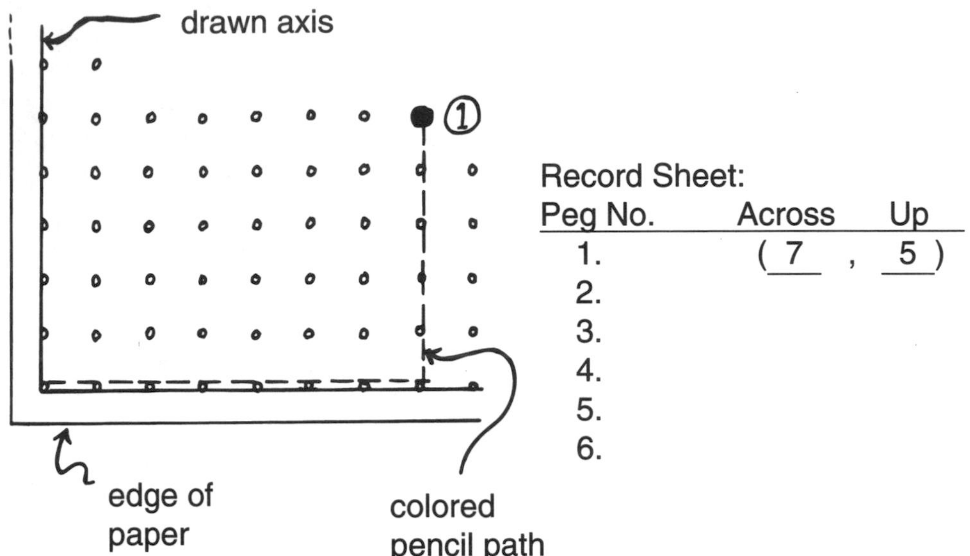

4. When all students are finished, have some of them come to the pegboard and use their finger to trace off the "across" and "up" paths for each numbered peg. They should also write the ordered pair on the chalkboard that describes the location of the peg they trace off.

Activity 3: HOPI KACHINAS

(Cooperative Groups)

Materials: Centimeter grid paper (see PATTERNS/GRIDS section)
Pencils
Colored pencils
Glue
Colored construction paper
Worksheet SP-2.3

Management: Teams of 4 students each (20–30 minutes)

Directions:

1. Background: The kachina doll is carved by Hopi craftsmen from dry roots of dead cottonwood trees found near the Little Colorado River or one of the Hopi mesas in the southwestern region of the United States. A nose, horns, ears, and the tableta or headdress are attached to the main piece of wood with small wooden pegs or glue. The doll is then ready to be elaborately painted and adorned with feathers. At special ceremonies Hopi men, masked to impersonate supernatural beings called kachinas, give the dolls to the children to help them learn about Hopi rituals.

The picture graph to be drawn in this activity depicts the old style of kachina doll. The body is in a standing position with the arms held close to the body. More modern styles may have the body carved in a dancing position. After students finish the picture graph, they might want to color the doll in bright colors and draw feathers at the top and corners of the headdress.

NAME ______________________________ DATE ____________________

RECORD SHEET SP-2.2
Marking Points

PEG NUMBER	ACROSS	UP
1.	(________ ,	________)
2.	(________ ,	________)
3.	(________ ,	________)
4.	(________ ,	________)
5.	(________ ,	________)
6.	(________ ,	________)
7.	(________ ,	________)
8.	(________ ,	________)
9.	(________ ,	________)
10.	(________ ,	________)

Sources for more information on Hopi kachina dolls:

Colton, Harold S. *Hopi Kachina Dolls With a Key to Their Identification.* Albuquerque, NM: University of New Mexico Press, 1959.

Krause, Marina C. *Multicultural Mathematics Materials.* Reston, VA: National Council of Teachers of Mathematics, Inc., 1983.

2. Give each team a sheet of centimeter grid paper, a list of ordered pairs, colored pencils, glue, and a sheet of colored construction paper (regular size). Using the lower left corner of the grid as (0,0), have students number the vertical and horizontal axes with consecutive counting numbers: 1, 2, 3, etc. Tell them that the shortest line segments on the printed grid are to be counted as the unit steps in the across and up directions for locating points.

3. Each of the following sets of points should be plotted and connected with drawn line segments in the order in which they are listed. (It is best to connect adjacent points as you plot them; this avoids confusion.)

(a) (6,3) (8,3) (8,0) (5,0) (6,1) (6,3) (4,3) (5,7) (4,8) (4,10) (6,11) (6,12) (4,12) (4,16) (6,16) (6,18) (7,18) (7,20) (9,20) (9,18) (10,18) (10,16) (12,16) (12,12) (10,12) (10,13) (11,14) (5,14) (6,13) (8,13) (8,11) (10,11) (12,10) (12,8) (11,7) (12,3) (10,3) (10,1) (11,0) (8,0)

(b) (5,7) (7,7) (7,8) (5.5,8) (5.5,9)

(c) (11,7) (9,7) (9,8) (10.5,8) (10.5,9)

(d) (6,3) (7,4) (6,5) (7,6) (6,7)

(e) This set consists of several separate segments: (6,1) to (10,1); (6,2) to (10,2); (8,3) to (10,3); (6,11) to (8,11); (10,11) to (10,12); (6,12) to (6,13); (6,12.5) to (7.5, 12.5); (8.5, 12.5) to (10,12.5); (8,13) to (10,13)

4. After students have completed their graph, have them color their kachina doll in bright colors and add "feathers" to the top and corners of the tableta or headdress. The drawing should then be mounted or glued on the colored construction paper and displayed on the classroom wall. Completed picture graph of kachina doll:

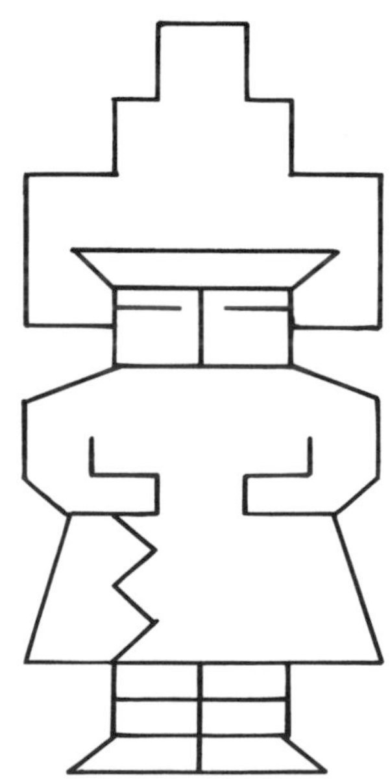

WORKSHEET SP-2.3
Sets of Ordered Pairs to Use for Hopi Kachinas

Each of the following sets of points should be plotted and connected with drawn line segments in the order in which they are listed. (It is best to connect adjacent points as you plot them; this avoids confusion.)

(a) (6,3) (8,3) (8,0) (5,0) (6,1) (6,3) (4,3) (5,7) (4,8) (4,10) (6,11) (6,12)
(4,12) (4,16) (6,16) (6,18) (7,18) (7,20) (9,20)
(9,18) (10,18) (10,16) (12,16) (12,12) (10,12) (10,13) (11,14)
(5,14) (6,13) (8,13) (8,11) (10,11) (12,10) (12,8) (11,7) (12,3)
(10,3) (10,1) (11,0) (8,0)

(b) (5,7) (7,7) (7,8) (5.5,8) (5.5,9)

(c) (11,7) (9,7) (9,8) (10.5,8) (10.5,9)

(d) (6,3) (7,4) (6,5) (7,6) (6,7)

(e) This set consists of several separate segments: (6,1) to (10,1);
(6,2) to (10,2); (8,3) to (10,3); (6,11) to (8,11); (10,11) to (10,12);
(6,12) to (6,13); (6,12.5) to (7.5,12.5); (8.5,12.5) to (10,12.5);
(8,13) to (10,13)

OBJECTIVE 3: Construct bar graphs where each cell represents multiple units.

Activity 1: SCALING DOWN

(Concrete Action)

Materials: One-inch grid paper (see PATTERNS/GRIDS section)
Colored paper squares (2" × 2"; 4 colors)
Colored markers (fine point)
Tape
Pencils

Management: Teams of 4 students each (40–50 minutes)

Directions:

1. Give each team 2 sheets of 1-inch grid paper, 2 colored markers (1 per color), and 6–8 paper squares of each of 4 colors. Two sheets of grid paper may be taped together to form a larger grid if necessary.

2. Ask the class to name the four most popular candy bars for their age group. Have each team survey themselves and 4 members of one other team for a total of 8 students surveyed regarding which of the 4 named candy bars each person likes best.

3. Using the longer side of the grid as the horizontal axis of a bar graph, students should mark off every 2 inches on the axis with one of the markers (color #1/marker #1) and label each such interval with the name of one of the 4 candy bars. Each team should assign one color of paper square to each type of candy bar. One paper square will represent one person's vote for a particular candy bar. A title should be given to the graph (e.g., *My Favorite Candy Bar*) and each axis should be named: *Number of People* (vertical) and *Type of Candy Bar* (horizontal).

4. Students should lay out the colored squares on their grid to show how the 8 people in their survey voted. With marker #1 they should mark off the vertical axis to show where each paper square's top edge falls and number these marks in order. That is, they should number every other grid line, beginning with the second line up. Students should also trace with marker #1 around each "vertical bar" formed by each color of paper square.

Example of the paper bars traced off on the grid:

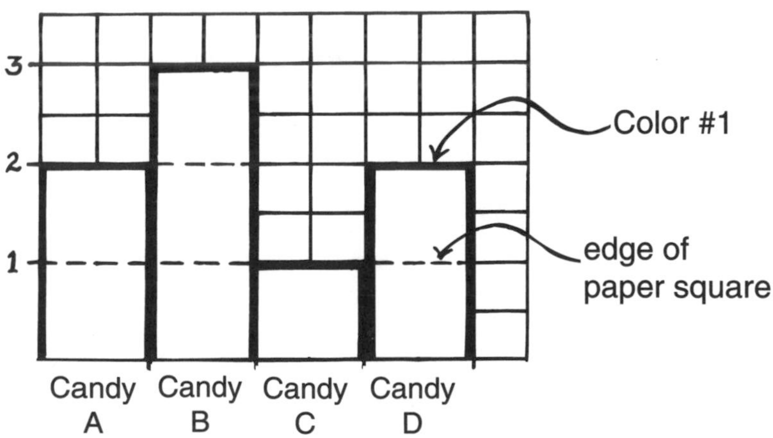

5. Now have students take each paper square used to make their bar graph and fold each one in half (fold top edge to bottom edge). Each 2" × 2" square becomes a 1" × 2" rectangle. Students should place the folded paper rectangles back on their grid in their original columns. Each paper piece still represents one person's vote in the survey.

6. Using marker #2 (color #2), team members should trace around the new paper bars they have formed and again number the vertical axis to correspond to the top edges of the folded paper rectangles. Parentheses should now be put around each number previously written with marker #1.

Example of the new paper bars traced off on the grid:

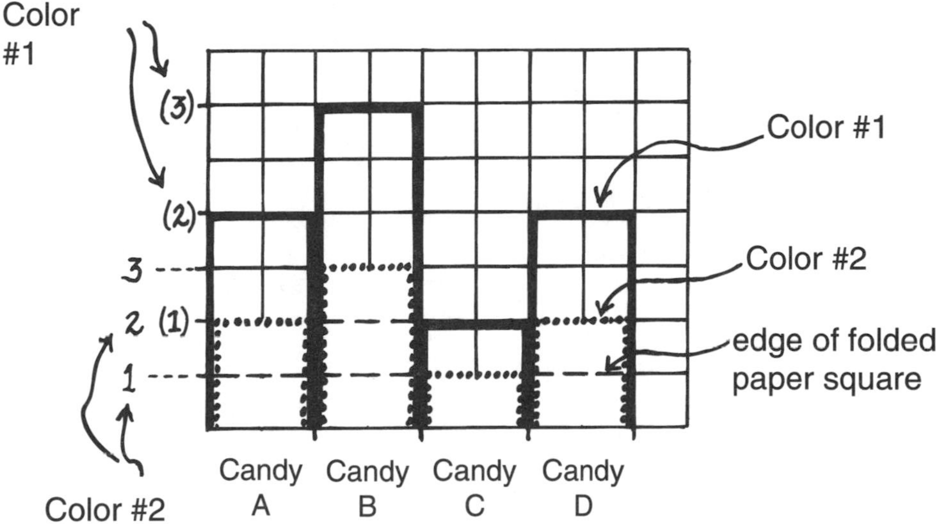

7. Ask each team to look at the bars drawn with marker #1 and compare them to the bars drawn with marker #2. Have students write a few sentences describing how the two bar graphs are similar or different. They should compare the *unit lengths* used on the two vertical scales as well as the *step patterns* created by the bars of the two graphs.

8. Have several teams read their paragraphs to the entire class. Some possible observations:

(1) Each bar on the new graph is half the height of its corresponding bar on the original graph.

(2) The original vertical scale has shrunk down—each new numbered mark is half as high as that same number was at first.

(3) The mark on the vertical axis that originally represented 1 person now represents 2 people.

(4) The step pattern is the same for both graphs, even though overall bar lengths have changed: the tallest bar on the original graph is still the tallest on the new graph, the shortest bar is still the shortest, etc.

(5) The number of people represented by each bar on the original graph remains the same on the new graph.

Activity 2: CHANGING THE SCALE

(Pictorial Action)

Materials: Bar Graph Worksheet SP-3.2
Pencils
Red pencils

Management: Partners (30 minutes)

Directions:

1. Give each pair of students a Bar Graph Worksheet and a red pencil. Ask various questions about the given bar graph and the number of spaces per bar to be sure that students know how to read the graph and use its scale.

2. Students are to draw a new bar graph on the worksheet's blank grid, which uses all the information found on the given bar graph, but they will change or shrink the original scale to make a new scale.

3. Tell students that every 4 votes shown on the original graph by 4 spaces will now be shown by 1 space on the new graph. Have students mark off in red pencil every 4 spaces on each bar of the given graph. They can then count how many groups of 4 spaces each are found in each original bar length; the number of *groups* in an original bar will be the number of *spaces* needed on the new graph to represent the same set of votes for a particular response choice.

Example of changing the scale of a particular bar:

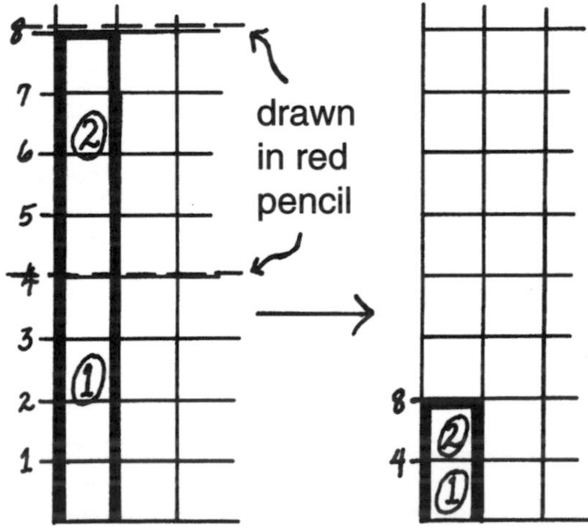

4. As students begin to shade the spaces on their new graph, they should also number their vertical axis. Since each space represents 4 votes now, the new scale will show 4 at the first mark, 8 at the second mark, etc. A title for each axis should also be written on the new graph.

5. After all are finished with their new graphs, ask different students to explain why they made their new bars the lengths they did. Ask the same questions used in step 1 with the original graph, but apply them to the new graph now. The answers should be the same if students have drawn their new graph correctly.

NAME ______________________________ DATE ____________________

BAR GRAPH WORKSHEET SP-3.2
Changing the Scale

Copy the given bar graph on the grid below. Change the vertical scale so that every 4 spaces of a bar on the original graph are shown by 1 space of a bar on the new graph.

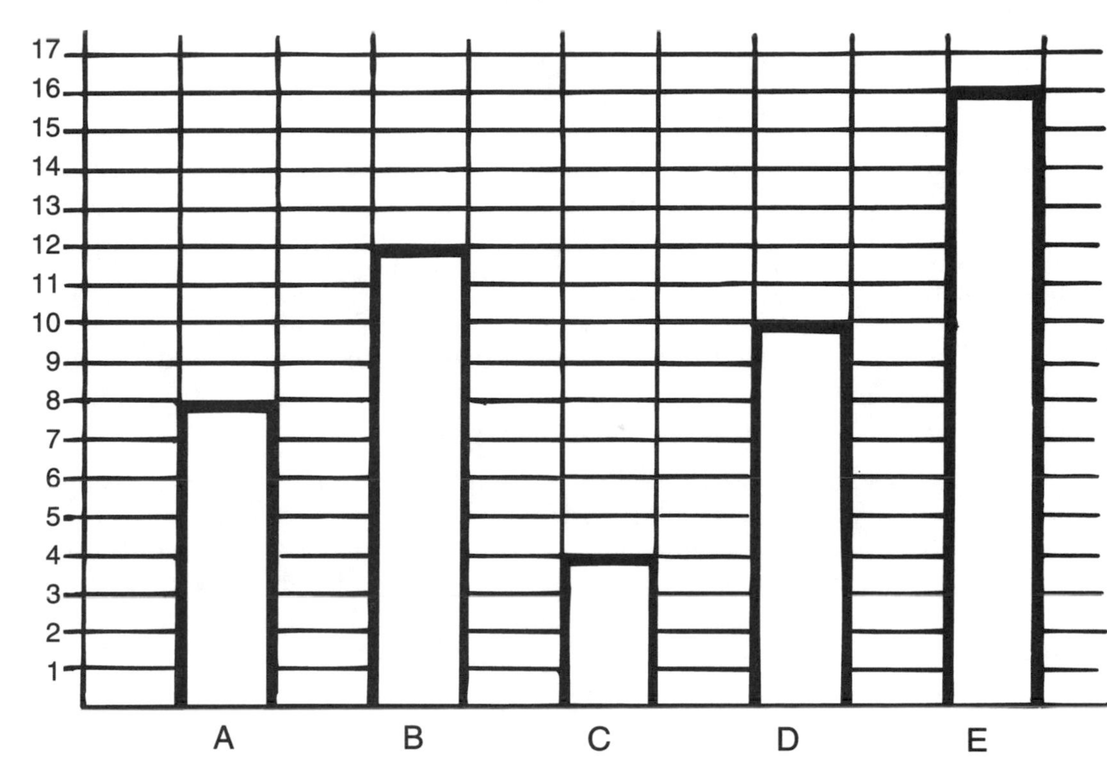

Activity 3: GRAPHING WITH LARGE NUMBERS

(Cooperative Groups)

Materials: Centimeter grid paper (see PATTERNS/GRIDS section)
Pencils

Management: Teams of 4 students each (40–50 minutes)

Directions:

1. Give each team a sheet of centimeter grid paper.

2. Write the following information on the chalkboard:

> Citizens of the tiny Island of Nivaro voted recently on the type of government they wanted. For many years they had been a commonwealth of a mainland nation. Here are the results of the voting: 110 wish to retain commonwealth status; 85 want statehood; and 30 want independence.

3. Each team is to construct a bar graph from the information given in step #2. Team members must select a title for their graph, names for the two axes, and a label to identify each bar. They must also decide on the scale they wish to use for the vertical axis. Each space, however, must represent a multiple amount (5 or more).

4. After students have constructed their bar graphs, have each team create three questions that can be answered by reading their particular graph. Encourage students to write questions that require higher thinking skills, that is, questions that cannot be answered by just reading a single number off the vertical axis or looking at the general heights of the bars. Higher-order questions will require students to use computation and logical reasoning. Such questions also tend to involve comparisons in some way. An example of such a question: *How many more people wish to remain a commonwealth than want statehood?*

5. Have different teams exchange graphs and sets of questions. Each team should try to answer another team's questions by reading that team's bar graph. If a graph is difficult to read, the team members who drew it should make corrections.

6. Extension: This might also be a good time to discuss *commonwealths, statehood, independence,* and the advantages and disadvantages of each form of government.

OBJECTIVE 4: Construct line graphs.

Activity 1: TRACKING CHANGES

(Concrete Action)

Materials: Large pegboard (approximately 20 holes × 20 holes)
10 pegs or golf tees
36-inch piece of colored yarn
Small index cards
Colored marker
Masking tape
Clock with second hand
Other materials (depending on topic selected)
Calculators (optional)

Management: Whole group (time period will depend on topic selected)

Directions:

1. With the class, select a topic to be represented by a line graph. The topic should involve collecting measurements over some time period. Here are some possible topics:

(a) Measure the temperature outside the school building at 9 A.M. every morning for 5 days.

(b) Measure the outside temperature every hour throughout one school day, e.g., 9 A.M., 10 A.M., . . . , 3 P.M.

(c) Count the number of times a student has thrown a small ball into the air and caught it (height of toss should remain constant) after 15 seconds, 30 seconds, 45 seconds, 60 seconds, 75 seconds, and 90 seconds. The recording at the end of each time interval is the accumulated total number of tosses completed up to that moment.

(d) Measure temperature of a freshly poured hot cup of coffee (or water) every 2 minutes for 14 minutes total.

(e) Compute the approximate volume in cubic millimeters of a melting ice cube sitting on a small saucer at room temperature every 15 minutes for 2 hours total.

2. Tape a strip of masking tape along the left edge of the pegboard just to the left of and touching the first column of holes. Tape another strip of masking tape along the lower edge of the board just under but touching the bottom row of holes. The strips of tape will serve as the vertical and horizontal axes for the grid, and the vertical or horizontal distance between two adjacent holes will be used to determine the size of the counting units or steps needed for locating points.

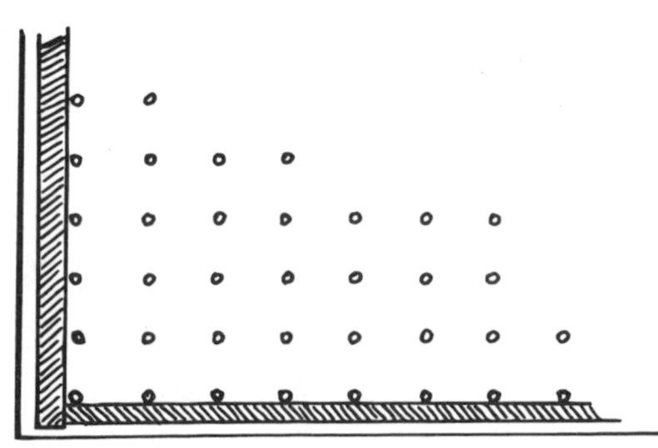

3. Place the pegboard on the chalkboard tray or an easel, or hang it on a bulletin board.

4. Use the small index cards and colored marker to prepare labels for the horizontal and vertical axes. Place specific time labels at every other hole along the horizontal axis of the pegboard. The sizes of the measurements taken at the end of each time interval will determine which labels to assign to the holes along the vertical axis. Also prepare a title for the graph and attach it at the top of the pegboard.

5. At the beginning of the experiment (or 0-time), take the initial measurement. For some topics, this measurement will just be 0; for others, it may be a number in the hundreds. A peg should be placed at the origin or at some upper point on the vertical axis to represent this initial measurement. Tie one end of the yarn around this first peg.

6. At each specified time interval thereafter, have students read the thermometer or take whatever necessary measurements are needed. Assign other students to serve as counters (if needed) or to record any data found.

7. After each measurement is taken, have a student go to the pegboard and place a new peg in the appropriate hole that represents that measurement and its corresponding time interval. Have that same student wrap the yarn around the new peg. The yarn will be used to connect the pegs together in the order that they are placed. Keep the yarn taut between pegs.

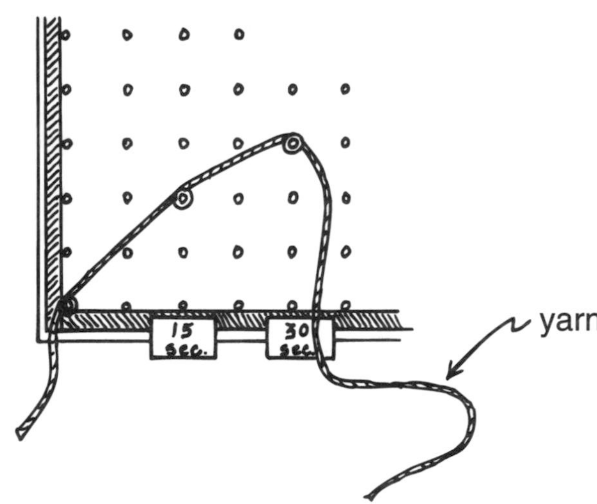

8. After all data are collected and all necessary pegs have been placed on the pegboard and connected with the yarn, discuss the line graph's results with the class. Observe any "peaks" or "valleys" that may appear in the yarn path. Ask students various questions that can be answered from the graph.

Activity 2: MAKING A LINE GRAPH RECORD

(Pictorial Action)

Materials: Rectangular dot paper (see PATTERNS/GRIDS section)
Red pencils
Regular pencils
Pegboard line graph from Activity 1

Management: Partners (30 minutes)

Directions:

1. Display the pegboard line graph completed in Activity 1 so that all students can see it.

2. Give each pair of students a sheet of rectangular dot paper and a red pencil.

3. Have students make a copy of the pegboard line graph on the rectangular dot paper. They should label the axes and title the graph according to the pegboard model. The yarn path should be shown with the red pencil.

4. Ask each set of partners to create three questions that can be answered from the graph. Encourage them to write higher-level questions that require computation in order to be answered. Have students share their questions with the entire class.

Activity 3: BOTTLES UP!

(Cooperative Groups)

Materials: "Flat Bottles" Worksheet SP-4.3
Centimeter graph paper (see PATTERNS/GRIDS section)
Paper
Pencils

Management: Teams of 4 students each (40–50 minutes)

Directions:

1. Give each team a "Flat Bottles" Worksheet and a sheet of centimeter graph paper.

2. Discuss item #1 on the worksheet with the class. At each fill level marked by an arrow, students should count the number of square units inside the bottle that are at or below that level. This number represents the units of capacity for this *flat bottle* when it is *filled* to this level. The capacity amounts found should be recorded in the table shown on the worksheet. The ordered pairs from the table will be (1, 7), (2, 12), (3, 15), (4, 16), and (5, 17). Team members should then use these ordered pairs to make a line graph on the grid provided on the worksheet.

3. After completing item #1, students should work item #2.

4. When all teams have finished the worksheet, ask them to look at their two line graphs and compare their shapes. Ask: *What does the steepness or lack of steepness at different places in the curve tell us about the way the 'flat bottle' fills up?* (Possible observations: For item #1, the curve is steeper between graph points at first because the bottle is wider near the bottom and requires *more filling* to change from one level to the next. The curve does not slope as much for the higher levels because the bottle narrows and requires *less filling* per level change. For item #2, the curve is not very steep between graph points at first because the bottle is narrow near the bottom and does not require much filling. To reach the upper levels where the bottle is wider, more filling is needed to make each new level, so the curve is steeper between graph points.) This discussion provides a readiness experience for the future topic of *slope* studied in secondary algebra.

5. Now ask each team to design its own *flat bottle* on the upper half of their sheet of centimeter grid paper. On the lower half, the team should draw a line graph that shows how their bottle's capacity changes as the bottle fills up. The graph's axes should be labeled just as the two previous graphs were. No student names or titles should be written on the graph paper that will identify the team members or connect the picture of the flat bottle to its line graph.

6. Have students cut their bottle picture and line graph apart and turn both sections in to you. Randomly number (1, 2, 3, etc.) all the bottle pictures and randomly label all the line graphs with a capital letter (A, B, C, etc.). Display all the bottle pictures together as a group on the classroom wall and all the line graphs together as another group.

7. During this same class period (if time permits) or at another time, have the teams look at the different bottle pictures and line graphs and try to match each bottle with its own graph. After all teams have completed the matching process, have various students share their answers and justify their choices.

NAME ______________________________ DATE ____________________

"FLAT BOTTLES" WORKSHEET SP-4.3
BOTTLES UP!

1.

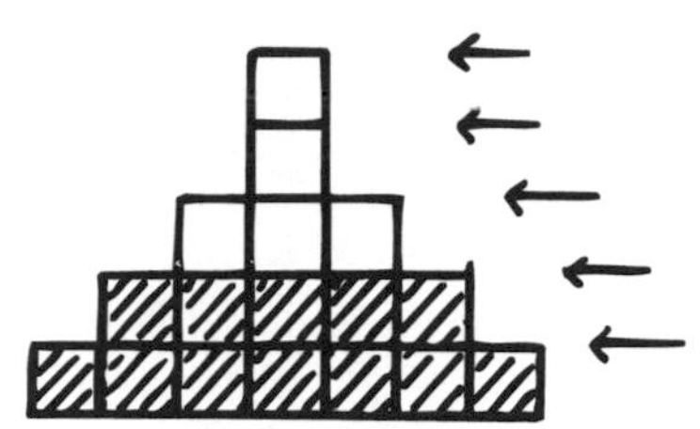

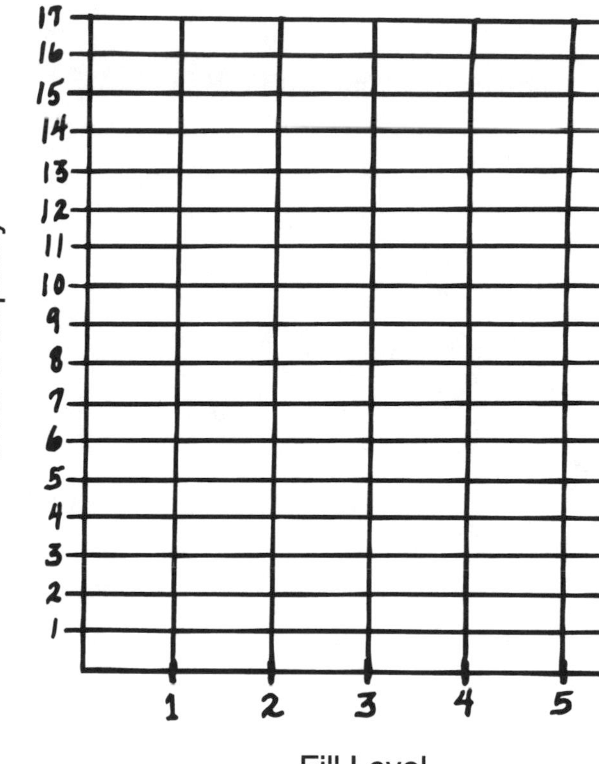

Fill Level	Capacity at Level
1	
2	
3	
4	
5	

2.

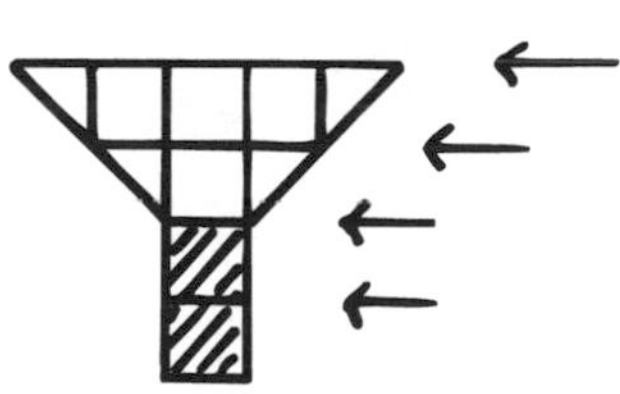

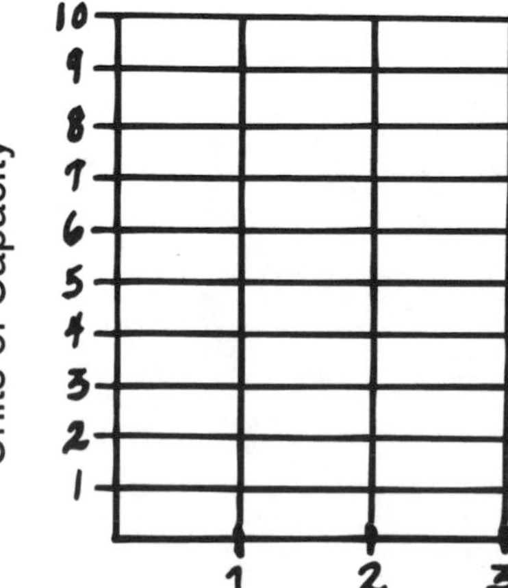

Fill Level	Capacity at Level
1	
2	
3	
4	

OBJECTIVE 5: List all possible outcomes of a given situation.

Activity 1: WHAT COULD HAPPEN HERE?

(Concrete Action)

Materials: 6 different hats/caps
Connectable cubes (or beads) in 5 colors
Paper
Pencils

Management: Whole class, then teams of 4 students each (40–50 minutes)

Directions:

1. In this activity we want students to explore the different ways a situation or an event could happen. That is, they will be finding the outcomes for different experiments. At this time we will not focus on whether one outcome is more likely than another, only those outcomes that are different from each other.

2. Place 6 different hats or caps in a box on a table at the front of the classroom. Do not tell students how many hats or caps are in the box.

3. Ask several students one at a time to go to the table, select a hat or cap, put it on, then return it to the box. Students may not choose a hat/cap that has already been chosen, so they must observe carefully to see what other students have selected before them. Repeat the process until all 6 hats/caps have been chosen.

4. Ask: *We have now seen all the hats or caps in the box. If we were to do this activity over again and a new student were to go to the box and take out a hat or cap, in how many different ways could this happen?* (Since there are only 6 different hats or caps in the box, there are only 6 ways a student could select a hat/cap and put it on.)

5. Now give each team of 4 students a bag of connectable colored cubes. Each bag should contain 5 different colors, 10 cubes per color.

6. Have students take out only the cubes of 2 colors that you specify. Cubes in the other 3 colors should be left in the bag.

7. Ask students to form pairs of cubes so that each pair consists of 2 different colors (the order in which the colors are connected within a pair is not important in this situation). Have them make as many different pairs as possible. (There should be only 1 pair made, since a color A-color B pair and a color B-color A pair are considered the *same* in this situation.)

8. Have students repeat the process of step 7, each time using a different number of colors. First have them take out only cubes of the 3 colors you specify; 3 different colors will yield 3 different pairs. Using only 4 colors, they should be able to make only 6 different pairs. Using all 5 colors in the bag, they can make 10 different pairs.

9. Now ask: *If we were to take all the cube pairs apart and ask a new person to connect a pair of cubes together, using 2 different colors in any order, in how many different ways could this happen if we gave them only 2 colors of cubes?* (There should be only 1 way the new person can make a pair, since there was only 1 such pair formed earlier.) Repeat this question, using 3 colors (3 ways), 4 colors (6 ways), then 5 colors (10 ways). *Note:* The sequence of total ways: 1, 3, 6, 10, . . . is the sequence known as *triangular numbers,* which is discussed in other chapters (e.g., Chapters 2 and 7) in this book.

10. This activity can be repeated several times by varying the materials used. The single-stage event of putting on a hat can be done in other ways, such as taking a colored pencil out of a box of colored pencils (each pencil a different color), taking a coin out of a bag (each coin being different), and throwing a dart at a dartboard whose scoring regions all have different values. The two-stage event of making pairs of colored cubes can be replaced by the following (conditions vary): making "outfits" by pairing cut-out paper shirts with shorts (the shirts and shorts being of different colors or designs), tossing 1 nickel and 1 penny together for different heads or tails combinations, making sandwiches, using different spreads with different breads.

Activity 2: WAYS TO DO IT!

(Pictorial Action)

Materials: Paper
Pencils
Colored pencils

Management: Partners (30 minutes)

Directions:

1. Give each pair of students colored pencils in 3 different colors. This activity will involve finding the outcomes of a two-stage and a three-stage experiment.

2. Tell them that the pencil colors represent different flavors of ice cream. Say: *Suppose there are only 2 flavors of ice cream in your freezer at home and you want to put two scoops on a cone. How many different ways can you do this if the two scoops could be the same or different in flavor?* In this situation the order of the scoops on the cone is to be considered; that is, chocolate as the top scoop is different from chocolate as the bottom scoop.

3. Students should choose 2 colors of pencils they want to use, then draw and color small circles arranged in vertical pairs to represent all possible ice cream cones they might make. They might even attach *cones* to their *ice cream* circles. When they finish, they should have 4 different 2-scoop ice cream cones drawn on their paper.

Examples of only 2 flavors used in 2-scoop cones:

4. Now have students repeat steps 2 and 3, using 3 different colors to make 3-scoop ice cream cones. This time each flavor can be used one or more times in the same cone or not at all. Remind students that having 2 scoops of chocolate as the top two scoops is different from having them as the bottom two scoops or as the top and bottom scoops with a different flavor between them. When students finish, they should have drawings for 27 different arrangements for a 3-scoop ice cream cone where each flavor is allowed to be repeated or not used at all.

5. Ask: *How many 3-scoop cones could be made if you wanted to use each flavor* ***at least once*** *for each cone? Cones with the same flavors, but with the flavors in different orders, are still considered as different cones. Which of the 27 cones you have just drawn would not be counted this time?* Have students look at their drawings for 3-scoop cones to see which ones meet the new criteria. (The three single-flavored cones and all 2-flavor cones found in step 4 would be excluded, leaving only the 6 cones where each flavor is used once.)

6. Ask: *If all the 3-scoop cones found earlier (the 27 cones drawn for step 4) were to be placed in bowls and the cones removed, leaving just the 3 scoops of ice cream* ***randomly placed*** *in each bowl, how many* ***different*** *combinations of 3 scoops of ice cream would you actually have? Would some of the bowls now look alike?* (There would be only 10 bowls whose ice cream combinations were different: 1 bowl having all 3 flavors, 6 bowls having 2 scoops of 1 flavor and 1 scoop of a second flavor, and 3 bowls where each bowl has only 1 flavor. All of the other bowls would look like one of these 10 bowls, because the ordering among the 3 scoops is no longer clear.)

7. For a pictorial activity that is a *single stage* experiment, prepare a sheet of paper with students' first names printed in block, capital letters in row-column form as in a word search. If necessary, names can be repeated or names might be used that are not your students' names in order to fill in all spaces. Ask: *If a person were to close his or her eyes and touch a single spot on this paper without looking, what are the different letters that might be touched?* Students must search through the rows of letters to find all the letters that are different from each other; any repeats will be excluded.

Activity 3: WHICH BAG IS WHICH?

(Cooperative Groups)

Materials: Paper bags (lunch-size)
Colored cubes (4 colors)

Management: Teams of 4 students each (20 minutes)

Directions:

1. Prepare sets of 3 bags each. Number each bag in a set as #1, #2, or #3. Each bag will hold 8 cubes. In bag #1, place 4 cubes each of color A and color B. In bag #2, place 3 cubes each of color A and color B, and 2 cubes of color C. In bag #3, place 2 cubes each of color A, color B, color C, and color D.

2. Give each team a set of 3 numbered bags filled with cubes.

3. Tell students they must decide which colors of cubes are in each bag without looking inside the bag. To help them decide, team members may take turns drawing a cube out of each bag, recording its color, and returning it to its bag. A team should draw out of the same bag 10 times.

4. After all teams have finished, ask each team to share its conclusions with the whole class. Ask students to give reasons for the color choices they make for each bag. Reasons will vary; accept any that seem logical. After each team has made its predictions of which colors are in each bag, have the students look in their 3 bags to see what colors were actually in there.

OBJECTIVE 6: Make all possible arrangements of a set of objects.

Activity 1: SCRAMBLE

(Concrete Action)

Materials: Colored tiles or counters (4 colors)
Paper
Pencils
Colored pencils or crayons (colors to match tile colors)

Management: Teams of 4 students each (30 minutes)

Directions:

1. Give each team tiles (or counters) in 4 different colors, 1 tile per color, and 4 colored pencils, 1 to match each tile color.

2. Ask students to select 2 of their colored tiles, then try to find all the possible ways to arrange these 2 tiles in a row. Have them record the arrangements they find by drawing and coloring each different row of tiles they build. (If a red tile and a green tile were selected, the only two possible arrangements or rows that could be built would be *red-green* and *green-red.*)

3. Have each team repeat step 2, but with 3 of the tiles instead. (If the tiles were red (R), green (G), and yellow (Y), the possible arrangements or rows would be RGY, RYG, YGR, YRG, GRY, and GYR.)

4. Have students repeat step 2, using 4 of the tiles. If the tiles were red (R), green (G), yellow (Y), and blue (B), then the possible arrangements would be as follows:

RGYB	GYBR	YBRG	BRGY
RGBY	GYRB	YBGR	BRYG
RBGY	GRBY	YRGB	BYGR
RBYG	GRYB	YRBG	BYRG
RYBG	GBRY	YGBR	BGYR
RYGB	GBYR	YGRB	BGRY

5. Ask: *As you were building the different rows of tiles, did you find special ways to decide which row to build next? How do you know that you have found all possible ways to arrange each set of tiles?* Have different students share their ideas and methods with the entire class.

6. Now have each team collect 4 different, small objects from some of its members (penny, paper clip, eraser, ring, key, earring, etc.). Ask them to make all possible arrangements (rows) as they did before, first with only 2 of the objects, then 3 objects, and finally all 4 objects. The students should develop their own ways to list the different arrangements they build. Recording methods might include drawing pictures of the objects in their different rows or listing the objects by name.

7. After all teams have finished building all possible arrangements with their various sets of objects, discuss the same questions given earlier in step 5. Ask students if they found themselves using the same organizational methods for building rows with their personal objects as they did with the colored tiles. Have different students compare or contrast the approaches they used with the different materials. There will be subtle differences in the ways students decide which arrangement they want to build next. It is this awareness of *organization* that causes students to believe that they have found *all possible* arrangements rather than just some random collection.

8. Note: In this objective the emphasis is on *experiences* with arrangements, not *computations*. Do not discuss the *counting principle* or *factorials* at this time; that is, do not present the counting of arrangements as a *string of multiplications*.

Activity 2: WALLPAPER DESIGNS

(Pictorial Action)

Materials: Paper
Pencils
Colored construction paper
Colored markers

Management: Partners (30 minutes)

Directions:

1. Draw 3 different, simple, geometric shapes on the chalkboard.

2. Ask each pair of students to draw on their own paper all the different ways the 3 shapes can be arranged together in a (vertical) column without rotating the shapes. There should be 6 different vertical arrangements in all.

3. Now draw a fourth shape beside the other three on the chalkboard. Using all four shapes without rotating them, students should draw all possible vertical or column arrangements. There should be 24 arrangements in all.

4. Give each pair of students a sheet of $8\frac{1}{2}$" × 11" colored construction paper and markers in four different colors (1 color per shape). Ask them to create a "wallpaper design" by redrawing the 24 different column arrangements of their 4 shapes on the construction paper in various ways. Several 4-shape columns might be connected together to make longer columns. Different orientations of the columns might be used as long as within a column, the original position and order of the shapes are preserved.

Samples of different orientations of 4-shape arrangements:

5. Once a design has been drawn on the construction paper, students should color the interior or the outline of each shape in its own color. When a design is finished, it might be displayed on the classroom wall.

Activity 3: NAME MIX-UP

(Cooperative Groups)

Materials: Paper
Pencils

Management: Teams of 4 students each (20 minutes)

Directions:

1. Have each team of students select a person's first name consisting of 4 distinct capital letters and list the 24 different "words" those 4 letters could make if arranged in various orders. Examples of names: JUAN, MARY

2. Team members should then print *all but one* of their different words randomly on a sheet of paper—along a curved path, upside-down, etc.—as long as the paper can be rotated to allow the word to be read from left to right and recognized as one of the 24 arrangements being sought. Each word used on the paper should appear only once.

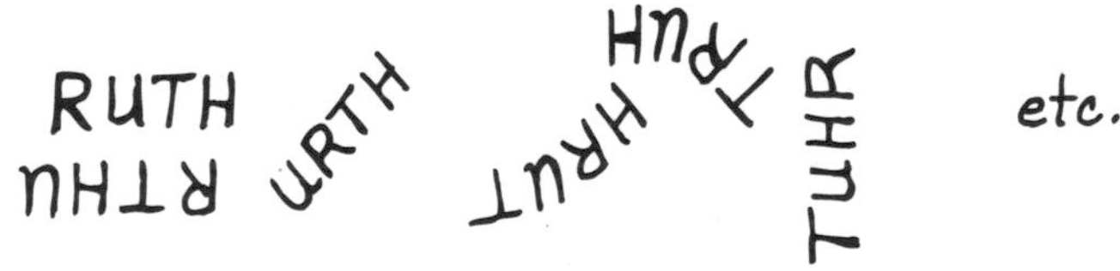

3. Teams should now exchange papers. Each team must try to discover which word or letter arrangement has been omitted from their new paper and also what name was originally used to form the words.

4. For extra excitement, teams looking for their missing word and name might enjoy racing against a 3-minute eggtimer.

5. For a super challenge, have teams select a 5-letter name and repeat steps 1–3. There will be *120* words possible this time.

OBJECTIVE 7: Find the mode of a given set of data.

Activity 1: WHAT'S THE FAVORITE?
(Concrete Action)

Materials: Students' shoes (or other common objects)

Management: Whole group (20–30 minutes)

Directions:

1. Ask each student to take off one shoe and place it on a table in front of the class.

2. Have two students serve as *shoe elves* to separate the shoes according to their different types (the "types" to be used are to be determined by the class members themselves). Several types are possible: Velcro® fasteners, sandals, high tops, slip-ons, loafers, buckles, boots, canvas uppers, tie-ons, etc. The class must decide when a shoe is to be considered a boot rather than a buckle shoe, etc. Limit the number of types used to *five at most*. The types must be distinct or disjoint from each other; that is, a shoe cannot belong to two different types at the same time.

3. Once the elves have separated all the shoes to the satisfaction of all class members, have them count the number of shoes of each type. List the types on the chalkboard and record the amount of shoes of each type beside its name.

4. Ask the class which type of shoe seems to be the most popular among the students in class today (the type that describes the most shoes). Tell them that this type of shoe is called the *mode* of all the types in their collection. If there are two types that have the same number of shoes and that number is more than any other type's amount, then we say that the shoe collection is *bimodal;* that is, it has two modes—the *two most* popular types of the class shoe collection.

5. This activity can be repeated many times by just changing the objects. The process involves sorting or classifying, then identifying the group or type with the most objects as the mode of the whole collection. It is important that the students make the decisions about what groups or types to use and which objects belong in which groups.

Activity 2: SHAPES AWAY!
(Pictorial Action)

Materials: Paper
Markers (medium or wide)
Masking tape

Management: Partners (20–30 minutes)

Directions:

1. Ask six different students to go to the chalkboard and draw a shape of their own choice; the 6 shapes must all be different. Encourage creativity. The shapes should be drawn beside each other and near the top of the board with at least a foot of space between each two adjacent shapes.

2. Give each pair of students a marker. Have them secretly choose one of the 6 shapes on the board and draw one to ten copies (their choice) of that shape on a sheet of paper.

3. After all have finished their drawings, have them go to the board and tape their paper under their chosen shape.

4. Have six students (different from those who drew the original shapes) each select a shape and count the number of copies of that shape shown on the sheets of paper taped to the board. The amount for each shape should then be written next to its original drawing on the board.

5. Ask the students which shape is the mode (i.e., has the most copies) of the six shapes on the board. Ask if there are two modes for the set of shapes; that is, are there two shapes that have the same number of copies and all other shapes have fewer copies? If so, the collection of all shapes (copies as well as originals) will be bimodal.

6. Have different students tell why they selected the shape they did (consumer preference) and why they drew the number of copies they did (by whim perhaps?). All reasons are good reasons.

7. This activity can be repeated several times throughout the year by changing the shapes used (geometric shapes, real object shapes, globs, etc.).

Activity 3: MODE DETECTORS

(Cooperative Groups)

Materials: Index cards (3 × 5 size)
Paper
Pencils

Management: Teams of 4 students each (20 minutes)

Directions:

1. Give each team 4 index cards. Have each team member write a random set of digits (digits 1–9) on one of the 4 cards. A digit can be repeated several times on the same card and may be used on 1 or more of the 4 cards being prepared by the same team. Each student may write 5 to 20 digits on his/her own card, counting repeats.

2. Once each team has completed a set of 4 cards, the members are to exchange their set for another team's set of cards.

3. Each team should now try to organize all the *different* digits on their 4 new cards. This might be done by listing each digit on a sheet of paper, then using tally marks to count the number of times a digit appears on all 4 cards. Encourage each team to find its own method for accounting for the different digits on the cards.

4. After each team knows how many of each digit it has, it should identify which digit is the mode of all the digits on the particular set of cards.

5. Have members from each team share the data (which digits and how many of each), describe the method used to organize the digits, and identify the digit that is the mode of the data.

OBJECTIVE 8: Find the mean of a given set of data.

Activity 1: FAIR SHARES
(Concrete Action)

Materials: Small counters
Paper
Pencils

Management: Teams of 4 students each (20–30 minutes)

Directions:

1. Give each team 48 counters.

2. Ask each member of a team to randomly take a handful of counters from the team's set. Each member should have some counters and all counters should be taken.

3. Have each team record how many counters each person has in hand at first. Then ask them to find a way to redistribute the counters they each have so that everyone on the team has the same amount (a *fair share*).

4. After they have formed equal shares, each team should write a short paragraph, describing the method they used to find the fair share for each member of the team. (If 48 counters are used, the fair share will be 12 counters.)

5. Have a *reporter* from each team read that team's paragraph to the whole class. Discuss any ideas that seem to be common to all the paragraphs. (Possible common ideas: (a) The four different amounts of counters were combined together in some way; (b) The four different amounts were regrouped, one counter at a time, until the four groups contained the same amount; (c) The four combined amounts were separated into 4 equal groups in some way, possibly by applying a division fact.)

6. If time permits, repeat the above procedure in steps 2–5 by having each team begin with a set of only 36 counters, 40 counters, 24 counters, etc. Since there are 4 students involved, be sure to use set totals that are multiples of 4.

7. Ask: *Can you describe in general the actions that seem to be taking place, regardless of the number of counters in a team's original set?* Let several students share their ideas. Hopefully they will notice that team members always started out with *different amounts* of counters, *combined* their counters together in some way, then *shared* them *equally* among the same members that began the process together. Tell students that the fair share they found each time is also called the *mean* of the original unequal shares with which they started.

Activity 2: DRAWING FAIR SHARES

(Pictorial Action)

Materials: Worksheet SP-8.2
Paper
Pencils

Management: Partners (30 minutes)

Directions:

1. Give each pair of students a *Drawing Fair Shares* Worksheet.

2. Discuss item #1 on the worksheet. Have the students discuss how they might redistribute the 4 unequal sets of circles on the left so that they form 4 equal sets of circles on the right. They might do this by marking out the circles one at a time and redrawing them one at a time into the new sets. They might also count how many circles in all there are, mentally divide this total by 4 to find the number needed for each new set, then draw the new sets, putting that number of circles in each set.

Example of marking-out method:

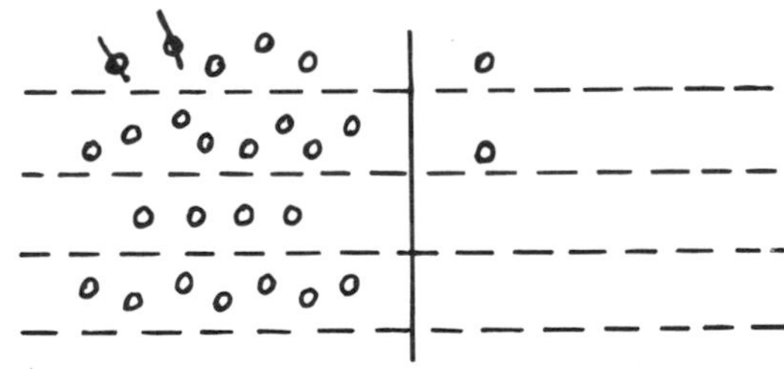

3. Students should now redraw their 4 sets to form 4 equal sets of circles. Have them draw a ring around one of the sets (or rows) and label that amount of circles as the *mean* of the original 4 sets of circles.

4. In the space to the right of the new sets, have students record number sentences that show the steps they used to find the mean for these first 4 amounts of circles. Discuss what each number sentence represents. Example of number sentences to record:

5 + 8 + 4 + 7 = 24 total circles (all circles combined = add 4 amounts)

$\frac{\text{24 total circles}}{\text{4 equal shares}} =$ 6 circles per share = mean of 5, 8, 4, and 7 (share all circles equally 4 ways = divide by 4)

5. Students should now complete the worksheet. Have some of the students share their results (the value of the mean) and their number sentences for each exercise with the entire class.

NAME ______________________ DATE ______________

WORKSHEET SP-8.2
Drawing Fair Shares

Unequal Shares	Equal Shares	Number Sentences
1.		
2.		
3.		
4.		

Activity 3: MEAN FLING

(Cooperative Groups)

Materials: Sets of numeral cards (28 cards/set; 1 number per card, using 1–99)
Calculators
Paper
Pencils

Management: Teams of 4 students each (20 minutes)

Directions:

1. Give each team of students a set of 28 numeral cards and a calculator. The cards might be small index cards with one number (1- or 2-digit) written on each card. Randomly select numbers from 1–99 for the cards.

2. Each team should shuffle their set of cards and turn them face down in the center of the table. For each round, every team member will draw a card off the top of the stack and place it face up beside the cards drawn by the other 3 team members.

3. The team members should look at the four numbers they have drawn and try to predict (without any computing with calculator or paper and pencil) where the mean of the 4 numbers will be with respect to the 4 numbers themselves. That is, between which 2 of the original 4 numbers will the mean lie? They should write their prediction on a sheet of paper in the form of an inequality. For example, if they think the mean will be between 5 and 12, they should write "$5 < m < 12$" where m will represent the value of the mean.

4. After recording their prediction, team members should calculate the actual mean, using the calculator or mental arithmetic.

5. If the computed mean lies between the two numbers that were predicted, the team earns 1 point. If not, they earn 0 points.

6. The team now draws 4 new cards and repeats steps 3–5. The goal is to make a "perfect 7" by the time all the cards are drawn from the stack.

7. If each set of cards prepared involves different numbers, then each time a team plays the game, the students will be able to use a different card set and gain more practice with their predicting.

OBJECTIVE 9: Find the median for a given set of data.

Activity 1: WHO'S IN THE MIDDLE?

(Concrete Action)

Materials: Large numerals (described below in step 4)
Calculator

Management: Whole group (30 minutes)

Directions:

1. Select seven students of different heights and have them stand beside each other at the front of the room, facing the rest of the class. At first their positions should be random so that their heights vary. [Note: This objective for finding the median assumes the prerequisite skill of finding the mean.]

2. Ask the seven students to rearrange themselves so that they are ordered by height. The other members of the class must approve the final order.

3. Have the seven now sit down by leaving a pair at a time, one person from each end of the group. Continue this "pairing off" until only one person is left standing. Tell the class that this person's height is called the *median* of the seven heights that were represented at the beginning.

4. Now have five new students stand side by side at the front of the room. Randomly select six numbers from 10–50 to write on $8\frac{1}{2}$" × 11" sheets of paper, using one number per sheet of paper. Give each student standing one of the numeral sheets in no particular order. There will be one numeral sheet unused.

5. Ask the five students to rearrange themselves according to their numbers so that the rest of the class can read the numbers in increasing order from left to right. Have those standing begin to sit down by leaving in pairs, one from each end as before. The student left without a partner now holds the median number of the 5 original numbers.

6. Now have the same five students return to the front and ask another student to join them, giving the new student the other numeral sheet.

7. Have the six students rearrange themselves in increasing order from left to right, then begin to sit down an "end-pair" at a time. Keep the last pair standing at the front of the room.

8. Discuss how there is not a single middlemost person remaining this time, but there are two instead. Ask: *If we were only looking for the middlemost height of the six original people, how might we find it?* Different ideas may be offered, but hopefully someone will suggest that a height needs to be found that is halfway between the heights of the two people left standing, assuming their heights are different. If they are the same height, then the middlemost height will simply equal their common height.

9. Ask: *If we are looking for the middlemost number of the 6 numbers we have here, how might we find it?* Hopefully, someone will suggest that a number must be found that is halfway between the last two numbers still being held at the front of the room. Discuss the idea that if the last two numbers are the same, then the middlemost number will equal that common number. Ask: *What method can we use that will equalize these last two numbers if they are not the same?* If necessary, remind students that when two different amounts are redistributed into two equal amounts, the new amount is the *mean* of the two different amounts. Have a student use the calculator to find the mean of the last two numbers. This number will be the median of the original 6 numbers.

10. Ask students if they think the mean of the last 2 numbers (i.e., the median of the 6 numbers just found) will be the same as the "mean" of all 6 numbers together. Let several students share their ideas, then have a student check their suggestions by using the calculator to compute the actual mean of the 6 numbers. For some sets of data, the mean and median will be the same, but not necessarily.

Activity 2: MEDIAN HUNT

(Pictorial Action)

Materials: Median Worksheet SP-9.2
Pencils
Red pencils
Calculators (optional)

Management: Partners (30 minutes)

Directions:

1. Give each student a median worksheet and a red pencil and give each pair of students a calculator.

2. Discuss item #1 on the worksheet with the students. They need to redraw all 5 bars from grid A onto grid B so that their lengths are in increasing (or decreasing) order from left to right. Have them put an X above the first bar at each end of the group of redrawn bars. They should continue to mark each "end-pair" with X's until they find the middlemost bar.

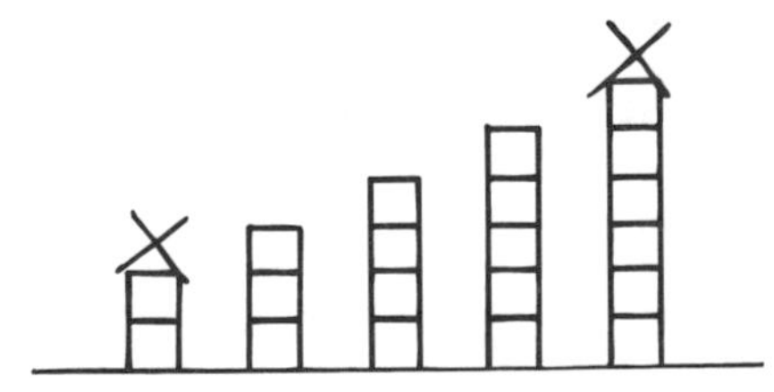

3. Have students draw a red ring around the middlemost bar and write the number of units in its length above the bar. The word *median* should also be written above the bar. The ringed bar (or the number for its length) is the median of this set of 5 bars (or their 5 lengths).

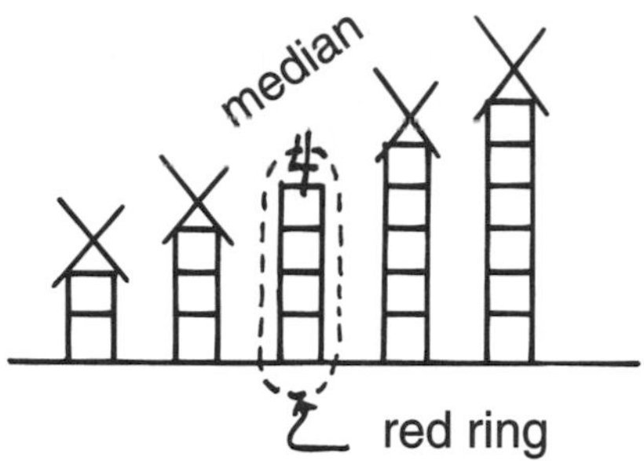

4. If a set of bars has 2 bars left in the middle after all other end-pairs have been marked with X's, students will need to write the number of units in the length of each of these 2 bars above them, draw a red bar between them so that its length falls halfway between their two top ends (or its length is the same as that of the 2 bars if they are equal). The word *median* and the number for the length of the red bar should then be written above the red bar.

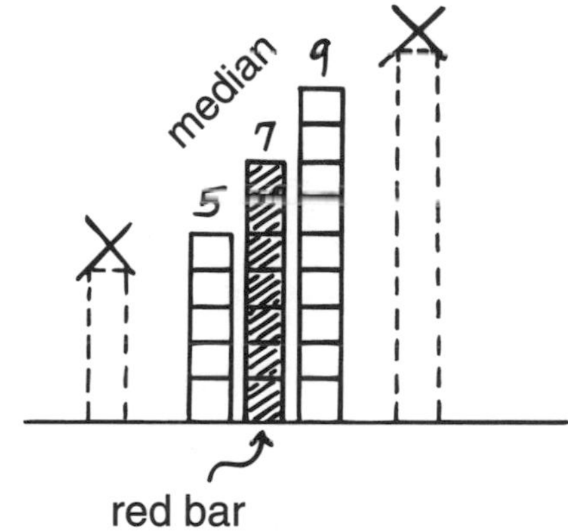

5. Discuss item #4 with the students. They are to redraw the 5 square-like groupings shown in area A in order of their increasing (or decreasing) size in the blanks shown in area B. Size is determined by the number of circles in each group. Have them mark out the end-pairs by drawing a slash through each group.

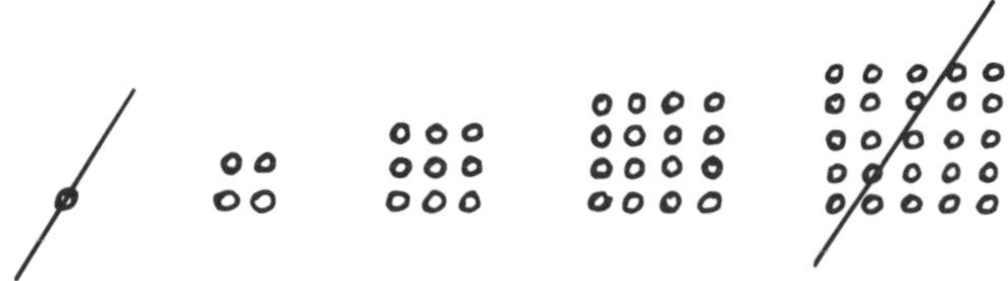

6. Have students draw a red ring around the middlemost group (the 3×3) that is left. They should also write the number for the amount of circles in the ringed group (9) and the word *median* above that group. This 3×3 group (or the number that shows its size) is the median of the 5 different sets (or amounts) of circles.

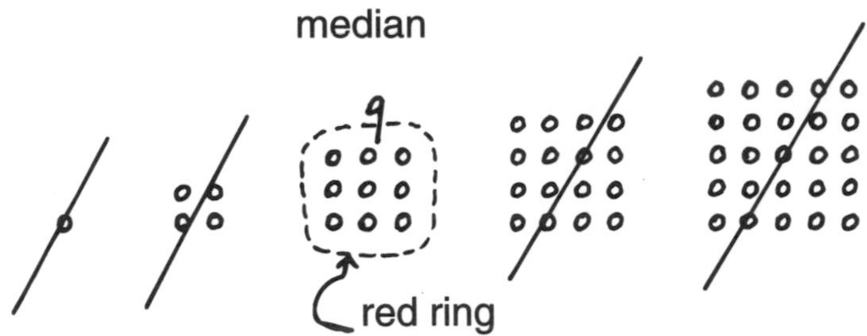

7. If two middlemost groups in a set remain after all other end-pairs have been marked out, then the number of circles in each of these last 2 groups should be written above its group. An *outline* of the type of group shape being used should be drawn in red between the two remaining groups, and the number of circles it *would* have (if it existed) should be written inside the red shape. This number should be the mean of the numbers of the two remaining groups. The word *median* should also be written above the red shape.

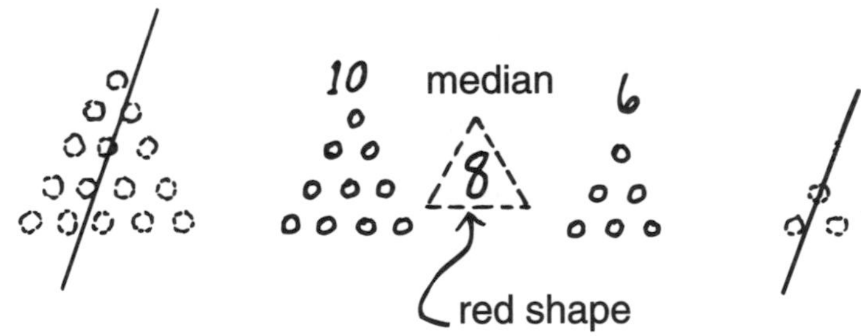

8. Have students complete the other items on the worksheet with their partners. When all are finished, have several students share their answers with the entire class, describing what the median numbers were and, if possible, what their shapes or groups looked like. It might be helpful to have a transparency of the worksheet available. Students can then draw their results on the transparency and show it on the overhead projector.

NAME ______________________________ DATE ____________________

WORKSHEET SP-9.2
Median Hunt

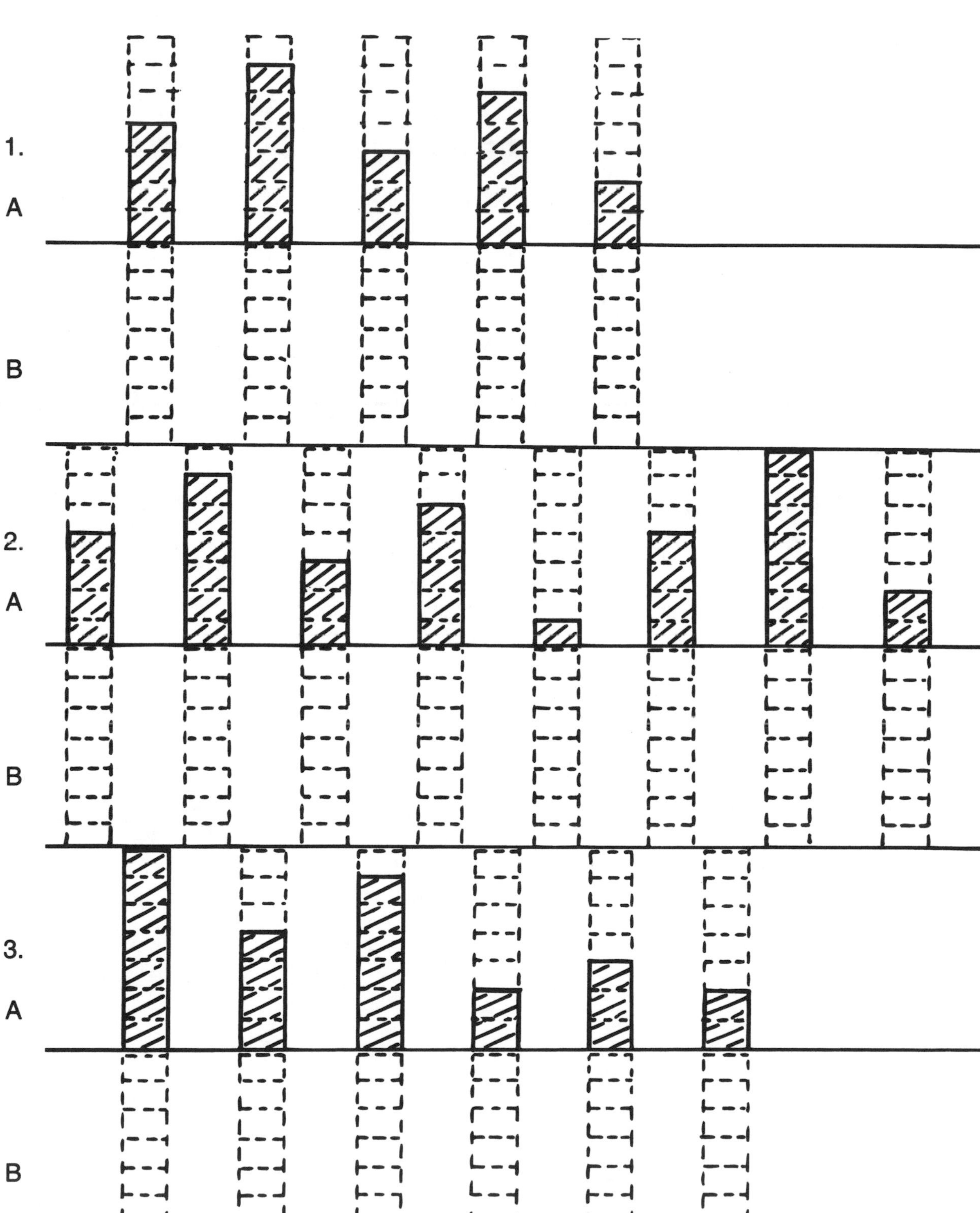

NAME ______________________ DATE ______________

WORKSHEET SP-9.2 (*cont.*)

4.

A

B

___ ___ ___ ___ ___

5.

A

B

___ ___ ___ ___ ___ ___

6.

A

B

___ ___ ___ ___ ___ ___ ___ ___

Activity 3: MEDIAN SPIN

(Cooperative Groups)

Materials: Spinner Pattern (Worksheet SP-9.3)
Sets of numeral cards
Paper clips
Calculators (optional)
Paper
Pencils

Management: Teams of 4 students each (20 minutes)

Directions:

1. Give each team a spinner pattern, a set of 24 numeral cards, a paper clip, and a calculator. For the spinner, the paper clip can be used as the spinner needle; one end of the paper clip can be held loosely with a pencil at the center point on the spinner pattern. Small index cards can be used for the numeral cards. For each set, randomly select 24 numbers from the numbers 5–99 and write them on the cards, one number per card. If you prefer, let each team make its own set of numeral cards.

2. Have each team shuffle a set of 24 cards and turn them face down in a stack in the center of the table. Team members will take turns finding the median of a set of numbers.

3. On each turn a student will spin the spinner to find out how many cards to draw off the top of the stack of numeral cards. The player will then arrange the drawn cards so that their numbers are in order, either increasing or decreasing, and identify which number is the median of the set of numbers on the cards.

4. If the median is one of the numbers on the cards (as will be the case when an odd number of cards is drawn) and it is correctly identified, the player will earn 1 point. If the median is not one of the numbers on the cards (as when an even number of cards is drawn), the player must compute the median by finding the *mean* of the two middlemost numbers. This computation might be done with the calculator to save time. If the other team members accept the computed median as correct, the player will earn 5 points.

5. After each round or whenever all cards have been drawn from the stack, the numeral cards need to be reshuffled and a new stack formed.

6. Play should continue until time is called or until one of the players has earned 12 points or more.

WORKSHEET SP-9.3
Spinner Pattern for Median Spin

OBJECTIVE 10: Use fraction names to describe the probabilities of simple events.

Activity 1: COMPARING THE WAYS
(Concrete Action)

Materials: Plastic bags of small objects
Paper
Pencils

Management: Teams of 4 students each (30–40 minutes)

Directions:

1. Prepare 1 bag of small objects per team, using 10–20 objects per bag. Objects in the same bag should be about the same size, but be different in color or some other aspect. Possible items: colored buttons, gummy bears, colored paperclips, lettered/decorated pencils, baseball cards, Teddy-Graham™ bears (cookies), Life-Savers™, assorted earrings, different flavors of bubblegum, colored drinking straws (shortened), plastic bugs or squiggly worms, cut-out paper shapes, erasers, etc.

2. Give each team a bag of objects. If possible, no two teams should have the same amount and type of materials.

3. Ask: *Out of the total objects in your bag, how many ways are there for you to choose each* ***kind*** *of object in the bag? You must decide what the kinds are for your particular bag, but one kind must be obviously different from another kind.* Objects might be separated by color, so that one kind of color for the objects is blue, another red, etc. Teddy-Graham™ bears (cookies) can be separated by flavor (how many are honey-flavored? chocolate? vanilla?) They can also be separated by the position of each bear's arms. Students must decide what characteristic they will use to separate their set of objects into smaller, disjoint groups (*kinds* of the chosen characteristic).

4. After each team has decided how to separate their objects, have them write comparison statements such as the following (assuming there are 15 cookie bears total in a bag):

Flavors (one possible characteristic to use)

6 out of 15 total cookies are chocolate.

5 out of 15 total cookies are vanilla.

4 out of 15 total cookies are spice.

Encourage teams to find a second characteristic for their set of objects and write comparison statements for it also.

Cookie Bear's Arm Positions (another possible characteristic)

8 out of 15 total cookies have arms up.

7 out of 15 total cookies have arms down.

5. Ask students to find the sum of the numbers they found for the different kinds of a particular characteristic. (The sum should be the same as the total number of objects in their bag.) In our example for flavors, we had 6 + 5 + 4, and for arm positions, we had 8 + 7. Each sum equaled 15, the total number of cookies we had.

6. Tell students that their comparison statements are sometimes called *probabilities.* A probability simply tells us that if a student takes one object out of a bag without looking, he or she has a specific number of ways to get a particular kind. For example, the probability of picking a chocolate cookie bear earlier was 6 ways out of the 15 total ways for taking a cookie out of the bag. Do not emphasize this terminology at this time. An introduction is all that is intended here.

7. If time allows, teams may exchange their bag with other teams and repeat steps 3–5.

Activity 2: COUNTING CHOICES

(Pictorial Action)

Materials: Probability Worksheet (SP-10.2)
Colored pencils
Regular pencils

Management: Partners (20 minutes)

Directions:

1. Give each pair of students a probability worksheet and 3 different colored pencils.

2. Discuss part (a) of item #1. There are 8 toy balls in a box. In how many ways can a striped ball be chosen if only one is to be picked randomly or without looking? Have students count the striped balls in the set, then record the amount in the blank as follows: *5 out of 8 balls or 5/8.* (Have students read *5/8* as *5 out of 8* during their study of probability.) Now have them complete part (b) and item #2. In item #2, the blanks within parts (a)–(c) should be completed with the 3 colors used.

3. Discuss part (a) of item #3. There is a giant, square, landing grid on which hot air balloons land. If the balloon descends to the grid without control (randomly), in how many ways could it land on a striped space on the grid? Have students count the striped spaces, then complete the blank as follows: *6 out of 16 total spaces or 6/16.* Now have them complete part (b) and item #4. In item #4, the blanks within parts (a)–(c) should be completed with the 3 colors used.

4. After all students have completed their worksheet, ask them to find the sum of the numbers of ways found in (a)–(b) or (a)–(c) of each exercise. How does the sum compare to the total ways for the same exercise? (The amounts are the same.)

NAME ______________________________ DATE ____________________

PROBABILITY WORKSHEET SP-10.2
Counting Choices

1. One of these toy balls is to be taken from its box:

(a) ways to get a striped ball? ______________________________

(b) ways to get a dotted ball? ______________________________

2. Randomly color the 8 toy balls above with 3 different colors. Make each ball only one color. Several balls will be the same color. Complete (a)–(c) for the 3 colors.

(a) ways to get __________? ______________________________

(b) ways to get __________? ______________________________

(c) ways to get __________? ______________________________

3. A hot air balloon is to land on this large grid on the ground.

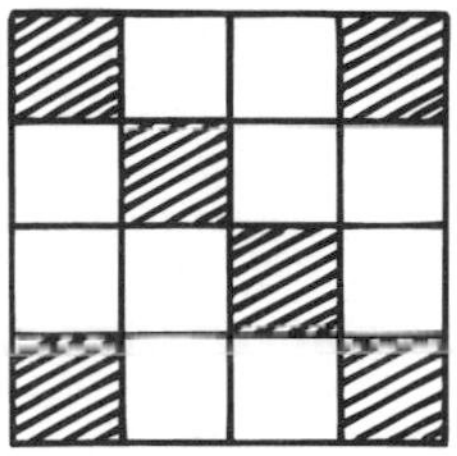

(a) ways to hit a striped space?

____

(b) ways to hit a plain space?

____

4. Color the 16 spaces in the above grid randomly with 3 different colors. Make each space only one color. Several spaces will be the same color. Complete (a)–(c) for the 3 colors.

(a) ways to hit __________? ______________________________

(b) ways to hit __________? ______________________________

(c) ways to hit __________? ______________________________

Activity 3: WHAT'S IN THE BAG?

(Cooperative Groups)

Materials: Colored tiles (4 colors)
Paper lunch bags
Paper
Pencils

Management: Teams of 4 students each (20–30 minutes)

Directions:

1. Prepare a lunch bag of colored tiles for each team. Place 10 colored tiles in each bag, using some combination of 4 different colors. Different color combinations might be used in different bags. Two or three bags might have the same combination, if necessary.

2. Give each team a lunch bag of colored tiles. Team members should not look inside their bag to see what tiles they have.

3. Tell students there are 10 tiles total in 4 different colors in each bag. Teams try to determine their four colors and to find the number of tiles of each color without looking in their bag.

4. Students should draw out a tile, record its color, and return it to the bag as many times as they wish, but without peeking inside the bag.

5. After the teams think they know the color combination in their particular bag, have them write down their predictions. Do not allow them to look in their bag yet. Ask each team to explain to the whole class why it predicted certain colors and amounts. Reasons will vary.

6. Now have the teams look in the bags to check their predictions.

7. Once students know exactly how many tiles of each color they *really* have, they should write a probability statement for each color in their bag. For example, if there are 4 blue tiles in a bag, students might write the following: *The probability of choosing a blue tile randomly from the bag is 4 possible ways out of 10 ways total or 4/10.*

OBJECTIVE 11: Construct circle graphs.

Activity 1: SURVEYING WITH CIRCLES

(Concrete Action)

Materials: Large Circle Pattern (Worksheet SP-11.1)
Scissors
Colored pencils or markers
Glue sticks
Colored construction paper
Regular pencils

Management: Teams of 4 students each (50 minutes)

Directions:

1. Give each team a circle pattern worksheet, scissors, 3 different colored pencils or markers, a glue stick, and a sheet of colored construction paper.

2. Each team should select a survey question that has three different response choices possible. Encourage students to be creative with their question, but limit them to three choices for a response. Some possible questions with their response choices:

"When is your birthday?" [January–April, May–August, or September–December]

"How long is your little finger?" [less than 4 cm, from 4 to 6 cm, or more than 6 cm]

"What TV cartoon do you like better?" [Bart Simpson, Ninja Turtles, or Batman]

"How fast do you think a NASA space shuttle is moving when it first lifts off from the earth's surface?" [less than 500 mph, 500–1000 mph, or over 1000 mph]

3. Each team should then survey eight different students in the class, using their chosen question and response choices. [Note: The noise level in the classroom may increase for a few minutes!]

4. Have students cut out the large circle pattern and fold the pattern in half three times to form eight equal sectors in the paper disk. A dark marker or colored pencil should be used to draw along the creases made in the paper.

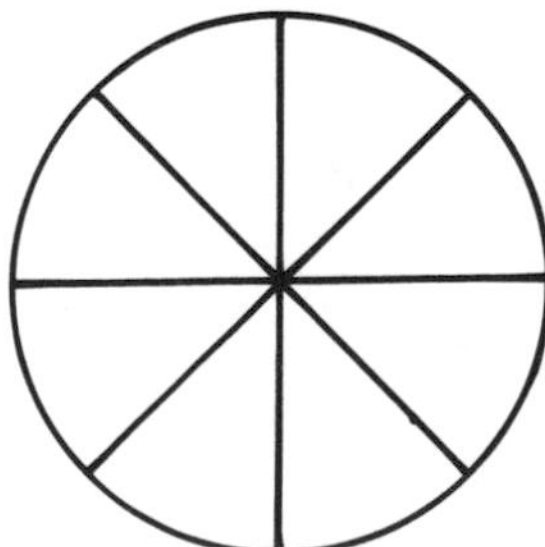

5. One sector should be colored for each person surveyed. Each type of response should have its own color. Thus, if 3 people answer with response #1 and blue is used to indicate that response, 3 adjacent sectors will be colored blue.

6. After a team has colored all eight sectors of the cut-out circle, they should glue it onto a sheet of colored construction paper and write a title for their new *circle graph* at the top of the construction paper. The title should reflect or might even state the survey question that was used. A color key should also be provided near the title above the graph that lists each color used and the response choice it represents.

7. Have each team create three questions about their circle graph, then write them on the construction paper below the graph. The mounted graph may now be displayed on the classroom wall so that other teams can read it and try to answer the questions about it. (This display phase of the activity might be used as *a learning center.* Teams might be allowed to read the different graphs and answer the questions over several class periods as the students have time. Then the final sharing time would be scheduled for a few minutes of another class period after all teams have read all graphs.)

8. Have several students share their answers to the various sets of questions with the entire class. Discuss any questions that might be confusing. Ask students to suggest changes if any question is not clear.

Activity 2: HUB AND SPOKES

(Pictorial Action)

Materials: Centimeter grid paper (see PATTERNS/GRIDS section)
Tape
Scissors
Colored pencils
Circle Graph Worksheet (SP-11.2)
Rulers (or straightedges)
Regular pencils

Management: Partners (50 minutes)

Directions:

1. In preparation for this activity, have each pair of students create a survey question that has 4 response choices. Partners should then use their question to survey 20 students in or out of class, during lunchtime, etc. The surveying will need to be done before the day of the actual graph work. Here are some possible questions and their 4 response choices:

"Which candy bar do you like best?" [use names of 4 candy bars popular with students]

"Who is your favorite TV sitcom star?" [use 4 names of actors/actresses suggested by class]

"Which canned drink do you like best?" [Coca Cola™, Dr. Pepper™, Sprite™, or Root Beer—or any 4 suggested by class]

"Whose advice will you take more often?" [parents, teachers, friends, or TV commercials]

2. Cut the centimeter grid paper into strips lengthwise; the strips should be over 20 cm long. Make each strip 1 cm wide.

3. Give each pair of students a centimeter strip, 4 different colored pencils, a circle graph worksheet, and a ruler.

4. One square on the centimeter strip should be colored for each person surveyed. A total of 20 adjacent squares will be colored, leaving only a few blank squares at one end of the

WORKSHEET SP-11.1
Circle Pattern for Surveying with Circles

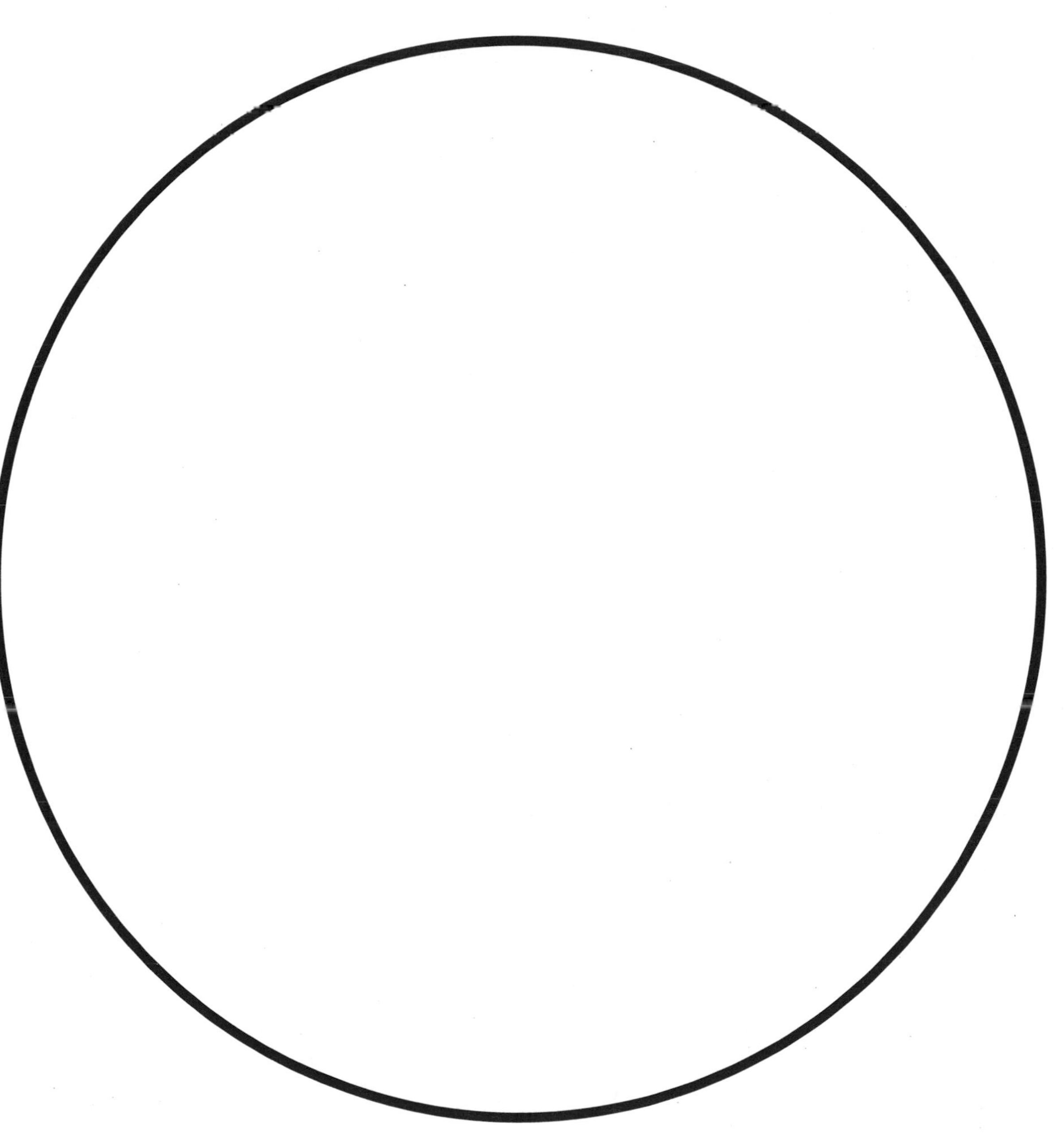

strip. A different color should be used to indicate each type of response. For example, if red is used to show response choice #1 and 8 people give that choice, 8 adjacent squares on the paper strip will be colored red.

5. After students have shown all their survey results on their centimeter strip, they should overlap and tape the two ends of the strip to form a loop. The square spaces must be showing on the outside of the loop, and only the 20 colored spaces will be exposed. The blank spaces will serve as a tab underneath the colored ones.

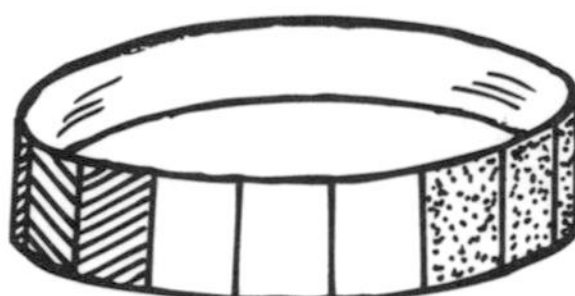

6. Have students now place their paper loop on their worksheet and position the loop so that it forms a perfect *circle* and its *imaginary center* corresponds with the center point actually marked on the circle on the worksheet. With one partner carefully holding the loop in place, the other partner should mark on the worksheet a point that indicates where the dividing line between a pair of adjacent colors on the centimeter strip intersects the surface of the worksheet. All such dividing line points should be marked.

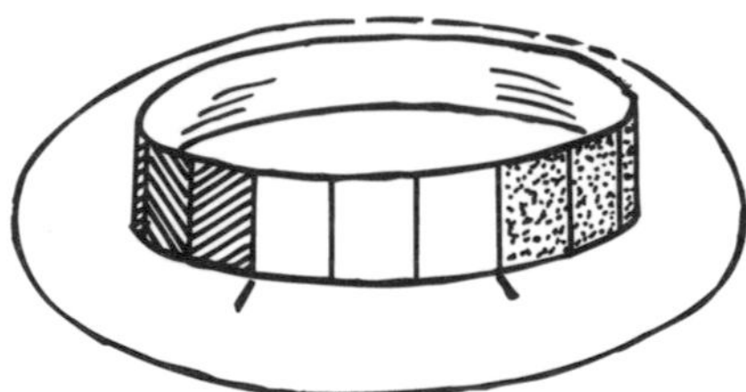

7. After all dividing line points have been located, the loop should be removed. Using the ruler, students should draw *radii* for their circle by connecting the center point to each dividing line point marked in the interior of the circle.

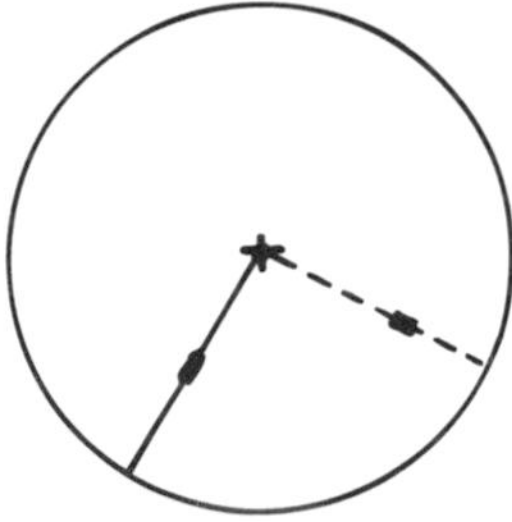

8. Each of the 4 new sectors that now appear on the circle pattern should be colored to match the section of colored squares on the centimeter strip to which the sector corresponds. In each sector, have students write the number of people it represents from the survey.

9. A title should be written above each circle graph and should reflect the survey question in some way. A color key should also be provided near the title above the graph that lists each color used and the response choice it represents.

10. Have students create three questions to go with their particular circle graph and record them on their paper below the graph. Encourage them to write higher-level questions that require computation in some way, rather than just reading a single number on the graph.

11. Have different pairs of students exchange papers with each other and try to answer the questions given with the new graph.

CIRCLE GRAPH WORKSHEET SP-11.2
Hub and Spokes

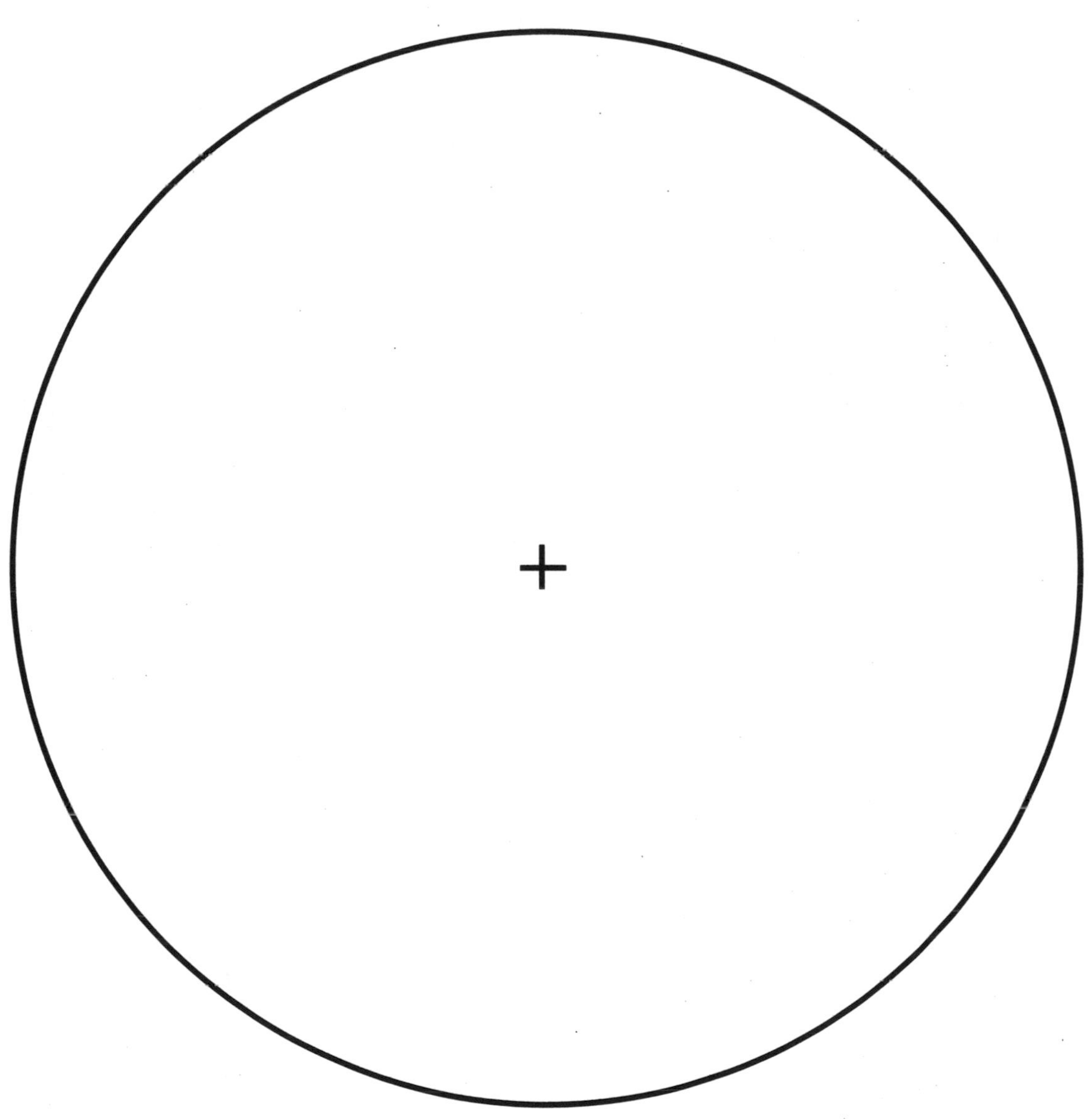

Activity 3: GRAPHING WITH ANGLES

(Cooperative Groups)

Materials: Circle templates (approximately 3" radius) or safety compasses
Protractors
Paper
Pencils
Calculators

Management: Teams of 4 students each (50 minutes)

Directions:

1. For this activity it is assumed that students already know how to construct angles with a protractor and that a complete rotation measures 360 degrees.

2. A few days before this graphing activity occurs, have the class select a question that they would like to have asked of students or teachers at their school. There should be five response choices this time. With the permission of other teachers, send 1–2 students to each of several classrooms to poll the students there regarding the chosen question. The polling may be just a quick counting of raised hands or the persons surveyed may record the number of their chosen response on a small piece of paper and give their *vote* to your students taking the survey. A total of 72 students or teachers should be polled. If extra votes are received, randomly delete that amount from the total number obtained in order to keep only 72. Have students in your class tally the votes for each response choice.

3. Give each team a protractor, a circle template (or safety compass), and a calculator. Write the survey data (number of votes per response choice) on the chalkboard for students to copy on their own papers.

4. Discuss the idea that in Activity 1, when 8 people total needed to be represented, a circle was subdivided into that number of sectors by folding. In Activity 2, when 20 people total needed to be represented, a circle was subdivided into sectors by "measuring" with the centimeter grid strip. In the latter case, we only marked off sectors for groups of people who had the same response choice. If necessary, we could have used each square on the grid strip to mark off a sector for each person who voted. Then our circle would have been divided into 20 sectors of the same size. Each time sectors of the same size are formed in a circle, their central angles are also equal.

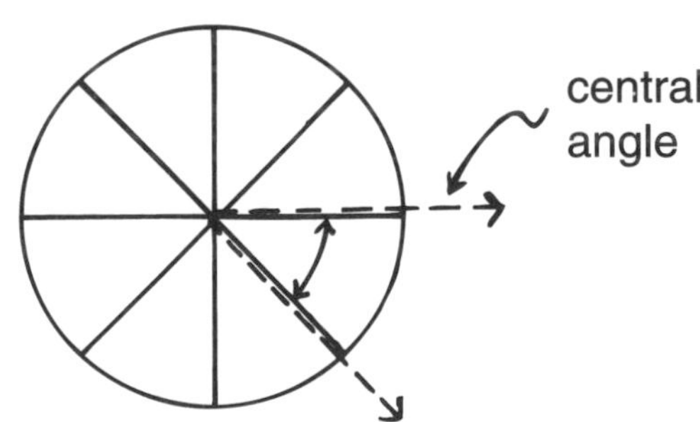

5. Have students now draw a circle on their own paper, using the circle template or a safety compass. The circle should have a radius of about 3 inches and should be drawn in the upper half of the paper, leaving room at the bottom of the paper for recording observations.

6. Ask: *In the earlier circle graphs you made, when 8 people were to be represented, you indirectly formed 8 equal central angles. When 20 people were to be represented, you used a grid strip that showed the positions of 20 equal central angles. Now we have 72 people to represent. How many equal central angles will we need to draw on our circle?* (72; 1 angle per person voting) *If a full rotation around a circle's center point measures 360 degrees, how many degrees will each central angle need to equal?* (360 degrees separated into 72 equal angles = 5 degrees for each angle) *If each person's vote is to be shown by a central angle measuring 5 degrees and 6 people have voted the same way, how many degrees total will their 6 combined central angles measure?* (6 central angles × 5 degrees per angle = 30 degrees total)

7. Have students now use the survey data written on the chalkboard to find the total degrees needed for each response choice if they want to combine all the central angles together for the people who selected that particular choice. They should write their equations, using both numbers and words. For example, if 16 people chose response #1, students should write the following on their own papers: *16 people × 5 degrees per person = 80 degrees total.* [Note: This very direct way of computing the needed angle measures seems easier for students to understand than the proportion method often taught.]

8. After each team has determined the degrees needed for each central angle that corresponds to each response choice, have them use the protractor to construct each central angle on the circle they have drawn. The first central angle can be placed anywhere around the circle's center; after that, each new angle must be constructed adjacent to the last angle drawn.

9. After all angles have been drawn, each sector needs to be labeled with the total

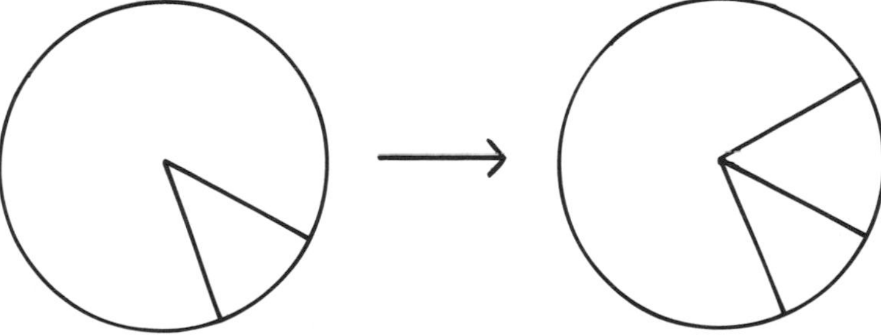

number of people the sector represents. (With older students, you might want to use percents as labels instead.) A title also needs to be given to the circle graph that reflects the survey question used. The total number of people surveyed (72 people) should be written under the title.

10. After all graphs are completed, ask each team to write three statements about the survey results that a person could discover by reading the specific circle graph. Have several teams share their statements with the rest of the class.

CHAPTER 7

NUMBER THEORY

INTRODUCTION

This chapter helps students understand basic number theory, including learning the differences between odd and even numbers. It introduces fundamental concepts, such as finding a common denominator, understanding the least common multiple, identifying factor pairs, and finding a number's prime factorization. Engaging activities and games are used to show students the principles of prime numbers and to help them differentiate between composite and prime numbers.

OBJECTIVE 1: Determine the evenness and oddness of whole numbers.

Activity 1: BUILDING ROWS

(Concrete Action)

Materials: One-inch square tiles
Paper
Pencils

Management: Partners (30 minutes)

Directions:

1. Give each pair of students a bag of 30–40 square tiles. If necessary, tiles can be made of construction paper or lightweight tagboard.

2. Ask them to count out 12 tiles, then try to arrange them in two rows with one row beside the other so that the rows have the same number of tiles. (They will be able to build two rows with six tiles in each row.)

3. Have the students draw a picture of their arrangement of tiles and record the number of tiles used beside the picture.

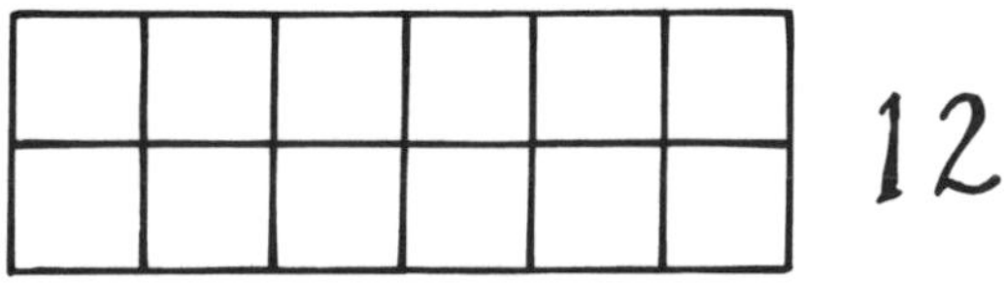

12

4. Now give them several other numbers to build, using two rows of tiles each time: 10, 15, 23, 18, 6, 9, 34, 11, 27, etc. Remind them to keep the two rows as close to the same length as possible each time they build.

5. After they have built several numbers, ask them what they notice about the two rows for the different numbers. (They should notice that sometimes the rows have the same number of tiles, but at other times one row is one tile longer than the other row.)

Activity 2: MATCHING ROWS

(Pictorial Action)

Materials: One-inch (or two-centimeter) grid paper
Colored markers
Scissors
Tape

Management: Partners (20–30 minutes)

Directions:

1. Give each pair of students two sheets of grid paper, a colored marker, tape, and a pair of scissors.

2. Assign three or four different numbers from 1 to 40 to each pair of students. Make certain an assortment of even and odd numbers is used throughout the class.

3. Ask partners to show each of their numbers by coloring two rows of squares on the grid paper. The rows should be equal in length if possible. For the larger numbers, students may need to tape two strips of the grid paper together before they color the rows of squares.

4. Have the students cut out their colored arrangements, then tape them to the chalkboard or bulletin board. They should tape the cutouts in a column under the heading *Equal Rows* if the two rows are the same length and in a column under *Unequal Rows* if their rows differ by one square.

5. After all cutouts are correctly displayed under the two headings, tell the students that all the numbers in the *Equal Rows* set are called *even* numbers (the rows of squares are evenly matched) and the numbers in the other set are called *odd* numbers (they have one unmatched square).

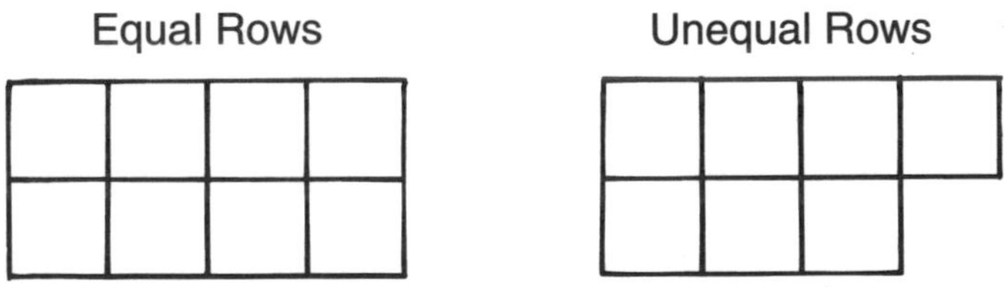

Equal Rows

Unequal Rows

6. List all the even numbers (in numeral format) on the board together, and list all the odd numbers together. Ask students what they notice about the numbers that are even. (Answers will vary, but hopefully they will notice that the *ones* digit is 0, 2, 4, 6, or 8.) Ask what they notice about the odd numbers. (Their ones digit will be 1, 3, 5, 7, or 9.)

7. Have students write word sentences to answer the following questions: *What test can you use to decide if a number is an even number? . . . an odd number?* Have several students share their answers with the class.

Activity 3: DESIGNING WITH ODDS AND EVENS

(Cooperative Groups)

Materials: Large sheets of construction paper
Colored markers
Pencils

Management: Teams of 4 students each (20–30 minutes)

Directions:

1. Give each team a sheet of large construction paper and several different colored markers.

2. Ask half of the teams to make an odd design, and ask the other teams to make an even design. This can be done in several ways. For example, to make an odd design, students can place a variety of odd numbers (in numeral form—large or small, fancy or plain) in different orientations on the paper and/or use pictures of geometric shapes that have been drawn in pairs of rows where one row is one shape longer than the other row. These should be *free-form* designs.

3. Have students create titles for their designs and display them on the classroom wall.

OBJECTIVE 2: Find the factor pairs for a whole number.

Activity 1: FACTOR FORMS
(Concrete Action)

Materials: Counters (e.g., square tiles, centimeter cubes, colored disks)
Paper
Pencils

Management: Partners (20 minutes)

Directions:

1. Give each pair of students a plastic bag of about 30 counters.

2. Ask them to randomly draw out a handful of counters and count them.

3. Have them arrange the counters in arrays, i.e., rows of equal length from left to right, and build as many different arrays as they can for their chosen set of counters. For example, if students have randomly selected 18 counters from their bag, they can build the following arrays: 1 row of 18, 2 rows of 9, 3 rows of 6, 6 rows of 3, 9 rows of 2, and 18 rows of 1 (arrays that are rotated forms of each other are considered different here).

Example of arrays for 8:

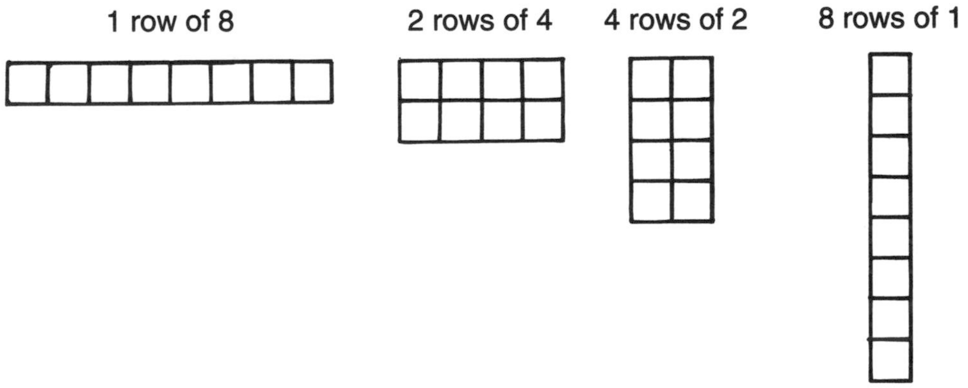

1 row of 8 2 rows of 4 4 rows of 2 8 rows of 1

4. Have students record each array they build in words, e.g., "2 rows of 9."

5. Encourage them to build arrays in an orderly way. For example, they should try to build one row first, then two rows, three rows, etc.

6. Also have them record the numbers of rows they *cannot* build with a given amount of counters. For example, for 18, they cannot build 4 equal rows, 5 equal rows, 7 equal rows, etc. (for this activity, have them try all the way up to 17 rows; do not stop at 9, the halfway value).

7. Have the partners repeat steps 2–6 with different amounts of counters for as long as time permits.

Activity 2: DRAWING FACTORS

(Pictorial Action)

Materials: Centimeter grid paper
Paper
Pencils

Management: Partners (30 minutes)

Directions:

1. Give each pair of students a sheet of centimeter grid paper.

2. Assign one set of numbers to half of the pairs of students in the class, and assign another set to the remaining pairs. Possible sets to use: [4, 9, 12, 17, 20, 24] and [5, 8, 13, 16, 21, 30].

3. Partners should shade in grid squares to make arrays for each number in their set, starting with 1 row, then 2 rows, etc. A *row* should be oriented left-to-right on the paper. On another sheet of paper, they should write the numeral name of the number they are *factoring* through this drawing process, then record each array found as a product of two factors (row and row size). That is, if 3 rows of 5 squares have been shaded to show the number 15, students will record *3 × 5*.

4. In this activity, ask students to draw only those arrays that will reveal *new* factors for them. For example, for 12, students will write 1 × 12, 2 × 6, and 3 × 4, but they will not need to write 4 × 3, 6 × 2, or 12 × 1 because those arrays do not reveal any new factors for 12. Discuss the idea that, if they have drawn 4 × 3, then they also know that 3 × 4 can be drawn (the rotated form).

5. After all partners are finished with their assigned set of numbers, have them exchange their drawings and lists of products with another pair who used a different set of numbers, so they can check each other's work for completeness.

6. When all lists have been checked, have different students record the numbers and the distinct factors (no repeats) found in their products. For example, for the number 12, a student will write the factors 1, 2, 3, 4, 6, and 12 on the board.

7. Ask students what the distinct whole number factors would be for the numbers 1, 2, and 3, if they built or drew arrays for them. (The number 1 only has the factor 1; 2 has factors 1 and 2; 3 has factors 1 and 3.)

Activity 3: FACTOR FRENZY

(Cooperative Groups)

Materials: Card sets (small index cards with a different numeral from 1–9 written on each to form a set)
Paper
Pencils
Calculators (optional)

Management: Teams of 4 students each (20 minutes)

Directions:

1. Give each team two sets of numeral cards, one set for each pair of students on the team.

2. The two pairs on a team will take turns laying down their numeral cards, two or three cards at a time. (If only one card is left, the pair cannot play.) Each pair decides which of their cards to lay down.

3. The numeral cards played represent factors (divisors), but not necessarily all of the factors, of some whole number. The pair playing must tell which whole number they wish to use, and they must find the number *mentally* (i.e., no paper and pencil or calculator allowed). This number becomes part of the pair's score, so the larger the better!

4. The playing pair may not use the calculator, but the other pair may use it, if they wish, to check the proposed whole number. Each factor card played on a turn must be able to divide the chosen number, or the playing pair does not score but loses 5 points. If the number works for all the factors played, it becomes points earned by the playing pair. Examples: If 2, 4, and 5 are played together, the whole number chosen might be 20 or 40; if only 3 and 5 are played, 15 or 30 might be used; 3 by itself cannot be played.

5. When a pair of students plays all of its remaining cards or has only one card left so cannot play, the game ends. The pair who has the larger total points at that time wins. (Each pair must find its own total score mentally or with pencil and paper; the other pair may check the sum with the calculator to see if they agree.)

OBJECTIVE 3: Identify prime and composite numbers using factor pairs or arrays.

Activity 1: BUILDING SPECIAL ARRAYS
(Concrete Action)

Materials: Counters (square tiles or centimeter cubes)
Record Sheet NT-3.1
Pencils

Management: Partners (20–30 minutes)

Directions:

1. Give each pair of students a bag of about 30 counters and a record sheet.

2. Assign each pair one number from each of the following two sets:

- Set A = [8, 9, 12, 14, 15, 16, 18, 20, 22, 25, 26] and
- Set B = [2, 3, 5, 7, 11, 13, 17, 19, 23, 29, and special number 1]

Two pairs of students may have the same number. If necessary, they can confirm each other's work. Assign a smaller number from one set and a larger number from the other set in order to balance out the building time needed.

3. Ask students to build all the possible arrays for each of their two numbers, including the rotated forms, and to record the products for the arrays on the record sheet. Also have them record how many different products are found for each number. (Example: 8—1 × 8, 2 × 4, 4 × 2, 8 × 1—4 products total)

4. Draw a copy of the record sheet on the chalkboard and have each pair record its results on the class record sheet. All students should copy the completed class record sheet onto their own personal copies.

5. Ask the students to look at the number of products found for each number and to decide if the amounts seem to group themselves in some way. Several groupings are possible; for example, numbers like 9 and 25 have only 3 products, whereas some have more than 5 products. The main groupings to seek are the following:

- numbers with more than 2 products (9, 12, 15, 18, etc.),
- numbers with only 2 products (2, 3, 5, 13, 17, etc.),
- and numbers with less than 2 products (the special number, 1).

6. Tell the students that numbers having more than 2 products are called *composite* numbers and those having exactly 2 products are called *prime* numbers. Since the number 1 only has one product (1 × 1), it is neither a composite nor a prime number; it is a special case.

NAME ______________________________ DATE ____________________

RECORD SHEET NT-3.1
Building Special Arrays

Number	Products Built	How Many Products?

Activity 2: PRIME SEARCH

(Pictorial Action)

Materials: Paper
Pencils

Management: Partners (20 minutes)

Directions:

1. Write several numbers on the board. Include several that are composite numbers and several that are prime numbers.

2. Ask the students to draw arrays of small circles/squares on their paper to help them decide which numbers on the board are composite and which ones are prime. Encourage them to be organized in their work: draw one row, then try to draw two rows, three rows, etc.

3. When all are finished, have several students share their answers and reasons. They must be able to explain their choices based upon how many products they found for each number (less than 2, exactly 2, or more than 2 products).

4. Ask them what they think the minimal information is that they need to know about a number in order to decide that it is *not* prime. Have them share their ideas with the entire class. (Basically all whole numbers greater than 1 will have at least 2 products, so if just *one more* product can be found for a number, it cannot be prime. Another way to describe a prime number is to say that its two products only involve two distinct factors: the number itself and the special number 1. So if a third factor besides these two can be found, the number must not be prime.)

Activity 3: SIEVE OF ERATOSTHENES

(Cooperative Groups)

Materials: Numbers Chart with numerals 1–100 (Worksheet NT-3.3)
Colored markers (4 different colors)

Management: Teams of 4 students each (30 minutes)

Directions:

1. Give each team a copy of the Numbers Chart Worksheet NT-3.3 and colored markers (4 different colors; 1 color per student).

2. Have students mark out with pencil the number 1 on their chart.

3. On each team, ask student #1 to use the first marker color to *underline* all numbers (except 2 itself) that have 2 as a factor while other teammates *identify* the correct numbers. Student #2 should then use the second marker color to draw a *square* around all numbers (except 3 itself) with 3 as a factor as others identify them. Some of these numbers will already be *underlined*. Student #3 will draw a *triangle* in a third color around all numbers (except 5 itself) with 5 as a factor. The next unmarked number in the number chart is 7, so student #4 will draw a *circle* in a fourth color around all numbers (except 7 itself) with 7 as a factor.

4. Let each team continue to develop its own code for marking numbers that have the same factor. The four colors can be repeated as often as needed. Each new factor to be considered will be the next unmarked number in the sequence of numbers. For example, after 7, the next factor should be 11.

5. After all teams have finished their charts and all possible factors have been tested by the above procedure, ask students to list all the numbers left unmarked on their charts. (Final unmarked numbers: 2, 3, 5, 7, 11, 13, 17, 19, 23, 29, 31, 37, 41, 43, 47, 53, 59, 61, 67, 71, 73, 79, 83, 89, 97)

6. Ask them what the unmarked numbers have in common. (Since they have not been marked, they do not have any factors except for 1 and themselves. Therefore, they are prime numbers. All the numbers greater than 1 that have been marked in a special way must be composite numbers.)

7. Ask them what it means for a number to have a circle, a triangle, and a square drawn around it. (It means that the number has the factors 7, 5, and 3.) Have them name the numbers having these three markings.

8. Ask students to find the numbers that share 7 and 2 as their factors. (Look for numbers that are underlined and circled.) Have them continue to explore by asking similar questions of their fellow students.

WORKSHEET NT-3.3
Numbers Chart for Sieve of Eratosthenes

1	2	3	4	5	6	7	8	9	10
11	12	13	14	15	16	17	18	19	20
21	22	23	24	25	26	27	28	29	30
31	32	33	34	35	36	37	38	39	40
41	42	43	44	45	46	47	48	49	50
51	52	53	54	55	56	57	58	59	60
61	62	63	64	65	66	67	68	69	70
71	72	73	74	75	76	77	78	79	80
81	82	83	84	85	86	87	88	89	90
91	92	93	94	95	96	97	98	99	100

OBJECTIVE 4: Find the prime factors of a whole number.

Activity 1: PRIME TIMES
(Concrete Action)

Materials: Centimeter cubes (or other counters)
Paper
Pencils

Management: Partners (20 minutes)

Directions:

1. Have students name the prime numbers from 2 to 19 as you list them on the board.

2. Give each pair of students a bag of about 40 centimeter cubes.

3. Have them randomly take a handful of cubes from the bag. Ask them to try to form two equal groups with the selected cubes. If they can, then 2 is a factor of this set of cubes. Since 2 is a prime number, it is a *prime factor.*

4. The students should record the number of cubes they have taken out of the bag and begin listing the prime factors they find, such as 2 in the example above.

5. Ask them also to try to form 3 equal groups, 5 equal groups, etc., forming a prime number amount of groups each time until they think there are no more ways to try for a particular set of cubes. Have them look at the list of prime numbers for more numbers to try. Example of a recording: 24 cubes—prime factors 2 and 3.

6. Have students randomly pull out another set of cubes and repeat the above process (steps 3–5) for forming prime amounts of equal groups of cubes in order to find the prime factors. Continue as long as time permits.

7. For closure, have students who used the same number of cubes compare their results to see if they found the same set of prime factors for that number.

Activity 2: DRAWING OUT PRIMES
(Pictorial Action)

Materials: Paper
Pencils

Management: Partners (20 minutes)

Directions:

1. Assign each pair of students a different composite number between 20 and 40. Write the prime numbers from 2 to 19 on the board for their use.

2. Ask students to try to draw equal groups of a "prime amount of circles" that will total their assigned number. The group size itself will be a prime number this time. For example, if the number is 20, they can draw 10 groups of 2 circles each—00 00 00 00 00 00 00 00 00 00, or 4 groups of 5 circles each—00000 00000 00000 00000. So the "prime factors" of 20 are 2 and 5.

3. After students have found all the possible prime factors for their assigned number, have them record their number with its prime factors on the board and also tell how many of each group size they needed, e.g., 10 of size 2 or 4 of size 5.

Activity 3: PRIME CHASE

(Cooperative Groups)

Materials: Sets of cards
(**Set A:** small index cards with a different black number written on each card—use 1 through 48; **Set B:** small index cards with a different red number written on each card—use 2, 3, 5, 7, 11, 13, 17, 19, 23, 29, 31, 37, 41, 43, 47; also for set B, include a card with a red smiley face on it and cards for the *distractor* factors 1, 4, 9, 10, 12, and 15)

Management: Teams of 4 students each (20 minutes)

Directions:

1. Give each team a set of A cards and a set of B cards. Students should shuffle their set of A cards and place them face down in the center of the table. Set B is also placed in the center, but it does not need to be shuffled. During each turn, one or more cards will be selected from and returned to the B stack without concern for order; the player has access to *all* cards in the B stack for that period of time.

2. The four team members take turns taking the top card off the A deck and placing it face up in a discard pile. The player then pulls out from set B those cards whose numbers are *prime factors* of the *number drawn from set A*. If the other members agree, the player earns 1 point for each correct prime factor. No points are lost for incorrect factors *when the A number is a composite number.*

3. If the number 1 is drawn from set A, the player must choose the smiley face card from set B to indicate that 1 has no prime factors and therefore earns 5 points. For each incorrect card played as a prime factor of 1, the player loses 1 point. If a prime number is drawn from set A, the player must choose the same prime number from set B, and *only* that number, for its factor in order to earn 5 points. If a player chooses any *incorrect* factor cards *when the A number is a prime number,* he or she will only earn 1 point for the correct factor and lose 1 point for each incorrect factor chosen.

4. Play continues until time is called or the stack of A cards is exhausted. The player with the highest score wins.

OBJECTIVE 5: Find the multiples of whole numbers.

Activity 1: NUMBER BUILDING
(Concrete Action)

Materials: Cuisenaire® rods (or equivalent colored paper strips—Rod Patterns Worksheet NT-5.1)
Paper
Pencils

Management: Partners (20–30 minutes)

Directions:

1. Give each pair of students a set of Cuisenaire® rods (or colored paper strips).

2. Ask the students to place a red rod on the desktop in front of them. Have them build different *trains* (rods placed end to end) with just the red rods. There should be a 1-rod train, 2-rod train, 3-rod train, etc.

3. The red rod is 2 cm long. Ask students to find the length of each red train they built and record their results as follows: 1 R = 2, 2 R = 4, 3 R = 6, etc. The total length of each red train is called a *multiple of the red or 2-rod.*

4. Have students repeat the above building process, using a different rod color each time (e.g., build trains with just light green rods or with just purple rods). Record as before, using these other letters, lengths and colors:

W or 1—white	Y or 5—yellow	N or 8—brown
G or 3—light green	D or 6—dark green	E or 9—blue
P or 4—purple	K or 7—black	0 or 10—orange

WORKSHEET NT-5.1
Rod Pattern for Number Building

Prepare on light tagboard for easier manipulation.

Color before cutting apart: O=orange, E=blue, N=brown, K=black, D=dark green, Y=yellow, P=purple, G=light green, R=red, and W=white.

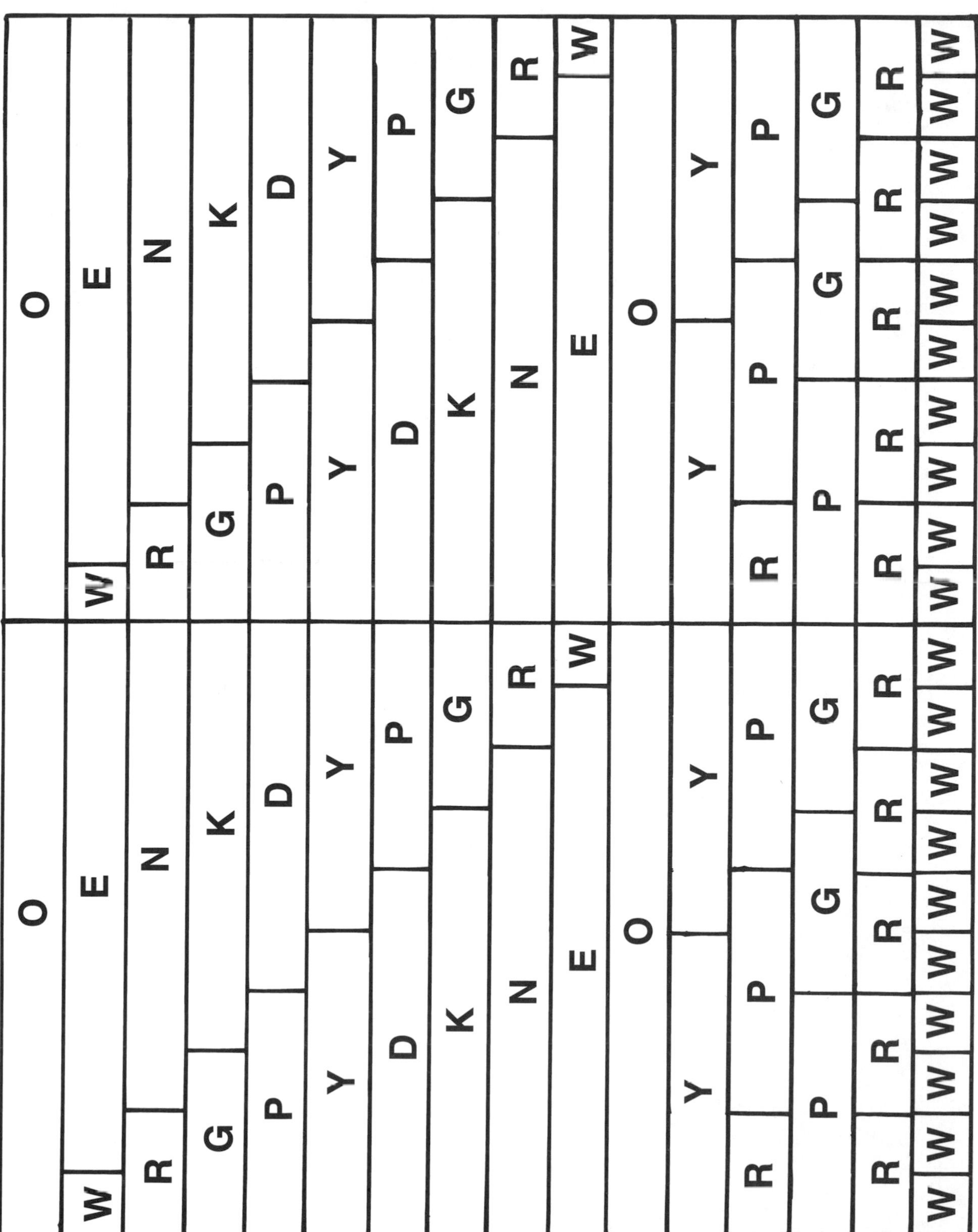

Activity 2: COLORING MULTIPLES

(Pictorial Action)

Materials: Centimeter grid paper
Colored markers (use Cuisenaire® rod colors, if possible)
Scissors
Tape
Glue sticks
Large construction paper

Management: Teams of 3–4 students each (30 minutes)

Directions:

1. Give each team 3–4 sheets of centimeter grid paper, colored markers (red, light green, purple, and yellow), scissors, tape, a glue stick, and a large sheet of construction paper.

2. Have them color red centimeter strips, using different amounts of 2-cm lengths. That is, color two grid squares to make a 2-cm strip, then color two of the 2-cm strip to make a 4-cm strip. Continue the process to make a 6-cm and an 8-cm strip. These four strips should be cut out, then placed horizontally and glued onto the construction paper, one below the other, and labeled in order of length as 1×2, 2×2, 3×2, and 4×2. Above the group of strips print "Multiples of 2."

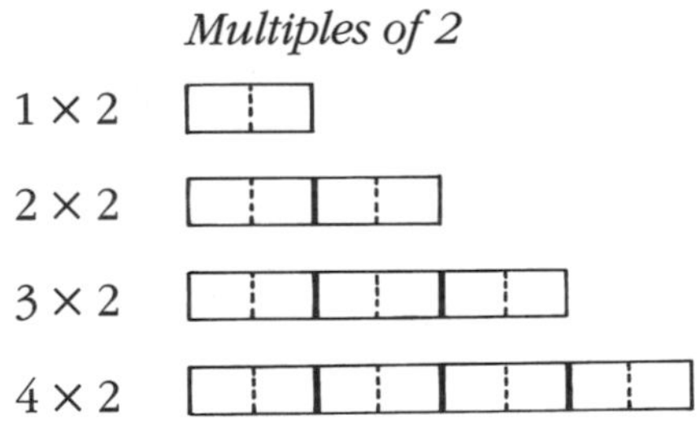

Multiples of 2

1×2

2×2

3×2

4×2

3. Have students repeat the procedure of step 2, using as the first strip of a new group each of the following: a 3-cm strip (light green), a 4-cm strip (purple), and a 5-cm strip (yellow). Strips may need to be taped together to make them long enough. Two sheets of construction paper may also need to be taped together to allow enough space for all the strips. The finished construction paper should contain four multiples of 2, four multiples of 3, four multiples of 4, and four multiples of 5.

4. When the teams are finished, ask them to look at their groups of multiples and see if any of the paper strips are the same length. Have them describe in writing any that they find in the following way: $4 \times$ *2* and $2 \times$ *4* have the same length, so 8 is a multiple of both *2 and 4* (often called a *common multiple* of 2 and 4). Also, $2 \times$ *2* and $1 \times$ *4* also have the same length, so 4 is a common multiple of *2 and 4,* etc.

5. Ask students if they think they would find other common multiples if they extended each group of cm-strips by making more multiples of 2, 3, 4, and 5. For example, ask: *Is there another strip longer than 8 that is also a multiple of 2 and of 4?* (yes; 12, 16, etc.) Discuss what some other common multiples might be.

6. Ask students if they can find a strip that is a multiple of *three* of the original cm-strips used. They may need to draw a few more strips to help them decide. (The number 12 is a multiple for 2, 3, and 4; the number 20 is a multiple for 2, 4, and 5; 30 is a multiple of 2, 3, and 5.)

7. Ask: *Of all the multiples common to 2 and 3, is there a smallest (least) multiple?* (yes, 6) If it is appropriate for your students, introduce them to the *notation* for the *least common multiple* of the numbers 2 and 3: *LCM(2,3)*. Be sure that they use the words, "least common multiple," and not the letters, "L C M," when reading this new expression.

Activity 3: MULTIPLES MATCH

(Cooperative Groups)

Materials: Sets of cards
(**Set A:** small index cards with black numerals 41–88, one two-digit numeral per card; **Set B:*** small index cards with red numerals 2–9, one numeral per card)
Small counters
Calculators (optional)
[*Alternative—a spinner with red numerals 2–9 may be used in place of card set B]

Management: Teams of 4 students each (20 minutes)

Directions:

1. Give each team one of each card set, A and B, and three small counters.

2. Students should shuffle each set of cards, then form 3 equal stacks of cards from set A, placing the stacks face down in the center of the table. Also, the cards from set B should be placed face down near the other 3 stacks.

3. The first player turns the top card of each stack face up. If any black numeral showing is a multiple of the red numeral, the player may collect that card for 1 point. On a single turn a player can earn up to 3 points if all three black numeral cards are multiples of the red numeral. If necessary, other team members may check a player's choice by using a calculator to see if the red numeral divides the black numeral a whole number of times.

4. If a top card is collected, the next card in the stack is turned face up for the next player. If a top card is not collected, it remains for the next turn and a counter is placed on the card. If a top card holding a counter is not collected on the next turn, it is to be removed to a discard pile and the next card in the stack turned face up.

5. After each red numeral is used, it should be placed at the bottom of its stack to be redrawn later.

6. If no top card is a multiple of the red numeral showing, the player must pass. The red numeral is then placed at the bottom of its stack and a new red card turned face up for the next player.

7. If two consecutive players are forced to pass, all three black numerals showing must be discarded and three new ones turned face up for the next player.

8. The game ends when no one can play or all black numerals have been either collected or discarded. The player with the most cards is the winner.

OBJECTIVE 6: Find the common denominator of two or more common fractions.

Activity 1: MAKING TRADES
(Concrete Action)

Materials: Cuisenaire rods® (or equivalent colored bars or strips)
Paper
Pencils

Management: Partners (50 minutes)

Directions:

1. Give each pair of students a set of colored rods.

2. Have students place 2 brown rods (N) on their desktops and place 1 purple rod (P) beside one of the brown rods and 3 red rods (R) beside the other brown rod.

3. Ask what part the purple is of the brown and have them show their answer by trading or exchanging one rod for rods of another color. The brown rod must be traded for 2 purple rods. This shows that the purple rod is *1 of 2 parts of the brown;* hence, the purple rod is *one-half* of the brown rod.

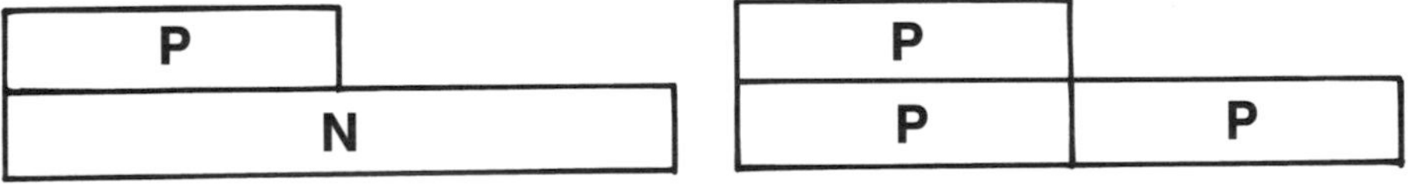

1 of 2 parts of the brown

4. Ask what part the 3 reds are of the brown. By trading the brown for 4 red rods, the students can show that the 3 reds are 3 of 4 parts of the brown; hence, the 3 red rods are *three-fourths* of the brown rod.

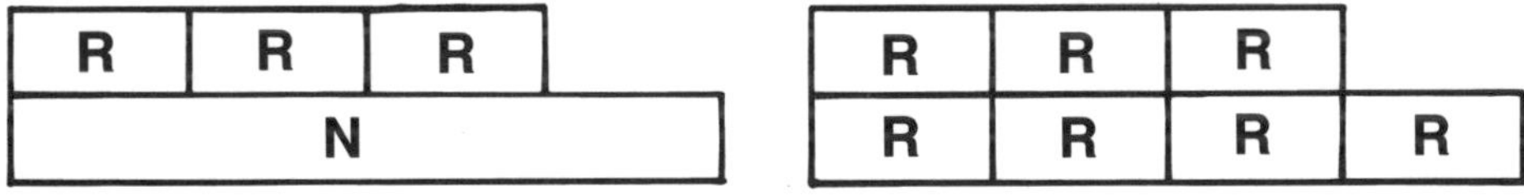

3 of 4 parts of the brown

5. Now ask students if they can make trades so that the purple and red rods can be compared to the brown rod in the same way (with the same part size). Each purple can be traded for 2 reds, so that a purple becomes 2 of 4 parts or *two-fourths* of the brown rod. Now the purple rod and the 3 red rods can be more easily compared and combined if necessary.

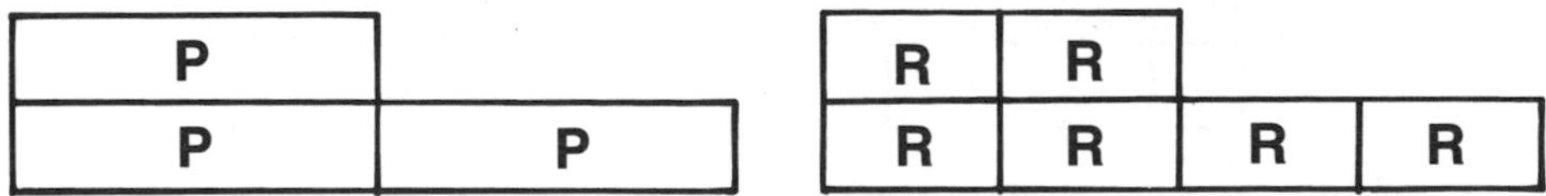

2 of 4 parts of the brown

6. Have students record *1 purple = 1 half = 2 fourths of the brown* and *3 reds = 3 fourths of the brown.* Some students may wish to trade each rod for white rods. If so, they will have the results: *1 purple = 1 half = 4 eighths of the brown* and *3 reds = 3 fourths = 6 eighths of the brown.* These answers are acceptable since we are not looking for the smallest common part size at this time.

7. Now give the students several other fraction pairs to change to a common part size, following the trading procedure used in steps 2–6. Have them record their results each time as in step 6 above. Here are some pairs to try: 1 light green rod to dark green (1/2) and 1 red to dark green (2/6); 2 light green rods to blue (2/3) and 1 yellow rod to blue (5/9); 2 red rods to dark green (2/3) and 1 light green to dark green (1/2); 1 yellow rod to orange (1/2) and 3 red rods to orange (3/5).

8. When all students are finished, ask them to compare the changes they made to the original fractional bar(s) [numerator] and to the whole bar [denominator] used. What happened each time they traded for a new part size? (Example: When the purple rod was shown as some part of the brown rod, to name the purple rod, both it and the brown rod were traded the same way, that is, for the same new part size. These new amounts were then compared as a ratio. We had either 1 P/2 P or 2 R/4 R.)

9. Discuss that when two fractions are based on the same whole bar and they are traded to the same new part size, the *number of new parts* that now make up the *whole bar* is the same for both fractions. For example, in the first example with the brown rod, when the purple rod trades to red rods, its brown rod changes to 4 red rods; for the fraction comparing 3 red rods to the brown rod, again the brown rod changes to 4 red rods. This *common number* (here, 4) is known as the *denominator* of the two new fractions.

Activity 2: MAKING LOOK-ALIKES

(Pictorial Action)

Materials: Worksheet NT-6.2
Pencils

Management: Partners (30 minutes)

Directions:

1. Give each student a worksheet, but have all students work with a partner.

2. Discuss the first example with the class. One unit bar is divided into 4 equal parts; the other is divided into 2 equal parts. The two bars must be subdivided again so that they have the same number of total equal parts. Each part of the 2-part bar can be traded for 2 new parts to make 4 parts total for the bar. The other bar already has 4 parts, so it is finished. Have students write a number sentence under each bar to show how it was changed to the new number of parts.

2 × 2 new parts = 4 parts total
4 × 1 old part = 4 parts total

Some students might want to change each unit bar to 8 new parts. Then each part of the 2-part bar trades for 4 new parts (2 × 4 new parts = 8) and each part of the 4-part bar trades for 2 new parts (4 × 2 new parts = 8). Other trades are also possible. Accept whatever trades will work.

3. Discuss the exercise involving 1/2 and 2/3. Have students decide how many new parts they want each unit bar to have, but this common amount can only be found through the trading process. So 6 parts can be used if the 2 parts (for 1/2) trade for 3 new parts each and the 3 parts (for 2/3) trade for 2 new parts each. Students should now draw the new parts and write the corresponding number sentences.

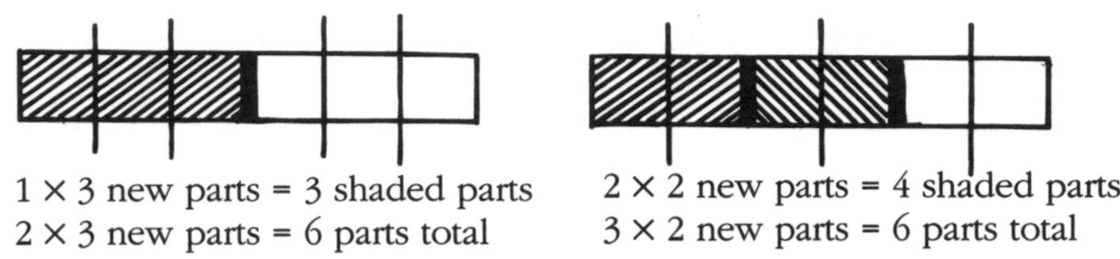

1 × 3 new parts = 3 shaded parts
2 × 3 new parts = 6 parts total
2 × 2 new parts = 4 shaded parts
3 × 2 new parts = 6 parts total

Some students might also notice that they can use 12 total parts for each unit bar. Then for 1/2 they will have 1 × 6 new parts and 2 × 6 new parts, and for 2/3 they will have 2 × 4 new parts and 3 × 4 new parts. Other amounts are also possible. We are not looking for the smallest number of total parts at this time.

4. Now have students complete the worksheet with their partners.

5. Discuss their results when all have finished. Ask students if they see a relationship between the two products found when they changed two unit bars to the same number of equal parts. For example, for the first exercise, the products were 4 × 1 and 2 × 2; that is, the common total, 4 parts, for both bars is just a *multiple* of the original 4 parts and 2 parts. If 4 × 2 and 2 × 4 were used, the common total of 8 parts is again a *multiple* of the 4 parts and of the 2 parts. Have students confirm this *common multiple* relationship for the other exercises on the worksheet.

Activity 3: DENOMINATOR SPIN

(Cooperative Groups)

Materials: Spinner Pattern (Worksheet NT-6.3)
Large paper clips
Red and blue markers
Paper
Pencils

Management: Teams of 4 students each (20 minutes)

Directions:

1. Give each team a Spinner Pattern Worksheet NT-6.3, a large paper clip to serve as spinner, and a red and a blue marker.

NAME ______________________________ DATE ____________________

WORKSHEET NT-6.2
Making Look-Alikes

Mark off new parts on the unit bars, so that each pair of unit bars will have the same number of parts.

1. 

2. 

3. 

4. 

5. 

6. 

2. Each team member takes a turn spinning two numbers with the spinner. These two numbers indicate the denominators for two unit bars. The player who spins the spinner draws two unit bars of *equal length* (4 inches or longer is best for drawing parts) and subdivides the bars according to the two spinner numbers. For example, if 3 and 6 were spun, one bar is marked off in 3 equal parts ("equal" by free-hand standards!) and the other is marked off in 6 equal parts. Note that if a player spins a *1,* then a unit bar must be drawn and left *whole,* i.e., not subdivided.

3. Now the next two players in order of play will each subdivide the two unit bars to get a common number of total parts and write the trades as products. One will use the red marker and the other, the blue marker. For example, for 3 and 6, one player with the red marker might divide each of the 3 parts of one unit bar into 2 new parts, leave the unit bar with 6 parts alone, and write the products $3 \times 2 = 6$ and $6 \times 1 = 6$. The player with the blue marker might divide each unit bar into 12 new parts total and write the products $3 \times 4 = 12$ and $6 \times 2 = 12$. In this latter case, the original 3 parts have 4 new parts each, as shown by blue markings, and the 6 original parts have 2 new parts each, also shown by blue markings.

4. The fourth player now gets to spin and the play continues until time is called.

5. Alternative: When a player spins the two numbers and draws the unit bars, he or she may also shade some of the parts on the unit bars. Then the other two players who subdivide the bars must also write the products for the changes in the shaded parts. For example, if a unit bar has 3 parts total and 2 parts are shaded, to make 6 parts total the products must be $2 \times 2 = 4$ shaded parts and $3 \times 2 = 6$ parts total.

WORKSHEET NT-6.3
Spinner Pattern for Denominator Spin

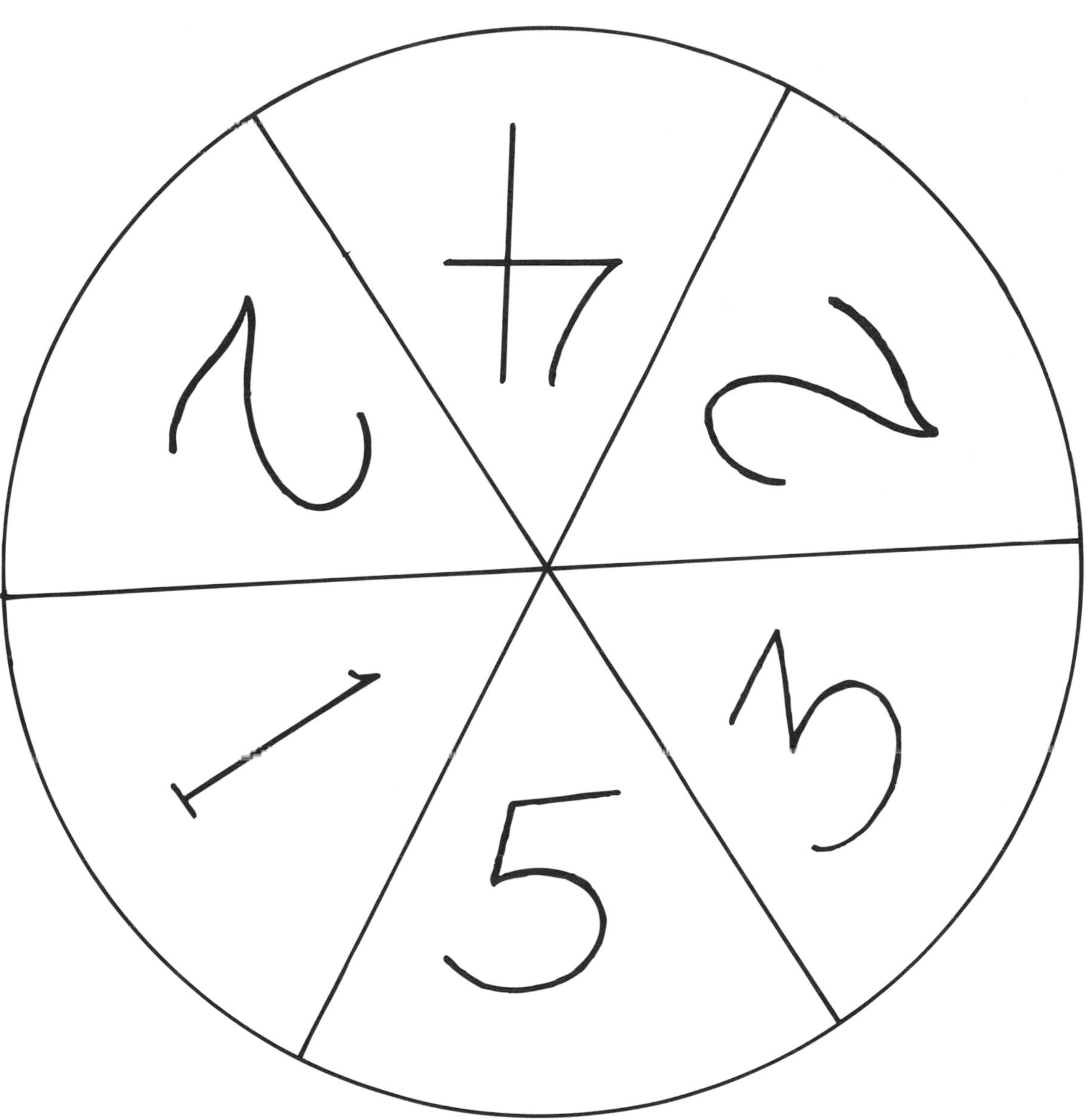

OBJECTIVE 7: Find the prime factorization of a whole number.

Activity 1: BUILDING WITH GROUPS

(Concrete Action)

Materials: Cuisenaire® rods (or equivalent colored rods or paper strips)
3" × 5" index cards
Paper
Pencils

Management: Partners (50 minutes)

Directions:

1. Give each pair of students 2 sets of colored rods and 5 index cards.

2. Have them make a *rod train* by placing one orange and one red rod end to end. This train is 12 cm or 12 white rods long and is described as (O + R).

3. Ask students to build another train the same length, using 3 of only one color of rod. (3 purple rods are needed.) Have them record their result: 12 = 3 × P for the purple train. *Note:* Do *not* write this as P × 3; the order of the factors is important here—3 is the multiplier or the counter for the purple rods and should always be placed on the left to prevent confusion in notation for future activities.

4. Have students place each new purple rod on a separate index card.

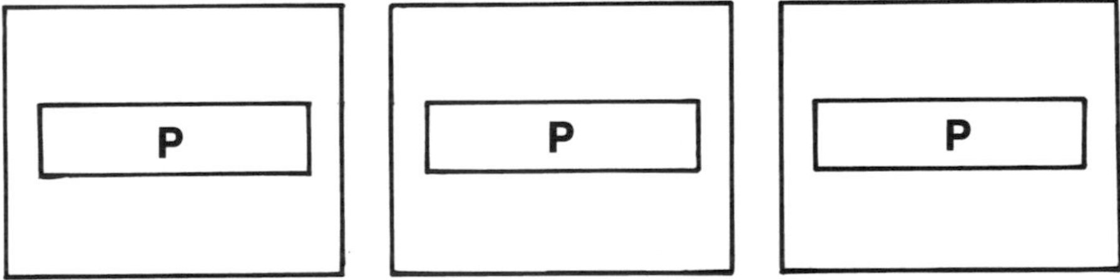

5. Now look at one of the purple rods and ask if it can be replaced by 2 rods that are alike. (Yes, 2 red rods) Have students replace each purple rod with 2 red rods. Since there are 3 index cards being used, 3 sets of 2 red rods each will be formed. Students should record this change as 12 = 3 × (2 × R) directly under 12 = 3 × P.

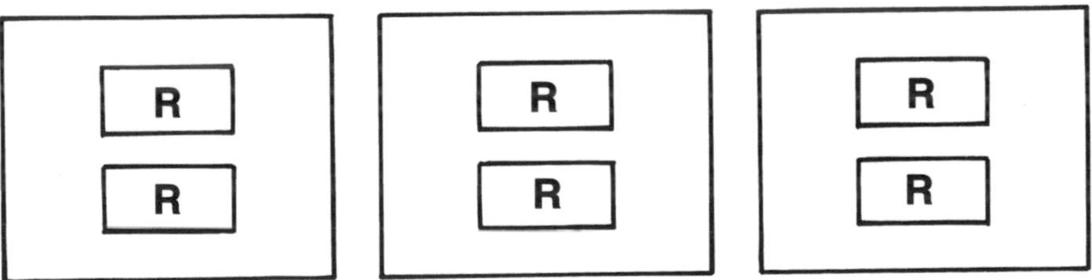

6. Since R is 2 cm long, it cannot be traded except for 2 white rods. Have the students trade each red rod for 2 white rods. Under the number sentence 12 = 3 × (2 × R), have them write the final sentence, 12 = 3 × (2 × 2).

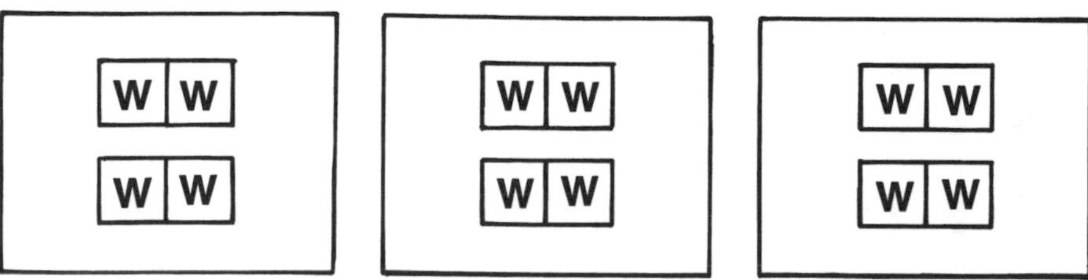

7. The amount of white rods, 2, within a single group is a prime number. The other two amounts of rod groups used, 3 and 2 (number of cards and number of rows on a card), are also prime numbers. Students have now expressed 12 as the product of three factors, all of which are prime numbers. This special product is called the *prime factorization* of 12.

8. Ask students to find another way to make prime amounts of groups for 12. This means only a prime number of cards and a prime number of rows per card can be used. The final row of white rods must also be a prime amount. Have them record a number sentence for each change they make. Other possible prime factorizations for 12: (D=dark green, G=light green)

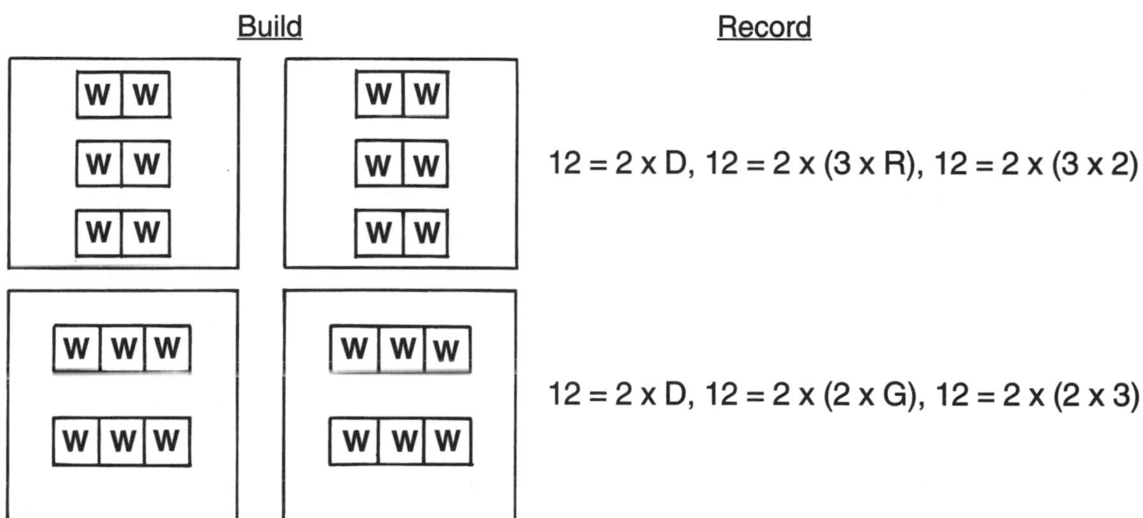

Build
Record
12 = 2 x D, 12 = 2 x (3 x R), 12 = 2 x (3 x 2)
12 = 2 x D, 12 = 2 x (2 x G), 12 = 2 x (2 x 3)

9. Ask them what they notice about the factors in the three different prime factorizations they found. (The factors are the same in all three factorizations: one 3 and two 2's, but their order is different.) So a *general form* to represent all three ways can be written by omitting the parentheses, e.g., $12 = 3 \times 2 \times 2$ or $12 = 2 \times 2 \times 3$. The order of the factors in the *general* prime factorization sentence does not matter because we now know the original number can be broken down in several different ways. If we want to factor the number in a specific way, then we must use parentheses.

10. Now have the students build prime factorizations for other numbers. Ask them to build two different factorizations for each one, write a specific number sentence for each change they make, then write a general prime factorization for the number. Here are some possible rods or numbers to use (with the general prime factorizations to be found):

10 as orange—2×5
9 as blue—3×3
14 as orange + purple (O + P)—2×7
8 as brown—$2 \times 2 \times 2$
18 as orange + brown (O + N)—$2 \times 3 \times 3$
28 as 2 orange + brown (2 O + N)—$2 \times 2 \times 7$

Examples of 2 × 5: 2 cards with 1 row of 5 white rods on each card, or 1 card with 2 rows of 5 white rods each on the card. (Since 1 is not prime, it is not included in the final factorization.)

11. As students share their results with the class, have them describe how they organized their rods. For example, if the factorization 28 = 2 × 2 × 7 is given, the student might say that 2 cards were used and each card held 2 of the black rods or 2 rows of 7 white rods each.

12. If time permits, ask students to find a prime factorization for 5, the yellow rod. Discuss their results. (Hopefully they will realize that 5 cannot be built as several groups of rods except for 5 of the white rods in one row on 1 card. Since 5 is already prime, it is its own prime factorization.)

Activity 2: PICTURING PRIME FACTORIZATIONS

(Pictorial Action)

Materials: Factoring Worksheet NT-7.2
Pencils

Management: Partners (20 minutes)

Directions:

1. Give each student a factoring worksheet.

2. Have students draw the prime factorization for 12 as their first exercise on the worksheet. Encourage them to *lightly* draw a group of circles together within a box to show the first separation, if it helps, before erasing and redrawing them in the rows. Have them record the final number sentence for their particular process. Below is a sample of what might be drawn if students decided to use 2 boxes and drew 3 rows of 2 circles per row in each box.

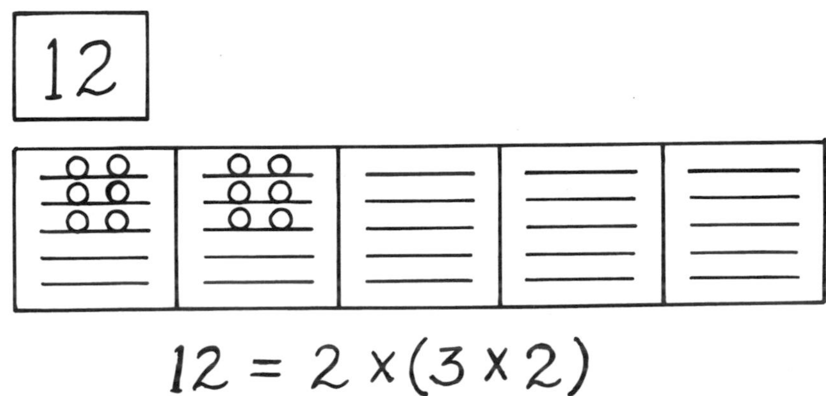

3. After all are finished, have several students draw their factorizations on the chalkboard and explain the steps they used. If two students have found different factorizations for the same number, have both drawings put on the board (e.g., 2 × (3 × 5) and 3 × (5 × 2)). For the number 21 on the worksheet, they might have 3 cards with 1 row of 7 circles on each card, or just 1 card with 3 rows of 7 circles per row, either of which reflects 3 sets of 7 or 3 × 7. To show 7 sets of 3, extra cards (or extra row lines on a single card) would need to be drawn.

NAME ______________________________ DATE ____________________

FACTORING WORKSHEET NT-7.2
Picturing Prime Factorizations

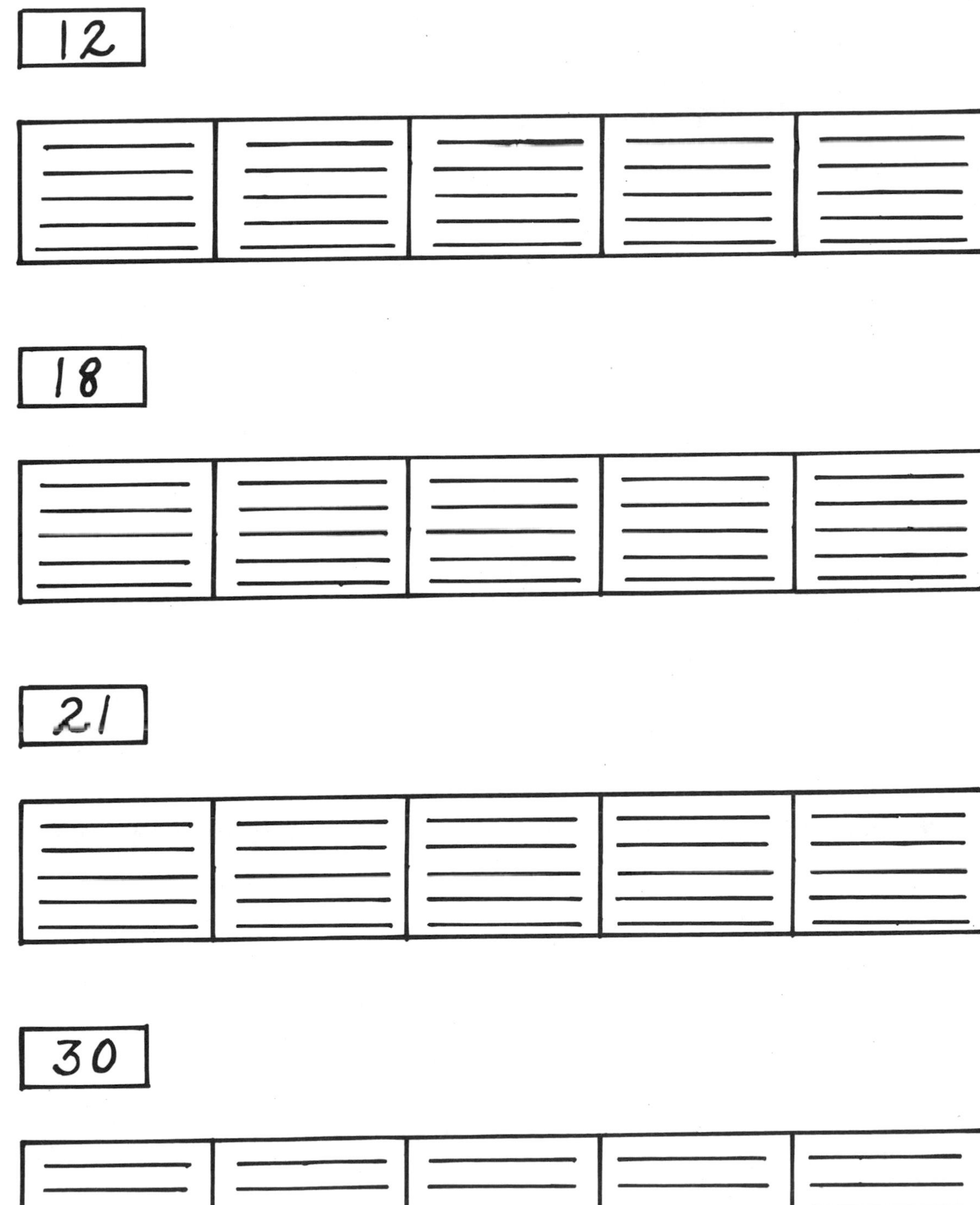

Activity 3: PRIMES CHECK

(Cooperative Groups)

Materials: Cuisenaire® rods
3" × 5" index cards
Sets of prime factorization cards

Management: Teams of 4 students each (20–30 minutes)

Directions:

1. Give each team two sets of Cuisenaire® rods, five 3" × 5" index cards, and a set of 20 cards made from small index cards. Each card has a particular prime factorization written on it; that is, parentheses are used to show how the product is to be built. Two- and three-factor products should be included. Here are some examples to use: 2×7, 5×3, 2×3, 5×2, 3×3, 5×5, 3×5, $3 \times (2 \times 3)$, $2 \times (5 \times 2)$, $5 \times (2 \times 2)$, $2 \times (3 \times 3)$, $3 \times (2 \times 2)$, $2 \times (2 \times 5)$, $3 \times (2 \times 5)$, $2 \times (3 \times 5)$, $3 \times (3 \times 2)$, $2 \times (3 \times 2)$, $2 \times (2 \times 3)$, $3 \times (3 \times 3)$, $2 \times (2 \times 7)$.

2. Team members take turns drawing a product card and building the product with colored rods and index cards. To do this, a player must start with the rightmost factor. For example, if $2 \times (3 \times 5)$ is drawn, the player finds the colored rod that is 5 white rods long—the yellow rod. Continuing with 3, the next factor to the left, 3 yellow rods must then be placed on each index card used; for the last factor 2, 2 index cards must be used. The total value of this product in white rods is 30. The other 3 team members may help the builder, if necessary.

3. Teams continue to build products until time is called.

4. Note that in all of the prime factorization activities, *commuting* (or changing the order of) *factors* within a product is *not allowed*. Even though commuted factors result in the same total value, the rod organizations they produce are quite different. Organizational differences are the focus at this time.

5. Challenge: Ask students to build with rods to show the prime factorization: $2 \times [3 \times (2 \times 3)]$. (Hint: For the leftmost factors 2 and 3, make 2 rows of 3 index cards per row. Then on each card place 2 of the light green rod, which is 3 cm long.) *What is the total value of all the rods?* (36)

OBJECTIVE 8: Use the prime factorization to find factor pairs of a whole number.

Activity 1: FACTOR FIND
(Concrete Action)

Materials: Cuisenaire® rods
3" × 5" index cards
Paper
Pencils

Management: Teams of 3–4 students each (30 minutes)

Directions:

1. Give each team of students two sets of colored rods and five 3" × 5" index cards.

2. Tell them to place 2 index cards in a row on their desktops from left to right with their short ends touching. On each card have them place 3 rows of 5 white rods each. The final arrangement should look like this:

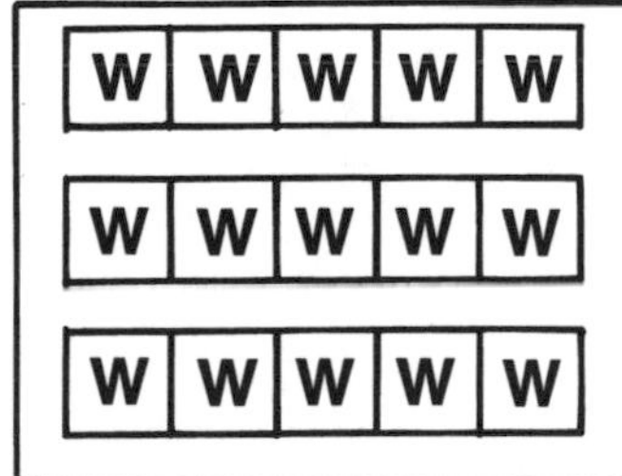

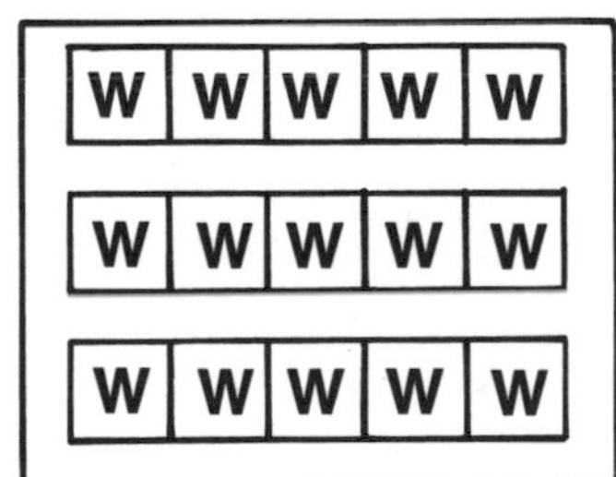

3. Ask students to decide how many white rods this arrangement equals and to tell what specific prime factorization it represents. (30; 2 × (3 × 5))

4. Now have the students combine the rows on each card and give a number sentence for what they have made. (Answer: 3 rows of 5 white rods mix together to make 15 randomly placed on the card, so the new sentence will be 30 = 2 × 15. This is a *factor pair* for 30.)

5. Ask students to rebuild the original arrangement of the rods. Tell them to move the different rows of white rods off the cards onto the desktop, keeping the rows intact but not necessarily the *grouping* by three rows at a time. Ask for a number sentence describing what they have made. (Since there are now 6 rows all together with 5 white rods per row, the number sentence is 30 = 6 × 5, another *factor pair* for 30.)

6. Have students collapse the separate rows and form just one group of all the individual white rods. The number sentence for this is 30 = 1 × 30 if we think of the rods as 1 group of 30 rods. If we think of the rods as 30 separate pieces, we can write 30 = 30 × 1.

7. Other factor pairs for 30, i.e., 5 × 6 and 10 × 3, can be found by building the factorization, 5 × (2 × 3), then by mixing the rods on each card or by moving all the rows off the cards onto the desktop. The factorization, 3 × (5 × 2), will yield the factor pairs 3 × 10 and 15 × 2. Have students try to find these different pairs by combining the rows on each card or by removing the cards but preserving the rows.

8. Give the class other prime factorizations (using three prime factors) to build then collapse the different parts in order to find various factor pairs for the total value of the white rods being used. For example, some specific prime factorizations for 20 are 5 × (2 × 2), 2 × (5 × 2), and 2 × (2 × 5). Have students build these arrangements, then find the factor pairs for 20 that could come from each.

9. Challenge: Ask students to find and build the arrangement of rods for 18 that can be used to find the factor pairs 9 × 2 and 3 × 6. (They must select the specific prime factorization, 3 × (3 × 2).)

10. Ask: *Is there a way to use a number's* ***general*** *prime factorization (where no parentheses are shown) to find its factor pairs?* Have students share their various ideas. Guide them to notice that two or more of the *prime* factors, regardless of their order in the general prime factorization, eventually are multiplied together to form a new factor for a factor pair. For example, we know that the specific arrangement 3 × (2 × 5) belongs to the general form, 2 × 3 × 5. So 2 × 5 becomes 10, which becomes a new factor to be combined with the remaining factor 3 to form 3 × 10 or 10 × 3. Similarly, from 2 × 3 × 3 × 5 we might use 2 × 3 as 6 and 3 × 5 as 15; the new factor pair becomes 6 × 15 or 15 × 6. Don't forget to multiply all *four* primes together to find 1 × 90 or 90 × 1!

Activity 2: FACTOR PAIR SEARCH

(Pictorial Action)

Materials: Factorization Worksheet NT-8.2
Pencils

Management: Partners (30 minutes)

Directions:

1. Give each student a copy of Worksheet NT-8.2.

2. Ask the students to find the factor pairs that come directly from each prime factorization shown on the worksheet. Only numbers having 3 prime factors will be used. Discuss the students' answers.

Example of finding factor pairs from a diagram of a specific prime factorization:

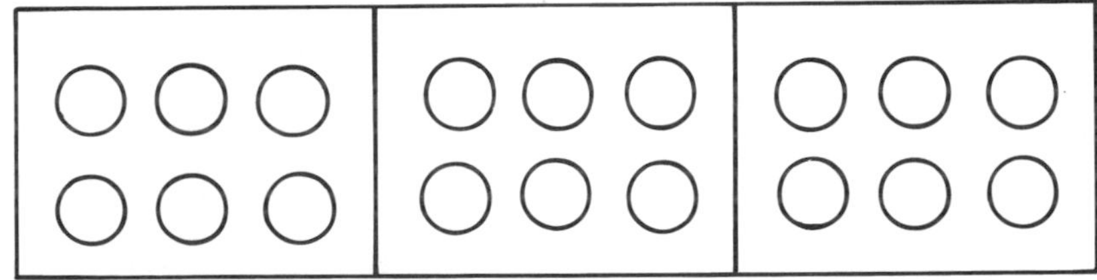

Specific prime factorization: 18 = 3 × (2 × 3)

Related factor pairs:

(a) remove cards, keep rows: 6 × 3

(b) mix rows, keep cards: 3 × 6

(c) remove cards, mix rows: 1 × 18 or 18 × 1

3. Now have each pair of students select a number and prepare their own factorization by drawing left-right rows of small circles on rectangles (like the rods on cards earlier) according to the rules for building prime factorizations from previous activities. They should draw arrangements different from those used on the worksheet. Different student pairs can then exchange their drawings and try to find the related factor pairs. To avoid choosing numbers with too many prime factors, which makes drawing more difficult, students might select a number from the following list: 18, 27, 28, 30, 42, 45, 50, 63.

Activity 3: FACTOR PAIR CHALLENGE

(Cooperative Groups)

Materials: Paper
Pencils
Calculators (optional)

Management: Teams of 4 students each (20 minutes)

Directions:

1. Each member of a team will have a turn at calling out either 3 or 4 prime numbers (repeats are allowed) that will serve as the factors in a number's (general) prime factorization. Use primes that are less than 20. The other three team members must use these numbers to record all the factor pairs of the original number, as well as find the original number. Consider *commuted* pairs as *different* pairs. When multiplying the larger primes, students may wish to use a calculator.

2. Example: One player calls out the prime factors 2, 5, and 7 for some number. Possible factor pairs are 2×35 or 35×2, 5×14 or 14×5, 10×7 or 7×10, and finally if all three factors are multiplied together, 70×1 or 1×70. The original number was 70.

3. Challenge the students by asking: *If a number has 3 distinct prime factors (no repeats this time!), can you predict how many factor pairs the number will have? Count commuted pairs like 2×3 and 3×2 as two different pairs.* Have the teams look at pairs they found earlier in this activity and try to find a pattern that will lead them to a prediction. (Did you get eight pairs?)

NAME ______________________________ DATE ____________________

WORKSHEET NT-8.2
Factor Pair Search

Find the specific prime factorization (s.p.f.) and its related factor pairs that are represented by each arrangement of circles shown below. Be prepared to tell how you found each factor pair.

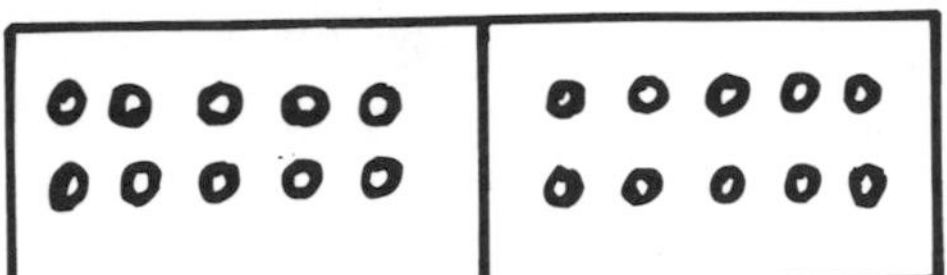

1. s.p.f. 20 = ____________________
   Related factor pairs:
   __________ __________
   __________ __________

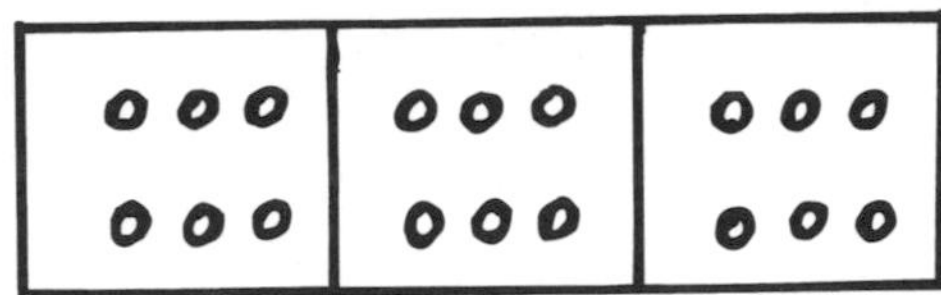

2. s.p.f. 18 = ____________________
   Related factor pairs:
   __________ __________
   __________ __________

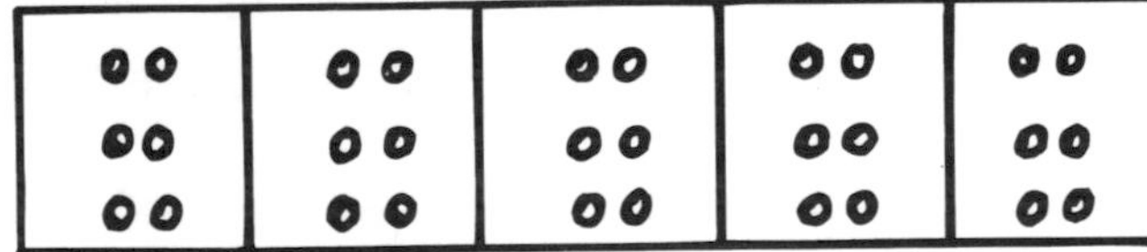

3. s.p.f. ____________________
   Related factor pairs:
   __________ __________
   __________ __________

4. s.p.f. ____________________
   Related factor pairs:
   __________ __________
   __________ __________

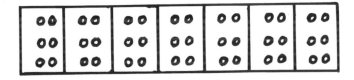

5. s.p.f. ____________________
   Related factor pairs:
   __________ __________
   __________ __________

6. s.p.f. ____________________
   Related factor pairs:
   __________ __________
   __________ __________

CHAPTER 8

ALGEBRAIC THINKING

INTRODUCTION

This chapter introduces students to algebra. Through fun activities and games, students learn to write algebraic expressions. They also learn to recognize and work with positive and negative integers. Students are shown how to use a sharing process to solve simple linear equations. In addition, they learn three basic algebraic techniques—take-away, separation, and add-on—and how to use each of these techniques.

OBJECTIVE 1: Write algebraic expressions for word phrases that reflect action in a story situation.

Activity 1: ACTING IT OUT!

(Concrete Action)

Materials: Colored one-inch cubes
Small counters

Management: Partners (30–40 minutes)

Directions:

1. Give each pair of students 6 cubes of each of two different colors and 20 small counters. Counters will be used to represent individual objects; cubes will be used to show containers of unknown amounts of objects.

2. Review the meanings of the four basic operations in terms of *action:*

- Addition is the joining together of two or more sets of objects.
- Subtraction may be the removal of objects from a given set or the finding of a missing part of a given set.
- Multiplication is the combining of several equal-sized sets of objects.
- Division is the separation of a given amount of objects into equal-sized sets.

3. Give students several different story situations that involve one or more of the above operations. Have them demonstrate the actions with their cubes and counters. Here are some possible examples:

(a) Addition: *There are 5 goldfish and several guppies in the aquarium. How many fish total are in the aquarium?* Students should place 5 counters (as "goldfish") on their desktops, then put a single cube beside them to represent the number of guppies to be joined to the 5. The number of guppies is unknown for the moment.

(b) Subtraction (removal): *Tonya had 6 bags of M&M® candies at first. She then gave 2 of the bags to Juan. If all the bags hold the same number of candies, how many candies does Tonya have now?* Partners should place 6 cubes of the same color on their desktop, then remove 2 of them. Each cube represents the unknown number of candies in one bag. Emphasize that this is all students can do at this time since they do not know the exact amount of candies per bag yet.

(c) Subtraction (missing part): *There are some marbles in a bag. Charles finds 4 more marbles. After combining all the marbles, how many does he have?* Students should place a cube on the desktop to represent the first amount of marbles in the bag, then place 4 counters beside the cube.

(d) Multiplication: *There are 5 envelopes in all. All envelopes hold the same number of coupons. How many coupons are there in all?* Students should place 5 cubes of the same color on the desktop, each cube representing the (unknown) number of coupons in one envelope.

(e) Division: *There are 6 CD storage cases full of CDs and 9 individual CDs that are to be shared equally by 3 friends. How many CDs total will each friend receive?* 6 cubes of one color should be placed on the desktop, along with 9 counters. Each cube represents the (unknown) number of CDs in one storage case; a counter is for 1 individual CD. Students should separate the cubes into 3 equal groups and also equally distribute the counters into the same 3 groups. The 2 cubes and 3 counters in one group show the CDs one friend will receive, i.e., an unknown amount of CDs in each of 2 cases plus 3 individual CDs.

(f) Addition-multiplication combination (one unknown): *Kim Lee has 3 boxes of pencils, each box containing the same amount. He has 6 extra pencils in his desk drawer. How many pencils does he have in all?* 3 cubes of the same color should be placed on the desktop to show the boxes of pencils; each cube represents the (unknown) number of pencils in one box. Then 6 counters should be placed beside the cubes to show the extra (known) amount of pencils.

(g) Addition-multiplication combination (two unknowns): *Joel has 2 packages of stickers. There are the same number of stickers in each of his packages. Sondra has 3 times as many packages as Joel. All her packages are alike, but they each hold a different amount of stickers than Joel's do. How many stickers do they have together?* Partners should put down 2 cubes of one color, e.g., red, then 3 sets of 2 cubes each or 6 cubes of the second color, e.g., blue. Each red cube represents the number of stickers in one of Joel's packages; each blue cube represents the number of stickers in one of Sondra's packages.

4. If time permits, have teams of 3–4 students create their own story situations, using known and unknown amounts. Actual numbers in the stories should be limited to the numbers of cubes and counters available to each team. Ask other students to represent the different amounts with their cubes and counters.

Activity 2: VISUALIZING UNKNOWNS IN EXPRESSIONS

(Pictorial Action)

Materials: Colored cubes and counters from Activity 1
Paper
Pencil
Colored pencils (same colors as cube colors)

Management: Partners (20–30 minutes)

Directions:

1. Give each pair of students 6 cubes each of two different colors, 20 counters, and a colored pencil for each color of cube they have.

2. Repeat the story situations described in Activity 1 (or use those created by students). Have students build the expressions with cubes and counters, then draw pictures to represent the different amounts of objects. They can use squares to represent the cubes. If two different colors of cubes are involved, they can color the squares accordingly. Small circles can be drawn for the counters.

3. Have students also write symbolic expressions for each pictorial expression. The symbols and their order should closely reflect what the students have drawn on their papers. Labels should also be used to identify the objects involved. Here are examples of pictures and symbolic expressions that might be used for the situations from Activity 1 (situations are identified by their letters in Activity 1):

(a) (5 + G) fish, G = number of guppies

○ ○ ○ ○ ○ □

(b) 6C – 2C or 4C candies, C = number of candies in one bag. Do not overemphasize the 6C-type of notation (i.e., a number beside a letter)—6C just means there are "6 of the C-amount of candies" or C + C + C + C + C + C

□ □ □ □ □ □

(c) (M + 4) marbles, M = number of marbles in bag at first

□ ○ ○ ○ ○

(d) 5C coupons, C = number of coupons in one envelope

□ □ □ □ □

(e) $\frac{(6D + 9)}{3}$ = (2D + 3) disks per person, D = number of CDs in one storage case

(f) (3P + 6) pencils, P = number of pencils in one box

(g) (2J + 6S) stickers, J = number of stickers in one of Joel's packages, S = number of stickers in one of Sondra's packages

Activity 3: MAKING SUBSTITUTIONS

(Cooperative Groups)

Materials: Colored one-inch cubes
Small counters
Paper
Pencils

Management: Teams of 4 students each (20 minutes)

Directions:

1. Give each team 4 cubes of each of 3 different colors and 50 small counters.

2. Write several algebraic expressions on the chalkboard. The expressions may involve 1–3 different unknowns (variables), and substitution values for those unknowns should be listed. Students should record the expressions and values on their own papers.

3. Team members must decide which color of cube to use for each unknown in an expression, then build that expression with the cubes and counters.

4. Students then exchange one cube at a time for its designated number of counters. After all exchanges are made, the final amount of counters should be recorded on the students' papers beside the appropriate expression. If preferred, the numerical exchanges may also be recorded.

Example: 3N + 5 + 2P = ______ when N = 4 and P = 3.

Choose the red cube for N and the blue cube for P. Keeping the order of the terms given in the expression, show 3 red cubes, 5 counters, and 2 blue cubes on the desktop.

Replace each red cube with 4 counters and each blue cube with 3 counters. Find the total shown in counters: 4 + 4 + 4 + 5 + 3 + 3 or 23 counters in all. Record 23 in the blank beside the expression. Optional recording: 3(4) + 5 + 2(3) = 23.

5. The total counters needed for each expression will be controlled by the number of counters each team has available to use (in this activity allow 50 counters per team). Students can also create their own expressions for other students to evaluate by substitutions. Here are some possible expressions to use:

N + R + 3 = ______ when N = 5 and R = 7.

P – 5 = ______ when P = 18. (Show 1 P-cube, exchange it for 18 counters, then remove 5 of the counters.)

2N + 7 = ______ when N = 8.

T + M – 9 = ______ when T = 4 and M = 15. (Show 1 T-cube and 1 M-cube at first; exchange them for counters, then remove 9 of the counters.)

P + 3B = ______ when P = 24 and B = 5.

T + W + N + 6 = ______ when T = 13, W = 9, and N = 16.

4B – B = ______ when B = 10. (Show 4 B-cubes, then remove 1 of them; replace all remaining B-cubes with 10 counters each.)

3P + 4 – P = ______ when P = 12. (First show 3 P-cubes with 4 counters, then remove 1 P-cube before replacing the remaining cubes with counters.)

2T + 3W + 2M = ______ when T = 7, W = 5, and M = 4.

4N – 2N + N – 8 = ______ when N = 3. (First show 4 N-cubes; remove 2 of them, then bring in 1 more of the N-cube before replacing all cubes with counters and removing 8 counters.)

OBJECTIVE 2: Determine the meaning of positive and negative units; order integers.

Activity 1: OPPOSITES
(Concrete Action)

Materials: Commercial algebra tiles or small counters in two colors
Paper
Pencils

Management: Partners (40–50 minutes)

Directions:

1. Give each pair of students 20 counters or tiles of each of two colors. (Various commercial counters are available; one-inch paper squares also may be used.) For convenience in our discussion here, we will use red and blue as the two colors. Red will be for positive integers and blue for negative integers.

2. Have two students stand at opposite ends of a small desk or table. Ask one student to push against the table to move it a few inches, then ask the other student to push the table, moving it in the opposite direction. Now ask both students to push against the table at the same time but in opposite directions to each other. They should try to match each other's force so that the table does not move in either direction. Discuss how both students are using force against the table, but their combined effect acts like a zero force since the table does not move. The two forces can be described as *opposites* or *inverses* of each other. When joined together (i.e., applied to the same object), they form a *zero-pair* in that they neutralize each other and produce no effect. One student's force can be called *positive one* (written as *+1*) and the other student's force, which is opposite in direction to the first force, can be called *negative one,* the *inverse of one,* or the *opposite of one* (written as *–1*). Numbers that can be used to count or measure such *opposite* forces are called *integers.*

3. Ask students to describe other pairs of actions in their daily lives that are opposites of each other. Such actions, when used together or following each other, appear to produce no change in the object they are affecting (although when done separately, each action does cause change). For example:

(1) *open* a closed door, then *close* the door again—the door finally looks like it did at the beginning

(2) *lift up* a light switch (light turns on), then *push down* the light switch—the light is off again or looks as it did at first

(3) *fold* in half, then *unfold* a sheet of paper

(4) *pick up* a book from the table, then *put down* the book on the table again

(5) *pour in* a quart of water to a bucket holding a gallon of water, then *pour out* a quart of water from the bucket—a gallon of water remains in the bucket

4. Now use the water in-water out example to help students place the integers in order. Discuss how +1 indicates that 1 cup of water has been placed in a bucket and –1 indicates that 1 cup of water has been removed from the bucket. You may even want to demonstrate these two opposite actions with real water, a cup, and a medium-sized, transparent container so that students may see how the water level in the container actually changes with each action. The size of the container should be such that the change in the water level is *visually* obvious when only *one* cup of water is added or removed. Ask: *Which action on the initial amount of water produces the higher water level in the bucket: +2 or –3?* The +2 means 2 cups of water have been added to the initial amount (water level raises); –3 means 3 cups have been removed from the initial amount (water level lowers). For many students the answer will be obvious, but we need to develop a thinking strategy here that can be applied later to more complex problems.

5. Have students show 2 red counters for +2 and 3 blue counters for –3. Whenever a red counter is brought in, this means the water level will be increased. First ask students to see if the –3 water level can be raised to the +2 level. Students can do this by bringing in a new red counter to match each of the 3 blue counters; this action represents putting 1 cup of water (red) back in the bucket to replace the 1 cup of water (blue) that has been removed. When 3 red counters have been matched to the 3 blue counters, this means that the water is *back* at its *original level* in the bucket. (Hence, –3 and +3 are *opposites* or *inverses* of each other.) So when 2 more red counters are brought in, the water reaches the +2 level. We then can say that the –3 < + 2, because the –3 water level could be *raised* to the +2 level, which shows that the +2 level is *higher* than the –3 level. (You might want to write this inequality on the chalkboard for students to record on their own papers.) Now begin again with just 2 red counters or +2. When other red counters are joined to these red counters, other positive amounts are found—not any negative amounts. Thus, the +2 water level cannot be *increased* to the –3 level; +2 will not be less than –3.

6. Give the students other integers to compare by means of the red and blue counters. For example, compare the two negatives, –1 and –4. Can the –1 level be increased to a –4 level? Students should join red counters to the 1 blue counter (–1) to first reach the 0 or initial water level, then other levels above the 0 level (i.e., positive amounts). So –1 cannot be *increased* to the –4 level; –4, however, can be increased to –1 by joining 3 red counters to the 4 blue ones. Thus, we have –1 > –4. For positive examples like + 3 and + 5, only +3 can be increased by more red counters to reach + 5, so +3 < + 5.

Activity 2: PICTURING INTEGERS

(Pictorial Action)

Materials: Paper
Pencils

Management: Partners (30 minutes)

Directions:

1. Have students draw a line segment, mark off steps on it, and label the middlemost mark as 0 (a number line without numerals except for 0).

2. Ask students to draw small circles with a large X inside each circle to represent negative integer amounts. Plain circles will represent positive integer amounts.

3. Have students draw circles for –2. Ask them to compare –2 to 0 to show which number is greater. They should draw and match plain or positive circles to the 2 negative circles until 0 is reached; only 0-pairs will be present. Two plain circles will be needed; this shows that 0 is 2 more than –2 or that –2 increased by +2 makes 0.

4. We will agree that larger numbers are to be written to the right of smaller numbers on the numberline (a mathematical tradition). Have students find a mark on their numberline that can be labeled as –2. This mark needs to be 2 *steps* (or spaces) away from 0. Since –2 < 0, the selected mark also needs to be to the *left* of the 0 mark. Have students record "–2 < 0" or "0 > –2" on their own papers.

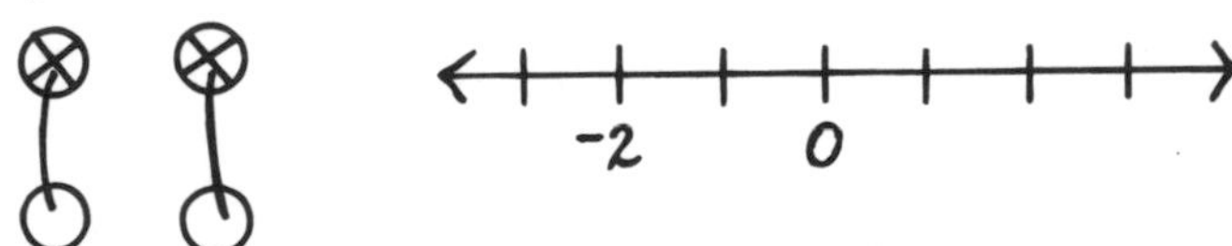

5. Have students repeat steps 3 and 4 with other randomly selected integers from –5 to +5. Randomness is necessary to prevent students from just labeling marks without regard for the meaning of the numeral names. Each integer to be located on the line must be compared to 0. When comparing a positive integer to 0, plain (positive) circles will have to be added to 0 (the absence of circles) in order to make the positive integer. Hence, each positive integer will be greater than 0 and should be placed to the right of 0 on the numberline (steps away from 0 = number of plain circles added on).

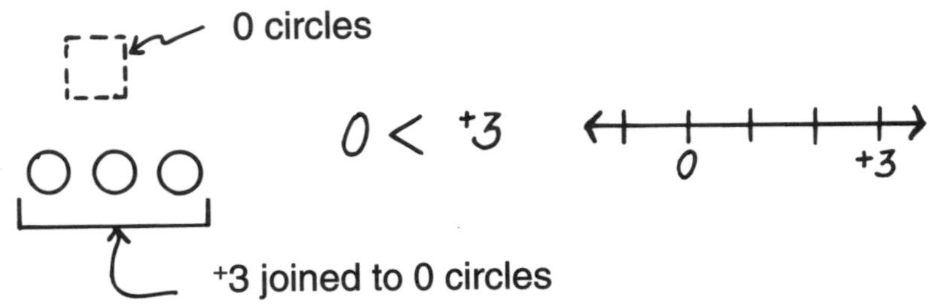

Activity 3: ORDO

(Cooperative Groups)

Materials: Sets of integer cards
(**Set description:** 32 small index cards with a different integer written on each card; randomly select numbers from –20 to +20, including 0; show each number's sign, whether + or –)

Management: Teams of 4 students each (20 minutes)

Directions:

1. Give each team a set of integer cards.

2. Students should shuffle their cards, then distribute them equally to all 4 team members. Each person's stack of cards should be placed face down on the table.

3. For each round of play, each player on the team will show his/her top card. The 4 players must then work together to place these 4 cards side by side in order left to right (as read) from smallest to largest. When they all agree, they may move the 4 ordered cards off to the side. The players may now draw the next top card from each stack and go to the next round of ordering the four new cards.

Example of a round of 4 ordered integer cards: [–15][–2][+7][+12]

4. Play continues until the stacks are gone. If time permits and the last cards have been drawn, all the cards can be reshuffled and new stacks formed in order to continue play.

OBJECTIVE 3: Apply zero-pairs in story situations that require combining of integers.

Activity 1: PAIRING UP
(Concrete Action)

Materials: Small counters (two colors)
Paper
Pencils

Management: Partners (30–40 minutes)

Directions:

1. Give each pair of students 20 counters of each of two colors. For convenience of discussion, we will use red and blue counters.

2. We will use the situation of pouring water into a bucket and removing it. Our red counter will represent 1 cup of water being added to the bucket; the blue counter will represent 1 cup of water being removed from the bucket.

3. Have students predict the outcomes (in terms of effect on water level in the bucket) and show the following situations with their counters:

(a) 1 cup in and 1 cup out (leaves water level in the bucket unchanged)—show this as 1 red counter joining to 1 blue counter to form a 0-pair; that is, together they have 0 or no effect. Record on the chalkboard: (+1) + (–1) = 0.

(b) 2 cups in and 1 more cup in (makes water amount increase by 3 cups)—show as 2 red joined to 1 red counter to make 3 red counters total. Record: (+2) + (+1) = (+3).

(c) 4 cups out and 2 more cups out (makes water amount decrease by 6 cups)—show as 4 blue joined to 2 blue counters to make 6 blue counters total. Record: (–4) + (–2) = (–6).

(d) 5 cups in and 1 cup out (makes water amount increase by 4 cups)—show 5 red joined to 1 blue counter; 1 red-blue or 0-pair can be formed, leaving 4 red counters. Record: (+5) + (–1) = (+4).

(e) 6 cups out and 5 cups in (makes water amount decrease by 1 cup)—show 6 blue with 5 red counters; 5 red-blue or 0-pairs can be formed, leaving 1 blue counter. Record: (–6) + (+5) = (–1).

4. If time permits, have students create their own water problems, then show them with the counters and record the results as number sentences.

Activity 2: DRAWING INTEGER COMBINATIONS

(Pictorial Action)

Materials: Paper
Pencil
Small counters (optional)

Management: Partners (30 minutes)

Directions:

1. Have students draw circles to show different integer situations. Use small circles with a large X inside each to show negative amounts and small plain circles to show positive amounts. Occasionally use the *water in-water out* language from Activity 1 to describe the integers being combined in an exercise. Some students may still need to work with the counters from Activity 1; this is quite acceptable. Have them show each exercise with their counters first, then draw pictures of the steps they used with their counters.

2. Begin with the combination: (–3) + (+5). Students should draw 3 negative circles and 5 positive circles, then form positive-negative pairs to make 0-pairs. 2 positive circles will be left unmatched. Record the result: (–3) + (+5) = +2.

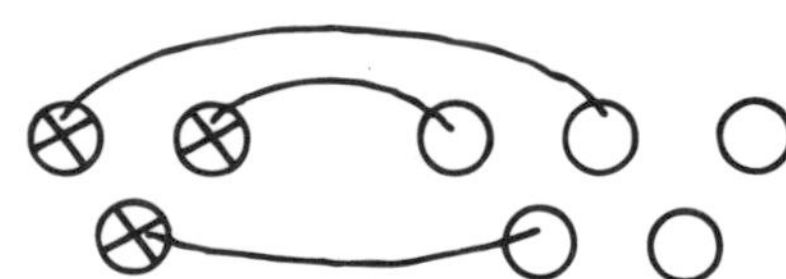

3. Write other combinations on the chalkboard for students to draw in order to solve. Number sentences can be written to record the results. Be sure to include all four (positive/negative) types. Here are some examples, one per type:

(a) (+2) + (+7) = ?

(b) (–5) + (–3) = ?

(c) (+4) + (–6) = ?

(d) (–5) + (+8) = ?

[Note: In (c) there are more negative units; in (d) there are more positive units.]

Also use exercises involving inverses like (–4) + (+4) = ?

4. After students have drawn models for at least two exercises of each type listed above, ask partners to write down any patterns they have discovered for combining or adding two integers. Have different students share their ideas with the entire class. Typical responses will be as follows:

(a) If two integers have the same sign, their amounts of units (positive or negative) are just totalled and keep that same sign.

(b) If two integers have different signs, then the two amounts of units are matched to form 0-pairs and the leftover units will have the sign of the integer representing the larger amount of units.

Allow students to develop their own wording for these relationships.

Activity 3: IS IT POSSIBLE?

(Cooperative Groups)

Materials: Small counters
Paper
Pencils

Management: Teams of 4 students each (20 minutes)

Directions:

1. Give each team 10 counters of each of two colors.

2. This activity further connects integer addition with physical experiences similar to the *water in-water out* situations used earlier. Students will be asked to determine whether or not given addition expressions correctly describe certain events.

3. Direct students to use their counters to find the overall effect of *opposite* actions. Have each pair begin with a piece of paper *already folded* in half. Ask: *If we decide that* ***positive one*** *means to fold the paper and* ***negative one*** *means to unfold the paper and we have performed 5 positive-one moves (or positive 5, +5) and 6 negative-one moves (or negative 6, –6) in all on the original folded paper, what is the final position of the paper? Let the red counter represent a positive one or folding move and the blue counter represent a negative one or unfolding move. Use 5 red counters and 6 blue counters to help you keep count of the different moves that you make on the folded paper. Each time you* ***fold*** *the paper, remove a red counter; when you* ***unfold*** *the paper, remove a blue counter.*

4. Students should experiment with their folded papers by making the two different types of moves and counting how many of each type they use. They must decide which move to make first. Have them share their findings. (Students will discover that they must start with the negative-one move or *unfolding* since the paper initially is in *folded* form. Then folding and unfolding actions alternate, ending with the final negative-one move or unfolding of the paper. The last counter removed is a blue one. Hence, the overall change to the paper is that it becomes *unfolded.* So in this example, when +5 and –6 are combined, their effect is equivalent to a single –1 move to the original folded paper. Have students record the number sentence: (+5) + (–6) = (–1.)

5. Discuss the idea that the actions represented by (+5) + (–6) were *possible* to perform on the folded paper, but what if the paper were initially unfolded? Would the integer expression still represent a possible set of actions? Ask students to repeat steps 3 and 4 with the same actions, but to apply them to an *unfolded* sheet of paper instead.

They will discover that they must *start* by *folding* the paper, which is shown by a red counter. After alternating the folding and unfolding actions a few times, students will finally remove all red counters, but have 1 blue counter left. This implies that the paper must be unfolded one more time, but it is already in an unfolded state. So the expression (+5) + (–6), as defined previously, does *not* apply to actions on an *unfolded* sheet of paper.

6. Have students now work with a book. +1 will mean to raise the book off the table and –1 will mean to lower the book back to the table. The book will initially be *resting* on the table. Ask students to test (–4) + (+5) to see if it will correctly describe actions on the book. (Yes, it will; the book will end up held by a student in a raised position above the table.) Ask students to find an expression that will work if the book initially is *raised* above the table. (Some possible examples: The expression (–3) + (+3) will leave the book raised above the table; (–4) + (+3) will leave the book resting on the table.)

OBJECTIVE 4: Apply take-away moves to constants to solve simple linear equations of the form n + a = b, where n, a, and b are positive integers.

Activity 1: WHAT'S HIDING?

(Concrete Action)

Materials: 3-ounce paper cups
Small counters (two colors)
Unlined paper (building mat)
Markers (dark colors)

Management: Partners (40–50 minutes)

Directions:

1. Give each pair of students 1 paper cup (3-ounce size), 25 counters of each of two colors, a colored marker, and a sheet of unlined paper ($8\frac{1}{2}$" × 11"). For convenience, we will refer to red counters (positive ones) and blue counters (negative ones).

2. Have students fold the paper in half from top to bottom and crease it. They should then unfold the paper and draw along the crease with a dark colored marker. This will be their building mat for this activity.

3. Students should place the mat on the desktop and turn it so that the length of the paper goes from left to right in front of them. Tell them that the mat represents a balance scale and that any counters placed on the left half must be balanced by an equal value in counters on the right. If counters are removed from one side of the balance scale, then the same amount (value) must also be removed from the other side to make the scale balanced again. If students have never worked with a 2-pan balance scale before, it will be necessary to show them a real one and to demonstrate how adding or removing objects from one or both pans affects the balancing of the pans. [*Note:* The real balance scale cannot be used to solve equations if both positive and negative integers are involved, since the counters all *weigh* the same, whether red or blue.]

4. Have them place their paper cup upside down on the left half of the mat, then hide 2 red counters under the cup. Ask how many red counters would need to be placed on the right half of the mat to balance the left side. (2) (*Note:* The paper cup is considered to have no weight.)

5. Students should now remove the 2 counters from under the cup. Discuss the idea that if the cup is on one side of the mat by itself and only 2 red counters are on the other side of the *balanced* mat, then 2 red counters must be hidden by the cup. This will be the basic strategy for finding hidden amounts of counters.

6. Ask them to place the cup and 3 red counters (+3) on the left side of the mat. (In later exercises the cup will be placed on the right side instead.) The counters will be beside the cup this time. Have them also place 8 red counters (+8) on the right side. Ask: *How many counters must be hidden under the cup, so that when they are combined with the 3 red counters, they will balance or equal the 8 red counters? Will the hidden counters be red or blue (i.e., positive or negative)? Decide and be ready to share your reasons with the class.*

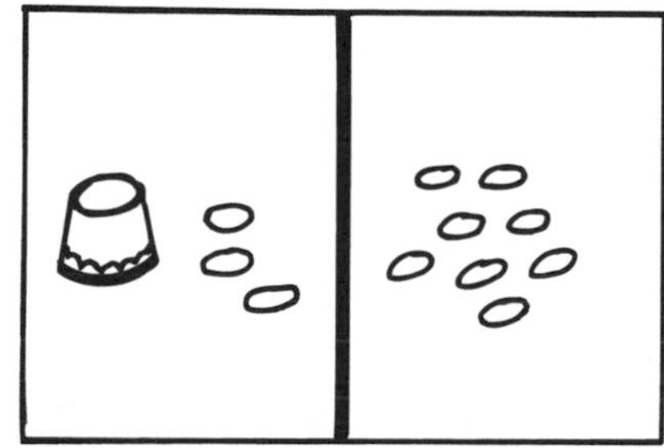

7. Have different students share their answers and methods. At this point many will just use a mental *trial-and-error* strategy. Since the main strategy being emphasized is to have the cup on one side of the scale balancing with only counters on the other side, guide students to remove the +3 from the left side, then repeat the process on the right side to keep the pans balanced. (Instead of removing +3 from the right side, some students will try to add +3 back to the left side in order to rebalance the scale; this just takes them back to where they started and does not help them find what is under the cup.) The cup is now alone on the left, and 5 red counters are on the right. So 5 red counters must also be hidden under the cup.

8. To confirm this, have students place 5 red counters under the cup, put 3 more red counters beside the cup, and place 8 red counters on the right side again. Ask them to remove the cup, leaving the 5 red counters in place, and look at the amounts (or values) of counters on both sides of the scale. Both sides of the scale contain 8 red counters, so the scale is balanced. Thus, 5 red counters is the correct answer for the amount hidden under the cup. This process of confirming the answer should be used with every equation solved by the students in this activity.

9. Write the following number sentences and expressions on the chalkboard to describe the steps used by the students:

$$\begin{array}{lcll} P + (+3) & = & +8 & \text{(P = amount of counters in cup)} \\ \underline{-(+3)} & & \underline{-(+3)} & \text{(3 red counters taken away)} \\ P & = & +5 & \text{(Cup is hiding 5 red counters.)} \end{array}$$

This notation has *not* been used to solve the equation for P; it only reflects what work has already been *done* to find the answer. Students must become comfortable with the *meanings* of different symbols before they begin to work with the symbols themselves.

10. Some students may solve the above equation by reasoning that the +3 beside the cup indicates that 3 objects have been *added on* to the cup's amount; therefore, the *opposite* action needs to be taken. This can be shown by combining the +3 with –3, as in the *water in-water out* activity. 3 blue counters will be combined with the 3 red counters on the left side of the mat. Since counters have been added to the left, *like* counters must be added to the right to maintain the balance. 3 blue counters are thus added to the 8 red counters on the right. Three 0-pairs will be formed on the left. Since 0-pairs have no effect on the overall action, they can be removed from the balance scale, leaving the cup on the left side by itself. The 8 red and 3 blue counters will join to form three 0-pairs also; these pairs can be removed, leaving 5 red counters on the right side. Once again the cup balances with 5 red counters, so the cup must be hiding 5 red counters in order to balance the scale. This approach can be recorded as follows:

$$\begin{array}{lcl} P + (+3) & = & +8 \\ \underline{+\,(-3)} & & \underline{+\,(-3)} \\ P & = & +5 \end{array}$$

(opposite action of +3 is used to return to P alone)

11. Now give the students other equations to solve for P, that is, to find how many red counters are hidden under the cup. Include some where P is on the right side of the equation. Have students confirm their answers (see step 8 for method to use). Here are some examples of equations to use:

P + (+2) = +6	P + (+5) = +12	+9 = P + (+9)
P + (+8) = +9	(+4) + P = +10	+12 = (+2) + P
+10 = (+7) + P	+11 = P + (+3)	(+5) + P = +5

12. Have various students share their results and encourage some of them to write number sentences on the board in order to record the steps they used. Note that in this activity we are only using positive integers for P since the focus is on the take-away method.

Activity 2: DRAW AND BALANCE

(Pictorial Action)

Materials: Paper
Pencils
Red pencils
Building mats from Activity 1 (optional)
Paper cups (optional)
Counters (optional)

Management: Partners (30 minutes)

Directions:

1. Some students may still need to work with the cup and counters on the building mat. This is quite acceptable. Have them first build each equation to solve it, then draw pictures to show the steps they used.

2. Have students draw the following diagram in regular pencil to represent the equation:

P + (+4) = +7.

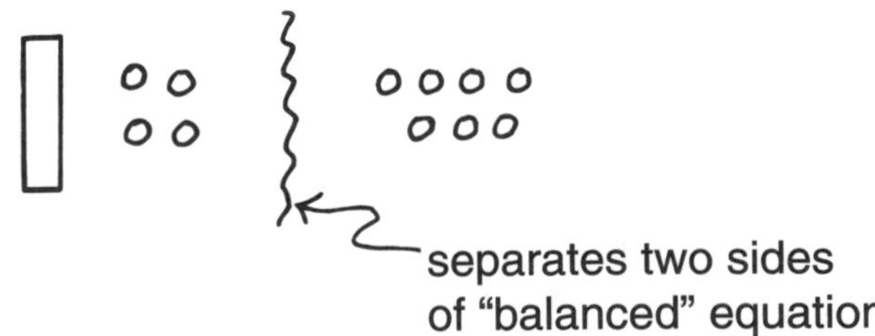

3. Ask students what the basic strategy is for finding the amount of counters hidden under the paper cup, which is represented by the rectangle. (The unknown, P—the paper cup—needs to be isolated on one side with only counters on the other side.) Ask them how to get rid of the counters on the left side. (Just mark through the 4 circles.)

4. Now that the counters have been removed from the left side, the scale is out of balance. Ask students to find a way to rebalance the scale (or equation). (They should mark out 4 counters on the right side.)

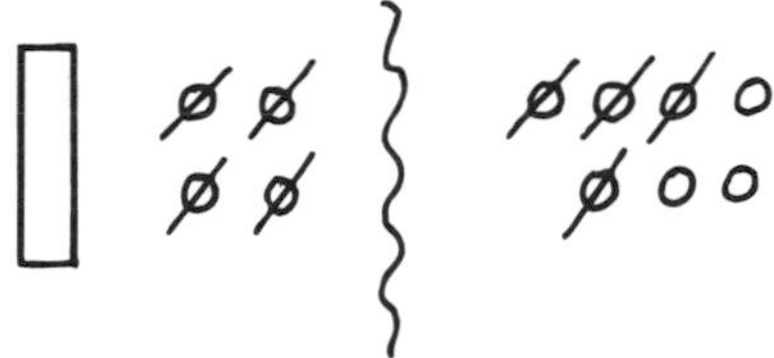

5. The rectangle is on the left side and 3 circles remain on the right. This tells us that our unknown P (the amount hidden under the cup) must be +3. Have students confirm this by redrawing the original diagram, replacing the rectangle with 3 circles drawn in red pencil. The original circles will still be drawn in regular pencil. There will now be 7 circles total on each side, indicating a balance. So +3 is the correct solution.

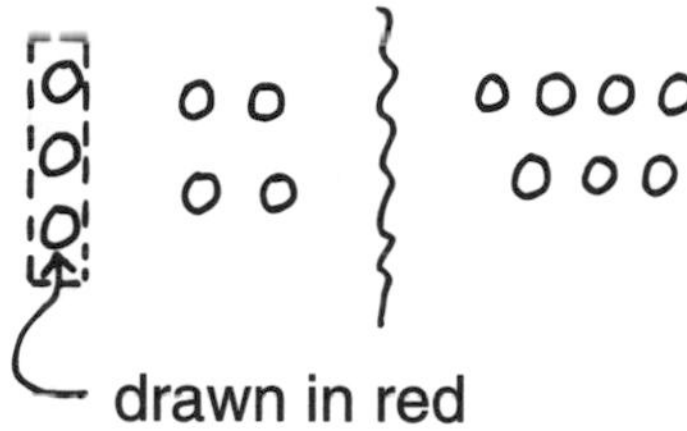

6. Have students record their steps in symbols as follows:

$$\begin{array}{lcr} P + (+4) & = & +7 \\ \underline{\quad -(+4)} & & \underline{-(+4)} \\ P & = & +3 \end{array}$$

7. If some students want to use the opposites method used in step 10 of Activity 1, they can draw circles with X's inside to represent the blue counters, then connect them to the plain circles to form 0-pairs. See the following diagram and numerical recording.

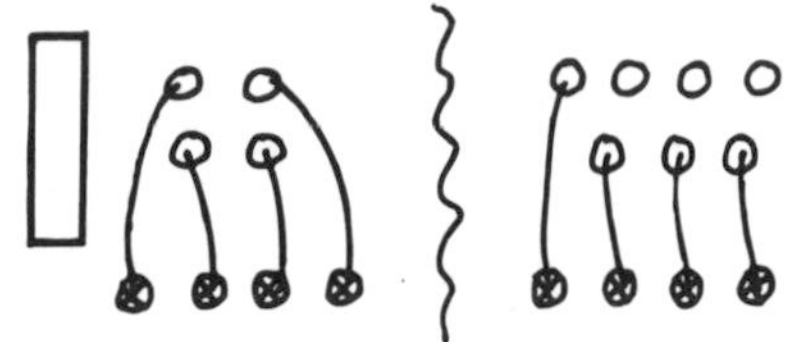

Recording:

$$\begin{array}{rcl} P + (+4) & = & +7 \\ \underline{+(-4)} & & \underline{+(-4)} \\ P & = & +3 \end{array}$$

8. Write other equations on the board for students to draw in order to solve. Include some where the unknown, P, is on the right side of the equation. Students should confirm each solution by redrawing the original diagram, replacing the rectangle with the solution circles. Have them also record their steps with symbols (i.e., letters and numerals). Ask several students to explain what the different written steps in symbols represent with regard to the different stages of their drawing for the same equation. Here are some possible examples to use:

$P + (+3) = +9$	$(+5) + P = +17$	$+10 = P + (+10)$
$+10 = (+7) + P$	$+11 = P + (+9)$	$(+8) + P = +8$
$P + (+5) = +13$	$+15 = (+10) + P$	$P + (+9) = +16$

Activity 3: EQUATION BASHING: TAKE-AWAY MOVES

(Cooperative Groups)

Materials: Paper cups
Counters
Building mats from Activity 1
Paper
Pencil

Management: Teams of 4 students each (20 minutes)

Directions:

1. Give each team a paper cup, a building mat, and the set of counters from Activity 1. If no students have used the opposites approach in Activities 1 and 2, only one color of counter will be needed here.

2. On each team one pair of members will play against the other pair. On each turn, one pair will set up an equation on the building mat, using the cup and positive counters. The amount of positive counters on the side with the cup should always be less than the amount of positive counters alone on the other side of the mat.

3. The second pair will then remove counters from the mat in order to solve for the value of the cup, that is, the amount of counters hidden under the cup that are needed to balance the equation. They will also write the numerical steps that describe what they did with the counters and cup.

4. The first pair will rebuild the original equation, then replace the cup with the number of counters found as the solution in order to confirm that the second pair's solution will keep the scale balanced. After the substitution, the total number of counters should be the same on both sides of the mat.

5. The second pair now builds an equation on the mat for the first pair of team members to solve and the next turn begins.

6. Play may continue as long as time permits.

OBJECTIVE 5: Apply separation moves to solve simple linear equations of the form kn = b where n, b, and k are positive integers.

Activity 1: FAIR SHARES

(Concrete Action)

Materials: Small counters
Building mats
3-ounce paper cups
Paper
Pencils

Management: Partners (30–40 minutes)

Directions:

1. Give each pair of students 5 paper cups (3-ounce size), a building mat (use mats from Objective 4, Activity 1), and 30 counters of one color. All counters will be considered as positive ones in this activity.

2. Have students place 3 paper cups upside down on the left half of the mat and place 6 counters on the right half. Discuss the idea that all the cups are the same, so each cup must have the same number of counters hidden under it.

3. Ask: *If the same amount is hidden under each cup and the total amount from the cups balances with the +6 on the right side of the scale, how many counters must be under each cup?* Students should place 6 other counters on the left side and try to distribute them to the 3 cups until the same number of counters (+2) is under each cup. Some will recognize this sharing situation as that of division and will know immediately that 6 objects shared 3 ways will result in 2 objects per share (or cup); they will just place 2 counters under each cup without experimenting.

4. Remind students that in this type of sharing process we want to know how many objects will be in *each* share. We want to know how many counters will be hidden under just *one* cup. So the answer is +2, or 2 counters per cup. Write the following number sentence on the board: 3P = +6, so P = +2.

5. Now have students place 4 cups on the right side of the mat and 12 counters on the left side. Students should separate the 4 cups from each other and line them up along the vertical line segment drawn on the mat. Since the cups have been separated into 4 distinct *equal groups,* the 12 counters on the left must also be separated into 4 distinct equal groups. Students can line up each group of counters beside a paper cup. This procedure will indicate how many counters must be hidden under each cup. On the board write the sentence: +12 = 4P, so +3 = P. Note that we are recording the sentences in the same left-right order in which they were built on the mat. Discuss the idea that +3 = P can also be written as P = +3.

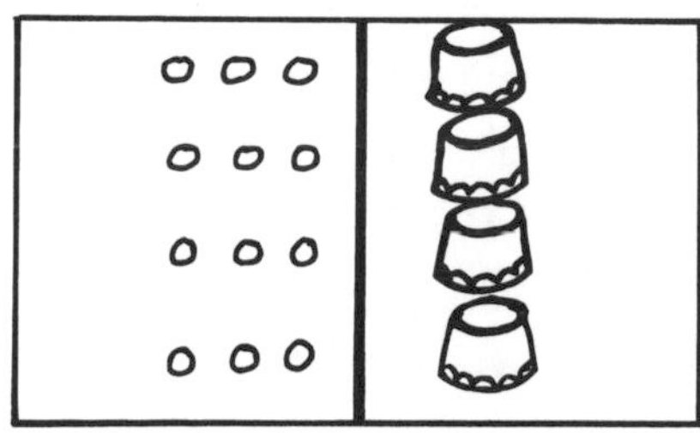

6. Have students confirm their solution of +3 by replacing each cup on the mat with 3 counters. The total number of counters on the right side of the mat should equal the total number of counters on the left side. Therefore, the solution of +3 is correct.

7. Now write several other equations on the board for the students to build on their mats, then solve by applying the *separation* process. Have them record number sentences for each equation and its result on their own paper. Remind them to confirm each solution found. Here are some possible equations to use:

2P = +10	5P = +15	+15 = 3P
+8 = 4P	2P = +14	+5 = 5P
2P = +12	+9 = 3P	4P = +4

Activity 2: PICTURING SHARES

(Pictorial Action)

Materials: Paper
Pencils
Red pencils
Building mats (optional)
Paper cups (optional)
Counters (optional)

Management: Partners (30 minutes)

Directions:

1. Some students may still need or want to work with the counters and cups on the mat; this is quite acceptable. Just have them build with the materials first, then draw a diagram of the construction steps they used. This time, however, they will need 9 paper cups in order to build some of the equations suggested in step 6. We will use tall rectangles to represent the cups and small circles to represent the positive counters.

2. First have students set up the equation, 3P = +12, by drawing the following diagram on their own papers:

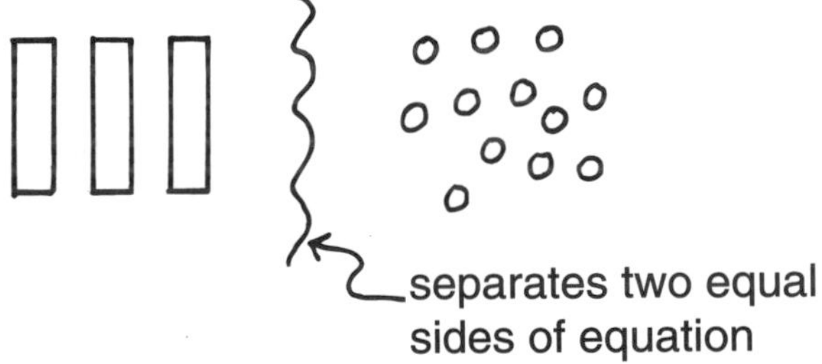

3. Now have them redraw the equation in a new diagram that shows the cups or rectangles separated and rotated (to save space) and the counters or small circles separated into 3 equal groups and lined up with the rectangles. A ring should be drawn around one row of figures to show the solution.

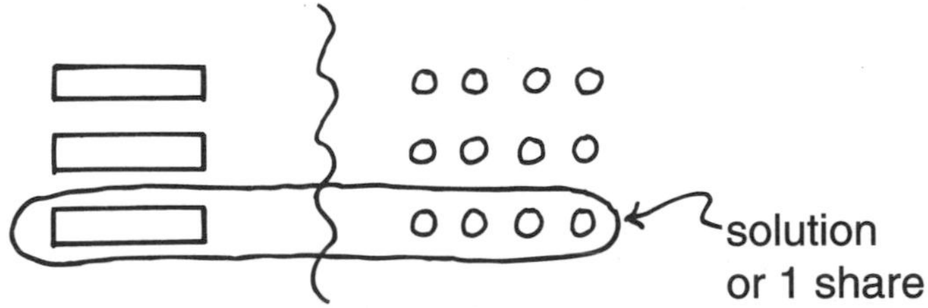

4. Have students record their steps in symbols with three separate sentences as shown below. The second number sentence should be recorded separately from the original equation in order to focus attention on the division or separation or sharing in equal groups that is occurring on both sides of the equation.

$$3P = +12 \quad \frac{3P}{3} = \frac{+12}{3} \quad P = +4$$

5. Students should confirm +4 as the solution for P by drawing 4 small circles in red pencil over each rectangle in the second diagram. The total circles in regular pencil or red pencil appearing on the left side of the diagram should equal the total circles shown on the right side. This test should be recorded as follows: TEST—3(+4) = +12.

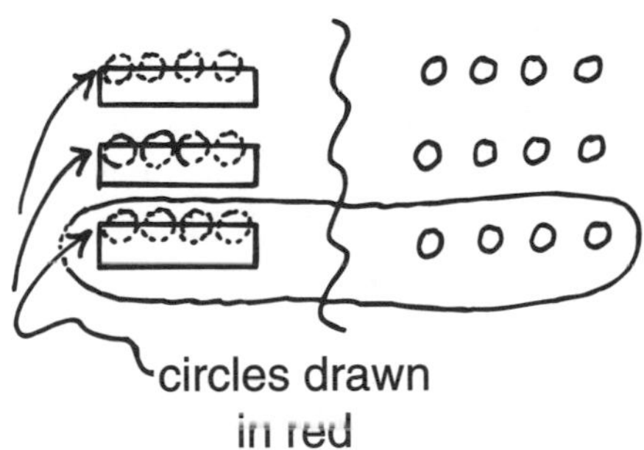

6. Now write other equations on the board for students to solve by drawing diagrams. Each exercise should be recorded with three number sentences, the third sentence indicating the solution for P (or the amount of counters hidden under each cup). Each solution should also be confirmed on its diagram and a number sentence written to record the TEST made. Here are some possible equations to use:

6P = +18	8P = +24	+16 = 2P
+25 = 5P	7P = +14	9P = +9
+15 = 3P	+20 = 5P	4P = +8

Activity 3: NAME CHANGING

(Cooperative Groups)

Materials: Paper
Pencils
Colored markers (optional)

Management: Teams of 4 students each (20–30 minutes)

Directions:

1. Give each team one or two different equations that involve the *separation* process. Other letters besides P will be used for the unknowns in this activity.

2. Students are to create a story problem to go with each equation. The name of the real object selected to be used in a story should begin with the letter given in the equation as the unknown. If preferred, students might also draw and color illustrations for their story problems.

3. After each team has created one or two story problems, they will exchange only their story problems (no equations or unknowns given) with another team, who will have to determine the correct equation and unknown to use for each problem, then solve the equation and describe the result. Solutions will be shared with the entire class in order to be checked for accuracy. The letter used for each unknown by the solving team might also be compared to the one originally used by the writing team; the letters may differ since the writing team will not have revealed their chosen letter in the story problem. Example of an equation and its story problem:

> 8K = +72 "Eight kangaroos went for a hop together. They spied a big patch of giant kuckaberries. Being quite hungry, they worked together to pick 72 kuckaberries in all, then shared them equally with each other. That helped some of the taller ones, who found it difficult to reach down to the low bushes. How many delicious kuckaberries did each fortunate kangaroo get to eat?" (K = number of kuckaberries per animal)

4. Here are some possible equations to use for this activity:

14G = +56	20J = +80	19M = +57	11B = +99
8T = +96	40A = +200	7E = +63	25H = +125
22N = +88	13K = +91	12V = +144	50C = +350

OBJECTIVE 6: Apply add-on moves to solve simple linear equations of the form n + (–a) = b where n, a, and b are positive integers.

Activity 1: PUT IT BACK!

(Concrete Action)

Materials: 3-ounce paper cups
Small counters (two colors)
Building mats (from Objective 4, Activity 1)

Management: Partners (30–40 minutes)

Directions:

1. Give each pair of students 1 paper cup (3-ounce size), a building mat, and 20 counters of each of two colors. We will use a red counter as positive one (+1) and a blue counter as negative one (–1) for the purpose of discussion here.

2. Have students place the paper cup upside down on the left side of the building mat (or "balance scale"). To show that the amount of counters hidden under the cup has been decreased by 3, have them place 3 blue counters (–3) beside the cup. This is similar to the actions used in the *water in-water out* examples discussed in Objectives 2 and 3. 5 red counters (+5) should be placed on the right side of the mat.

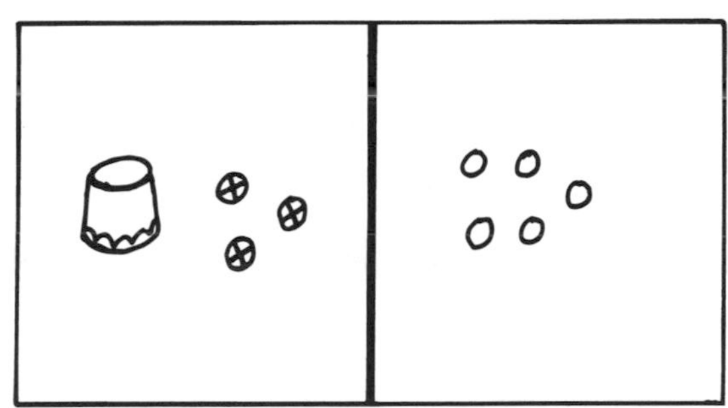

3. Ask: *If the red counters hidden under the cup have had 3 red counters removed from them (as shown by the 3 blue counters outside the cup) and the difference now balances with the 5 red counters on the other side, how can we find out how many red counters were originally under the cup?*

4. Allow students time to experiment with the problem, then have them share their ideas with the class. Hopefully, they will suggest that since 3 red counters were removed from the left side earlier, those 3 counters need to be replaced (like replacing 3 cups of water that have been removed from a bucket of water). Once these 3 are replaced on the left side of the scale, the amount there should represent only what was under the cup originally. This replacing can be shown by placing 3 new red counters on the left side beside the cup and 3 blue counters. The red and blue counters now pair up to form

0-pairs, so they can be removed from the scale, leaving only the cup on the left side. To keep the scale balanced, however, 3 red counters must also be added to the right side.

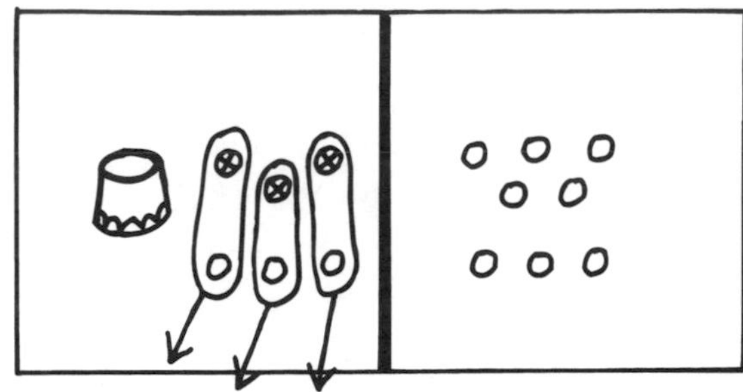

5. The mat now has 1 cup on the left and 8 red counters (+8) on the right. Hence, 8 red counters must have been hiding under the cup originally. Have students confirm this by building the original problem on the mat again, then replacing the cup with 8 red counters. After 0-pairs are formed and removed, there will be 5 red counters remaining on both sides of the scale. Thus, +8 is a correct solution for the original problem.

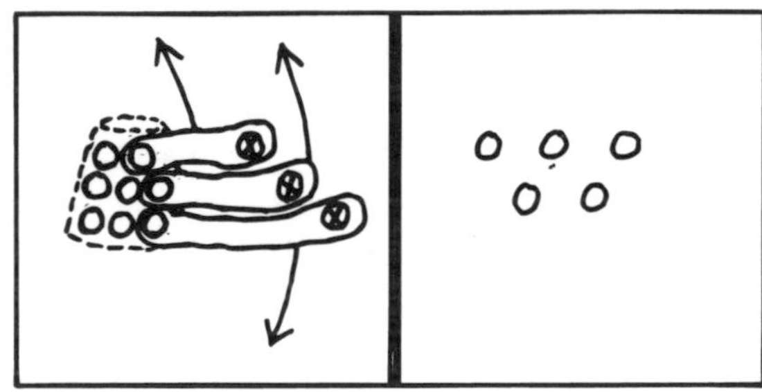

6. Write the following number sentences and expressions on the chalkboard to describe how the problem was solved:

$$\begin{array}{lcl} P + (-3) & = & +5 \quad \text{(P = amount of red counters hidden under cup)} \\ \underline{\quad + (+3)} & & \underline{+ (+3)} \quad \text{(3 red counters added to restore original amount of P)} \\ P & = & +8 \quad \text{(8 red counters were hidden under cup)} \end{array}$$

7. Now have students build other equations on their mats and try to solve them, using the *add-on* approach. Be sure to include some equations with the unknown P on the right side. Students should confirm each solution they find for P. P will always be positive in this activity. Here are some possible equations to use:

$P + (-5) = +2$ $\quad$ $P + (-2) = +1$ $\quad$ $+7 = P + (-6)$

$(-3) + P = +8$ $\quad$ $+4 = P + (-4)$ $\quad$ $P + (-7) = +3$

$+4 = (-8) + P$ $\quad$ $(-9) + P = +5$ $\quad$ $+5 = (-1) + P$

8. Encourage several students to try to write number sentences on the board to show the steps they used in solving some of their equations.

Activity 2: ADDING ON

(Pictorial Action)

Materials: Paper
Pencils
Red pencils
Counters (optional)
Paper cups (optional)
Building mats (optional, from Objective 4, Activity 1)

Management: Partners (30 minutes)

Directions:

1. Some students may still need or want to use the counters and cups; this is acceptable. Have them first build the equations and solve them, then draw diagrams of the steps they used.

2. We will use tall rectangles to represent the cup and small circles to represent the counters. Plain circles will be positive counters and circles with X's will be negative counters. Have students draw the following diagram to show the equation: P + (–5) = +3.

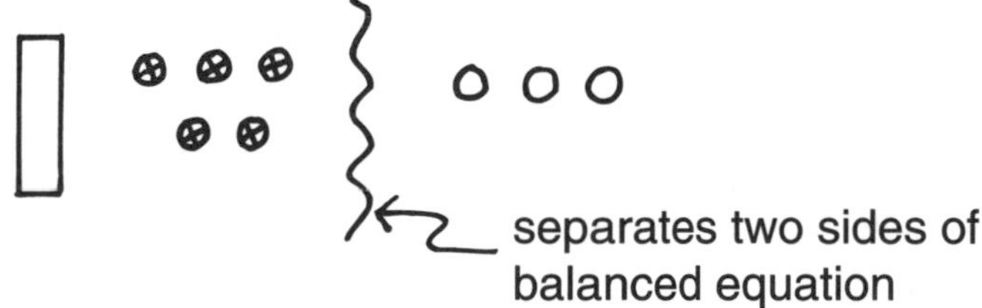

3. Ask: *How can we show that we are replacing the 5 positive counters that have been removed from the cup P?* Have students draw 5 plain (positive) circles below the 5 negative circles on the left side of the diagram. Ask: *Since we have added 5 counters on the left, how can we restore the balance of the scale?* Students should draw 5 plain circles on the right side of the diagram also.

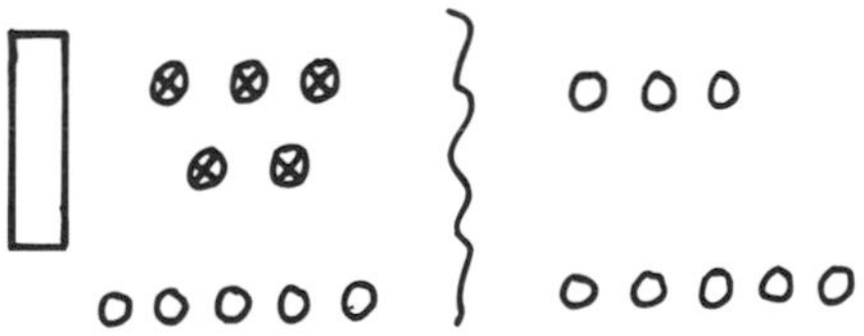

4. Students should now connect positive and negative counters together in pairs. Since these pairs are 0-pairs, they have no effect on the rectangle (or unknown). Thus, the rectangle on the left balances with the 8 positive counters on the right. The unknown P must equal +8.

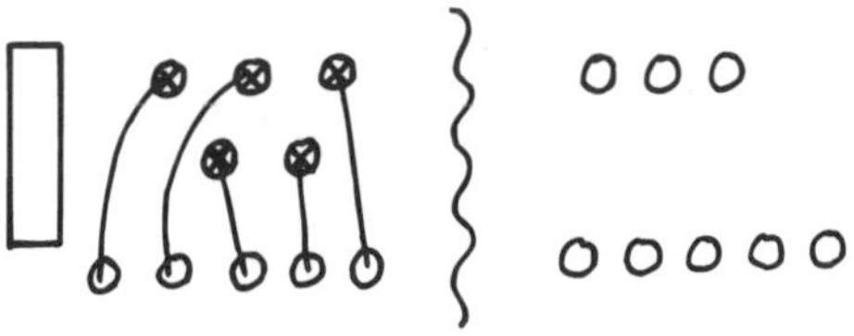

5. Have students confirm +8 as the solution by redrawing the original diagram for the equation, replacing the rectangle with 8 positive (plain) circles drawn in red pencil. The original circles will still be drawn in regular pencil. There will be 8 positive circles and 5 negative circles on the left of the diagram and 3 positive circles on the right. After 0-pairs are formed, 3 positive circles will remain on each side. So +8 is the correct solution.

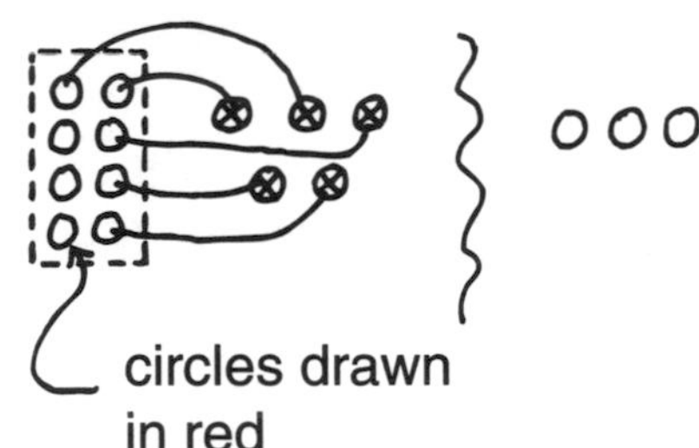

6. Have students record their steps with the following number sentences and expressions:

$$\begin{array}{lcr} P + (-5) & = & +3 \\ \underline{+ (+5)} & & \underline{+(+5)} \\ P & = & +8 \end{array}$$

7. Write other equations on the board for students to draw in order to solve. Include some where the unknown, P, is on the right side of the equation. Students should confirm each solution by redrawing the original diagram, replacing the rectangle with red solution circles. Have them also record their steps with symbols (i.e., letters and numerals). Ask several students to explain what the different written steps in symbols represent with regard to the different stages of their drawing for the same equation. Here are some possible examples to use:

P + (–3) = +9	(–5) + P = +8	+3 = P + (–10)
+13 = (–7) + P	+11 = P + (–9)	(–8) + P = +8
P + (–2) = +12	+14 = (–6) + P	P + (–9) = +5

Activity 3: EQUATION BASHING: ADD-ON MOVES

(Cooperative Groups)

Materials: Paper cups
Counters
Building mats (from Objective 4, Activity 1)
Paper
Pencil

Management: Teams of 4 students each (20 minutes)

Directions:

1. Give each team a paper cup, a building mat, and the set of counters from Activity 1.

2. On each team one pair of members will play against the other pair. On each turn, one pair will set up an equation on the building mat, using the cup and counters. Negative counters should always be placed on the side with the cup and only positive counters should be placed on the other side of the mat. Equation selection will be determined by the number of counters available.

3. The second pair will then place extra positive counters on the mat in order to solve for the *value* of the cup, that is, the amount of counters hidden under the cup that are needed to balance the equation. They will also write the numerical steps that describe what they did with the counters and cup.

4. The first pair will rebuild the original equation and replace the cup with the number of counters found as the solution in order to confirm that the second pair's solution will keep the scale balanced. The total number of counters should be the same on both sides of the mat after 0-pairs are formed and removed.

5. The second pair now builds an equation on the mat for the first pair of team members to solve and the next turn begins.

6. Play may continue as long as time permits.

OBJECTIVE 7: Apply take-away moves to variables to solve simple linear equations where the variable appears on both sides of the equation; the variable may also appear in more than one term on the same side of the equation.

Activity 1: BALANCING UNKNOWNS

(Concrete Action)

Materials: Small counters
3-ounce paper cups
Building mats (from Objective 4, Activity 1)

Management: Partners (30–40 minutes)

Directions:

1. Give each pair of students 8 paper cups (3-ounce size), a building mat, and 30 small counters in one color. We will use red in our discussion for positive counters.

2. Have students place 3 paper cups on the left side of their building mat and 2 paper cups and 4 red (positive) counters on the right side.

3. Ask: *What do we know about the amount of red counters hidden under each paper cup?* (Each cup hides the same amount.) *If we remove 1 cup (and the counters under it) from the left side, what can we remove from the right side in order to rebalance the scale? How can we be sure we have removed the same amount from both sides?* (We do not know *how much* is under each cup, but we do know that the *same amount* is under every cup. Thus, if we remove a cup from both sides, the same amount, whatever that may be, has been removed from both sides.)

4. Have students apply this method as often as possible. They should remove a total of 2 cups from each side, leaving 1 cup on the left and 4 positive counters on the right. Hence, there must be 4 red counters hidden under each cup.

5. Have students confirm +4 as the solution by rebuilding the original equation, then replacing each cup with 4 counters. A total of +12 should appear on each side of the mat. Therefore, +4 is the correct solution.

6. Write the steps used as equations and expressions on the chalkboard:

$$\begin{array}{rcrl} 3P & = & 2P+(+4) & \text{(P = amount of red counters hidden under cup)} \\ \underline{-(2P)} & & \underline{-(2P)\quad\;\;} & \text{(2 cups of counters removed from both sides)} \\ P & = & +4 & \text{(4 positive counters hidden under cup)} \end{array}$$

7. Discuss the idea that if the 4 counters in this exercise had been placed on the mat *between* the 2 paper cups, the following might have been recorded instead (actual position of objects on mat and the symbolic notation for them should be as closely correlated as is reasonable; when 2 separate cups exist, they may be recorded as P + P or combined as 2P):

$$\begin{array}{rcl} 3P & = & P+(+4)+P \\ \underline{-(2P)} & & \underline{-P \qquad\quad -P} \\ P & = & +4 \end{array}$$

8. Now have students build other similar equations and apply the take-away approach to the unknowns in order to find solutions. They should also confirm their solutions by rebuilding each equation on the mat, then replacing each cup with their proposed amount of counters. Both sides of the mat should hold the same number of counters if the solution is correct. Include some equations where, after several unknowns have been removed from both sides, the separation method of Objective 5 will have to be applied to the remaining unknowns. Here are some possible equations to use:

4P = 3P + (+1)	(+6) + P = 2P	2P + 3P = P + (+12)
2P + (+2) + P = 4P	P + (+3) = 4P	(+7) + P = 2P
3P = (+5) + 2P	4P = P + (+6) + P	P + (+10) = 6P

9. Encourage several students to try to write equations and expressions on the board that will describe the steps they used to solve some of their equations and also to explain orally what actual steps were taken.

Activity 2: TAKING OUT PARTNERS

(Pictorial Action)

Materials: Paper
Pencils
Red pencils
Paper cups (optional)
Counters (optional)
Building mats (from Objective 4, Activity 1—optional)

Management: Partners (30 minutes)

Directions:

1. Some students may still need or want to work with the paper cups and counters; this is quite acceptable. Have them first build each equation and solve it, then draw a diagram of the steps taken.

2. As in previous activities, we will use tall rectangles for the unknowns and small circles for the positive counters.

3. Have students draw a diagram to show the equation: 3P + (+3) = 4P.

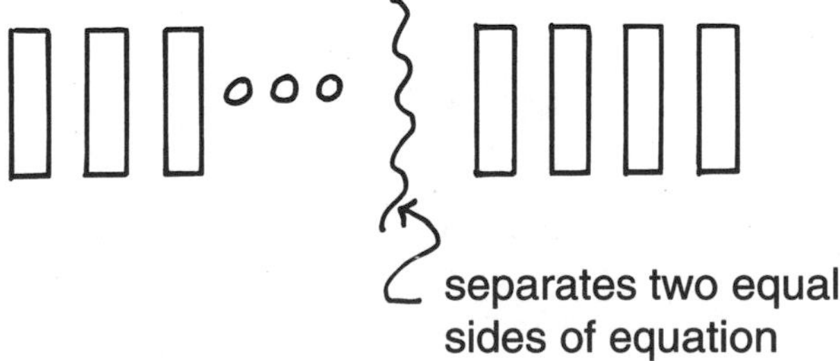

4. Ask: *What do we know about the amount of counters represented by each rectangle (or the amount hidden under each cup)?* (All rectangles represent the same amount of counters.) Have students mark out one rectangle on the left side of the diagram. Ask:

Now that one rectangle (i.e., a set of counters) has been removed, how can we rebalance the scale or equation? (Mark out one rectangle from the right side.) Have students continue to mark out matching (*partner*) rectangles from both sides until no more such partners exist.

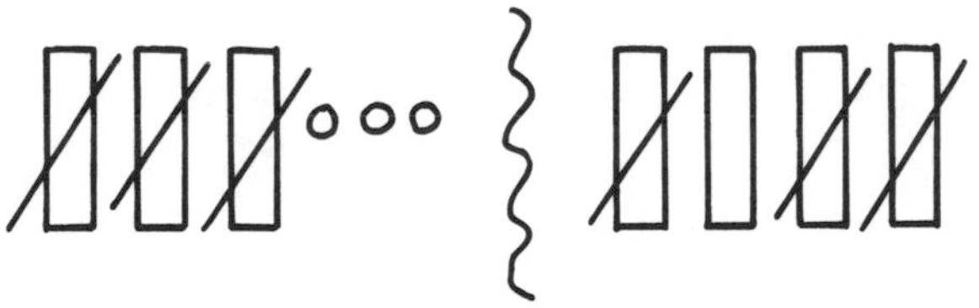

5. The diagram now shows the solution as +3 = P. Have students confirm their solution by redrawing the diagram for the original equation, replacing each rectangle with 3 small circles drawn in red pencil. The original 3 circles will still be drawn in regular pencil. The total circles or counters seen on each side of the equation should be the same.

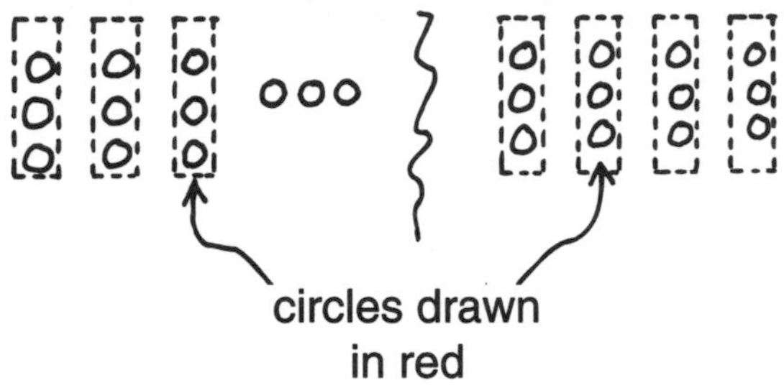

circles drawn in red

6. Have students record their steps with symbols:

$$\begin{array}{rcl} 3P & +(+3) = & 4P \\ \underline{-(3P)} & & \underline{-(3P)} \\ & +3 = & P \end{array}$$

7. Now write other equations on the board for students to solve by drawing diagrams. They should also confirm that their solutions are correct by replacing rectangles with red solution circles in their diagrams. Finally, they should record the steps they used with symbols. Be sure to include equations that have the unknown in more than one term on the same side of the equation. After all partner pairs of unknowns are removed, some equations might also require the separation approach used in Objective 5. Here are some possible equations to use:

4P = 3P + (+3)	(+3) + 2P = 4P + P	2P = P + (+7)
P + (+6) + 2P = 4P	P + (+6) = 4P	(+12) + P = 5P
3P = P + (+5) + P	4P = 2P + (+8)	P + (+10) = 2P + 4P

Activity 3: EQUATION CHALLENGE

(Cooperative Groups)

Materials: Index cards with an equation written on each card
Paper
Pencils

Management: Teams of 4 students each (20–30 minutes)

Directions:

1. Give each team 3 index cards. Each card should contain an equation like those suggested in Activities 1 and 2. However, other letters besides P should now be used for the unknowns.

2. Team members should work together to solve each of their equations, using only symbolic steps. If necessary, they may draw diagrams to justify their symbolic work. They should also confirm each solution they find. Here is a possible example (step sequence is not unique):

$$3G + (+12) = 2G + 4G$$
$$\underline{-(3G)} \qquad \underline{-(2G) - G} \quad \text{(Remove 3 unknowns from both sides.)}$$
$$+12 = 3G$$
$$\frac{+12}{3} = \frac{3G}{3} \quad \text{(Separate to find one unknown.)}$$

So +4 = G is the solution.

Another way students might record this equation is as follows:

$$3G + (+12) = 2G + 4G$$
$$\underline{-(3G)} \qquad \underline{-G - (2G)}$$
$$+12 = G + 2G$$
$$+12 = 3G \quad \text{(G's combined by simply recounting unknowns)}$$
$$\frac{+12}{3} = \frac{3G}{3}$$

So +4 = G is the solution.

Test the solution: $3(+4) + (+12) = 2(+4) + 4(+4)$

$$(+12) + (+12) = (+8) + (+16)$$

$+24 = +24$ True; therefore, G = +4 is correct.

3. After teams have completed their equations, have them share their steps or moves for solving one of the equations with the entire class. Encourage students to explain their procedures verbally and not just write the symbolic steps on the board. One team member might explain the take-away moves; another, the separation moves; and a third member, the testing process for the same equation.

4. Here are some possible equations to use (along with those already listed in Activities 1 and 2):

$5M + (+21) = 8M$	$7W = (+14) + 6W$	$B + (+18) = 3B$
$6J = J + (+24) + J$	$3N + (+15) + N = 9N$	$20A = (+50) + 10A$
$10R = 9R + (+17)$	$2X + 2X + (+32) = 12X$	$19C = 8C + (+56) + 3C$

OBJECTIVE 8: Apply combinations of the add-on (constants only), take-away, and separation moves to solve simple linear equations.

Activity 1: MAKING IT RIGHT!
(Concrete Action)

Materials: 3-ounce paper cups
Small counters
Building mats (from Objective 4, Activity 1)

Management: Teams of 4 students each (30–40 minutes)

Directions:

1. Give each team 8 paper cups, 20 counters of each of two colors, and a building mat. We will use a red counter for +1 and a blue counter for –1 for ease of discussion. A paper cup will represent each variable.

2. Have each team build the equation, 3P + (+4) = P + (+7). Ask them to try to solve the equation by using take-away, separation, or add-on (constants only) moves as needed. If a *positive integer* cannot be found for the solution (the solution for this equation is +3/2), ask the team members to *change* the original equation in some way(s) (by increasing/decreasing the amount of counters and/or cups) until they have a new equation whose solution will be a *positive integer*.

3. Many new equations will be possible, limited only by the number of paper cups and counters that are available. Have different teams share their results with the entire class. Ask other teams to build the team-proposed equations and solve them to confirm that the solutions are indeed positive integers.

4. As time permits, give the teams other equations to build, try to solve (but fail), then change, rebuild, and solve. In each case, have a few teams share their new equations for others to confirm. Here are some possible equations to try:

5P + (–2) = P + (+5) + P   (+4) + P = 4P + (–5) + P

2P + (+4) + 5P = (+12) + P + (–3)   (–7) + 2P + (+5) = 3P + P + (–5)

Activity 2: PREDICTING MOVES
(Pictorial Action)

Materials: Paper
Pencils

Management: Partners (30 minutes)

Directions:

1. On the chalkboard write four or five equations of the types that have been studied. Ask each pair of students to look at each equation and predict, without writing any mathematical notation down, which *types* of moves (take-away, separation, or add-on) will be needed to solve it. *Note:* The order in which moves are applied to solve an equation will not be unique. Also, the same move might be applied more than once during the process of solving an equation.

2. Discuss the predictions made by different students for each equation and their reasons for each prediction.

3. Have different students write on the board what they think are possible symbolic steps for solving each equation. Some equations might have more than one way for their solution steps to be recorded.

4. Then have the students draw diagrams to solve the equations in order to confirm the predictions of necessary moves and the symbolic steps suggested by students for each equation.

5. Here are some possible equations to use (the types of moves needed are indicated in brackets: T=take-away; S=separation; A=add-on):

$(+8) + 2P = 5P + (+2)$ [T,S]

$7P + (-4) = (+6) + 2P$ [A,T,S]

$2P + (+3) + 5P = (+12) + P + (-3)$ [A,T,S]

$(+7) + P = 3P + (-5) + P$ [T,A,S]

$(-6) + P = +13$ [A]

$3P + (+9) = 2P + (+14)$ [T]

$5P + (-4) = (+16)$ [A,S]

$3P + (+5) = 4P + (-5)$ [A,T]

$10P = +20$ [S]

$(-2) + 4P = (+12) + 3P$ [A,T]

Activity 3: MOVE MATCH

(Cooperative Groups)

Materials: MOVES and EQUATION Card Sets (described in step 1)
Paper
Pencils

Management: Teams of 4 students each (20 minutes)

Directions:

1. Prepare card sets made from small index cards or cut-out construction paper rectangles. Make the MOVES cards one color and the EQUATION cards another color. Each MOVES card will contain some combination of the name(s) of specific moves needed to solve simple linear equations; that is, a MOVES card might read *add-on & separation; take-away; separation, add-on, & take-away;* etc. There will be 7 different MOVES cards in a set, since there are 7 different ways to combine the 3 moves, using one or more moves at a time. Each EQUATION card will contain a linear equation that requires one or more of the 3 individual moves mentioned above. There will also be 7 of these cards, one for each move combination. Also include a *wild card* that shows an equation type that has not been studied yet.

2. Team members must match each EQUATION card to a MOVES card. The equation shown on the EQUATION card will require each move listed on the matched MOVES card to be applied *at least once* in order to be solved. One EQUATION card will remain unmatched—the wild card. This equation may require some of the moves listed here, but it will also need one or more moves that have not been introduced in this chapter.

3. Here are suggested equations to use along with the move combinations they would match:

COMBINATION OF MOVES:	EQUATION:
Take-Away, Separation	$(+7) + 2P = 5P + (+1)$
Add-On, Take-Away, Separation	$8P + (-6) = (+9) + 3P$
Add-On	$(-8) + P = +15$
Take-Away	$4P + (+9) = 3P + (+16)$
Add-On, Separation	$(+17) = (-8) + 5P$
Add-On, Take-Away	$3P + (+5) = 4P + (-7)$
Separation	$15P = +45$

Equation for wild card: $(3P + 9)/2 = +30$ (This particular wild card equation requires the making of multiple groups, or multiplication, in order to be solved. Such a move has not been introduced in this chapter.)

APPENDIX

PATTERNS/GRIDS

For your convenience, here is an assortment of patterns and grids that can be easily photocopied for the activities and games located throughout this resource. Included are:

- Pattern for FRACTION BAR Set
- Pattern for BASE 10 BLOCKS
- INCH GRID
- HALF-INCH GRID
- CENTIMETER GRID
- RECTANGULAR DOT PAPER
- TRIANGULAR DOT PAPER

Pattern for a FRACTION BAR set

Have each student color 4 sets of the FRACTION BAR Set to match the teacher's set for the overhead. The set may then be laminated (optional), cut apart and sorted in a reclosable plastic bag. Punch a small airhole in each bag for easy storage.

whole											
half						half					
fourth			fourth			fourth			fourth		
eighth		eighth		eighth		eighth	eighth		eighth	eighth	eighth
twelfth	twelfth	twelfth	twelfth	twelfth	twelfth	twelfth	twelfth	twelfth	twelfth	twelfth	twelfth
sixth		sixth		sixth		sixth		sixth		sixth	
third				third				third			

Pattern for BASE 10 BLOCKS

Make 4 copies of the pattern for each student set. Cut apart along solid lines.

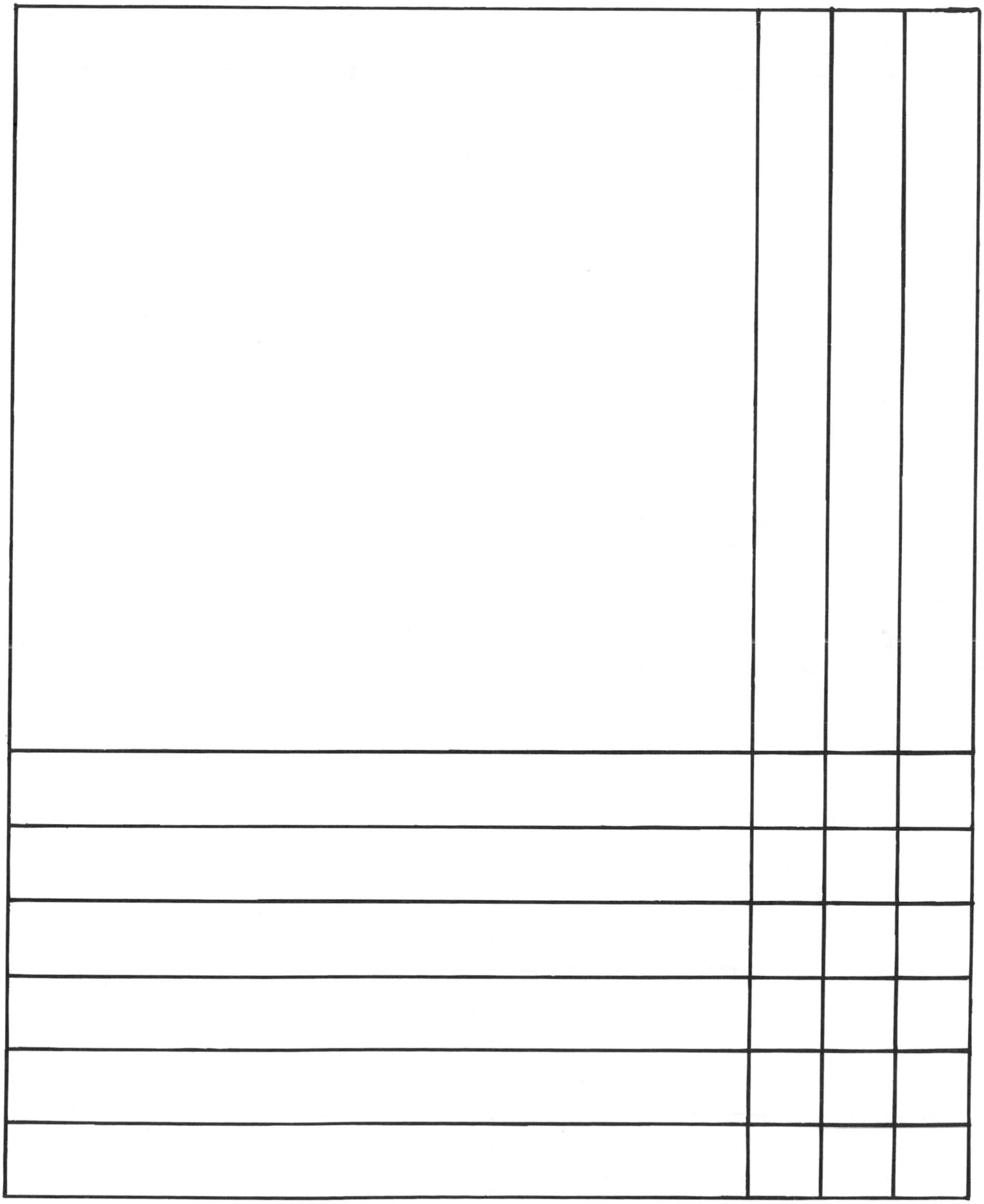

INCH GRID

HALF-INCH GRID

CENTIMETER GRID

RECTANGULAR DOT PAPER

TRIANGULAR DOT PAPER

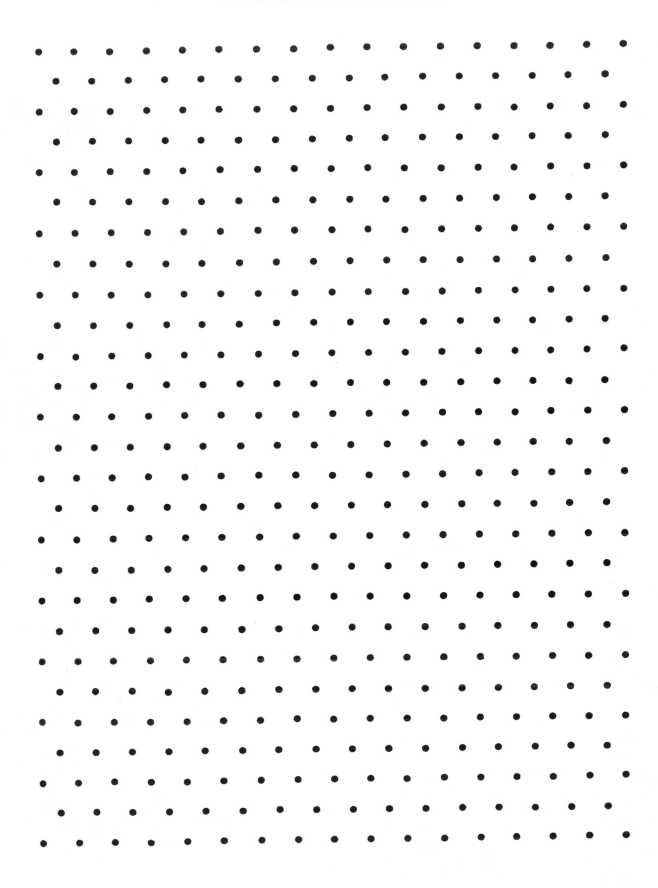